DATE DUE

PRINTED IN U.S.A.

The Draft

This book is based upon the Conference on the Draft, held December 4–7, 1966 at the University of Chicago with the aid of a grant from The Ford Foundation and includes papers by:

MARK ABRAMS

COL. MORDECHAI M. BAR-ON

ALBERT D. BIDERMAN

RICHARD W. BOONE

KENNETH E. BOULDING

LEON BRAMSON

BRUCE K. CHAPMAN

TERRENCE CULLINAN

DONALD J. EBERLY

ERIK H. ERIKSON

MILTON FRIEDMAN

RAYMOND L. GARTHOFF

COL. SAMUEL H. HAYS

GEOFFREY C. HAZARD, JR.

LT. GEN. LEWIS B. HERSHEY

MORRIS JANOWITZ

BERNARD D. KARPINOS

SEN. EDWARD M. KENNEDY

HARRY A. MARMION

BRIG. GEN. S. L. A. MARSHALL

WILLIAM H. MC NEILL

MARGARET MEAD

JOHN MITRISIN

WALTER Y. OI

JOHN DE J. PEMBERTON, JR.

PAUL A. WEINSTEIN

The Draft

A Handbook of Facts and Alternatives

EDITED BY SOL TAX

The University of Chicago Press
CHICAGO AND LONDON

Library of Congress Catalog Card Number: 67-25517

THE UNIVERSITY OF CHICAGO PRESS,   CHICAGO 60637

The University of Chicago Press, Ltd., London W.C. 1

© *1967 by The University of Chicago*

Third Impression 1969

Printed in the United States of America

. . . Then the officers shall say to the people, "Whoever has built a new house, but has not dedicated it, may leave and return home, lest he die in the battle, and another dedicate it. Whoever has planted a vineyard, but has not had the use of it, may leave and return home, lest he die in the battle and another get the use of it. Whoever has betrothed a wife, but has not yet married her, may leave and return home, lest he die in the battle and another marry her." The officers shall further say to the people, "Whoever is afraid and faint-hearted must leave and return home, so that his fellows may not become faint-hearted like him." As soon as the officers have finished addressing the people, the army commanders shall place themselves at the head of the people.

DEUTERONOMY 20:5

Preface

The problem of "who should fight?" is new every generation, as the verse from Deuteronomy shows. It was certainly new to most of us in May of 1966 when students at the University of Chicago (themselves not in the Armed Forces) objected to the use of course grades to decide who should stay in school and who should fight. Because nobody had satisfying answers, the faculty asked me to bring to a national conference those with the most relevant knowledge, so that we could all learn. The only important thing I myself knew was that Morris Janowitz, my colleague in sociology, was among the most knowledgeable in the land. He brought in Roger Little, who was coming to the University of Illinois from a teaching post at West Point and would join our committee. Arnold Weber, a labor economist, C. Arnold Anderson, an educationist-sociologist, and Ben Rothblatt, a philosopher, completed our committee. Lee Pravatiner undertook staff work. In a matter of weeks we had invited the people whose papers and discussion fill this book.

On July 1, 1966, President Johnson appointed a commission to study the problem of Selective Service, since the law was to expire a year later. The machinery of our conference preparations were put at the service of the commission members, advance copies of the papers in this book were mailed to them, and they were invited to attend the conference. In fact, the Executive Director of the Commission was a most attentive conferee, and carried back to Washington many pages of careful notes. He also made a brief report to open the discussions and a gracious statement at their close.

With the Selective Service system under fire, at least on the campuses, and under scrutiny by Congress and the administration, it was a strategic time for a conference; interest was intense and widespread. It seemed probable that what we put together in Chicago would have direct influence. Before the conference opened a reporter from Washington was surprised to hear—and found it difficult to believe—that I did not know the conclusions of the conference. In fact I was most curious. We would have a confrontation of knowledgeable people with very different views. There was no good answer in any case; only a series of less-than-good alternatives. I had studied the papers and considered the issues. There seemed no hurry to choose one of the bad answers; could a new and better one come from sober consideration by informed people?

The record is here and the reader can make his own judgment. The President's Message to Congress accepted the recommendations of his Commission, whose conclusions responded to the problems of Selective Service as they were discussed in Chicago. The Congress paid almost no heed. Although Senator Edward Kennedy, who participated in our conference, is the leading proponent of selection by lottery, the possibility was ruled out by Congress. Despite the fact that two of our participants are persuasive congressmen (Robert Kastenmeier, a Democrat, and Donald Rumfield, a Republican) who favor moving toward a voluntary army, the Commission, the President, and the Congress gave scant attention to what appeared to many observers at Chicago a striking new idea—that abandonment of conscription entirely might not be an outlandish alternative.

This book is therefore the beginning of the full discussion that an important public policy requires. It provides facts and views, leaving conclusions to be drawn by its readers. A university, established to search out the truth, is a place for learning and for teaching. It makes no pronouncements of what the truth is (which would end that part of the search): if there were an unchallenged truth it would hardly need to be pronounced. Rather, the academic tradition encourages development of all intellectually honest views, no matter how diverse. Meanwhile, public policy decisions properly take into account the interests of different segments of society; they lean heavily on what already exists in law, practice, and the preferences of people. These are sometimes outdated or based on misinformation or prejudice. This book—a university discussion—is intended to open eyes, correct misapprehensions, and provide new views, thus enabling the American people to form effective judgments on the issues with which it is concerned.

When the university called the conference, it did not know how it would be financed. The Ford Foundation quickly and generously provided funds so that our committee could devote all its efforts to intellectual matters. Because it was intended as the beginning of a national discussion, it seemed proper to invite major national organizations to listen (at their own expense) to the discussion among the experts and to participate where appropriate. Therefore invitations were sent to a wide cross-section of organizations in business, education, labor, religion, veterans affairs, and so on. We succeeded also in getting a cross-section of age groups; indeed twenty-eight of the 135 total registration were college students, and two were still in high school. It was possible in choosing the scholarly participants to achieve a fairly well balanced representation of different points of view. On the other hand those who accepted invitations to attend as part of the audience were necessarily self-selected; organizations and persons critical of the selective service system came in probably disproportionate numbers. Doubtless this accounts in some part for the sharp difference between the tone of the discussion here and the actions of the lawmakers, elected as they are with support from a different selection of organizations.

The papers that were prepared in advance of the conference arrived, of course, in miscellaneous order, and were so distributed to the working participants. The committee, in making up the sequence of the program, took into account what the papers said and implicitly ordered them. Only now, however, are they explicitly ordered. Another editor might choose a different order. I begin with seven papers which describe the Selective Service system and discuss the problems it faces. The next six papers accept the need for a system of Selective Service for military manpower procurement but propose means of making it less discriminatory and more positive by extending it to non-military service. Next follows a set of six papers which back away from the immediate technical and policy questions and put the problem in different perspectives. Finally there are eight papers which deny the validity or need for conscription, attacking the use of force from quite different points of view. Two of the papers depart again from the problem of military manpower procurement alone and propose broad programs of voluntary national service. The last paper was also written last. Erik Erikson was unable to come to Chicago, but having read all of the papers, he essayed his own conclusions before the conference opened. This is therefore a transition to the second part of the book, which discusses the papers and the issues.

There follows, in an Epilog, four post-conference documents: first, the President's message to the Congress; second, General Hershey's description of the changes in the law subsequently made by the Congress; third, a critical analysis of these changes made by Senator Edward M. Kennedy of Massachusetts, presented to the Senate in a vain appeal that these changes not be adopted; and last, a report from *Science* magazine of the events surrounding the emergence of the Selective Service Act of 1967.

The conference was well equipped with selective microphones, and the discussions were carefully recorded on tape and then transcribed. The transcript was edited with the expert help of Jean Block and Ruth Grodzins and reviewed for accuracy by all of the speakers who could be identified. Everything substantive that was publicly said is reported here, in the order in which it was said; only procedural matters and repetitions have been edited out. Although sentences are finished and grammar corrected, the intention is to maintain the style of oral presentation and preserve in the discussion as much of its life as is consonant with readability. The first discussion (after a dinner whose "invocation" was the passage from Deuteronomy) was a *tour de force* by Geoffrey Hazard, of the University's Law School. As one who had not been involved in the planning or the issues of the conference, he was asked by the committee to treat all the prepared materials as though they were the evidence developed in a court of law and to give us the equivalent of the judge's charge to the jury, stating the issues for discussion. He earned the gratitude of all for his labor (during a busy week) and his skill.

The conference itself was an exciting event, with "We won't go!" student meetings outside and a variety of political machinations inside. The chairmen often had difficult moments in keeping down attempts to turn the educational discussion into a parliamentary body. Somebody invented the expedient of passing around the room resolutions which people were free to sign so that the more politically oriented (and the press) could count the score on various issues. The conference threatened to split apart the last evening, when arrangements were made for a nationwide telecast of the next morning's concluding session; the issue was never settled because a local accident involving the fall of an elevated train from its trestle suddenly removed the television cameras to that scene. (The following afternoon and evening, however, the conclusions of the conference were reported to the general public at a downtown assembly, attended by a thousand people, which was televised both locally and nationally.)

If this book is good, we have the authors and discussants to thank. We all—but I especially—owe thanks also to the chairmen, to the committee, to the staff, and especially to Lee Pravatiner, whose labors are to be read between all the lines of this book.

SOL TAX

Contents

PART 2. The Discussions

PART 3. Epilogue

PART 1

Contributed Papers

PROBLEMS OF THE DRAFT

1

A Fact Paper on Selective Service

LT. GEN. LEWIS B. HERSHEY

The growing interest in the operation of the Selective Service System among people of prominence who have not previously participated in its study is providing the system with a unique opportunity to: (1) explore fresh areas of intellect for new ideas and new adaptations of old concepts, and (2) to correct misunderstandings and misinterpretations.

A lack of interest in Selective Service operations prior to the relatively recent increase in manpower calls has made it difficult for the system to tap new sources of thought except through intensive use of its own seminars among quasi-military businessmen, educators, professional men, and others who have military reserve affiliations. Since the close of World War II, the System in its continued search for new ideas has conducted 182 of these seminars. In all cases, however, many of the participants had a considerable knowledge of the current operation and its historical background and presumably approached the subject with some preconceived opinions.

The only other areas of intensive study of the Selective Service System operation during the period of relatively low calls has been the Congress, particularly the Armed Forces Committees, which have quietly and continuously required general and special studies and reports for evaluation. The assumption that rapid congressional action on extension of the Selective Service System law reflected a lack of adequate consideration of the Congress is not correct. It reflected, instead, a complete advance understanding.

This is only one of many areas of misinterpretation which should be clarified. If a conference such as yours is to have even a remote chance of producing really new ideas, it must start its thinking from fact, as you have indicated in your letter of invitation, rather than from faulty assumptions and misinterpretations which have deluged and warped discussions of Selective Service recently. Some pertinent statements of fact which in most cases are so elementary as to require no elucidation follow:

PURPOSE

The Selective Service System has three basic responsibilities:

1) To provide the Armed Forces with the number of men they need when they want them.

2) While doing this, to cause as little disturbance as possible in the civilian economy.

The author is Director of the Selective Service System.

3

3) To guide deferments into areas considered to be in the national interest by competent authority, such as the Department of Commerce, Department of Labor, scientific and educational groups.

All new ideas must be committed to the scope of these three objectives. Any innovation, no matter how spectacular, that does not support or enhance the effectiveness of these basic purposes, has missed the boat. Any proposal that would jeopardize or impair these functions is opposed to the reason for the system's existence.

"Personal" interest comes after "national" interest.

LIABILITY

The law places upon every registrant the liability and responsibility to register, to provide his local board with adequate evidence to permit a judgment "in the national interest" (not the registrant's interest), and to serve in the Armed Forces if found to be "available."

Every registrant is presumed by law, to be "available" (Class I-A) in the absence of convincing evidence to the contrary. It is not the function of the local board to create evidence. The local board is neither authorized nor directed to investigate. Much of the alleged variance between local board decisions is due to a registrant's failure to perform fully his legal responsibility to supply written evidence concerning himself.

A local board does not put a registrant in service. He is potentially there by law. The board can merely delay the beginning of the service through the instrumentality of deferment.

No registrant has a "right" to a deferment. His "right," by law, is a "privilege" to serve.

FOREIGN SYSTEMS

The Selective Service System maintains a library of all forms of conscription, historical, present, foreign, and domestic, ranging from exclusion by political fiat to the Chinese concept of the "seed son," and from military impressment to exemption by purchase. Many nations have sent representatives here for ideas.

REJECTIONS

The Selective Service System does not accept or reject registrants for military service. This screening is done by the Department of the Army as "executive agent" for the Department of Defense which by law fixes the physical, mental, and moral criteria. (The Selective Service System did not reject either Cassius Clay or Mickey Mantle.)

The Selective Service System determines "availability"; the Department of Defense determines "acceptability." The only exceptions are registrants who are badly crippled, obviously mentally retarded, and convicts—that is, manifest conditions.

UNCERTAINTY

Uncertainty can be eliminated by any registrant at any time at either a military recruiting office or by volunteering for immediate delivery through the Selective Service System. "Uncertainty" is usually confused with "probability."

Early physical examinations provide certainty only for those rejected. The status of those found acceptable remains unchanged.

FAIRNESS

As with the income tax and other comparable undertakings, popularity is not the primary consideration; fairness must be sought in the relationship between what an individual has that the nation needs at any particular time. Fairness, as a common denominator to the individual desires of each person, does not exist.

STUDENTS

Students have never been deferred just because they were students.

Students have never been deferred, or not deferred, solely because of class standing or intelligence tests. It is not now, and never has been, proposed that they should. The same goes for number of credits, part-time status, night classes, etc.

The Selective Service System did not create the class-standing-intelligence-test procedure. It was developed, and its use was requested, by nine of the leading higher education associations and groups in the nation. It is the basis upon which most participant educational institutions judge their own students for "kick-out" purposes.

Although there has been at least a year of implication that more specific criteria regarding students should be given local boards, not one proposal of this nature has been offered by any person or agency, educational or otherwise.

The issue regarding students is not whether they should or should not be drafted. There is not room in the Armed Forces for all of them, so mathematically they cannot all be taken. Conversely, if the calls are high enough, they cannot be filled without taking some students. "How" to obtain a varying number of students, depending upon the variable size of the current monthly calls (not a fixed number) is the issue.

APPEAL PROCEDURE

The Selective Service appeal procedure is open to all registrants. The appeal is simple to initiate and no reason for appealing need be given. It removes jurisdiction to a completely independent board for reconsideration.

ACCOUNTING RECORDS

Each local board maintains a current record of its available and acceptable registrants. State and national tabulations are made once each month, but can be made at any time by mail in less than ten days if there should ever be any need for it. The statistics used for distribution of calls are current, only three to ten days old.

PRORATION OF CALLS

Calls for delivery of registrants for induction are prorated to states mathematically from the national "stream" ("pool" is a seriously misleading term and results in misinterpretations). These calls would extract, if they were ever pursued that far, the last available and acceptable registrant from every local board at the same time.

Local boards do not place men in Class I-A in order to fill calls. Instead, the calls they receive are based upon the number of registrants they already have in Class I-A.

DATA PROCESSING

The Selective Service System has explored, and has experimented with, various forms of data processing since 1942. Although many experts have worked on it, none has been able to conceive a system or program to fit the function. Two basic approaches have been surveyed:

1) Extrapolations from local board decisions.
2) Replacement of local boards with machines designed to digest evidence and render judgment.

The first has always proved much slower and far more expensive than the present three- to ten-day reporting system. The second thus far has been too complicated, with fractional, contradicting, corroborated, and variable evidence, and vacillating objectives, for programmers to master. If a successful method were found and adopted it would destroy local autonomy, which is the greatest strength of the present system.

DEFERMENT UNIFORMITY

Most of what has been alleged to be a lack of uniformity between local board decisions has been found, upon inquiry into confidential evidence in registrant files, to be a recognition of actual difference in circumstances of the registrants involved.

CLASSIFICATION VARIANCE

A variance between local boards and states in the per cent of registrants they have in a specific classification does not indicate a variance in policy or difference in criteria. There is a greater variance in some of the classifications where judgment is excluded (fixed criteria on age, physical, mental, or moral qualities) than in some where judgment is the predominant factor. The variance is mostly a reflection of actual difference between registrants and their individual circumstances.

MARRIED VS UNMARRIED

For a short time some local boards delivered married registrants for induction while others did not. This is a national consequence whenever a new group of registrants is selected in small numbers—that is, less than the number of local boards. For example: if the total call from the Secretary of Defense in any month happened to be 2,000, about half of the 4,000 local boards in the nation would deliver a man and half would not.

BASIC MISCONCEPTION

There is a tendency to yield to the illusion that if more registrants are deferred, the number of men in the Armed Forces will reduce, and that if more are placed in Class I-A, more will go into the Armed Forces.

The determination of how many registrants are needed and authorized for induction is made by the Secretary of Defense. A call for zero men produces zero men regardless of how many or few are in Class I-A or deferred.

The Selective Service System remains ready to provide details wherever desired, and detailed papers on many of the subjects briefly mentioned here are available upon request to the Director, Selective Service System, National Headquarters, 1724 F Street, N.W., Washington, D.C.

2

A Military View of Selective Service

COL. SAMUEL H. HAYS

"To Mr. James Cook,
Sir, with the advice of the military officers select men and committee of this town you are draghted to do eight months service in the Continental Army from this date; and you are to furnish yourself for camp and be in readiness forthwith to muster and to march when and where ordered or otherwise you are to pay a fine of fifteen pounds in twenty four hours from the time of your being draghted. . . ."

WM PAGE, LT.

NEW SALEM, April 17th 1778

". . . The Congress hereby declares that an adequate armed strength must be achieved and maintained to insure the security of this nation. . . . The Congress further declares that in a free society the obligations and privileges of serving in the armed forces and the reserve components thereof should be shared generally, in accordance with a system of selection which is fair and just, and which is consistent with the maintenance of an effective national economy. . . ."—Universal Military Training and Service Act of 1951

The problem of providing manpower for our Armed Forces has been with us since the founding of the republic. For the past 188 years the ultimate source of military manpower has been the citizen selected from among his peers. Since the sound of gunfire faded away over the 38th parellel in Korea, the Armed Forces of the United States have been procuring from all sources between 600,000 and 900,000 men annually. The obligatory provisions of the Universal Military Training and Service Act of 1951 as amended have provided the incentives for both voluntary enlistments and officer procurement programs as well as providing from 13 per cent to 41 per cent of this annual intake. During this same period of time the numbers of young citizens eligible under the provisions of the act for military service grew steadily from 10,590,000 to 13,360,000, with a steadily decreasing percentage being required to perform some type of mili-

The author is Director, Office of Military Psychology and Leadership, United States Military Academy.
A substantial portion of this paper was published after the conference in the February issue of *Army* and is reproduced here with permission of the copyright owner.

tary service. As long as the monthly draft calls remained fairly low, little public attention was attracted to this situation.

The larger draft calls of early 1966, which placed students in a vulnerable position, aroused some of the more vocal and outspoken segments of our society and have stimulated a public debate over the inequities and problems surrounding the workings of the Selective Service System. As the debate has developed, not only have the inequities—always associated with selective service—been brought to light, but the fundamental philosophy and purposes behind the act have been seriously questioned for the first time in nearly fifteen years.

Through all the criticism and complaint runs a demand for uniformity of risk, equity, justice, and consideration for the individual. To citizens steeped in our liberal democratic traditions, this search for individual equity and justice has great emotional and logical appeal, a fact which the Congress fully recognized when it passed the act of 1951. The popular outcry in behalf of the traditional liberal creed should not obscure the fact that American society as a whole has a serious interest in the issues involved, nor should it drown out the viewpoint of the Armed Forces, which must use the products of the system in order to maintain their effectiveness. The purpose here is to analyze, in the light of current trends, the fundamental issues involved and to evaluate from a military viewpoint the results of the system and proposed alternatives as they might affect the efficiency of our Armed Forces.

Although on the surface the discussion over the operation of the Selective Service System appears to be largely over its mechanical operation, in reality there are fundamental social issues at stake. The principal issue is how best to raise and maintain in a democratic society the efficient and effective Armed Forces which our country needs in its present world position. Allied to this issue is the problem of the manner in which the Armed Forces should relate to the society which raised them. Finally, there is the issue of the relative value which should be placed on the overall welfare of society as compared to the demand for equal individual treatment. These are not easy issues to resolve. They have been the subject of discussion and controversy since the founding of the republic. Indeed the founding fathers in their day arrived at a general consensus on the subject which unfortunately we, today, are unable to apply to our greatly changed circumstances.

CHANGED CIRCUMSTANCES

Today, we find ourselves, willingly or not, in a position of preeminent world power during a period of rapid and accelerating technological and social change. These conditions directly influence the type and size of forces we must maintain and the problems involved in their recruitment. Most agree that our international position, with the extensive responsibilities which our power position places on us, requires the maintenance of Armed Forces of a much greater magnitude than in previous eras. Our experience in World War II and Korea taught us that the purposes of world peace and our national security were best served by maintaining professional land, sea, and air forces adequate to meet the international commitments we felt necessary in our national interest. Since the end of the Korean War the Department of Defense has felt that such forces must amount to over two and a half million men organized to cope with a variety of situations. Whenever we have tried to reduce these forces a crisis arose, such as those over Berlin or Cuba, which forced us to rebuild them. Further, the advent of nuclear weapons, the increased speed of communications and transportation have greatly reduced mobilization and readiness times and of necessity placed an increasing priority on immediate ready forces. The sequence of events in Lebanon, Berlin, Cuba, the Dominican Republic, and now Vietnam have clearly shown that if we are to contain conflict, keeping it within manageable proportions, we must be able to move our forces fast enough and in sufficient strength to influence the action at the earliest possible time. The organization of the Strategic Air Command and subsequently the STRIKE Command constitute an organizational response to the requirement.

The type and size of forces required are also affected by increasing qualitative requirements of military forces. The accelerated rate of contemporary technological advances dramatically portrayed in our space programs and missile weapons development is having a profound effect on the internal structure of our forces. Each year the weapons systems, vehicles, communications systems, and associated equipment become more sophisticated, more complex, and more specialized. The demand for skillful and highly articulated teamwork resulting from the development of nuclear-powered aircraft carriers, Polaris submarines, and the airmobile division are far beyond similar demands of World War II or Korea. At the end of World War II, the technical, mechanical and military administrative assignments in our services were less than half of all enlisted positions. By 1954, they had grown to nearly 60 per cent, and eleven years later they amounted to nearly two-thirds of all positions filled. While the basic requirements of the fighting man for endurance, emotional and physical stamina, leadership, courage and practical intelligence are still in demand, they alone are no longer sufficient to cope with the technical weaponry and complicated operational techniques of today.

Thus we find that the members of our forces must be more highly selected from the point of view of mental capacity, technical aptitude, and social maturity. More members must be sent to specialist schools for longer periods of time. Units require longer training times to develop the same degree of combat efficiency in the tactical employment of their weapons than they did in the past. In addition, these increasing complexities create an increasing requirement for adequate motivation, social solidarity and cohesiveness in our military units. Today's forces require a high degree of teamwork involving a wide variety of man-machine mixes capable of dealing with a wide spectrum of problems.

The increased size of the standing forces required, the necessity for more rapid action, and the increased lead times required for weapons production and personnel training have had an obvious effect on our traditional military posture. The concept of the small regular force as the base around which to mobilize the civilian soldiers of our reserve forces has faded more and more into the past. As the immediate show of force has become more frequent, partial or general mobilization has tended to become an increasingly less desirable alternative. We are thus being required to depend more and more on active duty forces and, short of a general emergency, able to place less reliance on large reserve forces or on long-term mobilization. While we must continue to retain our extensive reserve resources as insurance against the all-out emergency, we must also take into account our increased reliance on efficient combat-ready forces organized in proper proportions for such missions as can be anticipated. The first basic issue of how best to maintain such forces involves at least three major problem areas. One that taxpayers tend to think about most frequently is the cost. Our national budget provides evidence that our appropriations for defense and military forces absorb almost half of our programmed funds. The economic costs of the more complex weapons systems, the costs of education and training, the costs of maintaining larger numbers of higher paid personnel increase year by year as new developments and new situations create new demands. All would join in agreeing that one of our high priority goals should be to have the most effective Armed Forces possible for the least cost.

A second problem area which has plagued the services for the last decade is how to procure the high-caliber officers and men required and how to retain them on active duty at least long enough to amortize the investment in their education and training. By its very nature an armed force with its hierarchic structure and its innate requirements for combat readiness requires a reasonable turnover of officers and enlisted men in its lower grades. Combat conditions place a premium on youthful agility, stamina, audacity and courage in the junior grades, coupled with the stability, judgment and maturity of age normally associated with the more senior positions. Problems of career progression, promotion, rotational assignment indicate an annual turnover of about 15 to 20 per cent, largely concentrated in the junior grades. However, such a turnover should not denude the services of their skilled specialists or most promising leaders. Despite the extensive efforts to make the pay and career opportunities attractive, all services have had to rely heavily on other motivational factors in order to gain and retain the necessary level of talent. The rather negative view of liberal democratic society toward military careers tends to make recruiting difficult and has forced reliance on obligatory service to maintain both strength and skill levels.

A third problem area in maintaining efficient forces stems from extensive fluctuation in military strength levels, personnel procurement programs, and force deployment. The same recurring crises which require the existence of our standing forces tend to create problems in their maintenance. Vietnam, the Berlin crisis and the Cuban crisis were all reflected in increased draft calls, sudden changes of plans, family dislocations and not infrequently individual hardship. These fluctuations create many uncertainties in the plans of young men eligible for induction into the service as well as in the plans of those already serving. On the national level they make installation planning and programming subject to fits, starts, and frequent reversals. Such fluctuations underlie many of the basic inequities caused by the highly variable and frequently unpredicted draft calls. They create part of the difficulty in retaining highly trained people in the service.

THE ARMED FORCES AND SOCIETY

In considering the second fundamental issue, that of the relation of the Armed Forces to society, we must take notice that the same change which is transforming our Armed Forces is also affecting our society. The changes wrought in society by the technological revolution play an important part in our consideration of the relative position our Armed Forces should occupy. Military institutions are a reflection of the value system of the societies which produce them. In a technological world of growing interdependence on local, national and international levels, the interrelationship between economic, political, social and military institutions grows continually closer. Because of this growing interdependence, issues which arise in either national or international arenas become continually more complex and difficult of solution. Safeguarding Berlin or pacifying Vietnam are as far removed from guarding Tientsin or pacifying the Philippines a half-century ago as the Wright brothers' airplane is removed from Gemini XI.

This social and technological change, and the complexities and tensions which it engenders, places an additional emphasis on the motivaton, morale, teamwork, and loyalty of the Armed Forces. Our society places a heavy responsiblity on them and rightfully expects them to produce. Their motivation, morale and teamwork are affected by a wide variety of factors. The educational and social level of their membership, caliber of leadership, the severity of deprivation of the normal advantages of civilian life—all play a significant part. Underlying them all is the degree of social approval and recognition which each member thinks he receives in return for his deprivation, risk or sacrifice. While this recognition can be expressed to some degree in terms of pay, housing and fringe benefits, it is more importantly a function of prestige, status and public recognition. The motivation and morale of our forces is not a constant which can be taken for granted as it stems from individual and group needs over time and under varying conditions. In many ways it is easier to procure and develop the technical equipment used by the forces than it is to procure the men needed to put it into battle.

Today more than ever before the Armed Forces must relate positively to society. Their members must perceive that they are performing a vital social function and one which is recognized and awarded an appropriate status by the society as a whole. On the other hand it is perhaps equally important to the welfare of the society that this relationship be positively and continuously expressed. The rapid social change we are now facing with the weakening of community and isolation of the individual emphasize the importance of those institutions which can provide some elements of stability. The Armed Forces have been identified as agencies useful in inculcating social discipline, a sense of national purpose and in teaching individual responsibility and the requirements of group living.

It does not take extensive research to discover what has happened when the military forces of a society become estranged or isolated from the society which supported them. When citizens no longer feel responsible to perform military service, it is difficult for them to develop much interest in the military forces or their duties and responsibilities. In return, when soldiers no longer consider themselves understood by the community and not full citizens in the true sense of the word, the ensuing gap between military and society becomes difficult to bridge. Whatever solution might be chosen for the problem of manning military forces, it should include measures which would maintain the close relationship between the civilian society and the military institution which has been achieved during the past twenty-five years.

EQUAL INDIVIDUAL TREATMENT

The third basic issue, equity and justice for all individuals, must be given its true importance as has been indicated by the Congress. However, when equity for the individual and the welfare of society as a whole are inconsistent, decisions for society may be hard decisions to make and it may have to accept the resulting dissatisfaction and criticism. Unfortunately, true equity is hard to achieve in military operations. Inequity results when some serve while others escape. However, inequalities also occur even among those that serve. No one could find much equity between pounding a typewriter in the Pentagon and carrying the M-16 rifle in the jungles of Vietnam. Although the services do what they can to distribute risk, hardship, and discomfort through periodic rotation, the burdens and risks of military life are most unequally distributed both in peace and combat. In many ways the differences in sacrifice between those who are called to the service and those excused are less drastic than the differences which result from different assignments in the services. While we may not be able to do much about equality of sacrifice in the national interest we should do what can be done to see that the system of selection for service is efficient, just, and produces the best possible result for society as a whole.

THE SYSTEM

Examining our existing Selective Service System to determine how well it has filled our requirements, we are struck by the fact that it is essential in maintaining the strength of our Armed Forces. Despite our very best efforts during the 1948-1949 period, we were unable to maintain the relatively modest levels authorized during that period. Further, the quality and motivation of the personnel recruited during that period were too often marginal. In an infantry battalion during that period one might find only two or three high school graduates in nearly a thousand men. Technical proficiency was not at a high level; delinquency and court-martial rates were. The costs stemming from misuse of equipment, and from vehicle accidents as well as those associated with the administration of disciplinary punitive systems were proportionately high. These hidden costs were multiplied many times over when the forces raised under the volunteer system were committed suddenly to combat in Korea.

As the selective service brought in an increased volume of manpower needed for the Korean buildup, the personnel makeup of the services changed perceptibly. There was a marked increase in educational levels, skill levels, and efficiency among those brought into the service. During the months of continued high draft calls there was an increased number of volunteers who displayed many of the same characteristics as those who were drafted. However, disciplinary studies made during that period tended to show that military delinquents were more likely to be volunteers than draftees, have less education, be younger, come from backgrounds with fewer economic and social advantages, and have displayed more pre-Army delinquent behavior than draftees—factors generally related to unconcern with commonly accepted rules of behavior. A larger proportion of delinquents than draftees stated that they had planned to make the Army a career.[1]

Following the Korean War, as the draft calls declined, so too did both the number and quality of those volunteering. The numbers drafted amounted to the number required to provide sufficient incentive for the volunteers plus the number needed to fill the spaces they didn't fill. During the mid-Fifties the percentage of volunteers climbed slowly from about 60 to, in some years, over 80 per cent. However, once again the high school dropout became the typical volunteer and the frequency of delinquency with its associated human, material, and economic costs began to rise. In 1958, the Department of Defense sought and obtained authority to raise the mental and physical standards for draftees. The reasons for this move were the increasing demand for highly qualified men with the advent of new weapons, the growing surplus of eligible men in the draft "pool," and the desire to improve the effectiveness of military manpower through reducing costs incident to the administration of discipline and administrative discharges.

This increase in entrance standards brought in some dramatic changes. The Army was able to close down four out of five of its disciplinary barracks and the number it discharged for reasons other than honorable was reduced from 22 per thousand in 1957 to 16 per thousand in 1965. Noteworthy as these gains were, the most telling gains resulted from the increased proficiency and professionalization of the military units themselves. A significant result of the increase in quality input was the steady improvement in reenlistments during this period, reflecting higher morale, greater satisfaction with the service and improved primary group solidarity.

During most of this period of relatively low monthly calls, the Navy and Marine Corps and Air Force were able to supply all of their personnel needs by volunteers. However, the same draft calls that stimulated individuals to volunteer for the Army stimulated volunteers for other services. Draftees continued to be older and have higher educational levels than volunteers and this variation of distribution of accessions by educational level has tended to remain relatively constant. The statistics also suggest that the Army, at least, is getting somewhat better than an average cross section of the total population by educational group. This reflects, of course, the higher amounts of schooling achieved by those in the military age groups.

Age is another factor which bears directly on the quality of military accessions. The number of variables which influence this factor are difficult to unscramble. Physical agility and stamina are generally associated with youth. After screening out the physically disqualified, the optimum age for physical performance would appear to be from 18 to 25. Similarly the optimum age for military performance is difficult to gauge. Studies made following World War II tended to indicate that peak performance appeared to occur just over 25 years of age. Thus optimum military age seems to lie someplace between 19 and 30.[2] The age levels produced by our military procurement programs over the past fifteen years have stayed well within the limits defined by the study as shown in Table 1. The advancing ages after the Korean War can be attributed to increasing percentages of personnel in the regular forces age 40 and over and the somewhat advancing ages of those inducted due to reduced draft calls.

TABLE 1

Armed Forces Age Levels

	1950	1952	1954	1956	1958	1960	1962	1964	1965
Median age	23.6	22.9	22.7	23.0	23.8	24.5	24.2	24.0	23.9
Largest age group	20	21	21	20	20	20	20	21	21

Directorate for Statistical Services, Office of the Secretary of Defense, *Selected Manpower Statistics*, April, 1966, p. 38.

As the higher draft calls for the Vietnam buildup have called in successively lower age groups, they have provided incentives for increased volunteering among these same lower age groups. This can be expected to lower, in some degree, the educational levels and the civilian skills possessed by those inducted. In addition, both the Navy and the Marine Corps have had to request the allocation of some draftees to fill their requirements.

Officer procurement programs are affected by induction calls in much the same manner as are voluntary enlistments. As calls declined after the Korean War, ROTC enrollments tended to decline and officer candidate programs were drastically reduced. As the calls increase, more college students seek to enroll in ROTC, thus enhancing the program both in numbers and in quality. The Vietnam buildup has seen an extensive expansion of the officer candidate program.

Our commanders in Vietnam have been unanimous in their praise of the quality of the soldiers being provided. Even a cursory glance at our training centers today reveals ample evidence that we are producing a high quality of soldier. It is exceedingly doubtful whether we could have manned our modern air, sea, and ground units without this high quality. In terms of contributing to the efficiency of the Armed Services it would be safe to say that the Selective Service System as it stands today has successfully passed the ultimate test of battle.

In terms of relating the Armed Forces to society, the steady mixture of selective service men in the ranks and ROTC graduates among the officers has continued to maintain the integration of the military institution with society at large. As far as the services are concerned, they visualize themselves as a part of American society performing a vital service for the nation.

EQUITY OF SYSTEM

Has the system been just and equitable? This depends on the yardstick used to measure the results. If one uses the yardstick of uniformity or equality of risk, it has not been particularly equitable; equity in the military service can only be gauged in relative terms. If one measures justice in terms of adherence to law, regulation, and principle of local selection by one's neighbors, one could say that the system has been just. Perhaps equally vital to the national interest is the question of whether it has been the most efficient and best allocation of our human resources. This suggests still other questions: of deferment for vital occupational skills, age at induction, and quality of personnel inducted. Only too often these questions become entangled with the questions of equity.

Still another issue habitually inserts itself into any discussion of obligatory military service. Should the military services be used as an educational and socializing agency in our democratic community in order to provide educational opportunities, social discipline, and medical assistance to the less privileged elements of our society? Since the turn of the century this idea has repeatedly raised its head during discussions of military preparedness and universal military training. It lay behind the proposed STEP program and also behind recent programs to lower the induction standards in order to enlist personnel previously considered unqualified. To some extent it is implicit in a statement of the civic duty of military service. Those proposing such measures see the increasing percentages, now about 33 per cent of our young men who are considered unfit for military service, and feel that something should be done about it. They assume that providing military training for these young men will assist in their rehabilitation through providing them with medical assistance, increased educational opportunities, a vocational skill and perhaps a sense of social responsibility.

The military services can provide some assistance for these youths, although there is some evidence to indicate that special educational programs conducted by the services do not measurably improve the performance of such marginal personnel. Physical education and health programs coupled with a proper diet should greatly improve the physical condition of those young men with correctable deficiencies. Perhaps some of those who are alienated or feel little relation to society can be given a sense of purpose and understanding through their barracks experiences. Insofar as the provisions of the Uniform Code of Military Justice allow, some might be brought to a greater respect for the provisions of law and the rules of society.

It must be recognized, however, that there is considerable increased cost in such a program. There is an inordinate amount of administrative and training effort involved in handling marginal personnel. As we have seen, they have more disciplinary offenses, more vehicle accidents, go AWOL more often, have more personal problems and more mental breakdowns. They take longer to train for the same degree of skill. They are less flexible in their utilization. Their effect on the social solidarity and esprit of units to which assigned tends to be negative and destructive. In significant numbers, their ways of thought and habits of life make their barracks a less desirable place to live thereby tending to drive out the better qualified. The process would be somewhat analogous to a situation resulting from a requirement for state universities to matriculate and graduate not only every high school graduate who applied for entrance, but also those who graduated from reform schools. It would tend not only to drive out the good students but frustrate the faculty as well.

Skills can be taught if the student has the interest and desire. Unless there is some organic deficiency, physical condition can be improved through diet, exercise and proper medical care. But deficiencies in social and moral attitudes are another problem. The young man who has not made an adjustment to the standards of society in his community or who comes from an environment where such standards are ambiguous or non-existent is not very likely to adjust satisfactorily to the more rigorous demands of military life.

Without trying to evaluate the social advantages of having the military services undertake the task of the social rehabilitation of marginal personnel, it should be sufficient to point out that such an effort involves an associated cost. The bill for such a program must be paid in terms of the diversion of military resources of men, installations and equipment which could more profitably, from the military point of view, be employed in training qualified people. It would entail hidden costs in terms of lowering the status, attractiveness and efficiency of the organizations with which they serve. It would involve some degree of expansion in the administrative effort and installations required in the punitive and correctional area for the increased percentage of delinquency.

The costs, and the adverse effect on the military establishment raise the question of whether the military organization is in fact the most effective instrument. A pretty good case could be made for accomplishing the job under the aegis of the Department of Health, Education and Welfare. Control of such a program could be placed in the hands of retired military personnel to provide a military type of environment if such were desired.

Most of the proposals for revision or modification of the selective service laws revolve around the questions of social rehabilitation, individual equity and uniformity of criteria. As we have seen, no matter what alternatives one might choose, some element of inequity is going to remain. The Armed Forces for the foreseeable future are going to require an ever-declining portion of the increasing numbers of young men reaching military age each year. In examining the alternatives, one might examine first the relative merits of each proposal in terms of the national good; second, its efficiency of operation and in utilization of available human resources; and, finally, its effects on the military services.

The first alternative is universal military training. This proposal has been current off and on almost since before World War I. Many prominent personalities have endorsed it. It has been strongly pushed by the military services, particularly, on several occasions, by the Department of the Army. It has been said that it would perform the citizenship training and socializing mission previously discussed. By giving every physically qualified male three to six months of military training on active duty, we would provide a pool of trained manpower available for an emergency, and would provide trained personnel support for our reserve forces and reduce the requirement for active duty forces. The program would be more just and equitable for all than selective service. This proposal was seriously put forward and publicly discussed following World War II and was set aside as being unnecessary. After the Korean War broke out, it was again considered, basically accepted as a principle in the Universal Military Service and Training Act of 1951, and subsequently explored in great detail by a Presidential Commission which supported it and by the Congress which eventually did not. It has considerable appeal, not the least of which is the fact that it provides the closest approach to individual equity achieved by any of the proposals.

There are, however, a number of disadvantages which tend to make the plan exceedingly difficult to implement. Foremost among these is the problem of handling numbers. About 1,700,000 young men become 18 each year and the number is climbing. In 1952, it was estimated that the personnel required to support such a training effort, acting as the trainers, administrators, and housekeepers for the training installations, would demand the services of about one man for every two trainees. This would mean that we would have to devote something over 500,000 men of our current military establishment of about three million to the task of universal military training alone. This would either require a substantial addition to the size of our existing military establishment or a substantial reduction in its commitments and capabilites. In addition, the costs in terms of facilities, obligations for pay, medical care, clothing, food, bonuses, or reimbursements in case of service-connected disability would add substantially to our current military budgets without a proportional increase in our effective, ready military forces. On the one hand there is a limit to the amount of training that could be profitably provided in basic training camps, while on the other hand we do not have a military structure of sufficient size to absorb all of the recruits thus provided. The training time even if extended to a year is still too short to incorporate the trainees as fully trained members of combat-ready units. The combat units so used would have their readiness status seriously degraded by the necessity of absorbing a high proportion of new recruits once a year.

Experience with education and training generally indicate that while there is some carry-over of skills or knowledge acquired, it tends to dissipate with time and disuse. Thus the training given, while not enough for immediate use in a combat unit, would gradually fade once the trainees leave the service. Events, since universal military training was studied in 1952, indicate that whatever else we do, we need a combat-ready active force for immediate action in support of the national interest. As we have seen, such a force requires long training and a higher percentage of higher skill levels. The hope that universal military training could act to reduce our standing forces is not nearly as bright today as it appeared to be fourteen years ago. Despite its obvious advantages in terms of equity, its citizenship training and socializing mission, the overall cost of the program and its tendency to reduce the efficiency of our active forces by giving them an additional training requirement argue against the adoption of this proposal.

The alternate proposal—for national service—is similarly long standing, having been proposed in a different form and context by President Roosevelt during World War II. Like universal military training, it has the egalitarian ring of idealism, equity and justice for all, at least to a point. When one reaches the point of deciding whether it should be compulsory or voluntary, the equity begins to break down. The concept itself has much to recommend if it were put forward as a proposal distinct from the problem of raising, equipping and training our Armed Forces. Setting the requirement for selecting young men for military service to one side, the problem of national service, either voluntary or compulsory, should be examined on its own merits. Problems of educational and training facilities, useful employment opportunities, length of service required, all should be studied in detail, as should the necessity or desirability of such a program. It would still leave to be answered the problem of what to do with the marginal personnel—the ones no one would want. The military professional would probably support the concept providing that in its operation it did not detract from the quality or quantity of manpower allocated the services, or give them an additional training or administrative burden beyond those they already have.

A third proposal which has many strong supporters is to provide individual equity through selection of service inductees by lot. This proposal would appear to have considerable appeal. If coupled with selections from the 18- to 19-year-old age groups with minimal deferments, it should provide decreased uncertainty as to when the individual might be called and decrease fears of favoritism through substituting random selection of chance for the decentralized judgment of draft boards in the community.

General Hershey himself, after several experiences with lottery selection, has expressed opposition to it on both practical and theoretical grounds. Disregarding the mechanical administrative problems imposed, it is doubtful whether it would in fact be any more equitable to the individuals concerned than the present system. The reduction of uncertainty could be procured through other means. If it is meant to obtain more equitable distribution among social groups, that too, could be accomplished by other means. The problem of deferring special categories will arise under any system, as does the problem of standards of qualification for military service. Considering fluctuations in the monthly and yearly draft calls, the lottery system would appear to have many difficulties.

Perhaps the greatest problem with the lottery proposal lies in its rationale and psychological impact on the services. Efficient and scientific management of our personnel would not support random selection. No employer in industry, government or education would say, "Here are my basic criteria. Now let's select our employees from among those available by drawing straws." How would the selectee evaluate his selection? The potential damage to the public image of the Armed Forces and to the morale and motivation of both professional and inducted personnel could be extensive.

As previously pointed out, the motivation of military men and the morale of military units rests in some part on their perception of social approval by the community. Under the lottery system, the veteran officer or noncommissioned officer might well deduce that military service is considered a form of punishment rather than a privilege of citizenship. Recruiting could be expected to become more difficult. Morale could be more difficult to maintain and such honor and prestige as exists in the military service could tend to wither away.

A counter-proposal which has been put forward from time to time and which is still a contender for public attention is that of abolishing the draft entirely and committing our national security into the hands of paid professionals, hired for the job. This concept has a basic appeal and much can be said in its favor. It should provide the military forces with personnel who want to be there. It would relieve the government from the unpleasant and politically unprofitable requirement for sending its greetings in support of military recruitment, with all the uncertainties, inequities and problems that entails. It is also claimed that this solution would contribute to increased efficiency resulting from longer terms of service, less training load, and greater continuity. From the viewpoint of the professional, these arguments appear very attractive.

The other side of the coin, however, holds some basic drawbacks which would appear to rule out this solution at least for the foreseeable future. First, the Armed Forces as a whole have not been able, since World War II, to maintain an adequate force structure based on voluntary recruiting.

A recent study on this subject, made in the Department of Defense and presented by Assistant Secretary of Defense, Thomas D. Morris, in the Hearings before the House Committee on Armed Services, on June 30, 1966, concluded that an all-volunteer force under current policies would fall far short of any force level required since 1950 or projected for the 1970's, and that the quality of personnel procured including officers, medical personnel and skilled technicians would fall well below our increasing requirements. In pursuing the idea that higher pay or other incentives might bring forward an increase in volunteering, the study determined that pay alone is a much less potent motivator than might be supposed. Only 4 per cent of those questioned felt that pay equal to civilian standards would influence them, and only 17 per cent felt that considerably higher than civilian pay would provide an inducement. In determining how much pay increase would be required to stimulate voluntary enlistments, estimates indicated an order of magnitude of 20 to 50 per cent for officers and 80 to 280 per cent for enlisted men. There appeared to be no practical financial inducement sufficient to entice physicians or dentists to enter the services. Nor did the area of fringe benefits appear to be any more likely to produce results. Less than 3 per cent of those questioned indicated them as being important in career selection. Only in the area of education and training did special measures appear to have an effect on 8 to 29 per cent of the 16- to 19-year-olds questioned. However, since the "GI Bill of Rights" is already in law and operation, it was concluded that there was little more that could be added to increase inducements for volunteering above present levels. These findings pretty well corroborate the general feelings of those who have associated with our young soldiers over the years. Military motivation is not generally a commodity for sale. Even if it were, we might not elect to live with the results of such a program.

If we were to assume that we could raise a force for service in Vietnam on the basis of pay, the amounts paid would have to be competitive with those offered by civilian contractors or shipping lines in the same area. These rates are high. We could find ourselves enmeshed in problems of differential pay for different areas of the world with all the difficulties that would surround its administration: equitable assignments, rotation, living standards, gold flow and impact on local economies. Changing from a $110-a-month private to a $240- or $300-a-month private would amount to a quantum leap forward in problems that a professional company commander would shudder to contemplate in the field or in garrison. The morale, esprit and discipline of a fighting force would tend to be substantially undermined. The personal risks, deprivations and discipline of military service do not appear to be compatible with a financial motivation. How do we get men in large numbers to risk their lives for a monetary reward? History tells us that mercenary soldiers tended to exhibit considerable reluctance to undergo serious risks and hardship, and were frequently most difficult to discipline and control.

While Secretary Morris stated he felt the increased cost of a volunteer payroll might amount to about five to nine billion dollars, it could well come to much more if fringe benefits and combat bonuses were added and the services required of military personnel continued to be the high risk and high sacrifice variety now needed in Vietnam.

There are, of course, other disadvantages. A professional force envisages a long service, high pay, high investment per man, organization. This implies increasing ages with stagnation in the lower officer and enlisted grades, higher percentages of married men, more dependents, more household goods to move, higher standards of living expected, with greater impact on local economies.

We also could expect that there would be an increasing loss of contract and rapport between the American society and its defenders. This would work two ways. The military would lose sympathy or understanding of civilian attitudes and values, while the citizen would lose interest in the military problems facing the professional force. The abandonment of the requirement for the citizen to perform military service would have far-reaching effects in degrading social solidarity and patriotic commitment. It would also tend to deprive the country of any sizeable body of trained reserves. One could well foresee the pressure building up for the next step—that of hiring soldiers wherever we could hire them the most cheaply. Since they could be procured most cheaply abroad, we might soon find ourselves in the foreign legion business, with progressively fewer citizens interested in the risks, pay or working conditions of military service. The dangers and pitfalls in this approach have been pretty thoroughly explored; few would recommend it.

CONCLUSIONS

As one views the problem of military recruitment and its impact on society from the viewpont of the using agencies, the following points stand out:

a) The present draft system does accomplish its objectives although with some inequity and lack of uniformity. There may be ways in which the efficiency of the system could be improved.

b) Both universal military training and a volunteer professional force would involve an excessive expenditure of funds and incur other disadvantages which generally outweigh the advantages foreseen.

c) The lottery system would substitute chance for a rational system of selection, would not substantially increase equity for individuals, and could well have a most undesirable impact on military motivation and morale.

d) National service may be a most desirable concept when required in the national interest, but it is not, in fact, a reasonable substitute for the draft. It would not substantially improve the degree of equity for the individual but could have desirable effects in citizenship training and in providing services not otherwise obtained for our national commuinty.

After thus criticizing other proposals, the user of military manpower should be prepared to offer his version of how the selection should be made to fill his needs. Looking at personnel selection from its impact on the military services and the welfare of the nation they defend, one might propose something like the following:

The ultimate welfare of a democracy lies in the hands of its informed and educated citizenry. Its freedom depends on the amount of sacrifice they are willing to offer in its defense. To divorce military service from the duties of citizenship would be the height of folly, inviting ultimate disaster. At the same time the hard facts are that for the foreseeable future we will have an increasing number of our younger citizens with a decreasing percentage required for military service. It is obviously in the national interest to obtain the most efficient military forces possible at the least possible cost, while involving at least some portion of our citizens in the process. Efficient and effective teams and organizations depend on high-caliber personnel, while citizen involvement implies a degree of rotation and obligatory service.

We know from experience that not all of our best young men seek to serve their country in the military service We also tend to feel that those who eventually become our national leaders in government or business are somehow in a better position to evaluate national goals, objectives and problems if they have, in fact, performed duty in the Armed Forces. Social approval, recognition and status enhance the attractiveness and morale of the services. Good men in an organization tend to attract others while low-quality personnel tend to drive them out.

With these considerations in mind, it would appear that the selective service system should be retained essentially as presently constituted with such improvement in administrative efficiency, uniformity of criteria and equity as may be devised.

All young men should register for the draft at age 18 and be administered the appropriate mental, physical and aptitude examinations to determine their relative qualifications for service in the Armed Forces.

Those found best qualified for military service according to their mental, physical and aptitude tests would be inducted into the service in the order of their qualification.

Deferments should be granted for the purpose of completing high school, undertaking such college programs as may be necessary to provide officers, physicians or other specialists, or in isolated instances for severe hardship. All those so deferred should be required to perform military service on the completion of their educational program or termination of hardship.

Those inducted into the service and who satisfactorily complete the required term of at least two years should be provided educational assistance upon leaving the service, as is presently the case.

The annual call should be taken primarily from the 18-year-old group plus those who had completed their educational programs and were now ready for service. In most cases the annual call could be taken from that one year group. However, since emergencies may crop up, the 19-year group should be retained on a standby basis. If not inducted after their nineteenth year or not deferred for cause, they should be excused from further liability for military service. This would reduce uncertainty substantially since the majority would be selected the first year after registration.

Reserve forces would continue to be maintained, as at present, by volunteers with short periods of active duty for training and larger periods of reserve obligations, plus those draftees who had not completed their total obligations.

This system should be supported with modest and reasonable incentives for volunteering and reenlisting through the provision of adequate housing, supporting services, bonuses, and pay level sufficient to provide the standard of living appropriate to rank and responsibility.

Those not qualified for military service or those qualified but not sufficiently highly qualified to be called in any year would be available for a national service program, a citizens' rehabilitation program, further education or entrance into the labor pool. While undesirable, it might prove necessary to exempt from military service some highly qualified individuals for essential service in other areas. Such exemptions should be held to a minimum and based solely on national requirements.

The proposed system should have the following advantages:

a) It would be just, since the selection would be based essentially on qualifications of aptitude and ability. The spread of aptitude and ability should be sufficiently distributed through social strata to avoid criticism as to equity. It should be as least as fair as the lottery system and considerably more efficient and effective from the military point of view.

b) It should provide high-quality military manpower to the services, reducing training costs and administrative losses, and fostering more efficient operations, thus producing the most effective force for the least amount of money.

c) The high quality of personnel and the effectiveness of military units should enhance the attractiveness of the services, fostering voluntary recruitment. This should reduce to minimum levels the number of young men that might actually be required for induction.

Disadvantages might be predicted in the following areas:

a) Students desiring to enter educational programs not considered essential for military service might have to postpone their studies for two years while they performed their required active service.

b) It might be found that aptitude and ability were not evenly distributed through the various strata of society, thus denying some groups the opportunity to serve.

c) In order to provide greater equity, the acceptance of the 18- to 19-year-old group as the basis for selection involves accepting a group which on the whole are not as mature and reliable as those over 20 and who do not possess the same civilian skill levels.

In summary, regardless of the system selected, when considering the method of recruiting for the military services the most critical objectives of the nation as a whole should be given priority in the order of their critical relationship to the national welfare. In any assessment of critical objectives, national security must rank among the highest. The percentage of our national budget devoted to national security programs is a valid indicator of their relative importance. It would appear illogical and incongruous if we were to allocate our human resources in any different priority.

Second, it would appear unwise to confuse our purposes by assigning multiple objectives to one program. Social welfare and the rehabilitation of citizens are certainly worthwhile programs, but they should not be confused with programs to improve the efficiency of our Armed Forces.

Finally, we should not seek to avoid the hard facts of fundamental issues, basic requirements, available resources, and the demands of efficient procedure. The demand for equity and justice for individuals deserves due consideration in the hierarchy of requirements, but the requirements of the nation's welfare should come first.

NOTES

[1] George Washington University Human Resources Research Office, A *Preliminary Investigation of Delinquency in the Army*, Technical Report No. 5, April 1954, p. v-vi. See also U. S. Army Research Office, *Correlates of Disciplinary Record in a Wide Range Sample*, Technical Research Note 125, August 1962.

[2] American University Bureau of Social Science Research, "Optimum Age for Military Service," June 1951.

3

Occupational Crossover and Universal Military Training

PAUL A. WEINSTEIN

I. CAVEATS

The testimony submitted before the Armed Services Committee[1] on potential draft revision requires that attention be focused on some fundamental problems. The examination of these problems is a precondition to any constructive dialogue on the broader social and economic questions we face. Two particular geists, both at variance with each other, are relevant to the proposal of Section IV of this paper.

A romantic retelling of old war stories tends to inflate the experience in terms of its benefits while discounting its horrors. This finds expression in the pro-universal military service argument which emphasizes the moral fillip of the military. It forever has use as a tonic to a flagging moral capacity in the country. Posed in this way, the military invests not in the economists' "human capital" with market value, but in a more elusive stuff without which nations and civilizations fall.

While I do not doubt that there is a "good" produced by the military experience, the emphasis therein raises two problems. First, it broaches the legitimate question of the functions and influences of the military in a democratic society. To question the military as a source of virtue is totally appropriate. To restate it in the style of the economist: Could not this spirit be created in a better, more democratic and cheaper way? Second, the moral "value added" produced by the military is not measurable. That does not mean it should be dismissed, but it calls for a more rigid requirement to determine the appropriate weight in evaluating alternative programs.

This pro-military position is clarified when we join the anti-militarist argu-

The author is Associate Professor of Economics and Director, Military Training Study, University of Maryland.

The research underlying this paper was carried out under a grant from the Ford Foundation and augmented by a grant by the U.S. Office of Education. Richard Beaumont, formerly of Industrial Relations Counselors, was invaluable by offering encouragement, resources and access to strategic individuals. Assisting me in this paper are Eugene L. Jurkowitz, Richard Wertheimer, Elaine Greenbaum and Alice Weinstein. The views expressed herein are the responsibility of the author and do not represent either the Ford Foundation or the U.S. Office of Education. The quantitative data presented here are preliminary and incomplete.

ment and disassemble the civilian manpower contribution of the military. First, the military trains individuals who may transfer their training and job experience and economic perceptions to their civilian life, thereby enriching themselves, the economy, and society.[2] The former contribution is quantifiable and its specification is my primary research endeavor.

The use of the organized military structure and training system is not designed to encourage militarism, but merely a realistic acknowledgement that the military is a potent resource. It is only prudent that we try to use this asset for non-military purposes. I reject the use of the military to expand the internal value system.

I do strongly urge that we consider the use and development of by-products from the military system in a formal and structured way. The potentials of this use are now barely understood.

II. POTENTIALS OF THE MILITARY

The potentials for using the military can be developed through a large number of avenues. Broad political mandates dictate that the government create full employment, maximize economic growth, encourage political and economic growth of the world and maintain reasonably stable prices. Very specific ends that we wish to see produced supplement these broad goals. For example, an educated, healthy society residing in a favorable, unpolluted environment, safe in person and property both in home and outside are now part of the explicit goals of the United States.

To achieve the large array of public goals has always prompted the creation of non-private activity. The development of the free school system from the organization of the land grant college to the primary schools (and next, possibly, nurseries) has been partly prompted by the desire to increase a productive manpower pool.

Unfortunately the interrelations between the governments manpower activity and general goals like economic growth have not been clearly noted. Thus, one of the most crucial aspects of the growth of the United States economy in the nineteenth century was development of internal transport, particularly the railroad. This period of railroad building is viewed also as one of the significant accomplishments of the free market. It has not been noted that this accomplishment was significantly aided by the manpower contribution of the military. The technical requirements of manpower and material logistics were worked out by the only group with the experience and training to do the job: former military officers. Similarly, the "human capital" invested by the military proved *most* beneficial if not absolutely essential in the organization and command of the large work force necessary to construct the railroad. There is no need to labor the point that what was true in the United States then is plain to see in most underdeveloped areas today. It is less obvious that this phenomenon is still operative today in the United States.

The pursuit of better health and the preservation of law and order currently are two of the most clearly desired social goals. Manpower is a limiting resource in satisfying our needs in both safety and health. Efforts at bettering our lot in the form of new legislation authorizing expenditures of funds for medical aid may only serve to raise the prices of services and not increase the flow of real product—or the service may come, but only slowly and at great cost.

Protection is an excellent example of the type of potential we have for meeting our goals. The statistical details on crime dramatize our future needs. For example, there is an accelerated growth of crime against property in smaller cities and suburban areas. But even if the rates of crime for different types and sizes of communities were not to worsen, the demographic trend in our country would result in an increase of crime nationally. While considerable efforts need to be applied to the efficient use of the work force in the protection area through such devices as better telecommunications and transport, as well as in the quality of police, there is strong indication that the incidence of crime is universally related to the number of police.

We are already aware of the difficulties faced by communities in staffing their police forces. Many cities are recruiting nationally to get their share of the limited supply. While the demand for numbers of police have increased, our requirements for police are also on the rise. We desire a better quality of police, men who have no unhealthy, anti-social desires for uniform, and gun and club; who can do more complex jobs with a more sophisticated technology. To hire, screen and prepare this cadre is expensive and for many communities almost impossible. However, what a community purchases when it cannot buy adequate police is more crime.

The military in 1959 trained over 26,000 police. In the Army, for example, these men are carefully screened and have a minimum general aptitude above the mean score in the Army. After eight weeks of basic unit training, they receive eight weeks of advanced individual training and then further time is spent in basic unit training before they are sent out to work with supervisors as a member of the military police operating unit. Having observed the training and duties of the police in the military and in the civilian sector, I must conclude that there is little wanting on the military side. In fact, except for some of the more sophisticated metropolitan police, or state police systems, the teaching, curriculum and experience in the military cannot be duplicated in most local systems. In the two years in which they serve, they get an excellent background and experience. The question that we must ask is, what do they do with this experience after service?

An indication of the ease with which these trained people may transfer can be seen from the system that prevailed in New York City. Less than 10 per cent of the police force in New York have MP experience. There, a normal waiting period between passage of the Civil Service test and entry into the police academy is 12 to 18 months. In New York, no credit of any type either in terms of higher wages or better position is given to the candidate with MP background. (At the other extreme are communities that hire military police without further checking their background.) I would suggest that we have not as a nation tried to tap this source of human capital.

Health service improvement is another significant national goal. Our desires in this area have come up sharply against the reality of limited qualified personnel. The health professions in recognition of labor shortages in many occupations are experimenting with new modes of organization. In addition to the global deficit, this shortage has a geographic dimension that creates serious special problems.

Physicians, like all professionals, have a strong urge and need for togetherness. Hospitals, as the nodal point of the profession, tend to be clustered in urban areas. The density of demand permits the luxury of a variety of professional activity, as well as allowing the use of the most modern equipment, this in a field that is markedly changing its technology. Many of the sparsely settled areas in the United States are ill-equipped to meet their minimum medical needs, and the situation is unfortunately deteriorating. Without having to specify the exact needs, there appears to be a real shortage in the health field that precludes adequate medical care.

Public policy to overcome the problem is expressed in programs to increase the future supply of doctors, nurses and technicians. We support our existing medical schools more intensively, and we encourage new institutions to produce a greater supply of professionals at the top levels. At the same time, we initiate training under a burgeoning population of community colleges and technical centers to train for the expanding paramedical fields.

Despite those programs, a casual enumeration of some of our health goals and activities will illuminate the depth of the health manpower problem:

1) We are trying to stimulate increased medical care through localized service for our poor as a device to reduce poverty.

2) We encourage underdeveloped areas to increase their health facilities on a massive basis. This stimulus is projected through our lending programs.

3) We are dependent upon a supply of foreign doctors, interns and residents to fill the gap in our current demand for medical service. Even with a sizable importation of foreign doctors, our hospitals are woefully understaffed.

4) Nurses are in short supply. While the market is attempting to solve the problem, the supply is artificially restricted by professional organizations. This is further abetted by the teaching hospitals who require student nurses as a source of competent cheap labor.

5) Professionalization is increasing along with its normal by-product, controlled access to skill ladders.

When we put these observations together, they give adequate grounds for a pessimistic appraisal of programs to improve overall medical standards. Alongside this dismal picture, we have the simple fact that the military each year releases nearly 60,000 individuals who have served in the health professions. These individuals cover the broadest range of medical occupations. At the top of this professional ladder, the military provides training and experience to doctors, such as residency training at pay superior to non-military hospitals. At a slightly lower level the Army is initiating a nursing school to satisfy its voracious appetite for medical services. There is a remaining understructure of paramedical occupations that stand as a great potential for satisfying our goals in the health field.

The utilization of this resource requires solutions to some difficult problems. The medical system in the military has special characteristics that make it unique in the United States. The military, faced with a potential need for medical services that would be immediate, geographically dispersed, and frequently dispensed under hostile conditions, has had to improvise a structure for producing medical services and an occupational system to carry out the mission. Thus, the military provides two avenues to improve overall health needs.

First is the provision of a model of organization for a potential reorganization of production. Accompanying this is an array of production and manpower management techniques that are systematically altered by the military. And it must be noted that the military is not a monolith. The diversity of missions among the services provides a number of models that can be followed.

Second is the transfer of the military skills and experiences of the large number of paramedical personnel. Some of these occupations we know have immediate counterparts in the civilian area—primarily X-ray and laboratory technicians and a growing group of therapists. Other paramedical occupations are rich in medical experience. For example, medical corpsmen perform discretionary activities of diagnosis and medication. There is no occupation like the medical corpsman in the civilian sector, and the most difficult problems of crossover occur here. The problems focus on what role these veterans would play within the civilian medical structure and how they could be fitted within the existing pecking order. (Complicating the crossover is the fact that the wages of the non-professionals are dominated by females.)

From the scant data collected on the careers of retired military personnel, we know that medical occupations have the highest rate of transferability. Some 37 per cent of military officers transferred their skills compared to 25 per cent over all.[3] There is considerable bias in these figures, for some of these retired people are doctors and nurses who have of course stayed in their professional activities. The actual degree of transfer as well as the potential (under various specified conditions of wages and job structure) should whet the appetite of anyone concerned with meeting the problem of supplying health services.

What has been said about police and medical personnel holds true for a very large number of military occupations. The potential for expanding the trained work force in many occupational and industrial areas is related to the rate at which veterans transfer their skills from the military, as well as the rate in which the population is exposed to military training. In considering the overall educational goals of the United States, as well as the services which we wish to see produced, it is only prudent that we consider the military as a supply agent of these services along with other institutions. While we may ultimately reject the use of the military as a training institution, it would not be reasonable to eliminate them before we considered their potential.

III. CROSSOVER EXPERIENCE OF ARMY NON-CAREERISTS

The Defense Department faces a dilemma. Occupational linkage is apparently a strong variable in fostering enlistment, while a negative factor in reenlistment. This leads to ambivalence in the military's attitude toward crossover. The problems, while not insurmountable, cannot be perfectly resolved. I shall not concern myself with the retention problem.

The data for this section are derived from a longitudinal analysis of a sample of non-careerists in the Army. The broad occupational groups were chosen on the basis of degrees of potential crossover—largely through *a priori* analysis—as well as significance in the overall training effort of the services. The broad groupings are shown in Table 1.

The universe is composed of all reservists, non-careerists in these occupations who had been out of full-time service for a minimum of two years. From this universe a random sample was drawn. Extracted military records, as well as a telephone interview, provide the substance of the material that follows. These represent first and crude results, which I shall summarize for this conference.

TABLE 1

Occupational Groupings Used in Military Training Study

Group	Occupation
1.	Police (POL)
2.	Electronic Data Equipment Skills (EDP)
3.	Operatives—Construction and Repair (Ops)
4.	Trades Related to Telephone (Tel)
5.	Radio, Radar, TV and Auto Repair (TV)
6.	Teamster and General Warehousing (Teams)
7.	Esoteric Skills—High Formal Training (Eso)
8.	Combat Skills—Infantry (Inf)
9.	General Military—Duty Soldier (Duty)
10.	Business and Service Activities (Ser)

As anticipated, volunteers with some vocational preference had a good opportunity to gain experience in those occupations. Some 44 per cent of the volunteers served in their preferred activity, while only 19 per cent of the draftees were so benefited. Further, volunteers with an occupational preference at the time they entered the service had a 69 per cent assignment rate in those occupations compared to 45 per cent for draftees.

An examination of overall experience indicates some 30 per cent of non-careerists used their military occupations in their first post-service job. However, the rate varies between the draftees and enlistees. For example, draftees had a 33 per cent utilization rate as compared to 25 per cent for volunteers. (One should not rely too heavily upon these gross figures for drawing conclusions about transference.)

Inside the sample there is a high variance in utilization among the component occupational categories. A considerable percentage of the draftees' spillover from the military to the civilian is in occupations 2, 3 and 4, specifically the operatives, telephone trades and electronic data processing. We are unable at this time in our analysis to discern the relation between the military occupation of draftees and their pre-military experience. The assignment practices of most services, particularly the Army, is significant in interpreting the results. The Army draftees are older and therefore should be somewhat attached to an occupation. Policy dictates that the Army utilize pre-military skill within the service wherever possible. Thus, for plumbers, electricians and telephone repair people, it is quite likely these individuals would be given a direct duty assignment; that is, awarded an MOS immediately after basic training. Thus, we may be correlating the post-military with the pre-military experience. With these first data we are unable to weigh the impact of the military on human capital formation.

In comparing draftees and enlistees, different patterns emerge concerning the impact of time on usage. There seems to be a tendency for draftees to let their military skills atrophy with time. Thus 41 per cent of the individuals who had a preference for an occupation used their experience in their first job while the rate is only 34 per cent for the job changers. This experience is repeated for the group that served in their preferred occupation. In the first post-military employment, some 59 per cent used their skills as compared to 44 per cent for the switchers. Disaggregating the data by occupational groups, one sees a tendency for draftees who had worked in groups 2, 3 and 4 to transfer away from their military skills. One possible interpretation is that military experience encourages occupational mobility, even for individuals who had used their prior experience in the military.

A reverse trend appears to take place in group 1, police. Time encourages usage of these skills, possibly as a way of overcoming market barriers. This experience of ex-military police through time holds true for all draftees, whether they had a job preference, no preference, or had served in their preference.

Two final observations on the inter-temporal experience of draftees are in order. First is the experience with group 7 skills. These involve substantial formal technical training and are occupations that require careful screening for mathematical and mechanical aptitude. Draftees who had not thought of using these potentials move toward this activity. This category exemplifies how individuals exposed to an occupation transferred their experience to it, even though they have no vocational interest at entry. Interestingly enough, the military manuals claim these occupations have no civilian correlates.

This time pattern occurs again, but to a lesser extent for group 6, the general warehousing and teamster operations. The failure of that category to decline through time may be an indication of the wage rate paid to teamsters.

These movements are also observable in the volunteer group. For example, military police show very low transfer on their first post-service job for all groups. The group 1 switchers show a marked usage for all preference groups. The lag in utilization by military police may again be attributable to the barriers in the job market. The general inter-temporal trend appears to be similar for draftees and enlistees.

There is a marked difference in utilization between volunteers and enlistees. Draftees tend to use their skills more readily than volunteers. This is so for individuals who had job preferences, but is most striking for veterans who did not have job preferences. When these individuals were exposed to occupations in the military, they attempted to use the experience more readily. This is suggestive of the force the military may have in teaching individuals who are forced into a skill which is convertible.

The highest transference for any group is demonstrated for draftees who served in their preferred skill. A tentative conclusion is that forced service is not necessarily a deterrent to crossover. One must hold back on this conclusion generally, but restraint is most important for the draftees who served in their preferred field. Our conclusions await analysis of the pre-military, military occupational relations. Nevertheless, it is likely that the general trend of higher utilization by draftees should be of considerable significance in future draft and manpower policy.

The view most people have about the usage of military experience is confirmed with force for some groups. It is quite apparent that all groups serving in electronic data processing have in fact substantially transferred their skills. The group is highest for volunteers who had a desire and received some training in this field. It is slightly less for draftees, but one is encouraged to note there is a substantial increase in utilization through time for the draftees with no occupational preference.

Fabled in story are the millions of ex-G.I.'s who have gone into TV, radio and automobile repair. We do observe a tendency for this group to utilize their skills, but with a time lag.

We are not now prepared to speculate on the civilian activities of group 8.

That is, individuals who through time found a market use for their combat infantry training even though they had no prior occupational interest. It will be of no small interest both to this study and the general public to uncover the occupational crossover for light and heavy weapons infantrymen.

In order to fully investigate the alternatives of occupational transfer, respondents were questioned about secondary jobs. No strong relationships were found. One surprise was that the TV, radio and automobile repair group were a high moonlight group, but the percentage of moonlighting related to their military experience was inconsequential.

For policy reasons, two additional sets of information are useful. First, what use did the veterans who looked for jobs find for their experience in the market? Second, what factors discouraged crossover?

A first appraisal of the veteran's estimate of the job value of the experience is shown in Table 2. The entire sample is collapsed in this table. The base is all reservists who were hired for positions sought based upon their military experience. The results are inconclusive as the total is significantly less than the total numbers reporting crossover. The tentative implications are either that the market undervalues the training, or the experience has no convertibility.

TABLE 2

Veteran Appraisal of Benefit Derived in Obtaining a
Job Related to Military Experience

	Percentage	Number
Received better job title	37	45
Received better starting salary	14	17
No help	48	58
Don't know	1	1
	100	121

The relation of pay, retention in the military and civilian utilization are all intertwined. For example, for both draftees and enlistees low pay dominates in groups 1 through 7 and in 10 as the reason for non-transfer. This becomes even stronger when fringes and advancement are joined with pay. It would appear that the argument of military people with reference to losing technically trained first termers to higher pay civilian correlates is erroneous. The individuals who move out of these have skills, high ability and extremely broad job and income potential. They appear to use them. Groups 6 and 7, teamsters as well as esoteric skills, do not regard pay as the primary block, but a joint factor with poor market fitting. Fortunately, group 8 finds difficulty in locating jobs, and group 9—probably the lowest occupation—also shows poor fit. (The reason we suspect is low market perception by the individuals.)

All of the findings indicate that transference of specific training from the military and civilian can be enhanced. The policies that will facilitate the increased utilization of these skills basically fall into two categories. First, that there be a more systematic effort at job counseling prior to severance from the service; individuals should be made aware of the potentials which await them in the civilian market for their experience. Other labor market services should include attempts to educate employers on the basic skills of these veterans, as well as lowering the barriers which may retard transference; for example, a reduction of the police waiting period. The second major activity would be attention to wage rates paid in certain skilled occupations. It appears obvious that an ample supply of police can be obtained by raising wages. A lower real cost to the economy would result through crossover of skills rather than training *de novo*. Attrition may be minimized and therefore the value added of this training could exceed alternative forms of human capital formation. Having considered how transference might be altered, it is necessary to examine the broadening of the base of military training.

IV. MILITARY SERVICE AND HUMAN CAPITAL

The potential value that the military has for the economy is determined in part by the proportion of the population that serves the military. We have indicated that transfer can be effected for those who have served. We can now conjecture on the implications and consequences of spreading this experience across a larger population group.

The military acquisition policy should maximize the certitude of service. The known probability but high likelihood of different types of wars in the future implies a very low probability of certain non-service. Unstable manpower requirements yield an altered set of specifications at the induction centers. Therefore, we should warrant that all citizens will be put through the military system, leaving policy and operational flexibility in the age at which a person would serve, as well as the length of the tour and the compensation both while in uniform and subsequent to release. The surety of service underlies the following analysis.

It is useful to subdivide the universe of theoretically potential soldiers into appropriate categories on an *a priori* judgment of potential capital crossover. Considering those that do not serve currently, the physically and mentally unfit are probably of greatest interest. The lowering of barriers, as conceived in the thinking behind the STEP (Special Training Education Program) and other programs would open the military to a large number of individuals. The immediate interest are those individuals who, under current deferment policy, would not have been deferred for other reasons at a later date, such as a 4-F who would be eligible for a student or an occupational deferment. More specifically, we are interested in that part of the population discussed in *One-Third of a Nation* (a report of young men unqualified for military service, by the President's Task Force on Manpower Conservation, January 1, 1964). The program to eliminate the sources of poverty suggested in that document fostered the Job Corps which, as one would have expected, has had a checkered career.

Any scheme, like the creation of an ad hoc institution, such as the Job Corps, or the various programs suggested to guarantee income are not without merit, but it would be useful to know how successful these schemes may be relative to processing this group through the military. The costs and benefits should consider the long-run effect on the individuals, as well as their progeny.

The utilization by the military of 1-Y personnel would not be without cost to the defense establishment, both in the extra time required for training and the training resources that would be diverted from other activities. We know that bringing this group into the services would increase the discipline problem of the military and raise the unwarranted assertion that the military is a haven for marginals and misfits.

Programs for upgrading were employed extensively during World War II through the USAFI program as a means of providing increased supplies of man-power required to end the war. This program has been in effect almost contin-uously since the end of World War II. An examination of this experience, even with limited data, may be important in making successful policy for the 1-Y group. The benefits are quite obvious in this program for those who receive training. A considerable flow of general human capital was produced which could be transferred. It is also likely that some "occupational specific" human capital may be transferred. It is assumed that the costs of capital formation are at least comparable to the real costs outside the military.

Success with 1-Y's will not yield a maximum return to the military, but will yield a substantial product to the economy. This potential spillover points again to the deficiencies of cost effectiveness applied to restricted bureaucratic lines.

The conscripts or volunteers who are not benefited by the program are not likely to be hurt by it either. The chances of recovery for this group are almost nil. For these people, the negative income tax in some form should be considered as a powerful potential for meeting society's obligation.

All that has been said for the 1-Y group, those who should be called in only in an emergency, may also apply to category five individuals. However, some necessary exclusions are obviously required. Instead of the current standard for admission—the likelihood of adapting to military training in reasonable time—an alternative is required. That is, a new set of tests should be instituted that would predict for appropriate characteristics, the likelihood of average salvage-ability. In the health and moral area, new tests and requirements of salvageability are surely needed.

The current standards for entry into the military have performed yeoman service for their historic mission, but a considered change in assignment must be accompanied by some alterations. This revised standard should open for con-scription all those who are now not acceptable for physical or moral reasons, as well as those who do not measure up to the mental requirements. All too fre-quently, there is a high intercorrelation between deficiencies of health, aptitude and conduct. This group would, in fact, represent the greatest challenge—and potentially a very high incremental return to society.

There are difficulties in applying this analysis to those who for educational and occupational reasons are now bypassed for service. Too frequently schools are used as a sanctuary from military service. The current deferment policy en-courages this. The liberality of free higher education also encourages many to enter the university to forestall making a career choice, and/or to indulge in the consumer aspects of university life. In either case, the consequences are gener-ally undesirable; they foster a misdirection of resources through time. The student, by not being available for other projects, forces an immediate loss to the economy. The loss in the longer view is sustained through the misapplica-tion of skills in career choice. While we are ill-prepared to measure these losses currently, our judgment suggests that they are considerable.

These losses would unquestionably be reduced by universal service. For ex-ample, the exposure to careers not directly related to college preparation, coupled with the time spent in the military, should encourage men to leave the military for a related civilian occupation, or go through occupational paths that do not require higher education.

A universal system of military training, without deferments whereby college students could escape forever, should force people into the military at a younger age. High school graduates might well not consider college on their return and those who were in exile there before might not go back. Too frequently, both at the undergraduate and graduate level, individuals opt for higher education who for their own and society's welfare should be elsewhere. The policy of inescapable service would help relieve this pressure.

The veterans who enter universities or technical training programs after leaving the service might add the same tone to schools that followed World War II. It is not unreasonable to conclude that the net impact of universal service on this group may be positive. Unfortunately, insufficient attention has been given to measuring the effectiveness in human capital terms of the various G.I. bills. It is most reasonable that some post-service compensation program should accompany universal service.[4]

Educational and occupational deferments that lead to avoidance of service have raised some of the most difficult questions of equity for the current system, as well as for all other proposals. Whether and how individuals should serve raises difficult questions of economic equity and efficiency, as well as political and social justice. If individuals who pursue higher education are treated no differently from those who enter the military at a younger age, the economy suffers through a reduction in the current and future flow of resources. The military is also disadvantaged by not having an appropriate base of skills, which it must somehow overcome. On the other hand, if these individuals are to escape for all time, questions of class and race bias in service and the inequitable distribution of responsibilities of citizenship are raised. The following special programs are needed to yield an efficient, as well as an equitable and just service.

1) Service should be performed at the youngest age consistent with other goals. Thus, the main group of conscripts or volunteers would enter the military upon completion of high school. Deferment would be given to those accepted to college until completion of the program, provided they maintained a standardized level of performance, and individuals deferred for higher education would know that the military is inescapable. A revised R.O.T.C. program as suggested below should be introduced to help meet the military manpower needs.

Appropriate branches of government, such as the National Research Council, Department of Health, Education and Welfare, as well as the Department of Defense should define critical skills required in the military and in the economy, as well as determine the training needed to acquire these skills. For example, physicians and teachers may be so classified, and the military would issue elongated deferments to individuals in these programs. The doctor completing medical school, or internship, could then be inducted, or deferred even longer, to absorb the added training required for a residency certification.[5] The military and society would then have a more valuable asset at their disposal.

2) The reserve officers training corps should be revised to provide more intensive military work and drill during vacations and less emphasis upon military work during the school year. Students faced with assured service may be more willing to undergo R.O.T.C., particularly if it were connected with other incentives such as partial scholarships or some assured summer income. This program would help fill the growing need now and in the future for junior officers, a need expanded by universal service.

3) The induction of the entire age pool would permit a shortening of service time within bounds needed for military effectiveness. It would generate more trained individuals than could be used for the specific military mission. Assignment would be based upon the military's needs, but once these are satisfied, the group already put through some level of pure military training would be used in other activities as required by overall governmental policy both within the United States and abroad.

No one could escape some military experience, which is desirable on equity grounds, but individuals would be placed where their training would be most useful. The productivity in occupations would accompany some sacrifice of service. An allotment of doctors, teachers, and police to communities throughout the country is not unthinkable. The pay of these individuals and the length of tours would be determined by a centrally controlled authority to help create parity between those who served in purely military capacities within the military and those who pursue professional endeavors in a quasi-military role. While not unlike alternative service, it is at once more equitable and responsive to the communities' needs.

It is plain that there is no perfect solution to the military service problem. We face a need for increased specific manpower as well as military manpower. The utilization of the military for activities which are not purely defense-related has great historical precedent. To aid in the creation and transfer of skills is a rational approach to policy in a body politic that continually asks its government to do more for it—and therefore must be prepared to sacrifice more in meeting its own demands.

NOTES

[1] Review of the Administration and Operation of the Selective Service System, Hearings before the Committee on Armed Services, House of Representatives, Eighty-ninth Congress, Second Session (June 23-30, 1966).

[2] This is not to dismiss offsets to this gain; that is, the economic contribution of the military is the net discounted income stream of having gone into another activity.

[3] Bureau of Social Science Research Study on Retired Military Personnel, p. 203, Table 142.

[4] These benefit programs should be treated as a positive instrument of policy, i.e. to achieve increased crossover and/or service in particular occupations.

[5] Length of time in service, as well as pay-rank status could be adjusted to the specific temporal requirements of the military, much as adequate supply and demand are determined by price in a market system.

4

Mental Test Failures

BERNARD D. KARPINOS

No matter what policies or doctrines are advanced with respect to the draft, the following fundamental factors must be considered in the general problem: (1) Potential availability of youths for military service; (2) military manpower requirements; and (3) standards of acceptability; that is, determining the qualification of these youths for military service.

Potential availability of youths is a predetermined factor. By taking 1963 as the base-year, the number of 18-year-olds reaching the age of military liability increased in 1965 by some one-third, and at present their number fluctuates around one-fourth above that of 1963: some 1.4 million youths became 18 years of age in 1963; the number had increased to about 1.9 million in 1965; it is expected to be about 1.8 million from 1966 through 1970, 1.9 in 1971 and 1972. In other words, the potential manpower reservoir has increased by roughly half a million youngsters over 1963.

Military demand for manpower—the second factor—depends on our prevailing and future military commitments, which are, of course, outside my range of possible assessment.

As to the third factor, "standards of acceptability for military service," ideally these standards should be determined independently of the other two factors. Technological advances in military science and techniques, and advances in medical knowledge and techniques, should be fundamentally the determining factors for any changes. Actually, however, this is not the case. Standards have been changed according to the demands for manpower and its availability. This has been specifically true with respect to the mental standards; they were raised twice since 1958, and were recently lowered because of the Vietnam crisis.

These changes in the mental requirements have impinged upon the group of youths that is most likely to be called upon in case of manpower shortage, and it is this group that seems to be a major concern in discussions of the draft. For these reasons, the present analysis deals with the disqualifications for failing the mental tests.

Special investigations have indicated that those who could not qualify for mental reasons were principally youths who lacked sufficient education—dropouts and, in general, youths of low quantitative and qualitative levels of education; youths who came from poor economic groups, and who were mainly "job seekers" (that is, they had a relatively high rate of unemployment). These find-

The author is Special Assistant for Manpower, Office of the Surgeon General, Department of the Army.

ings reflect to a high degree the potential civilian productivity of these youths, as well as their future adjustment in civilian life. These findings are further accentuated by the fact that wide geographic and racial variations have been found in the disqualifications.

A proper evaluation of these findings certainly requires a full understanding of these mental tests: How did they originate? What are their objectives? What is the meaning of the mental test scores? What changes occurred?

The basic mental test for military service has been the Armed Forces Qualification Test (AFQT), supplemented beginning in August 1958 by the aptitude-area tests: ACB and AQB. The AFQT is discussed in the following section; the ACB and AQB in the section after.

ARMED FORCES QUALIFICATION TEST (AFQT)

Evolution of AFQT

The Armed Forces Qualification Test (AFQT) evolved from the experience gained by the Armed Forces with selection of men for military service in World War II and during the period immediately following the war—with the experience of the Alpha and Beta mental tests of World War I in the background. This accumulated experience strongly indicated a necessity of finding means by which the examinee's mental ability could be reliably assessed as to his potential trainability and usefulness for military service.

The Alpha and Beta tests of World War I may be thus regarded as the prototype of the AFQT, and the Army General Classification Test (AGCT), used in World War II by the military services, as its progenitor. After World War II, when each military service resorted again to its own recruiting of manpower, each of them developed its own mental tests for selection. Though different in structure, primarily with respect to cut-off scores, the tests were essentially the same with respect to content areas, relying on the time-honored items of vocabulary, arithmetic, and spatial relationships.

In 1948, anticipating a request for a uniform mental test as a result of the military unification provided by Congress, the services set up a working group for such a test to be used by all of them. This group agreed on the following with respect to objective and structure of the test: (1) the test should represent a "global" measure of mental ability; (2) it should, therefore, contain items like those used by the various services in their individual classification tests—namely, vocabulary, arithmetic reasoning, and spatial relations; (3) it should minimize the importance of speed so that mentally capable persons who are somewhat slower would not be penalized; and (4) it should reduce to a minimum, consistent with clarity, the difficulty of verbal instructions relating to test items. The AFQT is the results of the cooperative effort of this working group.

Its Objectives

The AFQT was delegated a dual function: (1) to differentiate the examinees who can effectively acquire military skill from those who cannot—in order to eliminate the latter group—and (2) to provide a general index of the potential usefulness for military service of those who qualified for military service, commensurate with their mental ability. The AFQT thus became wider in scope than the Army General Classification Test (AGCT) which was used in World

War II for assessing the mental ability of the examinees after they entered the Army. The latter function, accomplished in World War II at the reception centers, was thus transferred from these centers to the examining stations. The main purpose of this transfer was to provide a basis for an equitable qualitative distribution of manpower among the military services—a purpose now defunct.

In its dual function the AFQT is used thus both as a prescreening and a classification device. (There was no such prescreening in World War I, and in World War II prescreening was primarily an educational assessment.)

Early Phases

During two and one-half years (from July, 1950, through December, 1952) two equivalent versions of the test were in operation: AFQT 1 and 2. These versions consisted of 90 questions equally divided among the three content areas —vocabulary, arithmetic, and spatial relationships. By structure, it was a spiral omnibus type of test; that is, it was arranged in cycles of increasing difficulty and each cycle contained an equal number of questions of comparable levels of difficulty in each content area. The test was designed to emphasize power rather than speed.

The passing score, based on multiple-choice answers (with four alternatives to each question) varied—particularly in the earlier part of this period. From July, 1950, to July, 1951, the minimum AFQT requirement, regardless of the type of items answered successfully, was equivalent to 39 correct answers; from July, 1951, through December, 1951, the minimum was equivalent to 34 correct answers; from December, 1951, the passing score (10 percentile) established by the 1951 UMT&S Act was equivalent to 27 correct answers. (Examinees who failed the mental test prior to December, 1951, were reexamined in 1952 on the basis of the new minimum standards established by the 1951 Act.)

The minimum requirement was devised to have the effect of eliminating 10 per cent of the "total potential military population" of the lowest aptitude.

Current Versions

At the beginning of 1953, AFQT 1 and 2 were replaced by modified versions 3 and 4. A fourth content area—one relating to mechanized ability—was added to the new versions. The newly added content area, commonly referred to as "tool knowledge" or "tool function knowledge," presumably provided for measuring a wider range of abilities applicable to military service.

As in the previous versions of the AFQT, the content areas were arranged in multiple-choice manner, four alternatives to each question. With respect to "use of tools" the problem was to choose from four possible tools or objects that which "goes with" or is "used with" the tool or object given in the question.

The new versions of the AFQT consisted of 100 questions (instead of 90) equally divided among the four content areas and arranged as their predecessors in progressive order of difficulty. With the introduction of the new versions, the formula for scoring was modified to provide specifically for greater accuracy in the test scores close to the minimum standards of acceptance. Under the preceding tests, scores were based on the number of questions answered correctly. To counteract potential correct guessing, the new formula provided for subtracting a fraction (a third) of the number of questions answered wrongly from the number of questions answered correctly, not counting omitted questions.

The new scoring formula was not designed to affect the proportion of individuals that could qualify for military service but to insure that individuals who just barely pass the test could be utilized by the military service without extensive special training or schooling.

Under the new scoring procedure the required passing raw score was 25 (net) correct answers, but still equivalent to 10-percentile score established by law.

Since the mental test questions may become increasingly familiar or outmoded, and also because new research may suggest certain modifications in the questions, the tests are periodically revised or somewhat modified. Several versions of the test have been issued since AFQT 3 and 4 were instituted; at the present time, AFQT 7c and 8c are in use. Though the revised versions of the test have been somewhat modified in the arrangement of the cycles, their content areas, basic structure, and manner of scoring remain the same as in the initial AFQT 3 and 4.

Standard Population and Percentile Score

As previously stated, the test has been designed not only to measure the examinees ability to absorb military training—in order to eliminate those who do not possess such ability—but also to provide a uniform measure of general usefulness for the service of those who are qualified. Consequently, in order to supply meaning to the scoring for comparative analysis, the examinee's "raw score" (based on correct "net" answers) is converted into percentile score, which then establishes his relative standing in a "standard population" used as a frame of reference. This is done on the basis of specific conversion tables applicable to the particular version of the test. Thus, the percentile score of 10 on the basis of his "raw score" of the AFQT indicates that only 10 per cent of the standard population scored lower and 90 per cent scored as high or higher than the examinee. A percentile score of 90 means that only 7 percent in the standard population scored as high or higher than the examinee. Since the percentile distribution by AFQT was correlated and equated with that of the AGCT of World War II, the AFQT percentile scores reflect World War II mobilization population. Actually, the AGCT was standardized on the military personnel, officers and enlisted men, of all military services, as of the end of 1944. Since exemptions and deferments from military service were then at a minimum, it was assumed that the 1944 military population could be taken as "unbiased representation of the civilian manpower pool with respect to age, education, occupational status, and geographic distribution." The current mobilization population may differ in its distribution from that of World War II. However, inasmuch as all AFQT scores were standardized on the same basis, the present comparative analysis is not affected by it.

Mental Groups

In order to provide a more workable (operational) classification of the examinee's degree of trainability, the percentile scores on the AFQT have been condensed into five mental groups. The mental groups, the current required "net" correct answers and the percentile score on the AFQT included in each mental group, and the percentages of the standard population with each mental group are as follows:

Mental Groups	Required Net Correct Answers	Percentile Score	Percent within Standard Population of Each Group
I	89-100	93-100	7
II	74-88	65-92	28
III	53-73	31-64	34
IV	25-52	10-30	21
V	24 or less	9 or below	10

The mental groupings—from mental group V to I—obviously indicate progressive gradation of trainability. The examinee's mental group is recorded on his examination reports, alongside his percentile score.

Mental Subgroups

In addition to classification by mental groups, the mental tests also provided during the period prior to August 1958 for subclassification of those who failed to meet the prevailing minimum mental requirement (below 10 percentile). This subclassification was supposedly intended to identify and differentiate among disqualified examinees those who could be expected to learn to perform military duties, "if training programs were adopted."

Based on special tests used for this purpose, the following four subgroups of mental group V were distinguished: V-1—marginal literate; V-2—illiterate-high mental; V-3—illiterate-marginal mental; and V-4—substandard mentality.

Relationship to Educational Attainment and I.Q.

The current tests have been planned not to be excessively dependent on the amount of formal education—particularly as it concerns the minimum required for passing the tests. However, our findings on the relationship between the mental qualification of American youths for military service and their educational achievement clearly indicate a positive association between the two. The higher the educational achievements of the particular youths, the higher their average scores were found to be on the mental test. This holds true for whatever the quality of their educational achievements has been. However, wide geographic variations have been revealed by the data. For instance, while college graduates will on the average score higher than their high school companions (geographically and ethnically defined) within that area, their score may not be higher on the average than those of high school graduates in another geographic area. Likewise, high school graduates will have, on the average, higher scores than their companions who completed only elementary school; however, their average scores may not be higher than those of youths with elementary school education in other geographic areas.

The examinee's score on the tests depends on several factors: on the level of his educational attainment; on the quality of his education (quality of the school facilities); and on the knowledge he gained from his educational training or otherwise, in and outside of school. These are interrelated factors which obviously vary with the youth's socioeconomic and cultural environment, in addition to his innate ability to learn—commonly understood as I.Q.

The present mental tests are not I.Q. tests. They were not intended for that purpose. As in the case of the AGCT tests, the practical concern of the tests is not to establish "what a soldier's native intelligence was at birth, before his mental development had been facilitated in any degree by stimulating surroundings, or hampered by a stultifying environment. The assignment officer wants an index of what the new soldier can be expected to learn, rather than a figure which purports to tell what he might have been able to learn if only he had had a better home, no enfeebling illness, and a great deal more education."[1]

APTITUDE AREA TESTS: ACB AND AQB

Initial Standards

From the time it was initiated in 1950 until August, 1958, the AFQT was the only mental test (except for the equivalent test in Spanish administered to Spanish-speaking examinees in Puerto Rico) used for determining the examinee's mental qualification for military service, and the minimum requirement, as fixed by the UMT&S Act, was 10 percentile. It was thus the prevalent minimum mental requirement during the Korean War period and it continued to be for five more years.

In August, 1958, additional mental tests, and additional minimum mental requirements based on these new tests, were introduced by virtue of Public Law 85-564 (July 20, 1958) authorizing the President, except in time of war or national emergency, to raise the mental and physical qualification for induction into the Armed Forces. The Army Classification Battery (ACB), was thus added to be used concomitantly with AFQT.

The ACB tests were designed to determine the person's potential usefulness in particular kinds of military jobs or assignments ("aptitude areas"); specifically, in the eight major occupational categories into which the jobs for enlisted men have been grouped. (Formerly, these tests were administered to all qualified examinees at the reception centers—after induction.)

In mid-September of 1961, the ACB was replaced by an equivalent AQB-1 (Army Qualification Battery)—a shorter (timesaving) test which was presumably better adapted for measuring the narrower range of aptitudes required as a screening device at the Armed Forces examining station.

In July, 1962, a new version of AQB was adopted, and it is still in effect. The present AQB comprises the following seven aptitude areas: IN—Infantry; AE—Armor, Artillery, or Engineering; EL—Electronics; GM—General Maintenance; MM—Motor Maintenance; CL—Clerical; and GT—General Technical.

Only those who score in mental group IV (10-30 percentile) on the AFQT are subject to these additional tests. The initial minimum mental requirement for the examinees in mental group IV was a score of 90 in each of any two of these seven aptitude areas.

Raised Standards

Beginning in May, 1963, the minimum mental standards for the aptitude areas were raised by requiring that the examinees in mental group IV have a minimum score of 80 on the GT (General Technical) aptitude area, plus a minimum score of 90 in each of any two of the other (excluding GT) aptitude areas. Under these requirements, GT became mandatory as a qualifying aptitude area, in addition to any two other aptitude areas. GT measures general ability such as understanding of written instructions or directions. The purpose of this additional requirement was to gain further assurance that the examinee will be able to perform successfully in the aptitude areas for which he qualified.

Lowered Standards

Under the impact of the intensified Vietnam crisis three changes in the AQB requirements have occurred: one in November, 1965; one in April, 1966; and one in October, 1966—all directed toward lowering mental requirements.

In November, 1965, the minimum for the AQB requirements established in May 1963 for mental group IV was changed with respect to high school graduates who scored between 16 and 30 on the AFQT, within mental group IV. Such high school graduates qualified for military service without any AQB requirements.

In April, 1966, the mental standards were further modified. For high school graduates scoring between 16 and 30 percentile on the AFQT, the standards remained as before; and for non-high school graduates with the same scores, the minimum requirement was lowered to a score of 90 in any two aptitude areas on the AQB (GT was no longer mandatory, though it could be one of the aptitude areas). Examinees, high school and non-high school graduates alike, scoring between 10 and 15 percentile on the AFQT had the same minimum requirement on the AQB as before, namely, GT 80 (mandatory) and a score of 90 on any other two aptitude area tests.

In October, 1966, the GT was completely eliminated as a mandatory requirement. Under these new requirements, high school graduates scoring between 16 and 30 percentile qualify without any AQB requirements; high school graduates between 10 and 15 percentile and non-high school graduates within mental group IV (10-30 percentile included) have to meet a minimum requirement of 90 in any of two aptitude areas, but no GT requirement.

Draftees in mental group IV failing the AQB (or ACB) requirements have been designated as "Trainability Limited"—not qualified now but who would qualify under mobilization standards. It has been a changeable classification. For instance, examinees who qualified on these aptitude area tests prior to May, 1963, could be classified as "Trainability Limited" under the higher May (1963) standards. On the other hand, examinees classified as "Tranability Limited" under the May (1963) standards could be classified as mentally qualified under the current lower standards.

Marginal Men

In discussions of manpower utilization, reference is repeatedly made to the "marginal man." But this term is not an absolute concept. Its meaning depends on the period to which it relates and on the standards of acceptability prevalent during that period. When referring at present to the "marginal man" failing the mental test, the following periods are to be considered:

1) Prior to August, 1958, when the minimum mental requirements were determined by AFQT alone (10 percentile). During this period the term "marginal man" referred to examinees in mental subgroups V-1 (marginal-literate and V-2 (illiterate-high mental)—subclassifications of mental group V. Basic data indicate that some 45 per cent of the white examinees in mental group V were classified as V-1 and V-2 during the period from January, 1953, up to August, 1958, and 30 per cent of the Negro examinees in mental group V were so classified.

2) Since August, 1958, with the introduction of the aptitude area tests (ACB

TABLE 1

Results of Preinduction Examination of Draftees for Military Service, by Race

(July 1950 through June 1966)[a]

Results of Examination	July 1950-June 1966	July 1950-July 1958	August 1958 through June 1966				
			Total	August 1958-April 1963	May 1963-October 1965	November 1965-March 1966	April 1966-June 1966
			Total				
Examined	9,994,683	5,216,836	4,777,847	1,489,814	2,135,533	814,261	338,239
Found Acceptable	6,071,335	3,473,723	2,597,612	803,598	1,089,272	497,803	206,939
Disqualified	3,923,348	1,743,113	2,180,235	686,216	1,046,261	316,458	131,300
Administrative reasons	127,481	58,766	68,715	24,658	28,057	10,663	5,337
Failed mental requirements, only							
Failed AFQT	1,235,910	678,893	557,017	195,801	281,343	56,945	22,928
Failed ACB or AQB[b]	368,960	*	368,960	101,227	207,352	46,826	13,555
Mentally and medically disqualified	263,406	154,901	108,505	42,202	48,583	12,636	5,084
Medically disqualified only	1,927,591	850,553	1,077,038	322,328	480,926	189,388	84,396

42

White

Examined	8,504,602	4,441,477	4,063,125	1,248,129	1,782,441	303,617
Found Acceptable	5,534,126	3,135,216	2,398,910	736,802	1,003,749	193,137
Disqualified	2,970,476	1,306,261	1,664,215	511,327	778,692	110,480
Administrative reasons	106,613	48,555	58,058	19,984	24,075	4,523
Failed mental requirements, only						
Failed AFQT	654,642	361,637	293,005	106,531	141,098	32,251
Failed ACB or AQB[b]	233,785	*	233,785	56,671	134,810	33,155
Mentally and medically disqualified	172,886	101,141	71,745	27,603	31,624	3,558
Medically disqualified only	1,802,550	794,928	1,007,622	300,538	447,085	80,125

Negro

Examined	1,490,081	775,359	714,722	241,685	353,092	34,622
Found Acceptable	537,209	338,507	198,702	66,796	85,523	13,802
Disqualified	952,872	436,852	516,020	174,889	267,569	20,820
Administrative reasons	20,868	10,211	10,657	4,674	3,982	814
Failed mental requirements, only						
Failed AFQT	581,268	317,256	264,012	89,270	140,245	9,803
Failed ACB or AQB[b]	135,175	*	135,175	44,556	72,542	4,406
Mentally and medically disqualified	90,520	53,760	36,760	14,599	16,959	3,676
Medically disqualified only	125,041	55,625	69,416	21,790	33,841	9,514

aExcludes territories: Puerto Rico (including Panama Canal Zone and Virgin Islands) and Guam (including Mariana Islands).
bClassified as "Trainability Limited."
*No ACB or AQB requirements for mental group IV during this period (see text).

TABLE 2

Percentage Distribution of Results of Preinduction Examination of Draftees

(July 1950 through June 1966)[a]

Results of Examination	July 1950-June 1966	July 1950-July 1958	August 1958 through June 1966				
			Total	August 1958-April 1963	May 1963-October 1965	November 1965-March 1966	April 1966-June 1966
Examined	100.0	100.0	100.0	100.0	100.0	100.0	100.0
Found Acceptable	60.7	66.6	54.4	53.9	51.0	61.1	61.2
Disqualified	39.3	33.4	45.6	46.1	49.0	38.9	38.8
Administrative reasons	1.3	1.1	1.4	1.7	1.3	1.3	1.6
Failed mental requirements, only							
Failed AFQT	12.4	13.0	11.7	13.1	13.2	6.9	6.8
Failed ACB or AQB[b]	3.7	*	7.7	6.8	9.7	5.8	3.9
Mentally and medically disqualified	2.6	3.0	2.3	2.8	2.3	1.6	1.5
Medically disqualified only	19.3	16.3	22.5	21.7	22.5	23.3	25.0

44

White

Examined	100.0	100.0	100.0	100.C	100.0	100.0	100.0
Found Acceptable	65.1	70.6	59.0	59.0	56.3	63.8	63.6
Disqualified	34.9	29.4	41.0	41.0	43.7	36.2	36.4
Administrative reasons	1.3	1.1	1.4	1.6	1.4	1.3	1.5
Failed mental requirements, only							
Failed AFQT	7.7	8.1	7.2	8.5	7.9	4.4	4.3
Failed ACB or AQB[b]	2.7	*	5.8	4.5	7.6	4.6	3.0
Mentally and medically disqualified	2.0	2.3	1.8	2.2	1.8	1.2	1.2
Medically disqualified only	21.2	17.9	24.8	24.2	25.0	24.7	26.4

Negro

Examined	100.0	100.0	100.0	100.0	100.0	100.0	100.0
Found Acceptable	36.1	43.7	27.8	27.6	24.2	38.2	39.9
Disqualified	63.9	56.3	72.2	72.4	75.8	61.8	60.1
Administrative reasons	1.4	1.3	1.5	1.9	1.1	1.4	2.4
Failed mental requirements, only							
Failed AFQT	38.9	40.9	37.0	37.0	39.8	28.9	28.3
Failed ACB or AQB[b]	9.1	*	18.9	18.4	20.5	16.0	12.7
Mentally and medically disqualified	6.1	6.9	5.1	6.1	4.8	4.3	4.4
Medically disqualified only	8.4	7.2	9.7	9.0	9.6	11.2	12.3

[a] Excludes territories: Puerto Rico (including Panama Canal Zone and Virgin Islands) and Guam (including Mariana Islands).
[b] Classified as "Trainability Limited."
* No ACB or AQB requirements for mental group IV during this period (see text).

and AQB), the term refers to the Trainability Limited" group—a subclassification of mental group IV, a fully qualified group under the mental standards prior
to August, 1958. (The subclassifications of mental group V were dropped.)

MENTAL TEST FAILURES

The total results of the preinduction examination of draftees—registrants
forwarded by the local boards of the Selective Service System to the Armed
Forces examining stations to determine their qualification for military service—
are presented in Table 1 (numerical distribution) and Table 2 (percentage distribution). These distributions indicate the number and per cent of the examinees found acceptable for military service and the number and per cent of those
disqualified—the latter by disqualifying cause.

The data cover a 16-year period, from July, 1950, through June, 1966, and
are shown by race: white (non-Negro) and Negro. Some 10 million draftees
were given a preinduction examination during this period: 8.5 million white
draftees, and 1.5 million Negro draftees (Table 1).

About 3 million (35 per cent) of the white examinees were disqualified.
About 1 million (64 per cent) of the Negro examinees were disqualified.

While the ratio of white to Negro examinees was 17:3, that of white to Negro
disqualified examinees was 3:1. The disqualification rate for Negro examinees
was thus 80 per cent higher than for white examinees.

The primary difference in these disqualification rates by race are due to
mental test failures. As a matter of fact, with respect to the disqualification for
medical reasons, the Negro disqualification rates are more favorable than those
of the white examinees.

Nationwide Results, by Race

The analysis of the mental test failures relates to the period beginning with
August, 1958, when the aptitude area tests (ACB first, AQB later) were added
to the AFQT. The data are given for the total period ("Total"—from August,
1958, through June, 1966), and separately by selected periods, in accordance
with the changes in the AQB requirements. As indicated by these data, the disqualification rate for failing the AQB rose sharply in May, 1963, when these
standards were raised, followed by decreased rates, due at least in part to the
lower mental standards beginning in November, 1965.

During this period the following disqualification rates for failing the mental
tests were recorded for "Total" (undifferentiated by race) and by race:

Total: (a) Failed AFQT only (below 10 percentile)—11.7 per cent; (b)
failed ACB or AQB—7.7 per cent; (c) failed both types of tests (AFQT and
ACB or AQB), plus the "overlapping group" (failed mental tests and were
simultaneously medically disqualified")—21.7 per cent.

White: (a) Failed AFQT only—7.2 per cent; (b) failed ACB or AQB—5.8
per cent; (c) failed both types of tests, including the "overlapping group"—
14.8 per cent.

Negro: (a) Failed AFQT only—37.0 per cent; (b) failed ACB or AQB—
18.9 per cent; (c) failed both types of tests, including the "overlapping group"—
61.0 per cent (Table 2).

The disqualification rate for mental test failures among Negro examinees was thus four times as high as among white examinees. While one out of seven white draftees failed the mental tests, about three out of five Negro draftees failed—a disturbing cultural and socioeconomic phenomenon.

There is much interest in the number of examinees who failed the ACB or AQB ("Trainability Limited"), as these examinees are among those who are classified by the Selective Service System as I-Y ("Qualified for military service only in war or national emergency"). Table 3 includes not only examinees who were classified as "Trainability Limited" on preinduction examination, but also those who were so classified on induction examination. It also includes 18-year-olds who were examined separately ("early examination") under the "Conservation of Manpower" program.

TABLE 3
Draftees and 18-year-olds Classified as "Trainability Limited," by Race
(August 1958 through June 1966)*

	Total	Draftees, by type of examination		
		Preinduction	Induction	18-Year-Olds
Number				
Total	465,864	368,960	59,752	37,152
White	295,173	233,785	34,568	26,820
Negro	170,691	135,175	25,184	10,332
Percentage				
Total	100.0	100.0	100.0	100.0
White	63.4	63.4	57.9	72.2
Negro	36.6	36.6	42.1	27.8

*Excludes territories: Puerto Rico (including Panama Canal Zone and Virgin Islands) and Guam (including Mariana Islands).

When limited to preinduction examinations, some 369,000 examinees failed the ACB or AQB requirements: 234,000 white examinees, and 135,000 Negro examinees. By adding to these preinductees who failed the aptitude area tests the examinees who failed these tests on induction, and the 18-year-olds who so failed, a total of 466,000 examinees is obtained—295,000 white and 171,000 Negro examinees—in the "Trainability Limited" group.

The Negro examinees comprise about 37 per cent of the I-Y's—so classified for mental reasons (Table 3).

State and Regional Results, by Race

Due to certain technical causes, the data by individual states are for the period from August, 1958, through December, 1965. (The nationwide Tables 1 and 2 extend through June, 1966—6 months longer.) In all other respects, the state data are the same as the nationwide data. A wide variation by state with regard to disqualifications for failing the mental tests is most conspicuously reflected in the range of the disqualification rates for these reasons, especially when differentiated by race. Clearly, the differences are both regional and racial. The range in the disqualification rates by type of test were as follows:

Total: (a) Failed AFQT only—from 2.1 per cent (Oregon and Utah) to 40.1 per cent (Mississippi); (b) failed ACB or AQB—from 2.8 per cent (Washington) to 14.9 per cent (District of Columbia); (c) total mental test failures (AFQT and ACB or AQB plus the overlapping group)—from 6.3 per cent (Washington) to 57.3 per cent (Mississippi).

White: (a) Failed AFQT only—from 1.9 per cent (Oregon) to 17.4 per cent (Kentucky); (b) failed ACB or AQB—from 2.7 per cent (Washington) to 11.7 per cent (Hawaii); (c) total mental test failures—from 5.9 per cent (Washington) to 31.9 per cent (Kentucky).

Negro: (a) Failed AFQT only—from 14.7 per cent (Washington) to 60.7 per cent (Mississippi); (b) failed ACB or AQB—from 10.6 per cent (Washington) to 25.9 per cent (Nevada and Colorado); (c) total mental test failures—from 29.9 per cent (Washington) to 82.4 per cent (Mississippi).

In order to obtain a general pattern of the wide geographic and ethnic variations in the disqualifications for failing the mental tests, the state data were combined in geographic divisions and regions, by race. These data are presented in Tables 4 and 5. (The states included in each region are shown in footnote to Table 5.)

The following pattern emerges when the disqualification rates are differentiated by geographic region and race:

White: North Central: (a) Failed AFQT only—4.3 per cent, (b) failed ACB or AQB—5.0 per cent, (c) total mental test failures—10.6 per cent; West: (a) Failed AFQT only—6.0 per cent, (b) failed ACB or AQB—5.6 per cent, (c) total mental test failures—13.0 per cent; Northeast: (a) Failed AFQT only —9.3 per cent, (b) failed ACB or AQB—5.4 per cent, (c) total mental test failures—16.7 per cent; South: (a) Failed AFQT only—11.0 per cent, (b) failed ACB or AQB—8.4 per cent, (c) total mental test failures—22.1 per cent.

Negro: West: (a) Failed AFQT only—17.9 per cent, (b) failed ACB or AQB —20.5 per cent, (c) total mental test failures—41.6 per cent; North Central: (a) Failed AFQT only—25.0 per cent, (b) failed ACB or AQB—20.9 per cent, (c) total mental test failures—49.6 per cent; Northeast: (a) Failed AFQT only—28.1 per cent, (b) failed ACB or AQB—18.6 per cent, (c) total mental test failures—51.3 per cent; South (a) Failed AFQT only—45.1 per cent, (b) failed ACB or AQB—19.4 per cent, (c) total mental test failures—70.4 per cent.

A FINAL NOTE

In utilizing these data, we must not lose sight of the fact that they relate to a "draftee-population." Large numbers of young men are examined and accepted for voluntary enlistment, or officer training, at younger ages, before being reached as draftees for preinduction examinations. As a result, the Selective Service manpower pool ("draftee-population") tends to include a relatively smaller proportion of men who could meet the military qualification standards, which means a potentially higher proportion of disqualified draftees.

These limitations have been overcome by obtaining for various periods overall evaluations of all youths on a nationwide basis. For example, the 1965 data for draftees showed a disqualification rate of 44.0 per cent for all reasons (medical, mental, and moral) and 20.9 per cent for mental test failures, whereas the corresponding overall disqualification rates were calculated as 35.2 per cent for all reasons and 16.5 per cent for mental test failures.

Similar evaluations for 1965, differentiated by race, would indicate for: (a) White youths, overall disqualification rates of 31.3 per cent for all reasons and 9.5 per cent for mental test failures, versus disqualification rates of 39.7 per cent and 14.7 per cent, respectively, for draftees, and (b) for Negro youths, overall disqualification rates of 62.8 per cent for all reasons and 52.7 per cent for mental test failures, versus the disqualification rates of 70.8 per cent and 59.6 per cent, respectively, for draftees.

No such evaluation could be accomplished on a state basis, because of lack of appropriate data for this purpose.

It is obvious from these comparisons of the overall evaluation rates on a nation-wide basis with the corresponding rates of draftees, that the overall disqualification rates by state would differ from those presented here for draftees by state. Yet, judging from these nationwide comparisons, the presented disqualification rates for mental test failures by region and race may be considered as reliable indexes of the prevailing regional and racial differences. In general, it may be reliably inferred that the higher disqualification rates of draftees for mental test failure, the closer they would correspond to their overall rates. (Note that on a relative basis the overall disqualification rates for mental test failures differ much more from the draftee rates in the case of white draftees than in the case of Negro draftees.) If this be so, overall rates by state and race, if data were available for such computations, might reveal, on a relative basis, even more conspicuous regional and racial differences.

These relative shortcomings of the presented data with respect to "overall rates" do not detract, of course, from the relevant value of the quantitative distributions of the disqualifications for mental test failures by region and race. These numbers, as such, should prove very important for any planned draft policies or programs.

NOTE

[1] Walter V. Bingham, "Inequalities in Adult Capacity from Military Data," *Science*, 104 (August 16, 1946), 147-52.

TABLE 4

Results of Preinduction Examination of Draftees for Military Service, by Geographic Region and Division, and by Race
(August 1958 through December 1965)

Total

Geographic Region and Division[a]	Examined	Found Acceptable	Disqualified, by Disqualifying Cause						
			Total	Administrative	Failed Mental Tests Only			Failed Mental Tests and Medically Disqualified	Medically Disqualified Only
					Total	AFQT	ACB or AQB		
United States: Total	3,949,400	2,092,152	1,857,248	56,941	827,490	499,556	327,934	95,759	877,058
Northeast	984,942	524,639	460,303	16,008	177,320	111,018	66,302	22,153	244,822
New England	206,288	107,389	98,899	4,351	27,284	15,509	11,775	4,999	62,265
Middle Atlantic	778,654	417,250	361,404	11,657	150,036	95,509	54,527	17,154	182,557
North Central	1,006,169	616,044	390,125	11,530	127,219	61,977	65,242	15,314	236,062
East North Central	723,811	434,080	289,731	8,058	101,216	49,841	51,375	11,471	168,986
West North Central	282,358	181,964	100,394	3,472	26,003	12,136	13,867	3,843	67,076
South	1,351,828	610,423	741,405	14,465	444,567	286,510	158,057	49,175	233,198
South Atlantic	662,740	293,415	369,325	9,336	221,455	144,845	76,610	24,810	113,724
East South Central	333,321	140,443	192,878	2,121	122,967	81,736	41,231	13,711	54,079
West South Central	355,767	176,565	179,202	3,008	100,145	59,929	40,216	10,654	65,395
West	606,461	341,046	265,415	14,938	78,384	40,051	38,333	9,117	162,976
Mountain	139,268	83,114	56,154	1,986	17,065	7,835	9,230	2,350	34,753
Pacific	467,193	257,932	209,261	12,952	61,319	32,216	29,103	6,767	128,223

White

United States: Total	3,320,032	1,926,917	1,393,115	47,788	464,916	260,074	204,842	62,680	817,731
Northeast	883,617	492,316	391,301	13,246	130,050	82,567	47,483	17,513	230,492
New England	199,718	105,310	94,408	4,224	24,235	13,800	10,435	4,697	61,252
Middle Atlantic	683,899	387,006	296,893	9,022	105,815	68,767	37,048	12,816	169,240
North Central	913,571	582,362	331,209	10,056	84,708	38,860	45,848	11,906	224,539
East North Central	643,250	404,648	238,602	6,820	64,395	30,191	34,204	8,646	158,741
West North Central	270,321	177,714	92,607	3,236	20,313	8,669	11,644	3,260	65,798
South	946,767	522,412	424,355	10,553	183,446	104,048	79,398	25,103	205,253
South Atlantic	444,639	244,535	200,104	6,451	83,103	47,986	35,117	12,038	98,512
East South Central	238,827	121,877	116,950	1,630	59,586	35,734	23,852	7,914	47,820
West South Central	263,301	156,000	107,301	2,472	40,757	20,328	20,429	5,151	58,921
West	576,077	329,827	246,250	13,933	66,712	34,599	32,113	8,158	157,447
Mountain	136,107	82,097	54,010	1,923	15,541	7,005	8,536	2,201	34,345
Pacific	439,970	247,730	192,240	12,010	51,171	27,594	23,577	5,957	123,102

Negro

United States: Total	629,368	165,235	464,133	9,153	362,574	239,482	123,092	33,079	59,327
Northeast	101,325	32,323	69,002	2,762	47,270	28,451	18,819	4,640	14,330
New England	6,570	2,079	4,491	127	3,049	1,709	1,340	302	1,013
Middle Atlantic	94,755	30,244	64,511	2,635	44,221	26,742	17,479	4,338	13,317
North Central	92,598	33,682	58,916	1,474	42,511	23,117	19,394	3,408	11,523
East North Central	80,561	29,432	51,129	1,238	36,821	19,650	17,171	2,825	10,245
West North Central	12,037	4,250	7,787	1,236	5,690	3,467	2,223	583	1,278
South	405,061	88,011	317,050	3,912	261,121	182,462	78,659	24,072	27,945
South Atlantic	218,101	48,880	169,221	2,885	138,352	96,859	41,493	12,772	15,212
East South Central	94,494	18,566	75,928	491	63,381	46,002	17,379	5,797	6,259
West South Central	92,466	20,565	71,901	536	59,388	39,601	19,787	5,503	6,474
West	30,384	11,219	19,165	1,005	11,672	5,452	6,220	959	5,529
Mountain	3,161	1,017	2,144	63	1,524	830	694	149	408
Pacific	27,223	10,202	17,021	942	10,148	4,622	5,526	810	5,121

aSee footnote to Table 5.

TABLE 5

Percentage Distribution of Results of Preinduction Examination of Draftees for Military Service, by Geographic Region and Division, and by Race (August 1958 through December 1965)

Geographic Region and Division[a]	Found Acceptable	Disqualified, by Disqualifying Cause						
		Total	Adminis-trative	Failed Mental Tests Only			Failed Mental Tests and Medically Disqualified	Medically Disqualified Only
				Total	AFQT	ACB or AQB		
					Total			
United States: Total	53.0	47.0	1.4	20.9	12.6	8.3	2.4	22.3
Northeast	53.3	46.7	1.6	18.0	11.3	6.7	2.2	24.9
New England	52.1	47.9	2.1	13.2	7.5	5.7	2.4	30.2
Middle Atlantic	53.6	46.4	1.5	19.3	12.3	7.0	2.2	23.4
North Central	61.2	38.8	1.1	12.7	6.2	6.5	1.5	23.5
East North Central	60.0	40.0	1.1	14.0	6.9	7.1	1.6	23.3
West North Central	64.4	35.6	1.2	9.2	4.3	4.9	1.4	23.8
South	45.2	54.8	1.1	32.8	21.1	11.7	3.6	17.3
South Atlantic	44.3	55.7	1.4	33.4	21.8	11.6	3.7	17.2
East South Central	42.1	57.9	0.6	37.0	24.6	12.4	4.1	16.2
West South Central	49.6	50.4	0.8	28.1	16.8	11.3	3.0	18.5
West	56.2	43.8	2.5	12.9	6.6	6.3	1.5	26.9
Mountain	59.7	40.3	1.4	12.2	5.6	6.6	1.7	25.0
Pacific	55.2	44.8	2.8	13.1	6.9	6.2	1.4	27.5

White

Geographic area								
United States: Total	58.0	42.0	1.4	14.0	7.8	6.2	1.9	24.7
Northeast	55.7	44.3	1.5	14.7	9.3	5.4	2.0	26.1
New England	52.7	47.3	2.1	12.1	6.9	5.2	2.4	30.7
Middle Atlantic	56.6	43.4	1.3	15.5	10.1	5.4	1.9	24.7
North Central	63.7	36.3	1.1	9.3	4.3	5.0	1.3	24.6
East North Central	62.9	37.1	1.1	10.0	4.7	5.3	1.3	24.7
West North Central	65.7	34.3	1.2	7.5	3.2	4.3	1.2	24.4
South	55.0	44.8	1.1	19.4	11.0	8.4	2.7	21.6
South Atlantic	55.0	45.0	1.5	18.7	10.8	7.9	2.7	22.1
East South Central	51.0	49.0	0.7	25.0	15.0	10.0	3.3	22.1
West South Central	59.2	40.8	0.9	15.5	7.7	7.8	2.0	20.0
West	57.3	42.7	2.4	11.6	6.0	5.6	1.4	22.4
Mountain	60.3	39.7	1.4	11.4	5.1	6.3	1.6	27.3
Pacific	56.3	43.7	2.7	11.7	6.3	5.4	1.4	27.9

Negro

Geographic area								
United States: Total	26.3	73.7	1.5	57.5	38.0	19.5	5.3	9.4
Northeast	31.9	68.1	2.7	46.7	28.1	18.6	4.6	14.1
New England	31.6	68.4	1.9	46.5	26.1	20.4	4.6	15.4
Middle Atlantic	31.9	68.1	2.8	46.6	28.2	18.4	4.6	14.1
North Central	36.4	63.6	1.6	45.9	25.0	20.9	3.7	12.4
East North Central	36.5	63.5	1.5	45.3	24.5	21.3	3.5	12.7
West North Central	35.3	64.7	2.0	47.3	28.8	18.5	4.8	10.6
South	21.7	78.3	1.0	64.5	45.1	19.4	5.9	6.9
South Atlantic	22.4	77.6	1.3	63.4	44.4	19.0	5.9	7.0
East South Central	19.6	80.4	0.5	67.2	48.8	18.4	6.1	6.6
West South Central	22.2	77.8	0.6	64.2	42.8	21.4	6.0	7.0
West	36.9	63.1	3.3	38.4	17.9	20.5	3.2	18.2
Mountain	32.2	67.8	2.0	48.2	26.2	22.0	4.7	12.9
Pacific	37.5	62.5	3.5	37.2	17.0	20.2	3.0	18.8

aThe States within each geographic area are as follows: *New England*—Maine, New Hampshire, Vermont, Massachusetts, Rhode Island, Connecticut; *Middle Atlantic*—New York, New Jersey, Pennsylvania; *East North Central*—Ohio, Indiana, Illinois, Michigan, Wisconsin; *West North Central*—Minnesota, Iowa, Missouri, North Dakota, South Dakota, Nebraska, Kansas; *South Atlantic*—Delaware, Maryland, District of Columbia, Virginia, West Virginia, North Carolina, South Carolina, Georgia, Florida; *East South Central*—Kentucky, Tennessee, Alabama, Mississippi; *West South Central*—Arkansas, Louisiana, Oklahoma, Texas; *Mountain*—Montana, Idaho, Wyoming, Colorado, New Mexico, Arizona, Utah, Nevada; *Pacific*—Alaska, California, Hawaii, Oregon, Washington (Bureau of the Census).

5

A Critique of Selective Service with Emphasis on Student Deferment

HARRY A. MARMION

For almost two hundred years the United States had no experience with compulsory military service except in connection with major wars. Thus, compulsory service has been closely associated in the public mind with total national emergency. In 1948 this situation changed, and even though military strength requirements were not large, requirements were not met by voluntary enlistment. The situation was complicated by the aggressive tendencies of some nations which necessitated counter-measures by the United States. In 1948, for the first time in American history, Congress authorized the induction of men for a period of military service in peace time. This presented Selective Service with a completely new set of problems. Previously attained experience was no longer totally relevant. It has been necessary to renew the current Selective Service legislation every four years since 1951. During this period, because of the variety of cold and hot war pressures, the Congress has not been willing to try new approaches to manpower procurement.

Widespread criticism of the draft system is recent. During the two World Wars the system worked reasonably well because of the dangers facing the nation. During the Korean conflict there was no great outcry over the draft. As late as 1963, when the law was again extended, there were only perfunctory hearings and debate. The escalation of the war in Vietnam, beginning in the late spring of 1965, the unpopularity of the war, and relatively recent student militancy in the United States have brought the entire Selective Service System under close scrutiny from many quarters. Suddenly the draft has become uppermost in the mind of every American male between the ages of 18 and 26 and, in some cases, 35. As the *New York Times* said on August 10, 1966, "The army sends one out of three of its draftees to Viet Nam." However, the basic draft law has remained virtually unchanged since 1951, even though in the twenty years since World War II, America has undergone startling changes in other areas, such as education and the economy.

Many alternative proposals have been advanced: national service, a voluntary force, a lottery, and even universal military training. Finally there are those who favor a modification of the present Selective Service System as the best practical

The author is a Staff Associate, Commission on Federal Relations, American Council on Education.

alternative at this time. The primary reason for favoring the present system, with modification, is that during a wartime situation it is best, and even necessary, to continue a system that is providing the necessary manpower to meet the commitments of the nation.

This paper will focus on the present system, the most widely heard complaints about it, and, where feasible, possible changes.

MISNAMED UNIVERSAL MILITARY TRAINING AND SERVICE ACT

President Truman tried unsuccessfully for four years to have Congress pass a Universal Military Training Act. The proposed legislation would have provided one year of training for all American men. The issue always fostered bitter debate, but the adoption of a national defense depending upon air-nuclear deterrent cost the universal training concept much of its congressional support.

In 1948, the Congress did enact the Selective Service Act, which, for the first time in American history drafted men into the armed forces during peace time. The Selective Service Act of 1948 was succeeded by the Universal Military Training and Service Act of 1951. There were a number of significant changes in this Act which increased the sources of manpower available for induction, but the Universal Military Training provisions of the Act were debated but never passed.[1]

There has been confusion over the principle behind the legislation in question. For example, Kingman Brewster in his baccalaureate address to the 1966 Yale graduating class said:

> I realize that service to the nation has been mocked by a policy which offers no reason to justify the imposition of involuntary military service. . . . The carry-over of a manpower policy designed a generation ago seems heedless of the difference in both need and capability which have been brought about by change in population and military technique. The result has been to encourage a cynical avoidance of service, a corruption of the aims of education, and a tarnishing of the national spirit. . . . Selective Service in order to staff a two million man force from a two hundred million population has invited a cops and robbers view of national obligation. National morality has been left exposed to collective self-corruption by the persistent refusal of the national administration to take the lead in the design of a national manpower policy which would rationally relate individual privilege and national duty.

Another, Mr. John C. Esty, Jr., former associate dean at Amherst College and presently headmaster at the Taft School, has stated the case clearly in testimony before the Subcommittee on Employment and Manpower of the U.S. Senate Committee on Labor and Public Welfare in November of 1963:

> Present practice makes a mockery of the original intent that every able-bodied man serve his country. Our present difficulties arise from the strain of maintaining a semblance of universality while armed service needs dictate greater and greater selectivity. The time has come when we can no longer reconcile these opposites and must choose between them.

Many champion reform of the present legislation, feeling that the advantage of reform is that it need consider only those parts of the present system which need change whereas a complete alternative, to be feasible, must cover a variety of considerations during a period of serious world tension.

It appears that what started out as an attempt at Universal Military Training has fallen far short of the mark. The present draft system was fashioned to meet quickly the needs of a nation engaged in total war. It was continued because of world tensions and also because of the assumption that some form of universal service would be adopted. After it became clear that universal service would not be adpoted, the present law was amended in an ad hoc manner to meet short-range, changing manpower needs.

The first recommendation is that the legislation enacted have an unambiguous purpose which will be clear to the nation as a whole.

DECENTRALIZATION OF THE PRESENT SYSTEM AND ABSENCE OF NATIONAL STANDARDS

There are 4,061 local boards (over 16,000 local board members) where the fundamental operations of the Selective Service System are performed. There are 95 state appeal boards (one in each federal judicial district, with 23 extra panels in most heavily populated districts) which have over 500 unpaid board members. There are 56 state headquarters. All of these, plus the national office, make up the Selective Service System.

This "supervised decentralization" of the entire System has been criticized because decentralization creates apparently undemocratic situations. It leads to a lack of uniformity in interpretation. Draft boards throughout the nation have a wide latitude of action which in some cases may be used in an arbitrary manner. For example, one local board may induct part-time students before married men; another board's policies may be exactly the opposite. On the other hand, people using the same arguments, can come to the conclusion that the decentralization system is the essence of democracy.

During the first two days of testimony by General Hershey before the House Armed Forces Committee, June 22-23, 1966, the questioning by members of the Committee made it abundantly clear that many of the complaints by constituents concern the lack of uniformity. In one exchange, Congressman Schweiker noted that three civilian pilots doing the same job for the same airline were called: one board deferred two of them; another board classified the third as I-A. Two recommendations can be suggested to answer this criticism.

1) There should be an increased standardization of Selective Service System regulations and interpretation of these regulations without removing the concept of local board discretion.

2) Centralization of the Selective Service could be accomplished by modifying the law to make agency guidelines and Presidential Executive Orders *mandatory* rather than *advisory*. This could be done by modifying the final portion of Section 6(H) of the Act which states:

> Notwithstanding any provisions of this Act, no local board, appeal board, or other agency of appeal of the Selective Service System shall be required to postpone or defer any person by reason of this activity in study, research, or medical, dental, veterinary, optometric, osteopathic, scientific, pharmaceutical, chiropractic, chiropodial, or other endeavors found to be necessary to the maintenance of the national health, safety, or interest solely on the

basis of any test, examination, selection system, class standing, or any other means conducted, sponsored, administered, or prepared by any agency or department of the Federal Government or any private institution, corporation, association, partnership, or individual employed by an agency or department of the Federal Government.

DEFERMENT

Much of the criticism of the Selective Service System centers about present deferment policy. A number of people including students feel educational deferments should be discontinued. During fiscal 1965 educational deferments increased by nearly half a million to a total of over 1,600,000.

History of Student Deferment

Prior to World War I no serious thought had ever been given to deferment of students in America, except for their often being considered too young for service.[2] During the first World War, consideration was given to the importance of education and the possibility of deferment. At no time during this period were local boards even close to the bottom of the manpower pool available. In 1917 the Student Army Training Corps (145,000 men) was started to allow students under the age of 21 to be relieved from active military duty to attend college for three years. Over 500 college units were established but before the first enrollees began their courses of instruction, the Congress lowered the draft age to 18. After this change the period of instruction for these students was reduced to nine months. The first students were activated in October of 1917, but the Armistice was signed in November and all trainees demobilized before the end of the year. The principle of some type of student deferment was established.

Student Deferments—World War II

The Selective Training and Service Act of 1940 provided for the deferment of men whose activity was essential to the welfare of the nation. College students were in this category and by the end of 1941 more than 100,000 students were deferred. As the manpower situation tightened, student deferment was restricted to those preparing for critical occupations in essential industries to those preparing for critical occupations in essential industries. Students in engineering, science and medicine generally were deferred. Students in other areas were not deferred and by mid-1944 the male college population in the country declined to 30 per cent of the 1939-40 base. During the war both the Army and Navy had large numbers of students in uniform. Both services operated educational programs at colleges and universities and over 200,000 men were maintained as military students.[3]

Post-World War II Proposals for Student Deferment

The reinstitution of the draft together with a growing concern over shortages of scientific and other specialized personnel made draft deferment in the 1950's a real issue for the first time in our history. A variety of proposals were presented but finally the "Trytten plan," a composite of reports of six Advisory Committees to Selective Service, was adopted as the best alternative by the Selective Service System through executive order of the President.

The plan called for the maintenance of an uninterrupted flow of students through college.[4] Students would be selected for deferment on a basis of their performance in college and a nation-wide test administered by the Selective Service System. Presidential regulations, by executive order, may provide for further deferment of individuals whose education or employment may be in the national interest. Local draft boards have no obligation to defer students based on federally established guidelines. Each individual case may be examined in light of conditions facing local boards. Any man who obtained a deferment extends his liability for military service to age 35. Basically, this is the program currently in effect.

Arguments for and against Deferment

The argument against the deferment system is as follows: it defers those people who can afford higher education and remain in good standing while attending college or graduate school. As a result, the system drafts a disproportionately high number of economically deprived citizens, especially Negroes.[5] Hence, the present deferment system is inequitable and undemocratic. Further, the deferred student has more opportunity to reach age 26 without serving by receiving an occupational deferment, by continuing graduate study, or by acquiring dependents. Recently, however, Selective Service asked local boards to give physical examinations to men in the 26-35 category.

There are several distinctions that can be made concerning the argument presented. First, the universality of American higher education today places into question the use of the term "afford higher education," with the connotations intended. Low tuition rates at most public colleges, scholarships, work-study programs, loans, and various other sources make college available to almost all qualified students. Secondly, the rejection rate of males at a national rate of almost 50 per cent, mostly from the lower echelons of society, indicates that many economically deprived young men do not serve. Thirdly, General Hershey in his testimony before the Armed Services Committee of the House of Representatives indicated that a higher percentage of college men than non-college men serve in the armed forces. This statement was seemingly contradicted, however, by Assistant Secretary of Defense for Manpower, Thomas D. Morris, in his résumé of the Department of Defense study of the draft before the House Armed Services Committee on June 30, 1966.

There are several observations one can make concerning the deferment portion of the draft law. First, inequity will always be present in any draft system, at least until such time as all, rather than some, men are needed. Secondly, an attempt to correct or change one inequity could well create other inequities or be responsible for problems which could affect the economy of the nation. Thirdly, the armed forces look to civilian colleges for 90 per cent of their new officers. Finally, and most importantly, the need of an educated citizenry has never been denied. It is in fact essential to the future of our nation.

It seems possible that the argument against student deferment is not as strong as it might first appear. It is, however, difficult to defend a position which has connotations of establishing an elite group in our nation primarily based on intellectual or economic capacity.

There are two vital needs to be considered regarding deferments. First we need to provide military manpower, and secondly we must provide for the education and training of young men in a variety of areas. Currently, both of these vital necessities must be provided by our youth in the 19-26 age category.

Deferment policies and procedures have crystallized since World War I. The draft act itself has changed relatively little since its inception prior to World War II. The parameters withn which the act operates have changed dramatically. Today we have a partial or limited môbilization; initially the act was initiated to meet a total national effort. Decisions concerning the application of the act to individual cases during World War II were based on the potential of the individual's contribution to the "war effort." In the Sixties no such circumstances exist and therefore the needs of America's terribly complex society need to receive appropriate consideration. The needs of the nation should be paramount.

The most outspoken advocate for the continuance of the deferment system has been General Hershey. In his opening statement before the House Armed Services Committee, General Hershey said, "If the nation needs those who are trained, it should be prepared to defer them when the needs of the armed forces permit." The case for deferment has been the most clearly consistent theme in all his recent public statements on the Selective Service System. It is, in fact, the basis for the Selective Service System's concept of *channeling* to be discussed later.

The example General Hershey uses consistently when talking about allocation of manpower is the education of doctors and he feels there is wisdom in approaching the allocation question with the best judgments we can muster rather than by chance. He said, "I believe that virtually every student who seriously pursues training to become a physician be deferred to do so. The objections to chance rather than judgment as a method of selection, which are so obvious in the case of physicians, exist with respect to any category of registrants which might from time to time have some basis for deferment in the national interest."

A combination of two possible recommendations made earlier bears repeating at this point. Either there should be increased standardization of Selective Service System's regulations and interpretation of the regulations without removing the concept of local board discretion or the law should be modified to make agency guidelines and Presidential Executive Orders mandatory rather than advisory. This would make the deferment portion of the Selective Service Act more clearly understood and less open to criticism.

Channeling

A discussion of deferments is not complete without discussing a little known activity of the Selective Service System called the channeling function. "The term 'channeling' refers to that process through which registrants are influenced to enter and remain in study in critical occupations, and in other essential activities in the national health, safety, and interest by deferment or prospect for deferment from military service."[6]

> Further, Selective Service channels thousands of young men through its deferment procedures into those fields of endeavor where there are shortages of adequately trained personnel. . . . Many younger engineers, scientists, technicians, and other skilled workers have been kept in their jobs through occupational deferments. Young male teachers are induced to

remain in the teaching profession through deferment and additional students are attracted into the profession. The fields of medicine and dentistry also have benefited from student and occupational deferment channeling.[7]

The System appears to base its channeling function on the very general language in Section 1(e), Policy and intent of Congress, of the Universal Military Training and Service Act. The language states as follows: "Congress further declares that adequate provision for national security requires maximum effort in the fields of scientific research and development, and the fullest possible utilization of the nation's technological, scientific, and other critical manpower resources."

The most recent analysis of the Universal Military Training and Service Act released on March 1, 1966, by the Committee on Armed Services, U. S. House of Representatives, does not contain any reference to channeling or give any analysis of Section 1(e) of the Act indicating this as a function of the Selective Service System.

On the one hand, the System talks about blanket "channeling" into fields of endeavor where there are shortages of trained personnel. The language used in the 1965 Report of the Selective Service System is "induced to remain . . . in certain occupations," etc. On the other hand, the disposition of each case of individual deferment is the responsibility of the local draft board.

In this matter of channeling, some are of the opinion that explicit authority for this activity is not contained in the basic law and further, even though administrative interpretation over the years has created this function, the position of the Selective Service System on channeling and the language it uses to describe channeling are inconsistent with the decentralized decision-making authority of local boards. This is another compelling reason for a change in the wide discretion given to local boards. If channeling is to be accomplished, there should be definitive guidelines from Selective Service. Further, some question whether or not the Selective Service System is the proper agency for establishing and carrying out manpower policies.

There are those who take issue with the purported success of channeling because although the manpower pool is expanding, current draft calls are minimal, fewer men are affected, and the capacity of the system to channel diminishes. Finally and most importantly, to use the deferment-channeling device as an incentive for men to enter certain fields is highly questionable since it may motivate for the wrong reasons and reward evasive behavior.

SUMMARY

There are other areas of controversy in the present Act not touched upon but which should be mentioned. The status of part-time students should be clarified. The appeal procedure is not as fair or equitable as the Selective Service System indicates. The ten-day period is too short and the information the registrant receives is not clear cut. This information should spell out clearly what the rights and obligations of the registrant are in this regard. Finally, the whole question of manpower needs should be studied. As the number of availables increase, even with the relatively modest draft calls (at Vietnam levels) a smaller proportion of the eligible groups will actually be inducted. In the absence of a national emergency, a larger proportion of men will reach age 26 without serving.

CONCLUSION

In conclusion, the following are recommendations which might be considered. Their realization would necessitate new legislation:

1) The legislation enacted should have a clear unambiguous purpose.

2) Guidelines and Presidential executive orders concerning the operation of the Selective Service System should be *mandatory* rather than *advisory*.

3) The channeling concept should be clarified by law.

The following possible recommendations could be achieved by administrative action:

1) There should be increased standardization and clearer interpretation of Selective Service regulations.

2) Deferment policies should be standardized by making Presidential executive orders *mandatory* rather than *advisory*.

NOTES

[1] See pp. 266-72 of *Congress and the Nation* 1945-1964 for a good synopsis of the Congressional debate on the draft and on Universal Military Training.

[2] The material in this section comes from *A Working Paper: The Student Deferment Program in Selective Service* (prepared in the Planning Office, Office of the Director, National Headquarters Selective Service System, February, 1952).

[3] The National Manpower Council published a study, *Student Deferment and National Manpower Policy* (Columbia Univ. Press, 1952). Chapter I, pp. 23-38 discusses student deferment.

[4] M. H. Trytten, *Student Deferment in Selective Service* (Univ. of Minnesota Press, 1952). Although now dated, this book carefully analyzes the need for deferment in a period of "less than all out national emergency."

[5] The Negro induction rate is about 11 per cent, roughly proportionate to the Negro segment of the population.

[6] See p. 30 of *Selective Service and Chronology*, 1965 ed., U. S. Government Printing Office.

[7] *Annual Report of the Director of Selective Service*, 1965, U.S. Government Printing Office, p. 18.

6

The Search for an Ideal Solution in a Natural Game of Chance

BRIG. GEN. S. L. A. MARSHALL (RET.)

The subject of the Conference on the Draft concerns me very much. I am wholly opposed to the draft as it is now applied—in particular, I am opposed to the proposition that taking any kind of a ride through college should exempt from military service the youth while he continues his education. I do not object to the law primarily because it is unjust, inequitable, and that it works in general to the disadvantage of the underprivileged in this country. I am not sure that it does: entering military service may mean in the greater number of cases that the youngster in adversity gets for the first time a real break in his life, and may even go on to become college-educated and in a position to compete with anyone. Moreover, there is no way under heaven that a law can be written so that the obligations of military service, and the sacrifices sometimes entailed thereby, will fall equally and evenly on young Americans of military age.

That it can and should be done is mainly an illusion held dear by Congressmen and nourished by social scientists who advise them. As a practical matter it is a problem that is unadjustable, due to the very nature of military service. The demands of service itself can never be equalized. What happens to any person after he enters thereon is determined more by fate and by blind chance than by human computation. The individual is merely subject to the greatest lottery on earth. Possibly the initial demand could be equalized. What follows simply cannot. So the floods of oratory and the hours of calculation wasted on trying to make possible an ideal solution are pretty much beside the point. There is none.

I object to what is being done because I believe absolutely that it is the wrong thing for the nation as to what it augurs as to its prospects for long-time survival, and as to what is suggested as to the standards it upholds—the question being whether such standards are worthy of a free people, supposedly capable of determining, and righting, their own fortunes. It can profit the United States nothing to conserve and coddle a great reservoir (at least in theory) of brainy members of all professions if in the end our inheritance passes into the custody of a generation of men morally and spiritually flabby, in that they have been taught and trained to believe that any service to self is more proper, more correct, than being at the disposal of community work, the welfare of a group, the good

General Marshall's contribution was written as a personal letter to the Chairman of the Conference. Its title was given by the editor.

of the country. That certainly should not be the aim of a university as it deals with, and conditions, the young male. Its object should ever be the protection and furthering of the prospect of the general society, since it exists by their funds and sufferance.

Nor should it be the attitude of universities as a whole when they consider government policy. What is best for them is no more necessarily best for the nation at a particular point (and I speak here of the desire to keep enrollment figures ever spiraling up and on) than is the fortune of General Motors to be thought of as at one with the good of the country.

I hasten to add that in this particular the American universities are not uniquely disposed. The pressure they exert on government to help shape its draft policies in such a way that they will not themselves be hurt as to enrollment, future prospects, etc., does not make them singular. I do not mean that with them, as with business, industry, and government itself, doing things bigger is considered synonymous with doing them better, or is at least taken as an indication of continuing success. My point is rather that within all free societies, practically all institutions strain to keep the military requirement on manpower at the bare minimum while putting maximum reliance on all other factors entering into the common defense.

The frenzied pursuit of the secret weapon as a substitute for trained and ready forces continues into our day, as witness that the arrival of the time when we swung to Titan, Minuteman, and so on coincided with the decision that ROTC training in the land grant schools should become optional. What the weapon-change connoted was directly the opposite of what was done. Do we have a sufficient reserve of young officers today? The fact is we are scrambling to find them wherever we may. Not just the universities but the labor unions, churches, legislators, and even the veterans' organizations are loath to take an honest, well-considered stand on manpower programs, and the military sometimes go along with the mainstream too much, as when they continue to advocate, in inner councils, recourse to a stabilized professional army. That, under today's conditions, is like baying at the moon.

Thinking as an independent, I am not always sure of what I see. Being no longer in government, I cannot see the full spectrum, or even be certain this is a disadvantage. Before returning to Vietnam last May, I was for three days with the training center at Fort Bliss. That is where I started in the Army fifty years ago, and whenever I want to get a fresh measure of how we are doing, I return there. In this case, I was interested in learning whether we had weakened basic training because of the demand for strong combat leadership in Vietnam. I found that, to the contrary, the standard was being held high. Though other installations at Bliss are vast and time-proved, the center for turning civilians into soldiers has been going only since last October. The turnover is therefore a fair measure of the stuff filling today's army.

In six months, 14,000 recruits had schooled at Fort Bliss, and 19,000 had passed through the induction center, the 5,000 being sent to other bases. The average age of trainees was 19.8 years—quite young if not too young. The average education was 13.1 years—higher than in any past year. In the cycle I saw, 1,100 men were draftees and 2,600 regular Army, many of whom volunteered so that they could get their choice of a combat arm.

Now I get to the meat of the matter. Of the 19,191 recruits that had gone through the reception center since last November, only 630, or three per cent, were college graduates, a statistic hardly suggesting that the draft will get the college deferee in the long run. Every college graduate who came there was not only reminded that his degree gave him a claim on officership; he was given a sales pitch to the effect that commissioned status would be a big break, that he would at once draw $200 monthly as a candidate, and that he would not have to serve any longer than if he went the enlisted route. Yet of the 630 men, only 199, or less than one-third, applied for a chance at commission. At the same time, 4,372 high school graduates were going through the center and they, too, were given a pitch. Their diplomas made them eligible for warrant officer flight training, which means helicopters, Vietnam and all of that. More danger on the one hand, less prestige on the other. Even so, out of that number, 2,385, or more than half, saw it as a real opportunity and applied.

Granted that this is just one small sampling, I would like for social scientists to take a look at these figures and *tell me what they signify*. How does it happen that in the greater number the boys who only made it through high school responded when their manhood was challenged or their ambition stirred, while the college graduates, in the majority, did not? The aim of higher education, as I understand it, is not to reduce the male individual to gutlessness, to stress the importance of all things except character and acceptance of responsibility, and to grind out ground-up individuals just like a sausage machine. Yet the conclusion appears ineluctable that in the majority those 630 college men had to be either too smug, too dull-spirited, or too tied to the apronstrings to have a go at officership. They had a contempt for it or they were afraid.

I do not see how any reasonable person can doubt that the campus has become the last refuge of today's well-fed draft dodger though he has no more real promise of a productive professional life than had P. T. Barnum's Oofty-Goofty.

Last fall, following the President's decisions of July, the shadow of the Vietnam war fell heavy over the land. I was returning by air from New York and my seat companion was the head of one of the largest business administration colleges in the nation, located not far from where I live. He told me he had just finished dealing with 1,200 or so male students trying for the post-graduate school. Most had no real potential for it. He screened most of them carefully to get at their primary motivation. More than 90 per cent admitted that they were hoping to escape military service. He concluded: "Having served my time in the Army, I had no sympathy with that, but then I could not keep them all out."

On hitting the Pacific Coast when I returned from Vietnam, I saw an item in a newspaper which I cannot quote verbatim. It was datelined Ann Arbor. The University of Michigan had a problem. The policy was to make public the names of students belonging to campus organizations, but it happened that there were some 64 (I think that was the number) student groups protesting the war in Vietnam. They wanted these lists kept secret and the University bowed.

I have no sympathy with that. I had seen too many of our battalions come out of line after hard struggle and heavy loss. In the average rifle company, the strength was 50 per cent composed of Negroes, Southwestern Mexicans, Puerto Ricans, Guamanians, Nisei and so on. But a real cross-section of American youth? —almost never. I repeat that I see no way to equalize the burden. But so long as the universities hold to present ground and are upheld by national policy, there is no way to provide the fighting line with a sufficient number of intelligent young leaders. So the Army is filling more and more with Class 4 material, or those of lower IQ. By current estimate, it will go to 25 per cent.

More than any American living, I have watched the working of the draft at the fighting level, beginning in World War I, through two theaters in World War II, in Korea and finally, Vietnam. Theories of what men may be able to do interest me not at all; I want to know how a policy works out finally. It is peculiarly the case, however, that when policy is made on such a matter, only older generals, doctors, social scientists and manpower secretaries are called as expert witnesses—and what we do comes of what they say.

So the draft continues very much as it was from the beginning. The myth is accepted that only 18-, 19-, and 20-year-olds give the fighting line the energy and drive that is required. I assert that is absolutely false. Many American youths in those years are adolescent, uncertain, still growing. They lack stability under heavy pressure.

In World War I, I was 17 and a sergeant when first in combat. Being short, I had matured early and had no difficulty, though I would occasionally, despite every effort, fall asleep while walking post, though never caught at it. There were more than 100,000 underage volunteers in the AEF. Yet less than 250 of us were higher-rated NCOs. The others could fill in; but they could not be responsible for other men.

There is the trouble: fill an Army with such young numbers and it becomes shorted of a vigorous leadership. Many times in lecturing combat officers at Benning, Knox, Sill, and Leavenworth, I have asked the question: "How many of you would be willing to go into battle with a company formed, as to ranks, of men only 21 years old or younger?" I have never seen a hand go up. It is the man over 25 who has grace under pressure, steadies the line in crisis, and lasts longest. There are exceptions, but they are few. Five years ago at Fort Knox training center they held an experiment. Two companies were formed, one of volunteers under age 21, the other of former college men, drafted, age 24 or older. One company was completely self-organized by the end of the first week, and thereafter had no disciplinary problems. Moreover, in road marching, it was good for twice the distance of the other and its performance on the ranges was equally superior.

Yes, it was the company of the older men, which should have occasioned no surprise, but did.

7

Equality in the Exemption of Conscientious Objectors

JOHN DE J. PEMBERTON, JR.

The development of formal provision in our system of conscription for exemption of conscientious objectors is a credit to our democracy. But it is both unnecessary and unfair that the present law limits the exemption to those who (1) "by reason of religious training and belief" are (2) opposed "to participation in war in any form."

In earlier times exemptions for conscience were confined to members of traditional pacifist denominations. Since 1940 the statutory basis for exemption has been extended to include all religious pacifists, of whatever denomination. When conscription was reenacted in 1948—by adoption of the act whose successive renewals have given us our present law—a definition of "religious training and belief" was added, confining it to "belief in a relation to a Supreme Being involving duties superior to those arising from any human relation." The controlling interpretation of this definition, which was once thought to have confined the exemption to believers in God so as to discriminate against nontheistic faiths, was provided by the 1965 decision in *U.S. v. Seeger*, 380 U.S. 163, which held (with respect to a religious agnostic who claimed exemption):

> We have concluded that Congress, in using the expression "Supreme Being" rather than the designation "God," was merely clarifying the meaning of religious training and belief so as to embrace all religions and to exclude essentially political, sociological or philosophical views. We believe that under this construction, the test of belief "in a relation to a Supreme Being" is whether a given belief that is sincere and meaningful occupies a place in the life of its possessor parallel to that filled by the orthodox belief in God of one who clearly qualifies for the exemption. [380 U. S. at 166.]

The Seeger interpretation may be taken as a liberalization, but we are nevertheless left, after liberalization, with a recognition of conscience that is unwarrantedly limited to *religious pacifists*. The present law exempts one who objects in conscience to obeying conscription's command, *only* if he concurrently satisfies two collateral (and, I suggest, irrelevant) criteria:

1) That his conscience be religiously (though not necessarily theistically) informed, and
2) That his objection to conscription's present command extend as well to "war in any form."

The author is Executive Director, American Civil Liberties Union.

The first criterion imposes a qualification that is not only collateral, but is probably impossible to ascertain as well. The Seeger interpretation supplies a standard for determining what may be called the depth of an objector's belief, but it does not define which deeply held beliefs are religious (except by implication from the exclusion of those which are "essentially political, sociological or philosophical views"). Earlier decisions have attempted to define religion but offer only the alternatives of testing by orthodoxy or by depth of conviction. (See Barrett, *The Conscientious Objector in America*, pp. 4-6, especially quotation from *U.S.* v. *Kauten* on p. 5.) Since *Seeger* may be taken as rejecting the test of orthodoxy, the depth test may be the only acceptable alternative, despite its seeming tautology.

But if decision were required in the case of an objector whose depth of conviction unquestionably met the Seeger standard, who explicitly denied that his beliefs were religious, a clear conflict with constitutional standards would be posed. Not only would the denial of exemption to him prefer or "aid one religion [or] . . . all religions" (contrary to the nearly universally accepted dictum in *Everson* v. *Board of Education* 330 U.S. 1[1]), but its invidious discrimination against religious non-believers would seem to be beyond the permissible limits of reasonable legislative classification. That is, if Congress could validly prefer religion in the grant of this exemption, it could do so only to serve a proper secular purpose. It does not seem possible to demonstrate that such a purpose is served here.

The second criterion (opposed to "war in any form") seems to be a more reasonable one. It assumes a superiority to the moral position of pacifism; if a non-pacifist admits he might kill in different circumstances, killing in the present war would seem to do less violence to his conscience. But this assumption is open to question. It is not obvious that moral superiority may be assigned to an undiscriminating negative.

In the first place, the present exemption does not require absolute abjuration of all lethal violence. It is not a fatal inconsistency for a pacifist objector to acknowledge the propriety of a fully armed domestic police force, or to admit that he would be willing to serve in an international peace-keeping body. He may engage in other kinds of hazardous activities in which the taking of some human life may be predicted, with considerable statistical certainty, such as is true of air and automotive transportation and specially hazardous building construction.

Conversely his non-pacifist counterpart may only be refusing to answer dishonestly a series of hypothetical questions: He does not know what he would do if an invading army threatened his family and community. He was too young to face a decision to enter the armed forces in World War II; he cannot be sure he would have refused to use violence against Hitler. All he can know with certainty is that his deepest convictions tell him that for him to kill in today's war, or to participate in institutions that support this conflict, would be wrong and that it would be wrong as well for him to let his government decide *this* matter for him.

The heart of the matter is not whether an individual's conscience has been tutored by religion, for great numbers of the men who are inducted have been subjected to religious training similar to that of the objector and the inductees come from every one of the nation's traditional denominations. Nor is it whether the objector would take the same position with respect to every conceivable armed conflict, for he is usually a young man who has not had occasion to face and think through that many possibilities.

The heart of the matter—the circumstance that must govern the granting or denying of an exemption—is whether what conscription commands of the registrant *at the present moment* is, for him, a wrong that would do violence to his integrity, a wrong for which the command of government will not relieve him of personal responsibility.

There are sound reasons for exempting such objectors. It makes sense to do so because an attempt to force a man to violate such scruples would be destructive of his personality and demeaning to the government that made the attempt. It makes sense as well because his forced induction would contribute no advantage to the morale and effectiveness of the armed forces, while his imprisonment would be unnecessarily costly to both him and society.

This experience and these reasons apply as well to the non-religious and non-pacifist objector, presently denied exemption by statute. The destructiveness of forcing the alternatives of induction or imprisonment on either of them is essentially identical to that of the religious pacifist. The administrative experience gained in distinguishing genuine consciences from draftee reluctance is fully applicable to the administration of a broadened exemption. And the risk of fraud is minimal for it is unlikely that a man would choose to feign the conscience of a discriminating, non-pacifist objector when exemption as a religious pacifist was an available alternative.

Two difficult obstacles to achieving this extension do remain, however. The first is the fear that somehow the number of non-religious, non-pacifist objectors will be so much greater than the number of men presently exempted that a broadened exemption would overwhelm the system. To this fear there are two answers: The first answer is that the exemption does not involve merely dissenters from the war in Vietnam. It involves only (1) men whose convictions are such that, lacking the broadened exemption, they choose punishment (sometimes not until after induction) rather than obedience to orders they deem wrongful—and (2) men who will be morally crippled by this cruel choice and wear the uniform ineffectively, without advancing either the cause of their conscience or that of their country. However many of these there are, they are but a fraction of the number who are merely dissenters.

The second answer asks a question, one that is assuredly hypothetical if we may trust the inferences reasonably to be drawn from the data now at hand: What would the nation do if the number of conscientious objectors—non-religious and non-pacifist objectors included—rose to the point where it would impair the effectiveness of conscription? Real conscientious objectors, that is—not mere dissenters and reluctant draftees (who themselves constitute but a minority of the draft-eligible men today). Is it conceivable that policy itself would not be reconsidered as a result of such an expression of moral repugnance among those who are being asked to carry out that policy? Whether or not they were exempted, objections of conscience on the part of such numbers would render the conscription-based policy ineffective. An alternative would necessarily have to be found.

No such easy answers can be made to the second obstacle to an equitable broadening of the exemption. It is that the non-religious, non-pacifist objector seems threatening to other citizens in a more serious way than does the religious pacifist. Probably most citizens profess some kind of religious convictions, but only a few are guided by these convictions in forming or expressing their views about the conduct of the nation's foreign and military policy. In this respect the religious pacifist is sufficiently different from others to be relatively non-threatening.

Quakers have often been spoken of as "a peculiar people." So long as they remain thus differentiated from the rest of the community, conduct pursuant to the historic Quaker "peace testimony" has little impact upon the peace of mind of others. In this sense, the religious pacifist, who is popularly assimilated to the Quaker prototype, makes little dent upon either the public conscience or its consciousness.

But the non-religious, non-pacifist objector to organized violence is not so easily dismissed. He seems to take his stance from a similar background to that which others draw upon in thinking about war, and he acts upon data that is available to all. By his conduct he says, in a way no one from among the "peculiar people" can, that that which moved him ought similarly to move others. What he thus seems to say may be capable of refutation, but it cannot so easily be ignored. It is discomforting and the source of discomfort may easily become unpopular.

Perhaps the greatest obstacle to broadening the exemption, therefore, may be the unpopularity of the non-religious, non-pacifist objector. But the unpopularity of the object should not deter a democracy from doing equity to any one of its citizens. I submit that an overriding need for doing violence to the conscience of the non-religious, non-pacifist objector cannot be demonstrated, and equality of treatment with others who are similarly situated requires that the exemption be extended to him.

NOTES

[1] "The 'establishment of religion' clause of the First Amendment means at least this: Neither a state nor the Federal Government can set up a church. Neither can pass laws which aid one religion, aid all religions, or prefer one religion over another. Neither can force nor influence a person to go to or to remain away from church against his will or force him to profess a belief or disbelief in any religion. No person can be punished for entertaining or professing religious beliefs or disbeliefs, for church attendance or non-attendance. No tax in any amount, large or small, can be levied to support any religious activities or institutions, whatever they may be called, or whatever form they may adopt to teach or practice religion. Neither a state nor the Federal Government can, openly or secretly, participate in the affairs of any religious organizations or groups and vice versa. In the words of Jefferson, the clause against establishment of religion by law was intended to erect 'a wall of separation between Church and State.'" *Reynolds* v. *United States*, supra (98 U.S. at 164, 25 L ed. 249). 330 U.S. at 15-16.

BROADENING THE DRAFT

8

The Logic of National Service

MORRIS JANOWITZ

In the spring of 1966, public discussion of the draft became widespread and intense for the first time since 1940 when the legislation was initially passed. One of the groups most critical of current policies is composed of college students who are opposed to war in Vietnam. By opposing the way in which the draft is managed they believe that they have found an acceptable and popular issue for agitating about Vietnam.

Public debate about the draft has now come to involve the widest segments of American society. Leading senators and congressmen, newspaper editors and columnists, educators and civic leaders have made it an important issue. The appointment of a Presidential Commission on the Draft means that it is no longer a question of whether the policies of the Selective Service System should be modified, but along what lines they will be altered.

Recommendations for change usually rest on an admixture of arguments based on moral justification, economic costs and military efficiency, as well as on broad conceptions of national interest, both domestic and foreign. Three basic positions have emerged which contain some similar features but which express different conceptions of "who shall serve" in the armed forces of a political democracy.

First, there is the position that the armed forces should be a completely voluntary establishment based on a competitive pay scale, regardless of the costs. Immediate shortages in personnel should be made up by some form of lottery system. Selective service would be employed merely as a temporary device or to meet particular emergencies, and national policy should be to eliminate the Selective Service System as soon as possible.

Second, there is the position which seeks to reform the present Selective Service System. This approach assumes that the current system is inefficient as well as morally unjust because of the reliance placed on educational deferments. In this view, to rely exclusively on a "mercenary" army is politically risky and disruptive and it is probably not economically feasible. In the contemporary scene and in the foreseeable future, some form of selective service is required to produce manpower for the military establishment. To make use of educational deferments is to rely upon an unfair criterion which is biased against the lower classes, and immoral because it is a crude form of meritocracy which assumes that the intelligent should not serve their country. Moreover, it is disruptive of the operations of the university since it encourages many people to seek a refuge

The author is a professor in the Department of Sociology, University of Chicago.

in higher education and introduces excessive amounts of uncertainty into making career decisions. This position seeks to reform current practice mainly by a lottery to augument the number of those who elect to serve on a volunteer basis.

Third is the viewpoint that leads to some form of national service. In this perspective, the question of selective service cannot be detached from broader problems of American education and American policy in international relations. Effective education as well as the pressures of social and political change underline the desirability of broad involvement of young people for a period of one or two years in various types of national service, both domestic and international. Selective service is required, but it must operate in a moral and political setting which makes it legitimate. National service is based on the widest degree of voluntary choice, but to insure military needs, selective service would rely on a lottery plus differential incentives. Those who do not serve in the military either as volunteers or selectees would be expected (or, alternatively, required) to perform national service. The variety of forms of national service would be numerous and would involve many nongovernmental programs.

All three positions give a role to a lottery system, if only as a temporary or standby device. Civilians who urge this change must recognize that the idea of a lottery system strikes at a sensitive theme in the military self-image. The professional soldier often believes that he is perceived by civilians as one who has somehow failed in the occupational competition of the larger society. Many officers hold the view that a lottery for the selection of enlisted men would serve to strengthen and substantiate this stereotype of the military, that military service is a job for losers, as members of a luckless legion.

Moreover, the military services would still depend primarily on volunteers and professional soldiers, both as officers and enlisted personnel. Frequently the military contend that it would be difficult to incorporate men selected by chance with those whose service is based on choice. They believe that the motivation of the soldier selected by a lottery might contaminate the attitudes of regular personnel and thus weaken efficiency.

There is a deeper moral issue for the professional officer. Military service always involves a chance of death in combat or even in training. However, the professional soldier views such a contingency as much more than an occupational risk. It is for him a supreme sacrifice for the welfare of the society. The professional officer feels that a lottery system might produce a moral definition which is highly undesirable. The man drafted on the basis of a lottery is a loser, a man who has lost in a game of chance. Having lost once, he runs the risk of losing again as a casualty in combat. It is wrong, in their opinion, to define potential casualties as losers in a chance situation. What will be the attitudes of society toward sacrifice resulting from being a two-time loser? Will it view the loss as simply another contingency and thus fail to support the men who fight?

The civilian may not fully understand this point of view, but there exists here a difference between military and civilian perspectives. The sense of professionalism among the military officers would lead them to accept such a lottery if it were made the law. But to the extent that they understand the limitations of the present system, and to the extent that modification would produce a more diversified source of skilled manpower, they would be more prepared to accept such a change.

The purpose of this paper is to set forth some of the demographic and organizational issues involved in a national service system, which I believe to be the most desirable format as a long-term objective, even though it clearly could not be launched overnight. In exploring the logic of a national service system, two elements are of crucial importance, although the arguments for and against any one of the basic three formats are complex and contain highly problematic elements. First, in my opinion, the national service system supplies a sound basis for coping with the deficiencies of any draft system, including one that must rely on a lottery. In other words, I do not object to arguing that some form of national service would make the lottery, if it had to be used, more acceptable to all involved. Second, and more crucial, the argument will be developed that a national service program supplies a powerful weapon for preventing the creation of a predominantly or even all-Negro enlisted force in the Army, an "internal foreign legion," which would be disastrous for American political democracy.

THE HERITAGE OF SELECTIVE SERVICE

Demands for reorganizing the selective service are rooted, in part, in the strong public presumption that the system has worked with a definite social class bias. When selective service was reinstituted during the Korean conflict it was for a partial mobilization, in contrast to the more extensive mobilization of World War II. There was a military need for only part of the age cohorts from 19 through 26. There was also a belief in the necessity of continuing the flow of personnel into trained professional and scientific categories. In addition, selective service sought to remove itself from determining who should go on to higher education. As a result, occupational and educational criteria were used as the basis for deferment. In the public view, this had the result of placing the burden of military service on those who did not go to college, namely, on the lower socioeconomic groups, and has come to be viewed as unfair.

A set of demographic factors actually contributed to the validity of this perception. Steadily—since the Korean conflict until the period of the South Vietnam buildup—the size of the available manpower in age groups eligible for selective service has increased and the number to be drafted has decreased. The result was a greater and greater reliance on occupational and educational deferments. As a result, there is an important element of truth in the public's view of a selective service bias against the lower socioeconomic groups, but this view is so oversimplified as to be an inadequate and even dangerous basis for public discussion of selective service.

Unfortunately, social researchers have avoided serious and systematic analysis of selective service as a social and political institution. In fact, there is not a single major treatise on the subject. Nevertheless, as a result of the efforts of a handful of specialists, plus inferences that can be drawn from the operational statistics of government agencies and special government surveys, it is possible to piece together the social consequences of selective service. To this end, it is of prime importance to distinguish between the recruitment patterns of selective service and the allocation of manpower within the Armed Forces. For the period of the Korean hostilities, research has shown that the burdens of war, especially the incidence of casualties, fell disproportionately on lower socioeconomic groups. This was as much the result of the way manpower had to be utilized by the ground forces as it was of the social bias of selective service. At the officer level, casualties cannot be said to be distributed unequally as to social class. If anything, because of the emphasis on college graduation as a requirement for officers, there was a bias in the reverse direction. But among non-commissioned officers and enlisted men in the ground forces, where the bulk of casualties occurred, social scientists have documented the heavier incidence of casualties among lower socioeconomic groups. The division of labor in the military establishment meant that young men with better education (and higher socioeconomic position) were sent to advanced training and specialized units where the casualty rates were lower. Infantry units, those units which in the language of the military require "soft skills," were staffed with men of limited educational preparation. The result was that combat infantry units reflected a lower class and rural background.

After the Korean conflict, selective service, while it had definite biases, operated with a relative fairness, especially since there were no combat operations. The very few casualties occurred mainly in the Air Force among units engaged in routine aerial operations. These were officers of higher socioeconomic background and reflected the exposure to risks that a professional officer corps has to take.

The basic manpower requirements of the Armed Forces were met by two sources. Small quotas of young men were drafted and were assigned to the Army. The bulk of the requirements was met through volunteers who were responding in part to the pressure of the Selective Service System. This pressure generated not only contributions to the enlisted ranks but also men who joined the various short-term service officer programs. The Air Force and the Navy, because of their more attractive conditions of work and the specialized training they offered, could rely on volunteers exclusively. In fact, during the period after the end of the Korean conflict, standards of recruitment were being raised, thereby keeping out young men from low-income and Negro groups who would have served but who were ineligible because of educational requirements. The Marine Corps was also able to attract the personnel required because of its traditions and its image in American society. In addition, the Marine Corps had a two-year initial enlistment as opposed to the three-year term for the Army, which aided its recruitment. Since Vietnam, however, it has also drawn from Selective Service.

On the basis of available materials it is possible to describe the educational and social background of those who actually served in the Armed Forces during the period before the expansion of manpower for Vietnam. At this point we are interested in the incidence of all types of military service, whether a man volunteered or was drafted, whether he was an officer or an enlisted man, for all these types of military service are influenced by the operation of the Selective Service System. A good indicator is the military experience of men who were 27 to 34 in 1965; these men had already passed through the period of their eligibility for selective service. Of this group, those whose education ranged from having completed nine years of school to those who had completed college, roughly the same proportion (about 70 per cent) had had military service. At the lower end of the educational continuum the incidence of military service declines sharply; only one-third of those with less than grammar school education served in the military. At the upper end of the continuum, those who entered graduate and professional school, similarly only one-quarter entered active service.

The reasons are obviously different. Those with less than eight years of education were deferred on the basis of unfitness, a direct expression of their low educational achievement and related medical and psychiatric conditions. Graduate and professional study produced exemption on the basis of educational deferment, often supplemented by marital deferment. (This analysis does not include the limited number of agricultural deferments which tended to favor those with lower levels of education.)

Interestingly enough, we are dealing with the educational position of the son rather more than with that of the father. The relationship between father's education and son's military service is a much weaker relationship, although the same pattern holds true. In effect, the United States has moved more and more toward an achievement society via education, and this has had the effect of decreasing a young man's chances of serving in the Armed Forces to the extent that he applies his energies to extending his education beyond four years of college.

But education in the United States is unequally distributed, and therefore in order to understand the social risks of the military service it is necessary to analyze these issues in terms of socioeconomic categories, particularly in terms of the interplay of social class and race. This interplay has meant that in the recent past the Negro has been under-represented in the Armed Forces. This can be seen in two different ways. First, among men with less than 8th-grade education, Negroes have served to a lesser degree than whites. The same holds true among those with 9 to 11 grades of education—but among high school graduates, Negroes and whites have served in similar proportions. Second, among men of low socioeconomic background, the difference in military service between Negroes and whites has been marked, while the difference in military service between Negroes and whites with middle or medium socioeconomic background has declined.

Nevertheless, the integration of the Negro in the Armed Forces has been proceeding at a faster rate than in civilian society. This is the result of vigorous programs of desegregation and equal opportunity which have operated effectively despite the fact that until recently the criteria for selection based on education has served to depress the overall percentage of Negroes. Since 1962 the overall participation of Negroes has risen from 8.2 per cent to 9.0 per cent in 1965, and is most likely to continue to rise.

This rise needs to be related both to the procurement rate\ of new Negro personnel and more pointedly to the reenlistment rates of Negroes. During the period of 1962 to 1965, Negroes—both volunteers and inductees—were entering the Armed Forces at about their proportion in the civilian society or in slightly higher concentration for certain months. Given the attractiveness of a military career to low-income groups, this percentage still reflects the lack of educational preparation of Negroes. But the period 1962 to 1965 was one of an improvement in the quantity and quality of Negroes seeking admission to the Armed Forces. On the other hand, once there was an increase in Selective Service quotas because of Vietnam in the latter part of 1965, the procurement of Negroes by induction fell from 15.2 per cent during the month of July 1965 to 10.8 per cent in December 1965. A representative draft without college deferments would in the long run contribute to the elimination of any over-representation of Negro enlisted personnel.

However, more important in accounting for the representation of Negroes in the armed forces is the markedly higher reenlistment rate for Negro enlisted personnel. In 1965 the first-term reenlistments of white personnel was 17.1 per cent while for Negroes it was 45.1 per cent. Given their educational backgrounds and previous level of skills, Negroes have tended to concentrate in the combat arms of the Army where the opportunities are greatest for rapid advancement into non-commissioned officer positions. In some units such as the Airborne the percentage is near 40. Overall participation of Negroes in Vietnam was reported for the last part of 1965: the Army had the highest proportion of Negroes with 15.8 per cent, the Air Force 8.3 per cent, the Marines 8.9 per cent and the Navy 5.1 per cent.

The Armed Forces are aware of the dangers of creating units in which Negroes are concentrated. It is, of course, basic to their operations not to use racial quotas; on the contrary, they look with pride on the success of integrating the Negro into combat units, for success in combat units is the basis of military prestige. The armed services have a variety of personnel practices designed to distribute Negroes more equally throughout the services, but these are only slowly being implemented. Given the high rates of reenlistments among Negroes, it is not difficult to anticipate future trends.

Thus, in summary, it is clear that there have been distortions of the Selective Service System, mainly in the past, through the exclusion of low educational groups, especially Negroes, at one end of the scale, and through exclusion of persons following post-college education at the other. To some degree, exclusion at the lower levels will be modified as educational standards of the country rise and criteria for selection are altered. Efforts on the part of the Armed Forces to deal with this question by having special remedial battalions have not received congressional support, but special civilian or military programs are certain to emerge in the years ahead, not only because of the requirements of the military but because of broader social policy. Alternatively, distortions due to post-college education seem to be growing as the emphasis on such education increases. We must deal not only with the facts of distortion but with the growing public definition that educational deferments per se are morally undesirable.

Assessment of the past performance of the Selective Service System must encompass more than the social characteristics of those who entered military service. The system operated in the past with a considerable degree of administrative effectiveness in meeting immediate and short-term requirements. In fact, its concern with month-to-month procurement in part prevented the development of a longer-range perspective and a capacity to meet changing requirements.

The organization represents an effective balance between highly centralized policy decision-making and decentralized implementation. Selective Service has worked with an amazing absence of personal corruption. The use of local community personnel has reduced hostility to rules and regulations. Moreover, there is a general feeling that local boards have been fair in applying national directives to the local situation. Decentralized operating procedure thus reduces local friction, but it produces considerable variation in practice from state to state. These differences have become a new source of criticism.

Selective Service and its local boards do not proceed on the basis of a national manpower pool which would take into consideration wide discrepancies in population characteristics among communities. Moreover, there have come to be wide variations in quotas on a month-to-month basis. Selective Service has emerged more and more as a procurement agency for the Department of Defense, without adequately representing the interests of the registrants of the larger society. While local boards are civilian, all other officials, from national headquarters to State Directors, tend to be military in rank and orientation.

However, the Selective Service System as it operated after the Korean War was adapted to the realities of the American political system and to American strategic commitments during a period of international tension without actual military operations. First and most basically, it was seen as temporary. The resistance to a permanent Selective Service System remained pervasive even after the end of World War II. Second, Selective Service operated with minimal disruption of civilian society even while it obtained manpower for the type of Armed Forces the executive branch wished to create. During the period of gradual expansion of the military establishment after 1960, Selective Service operated without great social strain or disruption. In good part this was due to the career opportunities the military establishment offered to the socially disadvantaged. Third, a temporary Selective Service System coupled with an extensive reserve component helped keep alive the citizen-soldier concept which has strong roots in the American scene. More tacitly than explicitly, the Selective Service System is seen—and in fact does operate—as a force for civilianizing the Armed Forces and overcoming the sharp segregation of the military from civilian society that characterized the Armed Forces before World War II.

The temporary nature of Selective Service operated to inhibit both long-range planning and public discussion of its operations since there was a pervasive feeling that at some future date it would no longer be needed. In fact, in 1964 President Johnson authorized a study to probe the possibility of its ultimate elimination. Instead, Vietnam has demonstrated the rigidities and inequalities of present procedure. During this period of actual military operations, the system operates ineffectively and produces considerable social and political strain. The standards of procurement have been judged too rigid and too arbitrary. Selection criteria have been lowered, but the Armed Forces have not developed the kinds of remedial programs which operated during World War II to utilize manpower which civilian society had not adequately prepared for adult responsibility and service in the military establishment. On the contrary, college deferments had to be altered to meet manpower requirements. Selective Service turned to the American Council on Education. In retrospect it is incredible that the Council did not engage in wider consultation with its constituency, but merely endorsed the repetition of a system that was used during the Korean hostilities. The changed political circumstances and heightened sensitivity to issues of social justice, as well as the arbitrary character of the system of deferments based on academic performance, have led to the current agitation. Secretary Robert McNamara's proposal for a system of national service has created the conditions for a careful scrutiny of immediate military requirements and, for the first time since the end of World War II, public discussion has been generated, oriented toward long-range requirements and national objectives.

THE ORGANIZATION OF A NATIONAL SERVICE PROGRAM

To anticipate military manpower requirements for even a year or two in advance has been hazardous in the past. However, to describe the elements of a national service system, some assumptions must be made not only for the next two or three years but minimally for a ten- to twenty-year time period. While the military manpower aspects of national service could be introduced very rapidly, other elements would have to be developed over a five-year period.

In Table 1, the actual number of new personnel procured by the Armed Forces in 1965 is shown to be over 570,000. This includes the small number in the special federal programs of the Coast Guard, U.S. Public Health Service, and the Merchant Marine Academy. For 1966—with the Vietnam buildup—this is certain to have gone well over 800,000. As a point of departure for planning a national service program, it is assumed that the required level of manpower will be equal to that before the current buildup. This implies a reduction of international tensions and in particular some degree of stabilization in Southeast Asia, without which even larger amounts of military manpower will be required. For the purposes of this analysis, 550,000 to 600,000 men, obtained through all the various procurement programs for officers and enlisted men, is projected as the need for the next ten years and then slowly decreasing during the tenth to the twentieth year.

TABLE 1

New Military Manpower Actually Procured in 1965*

National military establishment		
Enlisted: First enlistments	318,209	
Inductions	102,555	
Reserves—active duty training	94,374	
Total		515,138
Officers: Commissioned	46,535	
Officer candidates		
Academy cadets (entering class)	2,449	
Aviation cadets and OCS	2,856	51,840
Total		566,978
Coast Guard		
Officers	385	
Enlisted: Regular terms	4,912	
Active duty training	3,038	
Total		8,335
U.S. Public Health Service		665
Merchant Marine Academy		200
Total new personnel		576,178

*Includes special federal programs (Coast Guard, U.S. Public Health Service, and Merchant Marine Academy).

Each year in the United States approximately 1,800,000 young men reach age 18, and this figure can be expected to increase slowly in the years ahead before it declines. To many manpower specialists this presents a real dilemma (see Table 2): We have too many young men to deal with only by a Selective Service System, yet military manpower requirements are too large to rely upon a voluntary system. Among other issues, a national service system is designed precisely to deal with this dilemma.

National service is based upon a dual concept. Military manpower must be met by a fair and flexible selective service system, recognizing that there will be hardships and imperfections in any system. At the same time all young men

TABLE 2

Number of Males Attaining Age 18 for Selected Years, July 1st

1966	1,791,000
1967	1,787,000
1968	1,775,000
1969	1,823,000
1970	1,871,000
1971	1,938,000
1972	1,974,000
1973	2,028,000

Source: *Current Population Reports*, Series P-25, No. 321, November 30, 1965, Table 4, p. 23.

should engage in some type of national service. The notion of national service applies to young women also, but for the purposes of this discussion it is given a second level of priority. For those young men who do not enter military service, either as volunteers or under a reformed system of selective service, national service would at the outset be voluntary. There must be a maximum amount of free choice in the type of national service and a heavy emphasis on the role of private and voluntary groups in developing opportunities to do national service. In short, our goal is to fuse together a reasonable selective service system with a broad concept of national service. The basic features and principles are strikingly simple.

First, each new group of 18-year-old men would be required to participate in a national registration at which each young man would make known his personal preference. He would have the opportunity to indicate his choice of three basic alternatives:

1) *Make known his intention to volunteer for military service* and indicate his interest in the various specialized procurement programs including enlistment in a reserve program with active-duty training.

2) *Declare himself subject to selective service* and indicate what type of alternative volunteer national service he prefers in the event he is not selected by lottery for military service.

3) *Apply for exemption* on the basis of being a conscientious objector by virtue of religious conviction or other criteria set forth in the decisions of the U.S. Supreme Court. There would be no marital exemptions and while there would be some family and financial hardship exemptions, a federal allotment system would be used wherever required to eliminate gross inequalities. Deferment on the basis of critical skill (as defined by the Department of Labor) would be kept to a minimum, handled as under present arrangements, and administered by local Selective Service boards.

Second, entrance into the military service would take place during the next year when the young man is 19, or in an orderly fashion on a basis of completing a given school year. Those who wished to volunteer for the Armed Forces would be directly incorporated on the basis of their preference and qualifications. Volunteers, of course, must be matched against the available openings. Deficiencies in military manpower requirements beyond those generated by voluntary choice would be met by the Selective Service System operating on the basis of a lottery system. Normally, a young man would be subject to the selective service lottery only once during this period of initial registration, at age 18. Such an approach would eliminate the great uncertainty which exists in the present system. In the event of a major national emergency, cohorts between the ages of 19 and 26 would on a systematic basis be liable for subsequent exposure to the Selective Service procurement system. It would also be expected that young men who did not enter the Armed Forces would have completed their alternative volunteer national service by the time they reached 26 years of age.

Third, it is clearly recognized that there would be differential incentives and rewards. Those who served in the Armed Forces would receive a GI Bill of benefits while alternative national service would not have such features, or very limited ones in the case of the Peace Corps. Alternative service might very well be longer than military service. The Peace Corps, for example, requires 27 months as against 24 months of military service, reflecting an appropriate differential incentive and differential obligation. The type of alternative national service would depend on the skill and qualifications of the man involved as well as his preference. Where the person would perform his national service would be determined by his convenience and the time at which he is best prepared for doing so.

This system does not imply that the Armed Forces will become the manager of large numbers of young men. Rather, the administration of selective service would rest in the present structure. Once military manpower needs are met, the Armed Forces have no involvement with the rest of the age group. For example, the Peace Corps would continue to operate as a volunteer organization; there would be no compulsion for any individual to enter, and young men could volunteer for it after they had been exposed to the lottery system. The same is true for all forms of alternative service described in detail below.

The national service concept emphasizes the maximum dependence on voluntary compliance along with the lottery which is designed to meet military manpower needs. But it is a system of voluntary service in the context of changing social and political definitions. It would be expected that when Congress modifies the Selective Service System it will express its intent and commitment to the idea that national service is a national goal. Expansion of the voluntary aspects would be based upon the creation of real and meaningful opportunities for fulfilling these goals which would require both public and private funds of noteworthy magnitude. This definition could become part of our educational system and its requirements. Thus, for example, Peace Corps volunteers are already given informal preference in selection for certain types of graduate school training programs. The basis of the national service concept could be that each young man be required by law to complete his service, but this seems to be unnecessary and would involve excessive compulsion. It may very well be that there are a limited number of types of national service activities which are either so burdensome, or so important to have done, that they could be specially designated as exempting an individual from the selective service lottery. This could be called substitute service and would include, as is presently the case, the U.S. Public Health Service, the Coast Guard, etc., as well as new programs such as a police cadet corps.

THE LOGISTICS OF NATIONAL SERVICE

The sheer number of young men reaching 18 each year sets the scope of a national service program. The Selective Service System based upon a lottery could be instituted immediately, while it would seem to require at least three and perhaps five years to develop the full range of opportunities for alternative voluntary service. These programs would have to be phased in year by year.

The initial step in examining the logistics of national service is to recognize that the existing standards of eligibility for selective servce—both medical and educational—are not relevant. In the past, of those young men who were subject to examination by Selective Service, 15 per cent were rejected on medical grounds. If one adds those rejected by reason of unacceptable educational standards and on administrative (moral and criminal) grounds, the percentage of rejection in specific years rose to over 45 per cent, the bulk of these falling in the educational category. Men who sought to volunteer for military service had, of course, a much lower rate of rejection. Thus, a more realistic rejection rate, on the basis of past military standards for the 18-year-old youth population, would be approximately 30 per cent ineligible. Thus under present arrangements the 1,800,000 young men of a given 18-year-old cohort would be allocated as follows: 600,000 enter military service; 600,000 rejected; and 600,000 surplus by various forms of exemptions and deferments.

But a basic objective of national service is to eliminate arbitrary educational standards, either through remedial efforts by the Armed Forces, or by substitute service in a National Job Training Corps. Thereby, these young men would have a second chance to enter the mainstream of American life. Some greater flexibility in medical and psychiatric standards is clearly possible both for military service and alternative forms of national service. However, it would be unrealistic to assume that all young men would be eligible by educational and medical and administrative standards to participate in some aspect of national service. There are those with severe medical problems, gross bodily deformities, incapacitating psychiatric maladjustments, mental retardation, or asocial personalities. There are, in addition, those young men who suffer from limited defects, especially medical ones, who would be better off not participating in any of the group experiences of national service. In all, we are dealing with approximately 15 per cent of the 18-year-old group, approximately 270,000 persons, leaving a total manpower pool of roughly 1,530,000. In Table 3, allocations of manpower to the various programs of a national service program are set forth on the basis of this figure. In addition to this reduction of eligibles for the volunteer programs, a goal of 80 per cent compliance within three years is set, although the figures presented are for the total group when it reaches age 19.

ARMED FORCES

If levels can be reduced to the size before the Vietnam buildup, the Armed Forces will require approximately 575,000 new men each year; 500,000 will be required for the normal intake of enlisted personnel, both volunteer and selected by a lottery system. Because of the impact of the operation of a lottery, the Air Force, Navy, and Marine Corps will be able as in the past to meet their military manpower requirements on the basis of volunteer three-year enlistments. The Army will have to rely on a mixture of volunteers and those procured by the lottery system.

In addition to meeting national security requirements, the manpower system of the armed services serves as a vast training system for basic technical skills as well as for a variety of more advanced occupations. In essence, the Armed Forces

TABLE 3

Manpower Allocations under Projected National Service Program

(Distribution for 19-year-old Age Cohort)

Total age group (19 years old)		1,800,000
Not eligible for national service		
(15 per cent medical and administrative)		270,000
Eligible annual manpower		1,530,000
Projected annual allocations:		
National military establishment		
Enlisted personnel	500,000	
Officer personnel*	75,000	575,000
Military remedial programs		40,000
Special federal programs (substitute service)		
U.S. Public Health Service, Coast Guard, Merchant Marine		10,000
Police Cadet Corps (substitute service)		100,000
National Teacher Corps		150,000
National Health Corps		50,000
Vista workers and Similar public programs		70,000
Private domestic programs		30,000
Peace Corps		50,000
Private Peace Corps programs		20,000
National Job Training Corps		400,000
Conscientious objectors		10,000
Not allocated		25,000
		1,530,000

*Does not include the 90,000 enrolled in high school ROTC programs.

are the main source of vocational education in the United States and there is every reason to believe this will have to continue during the next decade.

The majority of those who serve a term as enlisted men, including volunteers, do not reenlist. In 1964, only 25 per cent of all Armed Forces regulars, for example, reenlisted. The Armed Forces, because of the realities of the marketplace, still tend to lag behind civilian pay, especially for trained technicians. Some improvement in reenlistment rates might be expected, more in the case of second and subsequent reenlistments than for first-term reenlistments, by improving work conditions, etc. But a high rate of personnel turnover at the enlisted level is to be expected. If the situation were otherwise, it might be dangerous, indicating that the Armed Forces did not have flexible policies and were being burdened with personnel who could not find comparable positions in civilian life. Moreover, it should be recognized that the men who do not reenlist bring into the civilian sector crucial skills required for economic growth and personal mobility. Their training proceeds with a high effectiveness because of the organizational environment. Perhaps an important area of change would be to reduce the first term of volunteer enlistment in the ground forces to two years so it would be comparable to the period of service for those drafted. Specialized training would come wherever possible after the first period of two years of service.

An additional 40,000 young men would be taken on a volunteer basis into the proposed specialized training and educational program designed to supply remedial education and health services. This would be only ten per cent of those eligible for such training and the remainder would be allocated to the National Job Training Corps.

To meet officer manpower needs, 75,000 men would have to enter the various procurement programs. This would include new entrants into the military academies and into the various college ROTC programs. This does not include the 90,000 cadets in the high school ROTC since the bulk of these would enter into service as volunteers and become non-commissioned officers or, in a minority of cases, participate in an officer training program.

SPECIAL FEDERAL PROGRAMS

In the United States there are various national programs which provide substitutes for service in the Armed Forces. These include the Coast Guard, the Merchant Marine, and the Public Health Service. Entrance into these programs has been and should continue to be considered a substitute for involvement in Selective Service. In all, approximately 10,000 men each year are involved.

Police Cadet Corps

One hundred thousand young men could do substitute service in some form of police work. Increasing the number and quality of police officers is a pressing issue in the United States and resembles the issues of procurement of military manpower. Police departments require a broader base from which to recruit personnel, and professionalization would be enhanced if there were an increase in the flow of personnel at the lower ranks. The opportunity for promotion of career police personnel would be increased with a category equivalent to short-term military service.

A number of arrangements could be worked out. Youngsters could be taken at the age of 16 or 17 to serve four or five years on cadet tours of duty. This kind of a program would emphasize recruitment into the police service at the end of the cadet's duty. An alternative approach would be to take men at age 21 to serve three years as police officers. In all cases, personnel would volunteer for police duty and have to meet the qualifications of the police departments involved. Such substitute service would exempt the person from Selective Service.

National Teachers Corps

One hundred fifty thousand teachers could be recruited annually for work in the inner city. Present policies and resources make it impossible for the inner city to have an adequate supply of teachers and teaching personnel. The whole trend in teaching is to make use of more personnel with general liberal arts background and special summer training. The teachers corps concept would also make use of semi-professionals with two years of college, and teachers aides with a high school background.

Service in the national teaching corps would be an alternative for national service and would not exempt an individual from being subject to the lottery system. In particular it is important to emphasize that the national teachers corps would be extremely valuable in supplying men for the inner city. Organized by the federal government along the lines of the Peace Corps, it would involve about

27 months of service. It is not far-fetched to look forward to the day when, formally or informally, entrance to the teaching profession would include some service in the national teaching corps.

National Health Corps

Similarly to the national teachers corps, 50,000 young men could be utilized in the health service field.

Peace Corps

The present Peace Corps could be expanded to include 50,000 young men each year. The organizational procedures are well worked out and involve 27 months of service. Because of the small number involved, Peace Corps service could be either substitute service that exempts individuals from the lottery, or merely alternative volunteer service which the individual would perform if he is not selected by the lottery system. In addition, opportunities could be created for 20,000 men annually in private equivalents of Peace Corps operations abroad.

Domestic Vista Programs

Domestic equivalents of the Peace Corps under government sponsorship could employ 70,000. Private voluntary national service, under the auspices of church groups, voluntary associations, and the like, would involve another 30,000 young men in the United States.

Conscientious Objectors

Finally, there is the category of conscientious objectors. They, in effect, constitute a very small proportion of the population, even if present Supreme Court definitions are used which include both political and religious objectors. At a maximum, 10,000 men per year would be involved under the broadest definitions.

National Job Training Corps

Of special importance in a national service program is a National Job Training Corps along the lines of the Civilian Conservation Corps which would annually accommodate up to 400,000 young men. The United States is witnessing a crisis in the ability of its educational institutions to meet the needs of low-income groups. The entire thrust of federal aid to education has been thus far designed mainly for those entering college and those already prepared for various forms of specialized training.

We are faced by a problem of overwhelming magnitude. The public education system has been unresponsive to the needs of the most culturally depressed in the inner city. During the last three years we have witnessed an increase in social tension in the inner city to the point of outright explosion. It is unlikely that the schools can handle these problems. Initial halting steps have been taken by the Neighborhood Youth Corps and in some of the Job Training Centers. But the ideology of the professional educators and social welfare workers does not make possible the fundamental planning required to meet the needs of inner-city youths. We are particularly thinking of the years between dropping out or being forced out of school and of being available for employment. A National Job Training Corps under civilian jurisdiction with clear paramilitary elements would supply an opportunity for basic education and satisfactory achievement experience during this difficult period. In the past, the Armed Forces performed some of this job as a matter of routine. But this becomes more difficult as the Armed Forces become more automated and more technical. We are dealing with approximately 400,000 youths who have been failed by our society; at most 40,000 would have opportunities in the above mentioned special remedial programs of the armed services. A total of 360,000 would be eligible for this type of service. Service in a National Job Training Corps would be a substitute for military service. After successful completion of National Job Training Corps experience, however, the young man would be in a position to volunteer for the armed services.

LONG-TERM IMPLICATIONS

For the next five- to ten-year period, the national service concept must be evaluated against a purely voluntary armed force based upon competitive economic compensation. From an economic point of view, an Armed Forces based on "competitive" salaries is not a real possibility because of the imperfections of the marketplace. The military would always be disadvantaged relative to the private sector which could raise its prices and salaries more rapidly. Each official inquiry into these topics produces higher and higher cost estimates.

The argument against a purely volunteer force is not merely economic: it is also political and professional. The Armed Forces reflect the social structure and the basis of their recruitment. Their effectiveness is linked to their social composition and ties to civilian society. In a communist society, professional standards and political control are maintained by a system of party control. It should not be overlooked that this system operates with a considerable degree of effectiveness, although it is incompatible with the standards of a democratic society. By contrast, the armed services in a political democracy cannot operate without a variety of social links to civilian society; executive and congressional control at the top level is not sufficient. The military must find its place in the larger society through a variety of contacts and points of interaction and control. A widely representative military personnel contributes to a willingness to accept the controls of the outer society. A long-term and highly professionalized force, especially at the enlisted man's level, is likely to be less representative and have weaker civilian ties. The inflow and outflow of civilian recruits is both a control device and a basis for positive morale and incentive in the miltary establishment.

But the case for national service is not to be based on a refutation of the volunteer force concept. The arguments for national service involve positive ideas of institution-building and facilitating social change, although they fundamentally must deal with the task of selecting men for the armed forces.

First, national service is an attempt of a democratic society to find an equitable approach to sharing the risks of military service without disrupting the management of our universities. The present system is unfair because of its reliance on educational deferments and inefficient because of the exclusion of those who do not meet contemporary standards. The present system is dangerous because of the disruptive impact on the administration of higher education. It has led students into postgraduate study as a way of avoiding military service. If the universities and colleges are to perform their educational functions, they can do this best if they are free from excessive involvement in the administration of selective service. On the other hand, the present system cannot be defended on the grounds that it maintains a supply of trained professionals. The supply of professionals depends on many basic factors such as graduate-study subsidies, available training opportunities, and the like. Moreover, to interrupt training either before college or between college and professional school would not radically alter the long term supply of trained professionals.

Second, the present system cannot long endure regardless of the projected size of the military establishment. The United States is faced with the prospect of a segregated Negro enlisted men's ground force if the present trends are permitted to continue. In fact, the strongest argument against a volunteer force is that such a procedure would merely hasten this transformation.

A lottery system is an initial step toward the control of this form of disequilibrium. A national service system would be another important step, for it would both make the lottery system more meaningful and help bring the Negro into the mainstream of American life. To the extent that Negroes become integrated into the larger society and have the same medical and educational qualifications as their white counterparts, their concentration in particular sectors of the Armed Forces is likely to be reduced. Effective integration in the armed service requires in-service training and flexible personnel policies which would treat the armed services as a whole. Moreover, the armed services are abandoning an emphasis on merely retaining personnel in order to develop optimum policies of utilization which recognize the necessity and desirability of rotation and various forms of short-term service. These policies are likely to reduce the possibility of segregated units within the armed services. The case for a lottery and a system of national service can be made without reference to the position of the Negro in the Armed Forces, but this special problem only serves to emphasize the need for constructive reform.

Third, national service is an experiment in education. National service is more than an effort at rehabilitation and a second chance for those youngsters who come from the most deprived segments of our society. It is designed to deal with fundamental problems of personal maturation for all social levels. The present structure of American education is unable to supply those group experiences required for the socialization of successive generations. The search for personal development and individual identity in a social setting which has a narrow emphasis on individual classroom performance leads all too often to various forms of rebellion and withdrawal.

There is every reason to believe that the recent increased academic effectiveness of the American educational system, especially at the high school level, has been purchased at the price of complicating the process of personal development. In a democratic society it is particularly dangerous to make school and academic performance the exclusive route to social mobility. The results of this danger are already clearly manifested by the existing levels of hostility, negativism, and apathy toward "school." This is not to assert that the levels of hostility are higher than in the past; this is difficult to ascertain. Moreover, such a comparison is difficult to make since we are now keeping in school larger and larger segments of society whose education in the past was brief. Our problems derive from our higher aspirations and the necessity for more adequate levels of formal education.

National service should contribute positively toward innovation in education, broadly defined. Clearly, the military establishment has in the past performed educational functions, and continues to do so. It operates as the largest system of vocational education. It provides an avenue of social mobility for lower-class youth because it supplies social skills and a sense of self-respect to youngsters from the most deprived backgrounds. The Armed Forces, however, can have only a specific and delimited role in this process of social education. Professional requirements and organizational pressures in administering the military establishment preclude expansion. The United States is hardly an example of a nation which looks to its military to perform core tasks in education.

The Selective Service System and national service will nonetheless supply a system of national accounting of human resources. It will make clear how many young people are growing up without minimum health and education standards. In this sense national service will make a special contribution to the social welfare of the lowest income groups in our society.

But national service is designed to make contributions to the educational objectives of all social strata. It is designed to interrupt, at appropriate points, classroom experience so as to give the young man alternative educational experiences. These experiences are meant to develop intense and close group solidarity, based on collective rather than individualistic goals. They seem an essential aspect of personal maturing and are not supplied by classroom or academic education. In the complex and rapidly changing world, these experiences need to be intense and need to permit the expression of public service objectives.

It is particularly important to have these alternative life chances to overcome the boredom that comes from continuous exposure to classroom instruction. Young people particularly need exposure to a wide range of adults and teachers beyond subject-matter specialists. The broadening of the range of experience is crucial since at the university level there has been a rapid expansion of the faculty, a new large proportion of whom have achieved their teaching positions without any significant non-academic experience and who are therefore restricted in their capacity as effective teachers and role models.

Fourth, national service is an effort at "institutional building," to assist social change both at home and abroad. At home, it is an expression of the fact that traditional methods in education and social welfare need drastic adaptation. Abroad, it is part of the growing realization that United States foreign policy requires new approaches to produce economic, social, and political development.

National service is an innovation in the allocation of human resources, both of persons with motivation for labor-intensive jobs as well as for persons with highly trained skills. In dealing with the problem of the inner city and with selected aspects of overseas development, labor-intensive techniques have an important and crucial role to play. The terms volunteer, semi-professional and para-professional are prestigious words to describe the fact that there are limits to the number and effectiveness of highly trained professionals. We are dealing not only with the results of the restrictive policies in the education and training of professionals, but with the inescapable fact that many operational tasks are better performed by persons who do not have trained-in capacities. One way of organizing these work situations is to have persons perform them for short periods of time but without having to confront the issues of a career in that particular vocation. Such experience is also vital preparation for more fully

trained professional careers. The national service concept is designed particularly to meet this need, recognizing that there are limitations of the allocation
of labor by economic incentives.

On the other hand, the national service is a contribution to the reallocation of
the most highly trained professional skills. In recent years the gap between the
old nations and the new nations has not been closed rapidly. In fact, there has
been a drastic drain-off of professionals from the new nations, especially doctors
and scientists. The national service program is a device for making service abroad
part of the education and responsibility of each generation of highly trained
professionals. In the last analysis, national service is a form of enlightened self-
interest on a worldwide scope.

9

National Service and the American Educational System

TERRENCE CULLINAN

The continuing ferment over military service and the draft is essentially a search for a structure satisfying both military needs and the social-moral issues implicit in the raising of armies. The problem is twofold: who shall serve, and how can the service and opportunity base be shared by a maximum number of participants?

Universal military service, an old answer, has been almost completely rejected as both uneconomical and inefficient. It significantly fails as well to solve the newer non-military issues. Today, increasing attention is being given to the wider concept of national service.

National service by definition embraces non-military as well as military service and generally equates the two in terms of service to the nation and society as a whole. Conceptually at least, national service satisfies the dilemma cited in the opening paragraph. It fulfills military requirements as unpleasant but existent necessities. It devotes a portion—dependent both on military needs and the type of program adopted—of the nation's non-military manpower to social and moral issues of concern to the nation as well as the participant.

APPROACHES TO NATIONAL SERVICE

As an idea, national service has few detractors. The idealistic ethic is deeply implanted in the United States. Public and private non-military service already exists—the Peace Corps and local civic action organizations are representative of the former, and the Friends Service Committee and private social welfare groups typify the latter. The role of these activities in national service is the controversial matter.

Basically, there are three approaches to national service, differentiated by the respective roles of military and non-military service:

1) Compulsory national service—all young men serve the nation in either a military or non-military capacity.
2) Alternative national service—those men choosing non-military service would be exempted from military service.
3) Voluntary national service—non-military service would be encouraged but would provide no exemption from possible military duty.

The author is at the Stanford Research Institute.

Each approach requires that military needs be given first priority; under the second, some of those who would choose non-military service could be deprived of that option at times of heavy military needs.

Differences in the approaches are self-evident. Approach three is the current system in the United States. Approach two would permit individual choice as to service alternative, perhaps "forcing" some non-military choices as escape valves from military duty. It would also enable a percentage (who would neither select alternative service nor be selected for military duty) to avoid all service. The first approach would distribute the service responsibility among all individuals but would have the element of strong coercion which neither other alternative has.

NATIONAL SERVICE AS AN EDUCATIVE PROCESS

One increasingly common claim for national service, however approached, is that it is a continuation of a participant's education. For some, an interruption or interlude in the classical education pattern is seen as a beneficial change of educational pace. For others, national service is viewed as a means of broadening horizons when classical education is over. For still others, national service is viewed as the missing rehabilitation key for social dropouts.

Data exist against which to weigh these claims; some are historical, and some are based on recent studies. Some are of foreign origin. If the data are consistent, some useful conclusions may be possible.

An Enforced Interlude: World War II

World War II forcibly interrupted the lives of hundreds of thousands of young men. As the war ended there was much concern over the impact of the return of these men. Educators, for example, feared that colleges would be flooded with older men who had forgotten how to study and were merely taking advantage of the GI Bill. Lack of serious interest would drag down standards and corrupt the generation of students entering college directly from high school.

Exactly the reverse occurred. The GI students had experienced two to four years' interruption of their lives. They were intent on equipping themselves for their futures and careers. They worked harder, more seriously, and more effectively than their younger classmates, who were the ones most often unable to keep up with the pace. Academic standards went up instead of down.

Changes of both environment and activity had long been recognized in advanced programs of vocational adaption as a means of effecting enlarged perspective. Data from studies of postwar college classes now showed that interruption of the 16-year classical education cycle of first grade through college could bring marked improvement in achievement.

A Voluntary Interlude: The Peace Corps

More recently, some 15,000 young men have voluntarily interrupted their lives through Peace Corps service. Studies by the Peace Corps of the first 5,000 returnees[1] have found that academic faculties consistently cite strong similarities between ex-volunteers and the ex-GIs after World War II. These new returnees are also more mature, more serious, and more interested in education than their campus counterparts. The sense of purpose felt during their two years' service seems transferable to their continued education.

An Unfulfilled Interlude: The Pioneers

But national service would encompass all youth, not just the college-trained. Fewer data are available historically to indicate the influence national service might have on less-educated individuals. Average length of stay in the Job Corps is only nine months. However, even after this short period, 20 per cent of those leaving the Job Corps are accepted into the military; 60 per cent of these qualifiers previously had been rejected by the military on grounds of mental or physical inability. (The Defense Department's new program for upgrading marginal rejects to standards of acceptability will be another future data source.)

The most interesting analyzed data are provided by studies of 29 test cases in the only experimental Universal Military Training unit ever activated in this country.[2] These 29 were accepted into the Army by special arrangement. All were mentally unqualified by military standards. The official report on them summarized:

Nearly all had come from either broken homes or those in which argument and violence were common. Several of the young men had been affected by over-control, nagging, and excessive physical punishment. More had been affected by insufficient control. Almost all of them had found it necessary to go to work at an early age. Four had prison records. Only three of the 29 had ever learned to play baseball or other common games. A defeatist attitude in competition characterized the entire group. As a group they were easily swayed.

The 29 were placed in one unit and called the Pioneers. A six-month training cycle followed. In an as yet unpublished study of this Pioneer program, Edward F. Hall found that at the program's end:

Seventeen of the "graduates"—59% of the group—measured up to minimum Army standards on retesting. Five of them recorded scores between 80 and 87. From some point below the norm for 13-year-olds, these five had gained the equivalent of two years in a six-month period, their new scores being at the average level of developed intelligence of 15-year-olds.

The remaining twelve were discharged from the Army at the end of the course because of inaptness as defined in Army regulations. For them the six months had not sufficed to make up for the deficiencies of 18 years. Yet all twelve asked to be allowed to remain in the Army and receive further training. Hope had been awakened if not fulfilled.

Studies of CCC (Civilian Conservation Corps) men after their return home give further evidence that a pattern-breaking interlude may have long-run beneficial effects on "deprived" participants. A 1965 study of Selective Service rejects came to the same conclusion. The familiar pattern of broken homes and school dropouts had left the same record of discouragement and destroyed self-confidence. But of the two groups studied, 80 per cent of one and 90 per cent of the other expressed eagerness for a program of training and education.

MORE RECENT DATA: THE EDUCATIONAL DROPOUT

More than one million high school and college students will leave the American educational system in 1967 before graduating. Some will return; more will not.

Many, willingly or unwillingly, will experience military service. The majority will have no such organized experience.

From these latter will come the major percentage of our "hard core" drop-outs, the societal problem children. From these, too, will come most of our lost "soft core" dropouts, the unmotivated and rootless. Natinal service would pre-sumably absorb many from both these groups of incomplete students.

The College Dropout: An Educational Opportunity

Research on the college-level dropout has been going on since at least 1925. Perhaps surprisingly, attrition percentages have remained virtually constant up to and including the present time. Of any one entering freshman class, nationally: 50 per cent will drop out at some time in the four years after freshman admission; 40 per cent will never receive a diploma; 33 per cent of those who graduate will do so later from another institution than planned. Past dropout studies showed that up to 70 per cent of all dropouts were for "required" reasons; of these, about 85 per cent were academic or disciplinary. Today, however, causal statistics for dropping out are reported to be almost the reverse of what they were previously: today, nearly 70 per cent of all dropouts are for nonrequired reasons:

. . . the problems of poor motivation and immaturity are consistently noted as con-tributing to withdrawal. In most cases poor motivation was attributed to a general lack of interest ("just didn't want to study"), boredom, apathy, dislike for the cur-riculum, getting nothing out of college, a lack of goals, and a lack of certainty as to what to major in.[3]

There is also a steady increase in reports of definite effects of the interlude period on education when resumed. Survey respondents claiming "no effects" have sharply decreased. A corresponding rise in per cent reporting positive impact has been experienced. Trends in students' attitudes are thus consistent with the steady increase in the number of college deans and counselors who regard an interlude of dropping out as a beneficial part of the overall educative pattern for many students.

The High School "Dead End": An Educational Minus

Most American high school seniors leave the formal education system for good on graduation. Dr. Dorothy Knoell, educational consultant to the State of New York, has studied the psychological outlook of these students at time of graduation. Her most recent study, an in-depth attitude survey including 600 male students from urban areas of New York and about half the students' parents, showed that "going to college" was not the dream of the large majority of those interviewed, who had never experienced strong pressures for college attendance. Most had immediate job or military plans. Neither the students nor their parents had even minimal information about opportunities—academic or career-employ-ment—beyond their own limited economic and geographic horizons.

Dr. Knoell discovered one unexpected characteristic common to her student target group. Nearly all wanted an escape—most often temporary—from the environment in which they had grown up. A physical change of scene was the primary desire, usually accompanied by the wish for a change of "atmosphere." Little hostility to the historical environment was encountered. The desire was simply for a diversity of experience and an opportunity for independence.

Outside of those joining the military, the experience would not be attainable for most. Dr. Knoell concludes that:

. . . in each group of seniors [there] are some who have the potential to achieve goals they dare not dream of, if they can be given a second and sometimes still another chance. The way needs to be kept open for them to move up the educational ladder after high school as they demonstrate new potential . . . so that each may become all he is capable of being. There is a gap of monstrous proportions in the . . . services offered most youth during the years when they make critical decisions about education and life work.

CONCLUSIONS

Each of the three approaches to national service—compulsory, alternative, and voluntary—would as first priority satisfy the nation's military needs. Each would satisfy the social-moral issues implicit in the raising of armies by providing additional alternative service opportunities of a non-military nature. While voluntary national service would not give the same legal status to non-military activity, all three approaches would emphasize the merit and the positive social contributions of alternative duty.

Public approval of a national service type of structure was indicated by a Gallup Poll published July 3, 1966. Seventy-seven per cent of those responding favored a universal national service program including military and non-military options. More than five out of eight also said they would prefer military to non-military service for their sons. These data suggest that military needs would be met as efficiently under the new structure as under the old one.

There are at least three educational hypotheses relevant to the national service concept:

1) There is a potential benefit to almost any individual's growth and development from an interlude—occupational and geographical—during or after the classical educational process.

2) The number of youths taking such an interlude voluntarily will rise in the coming years, while the number of involuntary interludes will not diminish.

3) It is possible to structure workable programs from several different approaches and utilize these interlude periods in each case for the benefit of both participants and of society as a whole.

Historical and recent data previously outlined tend to validate the first hypothesis. The Princeton study, for example, showed that students returning to college after having dropped out are more likely to be graduated than students first entering college. At the other end of the dropout scale, psychologists and social scientists believe a large majority of social misfits could learn the skills and understanding that would enable them to lead useful and satisfying lives.

The Princeton survey also supports the second hypothesis, as does the growth of two-year colleges (which provide a natural break) and the apparent success of some interlude-encouraging pilot programs. For example, Yale's new five-year program includes an optional year of service abroad, and Western Michigan and Franconia College give students one year's academic credit for two years with the Peace Corps.

The experiences of foreign national service programs and those of many public and private programs in the United States tend to support the third hypothesis.

THE CRITICAL QUESTIONS

Two questions are critical to the development of the optimum program of national service for educational and service purposes:

1) The activities to be included will have to be determined and a means developed for channeling participants to activities of greatest value during the interlude period—to both participant development and society at large.
2) The extent of the program will have to be determined and the major question—compulsory or noncompulsory—answered.

The area of activities and assignments will require further study if a national service program is implemented in the United States. The experiences of the Peace Corps, VISTA, and many private organizations will be of assistance in the assignment question. As to activities, a coordinated national service program could be of real value in determining optimum use of activity resources. As yet, no one has optimally programmed some $9 billion raised annually in private funds (the Community Chest alone raises $1 billion per year—the same amount spent annually for all of VISTA).

The second question, that of extent, is largely political. To date, some thirty-five representatives and nine senators have offered resolutions in Congress on national service. Popular sentiments may be changing rapidly. In September 1966, Dr. Glenn Olds of the study center at Planting Fields, Long Island, reported an apparent campus trend in favor of compulsory universal national service of some kind. This to him was a complete change from the attitude of only six months earlier.

POTENTIAL IMPACTS OF NATIONAL SERVICE ON EDUCATION

The educational "fallout" from any possible national service program is evident from the foregoing. Compulsory national service, as it would affect everyone, would have by far the greatest impact on the educational establishment. Major benefit would accrue at the lower end of the educational spectrum: compulsory service would subject each individual to examination and hence to potential assistance. Alternative national service would have the next greatest impact, but would have the weakness of attracting chiefly the more educated: individuals of less education would be unlikely to seek out alternative programs, largely because of fixed habits and lack of knowledge. Voluntary national service would have the same disadvantage on an even greater scale.

Some have claimed that compulsory national service would encourage authoritarianism. Edward F. Hall, cited earlier, discounts this criticism. A study of rigorously disciplined air cadets showed an actual *decrease* in authoritarianism among the participants. Another study which followed a group of Army inductees through training found only a slight and statistically insignificant increase in this characteristic.

A positive effect of national service on education is partially evident from data on Peace Corps returnees. National service activities would emphasize the humanities and thus serve as a counterbalance to the current, perhaps exaggerated, emphasis in education on science. At non-college levels, given the rise in productivity of both industry and agriculture, shifts in employment from producing to service industries would be a net gain to society. Experiences in national service would be most likely to encourage this shift.

The case for a national service program incorporating the education of the deprived is strengthened by the experience of Israel as reported by Col. Bar-on in his paper for this conference. The educational level of a society is a determinant basis for its overall strength. By upgrading its least educated, the society can eliminate major retarding influences within itself and alleviate many of the social maladjustments that hamper social growth.

THE QUESTION OF COMPULSION

Compulsory National Service has been opposed by some as a possible invasion of individual rights—at best, contrary to the American tradition of voluntarism. This mid-twentieth century criticism is similar to the mid-nineteenth century questioning of compulsory education. The parallel is complete if the concept of national service as an extension of education is valid.

Education itself is not mentioned in the Constitution and, therefore, is not a function of the federal government. However, Congress has the constitutional prerogative to "provide for the . . . general welfare of the United States." Under this clause, the federal government has directly influenced education over the years. There has been no judicial challenge per se to this influence. In fact, the trend in Supreme Court decisions makes it clear that public education is related to "the general welfare of the United States" as a whole. Early court decisions defined the legal purpose of education as the development of a citizenry capable of participating effectively in self-government. It has become as much a legal duty as a privilege to become educated. The state, however, cannot require that all individuals be educated in the same precise manner; it can only establish the basic requirements and leave the individual to accomplish them after his own choice.

Compulsory national service, as proposed, follows a similar pattern. Both the suggested compulsory national service and the existing compulsory education systems have private and public options. Both allow reasonable exemptions: the ill, the physically or mentally incompetent, the special case. Both involve restrictions on individual freedom created and directed by the state. Both assume that universal participation is needed by the nation and cannot be attained by purely voluntary measures: an assumption proven by historical experience in the case of education and taken for granted with respect to national service.

The fact that compulsory education has received public approval does not, of course, mean that compulsory national service would be similarly accepted. However, the *legal* bases for both are similar, and the optimum approach to national service thus can be determined without constitutional complications.

TENTATIVE OPTIMUM PROCEDURE

Data and experience suggest that a national service program would have a significant, positive effect on education and development in American society. During their educational years, young men are a major underdeveloped national resource; it can be claimed that all would benefit from an interlude period during or immediately following those years. While this claim cannot be supported conclusively at present, it clearly cannot be rejected: historical, current, and international data lend it credence.

Perhaps instead of "interlude" the term used should be "interaction"—a counterpart, psychologically and physically, to classical education. Whatever term is used, the concept of national service clearly is relevant to development of any comprehensive articulated program.

A compulsory, nationwide program is not politically feasible at present; an experimental program on a smaller scale, however, appears desirable and feasible. For such a program, the idea of alternative voluntary service would be the more amenable concept, as input variables could be most easily regulated by changing the criteria (pay and length of service) for the non-military alternatives.

An experiment in this direction would not be out of place at present. The experience, whatever its results, would provide invaluable factual precedent for the continuing search for optimum position of both military and non-military service in the social structure.

NOTES

[1] Cited by Harris Wofford, Associate Director of the Peace Corps, at the National Service Workshop held Sept. 23-25, 1966, at Planting Fields, Long Island, under the leadership of Donald J. Eberly.

[2] The 692-man unit was disbanded during the Berlin crisis. The steady series of military crises since that time has prevented the military from resuming the experiment.

[3] Lawrence A. Pervin, "A New Look at College Dropouts," *Princeton Quarterly*, Winter 1964-65.

10

A *National Service System as a*
Solution to a Variety of National Problems

MARGARET MEAD

PROBLEMS OF THE COMPOSITION OF THE ARMED SERVICES

In considering the draft, it seems important to realize that the armed services
are not, as many critics believe, tied to types and levels of warfare which should
become progressively outdated. In the foreseeable future, every step toward
the elimination of major warfare is likely to be accompanied by an increase in
violence on a smaller scale. Types of conflict between small states, within states,
and within local communities which were formerly suppressed as the direct or
indirect consequence of the warmaking capacity of large nation-states prolifer-
ate under conditions within which massive nuclear weapons and major military
confrontations are barred.

At the same time, such worldwide conditions as the population explosion,
the spread of urbanization, the enormous increase in mobility and migration,
and a climate of opinion which hails the humanity of members of all races and
all classes inevitably result in a very large amount of social disorganization. Various forms of violence—border, warfare, riots, massacres, massive destructions
of life and property when urban concentrations and natural catastrophe are
combined, communal conflict, civil wars overtly or covertly supported from
outside the country, political coups, civil difficulties springing from unresolved
ethnic loyalties, and renascent irredentism—will have to be controlled.

It seems clear that the United States will have to maintain large mobile forces,
available for activities in different parts of the world—within international sanctions to the extent that international peace-keeping forces can be developed,
nationally dispatched to troubled areas in the world where international peace-
keeping forces cannot be used; and available for major domestic catastrophes
and disorders. Such forces will have to be composed of young men who are
physically and mentally fit, trained in combative activities, able to risk their
lives and to kill if necessary.

A crucial question thus becomes whether such a force should be composed of
volunteers for limited periods, of draftees, or of those who enter the armed services as a life career, or whether the three kinds of recruitment should be used in
various proportions. A nationwide draft helps to underline a sense of national

The author is Curator of Ethnology, The American Museum of Natural History,
New York City.

commitment and the ugency of total national involvement in the maintenance of an orderly world. A draft potentially touches every household in the nation, no matter how small the number who are actually drafted, and where it is conducted on any sort of lottery basis, it selects men of all types of temperament and character, and many kinds of social economic background and training. The substitution of volunteers for a limited period, even were it to provide a sufficient number of men, has the disadvantage of drawing on men with specific types of character and temperament. Armed services based on volunteers present a danger both to countries in which the population is as highly diversified as the United States, and to very homogeneous countries where the volunteer self-selection process is even more likely to select individuals to whom the particular ethos of the armed services, or of special branches of the services, is specially congenial. (Armed services in different countries have drawn historically on different kinds of character structure. In considering the Nazi period and the excesses of cruelty which occurred, the cruelty may be attributed to a selective process within which those who were willing to undertake careers of great responsibility were also those who were attracted to opportunities for excessive personal power, whereas in England, for example, responsibility was associated with requirements of impulse control and gentleness. The same kinds of differences can be found in the police forces of different countries; e.g., the contrast between those American police who were recruited from ethnic groups in which lawlessness had been a political virtue, and English police, who were selected for certain specific characteristics of strength and patience.)

However much they may differ from country to country, armed forces developed to defend against attack and control violence evolve a style that is antithetical to many of the values of ordinary democratic civilian society: discipline; uniform, unquestioning acceptance of orders; rank. Single items in the customary military repertoire may be removed or modified: excessive emphasis on polishing buttons may be diminished, over-insistence on rank at all times may be reduced, rank and routine requirements may be abrogated in front-line combat. But within our present cultural styles, the requirements for armed services are still differentiated from civilian life. And this holds for police forces also. The English policeman may carry nothing but a stick, but he wears a uniform and the force is hierarchically organized.

If the armed services—through some sort of nationwide draft—are continually faced with the task of absorbing recruits to whom the military way of life is basically uncongenial, or even repellant, there is a useful check on the development of a highly differentiated counter-civilian ethos. A professional army, with life-long career commitment, is even more cut off from civilian style, as those with inappropriate character can be cut off all through the recruitment and training and advancement process.

In summary, we will continue to need for the foreseeable future a sizable armed and disciplined force, however much it may become more acceptable to describe their activities as maintenance of order, peacekeeping or post-disaster control, inside and outside the United States. Under these conditions, armed services which draw at least in part upon the entire male population of the United States, within specified age limits, and which rule out complete self-selection—such as that which obtains in a purely volunteer or professional army —are more congruent with our national values. Acceptance of this fact means acceptance of the greater cost in time and energy of training draft armed forces.

If a draft is to be continued, then the question of the relationship of those who are selected to their contemporaries becomes an urgent question. The draft may be phrased as a lottery in which those selected become losers. Alternatively, the draft may be embedded in a system of universal national services in which all of the other elements involved in the draft—except specific military requirements of greater risk and the moral requirement to use arms—are shared. These other elements, which now play such a conspicuous part in judgments made on the fairness of the Selective Service System, are many. Perhaps chief among them are: arbitrary interference with an individual career, and with educational and personal plans, minimal pay, curtailment of freedom of movement in favor of directed activity, and compulsory association with a cross-section of the national population involving the hazards of reevaluating one's place in the national society. If, through universal national service, every young male shared all of these perceived disadvantages of the draft, except the requirement of military service, would this substantially reduce the present perception of the unfairness of the system?

Let us ask first how universal national service would affect the draft, and those purposes which the draft is expected to fulfill, without discussing the merits of universal national service on any other grounds. This question can be explored independently of other questions about universal national service, such as the cost, whether it should involve everyone of a fixed age or within a fixed age period, the reasons for including women, and the relations of such a service to our changing educational needs and changing economy. A basic question then becomes the way in which the sense of fairness or inequity would be met, and whether, within such a universal service, some lottery system would still have to be used.

Many of the discussions of universal national service seem to ignore the functions of a draft army when it is a question of military service within universal national service. Then assumptions are made which would produce in effect a magnification of the present pressure for volunteering—which comes from the draft—to the end that all those who served in the various branches of the armed services would ultimately be self-selected. If this were done, one of the essential elements in the compulsory participation in a citizen army—the inclusion of those who dislike bearing arms but are not morally opposed to it—would be lost.

AMERICAN ATTITUDES TOWARD CHANCE AND LUCK

The preservation of some element of chance, or lottery, among those from whom national service is required is the most immediately available method of assuring that the armed services would still be composed of draftees.

As a lottery would be a method of preserving the arbitrary character of the draft within universal national service, just as it is without universal national service, it is important to assay the way in which Americans view lotteries, prize winning, gambling and luck, and allegedly open competitions based on a mixture of luck and skill.[1] These are inextricably combined with notions of honesty and fairness, and with such ideas as having "pull," "the inside track," or "being born with a silver spoon in one's mouth." Americans handle the concept of luck itself in two ways: Those situations which give an individual an unfair advantage, such as ethnic origin, hereditary wealth, hereditary status or lack of status, are conceived of as either good luck or bad luck, but in either case essentially unfair, and inconsistent with the ideal of equal opportunity. On the other hand, when any individual outstrips his competitors to an extraordinary degree for which no unfair element in his past can be held accountable, or fails in spite of what looks like tremendous advantages, then the success or lack of success is again explained away by invoking luck. Luck can therefore be used both to excuse defeat and as a way of accepting one's own or another's success without challenging the ethic of equal opportunity. It is in these cases a way of affirming the reality of a system in which no one should win or lose unfairly in spite of apparently glaring exceptions.

Where a lottery is used, further considerations are involved. Because of our traditional ambivalence toward the ethics of gambling, many if not all forms of gambling have had to operate outside the law. Making an activity illegal almost inevitably produces corruption. The only form of gambling which could be completely regulated would be one in which no imponderables, such as the state of a race horse, the health of a jockey, or the fitness of a boxer, would be involved. The corruption involved in most gambling provides one of the principal attractions for gamblers who, far from being attracted by an impersonal fair system, combine their belief in its essential dishonesty with a hope that if they are lucky, they can beat the system.

So to the extent to which the American draft system is modeled on a gambling model, it will to that extent be invested with an expectation that it is intrinsically dishonest and that those who are involved will be working the system for their own benefit to evade the operation of the draft. (Veterans will be accused of working veterans' benefits in the same way.) The draft dodger who tries to beat the system and gets caught will be the scapegoat, and the man who is smart enough to beat the system will be envied and covertly admired. Those who are in line to be drafted, but are not drafted, will be subjected to certain kinds of hostility; their exemptions will not be credited to luck, even though the man who is drafted may try, along with his wife and parents, to assimilate this to his *bad* luck. The draft becomes personalized as a force which "catches up with you," or "gets you" if you aren't smart enough. When "Uncle Sam" is substituted for "the draft," the image of the federal government as a pursuing hostile figure out after young men becomes reinforced. When these attitudes are combined with the possibility of volunteering, instead of waiting to be caught because of a lack of skill, or with enough to escape, a man can volunteer and preserve the fiction of having made a free choice. Thus the draft does, in fact, increase the number of those who do volunteer by those who would never, without the pressure of the draft, have volunteered for military service. Such volunteers will have some of the characteristics which provide a useful challenge to the military ethos: an insistence on personal autonomy and an intolerance of submission to bureaucracy which is thought of as undue passivity or conformity. But the system of draft-induced volunteering also includes within it elements of resentment against those who are so sure they can escape military service altogether that they don't *have* to volunteer.

The less the lottery system contains elements which are seen as subject to manipulation, the less resentment there is. Ideally, therefore, what is needed is a draft system in which the lottery system works with impeccable impersonality.

Obviously all exemptions for education, marriage, parenthood, hardship, or participation in an essential occupation are elements which reduce the impersonality and therefore the intrinsic impartiality of the system. Even exemption for gross physical defect, such as blindness, deafness or crippling, can be seen as an element which makes it possible to beat the system.

Congruently, the exemption of anyone who can be regarded as likely to win the sympathy of a draft board and the drafting of anyone who is underprivileged or likely to alienate the sympathies of a draft board is also suspect. Categories of types of individuals who may expect exemption or draft vary from year to year; current gossip may advise making certain kinds of political speeches or abstaining from them, or spraying on perfume, or shaving the armpits. But there continues to be the belief that a draft lottery is a form of gambling, and that because it has so many human and variable components, it can be "fixed."

The lottery model also fits in with the extent to which Selective Service activities appear to be capriciously extended or reduced from month to month. Last month a given man would have been exempted; this month he is called up. This, in turn, fits into an undesirable picture of the Armed Forces as irrational, likely to fit square pegs into round holes, denying the capabilities of recruits and setting everyone to the performance of inappropriate tasks. The lottery model as a model for the route into the service is very easily extended to the whole of the services.

There were certain elements in the Korean War call-up, such as the recall of reserves, which increased the sense of the armed services as wantonly capricious, and this sense was expressed in stories of busloads of passengers abandoned in the wilds (sic) when the long arm of the government had plucked the bus driver off the bus. This sense of the capriciousness and unpredictability of the whole selective service mechanism was then expressed by parents and teachers in advice to the young, who were told that it was now impossible to plan for a consistent career. They insisted that it was impossible for a young man to make a rational career design for study, marriage, and occupation because this would be interrupted. Although the armed services have made extensive attempts to show how military service can be related to life-career plans, such irrational attitudes as those aroused by the Korean War and perpetuated in the communication between adults and adolescents have prevented the recognition that Selective Service regulations actually made it easier to plan ahead than it had been in either World War I or World War II.

In summary it may be said that some form of lottery is necessary in order to have a draft component in the Armed Forces which directly, or at least indirectly by creating pressure for volunteering, will provide a citizen component essential for our kind of democratic society. The more impersonal the lottery, the fewer the exemptions and exceptions, in fact the fewer human decisions involved, the less there will be a feeling that decisions are fixed and arbitrary, and the greater the acceptance of the chance results will be.

The problem then becomes how large the draft component based on some form of lottery need be, and what form it should take, in order to provide the conditions for a citizen army, most but not all of whom will be volunteers, and a small number of whom will be professionals. And how is the question of a feeling that forms of drafting and exemption are unfair to be handled?

Universal national service would provide a setting within which the sense of unfairness could be enormously reduced. If every young adult were subjected to the same initial form of arbitrary involvement, the feeling that no particular young adults were luckier or more unlucky than the rest would decrease the feelings of envy or guilt which are presently being expressed both by those who feel a disproportionate burden, and by those who feel—as many college students feel—that they are disproportionately privileged. Initially every individual, including the physically handicapped, the mentally defective, the emotionally disturbed, the totally illiterate, would be registered, and every one of these, according to their needs or potentialities, would be assigned to types of rehabilitation, education, and different kinds of services with different sorts of risks, benefits, and requirements. These categories, if seen in a national context, would be large. Within each category, including such categories as conscientious objectors, or those who desired to devote themselves to human welfare, or those who were determined to do something connected with aeronautics, there would again be choice, but at some point some element of chance could be preserved. A contrast can be drawn, for example, between the operation of chance in assignment to the Atlantic or Pacific theatres in World War II, and the use of the point demobilization system at the end of World War II, where a rational evaluation of services performed and hardships experienced was used as a basis for priorities. If all those groupings *within* which chance finally played a role were *initially* composed of individuals from all parts of the country, all races, all ethnic groups, all class levels, then the operation of chance would seem less arbitrary. When it was finally necessary to choose those who were actually most fit for military service within such a group, choice could again operate. Failure to reach a standard of performance which admitted to officer training school, or qualified a registrant for training as a pilot, would be the end product of long periods of equably shared sacrifice and opportunity.

As it is vitally important to change the present attitude toward selective service as involving extreme inequities, the creation of a situation within which such a sense of inequity would be almost abolished seems important.

UNIVERSAL NATIONAL SERVICE AS A NEW INSTITUTION

We may now turn to the other arguments in favor of universal national service. Universal national service would make it possible to assay the defects and the potentialities of every young American on the threshold of adulthood. The tremendous disparity in schools and health conditions in different parts of the country and in different socioeconomic groups which now results in the disqualification of such large numbers, both for military service and for participation in our society, could be corrected for the whole population. Currently, the bulk of the young people so handicapped are simply rejected and left to their own devices, or left to become the subject of inadequate and prohibitively expensive programs of reeducation or rehabilitation later.

Universal service would immediately do away with the present anomalous situation in which young people with a record are exempted. The juvenile delinquent is, in a majority of cases, a type of individual who most needs reeducation and rehabilitation. Where a professional army is compromised by a large number of members with court records, a universal national service could appropriately deploy young people into service specialties which would meet many of the unfulfilled desires which had led to their encounters with the law: a love of cars, speed, and risk.

Universal registration and evaluation would also serve to find the very extensive numbers of highly talented young people whose capacities are hidden by lack of education, medical care, or social experience, or by membership in deprived ethnic and racial groups. As our civilization becomes more and more technical, the demand for talent becomes ever more intense. Our present methods of talent search are terribly inadequate.

Universal national service would provide an opportunity for young adults to establish an identity and a sense of self-respect and responsibility as individuals before making career choices or establishing homes. At present a very large number go from dependency on their parents into careers that have been chosen for them, or use early marriage as a device to reach psuedo-adult status.

Universal national service would provide an opportunity for young adults to experience the satisfaction of services performed on behalf of the nation and of other fellow citizens—children, the sick, the aged, the deprived—which could serve as a paradigm for later social participation not immediately based on the standards of the marketplace. It should increase the capacity for dedication. Whatever methods are selected for distributing income in such a way as to separate productive ability from consumer need, universal national service could be set up as a suitable educational prelude. Universal national service, if set up in such a way that units were a cross section of the entire society, could compensate for the increasing fragmentation, ignorance, and lack of knowledge of their fellow citizens and the rest of the world which is characteristic of those reared in our economically segregated residential pattern, in which both the poor and the rich, the highly technologically gifted and those with obsolescent skills, the white collar and the blue collar, are each reared in almost total ignorance of the others.

Universal national service could be a preparation for later periods of reeducation and reevaluation which may become a necessary feature of a society faced with increasing longevity and rapid technological change.

Universal national service could be made into a tremendous system of incentives for pupils in elementary and secondary school. If it were widely known that every child would someday have to serve in a service unit, and that his skills and abilities would give him a chance at particular kinds of service, then the incentives, which now operate for the privileged group who know they must study in order to enter college, would be extended to the whole population. The present frequency of dropouts is due not only to poor backgrounds and poor teaching, but also to lack of incentive for those young people who have, at present, no vision of higher education. Higher education as an incentive to hard work on the part of privileged American students is not wholly an academic or economic incentive; it is primarily a promise that they will be able to participate for two years, or four, or six, in the kind of life that they want to live, associate with others with the same aspirations, and find the kinds of wives they want to marry. Universal national service could extend this kind of aspiration to young people who are not capable of or interested in higher education, but who are quite capable of dreaming of living in the city instead of the country, at the seaside instead of on the plains of Kansas, who want to work near airplanes instead of at mine pitheads, or in zoos, or forestry preserves, or in something connected with science or medicine. Just as the armed services have been able to make training for a chosen but often otherwise unobtainable vocation an incentive to the recruitment of young adults, the opportunities which would be opened for choice in universal national service could be widely disseminated to the young. The hopeless, unemployed young corner boys might never reach the corner if they knew that, no matter who they were, they would have a chance, at 18, at a wider world.

Universal national service would provide for an interval within our very prolonged educational system in which actual, responsible work experience would precede further educational and vocational choices. Our present changing society demands—instead of individuals who will learn one job and, driven by the fear of hunger will stick to it all their lives—people who are flexible, able to learn new skills and perform new tasks, who will be motivated by a desire to participate in work situations rather than a simple fear of starvation. Universal national service should prepare them for this kind of participation where parents and immediate elders, who have been reared in a world of scarcity and limitation of opportunity, are not able to give them the necessary training.

Universal national service would provide opportunities for service abroad in a variety of capacities, service in different parts of the country, service in different climes and conditions. It should broaden all young people in the way in which those who have taken full advantage of service overseas and of the Peace Corps have been broadened and prepared for responsible citizenship and wider understanding of national and world problems.

THE INCLUSION OF WOMEN

The inclusion of women on the same basis as men is absolutely essential for the accomplishment of the goals listed above. Universal national service for men only would be so handicapped that it might be wiser to retain the present system of selective service and the present numerically few minor activities like the Peace Corps and the Job Corps. It is necessary to include women because:

Women form half of the age group involved, and a failure to include them will promote a split in the experience of men and women at a time when it is essential that they should move in step with each other, economically and politically.

The position of women today has become so identified with ideas of non-discrimination, non-segregation, and equality of privilege that failure to include women will automatically touch off latent fears of other kinds of class, race, and ethnic discrimination. The association of women with disadvantaged minorities in recent legislation, and in the thinking of many developing nations, continually reinforces this attitude. Women are not, of course, actually a minority in the same sense as racially or ethnically disadvantaged groups, and there are cogent reasons for some discrimination between the sexes (which will be discussed below), but the national and world climate of opinion treats them as such.

One of the most important goals of universal national service is the identification and correction of physical and educational handicaps. These are as significant for women, as mothers of the next generation and as a large part of the labor force, as they are for men. If the women are left behind in isolated rural regions, in the slums or in ghettos, the broadening educational effects for men will be at least partially nullified because their wives will not be able to maintain the standards their husbands have learned to respect.

Universal national service will serve as a gigantic and effective talent search. Half of our intelligent and gifted citizenry are women. Because of the persistence of traditional ideas about women's aptitude, we are at present losing more highly gifted women than highly gifted men. Girls with mathematical ability are discouraged from going into the sciences or into any kind of technology; they are either shunted off into typewriting or, if they persist with academic interests, into the humanities. Furthermore, it has been found that women who reenter the work force later are more likely to follow up leads which they started in college than to enter entirely new fields. The chance to assay their abilities during universal national service would provide a background for appropriate career choices when they wish to reenter the labor market and are seeking additional education.

Women form a very substantial element in opinion formation and in political decision-making, especially at the local level. During the last two decades, much of the contra-suggestibility to scientific careers for men has come from women who have been alienated from the type of preparatory literature—science fiction and technical magazines—on which future scientists have been nourished. Failure to include women in universal national service would result in an imbalance in the capacity for advancement and higher standard of living which universal national service should give its participants, in a widening of the educational gap between men and women, and in a sharpening of irrational opposition both to the military and to the application of technology and automation. The two-party type of democracy rests upon giving women enough education so that children experience two parents, who often disagree, but who are both well informed and trustworthy.

WAYS IN WHICH UNIVERSAL NATIONAL SERVICE
WOULD DIFFER FOR WOMEN

Throughout human history, with very few and brief exceptions, women have never been given weapons or asked to take part in overt aggressive activity. Although women were given tools when tools were invented—the stone or bone knife, the needle, the scraper, the digging stick—we have no record of women in very technologically primitive societies wielding weapons of war. Either some very deep biocultural objection to giving weapons to women operated in all early societies, or those societies which did permit women to use weapons did not survive. History cannot, of course, provide a complete guide to the future and the fact that women have only very occasionally been given offensive weapons is not a conclusive proof that this would be an undesirable course for a society to take. But whenever such a cultural choice is very widespread, it is worthwhile considering its significance. Recent work on aggression in the animal world has emphasized the amount of ritual combat between males of the same species, in which competitive and rivalrous behavior was kept within biologically structured bounds. The females of the same species, when they fight, fight in defense of their young and fight to the death. The controls which operate on male aggression seem to be lacking in females. Among human beings, where cultural controls replace biological controls, the ability to use violence in a disciplined way seems to be dependent upon early experiences and learning how to subject aggressive physical behavior to rules of fair play and appropriateness. (It is notable that the massive killings within the same society which have occurred since World War II have occurred in societies in which open aggression is deprecated: India and Indonesia, especially Bali, where children of both sexes are restrained from any show of aggression whatsoever.)

The historical and comparative material at least suggests that it may be highly undesirable to permit women, trained to inhibit aggressive behavior, to take part in offensive warfare. Defensive warfare, on the other hand, does not have the same disadvantages, as it invokes the biological basis of defense of the nest and the young.

On the other hand, there seems to be no objection to permitting women to assume risks, and it is possible that defense of the young may be a very appropriate biological underpinning for risk. Nor does there seem to be any objection to women playing significant roles within the military establishment, as technicians, physicians, teachers, etc., except probably in the training of those special units where the whole emphasis is upon the development of techniques of face-to-face combat.

The other problem involved in including women in universal national service is the need to protect women as future mothers from inappropriate types of physical strain, and to protect them during a service period from pregnancy. Protection from pregnancy involves either adequate chaperonage or adequate contraception. In the present climate of opinion it should be possible for a choice to be made by each girl: for a sheltered and protected environment within which she could carry out her national service, caring for children or the sick or the aged under appropriate chaperonage; or for contraception. In either case, pregnancy could be treated as a severe breach of contract, comparable to going AWOL in males. Part of the institution of universal national service would be the postponement of marriage until the service was completed, if universal national service takes the form of a nationwide call-up at 18, or the possibility of the entry into national service as a working couple if proposals for extending the service period into the late 20's were to be adopted. Universal national service would replace for girls, even more than for boys, marriage as the route away from the parental home, and provide a period of responsible and directed reappraisal before marriage and parenthood were assumed. The postponement of marriage until the age of 20 would cut down on the number of divorces due to immaturity, reduce the number of fatherless families, and contribute to the control of the population explosion. Choice between chaperonage and contraception should meet the demands of religious groups who are still able to protect their young girls from premarital sex experimentation.

The coeducational aspects of the universal national services could be varied to suit the different circumstances, allowing for groups of both boys and girls who wished for time to mature before being forced into the continuous company of the opposite sex.

Others have dealt with the question of what types of services could be performed by the number of young people who would be called up each year, so this paper will not go into this except to suggest that any attempt to make part of the civilian services local and voluntary, without the mediation of a national agency, would defeat many of the purposes discussed here. Furthermore, a major part of the educational impact of universal national service is experience away from own home, own town, own class, own ethnic group, and an opportunity to gain a sense of independent identity and citizenship amid the diversities of the modern world. Any program of self-selection or local control which permitted immediate choice of locale or type of service would segregate young people into the kinds of groups that resident and non-resident colleges, low-level and high-level high schools, privileged rich communities and ghettos, slums and deprived rural areas, segregate them today. This is true of such organizations as the Peace Corps and the Job Corps. In any consideration of types of service, a primary emphasis should be on types of group residence and initial training which would serve to eliminate all deficiencies of experience due to various types of segregation.

Universal national service, in addition to solving the problem of fairness for those who are asked to serve in the military, in contrast to those who are not, is above all a new institution for creating responsible citizens alert to the problems and responsibilities of nationhood in a rapidly changing world.

NOTES

[1] M. Janowitz, in "The Logic of a National Service System" for this Conference, has discussed the attitudes of the military and those concerned with problems of morale on the undesirability of treating the drafted group as double losers. This is a special instance of the wider problem of how those who participate in a lottery, as either winners or losers, are viewed in American culture.

11

Guidelines for National Service

DONALD J. EBERLY

The concept of national service is based on the philosophy of the interdependence and hence reciprocal responsibilities of a society and the individuals who compose it. That is, each individual has a responsibility to enrich the society which has provided his educational and cultural heritage and, likewise, a society owes its citizens, on whom its growth and vitality depend, a maximum of opportunities to render such service and thereby to enlarge their range of experiences and to further their own personal development.

A concern with the present limited number and scope of service opportunities motivated the participants in the National Service Conference of May, 1966, to call for an expansion of service possibilities for all young citizens. At the same time, they rejected the prevailing misconception that national service would necessarily involve compulsory participation in non-military activities under an administrative structure similar to that of the Armed Forces—with the chain of command extending from Washington—and directed discussion toward the provision of the maximum degree of individual choice and decision.

In an informal survey of Conference participants, plus some additional persons particularly interested in national service, the National Service Secretariat asked that priorities be assigned to the various elements of the rationale for a national service program. Education defined in its broadest sense emerged as the primary consideration. Other purposes designated as essential included:

—Fulfillment of service obligation
—Reduction of draft inequities
—Cross-cultural experience
—Manpower for needed jobs
—Sense of civic worth

Some emphasis was given by a few respondents to providing an outlet for youths' energies, encouraging personal development, offering service alternatives for young people, improving the U.S. image, and contributing to world peace.

A flexible program of national service, as outlined in this paper, would enable an individual to serve his society in a manner consistent with his own talents and abilities and at the same time to extend his self-knowledge and understanding of others.

Before an operational mechanism for national service can be discussed, it is

The author is Executive Director, National Service Secretariat.

necessary to define the underlying assumptions which would be incorporated in any program of national service:

1) National security must always be the first consideration; therefore, *military manpower needs must have top priority*.

2) Citizens can be compelled to serve only in the Armed Forces and fire-fighting brigades, and a fairly strong case can be made for the volunteer spirit approach to non-military activities; therefore, *no one should be compelled to serve except in the Armed Forces*.

3) Accomplishment of needed tasks in non-military service would be in the national interest; therefore, *recognition should be given to persons who serve satisfactorily in approved non-military programs as well as in military activities*.

4) Legitimate objections have been raised by young men to the uncertainty of being drafted and to the limited range of choices open for serving their country; therefore, *any program of national service should be structured so that the social, economic and educational backgrounds of the young men in approved non-military programs would correspond to the backgrounds of young men in society*.

5) Tax money would be used to finance a sizable portion of the non-military activities, and national service must not degenerate into a make-work program; therefore, *the tasks undertaken in non-military service must serve the human and natural resources of the nation and non-military service must grow no faster than useful jobs are available*.

IMPLEMENTATION OF THE NATIONAL SERVICE CONCEPT

A beginning point for the operation of a national service program would be the establishment of basic criteria, which an activity must satisfy in order to qualify as an approved service within the framework of national service. Included in these would be the absence of political or religious proselytizing and the assurance that the proposed activity would not impinge on the legitimate interests of agriculture, business, or labor. Criteria such as the above would be determined by Congress for implementation by a body designated perhaps as the National Foundation for Volunteer Service.

The Foundation would be composed of representatives from both the private and public sectors and would be asked to approve projects proposed by agencies requesting national service volunteers. Thus, school boards could request teacher and clerical aides. Hospitals could request medical and nurse's aides. Church and community groups could request volunteers for social, recreational and other civic work. Present programs such as the Peace Corps and a revised Job Corps, in which volunteers perform a useful national service, would qualify.

After approving an activity, the Foundation would pay the volunteers through the sponsoring agency subsistence allowances at rates determined from the recommendations of the receiving agency. Generally, the service organization would be expected to meet any other costs. Finally, under certain specified circumstances, the national commission would also make grants to informational and placement programs, such as those outlined below.

National Service Summers

Youths aged 17 and 18, or having completed high school, could spend a summer at a camp in which they would perform an actual service function. They would be informed of opportunities in both military and non-military service and of opportunities in higher education. They would live and work with a heterogeneous group of young people. The inclusion of these basic elements in summer projects would open the door to a variety of useful programs which would prepare young people to meet their service responsibility in a constructive manner.

National Service Placement Centers

These centers would receive young men who wish to enter non-military service but have not yet found a place in a particular activity. Programs would last for three to six months, during which time persons would be tested, informed of appropriate service opportunities, given physical training and a service activity to perform, and perhaps trained in a specific skill. Here, also, a wide variety of arrangements would be possible and sponsorship could be shared among educational, fraternal, religious, business, labor, and other groups in the community.

The numbers entering these centers would be geared to the size of the requests for volunteers. In addition, most approved activities would themselves be responsible for training volunteers and receiving some of their volunteers directly and some through the placement centers.

A national service program so conceived could operate independently of the Selective Service System. However, the two programs could function complementarily if recognition were given to both military and non-military service as parallel elements of the national interest. As revealed in a recent congressional testimony by the Department of Defense, in 1966 only 46 per cent of men aged 26 had been called for military service. Assuming continuation of the current level in the Armed Forces, this percentage would drop to 42 per cent by 1974. Given the rate of approximately 35 per cent of age cohorts ineligible for military duty—for medical, mental, or administrative reasons—this means that today 19 per cent of the young men 26 years of age are qualified for but did not serve in military service. Nineteen per cent of the 26-year-old male population is approximately 230,000 young men.

In order to provide greater service opportunities for this expanding pool of young people, the 18-year-old, when he registers for the draft, could be allowed to choose between a definite commitment to military service and a definite commitment to non-military service. Those not wishing to opt for one of these forms of service would be liable for military duty by means of Selective Service, a lottery, or whatever mechanism is evolved. If this system had been operable in 1958 for men who became 18 during that year, it is evident that, on the basis of the military manpower needs for this period, 230,000 able-bodied young men could have engaged in non-military service at the same time that some 550,000 of their contemporaries were serving in the Armed Forces. Moreover, a sizable percentage of the 400,000 men unqualified for military service could have been given the opportunity to participate in useful non-military activities.

If a system of individual choices such as this were effected, and if recognition of the service obligation were extended to satisfactory completion of non-military activities, pressure would be exerted on young men to select a particular kind of service, corresponding most closely to their interests and abilities, rather than to submit themselves to an arbitrary draft pool. A possible consequence could be an increase in voluntary enlistment in the Armed Forces. A longer-range effect could be the evolution of a program of universal national service, achieved without legislated compulsory non-military service.

CONTROL OVER MILITARY MANPOWER REQUIREMENTS

Short and long-range military manpower needs would be compiled periodically by the Department of Defense and submitted to the President. These figures would be compared with the number of registrants who have declared an intent to enter military service at a particular time. To the extent possible, the President would establish conditions of service sufficiently attractive to draw the desired number of volunteers for the Armed Forces. If these indirect controls fail, young men would be drafted from the pool and, if necessary, a ceiling would be imposed on the number of persons allowed to enter non-military service.

ROLE OF WOMEN IN NATIONAL SERVICE

Women would be eligible to receive subsistence allowances from the National Foundation. While the questions of deferment and exemption would not apply to women, they would, in order to qualify for support, have to commit themselves to a period of service acceptable to the relevant agency and to the National Foundation.

SUMMARY

This paper is intended to suggest an appropriate balance among the several objectives of national service and to outline a mechanism that could implement the concept. An unanswered question, and one that needs very close study, is the appropriate phasing-in of national service. How big should the program be in 1968? in 1970? in 1980? Should present agencies such as Peace Corps and VISTA retain their independence or be subsumed under national service? Should the federal government establish new service agencies in areas of need where no private, community or state agencies exist?

The facing of such questions now, and the designation of a time scale for the various elements of a national service plan, are important factors in the kind of examination which the University of Chicago Conference on the Draft affords and which the concept of national service richly deserves.

PERSPECTIVES ON THE DRAFT

12

The Draft in the Light of History

WILLIAM H. McNEILL

As public discussion of the draft law assumes a new urgency it seems worthwhile to ask how other peoples in other times and places have regulated civil-military relations and defended themselves. Humanity's long experience with armed men ought to add to our wisdom in confronting the current dilemmas of American military policy.

To begin with, it is important to understand that an army is not simply a tool of foreign policy or an instrument of defense. It also and inevitably plays an important role in domestic politics, since no regime unacceptable to the military establishment can long endure. Divorce between those with the power to affect public policy and those who bear arms is at best precarious, being dependent on the good will of those who do control weapons. Viable political regimes have therefore tended throughout history to confine effective political rights to those who had arms and knew how to use them. A survey of the historical record may help to revive for us this cliché of eighteenth-century political wisdom.

In early times the relationship between military and civil communities was harsh but simple. Organized armies came into existence by conquest. Really successful conquerors overwhelmed local resistance by gathering an army that was too large to find food and other supplies for very long in any one place. Such armies lived by plunder. Accordingly, from the time of Sargon of Akkad (about 2250 B.C.) to that of Tamerlane (died 1405) and Wallenstein (died 1634) ever-victorious, predatory armies repeatedly arose whose numbers both guaranteed success in the field and required incessant campaigning year after year after year.

Seldom, however, did the cohesion of such an army long survive the captain around whom it formed. In relatively poor societies a more stable arrangement was to scatter small groups of warriors across the countryside. Such a "feudal" system made the armed establishment into a privileged class, supported locally by goods and services extracted from the inhabitants. In the relatively stable, face-to-face situations that resulted, law and custom soon defined who owed what to whom. The destructive and irregular depredation characteristic of primitive centralized armies could thus give way to relatively predictable rents and taxes, sustaining a military system which maintained most of the advantages of centralization. Tax collectors were able to concentrate enough goods and services at a single center to allow a monarch to maintain an armed establishment far superior to any merely local opposition. The ancient Assyrian, Persian, Chinese, and Roman empires sustained themselves on this principle. Indeed, as the

The author is a professor in the Department of History, University of Chicago.

subject peoples got used to paying taxes to an unseen and distant monarch, it became possible to station troops in outlying parts of the empire, far from the royal person. This simplified supply and improved frontier guard. It also invited rebellion, as the history of the ancient empires repeatedly demonstrated.

Nevertheless, from the iron age to the present, the prevailing form of military establishment among civilized states has been a tax-supported professional army, organized and supplied along lines first worked out by the ancient Assyrians. This kind of army prevailed quite simply because it was usually stronger than alternatives or rivals.

Needless to say, a tax-supported standing army was not a perfect solution to the problems arising from divergences between civilian and military interests. On the one hand, the sovereign had to guard against military usurpation. Court rituals designed to surround the person of the monarch with awe and mystery helped; so did the hereditary principle of succession and religious sanctions against rebellion. But these devices—the best which long centuries of imperial government ever discovered—were never effective for very long in any large state.

A second and almost equally difficult problem was how to prevent soldiers from oppressing the subject populations so harshly as to arouse their antagonism and persuade them to welcome almost any invader as a liberator. Here the principle of divide and rule came richly into play. Military bureaucracy could be paralleled by a civil bureaucracy, and the civil bureaucracy could be split up between administrative, judicial, and tax-collecting branches—each checking the others and each liable to inspection from above and vulnerable to appeals from below. In this fashion the army could be made to depend on supplies doled out by civilian officials, and any gestures on the soldiers' part toward helping themselves directly by plundering the civilian population could be detected from the start. But despite every administrative ingenuity, collaboration between local civil and military officials to fleece the population always remained possible. The history of all the world's great empires—especially during their later phases—demonstrates how widespread this phenomenon has been.

The conclusion to be drawn from such a survey of the historic record is that a citizen army of the sort we have been accustomed to taking for granted is rare and entirely atypical of civilized states. To be sure, most barbarian tribes expected every able-bodied man to bear arms. But such forces were militias rather than armies in the civilized sense. The Greek cities of antiquity did raise and train citizen armies during a period of about three hundred years; so did the Roman republic. In the corners and coulisses of history a considerable number of other tribal republics and city states can be discovered that depended for varying lengths of time upon a citizen army. This was the case, for example, in towns of medieval Italy and Germany, in parts of Japan before the Tokugawa period, in northern India before the time of Buddha, and in Palestine during the time of the Hebrew Judges.

However important some of these communities were for the world's cultural and religious history, in matters of war and politics they remained puny and of merely secondary significance. The reasons are not far to seek. An effective citizen army required (and requires) very special conditions to flourish. First, the technical level of warfare must be such that no elaborate or expensive equipment that is beyond the reach of ordinary citizens can have decisive effect in battle.

Until the introduction of firearms, this meant that infantry tactics and training had to be superior to cavalry—a circumstance only sporadically and locally the case. In the second place, a citizen army can only be effective as long as most citizens trust one another enough to fight side by side and back to back—not face to face against one another.

Since socioeconomic differentiation has been and continues to be a mark of civilized society, political or economic success with concomitant territorial expansion puts enormous strain upon such consensus. In fact, it proved easier to collect taxes from a disfranchised population than to maintain political consensus among a citizen majority. Accordingly, the great imperial states of history all fell back upon a professionalized army, separated from the general body of the subject population by a distinct ethos and, often, by distinct ethnic origin as well.

Western Europeans worked a remarkable variation upon these themes in the late eighteenth century. Prior to that time the European experience remained within the general patterns I have attempted to describe. With the invention of missile weapons that were effective against armor—first the cross bow and then guns—medieval feudal lords gave way to mercenary bands that lived mainly by plunder, just as Sargon of Akkad had done millennia before. In the course of the seventeenth century, royal bureaucratic administration converted these bands into royal standing armies that were organized along the same lines as the Assyrian army had been more than two thousand years earlier. The French revolutionaries broke away from these ancient patterns, however, by summoning all Frenchmen to the defense of the *patrie* in 1793. During the next twenty years innumerable French victories demonstrated the new power that mass armies could command in an age of incipient industrialism.

The subsequent military history of Europe is the history of more and more thorough mobilization for total wars—and the increasing awkwardness of citizen armies for the conduct of anything except all-out warfare. From this point of view the hesitations of the French, Austrian, and Prussian governments in military matters between 1815 and 1870 are most instructive. To fight limited wars abroad and maintain a dubiously popular regime at home clearly called for long-service professional troops. But such a force put a heavy strain on finances. A short-service conscript army cost less, since draftees did not get paid, but required the government to be popular or risk overthrow. Prussia's victories over Austria in 1866 and over France in 1870-71 seemed to prove that a conscript army of citizen soldiers could make even a conservative regime popular. This assuaged the scruples of aristocratic officers against more and more radical mobilization of social resources for war. The unparalleled efforts of World Wars I and II resulted.

British and American military experience departed from this European pattern in significant and important fashion. First of all, the British did not build up a large royal standing army. The seventeenth-century experience of Cromwell's military dictatorship soured king and Parliament, not to mention the people at large, against soldiers garrisoned at home. As a result, after the Glorious Revolution of 1688, the British army was legally subordinated to Parliament, not to the King; and its officers were recruited from the county families who simultaneously dominated Parliament and English society at large. Rank and file came mainly from the subject nationalities of the British Isles, the Irish and Scots, and secondarily from the English lower classes. The army was garrisoned abroad;

home stations were used for training recruits. The result was an imperial army that had remarkably little independent weight in politics. Coincidence between the social origins and consciousness of the officers and of the ruling classes of Great Britain was so close that no independent military interest ordinarily made itself felt; and nearly all of the rank and file were kept overseas where their behavior could bring no harm and their weapons could hold no threat to the social order of Great Britain.

As for the United States, until very recently we stayed close to the militia tradition characteristic of barbarian and simple agrarian peoples. Thirty years ago the professional army of the United States was minuscule—less than 100,000 in a population of 120 million. Local police forces, National Guard units commanded by state governors, together with widespread possession of firearms by ordinary citizens all meant that no centralized monopoly of armed force existed within the country. This, indeed, was the hope and intention of the Founding Fathers, among whom a close and indissoluble relation between the exercise of political rights and the possession of arms and practice in their use was taken for granted.

Nothing that has changed since the eighteenth century invalidates the wisdom of the men who fought the revolutionary war and drafted the Constitution. In the long run it still is true that the possession of arms and practice in their use must coincide with the effective exercise of political rights. This is so because the leaders of those who do have arms in their hands can always exercise a veto over any action proposed by public officials if they have the will to do so and command the support, or at least the obedience, of their troops.

Fortunately, the American officer corps has a strong tradition against involvement in politics, and as long as civilian government does nothing to offend the corporate interest or pride of the officer corps this tradition will undoubtedly continue to inhibit open intervention in political decision-making, as it has in the past. Yet the military veto is still there; hidden perhaps, but not so far from the surface as it used to be. This is the case not because army officers have changed or become greedy for power, but because, as the military establishment has become larger and more professionalized, it has become both more expensive and more distinct from the general body of the citizenry. This increases the risk of open divergence between civil and military interests in a way which the United States has not known in earlier times.

If such a confrontation should develop openly in future, citizens without arms obviously risk the loss of their political rights—in fact if not in form. In cases of stubborn disagreement between civil and military leaders it is simply not safe to cut off the pay and decree the dissolution of an aggrieved army. As Sulla and Caesar demonstrated to Roman republicans, such acts of civic virtue invite military usurpation. Nor does it require a great stretch of our imaginations to envisage a time when half a million disgruntled Americans might return from Vietnam, or from some future battleground, with the conviction that they had been betrayed by the fat cats at home. On high patriotic grounds some general might then refuse to defer to civilian authority—as General MacArthur was sorely tempted to do in Korea.

I conclude that military service is, always has been, and seems likely to remain, the ball and chain attached to political privilege. Political privilege, in this connection, means the exercise of an effective voice in the determination of public policy. It follows that either the armed services must remain very small or some sort of universal military service is required to provide a secure basis for democracy. And if it is true that technical conditions no longer permit a citizen army to attain high efficiency, then the democratic political order is at least potentially endangered by that fact.

If the United States decides nevertheless to accept the risks of relying upon long-term-service professional troops of the sort suited for conducting distant, low-grade wars and for garrison duty overseas, then devices must be found for linking military leadership more closely with the leadership of civil society. The existing policy of exempting the future leaders of civilian life from military service positively invites divergence of viewpoint and seems almost suicidal in a democracy. In case a selective draft continues to be necessary—assuming that we do not wish to invite a coup d'etat—then it is precisely those who go to college and are headed for the privileged places in our society who should be drafted. Unwillingness to qualify for social leadership at such a price amounts to abdication.

Preservation of democratic government will be difficult in future as it always was in the past. The success or failure of this enterprise in the United States will depend in very significant part upon the military policy we adopt. The debate now opening in congress should therefore command the very best wisdom and attention of citizens and legislators alike. No more important issue has confronted us since World War II.

13

What Is Military?

ALBERT D. BIDERMAN

The Selective Service System exists for the purpose of providing the Armed Forces with military manpower. Most of the discussions about the Selective Service System deal with the question of manpower. I would like to raise some fundamental questions concerning the other word in the defining phrase, the word "military." "What is military?" is a fundamental question that has to be answered to deal intelligently with many problems to which Conference is addressed.

If our need is merely neat statistics, we may define "military manpower" simply as those to whom a prescribed oath has been administered, who thereupon have been put into uniforms, and who receive pay for their services from the Armed Forces. But what kinds of roles, what kinds of work, what functions in our social world require that this be done by people in the uniforms of soldiers or sailors or marines?

THE PECULIAR FUNCTION

Transition from Military to Civilian

My most recent encounter with the question was in studies I have been doing on what happens to the professional soldier after retirement. More than ninety times out of a hundred, what happens to him after retirement is that he becomes a civilian; to all intents and purposes, he does a civilian job in the civilian work world. This is rather remarkable if we consider that, with relatively few and isolated exceptions, the man who has spent 20 or 30 years in the military establishment has been preponderantly, if not exclusively, trained and socialized to perform within a very distinctive and peculiar institution.

By and large, the retired military professional has been able to move fairly smoothly into a civilian "second career." The problem of effecting these transitions from military to civilian pursuits is often sufficiently problematic, however, to create at least a modicum of anxiety on the part of those having to make the shift. This results in a reversal of the pressures on self-identity, group identity, and institutional ideology on the part of those confronting the problem. Instead of being impelled to stress the distinctive and peculiar nature of the military calling, they are led to stress its identity with other worlds of work.

When he is out looking for a second-career job, the retired military man is

The author is Senior Research Associate, Bureau of Social Science Research, Inc.

likely to try to convince himself, and others, that he is no different, or at least not very much different, from any other qualified job applicant. His experience, he avers, has involved doing the same kinds of things in the same kinds of organizations as is true of civilian workers. The military, with the cooperation of the United States Employment Service, is ready to provide him with some instruction in translating esoteric military occupational specialties and job descriptions into verbal equivalents that will make familiar sense to a prospective civilian boss or, more usually, personnel office. Most retirees can muster in this fashion an imposing vita, documenting possession of the kinds of skills and experience needed for a host of core jobs in the civilian economy.

Perhaps one of the military retiree's major problems is that the job descriptions are often too rich. After 20-odd years of service, he may have had too much responsibility, supervised too many employees (both military and civilian), travelled a little too extensively, studied too many subjects, had specialized technical training in too great a range of skills, so that the placement officer of the large industrial concern or the counselor in the employment service is apt to be a little bit bewildered as to just where this man *should* fit.

From the standpoint of accumulating experience useful for finding a satisfactory second career in civilian life, relatively few retirees will suffer from the handicap of having spent the bulk of their military career doing things that involve skills useful only for the business of shooting at people or being shot at. Even with three wars having occurred during the career span of the cohorts currently retiring, there is on the whole a negligible net loss of time that would have been available for the development of skills transferable to the civilian economy which is attributable to time spent actually shooting at somebody or being shot at, or in situations in which this is the major business to be transacted. (I am forced to admit that I inferred this from my data and consequently did not bother to compute it.)[1]

As we look at the military careerist upon his exiting from the service, we find that even the time he spent in combat-type assignments involved essentially things other than firing weapons and avoiding hits from those being fired at him. They involved to a greater extent, getting people fed, housed, clothed, healed, schooled, bathed, pressed, liquored, paid, counted, bedded, wheeled, fueled, entrained and emplaned, tested, hired, fired, and so forth and so on. All of these things, as has been said many times, are things that have to be done among any group of people at any time, any place.

Presumably, however, most of these things, most of the time, were done in what is called "a military manner."

The Military Manner

Let us move next, then, to the question of what is the military manner. Why are the things that are done in the military done in that particular way? Why do the people who do them have to be adapted and changed in some way, so that they undergo the remarkable transformation from civilians to soldiers, sailors, or marines?

The way things are done in the Armed Forces follows from the way the military is organized. In turn, the rationale for the way it is organized derives from its special function. This special function is said to be warfare; most crudely put, the people-killing business. But in our society, many other roles, many other people—people who are not military—are also involved in warfare in various ways.

Fred Cook allows that we now have "The Warfare State," but a large proportion of all the nations that have ever existed as well as most other states of society that did not involve a political state have also been "warfare states."[2] Many of their members who were not warriors made weapons; organized, stored, and delivered supplies; sheltered and healed warriors; performed essential and sacred rites associated with the conduct of warfare. But the key function and the truly sacred one was usually combat.

It is "combatant" that the uniform signifies. Its function is to distinguish us good and fearsome fellows easily from those other guys, and, when the game is played according to the rules, to distinguish those who may kill and be killed from the bystanders.

Original Functional Problems

Military forms evolved from the problems of making effectively organized groups for combat.[3] Warrior organization presented special problems which differed from those of the bystanders. Essentially two types of problems are worth distinguishing: those of rational organization, on the one hand, and nonrational, emotional, and ideological organization, on the other.

Rational organization involved the need for integrating and coordinating the activities of very large numbers of people—larger numbers of people in one common activity than most societies usually have had to mobilize for any other purpose. Centralized decision-making, extended communication patterns, and extensive logistics are among the more obvious examples of the special needs of this large-scale activity.

That so large a number of people had to be organized for this activity stemmed, in turn, from its literally vital consequence to the society in many situations, and its very sacred nature in most.

The sacred quality of military functions leads to many of the nonrational elements of military institutions. Other aspects of organization that are nonrational at the individual level stem from the need to control, as need be, the possible propensities of the men involved to be afraid of being killed or to be squeamish about killing. Hence, we are told, soldiers have to be trained and arranged in such a fashion as to neutralize autonomic or nomic responses in battle, and to perform the soldierly roles automatically. These were the negative requirements. On the positive side is the activation of the sacred attachments of the warrior by organizing him in formations which allowed reinforcements by ceremony and sacred symbol in the heat of battle as well as by mutual allegiances.

LOSS OF DISTINCTIVENESS

Civil-Military Convergence

To a fantastic degree, these original differentiating conditions no longer peculiarly define "military." More and more civil society has had to cope with essentially the same problem of rationally organizing vast numbers of people for economic and other social functions. For doing so, civil society has borrowed to a degree probably even greater than we recognize, cultural and organizational innovations developed for meeting military requirements and adapted these forms to its own needs. One reason for military retirees usually fitting so well into civilian careers is that so much of the civilian work world is organized and carried on in a rather "military manner."[4]

Changed Requirements of Warfare

The other side of the coin is the change in the requirements set by modern warfare. With some oversimplifications. we can divide the contemporary military problem into two parts. One is misnamed "conventional warfare." The other is misnamed "strategic warfare."

To take the latter first, strategic warfare presents almost none of the elements that through history have given the military institution its peculiar character. The one exception is that it tends to be thought of as if it did. To illustrate, I think is is a matter of complete irrelevance in the event of missile war whether the men in the missile silo or the Polaris submarine perform their duty in uniform or in their underwear. The thrust of technology is to make them obsolete in any event. Most of the key functions that can culminate in the delivery of the weapon on target have been performed earlier by civilians in industrial plants, in R & D laboratories, computer centers, Washington cubicles and, yes, stretching all the way back to the activity in the corridors of the Capitol that affect appropriations. On the target side, the receiving end, militariness is perhaps even more inappropriate. Uniformed status has nothing whatsoever to do with being eligible to be killed. In short, the old distinctions between combatants and noncombatants, along with many of the old rules of the game, become irrelevant.

Indeed, to anticipate my next subject, being uniformed in strategic warfare may confer special rights and provisions for surviving for one's country and reduce chances of dying for it. I refer not only to the specially protected position of the rare bird in the hardened missile silo, or the elusive submarine (not the yellow one), but also to the probable viability of an organization geared for emergency survival.

This functionalist perspective requires recognition that combat was not always an instrumental activity oriented to extrinsic ends such as the gain of wealth or territory, or the protection of one's own. Often, it was a game played for its own sake—for the joy of winning in a test of one's mettle or of one's good standing with Fate. At other times, war was fought as expression of hostility toward the enemy. The venting of hatred, rage, contempt or other emotions was the dominant function. Speier labeled these three ideal types "instrumental war," "agonistic war," and "absolute war," respectively.[5] He noted that varying admixtures of the elements of each actually are what has usually been encountered historically, although examples of close approaches to the types can be pointed to. This has been true in the history of our Armed Forces, as well as other principal ones. Military organization and military culture, consequently, have incorporated elements from all three types of encounters. That each type of warfare (or aspect of any given war) calls for dispositions and capacities inconsistent with the two others complicates the problem of defining what is "military."

As examples, the knightly regard for the rules of the game appropriate to agonistic warfare is as incongruent with the calculated regard for the rules of profit and loss appropriate to instrumental war as it is to the indomitable depravity appropriate to absolute war. Much of the genius of military institutions has resided in the blending of these incongruities.

The fit of the historically developed forms of the military to the contemporary world has been disrupted not only by the change in technology but by the reasons for which wars are fought, or, in the case of nuclear war, contemplated. None of the three reasons defining Speier's types of war—for the game, for gall, or for gain—apply. The agonistic, the instrumental and the absolute elements of militariness become equally irrelevant to such wars. Such servomechanisms as the RAND Corporation are presumably as much better adapted to fighting them as they have been to designing them.

With regard to conventional warfare, Professor Janowitz[6] has examined exhaustively, but perhaps not as radically as I might, the change for rational military organization brought about by technological developments in the areas of communication, weaponry, firepower, surveillance methods, and mobility. Here I won't even try to illustrate these changes but will simply assert that they have rendered obsolete many of the traditional forms of military organization.

Operating in much the same direction are changes in the nature of the social and economic organization of the society from which the military draws its manpower. Here too, there is a degree of social differentiation and an elaborated skill structure that does not remotely resemble the undifferentiated pool concept of earlier days of mass levies.

Professor Janowitz also has indicated some of the changes that are associated with the politicization of warfare and of international conflict in general. He has indicated some of the implications of these changes for the ideological underpinnings of military institutions. He has also pointed to the changes in organizational structure that are needed to adapt armies to contemporary small-scale warfare.

The first implication of the changes he discusses can be summed up with the statement that the pyramid of pyramids is as obsolete as one might suspect of a form of organization that considerably antedates the pyramids of Egypt.

A second implication is the continuing decline in the ratio of combat line to support. The continued rapid change of this ratio is obscured by the fact that the support components increasingly are nonuniformed. (Some personnel are uniformed, but "civilian." In Vietnam, for example, some of the support elements may wear the uniform of Flying Tiger Airlines in ferrying troops across the Pacific, or the uniform of an airline company in the Far East performing various nontransport missions under contract with the U.S. Government.)

A third implication is illustrated by the high involvement of the Armed Forces in what the Army calls "civic action" missions. These activities, in Vietnam and elsewhere, are functions not traditionally conceived as military ones and, perhaps, are ones not ideally organized according to the most conventional of military lines.

Civil Functions of the Military

While "civic action" possibly looms larger in mass media than in actuality, those activities explicitly so designated constitute only a tiny fraction of the extensive involvements of the Armed Forces and of Armed Forces personnel in civil functions in the contemporary world. These activities are not confined to foreign areas. In the domestic sphere, however, the civil functions of the military perhaps may have declined rather than increased through time. In the early period of the republic, particularly during the time of the taming of the frontier, the Armed Forces probably played a greater part in what in the context of this Conference we might call "national service" than is now the case. But the Army engineers are still with us, and the military are with greater regularity than is probably recognized, called upon for a great variety of emergencies—to fight forest fires in California, to drop hay to starving cattle in Montana, to haul Washington, D.C., out of the snow, and to provide the logistics without which the American Red Cross would be a pathetically underequipped agency for dealing with a major hurricane. And, of course, both the National Guard, federalized or otherwise, as well as federal units have lately been used to deal with domestic disorder—essentially a police rather than military function in American society.

Partly because of a variety of external constraints and partly as a result of their own reluctance, the Armed Forces in the United States are probably used for domestic functions to a lesser degree than in most other nations. This despite the fact that there are many recurrent domestic problems to which their massive logistical, organizational and manpower resources are ideally suited. Inevitably, the sheer effects of increasing population density and interdependence should lead to much greater use of the military to meet recurrent emergencies, and to far more explicit and rationalized planning and provision for such use.

Overseas, there are similar emergency involvements of the Armed Forces—flying hospitals to Yugoslavia, stranded pilgrims to Mecca, or supplying the Congo.

If the world political community develops as many hope, such international activities of our military forces should become more prominent. The usefulness of the military in multilateral activities is enhanced by the great degree to which the military culture is an international one—armed forces are possibly the most uniform cross-nationally of all institutions. There are many reasons for this—the common evolutionary problems that have been mentioned here; the great extent to which culture contact has been contact with invading military forces; the great role that alliances have played in military affairs; and, most simply, that international warfare is itself a social encounter between the adversaries in which each party must adjust his thoughts and behavior to the others.

They Also Serve Who Only . . .

These nonmilitary emergency functions of the Armed Forces tend to be performed almost exclusively as "side shows." Planning for such crises does not have a prominent place in military staffs and the personnel engaged rarely have specific training for these types of missions. The great élan these missions appeal to evoke in those who perform them illustrates a core problem of military life—that almost every activity at most times is either a "dry-run" or in support of one.

Most theorists of the military presume that military organization and ideology derive from the problems of their ultimate function—combat. The predominant functions of the military, however, at least when the time spent is considered—are better described by the peacetime slogan words "preparedness" "readiness" or "deterrence." Most of the time for most forces, combat defines service less well than Milton's wisdom: "They also serve who only stand and wait."

The activities of peacetime have left the largest mark on present-day military organization. To a considerable extent, the military forms that develop in combat are temporary deviations from the normal form of these institutions—

cracks in the thick crust of custom that evolves during the more extensive periods when fighting is not taking place. The military may be contrasted in this respect with other rational-functional organizations, such as industrial, which more or less continuously consummate their manifest function. The elaboration of system-sustaining activities is inherent in the nonconsummatory state of affairs.[7]

Combat Risks

To pick up another strand, we have brought up several times the matter of killing and the acceptance of the risk of being killed as the quentessence of the military man. (I am now talking about combat in conventional encounters, air or ground, rather than in nuclear warfare.)

Strangely enough, considering its central human significance, military combat casualties have received remarkably little study. My own work is very much on the periphery since the most extensive attention given this field of inquiry has come from those with a medical interest, notably the group associated with the National Academy of Sciences—National Research Council Medical Follow-Up Studies Unit.

The first striking observation about combat casualties is that when stated as a ratio of deaths per 1,000 men per year they have steadily and continually declined throughout our history. The one exception to this trend is the Philippine insurrection. Table 1 taken from Beebe and DeBakey shows the steady decrease from the Mexican War where all deaths totaled 122 per 1,000 men per year through World War II, where it was approximately 13. I do not have a comparable figure for the Korean War, but stated as a percentage of those engaged, total deaths of Americans in the Korean War were under one per 1,000 in the armed forces as contrasted with 25 per 1,000 for World War II and a roughly similar figure for World War I. World War II involved considerably longer exposure, however.

Table 1 shows that the major part of the regularity of the decrease in casualties stems from a continual reduction in the percentage of nonbattle deaths, that is, fewer deaths from disease and injury. In the Civil War, nonbattle deaths totaled somewhat over twice the battle deaths. The two figures were close to equal in World War I while in World War II battle deaths were almost four times as great as nonbattle deaths. The Spanish War, of course, was the exception, nonbattle deaths comprising the lion's share of the total mortality.

The decreasing curve of casualties in relation to effectives despite the vast increases in the lethality of weapons reflects to some extent the improvement in the art of medicine—the percentage of wounded that died of wounds in recent wars is one-fifth to one-fourth of the rates of a century ago. But the decline reflects more particularly the changes in the ratio of support to line. In significant measure this change is due to the greater allocation of resources to those injured, but the greater share by far is attributable to the removal from the areas of greatest hazard that large proportion of personnel who have support functions or who engage in combat by means of remote weapons.

An Army source classifies 45 per cent of the 155,000-man force in Vietnam at the present time as support personnel. In the most combat-active divisional units, however, such as the 1st Cavalry Division, only 6,000 to 7,000 men of some 16,000 assigned are actually involved in combat operations.[8]

If being military is defined by the act of putting oneself in the position of

TABLE 1

Comparative Mortality in Various Wars, U. S. Army
Deaths per 1,000 Men per Year

War	Battle Deaths			Nonbattle Deaths			All Deaths
	Killed in Action[a]	Died of Wounds	Total	Disease	Injury[b]	Total	
World War II	9.0	1.1	10.1	0.6	2.2	2.8	12.9
World War I	12.0	4.4	16.4	16.5	1.4	17.9	34.3
Philippine Insurrection	2.2	0.6	2.8	12.9	2.8	15.7	18.5
Spanish War	1.9	0.8	2.7	34.0	2.0	36.0	38.7
Civil War							
North	21.3	13.6	34.9	71.2	3.4	74.6	109.5
South[c]	—	—	—	—	—	—	—
Mexican War	9.9	4.8	14.7	103.9	3.7	107.6	122.3

Source: Gilbert W. Beebe and Michael DeBakey, *Battle Casualties* (Springfield, Ill.: Charles C Thomas, 1952), p. 21.
[a]Includes deaths among prisoners and all the World War II battle categories except DOW.
[b]World War II data include the 2.4 per cent homicides, suicides, executions and drownings as death from injury.
[c]Data on the losses sustained by the South are incomplete.

getting killed for one's country, some classes of soldiers are many times as military as others. Others, by this criterion could hardly be called military at all. This is evidenced by the tremendous range in combat casualty rates by rank, military specialty, and type of military unit, and, although the data are scant here, by the characteristics of people that determine their placement in these categories.

As could be expected, the greatest range in casualty rates is that between deployed troops and those military specialties that are unlikely ever to leave safe Stateside berths or the equivalents in rear headquarters cities overseas. Within combat theatres, however, there has also been a vast range of casualties by arms and services.

Table 2 shows for World War II the range of wounded per 1,000 strength overseas per year by arm or service for all theaters in the European theater of operations. An enlisted man in the infantry had somewhat over 25 times the chance of being wounded as one in the Coast Artillery, better than 10 times the chance of one in the engineers or medical department, 25 times the chance of one in the Air Corps. The distinctive branch of the service in this table—"Other"— had the lowest casualty rate of all if we take it in the form of wounded, 4.8 per 1,000 per year for officers, 3.8 per 1,000 per year for enlisted men.

A similar range applied even within infantry divisions that were committed to combat when one considers variation by military occupational specialty. Table 3, also adapted from Beebe and DeBakey, presents battle casualties, killed, wounded and missing, by military occupation for combat units in the European and Mediterranean theaters of operations, Saipan and the Ryukyus in World War II. The rate of 35 casualties per 1,000 men per day in the case of the rifleman declines steadily as one moves through the specialties to where it is about less than half the rifleman's rate for a squad leader, less than one-third for a litter bearer, one-quarter for a scout, about one-ninth for a cannoneer, one-twentieth for a section chief and even lower for an auto mechanic. In these divisions the

TABLE 2

Wounded per 1,000 Strength Overseas per Year by Arm or Service,
December 1941 Through March 1945, all Theaters and ETO

Arm or Service	All Theaters		ETO	
	Officers	Enlisted Men	Officers	Enlisted Men
All Arms and Services	56.4	71.8	87.3	123.6
Infantry	251.0	264.9	422.2	454.4
Armored	—a	228.5	—a	327.7
Cavalry	165.1	163.1	235.7	191.6
Field Artillery	88.1	50.7	124.3	66.8
Air Corps	35.9	9.9	44.3	12.0
Chemical Warfare	31.0	29.6	35.5	34.2
Medical Department	9.2	26.7	13.2	41.2
Engineers	28.0	21.8	43.6	33.7
Coast Artillery	10.6	9.7	24.1	24.8
Other	4.8	3.8	6.4	4.5

Source: Gilbert W. Beebe and Michael DeBakey, *Battle Casualties* (Springfield, Ill.: Charles C Thomas, 1952), p. 38.

aDuring World War II officers assigned to armored units were carried under such arms as Infantry and Cavalry, and the designation "Armored" was used only for enlisted personnel.

rifleman casualty rate during combat was about 13 times that of all other enlisted men, and four and one-third times as great as that of officers.

Beebe and DeBakey also document quite extensively the inverse correlation of rank and battle casualties. This is shown in Table 4 for divisional and other combat troops in the Fifth Army Divisions. The very special hazard of the second lieutenant is shown most clearly. His chances of being a casualty were seven times that of the general or field grade officer. The jump to a silver bar reduced the second lieutenant's risk of being a casualty by 300 per cent. The most democratic aspect of the distribution of casualties is the fair parity between officers and enlisted men. Enlisted casualty rates were only half again as large as those of officers. That the difference is so small is largely due to the remarkable contribution of the second lieutenant to officer casualties.

These several tables show the very great range in casualties. Another way of looking at the same thing is that, even in the most terrible of recent wars, the total casualties as a percentage of all uniformed personnel involve fairly small proportions of those engaged—about 67 per 1,000 for all casualties and about 18 per 1,000 for battle deaths. But, for some, the statistical chances of surviving approached zero.[9]

Considered on an even longer-term basis, being a soldier as such is not a particularly hazardous occupation. Simple evidence of this is the fact that life insurance companies do not charge special premiums for military personnel, with the exception of those on flying or special hazardous duty. The policies they offer have no "war clauses." And, although the Vietnam war has affected somewhat the stock prices of companies that specialize in insuring military personnel at standard rates, some of them are nonetheless among the most touted items on the market.

One major conclusion, central to the topic of my paper, can be drawn from these remarks on casualty rates and their distribution among various types of

TABLE 3

Index of Relative Battle Casualties per Day by Military Occupation for U.S. Divisional and Attached Troops in Three World War II Campaigns

Military Occupational Specialty	Index of Relative Casualties— Percentage of Rate per Day for All Troops
Rifleman	432
Automatic Rifleman	280
Squad Leader	212
Platoon Sergeant	155
Section Leader	151
Litter Bearer	140
Gunner	134
Ammunition Handler	132
Scout	118
Messenger	108
Surgical Technician	70
Basic	68
Cannoneer	48
Lineman, Telephone and Telegraph	41
Radio Operator	34
Clerk-Typist	32
Orderly	32
Cook	29
Truck Driver	28
Supply NCO	27
Section Chief	22
Auto Mechanic	18
Other Enlisted Men	31
Total Enlisted Men	100
Officers	102
All Troops	100

Source: Gilbert W. Beebe and Michael DeBakey, *Battle Casualties* (Springfield, Ill.: Charles C Thomas, 1952), p. 42.

TABLE 4

Relative Battle Casualty Rates for Officers, by Rank

Rank	Percentage of Rate for All Officers
	Fifth Army Divisions
General or Field	35
Captain	52
First Lieutenant	78
Second Lieutenant	232
Warrant Officer	5
All Officers	100
Rate for all officers[a]	4.0

Source: Gilbert W. Beebe and Michael DeBakey, *Battle Casualties* (Springfield, Ill.: Charles C Thomas, 1952), p. 46.
[a]Casualties (WIA, KIA, and MIA) per 1,000 strength per day.

military personnel. If by militariness we mean putting oneself in the position of being killed or wounded in combat, we are faced with the paradox that those who are the most military with respect to this attribute most often are also the ones who are the least military when it comes to their socialization into the Armed Forces. I am referring here to the new recruit, or the relatively recently commissioned officer.

With respect to the current scene of combat, the Army calculated that a draftee currently entering the system has a one-in-three chance of serving in Vietnam, as compared with a one-in-seven chance for a man currently in the regular Army.[10] Unfortunately I have not been able to adduce data on the rate of casualty in the current combat operations or in previous wars by length of service, nor on the relative rates among draftees versus volunteers.

The question of the differential allocation of combat casualties surfaced recently in connection with publicity about disproportionate casualties among Negro personnel. I will not dwell on it, other than to remark that there is extraordinarily little good research on the social characteristics of casualties. Studies done completely independently of the Armed Forces show an inverse relationship between social class and combat fatality.

When the draft is being discussed, questions of the equitableness of the sharing of sacrifice for one's country tend to be considered in terms of who serves and who doesn't; who gets drafted, and who doesn't. The data I've presented on casualties suggest that the much more important differentiation probably takes place after induction. The major proportion of the variance between who gives his life for his country and who does not is not an allocation made by the operation of the Selective Service System, but is rather one that is affected by military decisions and policies after the Selective Service System has operated.

MILITARY AUTHORITY AND AUTONOMY

Circumscriptions of Military Authority

The autonomy of the military in deciding who among its members must accept what risks presents another definitional aspect of militariness; namely, the subjection of the military man to a system of authority that is more pervasive, rigid and arbitrary than that of ordinary life. Being military involves a sacrifice of freedom—freedoms of what one does, when, where, how and why. Of all the aspects of militariness that I have discussed, this is one that has lost least of its definitional significance of what is military.

This is true despite circumscriptions in the arbitrariness of military authority and the decreasing pervasiveness of its control over the lives and persons of men in uniform. In no small measure, these circumscriptions derive from the compromises the military must make when it draws upon a system of selective service. Self-conscious examinations of the operation of this system, such as those at this meeting, try to make involuntary military service more consistent with the values of the entire society. Pressures for changes in traditional military ways of doing things are generated. Further, Selective Service, by its nature, decreases the selectivity of military recruitment, and hence makes for broader permeation of the Armed Forces by the range of value considerations represented in the entire society.

Other changes mentioned here—changes in organization, technology and the manpower base—have also operated to modify the authority patterns of the military. They tend to make more readily assimilable the pressures for similar modifications that stem from the draft system. Nonetheless, the professional military have been most distressed by those demands which seek circumscription of the traditional authority system.

To repeat, of all the original defining characteristics of "militariness" I have discussed here, the authority patterns seem to me to have remained most intact. It is still largely autonomous decisions by military authority that determine who within it does what, when, and how. Thus, for many of those young men who confront with reluctance the prospect of military service, it is the certain loss of liberty that weighs most heavily, rather than the possible sacrifices of life or of property.

Preservation of Military Autonomy

But while the Selective Service System generates certain pressures that reduce the autonomy of the Armed Forces toward their personnel, the more objective consequence has been to preserve them from the erosion that would take place if a purely voluntary system were to be relied upon for enlisting such large numbers of men as at present. (For the purpose at hand, it is irrelevant how much of the manpower need stems from the body politic's setting of objectives for the Armed Forces or their own translation of these into means and requirements.)

This can be seen in the areas in which the military relies upon voluntary initial enlistment. For many classes of personnel, the military gains their services by agreeing, in advance, to surrender much of its freedom of action toward the individual. By awarding a commission, it may thus promise a certain status position or it may offer a certain type of training or job. The proliferation of roles within the military, and the increasing resemblance of many of these to civilian roles allows the military to offer increasingly broader ranges of self-selected career choices to entrants without strain to its structure.

The full extent of the adaptations it could make to accomodate to bargains with individual preferences is not discernible because of the coexistence of the involuntary recruiting system. It can fill jobs with draftees with small regard for their preferences and the bargaining power of the volunteer is low because being drafted is the alternative to striking a bargain.

The dimensions of "militariness" that I have sketched in this paper are pertinent to these bargains. There is some reason to suspect that volunteering relates to the poles of "militariness." For those who identify with traditional and central military values, the bargain is to be allowed entry into those select military groups that embody most fully these virtues. A greater number of bargains are struck with those who seek to serve in the military in as "unmilitary" a status as possible.

Converting "Military" to "Civilian" Jobs

It may be interesting, therefore, to speculate on the possible restriction of bargaining that may follow from the program of the Secretary of Defense for hiring 60,000 civilians to take the jobs of 75,000 military personnel.

This program is certainly the most prominent way in which the question "What is Military?" has been raised publicly of late. If we apply the kinds of elementary definitional criteria that I have applied in this paper, Mr. McNamara's five-figure goal for altering the civilian-military "mix" could be multiplied many fold. Before getting carried away, however, some other considerations need to be raised.

Special Dimensions of "Military"

The concentration of this discussion on elementary definitions of military has precluded my giving sufficient attention to more subtle and elaborate ones. In particular, by deriving my argument only from the general, fundamental, and elementary, I have neglected the specific and concrete concepts of what is military that are rooted in this particular time and in this particular society. The role of the military institution and of the military man is defined differently in the United States than in, say, Russia, Argentina or Israel. Definitions peculiar to America support and sustain the role of a very dangerous institution in our society. They are ones which set this institution off from the rest of society, however less so than was true in the recent past. These are definitions that imply peculiar constraints for the Armed Forces, special social psychological identities for those who are its members, and a high degree of insulation from many of the currents and conflicts of domestic life.

Effects of Loss of Self-Sufficiency and Autonomy

I wish to suggest that institutional controls on the military in American life have developed the particular forms they have at the present time in relation to armed forces that had the characteristics of what Goffman calls "total institutions." The application of simple functional criteria, particularly in light of various of the changes I have discussed earlier, has tended to strip the Armed Forces of many of the resources necessary to sustain this character. Now, to meet official and personal needs, the military must increasingly look to extra-institutional sources—to civilians.

The question needs to be posed of whether, and to what degree, new forms of control would have to substitute for the patterns of civil-military relationships that were afforded by the autonomy—indeed, the functional autonomy—of the military.

Caveats on Implications

Before stating some implications the main body of my paper may have for this Conference, I wish to generalize this caveat regarding the possible hazards of accelerating the already strong tendencies toward breaking down the distinctiveness and autonomy of the Armed Forces. In addition to the always pertinent cautionary attitude toward overly rapid social change, an additional caution is appropriate in attempting to apply narrowly rationalistic considerations to this particular institution. This is because, as I stated earlier, we have a propensity toward applying more refinedly rationalistic considerations in the area of military affairs than in most other spheres of life. At the same time, few other areas involve so essentially nonrational a function as warfare and few institutions are so permeated with nonrational-appearing forms that may have quite essential functional outcomes.

These caveats are particularly appropriate in that my approach leads to some quite radical thoughts.

SOME IMPLICATIONS

Should the Central Function Be Redefined?

The first suggestion I wish to raise is whether the concept of "national service" should be approached by thinking about the creation of some new, non-military institution, or by expanding the functions of what we now call the Armed Forces. First of all, at this particular juncture of the twentieth century, should a society sustain an institution for which systematic violence is the central and sacred goal—which is peculiarly specialized to the people-killing business or to the society-killing business? I have suggested that this kind of core value directly relates to most activities of most military personnel most of the time in the realms of ideology, myth and non-immediate contingency.

I have also suggested that, in actuality, the society relies on the uniformed services for many other functions, and will probably have to rely on them in the future for many more than at present.

Further, the military institution suffers from many disabling neuroticisms when it exists in a society and in a world that does not regard combat as one of the most honorable and exalted of human activities.

These considerations pose the question, I believe, of what would be the practicalities and consequences of redefining the functions of military forces to include many types of social emergencies, not only those involving violence. Along with this might go a renaming of them as "emergency forces," rather than armed forces. A partial model is posed by the police forces, for whom many varieties of service loom considerably larger than those involving violence. This is true, at least with respect to the demands on their time and energies. The model might be broadened by throwing in the fire department and the public health establishment as well (the latter already being one of the uniformed services).

Civilian Interventions

The second consideration I would like to raise is the extent to which either ethical or rationalistic criteria derived from the civilian ethos can govern the effects of the draft without direct intervention with matters that are now in the sphere of military autonomy. Much of my presentation has sought to illustrate that the major effects of a person's life chances that follow from the operations of the Selective Service System are determined *after* his induction, rather than by the decision as to whether he is to be inducted or not. Studies of the economic benefits associated with military service suggest that many may experience a very large enhancement of life chances through service, while others are selected for roles that involve an incredibly high risk of early termination of most or all life chances.

The question has also been raised here as to whether either functional or ethical criteria can be met when there is coexistence of voluntary and involuntary recruitment systems—where some can delimit markedly the control over their fates by the bargain they strike while others have scant bargaining position at all.

Lateral Entry

Yet another consideration raised by my remarks is that given a system of the lateral entry by military personnel into civilian institutions at the close of their military career, to what extent is there rationality in maintaining a military system that operates with almost no lateral entry whatsoever from other institutional areas?

I would submit that the military really has not operated as much in this way as it would like to believe. Rather, many of the seeds of what I have indicated as decay of its traditional form have occurred by ever-increasing reliance upon barely co-opted civilians. In civil service or contractor roles, these civilians perform functions that military recruitment and succession could not produce personnel to perform.

For the topic of this meeting, that would be the implications of rather broad lateral entry opportunities in the military establishment and, on the other hand, what would be the consequences for our national socio-political life of the undermining of the peculiar insulation and ideology of the military that consequential lateral entry at all levels would entail?[11]

Implications of Changes in Military Organization

Closely related to my suggestion regarding broadening Armed Forces functions, as well as to the preceding one, are the questions I've raised about the obsolescence of many forms of military organization; notably the dominance in theory, if not always in practice, of the pyramidal form (or to be more military about it, the py-ram'-i-dal). To what extent may changes in the kinds of organizations the military uses for its business, including the fighting business, result in increases in the effectiveness by which it can tap the manpower base provided by a transformed society? Would fundamental democratization of military organization help matters by encouraging a more heavily volunteer force, or a less reluctant involuntary one?

The ability of the military to undergo such structural change, I believe, will also be contingent upon the extent to which functional elaboration, such as I've alluded to, takes place.

One Additional Defining Characteristic

Since this latter contention, along with much else that I've had to say, partakes of a somewhat jaundiced, civilian's-eye view of the military, I would want to add that the military has proceeded considerably further along the line of rational and ethical reorganization than have most civilian institutions. That it has done so reflects the most general and central of the defining characteristics of what is military: it is a specialized institution for guarding and securing ultimate and sacred values of the society. The clearly recognized and clearly superordinate ultimate goal inherent in warfare contributes to the fundamental rationalization of military activity, including the rationalization of its use of personnel. The same grand social goals, however, also open it distinctively to influence from the common ethic.

NOTES

[1] There are some exceptions, these being principally men in military aviation. In technology and social organization, however, civil aviation is modeled so closely on the military model as to make even this time fairly applicable to a post-career civilian job.

[2] Fred J. Cook, *Warfare State* (New York: Macmillan, 1962).

[3] See Virgil Ney, *The Evolution of Military Unit Control, 500 B. C.—1965 A. D.* (No place indicated: Combat Operations Research Group, Technical Operations, Inc., September 10, 1965).

[4] Albert D. Biderman and Laure M. Sharp, "The Convergence of Military and Civilian Occupational Structures." Paper read at sixtieth Annual Meeting of the American Sociological Association, Chicago, Ill., 1965 (Washington D. C.: Bureau of Social Science Research, Inc. 1965).

[5] Hans Speier, "The Social Types of War," *American Journal of Sociology,* 46 (1941) 445-54.

[6] Morris Janowitz, *The Professional Soldier: A Social and Political Portrait* (New York: The Free Press, 1960). See also Charles H. Coates and Roland J. Pellegrin, *Military Sociology* (University Park, Md.: The Social Science Press, 1965), pp. 67-91; Walter Millis, *Arms and Men* (New York: G. P. Putnam, 1956).

[7] Albert D. Biderman, "Civilianizing and Militarizing Influences of Military Retirement Systems." Paper presented at the Sixth World Congress of Sociology, Evian, September 4-11, 1966 (Washington, D. C.: Bureau of Social Science Research, Inc., July 1966, mimeographed).

[8] John T. Wheeler, Associated Press, "Viet Chances of Survival Tops Korea," Washington *Post*, October 20, 1966.

[9] G. Haering, *The Impact of Attrition on Sustained Offensive Air Operations* (Washington, D. C.: Operations Evaluation Group, Center for Naval Analyses, November, 1962).

[10] Wheeler, "Viet Chances of Survival Tops Korea."

[11] The organized reserves do provide a mechanism for rather large-scale lateral entry in times of emergency. Also, in times of emergency, the direct commissioning route for officers and extraordinary rapid promotions for enlisted men produce required adaptations, although with rather considerable delay.

14

Education Processes in the
Israel Defense Forces

COL. MORDECHAI M. BAR-ON

The Israel Defense Forces (I. D. F.) maintains a widely spread system of educational and cultural activities; a range of schools, study circles, institutes for leadership training, publications, lectures, theater groups, choirs, etc. Nevertheless, though educational work in this narrow sense is highly intensive in comparison with the size of the army and its budgets, there is nothing in it that is specific for I. D. F. In one way or another, most of these activities exist in most armies. Moreover, with all the importance to be ascribed to the activities of the educational system, the educational influence of this machine on the progress of the individual and the creation of a general atmosphere is only marginal, compared with the influence exerted by army life as such.

The formative power of military service derives to a large extent from the highly varied range of actions performed by the soldier himself, and performed upon him in everyday life in the course of the performance of the army's job, which is fighting, training and routine.

Most of the educational influence of the army derives from the social *Erlebniss* that develops within it from the challenges facing its personnel and from the close ties between the army's work and the nation's destiny.

The purpose of this paper is to analyze the educational effect of the army in the context of its life, while educational activities in the technical sense of the word will only be described to the extent to which they are relevant to the general subject, or as examples for any particular theoretical point.

BACKGROUND

There has always been a consensus among the citizens of Israel that the I. D. F. is one of the primary educational factors in the country, that it serves as a highly important agency for social development and as a melting pot for integration and immigrant absorption. The State has even expressed its appreciation for the educational work of the Army by granting it the Israel Education Prize for 1966, the highest distinction in the country in this field.

What is more, during all the years of the I. D. F.'s existence, it has been highly evident that the larger part of the younger generation joins the army willingly and usually full of positive expectations, though they know full well that they

The author is chief Education Officer, Israel Defense Forces.

must expect a hard and even dangerous time as far as living conditions and physical hardships are concerned.

In a poll conducted by the I. D. F. among 17-year-old boys—that is to say, about a year before the draft—one of the questions asked was whether they would be prepared to volunteer for the army if the Compulsory Service Law should be abolished: 70 per cent of the boys answered in the affirmative, 20 per cent were doubtful and only 10 per cent answered in the negative. There is, of course, no certainty that the number of actual volunteers would be nearly so large, but the poll certainly bears out that more than three out of four boys regard military service as a positive factor from their own personal viewpoint, and the two years which they are about to spend in the army as a period which is likely to contribute in one way or another to the progress of their maturity. Even at this point we may say that the educational ability of the I. D. F. depends to a decisive extent on the positive attitude of the young people who join its ranks. Only the fact that the youngster does not enter the army with an antagonistic spirit, and even regards his service as being of benefit to himself, makes him accessible for positive influences effected by the environment. But the opposite is also true: the fact that the military environment has proved to be useful for the individual from an educational viewpoint is precisely what has created the positive attitude of those boys and girls.

Political Background

If we are to understand the processes which have created this situation, we must first become acquainted with some basic factors which give shape to the specific character of the Israeli army. The I. D. F. came into existence in the course of a war which was fought not only for the independence of Israel, but for the very existence of her people.

Since the War of Independence in the year 1948, and to this very day, the dangers of the Israel-Arab conflict have not grown less, and during this period, Israel was at least once more involved in an all-out military campaign—the Sinai Campaign of 1956. Much more frequently the army took part in limited operations, and light clashes along the borders are almost an everyday occurrence.

I feel that I will stand on sounder ground if I deal with this question by way of a subjective report: Though the tactical and operative doctrine of the I. D. F. is offensive, as befits a modern and efficient army and particularly a small army which must stand up against far larger forces, Israel's citizens are profoundly convinced that the I. D. F. is a definitely defensive instrument from the political and moral viewpoint. The word 'defense,' which forms part of the I. D. F.'s name, is not only a political slogan, but an expression of a basic trend of mind prevailing in Israel, whose influence on public morale and on the status of the army among the public is considerable. This conviction is the reason that a decisive majority of the Israeli public believes beyond any doubt in the justice of the I. D. F.'s wars and in the essential need for its existence.

Moreover, the political conditions under which Israel exists, and, what is even more important for our purpose, the image prevailing among the public about this existence, is that Israel is surrounded by enemies who will miss no opportunity to destroy it; that, from the viewpoint of relative demographic and military strength, Israel is in a chronic state of inferiority; and that the conclusions of those circumstances are that only the existence of a strong national army can assure not only the existence of the State, but also uphold deterrence, which means peace.

These remarks about the basic political conditions in which the State of Israel exists have not been written to note facts, but to note dominant trends of mind prevailing in Israel which have an effect on the positive image of the army and of military service in the eyes of the public and on the measure of personal and positive self-commitment of the soldier. The function of defense in the life of Israel is for most of the nation still of primary urgency and essentiality. The purposiveness of the army and its work, the obvious necessity of training and preparing for a defensive war, are something very concrete in Israel and are close to the home of all its citizens. They create one of the great advantages of the I. D. F.: the love and sympathy of the whole nation.

The Demographic and Cultural Challenge

When the State of Israel was established in 1948 it had 650,000 Jewish inhabitants. Even though most of these were actually immigrants who had come mainly from Eastern and Central Europe, they are regarded as the established population or, in terms of the atmosphere prevailing in Israel, as Israelis.

In the year 1963, 15 years after the establishment of the State, its Jewish population numbered 2 million. More than a million of them had immigrated since the establishment of the State. Among the large immigration waves of the early Fifties and even later, the lion's share was accounted for by groups originating from the Islamic countries—North Africa, Iraq, Syria, Egypt, Yemen and all the others. (In Israel they are customarily called the "Oriental Communities," but the term "originating from Islamic Countries" is factually more exact, though there is not necessarily any connection between this demographic description and the Moslem religion.)

The birth rate of this population is remarkably high. As a result, the Jewish population of Israel consists today of about 50 per cent of European and Western provenience, including Eastern Europe and North and Latin America or descendants of immigrants of those countries, and of about 50 per cent coming from the Islamic countries in Asia and Africa or children thereof. This demographic distribution causes one of the most basic social and cultural problems of Israel. In the educational field the need arose for learning Hebrew and for readjustment of the orientational structure of the immigrants to the needs of the new country, for adaptation to new trades, and the like. These problems are similar to those arising in any immigration country. However, to the extent that the original educational level of the immigrant is high and his culture in a general way more adapted to the needs of a modern western society, as was the case with the immigrants from Western Europe and the American countries, these questions are largely solved within about 10-20 years, and in respect of the second generation, they virtually do not exist. But from the viewpoint of Israel as a modern western society, many of the immigrants from Islamic countries brought with them the general, relative educational and cultural backwardness of their countries of origin. A situation arose in which definite correlations developed between the country of origin and the educational level and social standing deriving from the educational level. Figure 1 gives a visual expression of these correlations.

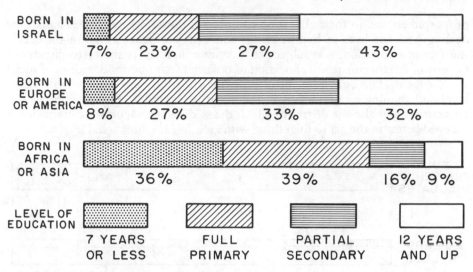

Fɪɢ. 1.—Formal education of soldiers (male only) according to country of origin (1960-61)

Moreover, statistics show that the problem tends, to some extent, to be inherited even by the second generation; although the gap has closed to a considerable extent, there are still signs of family deprivation even among native Israelis whose parents have come from Islamic countries (see Fig. 2).

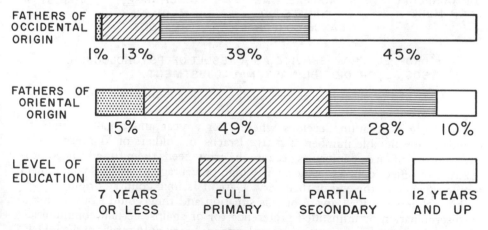

Fɪɢ. 2.—Formal education of native-born soldiers (male only) according to origin of fathers (1960-61)

Israel is still far from solving this problem. Nevertheless, in view of the demographic situation, it is remarkable to see how little social and political tension is generated in Israel around the communities question until now.

The situation in the I. D. F. is at first sight still more astonishing. The I. D. F., like any modern bureaucracy exposed day and night to public criticism, is extremely careful to pay attention to principles of achievement in the promotion of its soldiers and in their allocation to different duties. Moreover, as a machine dealing with the lives of human beings and with problems which might decide the fate of the nation, it is subject to a definite limit in its ability to distort the criteria of advancement and allocation of tasks in favor of considerations of social development. The establishment of a high correlation between the educational level and the degree of success in the army is inevitable. Figure 3 shows this correlation, and also the degree to which the soldiers with high educational levels succeed better in the army than those with an inferior educational level.

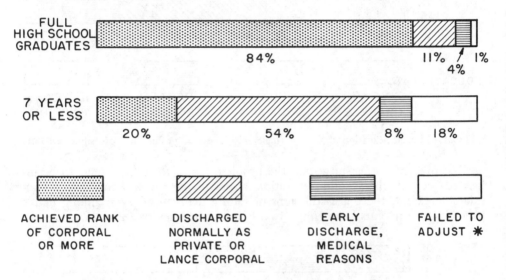

Fig. 3.—Success in military service (male only) according to formal education

Inevitably a situation develops where after a year and a half of military service a considerable number of native Israelis, or soldiers of Western origin, have left the infantry companies because the army needs them for advanced professional or officer courses, while a fairly high percentage of soldiers who remain simple riflemen to the end of their service are of Islamic country origin.

The soldiers are well aware of this situation and they could easily blame it on discrimination or unjustified preference for or against certain communities. However, as a matter of fact, such complaints are heard only rarely in the I. D. F.

An explanation of this phenomenon will be provided later. At this stage let it be sufficient to point only to the basic fact which determines a considerable part of the educational atmosphere in the army. There is a profound awareness in the nation as a whole that the education gap problem is one which requires a supreme effort in order to arrive at a rapid and definitive solution. This awareness arises from three causes:

1) *The extent of the problem:* Since the problem affects about 50 per cent of the population, no one can disregard it, and every individual is fully aware that he personally may be affected by the way in which it develops.

2) *Jewish tradition:* The Jewish people have always been highly conscious of the idea of the "Community of Israel." It is essentially pluralistic in conception. Moreover, every Jew has always regarded Jews of other countries, even if they were far away, as brothers. The inclination to mutual aid and the feeling of responsibility for the welfare of under-privileged Jewish communities-is a cornerstone of the tradition and mentality of the Jewish nation.

3) *The heritage of Israel in its renewal:* From the beginning, Israel was built on the principle of the Ingathering of the Exiles. The Law of Return, which opens the gates of the country to all Jews, is not only the first constitutional law of the State of Israel, but the large majority of the population who are either themselves immigrants or sons of immigrants regard it as a sacred value.

The Democratic Legacy

An additional factor which provides an important educational advantage derives from the historic development of the Jewish community in Israel and from the mentality of the people as it has been shaped by this development. We are referring to the fact that Israel is not only a democratic country, as far as its regime is concerned, but *Israeli society* is pervaded by a democratic and free atmosphere to a high degree. In speaking of a democratic society, we refer to the style of relations between people, the measure of social mobility, the measure of economic and social equality between the different classes, etc.

The very establishment of the State of Israel is connected with the ambition to liberate the Jew from outwardly enforced persecutions. "We are the last of slaves, and the first of the redeemed" writes Israel's national poet, Haim Nachman Bialik, and there is hardly any party in a kibbutz, any social evening in a youth movement, or any celebration in the army, where you will not find this quotation on a streamer on the wall. The Jew who comes to Israel expects in advance full freedom and social equality. From the moment he arrives, he is not ready to suffer any unjustified limitation of his freedom, or any intrusion into his private domain. His sensitivity to social inequality is extremely high. A Jew who only yesterday stood at the foot of the civic ladder in Baghdad or Casablanca, and would not have dreamt of protesting that situation, becomes in Israel overnight a daring fighter of his democratic rights. Moreover, while Israel has its poor and rich, the absence of hereditary classes, and the fact that no one in Israel has any definite vested right in anything except his personal achievements and his personal history, create a social atmosphere without class consciousness, and with far-reaching regard on the part of the citizen for his personal freedom.

The army in Israel is only the mirror image of the society in which it exists. The I. D. F. can therefore not disregard the atmosphere and social mentality of the country as a whole. This atmosphere in itself is sufficient to force the I. D. F. to shape its style of life in accordance with the expectations of the society.

There are two additional factors strengthening this process. First, the tradition of the underground movement. Most of the senior commanders of the I. D. F. received their basic military training in an underground movement that fought against the British and the Arabs before the establishment of the State. The underground movement was, in its time, a voluntary movement without any compulsive authority. Inevitably it turned to leadership methods based on social pressure on the one hand, and on motivation, idealism, and cooperation of the subordinates on the other.

Second, our numerical weakness and quantitative inferiority have from the very beginning induced us to adopt daring and original tactics and operative methods which leave a large measure of freedom and initiative to small units and even to individuals, and which are not subject to effective supervision by the higher echelons.

Night combat, flanking movement in depth, the use of forces spread thin over a large area, attacks relying more on surprise than on strength, and far-reaching reliance on improvisation are combat methods which demand that the soldier display highest standards of performance, and above all, the willingness to devote himself to his assignment, even in a situation where there is no supervision.

The I. D. F. is not the only army to show this development. It occurs everywhere and is due to the development of arms and modern methods of combat which lead to a democratization of the whole military institution. Many sociologists and historians have already noted this, but the particular conditions of Israel have impelled the I. D. F. to go much further in adopting democratic methods of leadership.

Such leadership is, of course, fertile soil for educational activity. Since we are used to a method of operation which relies very largely on the consent of the led, persuasion becomes one of the most essential instruments of leadership. The commander is first to understand that factors such as group cohesion and the soldiers' belief in the justice of their cause are basic elements in training good fighters, no less than order and discipline.

The commander must necessarily rely less on orders, and more on influence. He becomes less the boss and more the educator. Social norms and moral values become ammunition no less essential than shells or bullets. The satisfaction of the soldier with his unit and with the army becomes a major condition of his effectiveness as a soldier, and the personal example of the commander becomes the first commandment of combat leadership. Commanders are first to understand that they must also concern themselves with the integrative and normative functions of the unit, and not only with its operational function.

The I. D. F. is therefore an army which does not pay much attention to ceremonial and formal discipline. The privileges of officers, even in the regular army, are fairly restricted. The army uniform is simple and austere. Senior officers often take part in combat activities. The command "Forward!" has been struck out of the military dictionary, and replaced by the command "Follow me!"

This then is the social, political and demographical soil on which the army grows, and on behalf of which it has been given educational duties far beyond those necessary for the performance of its military assignments. This is also the background which enables the army to fulfill the educational mission which the nation has imposed on it.

THE DRAFT SYSTEM

The Universal Draft

One of the most important results of the strategic situation in which Israel finds itself is its draft system. The draft in Israel is according to the law universal for both sexes: all boys and girls are obliged to enlist in the army when they reach the age of 18. With respect to men, the principle of the universal draft is to a very large extent realized. An exception is made for two groups:

1) Persons with marked physical handicaps whose health would be endangered even by service in a rear-echelon unit. (For persons with professional or vocational qualifications, the cut-off point is even lower, since their profession or trade enables them to work efficiently even under conditions of extreme physical handicaps.) This regulation excludes from the draft pronounced cases of mental retardation, mental disorder, and serious chronic delinquency in accordance with the recommendations of probation officers.

2) Persons who combine lack of education, low intelligence standard, and lack of knowledge of Hebrew in such a severe degree that enlistment in the army becomes impossible without educational preparation, and where there is no possibility of the soldier's being integrated in military service; that is, where his enlistment would only make difficulties for the army and cause suffering to himself.

A low formal education standard or inadequate knowledge of Hebrew is in itself no reason for disqualifying a youngster from I. D. F. service.

Since the draft is universal, and a person needs to be a psychological or physical "case" to escape it, a situation arises in which not only a healthy and normal man does not even think of the possibility of evading the draft, and regards military service as something as simple and as self-evident as the rising of the sun, but in which rejection for military service is regarded as a social stigma. There are many youngsters with health handicaps who make desperate efforts to conceal their limitations, in order to be accepted by the army.

The fact of compulsory women's service, as such, underscores the universality of the draft and strengthens the feeling that being drafted into the army is something self-evident. If women are drafted, then men certainly have to accept the draft understandingly, if not willingly. Women perform those functions which do not require great physical effort, enabling the army to send the healthy men to combat units. Only soldiers with physical limitations are posted to backstage and auxiliary units, functions which, according to the prevailing values, carry inferior social status. In this atmosphere there is a widespread feeling that a job which a girl can do is not suitable for a young and healthy man.

As a result, not only enlistment in the army, but also going to combat units has become something desired and striven for.

The I. D. F. enlists less than 50 per cent of the women who reach the age of 18. (Nevertheless, the public and girls themselves are not under the impression that women's service is selective.) The Military Service Law provides two categories of women who are exempted from the service:

1) A girl who is married before reaching the age of 18 is not drafted, and a girl who marries during her military service is discharged immediately on marriage.

2) Among some of the traditional and religious families, particularly those that come from Islamic countries, it is still customary to keep the girls at

home until they marry. Accordingly, the law permits exemption of a girl from military service on the strength of her statement that enlistment is contrary to the religious moral principles of her family.

There is a high correlation between early marriage and educational standards, and between objection to military service on traditional grounds and educational standards. The result is that the I. D. F. in effect only drafts women with a comparatively high educational level. Nevertheless the women's draft of the I. D. F. is carried out according to objective criteria, so that among women with comparatively high educational standards, the feeling prevails that the draft is universal in the case of girls as well. For them, too, the draft appears to be a necessary and self-evident process.

In the I. D. F. girls do not perform combat functions; nevertheless they do serve in infantry and armored battalions, and at brigade H. Q. level. There they serve in office assignments and as education sergeants, welfare NCO's, nurses and telephone operators. In George Bernard Shaw's *St. Joan* we are told that when Joan came to the army camp, two miracles happened—the hens stopped laying eggs and the soldiers stopped swearing. The I. D. F. is not short of eggs and swearing has not completely stopped, but there is no doubt that the presence of girls in army camps has a restraining influence on the language and behavior of the boys.

The universal draft is not only the result of statistics, strategic conditions, and security needs. The military authorities and the government are fully aware of its educational and moral advantages and they are regarded as an important principle of public policy. A few years ago when the duration of military service was still 24 months for women and 30 months for men, the number of persons liable for service began to exceed the army's manpower needs. Considerations of efficiency and the interest of the army in the narrower sense might have led to the conclusion that it was desirable to introduce certain degrees of selectivity throughout. But the proposal to introduce a selective draft was rejected out of hand on the ground of public morale and educational impact. The duration of service was shortened by four months in order to preserve the sacred principle of the universal draft.

Promotion in Junior Command Ranks

The strategic situation which forces Israel to permanently maintain a large regular army cannot be reconciled either with the country's manpower potential or with the needs of its economy, and certainly not with financial possibilities of the State. In order to solve this problem, Israel has based its main military strength on its Reserves.

For peacetime purposes, in order to secure the borders continuously, and particularly in order to train the soldiers for the Reserves and provide a continuous supply of command cadres and trained crews, the I. D. F. relies on the draft, while the skeleton structure at senior command and expert level is provided by a small nucleus of professional soldiers.

For budget reasons the trend is to post draftees to every appointment possible. As a result, draft soldiers fill all junior commands and appointments at the level of squad and platoon commanders, and a wide range of staff and technical duties in the lower echelons. Since the training time of junior commanders is more than a year and since the duration of service is only 26 months at present, the situation arises in which corporals, sergeants, and second lieutenants in the I. D. F. have a regular one-year turnover.

This means that each year, tens of thousands of people in Israel have an opportunity for personal advancement and promotion in rank and status. Since statistics show that more than 50 per cent of all soldiers are discharged with the rank of corporal or up we witness a far-reaching social phenomenon which is extremely meaningful to the younger generation.

For the youngster who still stands at the beginning of his life and is full of hesitations about his abilities and value, even the promotion from private to private first class is an achievement which fills him with pride and self-reliance. Since promotion depends generally on the success of the soldier in realizing positive values from the military, professional, and even social viewpoint, the very fact of this success puts him largely under an obligation to continue and implement these values.

Thus, for instance, it is widely believed among regular soldiers that educational levels have an effect on chances of promotion. This has made study and intellectual advancement a generally accepted norm. Thousands turn to the secondary schools which the I. D. F. has opened in the main cities and in central camps and obtain the highest marks in the national matriculation examinations. The impulse which drives them to do so is no longer one of direct calculation, but rather part of the general atmosphere and the social norm.

The army, thus, in effect, created something like an effective mechanism of social mobility.

THE DRAFT AGE

Another factor deserving attention in any analysis of the educational potential of the military service in Israel is connected with the age of draftees. Draft policy in the I. D. F. is based on the assumption that the suitable age for military service is 18 years and no older. Consequently, the principle is that all draftees join the army at the age of 18, and there is a declared and closely observed policy of avoiding, as far as possible, any postponement of military service. Citizens who wish to continue their studies at academic levels do so in principle after and not before military service.

The Academic Reserve

There are, of course, exceptions. In Israel as in many other countries, there exists an academic reserve (similar to the R. O. T. C.), but it differs in a number of points of principal importance from the academic reserve in other countries. The choice whether to join this program and to study at the university before joining the military service is not that of the individual but of the army. Moreover, the army grants this privilege only to a limited number of draftees.

The academic reserve is maintained in order to train, for the benefit of the army, a limited number of academic professionals which it needs in order to solve its professional problems, and which it intends to place in professional jobs once they join the service. The advantage of this arrangement for the individual who can continue his studies without breaking their continuity is a by-product of the arrangement, and not its purpose.

Another difference derives from the fact that academic reservists in Israel first enlist in the army at the age of 18, pass an intensive course of recruit training, and only afterwards start their studies, as "soldiers on special leave." Throughout their study time, they are to a large extent subject to military discipline, and during the two summer holidays, between the first and second, and the second and third years, they must pass squad commander's and officer's courses. These courses are not held especially for the academic reserve, but are part of those taking place at the camps of the regular army, so that the officer candidate has an opportunity to absorb the military atmosphere, and to acquire, at least to some extent, the educational values which that atmosphere offers. At the age of 18 they look upon themselves as soldiers too, not only as students.

Even when all this is taken into account, the service of officers coming from the academic reserve in the I. D. F. is not always regarded as a success. As professional officers, they are very useful to the army, and fulfill important functions; the know-how which they place at the army's disposal is considerable. But the emotional identification of many of the academic reservists with military service and the values which it presents is small in comparison with ordinary officers who have won their rank in the course of the service itself, and at an earlier age. And of those few academic reserve graduates who have been posted to combat units, only a few have proved to be good officers and commanders. In general, their minds were occupied with quite other things. Some were already married or engaged, their intellectual level made them turn to spiritual worlds far from the army's affairs, while tactics and command duties such as they had to fulfill as platoon commanders appeared too simple and too lacking in intellectual challenge and sophistication to them.

From the social and intellectual viewpoint, their age separated them from their soldiers. At this level of platoon command, their comparative maturity proved a liability rather than an asset.

Service at the Age of 18

These observations have strengthened the prevailing opinion that the suitable age for military service, and particularly for service in combat units, is 18. At the age of 22, a man, particularly if he is a university graduate, has often found already the direction which he wants his life to take, and he is first and foremost concerned with entering into practical life, both in the professional sense, and in the social and sexual sense.

At present only 50 per cent of Israeli boys study regularly up to the age of 18. All the others have interrupted their schooling some time before reaching the draft age and have already had some opportunity to try and make a living for themselves.

Those who stay in school until they are drafted have long felt the need for detaching themselves from the dependence on their parents or on the school in which they have lived since childhood, and to try their strength in a direct and independent confrontation with society and with life. The army uniform frees them at long last from the painful and irritating need to pretend to be adult and provides them with the official admittance ticket to the adult world.

This phenomenon is conceived of in a still more positive way, both by the secondary school graduate and by the working youngster, because it does not require excessive moral and intellectual efforts. While finding a place in life in the civilian context always requires an effort of initiative and forces him to choose between alternatives and to shape his conduct according to his free choice, the youngster who joins the army acquires a label of adult while all his actions and ways of behavior are predetermined by factors outside himself. The range of free choice given to the individual within the context of military discipline is minimal. The army's work in the initial stages does not require particularly high intellectual ability. Everything is prescribed, laid down, and determined in advance, and all the individual is required to do is to obey. At the price of that obedience, he gains a feeling of self-confidence and mental relaxation which he has never felt before.

The process of ripening and maturing cannot really take place in full in the army. The army is not a context capable of training man to fulfill all those functions which he will be required to fulfill in adult life. Nevertheless, the feeling of finding one's identity in military service is not merely an illusion. This process is connected with three elements: finding a range of titles which one can attribute to himself, filing acts which he has performed within his personal "historical archive," and acquiring a certainty that these titles and acts are of positive value in the eyes of society.

We can therefore understand why at the age of 18 many soldiers regard the army as a way of life, with whose values it is worthwhile to identify. Since most healthy youngsters in Israel go to combat formations, it is important to note that under Israeli conditions, the younger age groups are considered also preferable from the viewpoint of their fighting ability. One of the great advantages of the I. D. F. as a fighting body consists of the fact that not only its soldiers, but also its squad and platoon commanders are below the age of 20 and its company commanders usually no older than 21 or 22.

Educational Absorptive Ability at the Age of 18

The same development which explains a large measure of the identification of the youth with military service also determines the soldier's capacity for absorbing educational influences, and provides the army with a considerable part of its educational impact. It is popularly believed that at the age of 18, men can be changed only very little because they are already "complete." The I. D. F.'s experience not only negates this belief, but shows that in the course of their military service, many youngsters have an additional and perhaps last opportunity for reshaping their personality.

The search for personal identity which we observed before from the viewpoint of the measure in which the army is capable of assuaging the feelings of frustration which derive from it also creates a large measure of accessibility to influence from outside. The youngster who wants to establish his world of values, who seeks to consolidate for himself ways of evaluation and judgement, who wants to shape his own view of the world in which he lives, who seeks a central nucleus around which he can organize his life, eagerly absorbs unambiguous and single-directed influences. This eagerness is known to lead the younger generation of some societies to subject themselves to the influence of extremist leaders with totalitarian doctrines whose main attraction is their simplicity and single-mindedness, and to be caught up in a wave of intolerance and stereotypism, cruelty and racialism. However, in a democratic system like that of Israel, the army served has positive values from the viewpoint of the society, and youth do not have to be dragged into social and political extremism and to adopt a rather destructive and fanatic attitude.

The high absorptive capacity of the 18-year-old for educational influences is underscored by a further factor. Under the age of 18, youngsters change the social environment in which they live only to a minor extent. This means that the group to which they belong initially has been formed at a comparatively early age.

On joining the army, the soldier is absorbed in a completely different social context. Not only is the human composition of this new primary group completely different, but it is also certain that the criteria according to which he will be judged will be of a different nature. This may work to his disadvantage, but more often to his advantage. In any case it will force him to struggle again for his place, and this time at an age when he has already a much greater measure of self-control and of consciousness of social processes which occur in his environment, and of mental processes which occur within himself.

Since the physical conditions of life in a military unit and the dangers to which it is exposed cause it to become by its very nature an environment which encourages solidarity and close personal relations, many youngsters have an opportunity to adopt a new starting line and a better one than the one on which they were placed in the past.

No wonder, therefore, that most soldiers, particularly those who found no satisfaction in their previous social context, greedily attach themselves to the new primary group which they have found in the army. This again causes the soldier to be highly dependent on his primary group and requires a much higher degree of conformity to its norms.

Social national and moral values which infiltrate into the system of group norms become therefore a powerful educational force. A considerable part of the patterns of behavior of many soldiers and the aspirations, the yardsticks, the conventions to which they are accustomed, will therefore undergo a far-reaching change under the influence of the group to which they belong in the army, to the extent that the army succeeds in imposing positive normals in its units. To the extent that the junior commanders maintain their social control and are themselves the bearers of positive values, a highly intensive process of profound group influence in an educational and positive direction will result.

NON-MILITARY FUNCTIONS OF THE I. D. F.

A further contribution to the educationally positive atmosphere of the I. D. F. results from the fact that the I. D. F., at the demand of the State and in accordance with needs of the nation, fulfills a range of functions which are of non-military nature, and assists in the development enterprises which are connected with the up-building of the nation and the country.

This circumstance enables many young men and women in Israel to opt for service in units which, though they will always involve a measure of military training, are mainly designed to provide an alternative national service, that is to say, an occasion for volunteering for national functions other than security.

Nahal and Gadna

From the outset of modern Jewish settlements in Israel, agricultural development as a matter of private enterprise existed only in the fertile coastal valleys. The fostering of settlements in the mountain regions, in the swamps, and in arid areas has always been so difficult that only public or idealistic elements could measure up to it. Lately, the more agricultural development progresses the more its continuation becomes still harder, because the better soils have long been occupied and it becomes necessary to turn to areas which are more and more problematic from the agricultural-economic viewpoint.

In addition, it should be kept in mind that Israel's defence, among other things, has always been based on a system of regional defence connected with settlements in border areas. New settlement has therefore always been considered important from the security viewpoint, the more so as agricultural development regions in recent years are mostly also sensitive areas strategically.

This combination of factors and the continuation of the old pre-state tradition has turned the I. D. F. into one of the central agencies among those engaging in the development of new agricultural settlements and in what in Israel is somewhat romantically called "the redemption of the soil."

This is the background for the existence of Nahal. Nahal, which obtains its name from an acrostic of a Hebrew phrase meaning "Fighting Pioneering Youth," is the most marked of I. D. F. activities with a non-military aspect, for it is a special corps which combines military training with agricultural training, and engages in the establishment of new settlements along the border.

Nahal soldiers are trained for combat duties, but at the same time, they are both vocationally and socially directed toward kibbutz life (a kibbutz being a type of cooperative agricultural settlement). Nahal units are based on coeducational youth groups which have already been socially consolidated for several years within youth movements and which intend to continue living together in agricultural settlements of different types, but mainly in kibbutizm. Toward their enlistment in the army, they have formed so-called "nuclei," part of which are designed to become new agricultural settlements.

The usual course of service in Nahal is as follows: First, initial training, which takes place in a special army camp. Girls take the normal recruit training in the same camp, but separately, while the boys spend a period of particularly intensive and hard training. Then the boys and girls of each "nucleus" join up again and are sent for a year's agricultural service to one of the old established kibbutzim. This is something of an incubation period for them.

Within the mother-kibbutz, they become acquainted with all branches of farming, consolidate themselves from the social viewpoint, become acquainted with the kibbutz way of life from the viewpoint of management, finances, economics, social life, and in all other respects, and prepare themselves for an independent existence. At the end of this year, the boys return to the army where they undergo parachute and commando training for a few months. (Since most boys in the Nahal are of a high educational and motivational level, they are regarded in the I. D. F. as excellent combat soldiers, and therefore the I. D. F. attaches them to its spearhead units in case of war.) At the end of their military service, a number of members are likely to leave the "nucleus," particularly those who wish to continue their academic studies, but some will remain and continue to live in the kibbutz for the rest of their lives.

The new settlements are called by the Hebrew name of "heachzuyot," which might conveniently be translated as "footholds." They are usually established in places which the army regards as important from the strategic viewpoint for the country's defense system. Nowadays such places are mostly found in particularly arid or mountainous areas, and they provide no opportunities for agriculturally viable settlement except after many years of soil reclamation, agricultural experimentation and other activities, such as the building of new roads, construction of housing, etc.

As long as the new settlement is not self-supporting, it remains connected with the army. Part of its development budget will, of course, be provided by the civilian authorities in charge of agricultural development, but it continues to be subject to Nahal discipline, just as Nahal is responsible for its maintenance, continued development, and regular reinforcement with new manpower. Only after several years, when the farm has developed and begins to show a profit, is it transferred by the army to the civilian authority. The settlement now becomes an independent economic unit that must support itself like any other settlement, while Nahal can invest the resources which have now become available in the establishment of a new settlement elsewhere.

The pioneering nature of Nahal expresses itself not only in the agricultural field. In recent years, after it became apparent that questions of immigrant absorption and the educational and cultural gap had become no less urgent problems than the establishment of border settlements, Nahal has begun to send "nuclei" to new immigrant towns. These "nuclei" settle within the new towns for a number of months and engage in educational and social activities such as teaching children, organizing youth clubs, developing courses for adults, dealing with welfare problems among poor families, and other public activities designed to create confidence among the new immigrants and to encourage them to shake off their inertia and to develop along modern lines capable of increasing their ability to adapt themselves and improve the prospects of their social and economic absorption in Israeli society.

Nahal is one of the most popular elements of the army and is known for the high standards of its soldiers, for its idealistic and cultural atmosphere, and for the pioneering spirit which inspires it. Another formation which has its place in the country's development work is Gadna. Gadna is the organization which deals with pre-military training within Israeli civilian schools and other educational institutes. This is of particular educational importance, both because the whole teenage generation of the country passes through this formation, and because this formation is unlike other military formations; essentially educational in its nature and purpose, it serves as a symbol and sign of the basic conceptions prevailing in the I. D. F.

In the Gadna, in addition to some military training, particular stress is placed on the incorporation of the youngsters in development enterprises. Gadna boys go from time to time for a number of weeks to help in forestation projects, road building, excavation of archaeological antiquities, or assistance to young kibbutzim on the border. Those who go for two or three weeks—to help uncover the past of the nation, to improve the country's landscape or to assure its future, while they become familiar with its old-new landscape—not only help with their own hands to further development as such, but first and foremost develop within their hearts a spirit of constructive patriotism. They identify the army, within which they carry out these activities, with building and not with destruction.

Teachers in New Settlements

The I. D. F. performs a range of additional non-military activities and functions in the course of its peacetime operations, not to mention such matters as assistance in flood disasters, retrieval of accident victims from inaccessible places, and similar matters which are well known in many armies. But one further activity deserves particular mention, because it affects the general educational atmosphere in the I. D. F. and because it is symptomatic for the manner in which the I. D. F. envisages the extent of its responsibility in the educational field, namely, the service of girl soldiers in teaching assignments in border settlements.

All girls who graduate from teachers' seminaries enlist in the I. D. F. on completion of their studies. Part of them serve in teaching assignments within the army, in soldier schools. The others are given short periods of recruit training, and are then dispatched to the Ministry of Education and Culture for two years and posted to ordinary primary schools in the border settlements where it is difficult to find salaried teachers. Their whole army duties for those two years consist of teaching immigrant children. The army continues to maintain contact with them, to deal with their personal problems, and to exercise disciplinary supervision over them, while their functional activation as teachers is entrusted to the Ministry of Education.

Therefore the I. D. F. provides in addition to hundreds of qualified teachers, several hundreds of girls who have graduated from high school and volunteered for teaching assignments among the civilian population on the border, and these girls are also posted to the same settlements in the Negev and in the Galilee, after taking short extension courses in adult education sponsored by the Ministry of Education. As a result, there are many hundreds of I. D. F. girl soldiers in uniform who live in all immigrant settlements and development centers of the country, teaching children in elementary schools or adults in night classes, organizing activities in youth clubs, and in many places bearing the main load of responsibility for education and cultural affairs and thus becoming the main agents in the process of acclimatization and acculturation of the new immigrants.

EDUCATIONAL RISKS

Risks

What we have said so far should be sufficient to enable us to draw one clear conclusion: Whatever may be the direction of the educational process in the I. D. F., the measure of its intensity is extremely high. We shall now turn to examine the direction of this educational impact, that is to say, we shall try to answer the question: Where does all this lead to? We shall begin with a number of negative elements or, to put it more cautiously, a number of educational risks.

Like every army, the I. D. F. is threatened by educational risks which are inherent in its very structure and in the nature of the work it performs. The first danger arises from the simple fact that we deal with the educational influence of an institution which is by no means "educational" by definition. One symptom of this situation is the measure of educational influence of the commander in the army, who is nothing but a man who has been chosen for his assignment by criteria other than education. Not all school teachers come to their job because of their suitability as educators, but that is at least the principle on which their selection and training is based; the army, however, selects its commanders according to criteria of ability to lead men in battle, such as courage, orientation in the field, tactical perception, etc. These qualities are not necessarily correlative with those required of the good educator. Hence it is perfectly possible that the situation may arise, and it does arise occasionally, in which a group of young people is entrusted to a man who by virtue of his position has a considerable influence on them, but is not possessed of any positive educational equipment and has no understanding of the educational aspect of his work. Such a man is not only liable to make serious mistakes but even to have a harmful influence.

The second risk arises from the military profession as such. Day after day, the soldier trains for combat and even if he does not actually fight, he is sure to imagine continually situations of killing, destruction, explosion and annihilation in the course of his training. A closely related matter derives from the nature of military discipline. Because of the need to make many people act in ways diametrically opposed to their nature, and to human reflexes, army commanders are given operative authority and at the same time far-reaching punitive power. The soldier is confronted with a situation of compulsion in which he must subject his will to the requirements of orders. There exists the possibility that the need to achieve uniformity of execution and to accustom the soldier to habits of discipline will be interpreted by commanders as the need to restrict the personal particularity of the individual, to lower his pride and to break his spirit. As a result, there is a real and present danger of such developments as sheer admiration for power assuming the shape of submission to force through self-negation in the case of the person subject to authority, of exceeding authority and exploiting force for its own sake in the case of the individual in command.

A third danger arises from the nature of everyday life in the army. A large part of the day-to-day activities of soldiers are repetitive and non-purposeful. The soldier storms the same hill for the seventh time, goes on a march for the tenth time, or lies in ambush for the twentieth time without meeting an enemy; he may perhaps understand the national necessity of these activities, but in everyday life he cannot escape the feeling that they are not too productive. In addition, it is difficult to carry out military training according to the premium system. In general, the soldier cannot escape the next round of training by excellent performance in the first round. The training program must be carried out in full and there never is any limit to the achievement of soldiers' combat preparedness. Consequently the soldier may well develop the feeling that it really doesn't make much difference, and that there is little point in making efforts. The famous slogan "Never refuse and never volunteer" expresses this characteristic soldier's mentality precisely.

Ways of Overcoming Risks

Firstly, though I. D. F. commanders are selected according to their suitability for leadership in battle, much attention is paid to the human and educational behavior of the candidate. Moreover, in the selection process of commanders, there is an increasing measure of reliance on sociometrical selection which in itself guarantees a certain degree of social suitability and sympathy of the subordinates for the commander, and these are fairly well correlated with positive educational ability and inclination. Furthermore, the I. D. F. has developed a widespread system of educational training that is provided for commanders at all levels. It is not mere chance that the whole subject of leadership training in the I. D. F. is the responsibility of the Chief Education Officer. The I. D. F. conception of leadership is whole, inclusive, and many-sided, and does not accept any division between leadership in combat and leadership in peacetime, or educational leadership. The prevailing opinion is that leadership in combat requires to a very large extent the same qualities required by general education responsibility.

The risk of the development of a cult of power in the I. D. F. is small because of the mental structure of the population, because of the political situation, and because of the basically defensive philosophy of the I. D. F. Under the conditions prevailing in Israel, soldiers are continuously aware that the necessity to train in the use of violence is forced upon them. As to the unjustified use of compulsion in the ranks of the army, certain excesses and distortions may be found in the I. D. F. and considerable efforts are made to eradicate these undesirable elements. From time to time detailed orders are published concerning what is permitted and what is forbidden in the field of authority for junior commanders, and regular extension courses are given on the subject. In addition, care is taken to make the soldiers acquainted with their own rights and duties, as well as with the limits of the authority of the commanders. This complex of measures has proved that it is possible to create an educational atmosphere even within the authoritative context which is essential for every army, and to prevent the abuse of the powers entrusted to commanders.

As for the danger of apathy, we do not meet it too often in the I. D. F., perhaps because the purpose of the army's activities is self-evident and every soldier can easily understand how essential it is for him and his family that he should make an effort to achieve high levels of performance and training.

The maintaining of high operative standards, the encouragement of *esprit de corps*, competition between units, and information on the purposes of the different activities are, of course, ways of preventing this danger which exist everywhere, and these are found in the I. D. F. as well.

VOCATIONAL TRAINING

We have now reached the point where we can make a more detailed and extensive examination of some of the positive educational contributions of the I. D. F., and we shall start with its contribution in the field of vocational training and the creation of the social overhead of the nation.

Types of Vocational Training

It will be recalled that a considerable number of the technical jobs in the I. D. F., including jobs that require a fairly long training period, are performed by draftees and not by regulars. This means that the turnover of manpower which has an opportunity for a vocational training and for a number of years of experience in work in a trade is very considerable, and the number of people who receive their vocational training in the army, or who at least consolidate their know-how by practical experience, is large in comparison with the compass of the economy. The army therefore does not fulfill a marginal place in the training of vocational cadres, but is, perhaps, the central agent in that process.

Moreover, the range of trades that are required in the army and which are likely to be relevant to the civilian economy expands and branches out continually—electronics, or motor mechanics, for example, which can be applied directly. Other trades are specific to the military as far as equipment and practices are concerned, but nevertheless provide the soldier with basic skills which will make it easier for him to convert after short training to a civilian trade and give him an initial advantage of considerable importance. Tank mechanics can adapt themselves without difficulty to tractor mechanics, and an armorer will find it easy to learn civilian metal-working trades.

In the conditions of the Israeli economy, which continuously expands and changes, and where there is, in any case, need for a continuous process of re-training, one may well go further and say that even the skills acquired in the army quartermaster's store will help the soldier when he becomes a grocer, while the soldier who has been a squad commander or an NCO has acquired leadership habits and self-confidence which will be of good service to him when he occupies a position as junior foreman or youth instructor. Offices in Israel are year after year filled with girls who learned basic office-work skills in the army at the expense of the nerves of their commanders, who took them into hand when they did not yet know how to put a finger on a typewriter or how to answer a telephone properly. And, surprisingly, the best Israeli stage actors of the middle and younger generations started their artistic careers in the military entertainment troops, and many well-known journalists and radio an-nouncers received their first professional training in army newspapers and in the army broadcasting station.

The vocational training provided by the I. D. F. may be classified into three groups:

1) Trades for which the training period is no more than a few months. Such trades are taught to soldiers even where they have had no previous con-tact with them. The short training period enables the army to derive bene-fit from the soldier's output for a comparatively long time after he has concluded his basic and vocational training.

2) Trades with a long training period, but which are not specific to the army. For this purpose the army usually draws its tradesmen from the boys who have been trained at civilian vocational schools, or as apprentices in the civilian industry. They are given short courses in which their know-how is adapted to the specific military equipment. These boys usually acquire their experience in practical work, while the army in turn cooperates with the civilian vocational schools in order to adapt their curricula, to the maximum possible extent, to the needs of the army without affecting the civilian character of the school.

3) Trades with a long training period which are specific to the army or for which the civilian industry and the civilian vocational training system do not provide sufficient candidates. For this purpose, the I. D. F. maintains its own pre-military technical training system. There are special technical schools for the Air Force, the Signal Corps, the Navy, the Ordinance Corps, and the Engineer Corps. These schools fill up year after year with thousands of boys of the age of 16 or 17 who stay there for a year or two and acquire specific vocational training and general education. Their years in national service will be applied to work in their trade.

Readaptation of Basic Skills

Vocational training acquires an additional dimension when it refers to new immigrant youth. In developing countries the army may fill a void created by the absence of other institutions capable of training the necessary cadres by serving as a large trade school for the purpose of supplying the enormous needs for technical know-how created in the wake of the modernization process. The importance of this process in Israel is particularly evident from the viewpoint of the individual, as part of the acculturation and readaptation process of people who have received their early education in undeveloped countries. New immigrants usually arrive in Israel without a trade or with trades which are unsuitable for the Israeli economic structure. For these immigrants, and particularly for those who have at the same time a low educational level, military service is a last opportunity to acquire not only a trade, but even those kinds of basic skills which are needed if they are to find their place at a later stage in the vocational structure of the modern Israeli society.

It is therefore not surprising that in the consciousness of the younger generation, the I. D. F. is widely conceived of as an opportunity for acquiring a trade plain and simple. The fact that many actually realize this ambition strengthens this positive expectation year after year, and since lack of a trade means the continuation of poverty and destitution in the family, or in other words the continuation of feelings of inferiority and foreignness, the activity of the I. D. F. in the field of vocational training and acquisition of skills contributes directly to raising the standards of part of the backward population, and to the solution of one of the basic problems of the social gap by enabling thousands of citizens to find themselves a respected place in the creative life of the Israeli society.

CLOSING THE EDUCATIONAL GAP

It is a matter of general knowledge that the existing education gap between the different classes of society is created and consolidated at an extremely early age and that most of the educational and employment institutions with which the educationally deprived youngster comes into contact in childhood, adolescence, and as an adult, do not narrow the gap. Unless special efforts are made to cater to the backward groups in order to elevate their educational standards, the elementary school will cause the child of the developed family to continue developing and acquiring knowledge and self-assurance against the background of his comparative success in the classroom, while the child from the deprived groups will soon become aware of his deprivation when he compares his ability and achievement with that of others. This feeling of inferiority is in itself enough to become a restraining element in further development, and the relative lag will increase as the years pass.

It has long been known that the achievement of equality as a goal in education requires a differentiating and not an egalitarian approach. Institutions which apply the principle of formal egalitarianism end up with more inequality.

We have already seen how the army, like any modern bureaucratic institution, applies a fairly rigid system of selection and job allocation, based on the principle of equal opportunity to every individual within every rank. What makes the situation still more acute and complements it dialectically is the fact that, on the other hand, the army stresses the differences between ranks by granting them authority and privileges and adding many status symbols. It concentrates attention on the rewards which derive from achievement and excellence. The egalitarian approach of the army to the question of promotion along principles of achievement, on the one hand, and the marked hierarchical character of its social structure, on the other hand, are liable to turn any army in which there is a mixture of population classes or ethic groups of different educational levels into a factor which perpetuates the deprivation, increases it, and thus also increases the bitterness that is the result of the gap.

How, then, has the I. D. F. been so fortunate in escaping this danger to a large extent? What are the factors which have prevented the development of feelings of discrimination and bitterness, and more than that, have even turned the I. D. F. into a positive factor in the development of the backward communities? Partial answers to this question have already been given when we discussed the questions of the draft age and of vocational training. Now we must uncover the full extent of the psychological and social processes which assure the comparative success in the solution of the question of the community gaps.

Experiments in Soldiers' Education

For many years there has existed a regulation in the I. D. F. requiring every soldier who in his youth had not completed primary school to spend three months out of his term of service in a school designed to complete his basic education. Studies in this school are highly intensive and at their conclusion a certificate is issued, which is recognized by the Ministry of Education, attesting that its holder has completed elementary school. This certificate is in great demand, because it enables the soldier to apply for better jobs. Eighty-five per cent of the soldiers attending the school are new immigrants from the Islamic countries and another 7 per cent are born Israelis whose parents came from Islamic countries. In other words, practically speaking, this school is one of the I. D. F.'s most important means of dealing with the closing of the education gap.

The practice had always been to let the soldier acquire his elementary education during the last three months of his service, after he had completed his Hebrew language studies in regional schools and in the course of the military service itself. In the year 1963, however, it was decided to make an attempt to transfer the study course to the beginning of the service. This decision was based on the assumption that there is a correlation between the educational standard and prospects of success in the I. D. F. and on the belief based on this assumption, that additional education would improve the youngsters' chances to make progress and achieve success in the I. D. F. So in the years 1963 to 1965 a number of experiments were undertaken in teaching the young soldiers immediately after their enlistment, even before they completed their basic training. The course of these studies was followed up scientifically and the prospects of success in military service of these soldiers were checked by means of a control group. To the surprise of many, these experiments proved to be a failure in all respects.

In the courses held at the beginning of the service, most soldiers demonstrated extreme opposition to the very idea of learning. Indifference proved to be the least evil, since its alternatives were interruptions, lack of discipline, an offensive attitude toward the teachers, and malicious interference during the lessons. It became necessary to send many soldiers to jail, and until the end of the course the cooperation of a considerable part of the pupils could not be secured. Motivation for studying was close to nil.

Still more surprising were the results of the comparative follow-up of the measure of success of the pupils during their military service. It was found that the groups of pupils who had been taught in the Military Education School at the beginning of their service proved subsequently to be somewhat worse than the soldiers of the control group; in other words, among the ex-pupils there were more who deserted, went to jail, were discharged for inadaptability, dropped out from combat units, or displayed other indicators of failure in service, and fewer of them were promoted or distinguished themselves as soldiers.

We shall confine ourselves to only one remark about the lack of success of the soldiers in the course of their service: It seems that additional knowledge in history of Bible as such does not make a better soldier. The existing correlation between the level of education and success in the service is only meaningful in the overall sense. The success of the educated soldier is due to understanding, emotional balance, self-assurance and overall mental factors acquired by way of slow assimilation during many years of learning at an early age. A concentrated dose of study given to the adult can be useful to him in many respects, but it cannot qualitatively change the intellectual capacity of the individual, and certainly not his character or his deeper mentality, the more so if it is provided in such a short time, and against the psychological opposition of the soldier himself.

The interesting phenomenon which we shall have to analyze for our purposes is the enormous difference between the learning motivation of the soldier at the beginning of his service and that at the end of his term. The difference is so large that it cannot be explained only by the age difference or by the small amount of knowledge which the soldier acquires during his service by way of diffusion. The only reasonable explanation is connected with the profound changes which military service makes in the soldier's inner self-assurance, in his willingness to try his strength again in different fields, in the way in which he looks upon himself, and upon his life, and in his orientations and thoughts toward the surrounding world. If we succeed in understanding the revolutionary change in the whole psychology of the soldier during the two years of his service, we shall be able to define the enormous educational contribution which military service gives the youngster, and to understand to its full extent the essential role played by the army in closing the gap between the communities.

The importance of the experiment is therefore not limited to the narrow confines of the schooling problem, but may serve as an indicator of basic processes which are set into motion as a result of military service at large.

The Problem of the Intellectual Criterion

With whom are we actually dealing? We are dealing with the lowest stratum of the population. We are dealing with a group of people who have dropped out of the learning process at a rather early stage in their lives, even before they have completed their elementary education, not necessarily because their parents were unable to pay for their education, but very simply because they were not able to learn. The socioeconomic causes of their educational deprivation are of course behind this, but their influence is always indirect and expressed in a real inferiority in the learning child, who is unable to concentrate and has difficulty with abstract thought and with formulating ideas in a precise manner, etc. That is to say, we are dealing with a group of persons for whom learning meant bitter suffering. Moreover, we are dealing with youngsters who during their whole lives up to the age of 18 had been subjected to one failure after another, and who had never been without a feeling of impotence and defeat, not because they were actually failures but because in infancy and adolescence they were usually measured by one criterion which is markedly preferred by adult society when it deals with education—the intellectual criterion.

But unfortunately the deprivation and inadequacy of youngsters is to a large extent connected with their intellectual inaptitude. The only way for them to defend themselves against the feeling of failure was to erect high walls of contempt for learning.

Military service confronts the youngster, at least for some time, with different criteria. The intellectual criterion will re-emerge as a factor of differentiation and selection when the youngster, a year and a half later, reaches the stage where his more educated comrades have been sent to officers' courses and he finds that the road to a commission is closed to him; but up to that time, the principles of military selection and distinction will attach no little importance to qualities in which he does not lag behind, such as physical ability, orientation, courage, ability to make friends, and even a certain measure of aggressiveness. Throughout the basic training period, it will be obvious to everyone that the best soldier is not necessarily the best educated soldier, but sometimes precisely the soldier who spent his childhood being naughty and playing games while his more intellectual comrades were busy with the principles of grammar and algebra.

Thus there arises a situation in which even after basic training the uneducated soldier has a very considerable number of opportunities to savor the sweetness of success and achievement and to win the visible recognition of the society and of the army as an institution.

In Israel we have already reached the situation in which the number of persons from the "oriental communities" in squad commander's courses is close to 50 per cent—that is to say, it corresponds to their share among the general population. Thousands of soldiers from these communities are therefore given the opportunity to occupy junior command assignments and to serve in situations which give them preferential social status. These feelings of achievement and success give the young soldier a gradually increasing new feeling of assurance, dilute his dense feelings of inferiority, and assuage much of the internal tension and gradually break down part of the defense mechanism which he has built up through childhood.

At the same time, his resistance to everything which smacks of school and education will weaken. If he really is somebody, if he has some value, even without being educated, then his other advantages, which he has so markedly discovered during the course of military service, will to some extent compensate for his intellectual shortcomings and make them less terrible and terrifying to him.

Now, after the youngster has experienced the sweet taste of progress in life, he also wants to continue making progress. Thus there arises in the soldier a desire for further education and an ambition to improve himself, which in itself is one of the best guarantees for the continued social development of the deprived classes. This, then, is the explanation for the fact which we discovered before, that at the beginning of his service, the youngster develops a desperate resistance to any attempt to put him on the school benches. His expectations from military service lie in other fields, and he is in a hurry to achieve them. He too wants to come into the open, to feel the relaxing sensation of adulthood which his elder brothers or his neighborhood friends have felt before him, and he is not prepared to postpone this.

At the end of his term of service, however, after he has grown up, relaxed and acquired new self-confidence, the same man is prepared to measure his strength once more against his intellectual problem.

Prejudices

It is obvious that if this process is to succeed, a number of further conditions are necessary. Considerable importance should be attached to the question of prejudices. In every society, there inevitably occur processes of social differentiation and stratification. The difficulties start when social and economic stratification are correlated with origin, that is to say when it appears at first sight that it occurs not according to the criterion of achievement, which in modern society is regarded as legitimate, but according to the criterion of ascription, which has long ago lost the legitimacy which it had in the traditional societies. In this case considerable importance is attached to the question in what degree the prejudices prevail within the society and to what extent the members of the higher classes give expression to these prejudices, even if there are no actual phenomena of discrimination.

Since a person usually finds it difficult to explain his social inferiority to himself on grounds of his poor achievements—since in doing so he would confess to actual inadequacy and backwardness—situations arise in which the existence of prejudice among the higher social stratifications enables the members of the deprived groups to attribute their social deprivation to limitations imposed on a basis of ascription and thus create a feeling of social injustice.

Israeli society is not free of prejudices. Nevertheless, the different factors connected with Jewish tradition and with the history of national revival have contributed to the fact that prejudices exist only in a limited extent and even less among younger generations. Moreover, just because the principle of achievement is much more marked in the army than in civilian life, even the simplest soldier understands its necessity and recognizes the military society as a framework in which social justice in the modern sense of the term prevails.

Social Friction

Social friction also has beneficial effects of its own. The army has a declared policy of preventing accumulations of one single ethnic group in one unit and composes its units from members of different communities and classes. One and the same squad will therefore, for a fairly long time, provide a meeting place for youngsters from the kibbutz with youngsters from the town, veteran settlers with newcomers, Moroccans with Rumanians, the poor with the rich.

By rubbing shoulders with each other in a context of mutual aid and friendship, such as is automatically established in the hard conditions of life of the army, the newcomers derive a new awareness of home and family, and when they leave the army they will no longer feel isolated and foreign in this country. All over the country they can find their good friends from army times.

This friction not only contributes to the soldier's self-assurance and social integration but also to the actuation of a wide basis of communications for the nation as a whole. Here new symbols are created, new expressions coined; here conceptions of belonging develop, and here a new national memory takes its shape.

As he draws closer to his fellow soldiers, the new immigrant also develops a profound change of values. Within the family and community context in which he largely belonged until the age of 18, he was subject to norms which were not always suited to the needs of the society on a larger scale. Attempts of the individual to break out of that circle are met with group dynamism. Society in general confronts the individual with low norms and is opposed to any deviation in the direction of personal progress. Moreover, the transition from one country to another and, even earlier, the process of urbanization to which the immigrants from Islamic countries were exposed in the old country led to complete destruction of the old standards and values. The youngster finds himself faced by an empty world and is caught up in circles of uncertainty.

In the army, after he is released from his community label and from the normative pressure of this community, he is open to the influence of new norms, and is eager to absorb them, since they seem to be the entrance ticket to a new life and a new society.

From this viewpoint the army becomes a new school of modernism and of the Israeli way of life for the new immigrant, where he will acquire new tastes, develop new expectations and understand the importance of new values.

Reservations

There is a not inconsiderable number of boys among the deprived communities for whom the opportunity which society offers them through military service comes too late. We must assume that a considerable part of the youngsters who are rejected for military service for mental reasons or for intellectual inadequacy come from these stratifications.

Part of the soldiers who drop out of the army before the normal completion of their term of service do so because of inadequate adaptation. These soldiers are usually discharged because of recurrent criminality, long terms in jail, or the appearance of psychotic symptoms. Many of these too belong to the deprived social and ethnic groups. From the psychological point of view this means that the mental and social distortions which have occurred in the mind of the youngster before he reached the army have proceeded to a degree where he can no longer be restrained by the framework of army life. Anti-social tendencies, insurrection, bitterness and inferiority complexes no longer allow him to acclimatize. For these youngsters the army will be an additional failure to a road paved with failures, and they will derive no benefit from their military service.

Research on the measure of adaptation of juvenile offenders to army life has shown that while minor offenders do not differ from all others, more than 50 per cent of those who were already notorious offenders in youth and had been in the hands of the police as a result of serious and repeated offenses, drop out of the army, which means that military service could no longer help them, and perhaps nothing will help them but psychiatric or legal treatment.

From time to time the army attempts to correct this. Twice a year the I. D. F. drafts a group of several hundred youngsters who have been found below minimum draft standards and who from all signs have no prospects of being absorbed in the army and therefore are not enlisted in the normal way. These youngsters are given a special three-month basic training course under a psychologist's supervision, within Nahal. After this they are sent for three months to the Central Military Education School for completion of their elementary education, and then they are attached to a Nahal "nucleus" in an old established kibbutz or to Nahal "footholds" on the border.

This is a project from which the army does not benefit; it is purely educational in intention. Many youngsters are saved in this way from a life of crime and social lawlessness, and are replanted in firm soil. Particular importance attaches to this project when these boys become fathers, for as parents they may be expected to see to it that their children will learn at the proper learning age, and up to a certain age they may even be able to check up on their children's schooling and to create that educational resonance within the family which is such an important condition for interrupting the deprivation process which tends to be reproductive.

If the I. D. F. were in a position to include all future mothers in the scope of its educational activities, its contribution to the closing of the education gap and the prospects of the future generation would be truly revolutionary, for of course in most families the mothers exert a more important educational function than the father. However, the army enlists girls only at a comparatively high educational level, while girls from the lower levels do not reach its ranks.

The Take-off Problem

Many of the beneficial prospects involved in the advancement process which takes place in the I. D. F. depend on the measure in which the economy and civilian society will be able to absorb the discharged soldier and give him an opportunity for continuing his personal progress and consolidation. To a large extent the army conducts the soldier only to the starting point, and one may well ask whether the society will be able to continue supporting his new aspirations and expectations. (The only riots with a community background which ever took place in Israel occurred about 10 years ago, around the personality of a man who reached the rank of sergeant in the I. D. F. and even served with distinction, but who was discharged in a period of austerity and unemployment and was not able to be absorbed in an occupation which in his eyes was becoming to an ex-sergeant.) In Israel there are numerous cases in which members of the oriental communities who had reached officer and NCO rank in the army occupy respectable and respected places in employment and in society, and some of them have found their places in the first ranks of the political leadership of the country.

The society must offer the discharged soldier and particularly the discharged commander employment in a position that will appear appropriate to the expectations aroused in him during his army service, and which fit the new image of himself which he has developed. The inability of the society to do so may cause a disastrous accumulation of social and political explosive.

Educational Encouragement Projects

Side by side with its organizational processes, the I. D. F. invests additional efforts in special encouragement projects. The project for the elementary education of soldiers has already been mentioned and space limitations do not allow me to describe the ideas and educational undertakings in all detail, but I shall mention two of them.

With the advancement of the national education system, the I. D. F. has also started to raise the standards of education which it provides for soldiers. This year for the first time, a number of courses for post-elementary education up to 10th-grade level have been opened. This particularly stresses the development of the ability to form abstract conceptions, the study of English, a more thorough acquaintance with the natural sciences, and a development of the pupil's ability to express himself. These courses also conclude with the issue of certificates which are recognized by the government and serve as a good-entrance ticket for all kinds of advanced vocational courses or for places of employment which offer jobs at higher-income brackets.

The second project is connected with the intention to encourage social and intellectual advancement in the deprived communities themselves, and the creation of an elite which in the future will be able to carry on the load of social development. Every year a group of youngsters originating from the Islamic countries, who have completed the secondary school, are sent to a special one-year extension course within their term of service and at the expense of the I. D. F. The purpose of this extension course is to enable them to be admitted to the university and to provide them with a better starting line, so that they may satisfy academic requirements and conclude their studies successfully.

Follow-up at Israeli universities shows that out of every 100 students who have received this encouraging education aid in the I. D. F., about 90 succeed in concluding their studies and achieving graduate rank, while no more than 5 would have been able to do so without the special program.

EDUCATION FOR PATRIOTISM

The values which guide the I. D. F. in its efforts to educate its soldiers are many and varied, and are geared both to prepare the soldier for combat and to educate him for good citizenship and humanity, two aspects which, according to the prevailing view in the I. D. F., are two sides of the same coin. Space does not allow me to discuss these values in full. Nevertheless, this paper would not be complete if it did not concern itself at least briefly with two facets of education which the military environment allows us to foster and turn into the main values of our educational activity: love of country and loyalty to democratic values.

Love of Country

The I. D. F. has no overseas assignments; all its activities take place in the homeland itself. Soldiers are given an opportunity to become acquainted with their country through the belly, not only through the windows.

The fact that Israel is only a small country has an enormous advantage from this viewpoint, because the individual can encompass it completely in his mind as if it were the large courtyard of his home. In a short time he can learn to know closely and intimately every river bed and every ruin, every settlement and every town, and to feel in all the limbs of his body the awareness of the overall landscape.

Israel is not a particularly beautiful country, but as the poet has put it, "There are many more beautiful, but there is none as beautiful." In the awareness of the people of this country, the "homeland" has three spheres of existence: that of the past, that of actuality, and that of hope. Israel is a country which is pervaded by the past. Every single stone has its story to tell. The Bible is concealed behind the slightest elevation of the soil, and ancient echoes may be heard clearly in its valleys and deserts.

Israel is very largely also a country of the present. The national revival in recent years, the dizzying pace of building, the ever stronger heartbeat of life, give it a dimension of actuality which stands in a strange contrast to its atmosphere of ancient history.

Israel is furthermore a country of hope, because there are always new development programs, because its existence is never something for its own sake but always an existence for the sake of achieving an ideal, because everyone lives here in a dynamic world and is accustomed to projecting onward into the future.

No wonder therefore that the army in Israel is one of the most active elements in encouraging awareness of the historical element of the landscape, and is highly active in publishing material, and in providing guidance and in research on the human and national meaning of the country.

Loyalty to the Democratic System

Not confined to love of one's country's landscape, the conception of "homeland" is in our day not only a geographical one, just as it is not merely a political one, but first and foremost a conception of moral values and emotional experience.

Paradoxical though it may seem, the I. D. F. is the place where many soldiers first learn to know and appreciate the values of Israeli democracy. They do not learn it in an academic manner, and certainly not as a philosophical formula. They meet those values in everyday life.

When the soldier arrives at the induction camp, he is received by the regimental sergeant-major who informs him what his duties as a soldier will be, but in the course of the same lecture also tells him of a long range of privileges to which he is entitled. The close and inseparable link between duties and rights, and particularly the absolute inviolability of rights which is upheld against all and any arbitrary action, accompanies the soldier throughout the course of his service.

The most important element in the development of democratic patriotism is the understanding of the conception of the State. In many systems of government, the citizen conceives of the State as something that belongs to the authorities, an external essence. It is "they" and not "we." In countries in which the Jews were persecuted because of their Jewishness, this conception was still more natural for Jews. In the I. D. F., the service itself arouses in the young generation a sense of belonging to the State and gives birth to the democratic conception of the State as the supreme embodiment of the personal sovereignty of every individual. For two whole years, the soldier will do many things, some of them demanding a great effort and even involving danger, which will be aimed at a transcendent matter, that is to say, the purpose of the soldier's activities will be directed toward a general and exalted cause. We therefore have a situation in which the soldier becomes, willy-nilly, an idealist.

In concluding, may I record some passages from a letter written by a young Israeli officer by the name of Uri to his girl, on the day of his discharge from the army. In a personal form, this letter gives an excellent expression to much of the theory and generalizations which this paper has attempted to express:

Well, this day is over too, this day to which I had looked forward so much wherever I was throughout the last three years. And now a new day has come. . . . I do not know whether I will have another day like this, that concludes a whole period with all that happened within it, with hard and tiring work, powerful experiences, moments of pain and worry, moments of expectation and fear, the friendship of many, occasional hatred, a thousand and one human experiences.

How often have I wanted to write and tell you about all that the army has given me, about how great the distance is between Uri of those times and Uri of now. I went into the army as a young boy, naïve, believing in many values with great snow-white expectations: the kind of man who grows up on the margin of life and who has hardly ever known what disappointment means. And who is Uri of today? Almost a totally different person. I come out of the army as an adult who has already gone through the first stages in his road through life, and with ideas which may perhaps even be regarded as new.

My hopes have remained the same, but much of what surrounds them has changed. The experience which I have acquired, the experience within the new society is enormous. It was a giant test of my strength, my balance, my ability to work with people, my ability to stand up without anybody pushing me from behind.

What kind of a person I am nowadays is hard to define, but I am much more than the boy of those days. Today I know that our world is a combination of colours and tints which no one can separate, that there is nothing in which there is not something positive and something negative all mixed together, that everywhere there are lights and shades, and that sometimes even people who differ from you in their views and in the background of their lives, may be right, each in his own way.

Out of myself and out of my observation and contact with others, I have learnt a little of what kind of creature man is. Sometimes he is petty and miserable, gives in to small things, and sometimes he achieves unimagined heights.

From the army, which is the forge of discipline to the very end for him who carries out the order as well as he who gives it, I have come with more understanding of what is really the true meaning of freedom and democracy.

15

Selection for Military Service
in the Soviet Union

RAYMOND L. GARTHOFF

Following the Bolshevik seizure of power in Russia, the first law on compulsory military service was enacted on May 29, 1918. On June 12, 1918, a decree ordered the conscription of certain age groups "of workers and peasants who do not exploit the labor of others." By the end of the Russian Civil War in 1921, over five million men were under arms. This large army was rapidly cut back to a little over half a million regular troops, and it was not until the latter half of the 1930's that the Soviet armed forces again increased substantially in numbers. During the 1920's and the 1930's a series of conscription laws succeeded one another. The 1936 Constitution of the USSR, which is still in effect, abolished class distinctions as a qualification for military service, and stated (in Article 132) that "Universal military obligation shall be law." On September 1, 1939, the Supreme Soviet passed a law "On Universal Military Obligation," which (with minor amendments) remains in effect today.

The law "On Universal Military Obligation" explicitly bases itself on Article 132 of the Constitution, and states (in Article 3): "All male citizens of the USSR without distinction as to race, nationality, religion, educational qualification, or social origin and position, shall be obliged to render military service in the ranks of the Armed Forces of the USSR." The law further spells out (Article 5) that: "Military service shall consist of active service and of service in the reserves of the army and the navy." In addition, the military establishment is accorded the right "to register and accept for service" women who have medical and special technical training, and in time of war to induct such women into the armed forces.

VOLUNTARY SERVICE

There is no provision for "volunteers" for military service (except for re-enlistees, and except for those choosing to enter military cadet and officer candidate schools). A voluntary youth organization, DOSAAF (The Voluntary Society for Support of the Army, Air Force, and Navy), conducts a large-scale preinduction training program in military-related activities such as parachute jumping, preflight training, marksmanship, and the like. Subsequent military service assignments are in part based on skills and premilitary training in

The author is Special Assistant for Soviet Bloc Politico-Military Affairs, U.S. Department of State.

DOSAAF. This organization is an adjunct of the Ministry of Defense, with the dual functions of preinduction training and civil defense training. In addition, a preservice military familiarization course is given in secondary schools (i.e., the 8th through 10th grades). This school course involves two hours of instruction per week, and includes brief summer field camp training between the 9th and 10th grades.

Since World War II, there have been a number of military and naval preparatory cadet schools. For a number of years some of these schools, established in 1943 and named "Suvorov" and "Nakhimov" (in honor of distinguished Imperial Russian military commanders), were open to boys at the age of ten with a seven-year course. These schools, which are military boarding schools, were opened primarily for the orphans and children of career military officers. However, at present all cadet schools are limited to the three-year secondary school level. Upon graduation, cadets are given preferential admission to officer candidate schools, which have an additional three-year curriculum.

During World War II, there was, in addition to the draft, a "Universal Military Training" program under which all men between 16 and 50 years of age were subject to a 110-hour course of military training supplementing their regular schooling or employment.

INDUCTION

Registration and induction for military service is administered through a network of rural and urban precinct "military commissariats." These commissariats, usually headed by a field-grade military officer, are associated with the local government authorities but are subordinate to the appropriate Military District of the Ministry of Defense.

All males register in January or February following the year in which they reach the age of 17 (lowered from age 18 in July, 1962). At the time of registration, each young man is presumably asked his preference for arm of military service, but—according to many former Soviet servicemen—in practice this preference is usually ignored. Those selected for induction are called up some time between June and December of the following year. Since August 1, 1960, the timing of induction varies according to the location and the arm of service in which the draftee would serve. Prior to that time (and for most conscriptees at present) the call-up is in September.

ACTIVE DUTY

The duration of active service for those conscripted depends upon the branch of service to which the man is assigned. In 1939, soldiers in the ground forces served for two years, in the air force for four years, and in the navy for five years. In much of the postwar period the term of active service was three years for the army, four years for the air force, and five years for the navy. At present, it is three years for all services except the navy, where the term of service is four years. Conscriptees serve not only in the regular army, navy, and air force, but also in the paramilitary internal security troops, border guards, and coast guard of the KGB (Committee for State Security).

The system of an annual age-class call-up, although slightly modified by the spread of induction over a several month period, is related to an annual training cycle in the armed forces. Since new trainees fill the places vacated by those leaving at the end of their three-year term, roughly one-third of the privates are new each year. By the same token, two-thirds are "veterans" of the repetitive annual training cycle, and in this manner the combat effectiveness of all units is presumably preserved.

SELECTION FOR SERVICE

It is evident that the number of young men conscripted each year will be a function of two factors: the size of the age class for call-up, and the personnel level desired for the armed forces. During the early 1960's, there was a manpower shortage of young men of military age caused by the "birth gap" of 1941-45. That gap has now been passed. As a very rough generalization, on the order of half of each age class is at present called up for active service. However, only a small minority are rejected on grounds of physical or mental disability.

Theoretically, the Soviet system of conscription is not a selective service system. But in fact, it is—a system based, however, on the principle of "selection out," rather than "selection in." Liberal deferments are granted for reasons of health, family hardship, and continued education. Marriage is, however, *not* a basis for deferment or non-selection. On the other hand, being the only support of a family (mother or brothers and sisters) is basis for non-selection. (Those who have been previously convicted of a crime by a legal court are also not drafted.)

Educational deferment is granted for secondary school pupils to age 20. Deferment is also granted to all full-time students enrolled in college-level schooling. Most college students serve after graduation in the ranks for one year, and are then commissioned in the reserve, but some (e.g., in engineering or medicine) are simply placed at once in the reserve. There also is a voluntary ROTC program in Soviet higher educational institutions.

Inadequate education is not generally a basis for non-selection. Those conscripted who do not have an eighth-grade level of education are given special after-duty schooling to bring them up to that level.

Those not called up for service are placed on the reserve rolls.

NON-COMMISSIONED OFFICER SERVICE AND REENLISTMENT

Some NCO's are career reenlistees, but conscripts during their initial obligatory three-year term of service comprise most of those of non-commissioned rank. The term of service of non-commissioned officers is the same as that for private soldiers. Reenlistment, particularly but not only by non-commissioned officers, is encouraged. A few privates, and a larger number of non-commissioned officers, do reenlist, and some continue to reenlist as career NCO's. Ordinarily, reenlistment brings a one-step promotion.

CONDITIONS AND PRIVILEGES OF ENLISTED SERVICE

Enlisted men receive, of course, all the necessities of life, plus very modest pay. Pay is based primarily on rank and position held, and to a lesser extent on length of service, with increments beginning with the third year of service and with each promotion. In addition, there is supplementary pay for specialist service of various categories. Pay of servicemen is tax free. Allotments are given to dependents only in cases where such dependents are unable by virtue of age, health, or other factors to be gainfully employed. Among the few statutory "fringe" benefits are accident insurance, reduced transportation charges, and free mail to and from servicemen.

RESERVE SERVICE

Under the basic military service law, obligations include enlisted reserve service up to age 50. Upon completion of the regular term of active duty, the conscript is automatically discharged into the reserve. Up to 35 years of age, the reservist is in the "first class" of the reserve, and is liable—apart, of course, from the possibility of call-up to active duty in time of emergency—to call-up six times for two-month refresher training tours (or, if he has been deferred and never served on active duty, nine such tours). From age 35 to 45 the reservist is in the "second class" and is subject to five additional calls for one-month refresher duty. Finally, from 45 to 50, the "third class" of the reserves may be called up for a single one-month refresher course. (Candidates for promotion within the reserve are liable for slightly longer periods of short-term active duty.) In practice, it appears that actual calls of reservists for short-term refresher duty are much less frequent.

The active and reserve service of officers differs according to rank, and reserve officers are kept in the respective grades of the reserve for longer periods than enlisted men. For example, a university student who has been commissioned into the reserve after completion of his deferred one-year service in the ranks would, if he had reached the rank of army captain in the reserve, be kept in the first class until age 50, the second class until age 55, and the third class until age 60. Upon reaching the age limit for being in the reserve, officers are retired, while enlisted personnel are simply discharged.

Until 1939, there existed "territorial troops" roughly along the lines of our National Guard. However, since that date there has been no equivalent of our National Guard.

CONCLUDING OBSERVATIONS

Soviet citizens appear to regard the system of conscription in the USSR as a reasonably equitable one. There has, of course, been no opportunity for public discussion of the subject. While there is no provision for alternative civilian duty for eligible young men who may not be needed for military service, as has been proposed in the United States, it should perhaps be noted that some components of the Soviet armed forces such as the construction troops and the railroad troops engage in what might be termed "paracivilian" activities. In addition, units of the regular army are on occasion shifted to meet non-military requirements such as "crash" harvesting. To date, probably largely by coincidence, the available pool of those eligible for induction into military service seems to have coincided reasonably well with the personnel requirements of the armed forces. When there has been a discrepancy, the slack (or squeeze) of the need for conscription has been met by tightening or loosening deferments and by evening out differences in annual age classes by postponing induction of some eligible men for a year or two. In the future, especially if the size of the Soviet armed forces should decline, it may be more difficult to avoid an evident selective service system. However, even in that case, the Soviet leadership would probably use indirect adjustments to regulate the flow of induction rather than alter the formal obligation—and image—of universal military service.

16

Some Effects of British Military Service on Education

MARK ABRAMS

Peacetime conscription in Britain has been limited to a few months before the outbreak of the Second World War and to the postwar years up to 1960. For most of the latter period, in each year all young men who reached the age of 18 became liable for military service for two years, while those reaching the age of 26 passed out of liability. In the average year approximately 300,000 young men reached the age of 18, but approximately 15 per cent of these anticipated the call-up by enlisting voluntarily in the Armed Forces. Of the balance (i.e., approximately 250,000) no more than two-thirds were, in fact, posted to the Armed Forces. Thus, in 1955 of those who registered (i.e., excluding volunteers), 67 per cent were posted to the Army, Navy or Air Force. The proportion of postings, however, fell sharply as the government planned to run down the size of Armed Forces, and by 1960 the proportion was less than 25 per cent. The difference between registrations and postings was accounted for by two main causes: each year approximately one-quarter of those registering were rejected on medical grounds; the balance was made up of those whose service was deferred on socioeconomic grounds, and as these were increased, the number of deferments grew. Thus, in 1955 deferments were granted to 500 men who joined the police forces, to 10,000 agricultural workers, 13,000 coal miners, 5,000 merchant seamen, and 300 fishermen. In addition, deferments were extended to young men who had entered into formal apprenticeships in skilled manual occupations, to articled pupils training for professional qualifications, and to most university students. In later years this list was extended by the addition of young men training to become school teachers. Broadly, as long as those deferred on occupational grounds remained in their exempt occupations deferment was continued until, on reaching their 26th year, their liability for military service ended. It is worth noting that applications for exemption on conscientious or religious grounds were usually negligible (e.g., 733 in 1955), and successful applications for deferment on grounds of exceptional family hardship were not much more numerous (in 1955, out of 4,400 applications, only 2,600 were successful).

The general position then in the mid-1950's was that with conscription at 18 (with liability extending to 26), of the 300,000 liable each year for service, 240,000 were judged to be medically fit, and of these 180,000 (or 75 per cent) entered the Armed Forces either as conscripts or as volunteers; the remainder

The author is with Research Services, Ltd., London.

had their service deferred on grounds of national economic needs—and, in fact, most of these postponements turned into exemptions. The main exception to this latter position were students—most of them fulfilled their service obligations after graduating. In other words, apart from the medically unfit, service in the Armed Forces was effective for at least three-quarters of the relevant population.

THE EDUCATIONAL SYSTEM

To assess the effects on education of the British system of conscription one has to consider briefly the British educational system itself during this period. From 1948 onwards the minimum school-leaving age enforced by the government was 15, and in the early 1950's almost 80 per cent of all boys had finished their schooling before reaching their 16th birthday. Beyond this point an additional year of schooling was possible in state secondary modern schools, an additional three or four in private and state high schools, and, of course, college and university education was available into the middle 20's.

In the early 1950's approximately 80 per cent of all boys aged 14 were attending state secondary modern schools. For the most part they were children who had failed to pass the selective examination at 11 for entry to high school and whose parents were too poor (or unwilling) to pay their fees at a private school. Almost without exception they all left school at the first legally possible opportunity. Among boys aged 16, only 16 per cent were still at school; for those aged 17, the proportion was little more than 8 per cent, and among the 18-year-olds, the ratio was less than 3 per cent.

In other words, opportunities and the effective demand for high school education affected only an extremely small minority of the population. The numbers concerned with full-time university and college education were even smaller. In the academic year 1952-53, the intake of full-time male students into all British universities was less than 16,000, and roughly 10 per cent of these were students from overseas.

On the educational side, therefore, the broad picture was that throughout the early 1950's, because of the very limited opportunities for higher education that then prevailed in Britain, the liability for military service at the age of 18 had extremely little relevance to the educational plans of the great majority of boys and young men. Two very different pieces of evidence support this generalization. In 1956 the Minister for Education asked the Central Advisory Council for Education to advise him on the education of boys and girls between the ages of 15 and 18. The Council, under the chairmanship of Sir Geoffrey Crowther, studied the matter for three years and then produced two substantial volumes; nowhere in them is there any discussion of the relevance of military conscription to educational policies. This is all the more remarkable since a large part of the second volume reports the findings of a large-scale survey carried out among conscripts in the Army and Air Force.

The second piece of evidence is an early postwar sample survey carried out among civilians to assess their attitudes toward service in the Army. Five groups of civilians were interviewed—youths aged 16 to 18 who had not yet registered for the Armed Forces; men aged 24 to 30 who had served in the Army; fathers with unmarried sons aged 14 to 30; mothers with unmarried sons aged 14 to 30; and wives or girlfriends of men who were under 30 years of age and had served or were serving in the Army. Among other things, respondents were asked to say what they considered to be the disadvantages of military service for young men. The average respondent mentioned between two and three disadvantages, but only 13 per cent of the total sample referred to the possibility that military service interfered with a young man's career; the frequency of these mentions was higher among middle-class respondents than among working-class respondents (19 per cent as compared with 11 per cent), and higher among youths than among those who had completed their military service (19 per cent against 6 per cent). Moreover, only a quarter of the 13 per cent mentioning career handicaps referred specifically to formal educational aspects of this situation; the majority simply had in mind the years lost in getting on with their normal progress in civilian occupations.

But if conscription in Britain seems to have had very little direct effect on the quality or quantity of education, it apparently affected modestly career choices—understandably since deferment was based on occupation.

CAREER CHOICES

As we have seen, at the beginning of the 1950's almost 70 per cent of all boys had left school before reaching their 16th birthday. At that point they had a little over two years before registering for military service. From the Census of Occupations the following reasonable inferences may be drawn about those who left school at 15:

1) A small minority (approximately 6 to 7 per cent) deliberately took dead-end jobs in order to fill in time; they became messengers, retail shop assistants, tea-makers, office boys, etc. In other words, they postponed a genuine career choice until after they completed their military service.

2) An unduly high proportion entered the deferred occupations—agriculture, coal mining and the merchant navy; here, again, however, the dimensions were comparatively small—although probably sufficient to aggravate the overmanning of these industries in the 1960's.

3) An unusually large number enlisted voluntarily in the Armed Forces on long-term service contracts and benefited from the industrial training courses provided for such long-term soldiers.

4) Despite the limits set by trade union rules, there was a very slight tendency for more early school leavers to become either apprentices in skilled manual occupations or articled pupils training for professional qualifications. For example, in 1952 of all boys aged 15 to 17 entering the labor force, 36 per cent were apprenticed or articled; in 1956 the comparable ratio had risen to 39 per cent; this, however, was a peak for the remainder of the conscription years.

Among boys attending high schools (both state and private) the age of starting compulsory military service was appreciably later than among those who attended a modern secondary school where the normal school leaving age was 15. According to a sample survey carried out by the Crowther Committee, only 33 per cent of the former were called up at the age of 18, while among the latter the rate of call-up at 18 years was over 50 per cent. This tendency for high school boys to enjoy deferment was not evenly spread among all social classes. During the early and mid-1950's a high proportion of boys in these schools were in fact "early-leavers," i.e., they left high school at either 15 or 16 years of age. For example, in 1954 and 1955 17 per cent of boys in these schools left before reaching their 16th birthday and another 16 per cent gave up before reaching 16¾ years of age, i.e., almost two-thirds could be described as early leavers. And parental social class played a large part in selecting these dropouts. Among the sons of middle-class parents, the dropout rate was 45 per cent; for the sons of working-class fathers, the loss rate was 75 per cent.

DROPOUTS AND DEFERMENTS

There were undoubtedly many reasons for this high dropout rate among working-class boys—lack of parental stimulus, the need to supplement family income as soon as possible, the desire to conform with neighborhood standards. It is probable that one reason was that some working-class boys lacked confidence in their ability to gain entrance into a university on completing their high school studies and thus gain further deferment. Insofar as this reason was operative, the result was a loss to society since the Crowther Report survey makes it clear that many working-class early-leavers from high schools were of high academic ability. On being called up, every conscript undertook five tests: non-verbal test of reasoning ability, measurement of mechanical knowledge and aptitude, test of simple arithmetic and mathematics, test of spelling, comprehension and verbal facility, test of ability to understand complex instructions and to carry them out rapidly and accurately. On the basis of the scores, each recruit was marked into one of six ability groups. Group 1 (the highest) contained 11 per cent of all army conscripts; 30 per cent were in Group 2; 17 per cent in Group 3; and 42 per cent in Groups 4, 5 and 6. Table 1 shows the distribution of these ability groups among the sample of Army recruits who left school at 16 or later and in terms of their social background. Briefly, what the figures indicate is that among middle-class boys of top talent (Group 1) only a quarter were early-leavers; but among working-class boys of the same ability, well over half (54 per cent) dropped out of school before reaching the pre-university classes. In the second level of talent, the discrepancy between the two social groups was even greater.

TABLE 1

Ability, School-leaving Age, and Parental Social Class
(among School-leavers Aged 16 or Later, Percentage Distribution)

Ability Group	Middle Class		Working Class			Total	All Ability groups
	Left at 17 or later	Left at 16	Left at 17 or later	Left at 16			
1	45	16	18	21	=	100	45
2	27	22	12	39	=	100	47
3, 4, 5, 6	21	20	10	49	=	100	8
All	35	19	14	32	=	100	100

Deferment for university and college students was the general rule; in most years it was granted to 80 per cent of those liable for military service. At most institutions of higher learning this postponement was almost automatic. The argument usually put forward to justify this arrangement was that a boy academically good enough to gain one of the very scarce university places was probably in his late teens, at the peak of his intellectual excitement about learning, and that a break in his studies at this point would irrevocably disturb his academic enthusiasm.

TABLE 2

Student Deferment Applications

	1955	1956	1957	1958
Granted	12,700	13,400	12,400	14,100
Refused	3,000	3,200	2,700	2,300
Total	15,700	16,600	15,100	16,400
Granted as Percentage of Total	81	81	82	86

The great majority of intending students who were deferred served their military service after graduation. The only significant exceptions were the few hundred first and second class honors graduates in science and engineering who took up school teaching or who entered employment approved by the Ministry of Labour.

To complete the student picture, it should be noted that each year a minority of intending students made no application for deferment. They accepted their liability at 18 years of age, served their two years in the Armed Forces and then entered university or college. It was generally believed (without much factual evidence) that these fatalists were, in their late teens, less bright academically than those who sought deferment, that their two years in the adult world made them more mature students and that during the two years of pre-college military service many of them changed their career intentions—schoolboys who had originally thought of becoming classical scholars and medieval historians decided, after service in Southeast Asia and West Germany, that they would prefer to be economists and engineers.

CONCLUSIONS

The general conclusion to be drawn is that the British system of compulsory military service had very little effect on education. Apart from those exempt on medical grounds, practically all those who were liable for service either entered the Armed Forces more or less as soon as they reached the age of 18 or else were granted deferment for two or three years. Roughly three-quarters of all boys completed their full-time schooling at the age of 15 and this left them three years in which to start on their adult jobs. For them, deferment was entirely on an occupational basis and a two-year deferment was sufficient for those entering skilled trades to complete their five-year apprenticeship. For the handful of young men planning a university education, the educational system was sufficiently flexible to allow a 20 to 25 per cent minority to take up their studies at 21 rather than the usual age of 18. It is possible that a few working-class boys of high intelligence forewent a university education since they could not afford to postpone the start of their careers for five years (three at the university and two in the Armed Forces). This social waste, however, is negligible when compared with the normal state of affairs in Britain in the 1950's when working-class boys constituted 65 per cent of all those judged by the Armed Forces to be in the two top ability groups, and yet 90 per cent of these talented working-class boys left school at the age of 16 or less. With wastage on such a scale, the only possible beneficial connection between the Armed Forces and education would have been if the Forces had developed an effective educational system of its own; no real effort was made along these lines and, indeed, as we have seen, anyone with formal training as a teacher was usually kept out of the Forces through the workings of occupational deferment. It is arguable that a great educational opportunity was then missed.

17

The High School Student, the Draft, and Voluntary National Service Alternatives: Some Survey Data

LEON BRAMSON

This is an era when, in the words of Erik Erikson, "youth are left high and dry by the ebbing wave of the past."[1] The effort to understand the adolescent has moved hand in hand with historical trends which have simultaneously increased his numbers and decreased both his autonomy and his responsibility. Survey data on adolescent "opinion" must therefore be assessed with utmost caution—a generalization which applies to survey data on most other subjects as well. For adolescents are quite likely to indicate "responses" which will be satisfactory to the adults who are doing the questioning, and they are at a stage of the life-cycle when they are notoriously sensitive to the opinions of others. Furthermore, observers such as S. M. Miller have indicated that lower-class high school students in particular have distorted views of their occupational future.[2] In spite of all these caveats, however, their surveyed opinions regarding the draft and national service are of potential interest to the members of this Conference; they are presented here without extensive interpretation since the data were made available only a few days before the Conference deadline.

Whatever merit there may be in surveying the opinions of high school students, it is not my merit. The research reported here was carried out by the Scholastic Research Center of Scholastic Magazines, Inc.[3] Scholastic has the advantage of a long-term familiarity with the interests of high school students, and their opinion surveys relevant to the topic of this Conference were carried out over a period of time which goes back to 1943.

What is reported first below—the responses to four questions—is the result of a survey carried out in October, 1966. Individuals polled represented a probability sample encompassing the in-school adolescent population of the United States between the ages of 14 and 18. It was a two-stage sample, utilizing first a cross-section of high schools broken down according to public, private, and parochial, and also geographically according to the number of schools in a region. One hundred high schools were then selected randomly from these strata. Differences such as those between urban and rural schools were thus

The author is Associate Professor of Sociology and Chairman, Department of Sociology and Anthropology, Swarthmore College.

accounted for. A careful random sample of students was taken within each school chosen for study. The questionnaire was administered during school hours by an administrator or teacher—which increased the likelihood that students might respond in a way which they thought appropriate in such a setting. Finally, there was a cross-check on the proportional representation of the different religious groups through inclusion of an item on religion in the questionnaire. There were a total of 2710 responses (five of the 100 schools did not respond).

Although the sampling process was extremely careful, it should be pointed out that a large proportion of the adolescent population is not represented—the dropouts. This group is one which would figure importantly in any program of voluntary national service alternatives. (One need only be reminded of the fact that half a million applicants responded to the creation of the Job Corps, though there were only thirty thousand places available.) The questions, with their tabulated answers, are given in the accompanying tabulation.

In spite of the astonishing numbers of students who appear to welcome the opportunity to engage in national service, even involuntary service for females, I am inclined to view the results with considerable skepticism. There is always a question as to what element in a forced-choice questionnaire the individual is responding to. How many of the girls who were asked question 3 above could define the word "involuntary"? The emotional coloration of "protecting, conserving, and developing" as expressed in that question probably accounts for part of the high positive response, and such difficulties are endemic to this type of research unless appropriate checks are built into the questionnaire itself. Other recent polls in the United States have indicated a positive response among the general public. A Gallup report in July, 1966, showed seventy per cent "favoring" Secretary of Defense McNamara's proposal that young Americans give two years of service to their country, in either military or non-military capacities. Louis Harris & Associates reported in early November, 1966, that "by nearly four to one, people favor the idea of a universal service program for all young men between 18 and 26, under which they could choose between a two-year stint in the armed forces, the Peace Corps, or in some other public service." However, we need to know a good deal more about what such "favoring" means to the people behind the poll results.

The results of the following surveys are included here in spite of the great variations in methodological sophistication between 1943 and 1965. They represent an unusual source of longitudinal data, the importance of which was recently reemphasized by Peter Rossi of NORC. All surveys carried out by Scholastic represent sampling of junior and senior high school students at all grade levels. In the earlier surveys, the point of contact was the faculty advisor to the student newspaper. He or she distributed questionnaires to samples of students within the school at each grade level. Results reflect the bias of excluding dropouts but are probably a reasonably good reflection of the responses of high-school students, with some under-representation among those students who were incapable of dealing with such questionnaires.

The first survey was conducted in November, 1965, among a scientifically selected sampling of 3,455 junior and senior high school students in public, private and parochial schools throughout the country. The sampling included 1,695 boys and 1,760 girls.

1) Do you favor the U.S. adopting a National Service Program under which young men could meet their service obligations through approved non-military activities such as service in the Peace Corps, Medical Corps, VISTA, Job Corps and related programs whether sponsored by government or private organizations?

(answered by boys and girls)

	Percentage		
	Total	Boys	Girls
yes	78.7	76.0	81.0
no	18.4	22.6	14.8
no answer	2.9	1.4	4.2
	100.0	100.0	100.0
BASE:	(2710)	(1260)	(1450)

2) Would you prefer to meet your own service obligation through military or non-military service?

(answered by boys)

	Percentage
	Boys
military	55.4
non-military	26.3
unsure	18.0
no answer	0.3
	100.0
BASE:	(1260)

3) Do you think a National Service Program should include involuntary service for women, for the tasks of protecting, conserving and developing our country or those countries we wish to aid?

(answered by girls)

	Percentage
	Girls
yes	46.6
no	33.2
unsure	20.2
no answer	—
	100.0
BASE:	(1450)

4) If a National Service Program is adopted, do you think stricter requirements should be imposed on those entering the non-military, such as longer duration (three years) and lower salary?

(answered by boys and girls)

	Percentages		
	Total	Boys	Girls
yes	34.2	43.8	26.0
no	63.2	54.7	70.6
no answer	2.6	1.7	3.4
	100.0	100.0	100.0
BASE:	(2710)	(1260)	(1450)

Students were given an opportunity to express their views as to why such a large number of young men of draft age are declared unfit for military service. The SRC survey also asked students if they thought this country's present draft system was a fair one, and if not, to discuss why.

Of the total number of students participating in the survey, more than half (56 per cent) feel that the reasons most men are declared ineligible for the draft are legitimate ones; i.e., physical fitness and inability to pass intelligence and literacy tests.

But more than one-fourth of the students (28 per cent) believe deliberate evasion is also involved as a major factor for rejections. Of this percentage, 19 per cent cite deliberate failing on intelligence tests, and 9 per cent cite exaggeration of physical unfitness as methods of draft evasion. Boys for whom the draft is more imminent (18-year-olds) are more likely than younger boys to cite deliberate evasion as a possible cause of draft board rejections.

While 61 per cent of the total number of students polled think this country's present draft system is basically fair, a good proportion (29 per cent) disagree. Among the age groups questioned, boys and girls 18 years of age most seriously question the fairness of the present draft system.

Boys are more willing to accept the procedure of the present draft system than girls. Girls 18 years (33 per cent) and girls 12 to 14 years of age (31 per cent) are most critical of the present system.

When the groups of students who think the draft system unfair were asked to give their reasons, the greatest percentage (38 per cent) pointed to the present policy of drafting married men without children. Strongest objection to this policy is voiced by junior high school students, ages 12-14 (47 per cent), with least objection from the 18-year-old boys (33 per cent).

Another objection to the present system is grounded in the feeling that certain groups receive preferential treatment. Almost a quarter of the students (24 per cent) feel that deferment of college students is not equitable, with 18-year-old boys finding least fault with this policy.

Here are the results of the November, 1965, survey:

1) You may have heard that a large number of our young men of draft age are declared by the draft board to be unfit for service. What do you think is the main reason for this?

	(Percentage Distribution)			
	All Students	*Boys*		
Reasons for Rejection		*12-14*	*15-18*	*18 yrs.*
Physical unfitness	40.8	37.4	38.0	31.9
Deliberate giving of false answers on intelligence and literacy tests	19.0	19.5	21.3	27.4
Inability to pass intelligence and literacy tests	15.4	23.5	13.5	12.6
Deliberate exaggeration of physical unfitness	8.6	4.8	10.1	10.4
Physical and mental standards too high	5.6	4.5	5.9	5.2
Other	2.9	3.5	3.7	6.7
Don't know	7.6	6.7	7.5	5.9
BASE:	(3455)	(374)	(1312)	(135)

2) Do you think this country's draft system is a fair one?

	(Percentage Distribution)					
					Girls	
Fairness	*All Students*	*All Boys*	*All Girls*	*Boys 18 yrs.*	*18 yrs.*	*12-14*
Yes	61.0	64.5	57.7	58.7	54.3	52.4
No	28.7	28.0	29.5	35.5	32.6	30.6
Don't know	10.1	7.4	12.8	5.8	13.0	17.0
BASE:	(3455)	(1695)	(1760)	(138)	(46)	(481)

3) If you answered "No" to Question 2, please answer the following: What do you feel is unfair about the present draft system?

	(Percentage Distribution)			*Jr. High Students Ages 12-14*
	All Students	*Boys*		
		15-18	*18 yrs.*	
Married men without children are drafted	38.0	34.5	33.3	46.6
College students are deferred	24.3	20.6	18.7	27.7
Draft boards around the country vary in the way they apply the draft laws	20.4	19.0	18.7	21.4
Draft reaches younger age groups; under 21, etc.	7.9	6.2	12.5	6.7
The service is disruptive of people's lives	3.0	3.8	2.1	1.3
Married men with children are now drafted	1.5	.8	2.1	1.7
Part-time students and night students are drafted	1.3	.5	—	1.3
The system in general is unfair or poor	.5	.8	2.1	—
Too easy to be deferred for physical disabilities	.5	1.4	4.2	—
Other reasons unspecified	21.0	28.5	25.0	13.9
BASE:	(965)	(368)	(48)	(238)

In February, 1963, 5,297 students were polled: Which field would you like to make your career?

Boys (Percentage Distribution)

1st Choice		2nd Choice	
Engineering	19.96	Science	11.98
Sports	9.69	Engineering	11.67
Armed Forces	*7.74*	*Armed Forces*	*11.09*
Business	7.70	Sports	7.65
Science	7.43	Business	7.61
Medicine	7.24	Skilled Trade	6.44
Teaching	5.88	Teaching	6.21
Skilled Trade	5.60	Law	5.89
Law	4.52	Medicine	5.15
The Arts	3.89	Farming	3.75
Farming	3.12	Government	3.49
Government	1.95	Sales	2.46
Church	1.71	Financial	2.42
Financial	1.44	Journalism	2.42
Sales	1.13	Advertising &	
Advertising &		Public Relations	2.34
Public Relations	1.12	Office Work	2.30
Journalism	1.05	The Arts	2.30
Office Work	.86	Church	1.01
Homemaking	.07	Homemaking	.23
Other	3.93	Other	2.15
Undecided	3.97	Undecided	1.44

Girls (Percentage Distribution)

Medicine (including		Homemaking	18.83
Nursing)	19.06	Teaching	13.11
Teaching	16.98	Office Work	12.60
Office Work	16.76	Medicine	8.81
Homemaking	9.88	The Arts	6.78
The Arts	7.14	Science	5.97
Business	4.72	Business	5.90
Science	2.63	Journalism	3.91
Church	2.20	*Armed Forces*	*3.45*
Journalism	1.90	Government	3.02
Armed Forces	*1.72*	Advertising &	
Advertising &		Public Relations	2.45
Public Relations	1.61	Church	2.45
Law	1.54	Sports	2.24
Government	1.35	Law	1.99
Sports	1.24	Sales	1.60
Skilled Trade	1.06	Financial	1.49
Farming	.55	Engineering	.64
Financial	.55	Farming	.53
Sales	.40	Other	2.45
Other	5.53	Undecided	1.14
Undecided	2.78		

In February-March, 1961, nearly 10,000 students were polled—grades 7 through 12—in junior and senior high schools of all sizes—both public and private—in 45 states, the questions being:

1) A prominent educator has proposed that young women be drafted for selective service. Instead of serving in the military, however, women would serve as teachers' assistants, nurses' aides, or social workers, either in the United States or overseas. Do you favor such a plan of compulsory service for one year?

	(Percentage Distribution)		
	All Students	Boys Only	Girls Only
I am definitely in favor of it	18.9	18.7	19.1
Offhand, I think it's a good idea	43.9	42.9	44.9
I am definitely opposed to it	14.2	13.0	15.3
Offhand, I think it's a poor idea	16.8	17.7	16.0
No opinion	6.2	7.7	4.7

2) During the recent Presidential campaign, President Kennedy proposed the establishment of a "peace corps of talented young men." As a substitute for military service, these men—all volunteers—would spend three years abroad as technicians in underdeveloped countries. They would include doctors, teachers, engineers, agricultural experts, lawyers, and civil servants. They would be young men who have been trained in the language and customs of the foreign country to which they are assigned. Only a limited number of young men could qualify for such a program. What do you think of this idea?

	(Percentage Distribution)		
	All Students	Boys Only	Girls Only
I am definitely in favor of it	48.4	54.8	41.3
Offhand, I think it's a good idea	37.4	31.7	43.6
I am definitely opposed to it	3.3	3.5	3.0
Offhand, I think it's a poor idea	4.6	4.8	4.5
No opinion	6.3	5.2	7.6

In September-October, 1960, the following question was asked of 5,504 boys: Which of the following statements most nearly expresses your opinion of the present system of selective service?

	(Percentage Distribution) Boys
It is absolutely necessary that the United States be ready to defend itself at all times. Therefore, a system of selective service such as we now have must always be in operation.	62.3
Selective service may be necessary, but I feel that we should spend more money for the most modern weapons and less for maintaining large Armed Forces. I feel that selective service calls should be cut down.	27.8
Selective service is unnecessary in the Age of the Atom and should be discontinued.	2.8
None of these. (No opinion)	7.1

In December, 1959, the question was asked: What are your personal plans regarding service in the Armed Forces?

	Total	Boys
Total number of students taking the poll	10,763	5,165
Percentages based on total replies of	5,021	5,021
	(Percentage Distribution)	
Enlist for six months and then serve in the Reserve or National Guard	8.4	8.4
Wait for induction for two years of service	12.7	12.7
Enlist for three or more years in order to choose branch of service	22.2	22.2
Join ROTC in college	12.0	12.0
Enlist in the Reserve or National Guard	3.4	3.4
Make the military service a career	7.2	7.2
No plans	33.8	33.8

In April-May, 1958, the question was asked: Which one of the following fields would you like to make your final career?

	Total	Girls	Boys
Total number of students taking the poll	11,416	5,590	5,826
Percentages based on total replies of	10,868	5,610	5,258
	(Percentage Distribution)		
Clerical	13.7	25.4	1.3
Engineering	12.4	1.6	24.3
Medicine	12.0	17.1	6.9
Teaching	10.1	15.8	4.2
Armed Forces	6.4	2.6	10.5
Business	6.3	5.9	6.6
Science	6.1	3.4	8.3
Skilled trade	4.2	1.4	7.1
Farming	3.2	.6	5.9
The Arts	3.1	3.6	2.5
Law	2.5	1.1	3.9
Entertainment	2.0	2.5	1.4
Journalism	1.8	2.4	1.1
Financial	1.7	2.0	1.4
Social service	1.5	2.2	.7
Church	1.5	1.6	1.4
Civil service	1.1	.8	1.5
Advertising, public relations	.8	.8	.9
Sales	.7	.5	.9
Other	8.9	8.7	9.2

Finally, here are results of a number of different polls on universal military training conducted by the Institute of Student Opinion under the sponsorship of Scholastic Magazines, Inc., over the ten-year period from 1943 through 1953:

Poll No. 2, October, 1943: Are you in favor of a year's compulsory military service by 17- to 21-year-old boys after the war?

	BASE	(Percentage Distribution)		
		For	Against	No Opinion
Boys	(60,877)	47.39	44.99	7.62
Girls	(69,081)	31.21	59.21	9.58
Total	(129,958)	39.00	52.00	9.00

Poll No. 6, September, 1944: Are you in favor of one year's compulsory military training for 17- to 23-year-old boys after the war?

	BASE	(Percentage Distribution)		
		For	Against	No Opionin
Boys	(52,965)	58.5	30.5	11.0
Girls	(60,555)	38.5	44.5	17.0
Total	(113,520)	48.5	37.5	14.0

Poll No. 16, February, 1948: Are you for or against the United States having a plan of compulsory military training for all boys at some time between the ages of 16 and 21?

	BASE	(Percentage Distribution)		
		For	Against	No Opinion
Boys	(41,174)	65.08	27.09	7.83
Girls	(43,358)	62.36	26.94	10.70
Total	(84,532)	63.60	27.00	9.40

Poll No. 20, March, 1952: Are you in favor of Universal Military Training for every able-bodied young man?

	BASE	(Percentage Distribution		
		For	Against	No Opinion
Boys	(55,990)	53.36	35.88	10.76
Girls	(50,560)	55.66	31.50	12.84
Total	(106,550)	54.45	33.80	11.75

Poll No. 21, January, 1954:

A) Under present world conditions, do you favor the general principle of compulsory military training?

	BASE	(Percentage Distribution)		
		For	Against	No Opinion
Boys	(24,507)	65.76	27.74	6.50
Girls	(23,892)	65.45	24.64	9.91
Total	(48,399)	65.61	26.20	8.19

B, 1) Do you favor the plan as recommended by the National Security Training Commission?

	BASE	(Percentage Distribution)		
		For	Against	No Opinion
Boys	(23,342)	37.26	52.48	10.26
Girls	(22,632)	37.80	48.53	13.67
Total	(45,974)	37.52	50.54	11.94

B, 2) Would you favor compulsory training for six months, followed by 7½ years in the *Ready Reserve*, provided it was required of all fit young men?

	BASE	(Percentage Distribution)		
		For	Against	No Opinion
Boys	(20,943)	31.23	54.03	14.74
Girls	(19,901)	30.36	49.87	19.77
Total	(40,844)	30.80	52.01	17.19

B, 3) Would you favor two years of active duty followed by six years in the *Stand-by Reserve*, provided it was required of all fit young men?

	BASE	(Percentage Distribution)		
		For	Against	No Opinion
Boys	(19,725)	41.64	39.93	18.43
Girls	(18,815)	40.74	36.67	22.59
Total	(38,540)	41.40	38.34	20.46

NOTES

[1] "Wholeness and Totality," in Carl J. Friedrich (ed.), *Totalitarianism* (Cambridge, Mass.: Harvard University Press, 1954), 170.

[2] "The Outlook of Working-Class Youth," in Arthur B. Shostak and William Gomberg (eds.), *Blue-Collar World* (Englewood Cliffs, N. J.: Prentice-Hall, 1964), pp. 122-34.

[3] These data were made available through the kindness of Mr. Maurice R. Robinson, Chairman of the Board, and Dr. M. Prince, of Scholastic Magazines, Inc., and their generosity is gratefully acknowledged. Questions on national service were included in a larger study at my suggestion.

ALTERNATIVES TO THE DRAFT

18

The Impact of the Draft on the Legitimacy of the National State

KENNETH E. BOULDING

THE RISE AND FALL OF LEGITIMACY

One of the most neglected aspects of the dynamics of society is the study of dynamic processes which underlie the rise and fall of legitimacy. This neglect reflects, in the United States at least, not merely a deficiency in social sciences and social thought; it reflects a grave deficiency in what might be called the popular image of the social system. We all tend to take legitimacy for granted. Thus, the economist hardly ever inquires into the legitimacy of exchange, even though this is the institution on which his science is built. The political scientist rarely inquires into the legitimacy of political institutions or of the institutions of organized threat, such as the police and the armed forces. Consequently we are much given to discussions of economic development as if this were a me-chanical or quasi-automatic process without regard to the conditions of legiti-macy of various activities and institutions. Similarly, in our discussions of the strategy of threat we rarely take account of the legitimacy of the institutions which either make the threats or provide their credibility. To put the matter simply, we tend to regard both wealth and power as self-justifying and this could well be a disastrous error.

The truth is that the dynamic of legitimacy, mysterious as it may seem, in fact governs to a remarkable extent all the other processes of social life. Without legitimacy no permanent relationship can be established, and if we lose legiti-macy we lose everything. A naked threat, such as that of the bandit or the armed robber, may establish a temporary relationship. The victim hands over his money or even his person at the sword's point or the pistol's mouth. If we want to establish a permanent relationship, however, such as that of a landlord demanding rent or a government demanding taxes, the threat must be legitimized. The power both of the landlord and of the government depend in the last analysis upon the consent of the rentpayer or the taxpayer and this consent implies that the whole procedure has been legitimated and is accepted by everyone concerned as right and proper. Legitimacy may be defined as general acceptance by all those con-cerned in a certain institution, role, or pattern of behavior that it constitutes part of the regular moral or social order within which they live. Thus legitimacy is a wider concept than the formal concept of law, even though the law is a great

The author is a professor in the Department of Economics, University of Michigan.

legitimator. At times, however, law itself may become illegitimate and when it does so its capacity to organize society is destroyed.

Legitimacy has at least two dimensions which might be described as intensity and extent. Its intensity refers to the degree of identification or acceptance in the mind of a particular individual, and it may be measured roughly by the extent of sacrifice which he is prepared to make for an institution rather than deny it or abandon it. The extent of legitimacy refers to the proportion of the relevant population which regards the institution in question as legitimate. An overall measure of the legitimacy of any particular institution might be achieved by multiplying its intensity by its extent, but such a measure might easily obscure certain important characteristics of the system. A case in which an institution was regarded with intense allegiance by a small proportion of the people concerned would be very different from one in which there was a mild allegience from all the people; the former, indeed, would probably be less stable than the latter. In considering any particular case, therefore, it is always important that we consider both dimensions.

The creation, maintenance, and destruction of legitimacy of different institutions presents many difficult problems. Legitimacy is frequently created by the exercise of power, either economic power in the form of wealth or political power in the form of threat capability. Legitimacy, furthermore, frequently increases with age so that old wealth and old power are more legitimate than new. The nouveau riche may be looked upon askance but their grandchildren easily become aristocrats. The conqueror likewise is illegitimate at first, but if his conquest is successful and his empire lasts, it eventually acquires legitimacy. All these relationships, however, seem to be non-linear, and reverse themselves beyond a certain point. Thus, the display of wealth tends to become obscene and damages the legitimacy of the wealthy. In order to retain legitimacy they often have to diminish their wealth by giving it away, establishing foundations, or at least by abstaining from ostentatious consumption. Similarly, political power often seems to lose its legitimacy when it is apparently at its very height. It is at the greatest extent and power of a regime, nation, or empire that it often suddenly collapses through sheer loss of belief in it. Even age does not always guarantee legitimacy. After a certain point an ancient person or institution simply becomes senile or old-fashioned and its legitimacy abruptly collapses.

There have been enough examples of collapse of legitimacy of apparently large, prosperous and invincible institutions to suggest that we have here a general, though not necessarily a universal, principle at work. It is perhaps an example of another much-neglected proposition, that nothing fails like success because we do not learn anything from it. Thus in Europe the institution of the absolute monarchy seemed to be most secure and invincible at the time of Louis XIV, yet only a few decades later it was in ruins. Similarly, in the early years of the twentieth century the concept of empire seemed invincible and unshakably legitimate, yet in another few decades it was discredited, illegitimate, and the empires themselves collapsed or had to be transformed.

It looks indeed as if there is some critical moment at which an institution must be transformed if it is to retain its legitimacy and transformed, furthermore, in the direction of abandonment of either its wealth or its power in some degree. Thus, after the eighteenth century the only way in which the institution of the monarchy could retain its legitimacy was to abandon its power and become constitutional. By abandoning his political power, that is, his threat capability, the monarch was able to become a symbol of the legitimacy of the state and hence was able to preserve his role in the society. Where the monarch did not make this transition, as for instance in France, Germany, and Russia, the incumbent frequently lost his head, the whole institution was destroyed, and the role simply abandoned. Similarly, in the twentieth century, if any semblance of empire was to be maintained, the political power had to be abandoned and the empire transformed into a commonwealth or community based on sentiment rather than on threat. Even the church in the twentieth century has largely had to abandon the fear of hell, that is, its spiritual threat system, as the prime motivation in attracting support. In most countries, furthermore, it has likewise had to abandon the support of the state and the secular arm, that is, the secular threat system, in an attempt to enforce conformity. Here again we see an example of the abandonment of power in the interests of retaining legitimacy.

THE NATIONAL STATE

At the present time by far the most wealthy, powerful, and legitimate type of institution is the national state. In the socialist countries the national state monopolizes virtually all the wealth and the threat capability of the society. Even in the capitalist world the national state usually commands about 25 per cent of the total economy and is a larger economic unit than any private corporation, society, or church. Thus the United States government alone wields economic power roughly equal to half the national income of the Soviet Union, which is the largest socialist state. Within the United States government the United States Department of Defense has a total budget larger than the national income of the Peoples Republic of China and can well claim to be second largest centrally planned economy in the world. It is true that the great corporations wield an economic power roughly equal to that of the smaller socialist states; there are, indeed, only about 11 countries with a gross national product larger than General Motors. Nevertheless, when it comes to legitimacy the national state is supreme. All other loyalties are expected to bow before it. A man may deny his parents, his wife and his friends, his God, or his profession and get away with it, but he cannot deny his country unless he finds another one. In our world a man without a country is regarded with pity and scorn. We are expected to make greater sacrifices for our country than we make for anything else. We are urged, "Ask not what your country can do for you, ask what you can do for your country," whereas nobody ever suggests that we should "Ask not what General Motors can do for you, ask what you can do for General Motors."

An institution of such monumental wealth, power and legitimacy would seem to be invincible. The record of history suggests clearly, however, that it is precisely at this moment of apparent invincibility that an institution is in gravest danger. It may seem as absurd today to suggest that the national state might lose its legitimacy as it would have been to suggest the same thing of the monarchy in the days of *le Grand Monarque*. Nevertheless both monarchy and empire have lost their legitimacy and that at the moment of their greatest power and extent. If history teaches us anything, therefore, it should teach us at this moment to look at the national state with a quizzical eye. It may be an institution precisely filling the conditions which give rise to a sudden collapse of legitimacy, which will force the institution itself to transform itself by abandoning its power or will create conditions in which the institution cannot survive.

These conditions can be stated roughly as follows: An institution which demands sacrifices can frequently create legitimacy for itself because of a strong tendency in human beings to justify to themselves sacrifices which they have made. We cannot admit that sacrifices have been made in vain, for this would be too great a threat to our image of ourselves and our identity. As the institution for which sacrifices are made gains legitimacy, however, it can demand more sacrifices, which further increases legitimacy. At some point, however, the sacrifices suddenly seem to be too much. The terms of trade between its devotees and the institution become too adverse, and quite suddenly the legitimacy of the whole operation is questioned, and ancient sacrifices are written off and the institution collapses. Thus men sacrificed enormously for the monarchy, and the king was able to say for centuries, "Ask not what I can do for you, ask only what you can do for me," until the point when suddenly people began to ask. "What can the king do for me?" and the answer was "Nothing." At that moment the monarchy either died or had to be transformed.

We may be in a similar moment in the case of the national state. The real terms of trade between an individual and his country have been deteriorating markedly in the past decades. In the eighteenth century the national state made relatively few demands on its citizens, and provided some of them at least with fair security and satisfactory identity. As the nation has gathered legitimacy however from the bloodshed and treasure expended for it, it has become more and more demanding. It now demands ten to twenty per cent of our income, at least two years of our life—and it may demand the life itself—and it risks the destruction of our whole physical environment. As the cost rises, it eventually becomes not unreasonable to ask for what. If the payoffs are in fact low, the moment has arrived when the whole legitimacy of the institution may be threatened.

We must here distinguish the internal from the external payoffs of the national state. Internally the payoffs may still be quite high, though it is perhaps still a question whether governments today, like the medical profession a hundred years ago, really do more good than harm. In the external relations, however, there can be no doubt that the system of national states is enormously burdensome and costly. It is not only that the world-war industry is now about 140 billion dollars, which is about equal to the total income of the poorest half of the human race, it is that this enormous expenditure gives us no real security in the long run and it sets up a world in which there is a positive probability of almost total disaster. It is perfectly reasonable indeed to ask ourselves this question: After a nuclear war, if there is anybody left, are they going to set up again the institutions which produced the disaster? The answer would clearly seem to be "No," in which case we may say that as the present system contains a positive probability of nuclear war it is in fact bankrupt and should be changed *before* the nuclear war rather than afterward. It can be argued very cogently indeed that modern technology has made the national state obsolete as an instrument of unilateral national defense, just as gunpowder made the feudal baron obsolete, the development of the skills of organization and public administration made the monarchy obsolete, and economic development made empire obsolete. An institution, no matter how currently powerful and legitimate, which loses its function will also lose its legitimacy, and the national state in its external relations seems precisely in this position today. Either it must be transformed in the direction of abandoning its power and threat capability or it will be destroyed, like the absolute monarchy and the absolute church before it.

THE IMPACT OF THE DRAFT

What then is the role of the draft in this complex dynamic process? The draft may well be regarded as a symbol of a slow decline in the legitimacy of the national state (or of what perhaps we should call more exactly the warfare state, to distinguish it from the welfare state which may succeed it), that slow decline which may presage the approach of collapse. In the rise and decline of legitimacy, as we have seen, we find first a period in which sacrifices are made, voluntarily and gladly, in the interests of the legitimate institution, and, indeed, reinforce the legitimacy of the institution. As the institution becomes more and more pressing in its demands, however, voluntary sacrifices become replaced with forced sacrifices. The tithe becomes a tax, religious enthusiasm degenerates into compulsory chapel, and voluntary enlistment in the threat system of the state becomes a compulsory draft. The legitimacy of the draft, therefore, is in a sense a subtraction from the legitimacy of the state. It represents the threat system of the state turned in on its own citizens, however much the threat may be disguised by a fine language about service and "every young man fulfilling his obligation." The language of duty is not the language of love and it is a symptom of approaching delegitimation. A marriage in which all the talk is of obligations rather than of love is on its way to the divorce court. The church in which all worship is obligatory is on its way to abandonment or reformation, and the state in which service has become a duty is in no better case. The draft therefore, which undoubtedly increases the threat capability of the national state, is a profound symptom of its decay and insofar as it demands a forced sacrifice it may hasten that decay and may hasten the day when people come to see that to ask "what can your country do for you" is a very sensible question.

The draft, furthermore, inevitably creates strong inequities. It discriminates against the poor, or at least against the moderately poor; the very poor, because of their poor educational equipment may escape it just as the rich tend to escape it, and the main burden therefore falls on the lower end of the middle-income groups. As these groups also in our society bear the brunt of taxation—for a great deal of what is passed as "liberal" legislation in fact taxes the poor in order to subsidize the rich—an unjust distribution of sacrifice is created. Up to now it is true this strain has not been very apparent. It cannot indeed be expressed directly because of the enormous legitimacy of the national state, hence it tends to be expressed indirectly in alienation, crime, internal violence, race and group hatreds and also in an intensified xenophobia. This is the old familiar problem of displacement. We dare not vent our anger at frustrations upon their cause and we therefore have to find a legitimated outlet in the foreigner, or the communist, or whoever the enemy happens to be at the moment. What is worse, the frustrated adult frequently displaces his anger on his children who in turn perpetuate the whole miserable business of hatred and lovelessness.

Like compulsory chapel or church attendance, which is its closest equivalent, the draft has a further disadvantage in that while it may at best produce a grudging and hostile acquiescence in the methods of the society, it frequently closes the mind to any alternative or to any reorganization of information. The psychological strains which are produced by compulsory service of any kind naturally result in displaced aggressions rather than in any reform of the system which created them. Consequently the draft by the kind of indoctrination and hidden frustrations which it produces may be an important factor in preventing that reevaluation of the national policy and the national image which is so essential in the modern world if the national state itself is to survive. The draft therefore is likely to be an enemy of the survival of the very state in the interests of which it is supposedly involved. It produces not a true love of country based on a realistic appraisal of the present situation of human society but rather a hatred of the other which leads to political mental ill health, and an image of the world which may be as insulated from the messages which come through from reality as is the mind of a paranoid.

Perhaps the best thing that can be said in defense of the draft is that the alternative, namely, raising a voluntary armed force by offering sufficient financial inducements, or by persuasion and advertising, would involve even more the whipping up of hatred of the foreigner and the reinforcement of paranoid political attitudes. The draft by its very absurdities and inequities at least to some extent helps to make the whole operation faintly ridiculous, as we see it in comic strips like Beetle Bailey or in movies such as *Dr. Strangelove*, and hence makes the operation of national defense commonplace rather than charismatic. The draft certainly represents the institutionalization of the charisma of the national state, to use an idea from Max Weber, and this may be something on the credit side. Even this merit, however, is dubious. Insofar as the draft leads to widespread commonplace acceptance of mass murder and atrocities, and an attitude of mind which is blind to any but romantically violent solutions of conflict, its influence is wholly negative. Certainly the political wisdom of the American Legion is no advertisement for the political virtues of having passed through the Armed Forces.

It seems clear therefore that those of us who have a genuine affection for the institution of the national state and for our own country in particular should constantly attack the legitimacy of the draft, and the legitimacy of the whole system of unilateral national defense which supports it, in the interest of preserving the legitimacy of the national state itself. The draft, it is true, is merely a symbol or a symptom of a much deeper disease, the disease of unilateral national defense, and it is this concept which should be the prime focus of our attack. Nevertheless, cleaning up a symptom sometimes helps to cure the disease, otherwise the sales of aspirin would be much less, and a little aspirin of dissent applied to the headache of the draft might be an important step in the direction of the larger objective. Those of us, therefore, who are realistically concerned about the survival of our country should probably not waste too much time complaining about the inequities and absurdities of the draft or attempt the hopeless task of rectifying it when the plain fact is that the draft can only begin to approach "justice" in time of major war, and a peacetime draft has to be absurd and unjust by its very nature. The axe should be applied to the root of the tree, not to its branches. An attempt to pretty up the draft and make it more acceptable may actually prevent that radical reevaluation of the whole system of unilateral national defense which is now in order. We are very close to the moment when the only way to preserve the legitimacy of the national state will be to abandon most of its power. The draft is only a subplot in this much greater drama.

19

The Draft in a Democratic Society

RICHARD FLACKS

I do not see how it can be denied that the institution of conscription is by definition alien to a genuinely free society. Therefore, I want to stress at the outset my view that the abolition of this institution ought to be a very high priority for Americans. This goal is, however, utopian so long as the United States continues to follow a policy based on the assumption that the status quo in every part of the world must be maintained by American military power. Thus, the only really worthwhile question to ask about conscription—how we can get rid of it—cannot be answered without debating the whole scope of American foreign policy.

It is, however, not entirely fruitless to raise some questions about the way in which conscription is used by our society, assuming that some form of selective service is going to be with us indefinitely. This may be particularly necessary for those of us who oppose the draft altogether, since much of the present discussion concerns how best to *extend* the scope of military training institutions, and how better to *integrate* them into the fabric of American life. My concern here, then, will be not with the many inequities of the present draft system, but with discussing ways of limiting the impact of this alien system and of preventing or diluting some of its more pernicious effects.

In my view, a fundamental flaw in the current draft system is that it reinforces and exacerbates a serious constitutional weakness in American political life, namely, the enormous delegation of power in international affairs to the Executive. This Presidential power to make international commitments, wage war, and mobilize national resources and public consent is not substantially checked or limited by any countervailing governmental or private power. The institution of permanent, compulsory military service facilitates the freedom of the President in this regard and enables him to deploy military forces on a very large scale without achieving prior popular consent. Such built-in presidential irresponsibility is intrinsically repugnant; from a pragmatic point of view, its consequences can be read in Vietnam.

It is my hope that serious study will be given to ways in which Presidents can be made responsible for their international policies and to mechanisms by which the presidential ability to mobilize for war can be balanced and checked. Many of the most important considerations in this regard lie outside the scope of this paper. But, it seems to me, there are ways in which the contribution of

The author is an Assistant Professor of Sociology at the University of Chicago.

the Selective Service System to presidential irresponsibility can be reduced or reversed.

First, it seems to me inadmissible that those most likely to be compelled to kill and die for often highly questionable policies do not even have the right to vote. If we are going to draft 18-, 19-, and 20-year-old men, then we ought to allow them access to the ballot box. This, I think, would not be merely a formalistic reform, permitting young men to ratify their own induction, although it might turn out to be only that. Rather, it seems plausible that the introduction of large numbers of young people into the political arena would create a substantial new constituency for policies of restraint and internationalism—a constituency which might provide some check on the patriotic hawking of elderly politicians.

Second, I think we should adopt the notion, which prevails in other countries such as Canada, that conscripts ought not to be used indiscriminately in foreign wars. The only legitimate use for draftees ought to be for the defense of the nation's most vital interests. The proposal of Senator Ernest Gruening of Alaska to prevent the President from using conscripts involuntarily in combat without specific congressional mandate seems to me to be a reasonable, if minimal, way to ensure some congressional check on Presidential power. A stronger, and in my view more legitimate, proposal would be to prevent the use of draftees who do not volunteer in combat, without a specific declaration of war. In any case, some mechanism of this sort would be a desirable way of bringing the power of the President to escalate conflicts under some degree of democratic control, while establishing conscription as an institution for national defense rather than an instrument for imperial adventure.

Third, it seems to me necessary to increase the freedom of citizens to resist being mobilized for wars of questionable justification. One way to do this is to broaden the grounds for conscientious objection. Conscientious objection can be founded on philosophical and political grounds as well as religious ones. Moreover, if there is any sense to the distinction between just and unjust wars, then it is improper to deny the possibility of conscientious objection to particular wars. As far as I can tell, any practical difficulty in establishing whether a young man is a sincere objector on non-religious grounds is already contained in the present definition of conscientious objection. It seems to me inconsistent with our best traditions to compel a young man to fight a war against his conscience, even if his basic values have been shaped by philosophical or political rather than religious influences. And it would seem to me desirable, from the point of view of limiting presidential power, if each inductee had the freedom to test whether his conscience would be violated by serving or fighting in behalf of current policy.

Finally, I would argue that the traditional view of the draft as an alien institution must be preserved, and all attempts to make conscription a permanent, integral feature of American society must be firmly resisted. The goal of democrats in the coming period ought to be to reduce rather than enhance areas of compulsion in American life. There is serious danger in some of the proposals now being offered to reduce the inequities of Selective Service. I refer here not only to attempts to revive universal military training, but to suggestions for universal conscription for "national service." The idea of national service for youth is an interesting one, but the notion that it should be compulsory or tied to conscription is literally totalitarian. Similarly, the proposals to expand the scope of induction to include unqualified youth, so that they may receive the educational benefits of the armed services, is highly reminiscent of the procedures of a garrison state. It is not a matter of pride that the best opportunities for self-improvement for underprivileged youth are offered by the military, or that the only fully integrated educational institution in our society is the army. This situation is a measure of the default of the larger society; the war on poverty is not going to be won by giving the military even more control over the lives of young men.

The only really worthwhile goal of an affluent society with respect to its youth is to promote the maximum possible freedom and opportunity for self-development. At present, upper-status youth have enormous opportunity for years of higher education, and many avenues open for cultural enrichment and personal fulfillment. These opportunities are widely buttressed by public subsidies in the form of scholarships, fellowships, loans, and so on. In the long run, the only way to reduce the inequities of the draft and to offset present trends toward a quasi-caste system among youth is to extend these privileges, opportunities, and subsidies to all youth. What appears to be needed is a massive opening up of the range of choices for youth so that each has a chance to select experiences of service, of education and training, of cultural enhancement and self-realization.

I want to conclude by indicating an important problem posed by these suggestions for limiting the uses of conscription. The present system has the apparent virtue of permitting a partial mobilization for wars as large as Vietnam, without substantially increasing the militancy of the population, without developing major war fever, without very widespread suppression of dissent. It may well be that mechanisms such as those proposed here, which would limit the Executive's freedom of action in this regard, will backfire, and produce more systematic efforts to engineer full popular support for war efforts. This situation would be dangerous domestically; it could also lead to more rapid escalation of conflicts. Such considerations should be given due weight; on the other hand, we need to ask whether the costs added by these constraints might not make Presidents more cautious and rational when they make decisions about the deployment of military forces.

At any rate, these proposals to limit the uses of conscription and to resist its integration into American society seem to run counter to the drift of present policy. The likelihood of their adoption by Congress in the near future seems very small. In this situation, it is heartening that a significant number of inductees have decided to risk jail by undertaking legal tests of the current definition of conscientious objection, by refusing induction during a war which they perceive as unjust and illegal, and by publicly refusing to report for combat duty in such a war. These men may well be speaking for a sizable portion of their generation in questioning the legitimacy of conscription. They deserve the highest degree of support from those concerned to preserve and extend democratic values.

20

Why Not a Voluntary Army?

MILTON FRIEDMAN

Manning our military forces currently requires the services of only a minority of young men. At most, something like one-third will have seen military service by the time they reach age 26. This percentage is scheduled to decline still further as the youngsters born in the postwar baby boom come of age. Hence, some method of "selective service"—of deciding which young man should serve and which two or three should not—is inevitable. However, the present method is inequitable, wasteful, and inconsistent with a free society.

On this point there is wide agreement. Even most supporters of a draft like the present one regard it as at best a necessary evil. And representatives of all parts of the political spectrum have urged that conscription be abolished —including John K. Galbraith and Barry Goldwater; the New Left and the Republican Ripon Society.

The disadvantages of our present system of compulsion and the advantages of a voluntary army are so widely recognized that we can deal with them very briefly. The more puzzling question is why we have continued to use compulsion. The answer is partly inertia—a carryover from a total war situation when the case for a voluntary army is far weaker. But even more, the answer is the tyranny of the status quo. The natural tendency of an administrator of a large, complex, and ongoing activity is to regard the present method of administering it as the only feasible way to do so and to object strenuously that any proposed alternative is visionary and unfeasible—even though the same man, once the change is made and it becomes the existing method, will argue just as strenuously that *it* is the only feasible method.

This bureaucratic standpattism has been reinforced by a confusion between the apparent and the real cost of manning the armed forces by compulsion. The confusion has made it appear that a voluntary army would be much more expensive to the country and hence might not be feasible for fiscal reasons. In fact, the cost of a voluntary army, properly calculated, would almost surely be less than that of a conscripted army. It is entirely feasible to maintain present levels of military power on a strictly voluntary basis.

The other disadvantages that have been attributed to a voluntary army are that it might be racially unbalanced, would not provide sufficient flexibility in size of forces, and would enhance the political danger of undue military influence. While the problems referred to are real, the first and third are in no way connected with the use of voluntary or compulsory means to recruit en-

The author is a professor in the Department of Economics, University of Chicago.

listed men and do not constitute valid arguments against abolishing the draft. The second has more merit, but devices exist to provide moderate flexibility under a voluntary as under a compulsory system.

There is no reason why we cannot move to volunteer forces gradually—by making conditions of service more and more attractive until the whip of compulsion fades away. This, in my opinion, is the direction in which we should move, and the sooner the better.

THE DISADVANTAGES OF COMPULSION AND
ADVANTAGES OF A VOLUNTARY ARMY

Military Effectiveness

A voluntary army would be manned by people who had chosen a military career rather than at least partly by reluctant conscripts anxious only to serve out their term. Aside from the effect on fighting spirit, this would produce a lower turnover in the armed services, saving precious man-hours that are now wasted in training or being trained. It would permit also intensive training and a higher average level of skill of the men in the service. And it would encourage the use of more and better equipment. A smaller, but more highly skilled, technically competent, and better armed force could provide the same or greater military strength.

Individual Freedom

A voluntary army would preserve the freedom of individuals to serve or not to serve. Or, put the other way, it would avoid the arbitrary power that now resides in draft boards to decide how a young man shall spend several of the most important years of his life—let alone whether his life shall be risked in warfare. An incidental advantage would be to raise the level and tone of political discussion.

A voluntary army would enhance also the freedom of those who now do not serve. Being conscripted has been used as a weapon—or thought by young men to be so used—to discourage freedom of speech, assembly, and protest. The freedom of young men to emigrate or to travel abroad has been limited by the need to get the permission of a draft board if the young man is not to put himself in the position of inadvertently being a law-breaker.

A conspicuous example of the effect on freedom of a voluntary army is that it would completely eliminate the tormenting and insoluble problem now posed by the conscientious objector—real or pretended.

Arbitrary Discrimination

A by-product of freedom to serve would be avoidance of the present arbitrary discrimination among different groups. A large fraction of the poor are rejected on physical and mental grounds. The relatively well-to-do are in an especially good position to take advantage of the possibilities of deferment offered by continuing their schooling. Hence the draft bears disproportionately on the upper lower classes and the lower middle classes. The fraction of high school graduates who serve is vastly higher than of either those who have gone to college or those who dropped out before finishing high school.

Removal of Uncertainty for Individuals Subject to Draft

A volunteer army would permit young men, both who serve and those who do not, to plan their schooling, their careers, their marriages, and their families in accordance with their own long-run interests. As it is, the uncertainty about the draft affects every decision they make and often leads them to behave differently from the way they otherwise would in the correct or mistaken belief that they will thereby reduce the chance of being drafted. This disadvantage could be avoided under a compulsory system by, for example, a universal lottery that at age 16, say, assigned youngsters categories such as: certain to be called, likely to be called, possibly will be called, unlikely to be called, certain not to be called. The size of each category would be determined by estimates of future military needs.

Effect on Rest of Community

Substitution of a voluntary army (or of a lottery) for the present draft would permit colleges and universities to pursue their proper educational function, freed alike from the incubus of young men—probably numbering in the hundreds of thousands—who would prefer to be at work rather than in a school but who now continue their schooling in the hope of avoiding the draft and from controversy about issues strictly irrelevant to their educational function. We certainly need controversy in the universities—but about intellectual and educational issues, not whether to rank or not to rank.

Similarly, the community at large would benefit from the reduction of unwise earlier marriages contracted at least partly under the whip of the draft and from the probable associated reduction in the birth rate. Industry and government would benefit from being able to hire young men on their merits, not their deferments.

Defects Unavoidable under Compulsion

So long as compulsion is retained, inequity, waste, and interference with freedom are inevitable. A lottery would only make the arbitrary element in the present system overt. Universal national service would only compound the evil —regimenting all young men, and perhaps women, to camouflage the regimentation of some.

THE SITUATION IN TIME OF MAJOR WAR

If a very large fraction of the young men of the relevant age groups are required —or will be used whether required or not—in the military services, the advantages of a voluntary army become very small. It would still be technically possible to have a voluntary army, and there would still be some advantages, since it is doubtful that literally 100 per cent of the potential candidates will in fact be drawn into the services. But if nearly everyone who is physically capable will serve anyway, there is little room for free choice, the avoidance of uncertainty, and so on. And to rely on volunteers under such conditions would then require very high pay in the armed services, and very high burdens on those who do not serve, in order to attract a sufficient number into the armed forces. This would involve serious political and administrative problems. To put it differently, and in terms that will become fully clear to non-economists only later, it might turn out that the implicit tax of forced service is less bad than the alternative taxes that would have to be used to finance a voluntary army.

Hence for a major war, a strong case can be made for compulsory service. And indeed, compulsory service has been introduced in the United States only under such conditions—in the Civil War, World War I, and World War II. It is hardly conceivable that it could have been introduced afresh in, say, 1950, if a system of compulsory service had not so recently been in full swing. As it was, the easiest thing to do when military needs for manpower rose was to reactivate the recent wartime technique.

POSSIBLE DISADVANTAGES OF A VOLUNTARY ARMY

Is a Voluntary Army Feasible?

Under present conditions, the number of persons who volunteer for armed service is inadequate to man the armed forces, and—even so—many who volunteer do so only because they anticipate being drafted. The number of "true" volunteers is clearly much too small to man armed forces of our present size. This undoubted fact is repeatedly cited as evidence that a voluntary army is unfeasible.

It is evidence of no such thing. It is evidence rather that we are now grossly underpaying our armed forces. The starting pay for young men who enter the armed forces is now about $45 a week—including not only cash pay and allotments but also the value of clothing, food, housing, and other items furnished in kind. When the bulk of young men can command at least twice this sum in civilian jobs, it is little wonder that volunteers are so few. Indeed, it is somewhat surprising that there are as many as there are—testimony to the drives other than pecuniary reward that lead some young men to choose military service either as a career or for a few years.

To man our armed forces with volunteers would require making conditions of service more attractive—not only higher pay but also better housing facilities and improved amenities in other respects. It will be replied that money is not the only factor young men consider in choosing their careers. That is certainly true —and equally certainly irrelevant. Adequate pay alone may not attract, but inadequate pay can certainly deter. Military service has many non-monetary attractions to young men—the chance to serve one's country, adventure, travel, opportunities for training, and so on. Not the least of the advantages of a voluntary army is that the military would have to improve their personnel policies and pay more attention to meeting the needs of the enlisted men. They now need pay little attention to them, since they can fill their ranks with conscripts serving under compulsion. Indeed, it is a tribute to their humanitarianism—and the effectiveness of indirect pressures via the political process—that service in the armed forces is not made even less attractive than it now is.

The personnel policies of the armed forces have been repeatedly criticized— and, with no spur, repeatedly left unreformed. Imaginative policies designed to make the armed forces attractive to the kind of men the armed services would like to have—plus the elimination of compulsion which now makes military service synonomous with enforced incarceration—could change drastically the whole image that the armed services present to young men. The Air Force, because it has relied so heavily on "real" volunteers, perhaps comes closest to demonstrating what could be done.

The question of how much more we would have to pay to attract sufficient volunteers has been studied intensively in the Department of Defense study of military recruitment. Based on a variety of evidence collected in that study, Walter Oi estimates in his paper that a starting pay (again including pay in kind as well as in cash) of something like $4,000 to $5,500 a year—about $80 to $100 a week—would suffice. This is surely not an unreasonable sum. Oi estimates that the total extra payroll costs (after allowing for the savings in turnover and men employed in training) would be around $3 billion to $4 billion a year for Armed Forces equivalent to 2.7 million men under present methods of recruitment and not more than $8 billion a year for Armed Forces equivalent to the present higher number of men (around 3.1 or 3.2 million men). Based on the same evidence, the Defense Department has come up with estimates as high as $17.5 billion. Even the highest of these estimates is not in any way unfeasible in the context of total federal government expenditures of more than $175 billion a year.

Whatever may be the exact figure, it is a highly misleading indication of the cost incurred in shifting from compulsion to a voluntary army. There are net advantages, not disadvantages, in offering volunteers conditions sufficiently attractive to recruit the number of young men required.

This is clearly true on the level of individual equity: the soldier no less than the rest of us is worth his hire. How can we justify paying him less than the amount for which he is willing to serve? How can we justify, that is, involuntary servitude except in times of the greatest national emergency? One of the great gains in the progress of civilization was the elimination of the power of the nobleman or the sovereign to exact compulsory servitude.

On a more mundane budgetary level, the argument that a voluntary Army would cost more simply involves a confusion of apparent with real cost. By this argument, the construction of the Great Pyramid with slave labor was a cheap project. The real cost of conscripting a soldier who would not voluntarily serve on present terms is not his pay and the cost of his keep. It is the amount for which he would be willing to serve. He is paying the difference. This is the extra cost to him that must be added to the cost borne by the rest of us. Compare, for example, the cost to a star professional football player and to an unemployed worker. Both might have the same attitudes toward the army and like—or dislike—a military career equally. But because the one has so much better alternatives than the other, it would take a much higher sum to attract him. When he is forced to serve, we are in effect imposing on him a tax in kind equal in value to the difference between what it would take to attract him and the military pay he actually receives. This implicit tax in kind should be added to the explicit taxes imposed on the rest of us to get the real cost of our Armed Forces.

If this is done, it will be seen at once that abandoning the draft would almost surely reduce the real cost—because the armed forces would then be manned by men for whom soldiering was the best available career, and hence who would require the lowest sums of money to induce them to serve. Abandoning the draft might raise the apparent money cost to the government but only because it would substitute taxes in money for taxes in kind.

Moreover, there are some important offsets even to the increase in apparent money cost. In addition to the lower turnover, already taken into account in the estimates cited, the higher average level of skill would permit further reductions in the size of the army, saving monetary cost to the government. Because manpower is cheap to the military, they now tend to waste it, using enlisted men for tasks that could be performed by civilians or machines, or eliminated entirely. Moreover, better pay at the time to volunteers might lessen the political appeal of veteran's benefits that we now grant after the event. These now cost us over $6 billion a year or one-third as much as current annual payroll costs for the active armed forces—and they will doubtless continue to rise under present conditions.

There are still other offsets. Colleges and universities would be saved the cost of housing, seating, and entertaining hundreds of thousands of young men. Total output of the community would be higher both because these men would be at work and because the young men who now go to work could be used more effectively. They could be offered and could accept jobs requiring considerable training instead of having to take stopgap jobs while awaiting a possible call to service. Perhaps there are some effects in the opposite direction, but I have not been able to find any.

Whatever happens to the apparent monetary cost, the real cost of a voluntary army would almost surely be less than of the present system and it is not even clear that the apparent monetary cost would be higher—if it is correctly measured for the community as a whole. In any event, there can be little doubt that wholly voluntary armed forces of roughly the present size are entirely feasible on economic and fiscal grounds.

Would a Voluntary Army Be Racially Unbalanced?

It has been argued that a military career would be so much more attractive to the poor than to the well-to-do that volunteer armed services would be staffed disproportionately by the poor. Since Negroes constitute a high proportion of the poor, it is further argued that volunteer armed forces would be largely Negro.

There is first a question of fact. This tendency is present today in exaggerated form—the present levels of pay are *comparatively* more attractive to Negroes than the higher levels of pay in voluntary armed forces would be. Yet the fraction of persons in the armed forces who are Negro is roughly the same as in the population at large. It has been estimated that even if every qualified Negro who does not now serve were to serve, whites would still constitute a substantial majority of the armed forces. And that every qualified Negro who does not now serve *would* serve is a wholly unrealistic possibility. The military services require a wide variety of skills and offer varied opportunities. They have always appealed to people of varied classes and backgrounds and they will continue to do so. Particularly if pay and amenities were made more attractive, there is every reason to expect that they would draw from all segments of the community.

In part, this argument involves invalid extrapolation from the present conscripted army to a voluntary army. Because we conscript, we pay salaries that are attractive only to the disadvantaged among us.

Beyond this question of fact, there is the more basic question of principle. Clearly, it is a good thing not a bad thing to offer better alternatives to the currently disadvantaged. The argument to the contrary rests on a political judgment: that a high ratio of Negroes in the armed services would exacerbate racial tensions at home and provide in the form of ex-soldiers a military trained group to foment violence. Perhaps there is something to this. My own inclination is to regard it as the reddest of red herrings. Our government should discriminate neither in the civil nor in the military services. We must handle our domestic problems as best we can and not use them as an excuse for denying Negroes opportunities in the military service.

Would a Voluntary Army Have Sufficient Flexibility?

One of the advantages cited for conscription is that it permits great flexibility in the size of the armed services. Let military needs suddenly increase, and draft calls can be rapidly stepped up, and conversely.

This is a real advantage—but can easily be overvalued. Emergencies must be met with forces in being, however they are recruited. Many months now elapse between an increase in draft calls and the availability of additional trained men.

The key question is how much flexibility is required. Recruitment by voluntary means could provide considerable flexibility—at a cost. The way to do so would be to make pay and conditions of service more attractive than is required to recruit the number of men that it is anticipated will be needed. There would then be an excess of volunteers—queues. If the number of men required increased, the queues could be shortened and conversely.

The change in scale involved in a shift from conditions like the present to a total war is a very different matter. If the military judgment is that, in such a contingency, there would be time and reason to expand the armed forces manyfold, either universal military training, to provide a trained reserve force, or standby provisions for conscription could be justified. Both are very different from the use of conscription to man the standing army in time of peace or brushfire wars or wars like that in Vietnam which require recruiting only a minority of young men.

The flexibility provided by conscription has another side. It means that, at least for a time, the administration and the military services can proceed fairly arbitrarily in committing U. S. forces. The voluntary method provides a continuing referendum of the public at large. The popularity or unpopularity of the activities for which the Armed Forces are used will clearly affect the ease of recruiting men. This is a consideration that will be regarded by some as an advantage of conscription, by others, including myself, as a disadvantage.

Is a "Professional Army" a Political Danger?

There is little question that large Armed Forces plus the industrial complex required to support them constitute an ever-present threat to political freedom. Our free institutions would certainly be safer if the conditions of the world permitted us to maintain far smaller armed forces.

The valid fear has been converted into an invalid argument against voluntary armed forces. They would constitute a professional army, it is said, that would lack contact with the populace and become an independent political force, whereas a conscripted army remains basically a citizen army. The fallacy in this argument is that the danger comes primarily from the officers, who are now and always have been a professional corps of volunteers. A few examples from history will show that the danger to political stability is largely unrelated to the method of recruiting enlisted men.

Napoleon and Franco both rose to power at the head of conscripts. The recent military takeover in Argentina was by armed forces recruiting enlisted men by conscription. Britain and the U. S. have maintained freedom while relying primarily on volunteers; Switzerland and Sweden, while using conscription. It is hard to find any relation historically between the method of recruiting enlisted men and the political threat from the armed forces.

However we recruit enlisted men, it is essential that we adopt practices that will guard against the political danger of creating a military corps with loyalties of its own and out of contact with the broader body politic. Fortunately, we have so far largely avoided this danger. The broad basis of recruitment to the military academies, by geography as well as social and economic factors, the ROTC programs in the colleges, the recruitment of officers from enlisted men, and similar measures, have all contributed to this result.

For the future, we need to follow policies that will foster lateral recruitment into the officer corps from civilian activities—rather than primarily promotion from within. The military services no less than the civil service need and will benefit from in-and-outers. For the political gain, we should be willing to bear the higher financial costs involved in fairly high turnover and rather short average terms of service for officers. We should follow personnel policies that will continue to make at least a period of military service as an officer attractive to young men from many walks of life.

There is no way of avoiding the political danger altogether. But it can be minimized as readily with a volunteer as with a conscripted army.

THE TRANSITION TO A VOLUNTEER ARMY

Given the will, there is no reason why the transition to volunteer armed forces cannot begin at once and proceed gradually by a process of trial and error. We do not need precise and accurate knowledge of the levels of pay and amenities that will be required. We need take no irreversible step.

Out of simple justice, we should in any event raise the pay and improve the living conditions of enlisted men. It if were proposed explicitly that a special income tax of 50 per cent be imposed on enlisted men in the armed services, there would be cries of outrage. Yet that is what our present pay scales plus conscription amount to. If we started rectifying this injustice, the number of "real" volunteers would increase, even while conscription continued. Experience would show how responsive the number of volunteers is to the terms offered and how much these terms would have to be improved to attract enough men. As the number of volunteers increased, the lash of compulsion could fade away.

This picture is overdrawn in one important respect. Unless it is clear that conscription is definitely to be abolished in a reasonably short time, the armed services will not have sufficient incentive to improve their recruitment and personnel policies. They will be tempted to procrastinate, relying on the crutch of conscription. The real survival strength of conscription is that it eases the life of the top military command. Hence, it would be highly desirable to have a definite termination date set for conscription.

CONCLUSION

The case for abolishing conscription and recruiting our armed forces by voluntary methods seems to me overwhelming. One of the greatest advances in human freedom was the commutation of taxes in kind to taxes in money. We have reverted to a barbarous custom. It is past time that we regain our heritage.

21

Politics and Conscription:
A Proposal to Replace the Draft

BRUCE K. CHAPMAN

Americans in the past decade have become increasingly aware of the injustices of life in the nation's poverty pockets—an awareness made possible, it should be noted, by the virtual disappearance of poverty as a threatening norm. The intelligent public, at least, also has become increasingly sensitive to the seriousness of secondary forms of racial discrimination which previously went largely unnoticed because of the prevalence of more gross forms.

But if, in several areas, injustices once considered secondary and qualified have now in the national conscience assumed first prominence (and quite properly so), the fundamental injustice of military conscription, which any previous generation of Americans recognized instantly, has now become a moral issue compromised, sidetracked and interpreted—devastatingly—as subtle. After 15 years the draft is at last again a public question, but the focus upon it is woefully fractured. Many supposed reformers of the draft seek merely to build a greater conscription on top of the one that serves the military, thereby exploiting the plight of the draftee rather than ameliorating it. Critics who would never have been so naïve as to accept at face value government statistics on, say, the contribution of public housing to the elimination of poverty or the apologetics of segregationist authorities on the happy state of southern Negroes, quite readily accept the most shoddy, hollow and self-incriminating rationalizations for continuation of a draft propounded by interested departments of the Pentagon.

It is remarkable that the present conscription program has been so little scrutinized. Although the draft is the only institution in society other than prisons to appropriate in full the liberty, time, productivity, and security of an individual, many persons have come to view it as a permanent feature of our life. Yet a draft, by definition, is antithetic to a free society. The "nation in arms" traditionally has been a Napoleonic and Prussian ideal, while in Britain and the United States impressment has always been seen as unjustifiable except when the security of the state requires it. That principle lay behind the drafts of the Civil War, World War I and World War II. It was understood in each case that when national security could be maintained without conscription the draft would be terminated.

Adapted from a paper of the Ripon Society. The author is Ripon Society representative to the Conference and author of *The Wrong Man in Uniform*.

Today we are arguing in America whether this deferment or that is more "fair"; whether the Selective Service System is consistent from board to board; whether this or that prominent individual deserves his deferment; whether draft-card burners and other protesters should be tried and punished by the courts or tried and drafted by the Selective Service, and so on. Indeed, what should be apparent by now in the debate over fairness in our present draft system, or under the alternative drafts being proposed, is that the only truly fair system of man-power recruitment in a nation that has reached the point of not needing a draft is no draft at all. Today, as the result of a burgeoning manpower supply, burgeoning federal revenues, and the rising sophistication of military skill requirements, we have reached that point.

THE DRAFT AND POLITICS

The confused focus of the draft issue is as much a product of political indifference and political manipulation in recent years as of misguided criticism from some reformers in recent months. Leaders as diverse as Adlai Stevenson and Barry Goldwater advocated abolition of the draft in their Presidential campaigns, but Congress, with responsibility every four years for extending or ending the draft, has given the matter only the most perfunctory attention, holding ten minutes of debate on it in the Senate in 1963, for example. General Lewis B. Hershey, Director of the Selective Service System, has asserted that the reason for so little debate is that the Armed Services Committees have always done their homework on the issue and found no reason for changes. However, there is little evidence that such homework ever really probed deeply into the draft since the present so-called Universal Military Service and Training Act was written in 1951. The inequities that are now public knowledge existed in the system for years without Congress concerning itself with them, the best evidence that the real cause for lack of debate on the draft was lack of information. The tightly controlled hearings held briefly last summer by the House Armed Services Committee, after some six months of public prodding by other Congressmen and the press, further demonstrated how really out of touch with the problem Congress has been. At no time during those hearings did the Committee seriously ask itself whether the draft is necessary at all. Indeed, Representative L. Mendel Rivers (D-S.C.), Committee Chairman, opened the hearings by declaring that a draft of some kind is necessary.

Where the Congressional leadership has tended towards indifference, the Administration has tended to sidetrack the issue into closed studies. The first time the call for draft reform was forcefully brought before the public was in a series of speeches on the subject presented on the House floor by a group of Republicans in early 1964. However, three days before their scheduled presentation, the White House announced a committee on the draft reform to be set up within the Pentagon and which was to report within a year, by spring of 1965. This move had the effect of thwarting the draft reform movement for nearly a year and a half, for it took that long for critics to realize that the Pentagon had no intention of releasing its study.

There are now indications that the Defense Department study as of May, 1965, had come to the tentative conclusion that the draft could be abolished and an all-volunteer modern military instituted. One can only speculate on the reasons for the suppression of that report at that time: the escalated Vietnam

War, which didn't so much indicate the need for a draft as the need to appear before world opinion as "determined" and "willing to sacrifice."

In early 1966 criticism of the draft again became widespread, with various povertarians charging that Negroes were bearing an unfair share of draft quotas (a charge later effectively rebutted) and with largely the same group of Republicans as had protested the draft's operations in 1964 now producing evidence of inconsistent applications of policy from board to board and state to state and demanding that the Pentagon report be released and a full congressional study undertaken.

The Administration responded not by releasing the Pentagon report, but by issuing what Rep. Thomas B. Curtis (R.-Mo.) appropriately called "a report on a report." The 22½-page, double-spaced, wide-margined release barely got into the draft problem and raised far more questions than it answered. Rejecting a volunteer military, the Pentagon estimated its cost at from $6 billion to $17 billion with no breakdown of those figures to explain why such large sums would be needed. (Secretary McNamara in 1965 estimated the cost of a volunteer military at $4 billion on one occasion and at $20 billion on another.[1]) Just how such conclusions were reached was left a mystery. For example, to justify its apparent decision that higher pay would not have much effect on enlistments the Pentagon paper described part (and just a part) of a survey of boys 16-19 which asked whether "pay alone" would induce them to join the military if there were no draft. The "surprising" findings were that "equal pay with civilian life was considered the most important inducement by less than 4 per cent."[2] But, of course, "pay alone" is not the "most important inducement" to persons planning almost any career, and especially to 16- to 19-year-olds, who not only are idealistic but have no idea how really low military wages are now. Good wages unquestionably are *an* important inducement to any career, and previous surveys of public opinion made by the military cited low pay as a major reason for the relative unattractiveness of the military life in the eyes of civilians. (It would have been interesting to see the question of influences turned around. A 1962 survey of first-term enlistees in the Army revealed that 63.3 per cent counted the draft "very little or no" influence on their decision to enlist, while 17.4 per cent said it was only of "some influence." Only 19.3 per cent said they were "very much influenced" by the draft.[3]

Later attempts by Congressmen and other critics to pry loose the Pentagon calculations were unsuccessful. But before critics could launch a full attack on the Pentagon's "report on a report," the White House once again stymied reformers by announcing a blue-ribbon Presidential "National Advisory Commission on Selective Service."

The Presidential Commission is less vulnerable to attack than was the Pentagon study, but considering its origins and the fact that several of the same people who worked on the Pentagon study staff are working as staff on the Commission study, there is reason to believe that at least part of its motivation is similarly political. Undoubtedly the distinguished Commission members are sincere in their desire to find ways to improve the draft system. However, a Commission source indicated in mid-October—just two and one-half months before the Commission's report was scheduled to be on the President's desk—that only two "official" meetings had been held. Perhaps the very skilled staff men have gleaned information and opinions from knowledgeable people on all sides of the draft question. However, there has been no opportunity for knowledgeable draft critics—particularly proponents of a volunteer military—to examine, challenge, or debate the premises, facts, and theories with which the Commission is working. It is hard to imagine the suppression of this latest study (it was due in January), but its value certainly will be lessened by the fact that its operations were clothed in mystery.

Meanwhile, in the course of these developments, the unexplained conclusions of the Pentagon's "report on its report" have detoured many critics from the question of whether in fact America could dispense with the draft. Fifteen years ago—indeed at any previous time in American history—the necessity of any draft would have been the first point of contention.

Now, however, the draft critics have scattered their attacks and proposals in so many directions that it will be difficult for any reform to overcome resistance of the still very strong lobby for the present system. Indeed, most of the proposed reforms would not really provide a system more effective militarily or more equitable than the one we have today.

THE DEFICIENT ALTERNATIVES

The most common alternatives proposed are a lottery and a national service. The lottery, as General Hershey has observed, would merely substitute impersonal injustices for human injustices. Some people find such a system neater, more abstractly pure, more principled. But to the young married father taken instead of a school dropout, or the future but as-yet-untrained doctor taken instead of the unemployed worker, the system's orderliness would seem small solace. Nor would the country's interest in obtaining skilled technicians and other specialists for the military while leaving the civilian sector with its critical personnel be served by a lottery.

Some lottery proponents protest that certain deferments would be allowed after all under a lottery, but since the nation has millions more young men of draft age than it needs in the service, those deferments would have to be broad indeed to maintain a semblance of universality, and the only difference between that kind of system and selective service would be in the "Russian roulette" irrationality of the lottery.

The lottery still would not solve the problem of resentment caused by some young men being drafted and others missing service. By what might be called its method of planned capriciousness, the lottery would merely build one more anxiety into lives already troubled by the absurdities and dehumanizing impersonality of modern society.

"National Service" is even more problematical than a lottery. Like a lottery, it would not even pretend to deal with the backward manpower policies that underpin the draft. Indeed, institution of national service would make replacement of those policies even more difficult by building upon them. The example problem always foremost in the minds of national service proponents as they imagine the benefits of their system is the young college graduate who would like to go into the Peace Corps but cannot do so without also (possibly) serving two years in the draft. However, no national service proponent has yet worried about the men of many skills and patriotic perspectives—including ones with ability and desire who would like to join the Peace Corps, to use the national service prototype—who still would be drafted under national service to fill up the Armed Forces. While options for service would increase for some, their good fortune would simply mock those unwillingly channeled through an unreformed military draft.

National service springs less from a desire to reform the draft than to reform society. Men and women who have experienced the fulfillment of volunteer service to mankind understandably would like everyone to have such an experience, even though the voluntary element might have to be removed to accomplish it. Moreover, national service proponents are concerned that many young men who might otherwise enjoy such an experience on their own (the Peace Corps prototype) are discouraged by the draft today and should be given another option.

It has been charged against national service that to achieve its objectives would require wholly unparalleled state control of human endeavor, far beyond the constitutional provision for conscription to provide for the common defense. Originally, proponents argued in reply that "assignments" to various social projects bearing the government stamp of approval would take into account individual interests and abilities. But the same might be said of the Communist system, the only difference being that national service proposed to conscript persons for only two or three years (though longer periods have also been suggested). Lately, however, some key advocates apparently have decided that the non-military alternative service would be "voluntary." Essentially, in terms of human freedom, that is scant improvement, for while the practical choice would no longer be merely the indication of a desire for work in a social project of one kind or another, it would still be to join national service or be drafted by the military. So instead of a system of total compulsion, we would have one that is compulsion for some and mere coercion for others, but which still is an infringement on human liberty if, in fact, no draft is really necessary.

The administrative problems of national service are no less staggering than the philosophical problems. Since many of the projects proposed would be of a social service nature, there would be little fairness in coercing young men into them while letting young women go free. With 2 million men turning draft age each year (by the mid-Seventies), 1.2 million of them unneeded by the military, and with 2 million women a year, and assuming a three-year term for men and two years for women, a pool of 7.6 million, largely drained from an already tight labor market, would be potentially available for national service. Obviously, there are not nearly enough jobs to be done through VISTA, the Peace Corps, etc., to occupy any appreciable percentage of such a number, nor money enough to pay them. (Training costs for one Peace Corps volunteer: $7800.)

National service advocates calculate manpower supply differently, of course, and usually, when pressed, some decide (though not Dr. Margaret Mead) to exempt women after all. They also point out that perhaps 15 per cent of young people are unfit for any service. But then the advocates also use present manpower figures (1.8 million men a year) even while admitting national service could not be instituted until the early Seventies, by which time the yearly 18-year-old pool will be up to 2 million.

Also, the figures of men to be allocated to various approved national service projects are computed on a yearly basis, as if one year's supply of manpower were all national service was asking, instead of two, three, or more. The favorite Peace Corps program is always increased in national service projection to four or five times its present size, failing even then to note that less than a third of the Peace Corpsmen now serving are draft-age and that Peace Corps selectivity in choosing volunteers is far too tight, even now, to permit wholesale expansion, especially through a system of coercion.

Many new thousands of men also are seen "serving" in the Job Corps, although how the Job Corps can be considered the moral equivalent of either the Peace Corps or the military itself remains a mystery.

It is indicated by national service advocates that many projects would be privately operated by such organizations as churches and civil rights groups, but publicly subsidized. No indication, however, is given as to how such projects will be selected. If an NAACP project is all right, why shouldn't an SNCC project be? If the Friends or the Catholics are acceptable, why aren't the Black Muslims?

Finally, national service offers no fair outlet for the man whose service to his country simply does not fit into some bureaucratic scheme. It is said that the future doctor would be helped in understanding his career if before medical school he worked as a hospital menial through national service. That is certainly questionable, both from the standpoint of the individual and the country's need for practicing physicians. But in any case, what similarly valuable training does the national service offer the future but as-yet-untrained painter (highway beautification?) or poet (editing the Job Corps yearbook?) or musician? Such people in our society of diversity would be just as misused by national service as by the draft, and maybe more so.

National service would not end the draft's injustices but compound them. There would still be deferments, not only for the physically or mentally unfit, but for young fathers, men with occupations critical to the national security and probably farmers. Some men would serve and some would not.

One would not want to depreciate the social goals cited by national service or the contributions, present and potential, of the Peace Corps, VISTA, the Job Corps, the proposed Teachers Corps or Health Corps. But meeting social needs and opportunities by grafting a national service onto the draft would be like taking cough medicine to cure an earache. It would be an inappropriate way of dealing with social needs as well as a counterproductive way of treating draft inequities. Its very proposal is a case of displaced social concern.

Voluntarism is a much more powerful instrument for social advance. It is as hard to imagine Peace Corpsmen who joined only to avoid the draft as it is to imagine "assigning" men to the clergy. If certain social objectives are worthwhile, they are worth pursuing by means of a joint government-private effort. What is needed is a semi-public foundation that would finance on a subsistence basis volunteer work of social worth. Such opportunity for service would be available not only on a yearly basis, but for college and high school students during the summertime.

However, a gargantuan Brook Farm, spurred by compulsion, as Harvard President Nathan Pusey has said, would be "a colossal waste of time."

Unhappily, the waste of time occurs in even considering national service, or a lottery, as alternatives to today's draft. Congress for good reason is unlikely to adopt either, beyond perhaps a marginal change or two in the present system.

But such changes, whether giving an outright exemption to Peace Corps-men or drafting from the lower age groups first, would not constitute truly relevant reform.

What the national service and lottery schemes do accomplish is to confuse the issue.

WHY VOLUNTARISM?

The practical case for a volunteer military rests in largest part on the new man-power and financial possibilities for the complete replacement of conscription. Not since the early part of the nineteenth century has America had such a high percentage of its population in the draft-age category. As the post-World War II baby boom comes of age, the number of young men is doubling. The Ameri-can generational revolution reordering political life thus has tremendous rele-vance to the military institution as well. Where some 1,100,000 men turned draft age each year in the early Fifties, some 1,800,000 are turning draft-age this year, and in 1975 the figure will be up to 2,100,000. That means an immensely expanded pool of potential volunteers.[4]

Secondly, the increasing sophistication of military technology has restruc-tured the nature of manpower needs. A radar technician is several times more expensive to train and several times more expensive to lose. The draft does not attract such people and draftees do not ordinarily become highly skilled tech-nicians. (The benefits of the military's famed training schools usually are not lavished on men who will serve only a year and a half after processing through them.) It is said that the draft does tend, through its threat, to get men suitable for technical training to enlist on their own. But these men too are largely a man-power waste for the military. While the turnover rate of draftees fluctuates from 90 to 97 per cent, the turnover rate for first-term enlistees (and officers) is also very high, ordinarily over 75 per cent.

Indeed, in a normal year, over 500,000 men—out of a total force of between 2,700,000 to 3,200,000 men—leave the military. That is one out of every six men; it is hard to imagine a business operating with such a high annual loss. According to Brigadier General Lynn D. Smith (Army), even before the Vietnam buildup, some 43 per cent of Army men at any given time had less than a year's experi-ence.[5]

According to General Smith, "the basic problem of the Army (is) too much personnel turnover." Commanders complain, says Smith, that "As soon as we are able to operate as a unit, the trained men leave and we have to start all over again."

The equivalent of ten divisions of men are in training at any given time. They tie up the energies not only of themselves, but also of thousands of career men who must do the training. A military efficiency report by Ralph J. Cordiner, former Chairman of General Electric, to President Eisenhower in 1957 described the situation at many training camps: "I found antagonism and bitterness over the draft. They were checking off the days until they get out. We must devote 25 per cent of our military effort to training men who don't stay. The trainers are discouraged. They resemble the poor teacher whose every class flunks."[6]

Interviews with servicemen, trainers and draftees alike, indicate that the situa-tion has not much improved in the last few years. Cordiner's conclusions of 1957 seem even more valid now, with our increased pool of potential volunteers: "Reduced to its simplest terms, the personnel problem appears to be a matter of quality as opposed to quantity. It is not a matter of the total number of people on hand, but it is a matter of the level of retention of those possessing a high degree of leadership quality and those with the technical training and experience the services so urgently need. It is a matter of not being able . . . to keep and challenge and develop the kinds of people for the periods of time necessary for them to make an effective contribution to the operation of the force. . . . It is foolish for the armed forces to obtain highly advanced weapons systems and not have men of sufficient competence to understand, operate and maintain such equipment."

The cost of the draft in money and manpower is enormous, and in the last analysis, perhaps incalculable. But it is worth noting that the turnover rate for career men is only 15 per cent per year. If that sort of rate, common in Canada's volunteer system, could be maintained throughout our military, we could effect an annual savings numbering in the hundreds of thousands of personnel and all the time and money required to train them.

The draft is the biggest obstacle to lowering the turnover rate and, hence, an obstacle to increased military efficiency. Low wages are behind much of the problem. Because of the costly draft and the sure supply of manpower it provides (in terms of quantity, not quality), Congress has long held down the wages of the military and particularly of the first-termers. Today an entering private in our military makes slightly more than a Rumanian peasant on a collective farm: $90.60 per month.[7] That amount is only 20 per cent more than he would have earned per month just after World War II, 20 years ago, despite the fact of 60 per cent inflation of the dollar in that period.

The American private also makes substantially less than his counterparts in Canada or Britain—where volunteer systems operate—or his counterpart in Germany, with its selective service system. The difference in pay is magnified by the gap in standards and costs of living between these other nations and ours. Nor, it must be added, has any of them the great productive margin of the United States to financially support its military.

Draft defenders protest that the American private's pay does go up after only four months, which is true, but it only goes up $4.30 a month and stays at that level for the rest of his two-year term. Then and only then do the Armed Services hold out the promise of a bonus, and of course by that time a soldier who barely has had pocket money for two years has already decided to leave the services for good.

The sad fact is that our military, wittingly or not, often discourages perfectly worthy people from making a military career. They are propagandized against marrying early and if they do marry while still in the lower four pay grades and with under four years of service they are unlikely to get dependency allowances. The average man who wants to start a family cannot afford to remain in the military.

If a man does make a career of the service he and his wife find themselves living in often unattractive quarters in often poorly planned military communities. Whether from ignorance of modern planning techniques or from some misguided worship of the spartan mystique, the military has constructed some of the most sterile and unesthetic communal agglomerations in the country. Psychologically, such an environment cannot help but have an influence on a potential careerist's attitude toward the services.

Another negative psychological influence is the draft's own aura of compulsion which carries over to the military as a whole, making it seem less desirable a career to many people than it need be. It is not affirming to a mechanic, for example, to know that the job he enjoys and to which he has committed himself by choice is done by his fellow worker, a disgruntled draftee, under compulsion. A volunteer system would improve military morale and the popular attitude towards the military career enormously; more volunteers would be the result.

Yet another manpower policy change that would abet a volunteer system would be a substantial lowering of our unrealistic induction standards, particularly in regard to physical requirements. Rejection rates among our NATO allies are 18 per cent in Italy, 18 per cent in France, 25 per cent in Norway, as examples, compared to the 47-52 per cent which is the fluctuating average in the United States. A year or two ago many well-meaning observers saw in the then rising draft rejection rates a sign of increasingly poor physical condition of our nation's young people, but the truth was that, faced with an overabundance of available manpower and already having loosened requirements for other deferments, the Pentagon and the Selective Service simply were increasing their "selectivity," both in terms of objective criteria and of interpretation of data. Some months rejections ran as high as 57 per cent. However, with the advent of the Vietnam buildup in the middle of 1965 the rejection rate began to drop, until by the summer of 1966, it was down to 39 per cent, the Korean War level.

Such manipulation of standards, of course, is one of the inequities of the present draft. Not only do deferment and induction physical test standards vary from board to board, but they vary from time to time. Under a volunteer system, the standards would be much lower than the norm of the past few years. Positions and work would be found for men now being judged unfit because they are unusually tall or short, thin or fat, or have some chronic physical problem that would make them unsuitable for combat. Since only one in five military jobs is of a combat nature, there is no good reason to apply standards of combat fitness to every man who volunteers for service. Indeed, there obviously are many career men in the military right now who could not meet those entering standards, though, of course, they once did. But fat or thin they still make quite good supply officers, clerks and—presumably—Pentagon generals.

Similarly, the sophistication of new skills required by the military also makes possible and desirable the greater use of civilians in technical, non-combat positions and, at the other end of the skill spectrum, for maintenance work. There is nothing radical or untried about such a proposal; the Seabees of World War II are merely one classic example of trained men recruited from civilian life. The principle of hiring people who already are trained is well-established, but it could be much more widely applied.

All of these proposals, however, would cost money; funds for better recruitment programs, better college scholarship programs for potential officers, more attention to side-benefits and, particularly, higher salaries.

However, the upper estimate of $17 billion given by the Penatgon as the cost of a volunteer military can be dismissed as a scare figure; it would mean an *average* increase of $6,000 a year for everyone in the services. A much more reasonable estimate is suggested by Dr. Walter Oi, Professor of Economics at the University of Washington and a participant in the original Defense Department study of 1964-65. With a decreased need for approximately 200,000 personnel as the result of an all-professional system, and a turnover of no more than 650,000 per year (which seems very high indeed), Oi believes the volunteer service could be ushered in for considerably less than the $6 billion figure cited as a minimum by the Pentagon.

Other draft experts, such as Rep. Thomas B. Curtis, believe that increased efficiency and higher morale would in the long run actually mean a savings rather than a loss, and that regaining hundreds of thousands of men for civilian productivity who otherwise would have passed through the draft would mean a considerable help to the general national economy.

A full-scale Congressional probe, made up of members of the Labor and Education, Joint Economics and Appropriations Committees as well as the Armed Services Committees is required to fully explore the economics of a volunteer system. It should be undertaken in January by the new Congress. But even the result of such a probe would be more to set boundaries of cost than to establish a hard figure, for too many intangibles of attitude obtain and cannot be programmed in anyone's computer.

However, at this point it does seem appropriate to note that America's national government treasury is growing by more than $6 billion *per year*. The United States can well afford an improved military system and the abolition of the draft.

Obviously, many other practical questions and accusations about a volunteer military still remain to be answered. The principle of freedom against conscription is no longer sufficient in many minds to justify alone the draft's abolition.

General Hershey, for instance, has charged that a volunteer, all-professional military would be made up of "mercenaries" and should therefore be prevented. But "mercenary" also, then, could be applied to those men who are "careerists" today. It could be applied to the men who have served in the Armed Forces during the overwhelming proportion of our history when we had no draft. And it could be applied to General Hershey.

If a "mercenary" is someone who is paid for his living, then we are all mercenaries. If a "mercenary" is someone who is paid an inordinately large sum for his work, then the word still does not apply to the men who would make up a volunteer service; no one has proposed paying military men more than a competitive wage.

Another charge leveled against the volunteer service is that it would soon become predominantly Negro, just for the very reason that it would be relatively attractive financially. However, already there are proportionately more Negroes than whites who reenlist in the services. That is because of the military's lack of racial discrimination, but also because the present low wages are more attractive to Negroes than to whites. The raising of wages would tend to attract whites as well as Negroes.

But even if the undue concern that Negroes would be more attracted than whites were based on a correct appraisal of the employment market forces at work, there would be no threat of an all-Negro military: There wouldn't be enough Negroes to fill it. Negroes tend to have a higher unfitness rejection rate than whites, but even if *every single Negro male*, fit or not, interested or not, upon turning 18—approximately 250,000 next year—were the join the Armed Forces each year, there would not be enough to meet the annual personnel turnover, even under the volunteer system. Significant Negro over-representation in a volunteer service, then, is more than an exaggerated problem; it is a nonexistent one.

Another dubious assertion is that a volunteer military would be unfair because poor people would be attracted to it and would, as Congressman Charles S. Joelson (D.-N.J.) puts it, "be sent off to be killed." This argument ignores the fact that wages would be raised for officers (mostly college educated) and other highly trained men along with everyone else and, therefore, that the services would be as socially representative under a professional system as they are now. It also ignores the fact, previously stated, that four-fifths of the military's jobs are noncombat, and also that the actual statistical chance of a man dying while in the service is exactly the same, based on 1965 figures, as in civilian life: 2.5 in 1000. A policeman's job is probably more hazardous than most soldiers', but no one proposes (yet) that we conscript for the police force, or for that matter, the fire department. Indeed, if a man wants a military career and finds he can enter one with hope of reasonable financial compensation, who can be so condescending as to suggest he is being exploited?

A more reasonable argument than any of these against a voluntary service is that such a system would be a less flexible tool for manpower recruitment than would the draft. In answer, it must be said that to some extent such inflexibility of numbers would be compensated by the greater flexibility and reliability of trained, seasoned personnel. However, any further problem could be corrected by maintaining a slight margin of surplus manpower above that required under normal circumstances. This surplus might be made up from the saved manpower in training units under a volunteer system; it might be made up through over-recruitment, even though that would mean a higher overhead in wages; or, it might be made up of a truly ready reserve system, consisting of well-paid veterans whose call-up would be considered routine in times of manpower expansion and not as signifying a "national emergency" as does the call-up of our very unready ready reserves today. In any case, the surplus would cushion any minor military manpower reorganization or any major transition to a massive land-war strategy (e.g., World War II) and the temporary restoration of the draft.

REACHING THE VOLUNTEER GOAL

Implementation of a volunteer manpower recruitment system would require a transitional period during which a draft would operate. However, the transitional draft should be quite different from the present system, with methods and planning that would encourage the development of the new system rather than retard it. The present draft, attempting to perpetuate the myth of "universality" in its application, uses deferments and rejection standards to regulate the pool of available manpower to the immediate need for new bodies. The transitional draft would seek through incentives and lower rejection standards to widen the flow of volunteers as much as possible. The rehabilitation program for men who have failed the military entrance examination for education, instituted under the pressure of the rapid Vietnam manpower buildup, would become (for volunteers only, however) a permanent manifestation of that policy. So too would a completely new project designed to utilize those men who fail the physical tests through special noncombat-oriented training programs.

Simultaneously, military pay would be increased, with volunteers paid more than draftees. Congress understandably has opposed such discrimination in the past, but the procedure seems more justifiable when used over a brief period of a year or two as a help in priming the increased flow of volunteers. The present "bonus" program for reenlistment would be somewhat curtailed as a less effective means of gaining a man's commitment to a military career. A systematic improvement of living conditions for volunteers would be undertaken, as would a special recruitment program for utilizing more civilians in noncombat positions.

Meanwhile, the draft system itself would reverse its priorities, drafting younger men first, as, in fact, the Pentagon now recommends. The same deferments as are now available would obtain, though of course fewer men at that age would be physically unfit, fathers, employed in jobs critical to the national security, etc. Students, however, would be deferred only after they had been notified of their induction; at that time they would be allowed to sign a commitment to serve in a branch of their choice after completion of their college careers and given a deferment on that basis. Of course, they also could opt to serve at once.

Under the transitional draft, the Selective Service System would publish and distribute to all registrants a booklet fully explaining all the options before them and broadly describing the career opportunities in the various services. (Today, except for a skimpy fold-over flyer whose information is couched in a kind of scolding bureaucratese and merely made available to registrants who request it, the Selective Service System makes virtually no attempt to educate young men in their obligations and choices. For example, one is told he has the "right" to appeal, but he is not given a clue as to how to handle that appeal.) Even when the volunteer system was completely implemented, the Selective Service would continue to register young men and to classify them, against the day when massive conscription might have to be reinstated. The physical examinations given all young men would be designed—as they are only theoretically designed today —as much to provide all young men, including those from disadvantaged backgrounds, with advice on their state of health and to direct the sick ones to help, as to provide the military with an account of their fitness for potential induction.

Finally, during the transitional draft, the registration and classification of men would remain the responsibility of local boards, though under tighter national guidelines. But actual selection of men would be conducted through a national pool, to end the inequities that result when categories of registrants are inducted in some areas but not in others. Data-processing computers would be initiated into the national procedure.

The transitional draft described here really would be an improved *permanent draft* over what we have today, or, for that matter, over national service or a lottery. But some men would still serve under compulsion while others served by personal choice and still others served not at all. Such inequity, inevitable under any system of compulsion, and the new reality of manpower surfeit make the real virtue of the transitional draft just that—it is transitional, planned to smooth the way to an all-volunteer, all-professional military.

NOTES

[1] "In answer to a question at a Congressional hearing on the defense budget on February 26, 1965, McNamara estimated $4 billion. . . . In an interview with *This*

Week, December 5, 1965, he said at least $20 billion." Cited by George F. Gilder and Bruce K. Chapman, *The Party that Lost its Head* (New York: Knopf, 1966), p. 314.

[2] Statement of Thomas D. Morris, Assistant Secretary of Defense (Manpower), June 30, 1966.

[3] A 5 per cent Army-wide sample as of November 2, 1962.

[4] U. S. Census, interview, June 8, 1966.

[5] Brigadier General Lynn D. Smith, "The Unsolved Problem," *Military Review*, June, 1964.

[6] Report of the Defense Advisory Committee on Professional and Technical Compensation, "A Modern Concept of Compensation for Personnel of the Uniformed Services," March, 1957.

[7] Pentagon figures, August, 1966. A pay raise of 3½ per cent this past summer will be eaten up in one year's inflation alone.

22

The Costs and Implications of an All-Volunteer Force

WALTER Y. OI

The draft constitutes one means of supplying the Armed Services with qualified personnel.* Except for a brief lapse from March, 1947, to June, 1948, a military draft has been in continuous operation in the United States since 1940. Under provisions of the current draft law, every qualified male incurs a liability to serve for two years in active military service and up to six years in the standby reserves. Some men obtain deferments or exemptions from this liability, while others discharge it through voluntary entry into military service. The remaining qualified youths have, however, been involuntarily inducted into active duty service.

In times of war when nearly everyone must serve, alternatives to a draft are judged to be too costly or infeasible. The peacetime demands for military personnel are, however, considerably smaller, with the consequence that a draft becomes selective. Rules must therefore be established to determine which qualified youths will be involuntarily selected. The equity of the selection process (which under the current draft translates into deferment policies) is then questioned. These debates over the equity of a draft are testimony to the fact that some alternatives should be given serious consideration and perhaps even adopted.

One of several proposed alternatives to the current draft is the establishment of an all-volunteer force.[1] To say that a particular alternative such as an all-volunteer force is preferable to the current draft implies that the cost of the

The author is a professor in the Department of Economics, University of Washington.

* A considerable amount of the research for this paper was done while I served as a consultant for the Office of the Assistant Secretary of Defense from June, 1964, to July, 1965. I am deeply indebted to many members of the OASD staff who provided assistance and information. The opinions and conclusions which appear in this paper are solely my responsibility and do *not* in any way reflect the position of the Department of Defense. I am especially indebted to Mr. William A. Gorham, Dr. Harold Wool, and Prof. Stuart H. Altman who provided counsel and advice in my year of service on the manpower study. They are absolved of responsibility for any errors of fact or interpretation which may still remain in this paper. A shorter version of this paper which emphasizes the economic cost of the draft appears in the *Papers and Proceedings* of the American Economic Association.

alternative is, in some sense, lower than the cost of procuring military personnel with the present Selective Service System. If the draft were abolished, military pay and other recruitment incentives must be improved to attract enough recruits to meet prescribed manpower objectives. In his statement before the House Armed Services Committee, the Hon. T. D. Morris (Assistant Secretary of Defense) indicated that an all-volunteer force of 2.65 million men would increase the military payroll budget by 4 to 17 billion dollars per year.[2]

The budgetary cost of the Department of Defense (hereafter abbreviated DOD) is *not* the economic cost of labor resources which are allocated to the uniformed services. The presence of a draft has affected both the level and structure of military pay. Moreover, the men who are in the Armed Forces were recruited and conscripted through manpower procurement programs which rely in differing degrees on the coercion of a draft liability. Adoption of a purely voluntary force entails increases in pay as well as substantial changes in the procurement channels through which men are recruited. The composition and structure of an all-volunteer force would thus differ significantly from that of the present force containing many men who were enlisted under the pressure of a draft liability. The structure of the Armed Forces is thus a product of manpower procurement and retention policies. In this paper, I shall compare the costs of two procurements systems; a purely voluntary system, and the system which has evolved under the current draft law.

The implications of projected military manpower demands are first examined in Parts I and II for the two cases—a mixed force under a continued draft and a voluntary force. Part III presents estimates of the financial cost of the Armed Forces in terms of the value of civilian goods and services that could have been produced by men in the Armed Services. The full economic cost of the draft acknowledges the occupational preferences of prospective recruits. If a youth has an aversion to service life, he could in principle be compensated by enough to induce him to become a volunteer. Presently, many men who would demand such compensations are involuntarily inducted, while others reluctantly volunteer before they are drafted. The magnitude of these costs which are imposed on reluctant service patricipants is estimated in Part IV. Finally, the mechanics of the current draft create uncertainties about the incidence and time of involuntary induction. Some of the costs associated with these uncertainties are briefly discussed in Part V.

I. FORCE STRENGTHS AND MILITARY MANPOWER REQUIREMENTS UNDER A DRAFT

The labor resources demanded by the Armed Services can be approximated by force strength which is simply a stock demand for military personnel unadjusted for the quality of servicemen or for the proportion in an effective (non-training) status. The total defense establishment is conveniently divided into three force strengths: (1) officers on active duty, (2) enlisted men on active duty, and (3) paid drill reservists. The last component engages in active duty mainly for training and is rarely used to bolster active duty strengths.[3]

The average force strength in all active and reserve components for the six years prior to Vietnam was just under 3.7 million men of whom 2.6 million were on active duty. The fluctuations in force strengths which are shown in Table 1 are largely explained by international tensions. Since a discussion of factors de-

TABLE 1
Force Strengths and Accessions From Civil Life
(Actual FY 1960-65 and Projected FY 1970-75, in Thousands)

	1960	1961	1962	1963	1964	1965	Annual Averages	
							1960-65	1970-75[a]
Force strengths[b]								
DOD (active duty) total	2476.4	2483.8	2807.8	2697.7	2685.2	2653.1	2634.0	2650.0
Officers	316.7	314.8	343.1	333.4	336.4	337.6	330.3	340.0
Enlisted	2159.7	2168.9	2464.7	2364.3	2348.8	2315.5	2303.7	2310.0
Army (active duty) total	873.1	858.6	1066.4	975.2	972.4	968.3	952.3	969.5
Officers	101.2	99.9	116.1	107.8	110.3	111.5	107.8	112.5
Enlisted	771.8	758.7	950.4	867.4	862.2	856.8	844.6	857.0
Reserves and National Guard (paid drill)	1079	1086	958	964	1048	1006	1023.5	—
All components total	3555.4	3569.8	3765.8	3661.7	3733.2	3659.1	3657.5	—
Accessions from civil life								
DOD total	469.8	475.3	622.4	488.0	569.3	495.0	520.0	507.7
First enlistments[c]	349	386	423	373	377	352	376.7	416.7
Inductions[c]	90	60	158	74	151	103	106.0	55.3
Officers[d]	30.8	29.3	41.4	41.0	41.3	40.0	37.3	35.7
Army	206.3	188.6	303.2	203.0	285.8	221.0	234.6	228.5
First enlistments[c]	106	118	127	113	117	103	114.0	159.0
Inductions[c]	90	60	158	74	151	102	105.8	55.3
Officers[d]	10.3	10.6	18.2	16.0	17.8	16.0	14.8	14.2
Reserves and National Guard[e]	130.0	130.0	90.0	110.0	170.0	120.0	125.0	—
Total entries all components	599.8	605.3	712.4	598.0	739.3	615.0	645.0	—

[a]Source: *House Hearings*, p. 9954.
[b]Active duty force strengths include both sexes as reported in *Statistical Abstract of the United States, 1966*, Table 365, p. 261 (Government Printing Office: Washington, D.C., 1966). The paid drill Reserve and National Guard strengths were obtained from unpublished data, DOD Statistical Office.
[c]First enlistments include two-year reserve enlistments but exclude reserves recalled to active duty. See *Statistical Abstract*, Table 366, p. 862.
[d]Data for officer accessions taken from a special tabulation prepared by the DOD Statistical Office.
[e]*House Hearings*, p. 10001.

termining force strength objectives is clearly beyond the scope of this paper, the peacetime force strength objectives are taken to be exogenous.

A more meaningful concept of demand is provided by the gross flow demand for new accessions from civilian life. The gross flow demand is the number of required accessions A_t that must be recruited or conscripted to replace losses during the year L_t and to achieve prescribed changes in strength objectives, $(S_t - S_{t-1})$.

$$A_t = L_t + (S_t - S_{t-1})$$

If force strength is kept stable, $(S_t - S_{t-1})$ will be zero. In this case, the gross flow demand is simply a replacement demand for losses which arise during the year because of voluntary separations upon completion of obligated tours of duty, retirements, deaths, and other discharges for medical or unsuitability reasons. The actual accessions between FY 1960-65 are shown in the lower panel of Table 1.[4]

An annual average of 645 thousand men were recruited or conscripted from civil life to maintain the average strengths which prevailed over the period FY 1960-65. The ratio of annual accessions to force strengths provides a rough measure of military personnel turnover. Using the six-year averages, FY 1960-65, from Table 1, the data indicate the following implicit turnover rates (Table 2). Since the obligated tour of a draftee is considerably shorter than that of a regular voluntary enlistee, the Army—with larger inputs of draftees—necessarily experiences a higher turnover rate. For prescribed peacetime force strength objectives, turnover rates determine the gross flow demands for new recruits. Elimination of the draft and policies which raise reenlistment rates thus operate to lower the gross flow demand corresponding to a given stock demand. (This point is amplified by Part II below.)

The manpower procurement channels which have evolved under a draft have strongly influenced the characteristics of servicemen. Of the 645 thousand annual accessions to military service in FY 1960-65, 539 thousand (83.6 per cent) entered through a variety of voluntary programs. An individual can discharge his draft liability by serving as an enlisted man or officer. He can accomplish the former in any of three ways: (1) as a regular voluntary enlistee, (2) as a volunteer to a two-year active duty reserve program in the Navy or Marine Corps, or (3) as a draftee.[5] Except for the draft of doctors and dentists, all officer procurement programs are voluntary. Finally, the draft liability can be satisfied by volunteering for a Reserve or National Guard program requiring active duty only for training. Many men who discharge their draft liabilities through voluntary entry into military service can properly be called reluctant volunteers who entered a particular program in preference to being involuntarily drafted. In order to extrapolate the characteristics of men who are likely to enter military service in the future, it is convenient to study the military service experience of age classes born in specific years.

The disposition of military service obligations by men born in 1938 was estimated from a sample of Selective Service registrants. By July, 1964, this age class reached the age of 26 at which the draft liability is effectively terminated.[6]

According to the data of Table 3, the incidence of military service was highest for men with some college education, 59.5 per cent, and lowest for college graduates, 40.3 per cent. Only 18 per cent of this age class were formally rejected and placed into draft classifications IV-F and I-Y. This low rejection rate is probably due to the fact that men obtaining dependency and occupational deferments were never examined.

Physical and moral standards for military service have remained quite stable and appear to be unrelated to educational attainment. Mental qualification standards which are based on the Armed Forces Qualification Test (AFQT) scores have, however, been varied in response to changing manpower demands. If the minimum mental standard is set equal to the 16th percentile on the AFQT, I obtain the estimated rejection rates given in Table 4.[7]

TABLE 2

Implied Actual Turnover Rates by Component, FY 1960-65 (Percentages)

Total DOD (active forces)	19.7
Officers	11.3
Enlisted men	21.0
Army (active forces)	24.6
Officers	13.7
Enlisted men	26.0
Reserves and National Guard	12.2

The population of men who were physically and mentally qualified for military service was thus estimated by applying these rejection rates. The incidence of military service in relation to the base of qualified males is now highest, 85.5 per cent, for men with less than 12 years of education. Only 74.3 per cent of qualified males with some college (13-15 years) experienced military service.

TABLE 3

Estimated Military Service Status of 26-Year Age Class,[a]

by Educational Level, July, 1964 (In Thousands)

Status	Total[b]	Less Than High School	High School	Some College	College
Total	1190	495	355	131	154
Entered military service	614	247	203	78	62
No military service, total	576	248	152	53	92
Available for Service (I-A)[c]	13	3	3	1	5
Not available for service—					
Disqualified (I-Y & IV-F)	217	126	43	18	18
Student deferments (I-S & II-S)	12	—	(d)	2	9
Occupational deferments (II-A & II-C)	20	1	1	1	17
Dependency deferments (III-A)	296	116	103	30	38
Other deferred & exempt groups	20	3	2	1	4
Estimated Qualified Male Population	828	289	267	105	124
Military Service Participation					
Per cent of total population	51.6	49.9	57.2	59.5	40.3
Per cent of qualified population	74.2	85.5	76.0	74.3	50.0

Source: *House Hearings*, Table 7a, p. 10011

[a]Includes individuals born in calendar year 1938 and who were therefore approximately between 25½ and 26½ years old in July, 1964.

[b]Also includes registrants whose educational attainment is unknown.

[c]Includes individuals between 25½ years and their 26th birthday who were still liable for induction until they attained age 26. It is probable that most of the small number of qualified, unmarried men in this group were reached for induction before their 26th birthday.

[d]less than 500 persons or 0.5 per cent.

TABLE 4

Estimated Rejection Rates by Education

Reason for Rejection	Years of Education				
	Less than 12	12	13-15	16 and Over	Total
Physical	16.0	16.0	16.0	16.0	16.0
Moral	2.5	2.5	2.5	2.5	2.5
Mental[a]	28.4	7.6	2.0	0.9	14.6
All reasons	40.8	24.7	20.1	19.1	30.4

[a]The mental rejection rate is applied to the population of physically and morally qualified males. This procedure assumes that the incidence of mental rejections is uncorrelated with the other two causes for rejection.

The avenues by which men entered military service cannot be identified from Table 3. A study by the DOD Statistical Office developed estimates of the age and education distribution of new accessions to all reserve and active duty components during FY 1963. The results of this study are summarized in Table 5. This pattern of military service participation appears to be representative for the age classes born in 1936-40.[8] If peacetime force strengths return to their pre-Vietnam levels, future accessions to military service in FY 1970-75 are likely to be distributed in a similar fashion.

Of 563,159 accessions in FY 1963, 53.5 per cent volunteered for regular enlisted ranks. Fully 78.8 per cent of these did so before their 21st birthday, and a majority had, at most, a high school degree. A similar pattern is observed for entrants to the two-year active duty reserve programs.[9] Since the oldest liable men are taken first in the Selective Service System's order of call, low draft calls raise the average age of draftees. The draftees in 1963 (a year of low draft calls) are thus considerably older than regular enlistments.

Nearly all new officers (96.2 per cent held college degrees. During the Korean War, candidates without degrees could qualify for many aviation cadet programs. Finally, the initial enlistments to Reserve and Guard components are somewhat older and more educated than accessions to the active force.

An independent estimate of the pattern of military service participation can be constructed from the data of Tables 1 and 5. The male population was distributed by education according to the educational distribution of the male labor force, 25-34 years of age as reported in the 1960 Population Census. The qualified populations were obtained by applying the rejection rates developed above. Since men born in 1938 entered military service between 1956-64, the average annual accessions in the next-to-last column of Table 1 indicate the major components which they entered. The 614 thousand men who reported some military service were thus allocated to active duty and reserve components (see the first column of Table 6). The entrants to each component (say voluntary enlistments) were distributed by education on the basis of the percentage distributions of Table 5.

The estimated pattern of service participation in the upper panel of Table 6 differs from the Selective Service sample of Table 3 in one notable respect. In my estimates of Table 6, there are too few servicemen with 0-11 years of education. This discrepancy is partially due to the upgrading of mental qualifica-

TABLE 5

Non-Prior Service Accessions to Active Duty and Reserve Components, FY 1963

(Percentage Distributions)

Education and Age at Enlistment	Grand Total All DOD	Accessions to Active Duty Forces					Reserves and Nat'l Guard
		Total	Officers	Voluntary Enlist	Two Year Reserves	Inductions	
Less than high school graduate—total	32.90	33.85	.01	32.75	70.75	35.32	29.30
20 & under	26.58	27.51	0	29.33	69.13	11.99	22.99
21-23	3.79	3.52	0	2.97	1.46	8.35	4.82
24 & over	2.53	2.81	.01	.44	.17	14.98	1.48
High school graduate—total	43.74	45.82	.43	55.39	21.53	39.57	35.79
20 & under	29.51	33.14	.01	45.11	18.32	6.91	15.67
21-23	10.10	8.41	.14	9.56	2.95	10.18	16.59
24 & over	4.12	4.28	.28	.73	.26	22.48	3.53
Some college, no degree—total	13.14	10.98	3.39	10.59	4.87	19.00	21.39
20 & under	3.69	3.39	.01	4.38	1.92	1.62	4.84
21-23	6.70	5.01	1.74	5.55	2.71	5.44	13.14
24 & over	2.75	2.58	1.64	.66	.24	11.94	3.41
College graduate—total	10.22	9.36	95.18	1.26	2.86	6.11	13.52
20 & under	.01	.01	.04	.01	.01	0.00	.03
21-23	5.12	4.37	43.88	.61	1.70	.79	7.99
24 & over	5.09	4.98	47.26	.65	1.15	5.31	5.51
All education—total	100.00	100.00	100.00	100.00	100.00	100.00	100.00
20 & under	59.79	64.05	.05	78.83	89.37	20.53	43.53
21-23	25.71	21.30	50.76	18.68	8.82	24.76	42.54
24 & over	14.50	14.65	49.18	2.48	1.81	54.71	13.93
Total number	563159	446334	33638	301503	36806	74387	116825

Source: Unpublished tabulations from DOD statistical office.

tion standards. Because of the higher mental standards which prevailed in 1963, many high school dropouts who could have qualified as volunteers in FY 1956-58 were denied entry in FY 1963. However, if mental standards are held constant into the future, the characteristics of initial accessions shown in Table 5 should apply.

The participation rate in active duty forces (in relation to the total population) was 59.2 per cent for the age class of 1938. The uneven incidence of active military service is evident from the qualified participation rates shown in Table 6. Over three-fourths of qualified high school graduates served in the active duty forces, while less than one-third of college graduates discharged their draft liabilities in this way.

TABLE 6

Estimated Military Service Participation of Two Age Classes

(in Thousands)

	Total	*Years of School Completed*			
		0-11	*12*	*13-15*	*16+*
Age class born in 1938					
1. Total male population	1190.0	464.1	392.7	154.7	178.5
2. Less rejections	355.8	193.2	97.1	31.1	34.4
3. Qualified male population	834.2	270.9	295.6	123.6	144.1
Entered active military service as:					
4. Voluntary enlistment	366.7	133.4	191.2	36.9	5.2
5. Induction	90.0	31.8	35.6	17.1	5.5
6. Officers	37.3	0.0	0.1	1.3	35.9
7. Total accessions to active duty	494.0	165.2	226.9	78.1	82.6
Accessions to active duty as:					
8. Per cent of total population	41.5	35.6	57.8	35.7	26.1
9. Per cent of qualified population	59.2	61.0	76.8	44.7	32.3
Age class born in 1947					
1. Total male population	1880.0	733.2	620.4	244.4	282.0
2. Less rejections	562.1	305.2	153.4	49.2	54.3
3. Qualified male population	1317.9	428.0	467.0	195.2	227.7
Entered active military service as:					
4. Voluntary enlistment	416.7	136.5	230.8	44.1	5.3
5. Induction	55.3	19.5	21.9	10.5	3.4
6. Officers	35.7	—	.2	1.2	34.3
7. Total accessions to active duty	507.7	156.0	252.9	55.8	43.0
Accessions to active duty as:					
8. Per cent of total population	27.0	21.3	40.8	22.8	15.2
9. Per cent of qualified population	38.5	36.4	54.2	28.6	18.9

To determine the financial cost of the Armed Forces, it is necessary to estimate the age and educational distribution of the entire force. Special tabulations provide estimates of the percentage of enlisted men with high school degrees and officers with college degrees; these data for selected dates apply to total DOD active forces (Table 7).

Secular improvements in the educational attainment of the entire population and higher qualification standards both contribute to the upward trend in the education of the Armed Services. A more detailed description was obtained from the 1960 population Census and is described by the data of Table 8.[10]

Attention is next directed to projections of military service participation under two vastly different procurement systems corresponding to a mixed force

TABLE 7

Educational Attainment of Servicemen on Active Duty

(Total DOD, selected dates)

Date	Percentage of Enlisted Men with High School Degrees	Percentage of Officers with College Degrees
31 December 1952	52.7	46.2
31 May 1956	55.2	55.5
29 February 1960	66.1	56.8
31 December 1963	72.8	69.4

Source: Special tabulations, DOD Statistical Office.

of volunteers and conscripts and a purely voluntary force. In this section, I examine the mixed-force case, in which the current draft law is assumed to be continued. Flows of volunteers and draftees are demanded to maintain the assumed force strength of 2.65 million men. Projections of required accessions (gross flow demands) over the period FY 1970-75 were developed for this case in the DOD study; the annual averages for the six years appear in the last column of Table 1.[11] In the light of the expanding population base, it is projected that the other Services (Air Force, Navy, and Marine Corps) will enjoy excess supplies of enlistment applicants. A statistical analysis of time series data on regular Army enlistments suggested that the appropriate base from which such recruits are drawn is the population of 18- to 19-year-old males not enrolled in school. Since the proportion of an age class that remains in school is increasing, Army enlistments do not grow in proportion to the growth in the population of qualified males.[12] Army enlistment rates were also found to be correlated with unemployment. If the unemployment rate falls from 5.5 to 4.0 per cent, voluntary enlistments are expected to decline by 16 per cent.

In a steady state, the required accessions to sustain the assumed force of 2.65

TABLE 8

Distribution of Armed Forces by Age and Education

(For Force Strength of 2,650; Figures in Thousands)

Age	Years of School Completed					
	0-8	9-11	12	13-15	16+	Total
TOTAL DOD						
17 or less	11.3	55.2	6.7	.4	—	73.7
18-19	21.7	141.3	218.6	14.3	.2	396.2
20-21	18.4	111.3	235.1	48.3	2.7	415.8
22-24	30.8	97.9	238.3	81.1	79.6	527.7
25-29	34.7	89.3	181.0	47.4	63.1	415.5
30-34	38.2	67.8	124.3	34.7	28.5	293.5
35-44	44.2	67.2	178.2	81.2	59.9	430.8
45-54	12.3	12.0	21.2	14.9	21.3	81.8
55 & over	2.8	3.2	4.3	1.6	3.2	15.1
Total	214.5	645.2	1207.8	323.9	258.5	2650.0

Source: Derived from *U.S. Census of Population, 1960:* Subject Report: "Educational Attainment," Code No. DC(2) 5B, Table 4, p. 54.

TABLE 9

Estimated Retention Profiles of Enlisted Men by Service

(Proportion on Active Duty after N Years)[a]

Years of Service, N	Total DOD	Navy, Marines & Air Force	Regular Army	Army Draftees
0	1.0000	1.0000	1.0000	1.0000
1	.9149	.9289	.9001	.9001
2	.6494	.8354	.8291	.0540
3	.4710	.8315	.1743	
4	.1631	.2373	.1645	
5	.1563	.2281	.1564	
6	.1456	.2202	.1295	
7	.1407	.2133	.1243	
8	.1365	.2073	.1196	
9	.1281	.2021	.0968	
10	.1125	.1734	.0936	
11	.1098	.1696	.0907	
12	.1068	.1660	.0860	
13	.1045	.1626	.0835	
14	.1023	.1595	.0812	
15	.1002	.1565	.0790	
16	.0982	.1537	.0768	
17	.0964	.1511	.0748	
18	.0945	.1484	.0728	
19	.0927	.1459	.0709	
20	.0818	.1255	.0690	
21	.0527	.0797	.0469	
22	.0439	.0654	.0411	
23	.0372	.0546	.0366	
24	.0321	.0464	.0330	
25	.0283	.0406	.0297	
26	.0249	.0355	.0267	
27	.0220	.0312	.0238	
28	.0195	.0276	.0211	
29	.0172	.0244	.0186	
30	.0150	.0213	.0163	
Sum	5.2981	7.0430	4.8667	1.9541

[a]The estimated survival rates are based on the retention experience in the late 1950's.

million men are equal to losses during the year. Losses can be approximated from retention profiles which indicate the proportion of men remaining on active duty N years after entry. Retention profiles estimated from the experience of the late 1950's are shown in Tables 9 and 10. The sum of retention rates in a column represents the force strength that could be maintained by an input of one man per year; it is simply the integral under the retention profile. The length of the first term of service is evident in these profiles by the sharp drop in the retention rate. It is convenient to divide the area under the profile into two parts. Let F be the sum of retention rates over the first term, while C is the sum for the career force on their second and later tours. The maintainable force from an annual input of one man is simply $F+C$. The turnover rate for a stable force is simply the reciprocal of $(F+C)$. The turnover rates implied by the DOD projections are obtained by taking the ratio of accessions to strengths from the last column of Table 1 (see Table 11). The discrepancy between the two estimates of turnover rates is small, especially for the Army enlisted men.

TABLE 10

Estimated Retention Profiles of Regular and Non-Regular Officers

(Proportion on Active Duty after N Years)

Years of Service	All Officers	Reg. Officers	Non-Reg. Officers	Years of Service	All Officers	Reg. Officers	Non-Reg. Officers
0	1.000	1.000	1.000	16	.242	.548	.111
1	.973	.977	.971	17	.240	.540	.111
2	.931	.950	.923	18	.238	.535	.111
3	.533	.920	.367	19	.234	.531	.106
4	.428	.826	.257	20	.206	.460	.097
5	.384	.786	.212	21	.171	.407	.070
6	.366	.761	.196	22	.159	.395	.058
7	.350	.731	.186	23	.144	.378	.044
8	.336	.708	.176	24	.135	.360	.038
9	.329	.696	.172	25	.121	.339	.027
10	.310	.658	.161	26	.096	.265	.024
11	.303	.646	.156	27	.086	.243	.018
12	.269	.593	.130	28	.057	.178	.005
13	.263	.580	.127	29	.056	.175	.005
14	.251	.560	.118	30	.012	.041	.000
15	.247	.554	.115	Sum	9.467	17.341	6.092

The retention profiles were also compared to the actual active-duty forces as of 30 June 1965 which appears in Table 12. The two conform quite closely. The percentages of enlisted men with less than ten years of service were 73.4 per cent in Table 12 and 73.7 per cent as implied from the retention profile. Likewise, 51.5 per cent of officers in 1965 had less than ten years of service as compared to an implied 59.5 per cent from the profile of Table 10.

In order to infer the incidence of future military service under a continued draft, the projected accessions were juxtaposed to a typical age class born in 1946-48 which according to Census projections will contain 1,880 thousand males. Some 562 thousand, will, however, be rejected for military service. By applying the pattern of military service participation shown in Table 5, I distributed the accessions across education groups. In this manner, I constructed the data shown in the lower panel of Table 6.[13]

TABLE 11

Comparison of Turnover Rates from Retention Profiles and DOD Projections[a]

Component	F	C	F+C	Turnover Rates	
				1/(F+C)	Implied
Enlisted Men					
Total DOD	2.9252	2.3728	5.2981	18.9	20.4
Other services	3.5958	3.4472	7.0430	14.2	17.7
Regular army	2.7292	2.1375	4.8667	20.5	
Army draftees	1.9001	0.0540	1.9541	51.2	25.0
Officers					
All officers	3.064	6.403	9.467	10.6	10.5
Regular officers	3.847	13.494	17.341	5.8	
Non-regular officers	2.894	3.198	6.092	16.4	

[a]The first three columns are sums of retention rates from Tables 9 and 10. The last column is derived from the projected accessions and strengths in the last column of Table 1.

TABLE 12

Active Duty Force Strength by Years of Service

(As of 30 June 1965, in Thousands)

Years of Service	Total	Officers	Enlisted
0	427.7	28.4	399.3
1	488.4	34.1	454.3
2	301.6	25.0	276.5
3	226.3	20.1	206.2
4	99.8	12.9	86.8
5-9	321.6	54.0	267.7
10-14	338.6	51.1	287.4
15-19	291.0	58.4	232.6
20-24	131.4	45.4	86.0
25 and over	17.7	9.4	8.1
Total	2643.8	338.8	2304.9

Although 41.5 per cent of males born in 1938 are estimated to have entered active military service, only 27.0 per cent of men born in 1947 are projected to be required to sustain an active-duty force of 2.65 million men. The participation rate in relation to the qualified population falls from 59.2 to 38.5 per cent. Only 18.9 per cent of qualified college graduates are projected to enter active duty forces in FY 1970-75.

II. SUPPLIES OF MILITARY PERSONNEL IN THE ABSENCE OF A DRAFT

The task of estimating the cost of an all-volunteer force was approached in two steps. It was first assumed that the draft would be abolished with no accompanying changes in pay or other recruitment incentives. An implication of this exercise is that supplies of volunteers fall short of requirements for a force of 2.65 million men. In the second step, military pay was advanced to attract enough recruits to meet the prescribed force strength objective.

If the draft is eliminated, the services would obviously lose the draftees who had accounted for 21 per cent of accessions to enlisted ranks in FY 1960-65. In addition, the flow of new accessions is likely to be reduced by nonparticipation of the reluctant volunteers who enlist in preference to being drafted. To determine the probable number of reluctant volunteers, the Department of Defense conducted a survey in the fall of 1964 of men on active duty and male civilians who were 16-34 years of age. Regular enlisted men in their first term (all of whom had volunteered between 1960 and 1964) were classified as true or reluctant volunteers on the basis of their response to the question,

If there had been no draft, and if you had no military obligation, do you think that you would have volunteered for active military service?

Those replying "No, definitely" or "No, probably" were classified as reluctant volunteers. Percentages of true voluntary enlistments in sub-groups identified by age and education are shown in the first column of Table 13. The incidence of true volunteers is highest in the youngest and least-educated group and declines as age and education are increased. The projected flows of enlistments under a continued draft appear in the fourth column. If these are multiplied by the respective percentages of true volunteers, one obtains the estimated flows of true volunteers if the draft were abolished with no pay changes.[14]

TABLE 13

Effect of the Draft on Voluntary Enlistments—Survey Responses

(Classified by Age and Education)

Age at Entry and Education	Percentage of True Volunteersa	Number in DOD Sampleb		Voluntary Enlistments in FY 1970-75 (in Thousands)		
				With Draftc	No Draft	
		Number	Per cent		Numberd	Per cent
17-19 years of age						
Less than high school	79.3	167.8	27.7	122.2	96.2	36.6
High school graduate	63.7	247.1	40.8	188.0	119.7	45.5
Some College	55.9	44.0	7.3	18.3	10.2	3.9
Total	68.7	458.9	75.8	328.5	226.1	86.0
20 and over						
Less than high school	60.2	20.2	3.3	14.3	8.6	3.3
High school graduate	42.3	61.7	10.2	42.8	18.1	6.9
Some college	32.7	64.4	10.6	31.1	10.2	3.9
Total	40.5	146.4	24.2	88.2	36.9	14.0
All ages						
Less than high school	77.4	31.1	31.1	136.5	104.8	39.8
High school graduate	59.5	51.0	51.0	230.8	137.8	52.4
Some college	42.1	17.9	17.9	49.4	20.4	7.8
Total	61.9	100.0	100.0	416.7	263.0	100.0

aBased on responses of regular enlisted men in their first term of service to the question, "If there had been no draft and if you had no military obligation, do you think you would have volunteered for active military service?" Entries denote the percentage who responded, "Yes, definitely," or, "Yes, probably."

bFigures may differ from force strength statistics due to elimination of non-respondents and sampling variability.

cEstimates of voluntary enlistments In FY 1970-75 if the draft is continued.

dObtained by multiplying columns 1 and 4. Assumes that the draft is eliminated, but pay and recruitment incentives are unchanged.

This question on draft motivation was also asked of officers on their first obligated tours. Percentages of true volunteers classified by source of commission are shown in the first column of Table 14. The direct appointments which include doctors and dentists exhibit the lowest incidence of true volunteers, followed next by the college graduate procurement programs. The "Other" category, mainly composed of men without a college degree, reveals the smallest fraction of reluctant, draft-motivated volunteers. The estimated flows of officer accessions in the absence of a draft (the fifth column of Table 14) should be regarded as only representative.[15]

TABLE 14

Effect of the Draft on Officer Accessions—Survey Responsesa

(Classified by Source of Commission)

Source of Commission	Percentage of True Volunteers	Number in DOD Sample		Actual Average 1960-64	Accessions with No Draft 1970-75	
		Number	Per cent		Number	Per cent
Academy	89.1	583	7.6	2776	3000	10.5
OCS	48.6	2133	27.8	7779	5300	18.5
ROTC	54.6	2764	36.1	13769	10500	36.6
Direct appointment	42.2	862	11.3	6359	3800	13.2
Otherb	80.3	1320	17.2	6068	6100	21.3
Total DOD	58.7	7662	100.0	36751	28700	100.0

aSee notes to Table 13.

bIncludes officer accessions from enlisted ranks and from non-college programs for aviation cadet training.

TABLE 15

First-Term Reenlistment Rates for Mixed and Voluntary Forces by Service

	Percentage of True Volunteers	Actual Reenlistment Rate Avg. FY 1957-64 Ra	Voluntary Reenlistment Rate Rvb
Regular enlisted men			
Army	56.8	22.06	33.0
Navy	67.4	22.14	29.1
Marine Corps	69.6	18.28	22.9
Air Force	57.1	34.64	54.9
DOD	62.0	25.58	36.6
Army inductees	0	7.67	
Total DOD	—	20.26	

aFigures are weighted averages of adjusted first-term reenlistment rates weighted by the number eligible for reenlistment. The adjusted reenlistment rate applies to a cohort and takes account of early discharges for reenlistment.
bThe voluntary enlistment rate is defined as,
$$R = kR_v + (1-k)R_d$$
where R_d = 7.67 per cent, the reenlistment rate of draftees.

The reduction in active-duty force strength will be less than the fall in voluntary accessions because of offsetting improvements in retention. Air Force studies reveal that first-term reenlistment rates were higher for Airmen whose primary reason for entry was unrelated to the draft.[16] The data of Table 15 show that the reenlistment rate of draftees in FY 1960-65 was only a third as large as that of regular enlisted men. If the reenlistment rate of draftees, R_d, is assumed to apply to reluctant volunteers, one can estimate the reenlistment rate if all recruits were true volunteers. The observed reenlistment rate, R, of regular enlisted men in FY 1960-65 is simply a weighted average of the rates applicable to true and reluctant volunteers.

$$R = kR_v + (1-k)R_d,$$

where k is the proportion of true volunteers. Setting $R_d = 7.67$ per cent (the average rate for draftees), one can solve for R_v. The results are shown in Table 15.

Similar improvements in retention can also be expected of officers. Since all officers (except doctors and dentists) are obtained from voluntary programs, we have no data corresponding to R_d. However, from a survey of intentions to remain on active duty, it proved possible to develop estimates of retention rates in an all-volunteer force (see Table 16).[17]

TABLE 16

Comparison of Officer Retention Rates (Percentages)

Source of Commission	Mixed Force (Actual 1960-64)	Voluntary Force (Estimated)
Academy	82.1	82.1
Officer Candidate School	26.0	48.5
ROTC	35.3	53.9
Direct appointments	n.a.	33.0
Other	82.1	83.1
Total DOD	41.9	59.3

The substitution of true volunteers for draftees and reluctant volunteers operates to raise retention rates in an all-volunteer force. Annual losses for a given strength will thus be smaller, implying a lower gross flow of required accessions. If one ignores the transitional problems of moving from a mixed to a voluntary force, required accessions can be estimated from the new retention profiles. The impact of lower turnover rates on required accessions is indicated by the comparison in Table 17.

TABLE 17

Gross Flow Demands (Required Accessions) for a Strength of 2.65 Million (in Thousands)

Component	Voluntary Force (No Draft)	Mixed Force (With Draft)	Ratio
Total required accessions to enlisted ranks	333.5	472.0	.707
Other services	188.9	257.7	.733
Army—total	144.6	214.3	.675
Volunteers[a]	144.6	159.0	.909
Inductions	0	55.3	
Required accessions of officers	28.4	35.7	.796
Total gross flow demands	361.9	507.7	.713

[a]Assumes a 5.5 per cent unemployment rate.

Voluntary supplies in the absence of a draft (compare the fifth columns of Tables 13 and 14) fall short of these requirements. Hence, if the draft were eliminated with no pay changes, the sustainable force strength would fall to around 2.2 million men. Moreover, the reduction in force strength would be largest for the Army, which accepts the largest number of draftees and draft-motivated volunteers.

These deficits in voluntary supplies could be eliminated by raising military pay. The responsiveness of voluntary supplies to pay changes was estimated from cross-sectional data for nine census regions. From the DOD survey, it was possible to estimate voluntary enlistment rates, E, in the absence of a draft.[18] Although first-term military pay, M, is the same for all recruits, relative pay in relation to alternative civilian employment varies because of regional differences in civilian pay C. Relative military pay, $Y = (M/C)$, is higher in regions such as the South where C is low. Data for the nine regions indicate that the hypothetical voluntary enlistment rate is positively correlated with relative pay Y.

Of several functions which were fitted to the data, the most consistent fit was provided by a complement supply equation given by

(1) $$(1 - E) = \alpha Y^{-\beta},$$

where α and β are parameters. According to this equation, a 1 per cent increase in relative pay, Y, leads to a β per cent decline in the remainder of the population $(1-E)$ *not* in military service. The elasticity of supply, ϵ, is given by

(2) $$\epsilon = \beta \left(\frac{1-E}{E} \right).$$

As the enlistment rate E approaches unity, the elasticity of supply approaches zero. The parameters of this equation were estimated by least squares for two groups: (1) all enlistments to total DOD in mental groups I to III and (2) Army enlistments in mental groups I to III.[19]

An upper bound to the cost is obtained by estimating the necessary pay increase to fill the deficit in Army enlistments. According to DOD projections, annual inputs of 214.3 thousand are required in FY 1970-75 to sustain an Army enlisted strength of 857 thousand. The turnover rate for the mixed input of draftees and regular enlistees is 25 per cent. If all inputs were three-year enlistees, the retention profile of Table 9 (applicable to inputs of true and reluctant volunteers) implies that the turnover rate could be reduced to 20.6 per cent. Next, the substitution of true for reluctant volunteers in an all-volunteer force leads to a further gain in retention. The first-term reenlistment rate can be expected to climb from 22.1 per cent (for mixed inputs of which only 56.8 per cent are true volunteers) to 33.0 per cent in a voluntary force: see Table 15. Hence, when all recruits are true volunteers who freely choose military service over alternative civilian jobs, the turnover rate is reduced to 16.9 per cent.[20] In a steady state, this turnover rate determines the required accessions of 144.6 thousand to sustain a voluntary Army strength of 857 thousand enlisted men. If the draft were abolished, Army enlistments are projected to fall by 43.2 per cent (the percentage of draft-motivated reluctant volunteers) to annual flows of 90.3 thousand. The ratio of required accessions to enlistments, $(A/E) = (144.6/90.3) = 1.601$, describes the magnitude of the deficit. The necessary pay increase, (Y_1/Y_0), was then calculated from the complement supply curve, equation (1).

$$(3) \qquad \left(\frac{1-A}{1-E}\right) = \left(\frac{Y_1}{Y_0}\right)^{-\beta},$$

where $Y_0 = M_0/C$ is the initial relative military pay, and $Y_1 = M_1/C$ is the new pay scale that is required to eliminate the deficit. The Army enlistment rate, E, before a pay increase was found to be 8.33 per cent of the labor force for a specific age class, while A was 13.33 per cent. The least squares estimate for β in the Army supply curve $\beta = .108$ implying an elasticity of $\epsilon = 1.36$. By substituting these values in equation (3), the necessary pay increase was found to be $(Y_1/Y_0) = 1.68$.[21]

Since pay increases apply to men in their first term, it is essential to discuss briefly the mechanics of implementing this pay increase. The income of a serviceman includes money payments for various items and some income in kind. In this paper, I shall use the concept of tax-equivalent income consisting of (1) base pay, (2) quarters, subsistence, and uniform allowances when received in money, or (3) the imputed value of quarters and subsistence when no money payments are received, and (4) the tax advantage.[22] Annual tax-equivalent incomes for enlisted men classified by years of service are shown in Table 18. Military pay in the first two years of service is extremely low because pay increases which were legislated prior to 1964 applied mainly to the career force. Since the supply of new accessions could be assured by the draft law, there seemed to be no need to raise entry level pay. In implementing the 68 per cent increase in first-term pay, I assumed that the discontinuity in the pay profile would be eliminated. Consequently, the average military income over the first

TABLE 18

Annual Incomes of Enlisted Men

(For Pay Scales of FY 1963)

Years of Service	Total Income DOD	Army			Base Pay as Percentage of Total Income
		Total Income	Taxable Income	Base Pay	
1	1830	1900	1058	1055	55.5
2	2143	2304	1359	1382	60.0
3	2991	3247	2199	2002	61.7
4	3344	3711	2392	2433	65.6
5	4130	4248	2691	2575	60.6
6	4462	4465	2792	2725	61.0
7	4649	4596	2937	2858	62.2
8	4741	4797	3037	3003	62.6
9-12	5235	5377	3409	3280	61.0
13-16	5926	6043	3918	3885	64.3
17-20	6387	6414	4245	n.a.	

three years of service climbs from $2,500 to $4,200 per year. In order to prevent reversals in the pay structure by years of service, men in the career force would receive pay increases which average around 17 per cent.

With these pay increases, the Armed Forces should be able to meet their strength objectives with voluntary supplies of new accessions. Since the incidence of reluctant volunteers was highest for older, more educated men, the voluntary force is likely to have a lower educational attainment. From the estimated flows of true volunteers in Tables 13 and 14, I constructed a plausible pattern of military service participation in the absence of a draft which appears in Table 19. The voluntary force with its higher retention requires fewer accessions to sustain the same active-duty strength. Consequently, the qualified participation rate falls from 38.5 per cent in the mixed force to 27.5 per cent. Relative de-

TABLE 19

Estimated Military Service Participation in an All-Volunteer Force

(Hypothetical for an Age Class Born in 1946-48, in Thousands)

	Years of School Completed				
	Total	0-11	12	13-15	16+
1. Total male population	1880.0	733.2	620.4	224.4	282.0
2. Less rejections	562.1	305.2	153.4	49.2	54.3
3. Qualified male population	1317.9	428.0	467.0	195.2	227.7
Volunteered for active military service as:					
4. Enlisted man	333.5	139.5	169.4	23.4	1.2
5. Officer	28.7	—	—	8.7	20.0
6. Total	362.2	139.5	169.4	32.1	21.2
Accessions with no draft as:					
7. Per cent of total population	19.3	19.0	27.3	13.1	7.5
8. Per cent of qualified population	27.5	32.6	36.3	16.4	9.3
Accessions under continued draft as:					
9. Per cent of total population	27.0	21.3	40.8	22.8	15.2
10. Per cent of qualified population	38.5	36.4	54.2	28.6	18.9
11. Ratio 8/10	.71	.89	.67	.58	.49

clines in qualified participation rates which appear in the last row of Table 19 reveal that the largest decline is for college graduates. These changes in the probable educational mix of recruits will, in a steady state, be reflected in the educational attainment of the entire force.

The move to a voluntary force is likely to be accompanied by considerably higher first-term reenlistment rates. Each voluntary recruit is expected to have a longer tenure of active duty. If marginal retention rates are assumed to remain stable, one can construct new retention profiles from the anticipated higher first-term reenlistment rates. The projected age structure of an all-volunteer force was developed from the new retention profiles and appears in Table 20.

TABLE 20

Active Duty Force Strength by Years of Service

(Hypothetical Voluntary Force, in Thousands)

Years of Service	Total	Officers	Enlisted
0	355.3	34.5	320.8
1	327.5	33.6	293.9
2	299.2	32.1	267.1
3	204.4	20.2	184.2
4	108.0	16.0	92.0
5-9	455.6	65.4	390.2
10-14	343.3	51.5	291.8
15-19	304.6	44.1	260.5
20-24	165.2	28.1	137.1
25 and over	86.9	14.5	72.4
Total	2650.0	340.0	2310.0

Finally, the age and educational distribution of a voluntary force was inferred from the educational mix of new accessions. It was assumed that officer procurement programs for non-college graduates would be expanded. The proportion of enlisted men with 0-8 years of education is small for two reasons. First, the population base of men in this group is growing only slightly because of secular improvements in overall educational attainment. Second, mental standards are assumed to be held at a minimum AFQT score of 16. The hypothetical distribution of the voluntary force by age and education is shown in Table 21.

In estimating the cost of an all-volunteer force, I neglected at least three pertinent factors: (1) the transitional period, (2) the savings which obtain from lower personnel turnover, and (3) possible substitutions of civilians for uniformed men. The required accessions, A, were estimated for a steady state in which the retention profile of a voluntary force prevails. In order to maintain force strengths in the transition, required accessions are likely to be around 10 per cent higher. The necessary pay increase to supply this higher gross flow demand is estimated to be 94 per cent as compared to the previous 68 per cent increase in first-term pay. If, however, pay is advanced prior to eliminating the draft liability, losses (and hence required accessions) can be reduced during the transitional period.

At least 10 per cent of the mixed force with its high personnel turnover is engaged in training. Since initial accessions to a voluntary force of the same size are some 30 per cent smaller, the voluntary force could be reduced by 3 per cent and still retain the same number of men in an "effective" status. In addition, men currently engaged in training others can be moved to other assignments, producing further savings. Neglect of these savings from lower personnel turnover thus imparts an upward bias to my estimate of the necessary pay increase.

Many clerical, medical, food-service, and maintenance positions now staffed by servicemen could be assigned to civilians. Given the low levels of first-term military pay, the assignment of uniformed personnel to these jobs may well produce the lowest budgetary cost. However, if military pay is sharply advanced it

TABLE 21

Active Duty Force Strength by Age and Education

(Hypothetical All-Volunteer Force, in Thousands)

	Years of School Completed					
Age	0-8	9-11	12	13-15	16 and over	Total
Total DOD						
17-19	25.7	145.1	212.1	18.0	—	400.9
20-21	30.3	170.8	248.6	26.5	4.8	481.0
22-24	28.8	133.9	194.0	31.8	41.1	424.6
25-29	22.6	127.3	188.7	41.0	84.6	464.2
30-34	17.1	100.5	147.5	29.7	52.5	347.3
35-44	20.7	124.1	182.7	39.6	74.5	386.9
45-54	3.1	19.1	28.8	8.6	30.2	89.7
55 and over	—	—	0	0	0.7	0.7
All ages	143.3	820.8	1202.4	195.2	288.3	2650.0

becomes economical, even from the viewpoint of budgetary cost, to substitute civilians for military personnel.[23] By implementing such substitutions, the size of the active-duty Armed Forces could be reduced without changing the tasks performed by the totality of civilians and uniformed men. A careful study of the possibilities for substituting civilians should, in my opinion, be an essential part of moving toward a voluntary force.

III. THE FINANCIAL COST OF THE ARMED FORCES

There are at least three senses in which the Armed Forces entail a financial cost: (1) the budgetary cost, (2) the cost to the economy, and (3) the cost to reluctant military service participants. In this paper, I propose to compare these costs for mixed and voluntary forces with the same active-duty strength of 2.65 million men.

According to the defense budget for FY 1965, the cost of active-duty military personnel was $12,662 million plus an additional $1,384 million for retirement benefits.[24] Another estimate of the payroll cost can be derived by applying the annual military incomes of Table 18 to the 1965 force shown in Table 12. This estimate of $12,049 million differs from the DOD budget because my measure of annual military incomes excludes many pay items.[25] This latter approach is, however, the only convenient way to estimate the budgetary cost of a hypothetical voluntary force.

In order to achieve a voluntary force, the entire pay profile must be shifted upward with the largest pay increases applying to men in the first few years of service. Moreover, the longer service life of recruits to a voluntary army implies that the higher incomes of the career force receive more weight. If the higher pay profile is applied to the age structure of a voluntary force (Table 20), the budgetary cost is estimated to be $16,103 million.[26] My estimates suggest that the defense budget for active-duty military personnel would rise by $4 billion per year to acquire recruits and new officers on a voluntary basis. It should be repeated that the additional budgetary cost of an all-volunteer force neglects the higher cost during the transition, and the savings from lower personnel turnover and possible substitutions of civilians.

Turn next to the financial cost of the Armed Forces to the economy as a whole. In both mixed and voluntary forces, 2.65 million men are allocated to maintaining the defense of the nation and are thereby kept out of the civilian labor force. The alternative cost of these labor resources is the value of civilian goods and services that could have been produced by these servicemen. An ideal measure of this cost requires data on the marginal value products of the particular men in service. A useful approximation is obtained by assuming that servicemen could have earned the incomes of civilians of comparable ages and educational attainment. The 1964 annual civilian incomes classified by age and education and adjusted for unemployment are presented in Table 22. The tacit assumption is that if servicemen were relocated to the civilian economy, they could earn the same incomes as their civilian counterparts.[27]

TABLE 22

Median Incomes of Civilian Male Labor Force, 1964

Age	Years of Education Completed				
	0-8	9-11	12	13-15	16+
17-19	2010	2926	3196	3147	—
20-21[a]	2391	3314	3924	4668	—
22-24[b]	3160	4026	4789	5168	5280
25-29[c]	3673	4500	5366	5502	6213
30-34	4296	5339	6167	6910	8353
35-44	4710	5860	6528	7389	9853
45-54	4717	5636	6549	7855	10846
55 and over	4229	4944	6135	6642	9883

[a]Incomes for males 21 years of age and under estimated from DOD Survey of civilian non-veterans, 16-21 years of age. Adjusted for unemployment.

[b]Incomes interpolated from data for ages "20-21" and "25-29."

[c]Median total incomes taken from *Statistical Abstract of the United States, 1966*, Table 157, p. 115. Figures were adjusted for unemployment rates of 2.8 per cent for males 25 and older and with more than 8 years of education, and 4.7 per cent unemployment for males with less than 8 years of education.

Age and education are the best available surrogates for measuring the alternative incomes (representing the value of civilian goods and services) that could have been earned by servicemen. The estimated age and educational distributions of mixed and voluntary forces are respectively shown in Tables 8 and 21. If the draftees and volunteers in the mixed force received the civilian incomes of Table 22, their aggregate income would have been $13,041 million. The corresponding sum for an all-volunteer force is $14,233 million, or 9.1 per cent more than that for the mixed force. Although the voluntary force has more men without a high school degree, it also contains older men, and on balance, the age effect outweighs education. These financial costs ignore the effects of personnel turnover. In a mixed force, larger flows of men from each age class enter military service for shorter periods. The critical question is, "Are civilian incomes in later life reduced or enhanced by short (two to four years) tours of active military service?" The relationship of income to age (given education) can be explained in two ways. One is that older men acquire on-the-job training which is reflected in their incomes. The other argues that income is a proxy for maturity and stability, which command more income.[28] If the first explanation is correct, and military training is only an imperfect substitute for civilian job experience, the financial cost of the mixed force would be higher than $13,041 million. Finally, it should be noted that these financial costs disregard the occupational preferences of individuals, some of whom are involuntarily drafted to serve.

TABLE 23

Projected Accessions to Enlisted Ranks under a Continued Draft, FY 1970-75

(By Age at Entry, Education, and Draft Motivation)

		Years of School Completed				
	Total in Thousands	0-8	9-11	12	13-15	16 & over
Voluntary enlistments under a continued draft						
17-19 years	328.5	15.0	107.2	188.0	18.3	0
20 years and older	88.2	1.4	12.9	42.8	25.8	5.3
All ages	416.7	16.4	120.1	230.8	44.1	5.3
Reluctant volunteers						
17-19 years	102.4	3.0	23.0	68.3	8.1	0
20 years and older	51.3	0.4	5.3	24.7	17.8	3.1
All ages	153.7	3.4	28.3	93.0	25.9	3.1
Inductions	55.3	4.3	15.2	21.9	10.5	3.4
Reluctant military service participants						
17-19 years	102.4	3.0	23.0	68.3	8.1	0
20 years and older	106.6	4.7	20.5	46.6	28.3	6.5
All ages	209.0	7.7	43.5	114.9	36.4	6.5

Source: Derived from Table 13.

The third concept of financial cost measures the monetary losses suffered by individual military service participants who were coerced into active-duty service by the draft liability. By FY 1970-75, it is projected that annual draft calls will fall to 55.3 thousand. If the survey responses of Table 13 are valid, they imply that another 153.7 thousand men will enlist each year because of their draft liabilities. The annual flows of these reluctant service participants to enlisted ranks are distributed by age and education in Table 23. In his first two years of service, a draftee receives an annual military income of $2,100, while the reluctant volunteer who serves for a longer period earns an average income of $2,500; these figures apply to the 1963 pay scales. The alternative civilian incomes for these men were estimated from the data of Table 22 and reveal the averages shown in Table 24.

The differential between civilian and military incomes is obviously larger for older, more educated men. The infrequent college graduate who is drafted into the Army can expect to lose more than $6,000 over his two years of service. If each draftee serves for 1.9 years, and each reluctant volunteeer for 3.5 years, the aggregate financial loss for reluctant participants from an age class is $691 million. This is surely an obvious tax placed on those who are coerced to serve. To the extent that many officers (especially doctors) reluctantly serve an initial tour of obligated duty, this financial cost is even larger. If the discontinuity between first-term and career military pay is eliminated, most of this financial cost would disappear.

TABLE 24

Estimated Annual Incomes of Draftees and Reluctant Volunteers

	Annual Accessions (In Thousands)	Civilian Income	Military Income	Ratio
Draftees	55.3	$3,810	$2,100	.55
Reluctant volunteers	153.7	3,450	2,500	.72
Total	209.0	3,545	2,400	.68

IV. THE ECONOMIC COST OF A DRAFT

The full economic cost embraces the principle that equalizing income differentials are properly included in the opportunity cost of acquiring men for military service. Since pay cannot be separated from the working conditions of a job, workers' preferences (the utilities and disutilities of the job) necessarily affect supplies of labor to particular occupations. In this paper, military service is regarded as an occupation. Suppose that individual A could earn an income C in the civilian labor market. If A has an aversion to military service, he would remain a civilian even if first term military pay, M_0, were the same as C. Military pay could, in principle, be advanced by enough to compensate him for his disutility, thereby attracting him into military service. There is some minimum supply price M (military pay) with its accompanying differential δ which would make A indifferent between employment in the military or in the civilian sector. If first term military pay were M_1, where $M_1 > M = (1 + \delta)C$, A would become a true volunteer. If $\delta > 0$, the individual must be compensated to induce him to enter military service. It is possible that some men prefer military service, in which case δ would be negative. The supply curve of volunteers in the absence of a draft would thus be determined by the joint frequency distribution of alternative civilian incomes C and equalizing differentials δ which summarize workers' preferences. The supply of volunteers with no pay changes consists of those individuals for whom current first-term pay M_0 is greater than $(1 + \delta)C$. As pay is advanced, the Armed Services attract men with higher alternative incomes or with greater aversions for service life.

Manpower procurement under a draft imposes costs on men in the Armed Forces in at least three ways. First, more men from an age class are demanded under a draft because of the high turnover of draftees and reluctant volunteers. Second, some men are coerced to serve by the draft without being compensated for their aversion to service life. At sufficiently high levels of military pay, all of these reluctant, draft-motivated men could have been induced to become true volunteers. Finally, true volunteers who enlist at low levels of pay irrespective of the draft law are denied the higher pay that would have prevailed in an all-volunteer force.

In the years ahead, FY 1970-75, it is projected that under a continued draft 209 thousand accessions to enlisted ranks in each year can properly be called reluctant service participants (see Table 23). Not all 209 thousand men would be demanded by a voluntary force, which enjoys lower personnel turnover. In fact, the supply of true volunteers need only be increased by 75 thousand to sustain a force of 2.65 million men—55 thousand in the Army and 20 thousand in the other services.

An ideal measure of the economic cost of the draft requires data on the minimum supply price, M, at which each draftee and reluctant volunteer could have been attracted into active military service. Such data are clearly unavailable and some simplifying assumptions were made to arrive at an estimate of this cost. It seems reasonable to suppose that the 153.7 thousand reluctant volunteers who enlist in preference to being drafted have less aversion to military service than do draftees or men who never enter military service. Indeed, if the draft were abolished and military pay advanced, I suspect that most of these men would become regular volunteers to enlisted ranks. A lower bound to the economic cost is thus obtained by assuming that these men have the lowest minimum supply prices above the current first-term pay M_0. According to the complement supply curve for enlistements to total DOD, first-term pay must be raised by a factor of 1.88 to attract an additional 153.7 thousand recruits on a voluntary basis.[29]

The exposition is facilitated by referring to the supply curve of Fig. 1. When the draft is eliminated, the annual supply of enlistements is projected to be 263 thousand men at the current and unchanged level of first-term pay $M_0 = \$2,500$. If pay is increased by a factor of 1.88 to $M_1 = \$4,700$, the annual supply increases to 416.7 thousand men; i.e., from $0A$ to $0B$ accessions. The reluctant volunteers (the line segment AB) are projected to enlist at the lower pay because of the threat of a draft. Differences between minimum supply prices (indicated by the height of the curve along DE) and current first-term pay M_0, represent the implicit taxes levied against these men. The aggregate annual cost is given by the area of the triangle, $DB'E$, which is equal to \$141 million. This estimate assumes that each reluctant volunteer would be compensated in a discriminatory fashion without compensating others. If, however, pay were raised to \$4,700 for all recruits, the annual cost is increased by the quadrangle, M_0DEM_1 or \$917 million.[30] The lower annual cost of \$141 million which excludes rents constitutes a lower bound to the tax implicitly placed on reluctant volunteers who were coerced to enlist by a draft liability. In a sense, each reluctant volunteer pays an annual implicit tax of \$915 during his first term of service. If the point estimate of β had been used (implying a steeper supply curve), the annual cost climbs to \$192 million.[31] Since each reluctant volunteer serves for 3.5 years, the total implicit tax levied on reluctant volunteers from a given age class is estimated to be \$493 million; the best estimate is \$672 million.

The economic cost of conscripting men is hard to assess. The Selective Service System does not attempt to draft men with the least aversion to military life.

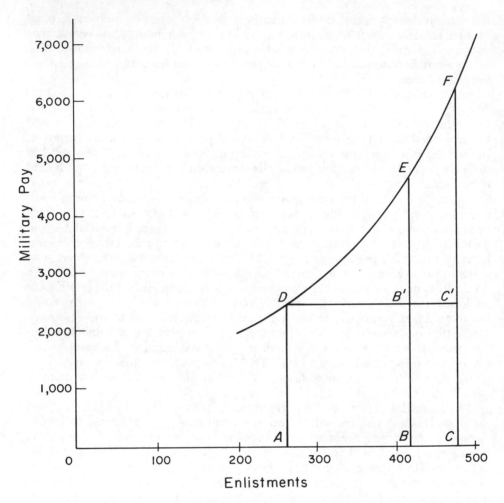

Fɪɢ. 1.—Supply curve of voluntary enlistments to total DOD

An assumption that draftees would be next in line above the point E in Fig. 1 (implying that they have the next lowest minimum supply prices) is less plausible. However, a lower bound estimate of the cost is again obtained by invoking this implausible assumption. The complement supply curve of Fig. 1 indicates that first-term pay must be raised from $M_1 = \$4,700$ to $M_2 = \$5,600$ in order to attract 55.3 thousand more recruits on a voluntary basis. If each conscript (the line segment BC) is compensated in a discriminatory fashion, the implicit annual tax placed on draftees is $175 million, the area of the trapezoid $EB'C'F$.[32] Since the average active-duty tour for a draftee is 1.9 years, the total implicit tax for draftees in an age class is $333 million.

V. CONCLUDING REMARKS

A manpower procurement system predicated on a draft liability compels some men (draftees) to serve, while others (reluctant volunteers) are coerced to enlist at abnormally low pay scales. Each draftee and reluctant volunteer could, in principle, have been induced through higher pay to volunteer for the Armed Forces. The difference between his minimum supply price and current first-term pay is surely a tax implicitly paid by each reluctant service participant. A lower bound estimate of the economic cost of the draft for those who serve as enlisted men is provided by the area $DC'F$. The cost to members of an age class is conservatively estimated to be $826 million. Where the best estimate of the supply elasticity has been used, I obtain the estimates in the last column of summary Table 25.

TABLE 25

Estimates of the Economic Cost of the Draft

(For Reluctant Participants Serving in Enlisted Ranks)

	Low Estimate $(\beta = .402)$	Middle Estimate $(\beta = .315)$
Annual first-term pay		
M_0	$2,500	$2,500
M_1	4,700	5,600
M_2	5,900	7,450
Annual cost excluding rents (millions)		
Reluctant volunteers ($DB'E$)	141	192
Draftees ($EB'C'F$)	175	243
Aggregate cost for members of an age class (millions)		
Reluctant volunteers	493	672
Draftees	333	462
Total	826	1,134

These estimates are biased downward because the men (reluctant service participants) who bear the cost are assumed to have the lowest supply prices in the absence of a draft. Put in another way, I have assumed that if the draft were abolished, the reluctant participants would be the ones who would be induced to enter an all-volunteer force. Under a draft, the true volunteers are denied the higher military pay that they would have received if the Armed Forces were obliged to acquire labor in a competitive labor market. By including these rents to true volunteers, the full economic cost rises to $5,364 million.[33]

In this paper, the economic cost has been estimated only for men who serve in the active-duty enlisted ranks because of the draft law. A fuller analysis must include the costs borne by draft-motivated accessions to officer ranks and to reserve components. According to the 1964 DOD survey, 41.3 per cent of newly commissioned officers indicated that they probably or definitely would not have volunteered if there had been no draft. Available evidence suggests that reservists have even higher aversions to service life.[34] If we had estimated the cost of military service for these individuals, the economic cost of the draft would be considerably greater.

In addition to the direct costs borne by those who ultimately serve in the Armed Forces, the draft allegedly creates other indirect costs which derive from the mechanics of the selection process. Under the current Selective Service system, a youth can remain in a draft-liable status for seven and one-half years. Some evidence suggests that employers discriminate against youths who are still eligible to be drafted.[35] The youth who elects to wait and see if he can avoid military service is likely to suffer more unemployment. He may be obliged to accept casual employment which does not provide useful job training for later life. Moreover, long periods of draft liability encourage youths to pursue activities which might bestow a deferment. When married non-fathers were placed in a lower order of call in September, 1963, the action was followed by small increases in marriage rates of males in the draft-liable ages. It is also alleged that the draft prompts men to prolong their education or to enter occupations which grant deferments. These costs deriving from the uncertainty of the present draft are, in my opinion, small when compared to the direct economic costs incurred by those who are involuntarily inducted or who become reluctant volunteers.

If the current draft law is extended into the decade ahead, it is projected that only 38.5 per cent of qualified males will be required to staff a mixed force of 2.65 million men. Since the draft assures adequate supplies of initial accessions, military pay can be kept at artificially low levels. Many servicemen on their first tour can correctly be called reluctant participants who pay substantial implicit taxes because they were coerced to serve. A conservative estimate of the economic cost (excluding rents) is $826 million—the amount of compensation which would have induced these men to enter on a voluntary basis. If all recruits received the first-term pay needed to attract the last draftee, the opportunity cost of acquiring new accessions would exceed $5.3 billion.

An all-volunteer force offers a polar alternative to the draft. With its lower personnel turnover, a voluntary force of the same size could be sustained by recruiting only 27.5 per cent of qualified males. The budgetary payroll cost would, however, have to be raised by $4 billion per year.

It should be emphasized that the figures appearing in this paper represent my estimates. The two crucial ingredients are (1) the supply curve of voluntary enlistments in the absence of a draft and (2) required accessions as determined by the assumed force strength and personnel turnover. Complement supply curves were estimated from cross-sectional data on estimated voluntary enlistment rates.[36] The new retention profiles used to derive gross-flow demands for an all-volunteer force generated an age structure of the force which closely resembles those of smaller professional armies in Canada and the United Kingdom. In the light of the data examined, I am reasonably confident of my cost estimates, at least for the assumed force strength of 2.65 million men.

If peacetime military requirements necessitate larger active-duty forces, all costs necessarily climb. In order to sustain a force strength of 3.3 million men on a voluntary basis, required accessions must be increased by roughly 30 per cent. The additional budgetary cost of a voluntary force over a mixed force of the same size would be in the neighborhood of 8 to 10 billion dollars.[37] The high budgetary cost of a voluntary force is not the only relevant consideration. If men are procured by a draft, the high turnover of draftees implies that over 60 per cent of qualified males would be demanded to maintain a mixed force of 3.3 million men. Annual accessions under a draft would rise by more than 50 per cent in the mixed-force case.

The alternative of a voluntary manpower procurement system has been criticized because of its inflexibility to changing military demands. If, for example, force strengths must be increased from 2.65 to 3.3 million men within a single year, it would be difficult to accomplish this through higher pay. The criticism is, in my opinion, valid for changing demands of this magnitude. However, a voluntary procurement system could be designed to accommodate minor fluctuations in stock demands—say from 2.65 to 3.0 million men. Entry level and career military pay could be set to provide excess supplies of enlistment applicants and servicemen who wish to reenlist. The number of men accepted (either as new recruits or as reenlistments) would be determined by the stock demand, meaning the force strength objective. In response to a short-run increase in strength objectives, the services would accept more of the excess supplies. The criticism of inflexibility is valid only if "peacetime" military demands are so highly variable that they involve increasing force strengths by more than 10 per cent in a single year.

The defense budget for active-duty military personnel is obviously lower with a draft. However, the conscription of military personnel simply substitutes implicit taxes levied on those men who serve for explicit taxes on all citizens to finance the higher payroll of an all-volunteer force. The real economic cost of maintaining a defense establishment is partially concealed because these implicit taxes never appear in the defense budget. The real opportunity cost of acquiring military personnel must include the full economic cost of the draft.

NOTES

[1] The three leading alternatives to the current draft are (1) an all-volunteer force, (2) lottery at a younger age, and (3) equivalent service. In the third alternative, men could discharge their draft liability by equivalent service in some other endeavor such as the Peace Corps or VISTA. Given the projected growth in male population, these "other endeavors" would have to be greatly expanded if all qualified youths are to serve their country. Adoption of this alternative would put the federal government into many new activities as well as entailing a sizable rise in budgetary costs. The cost of a lottery selection system cannot be evaluated until its specific details are clarified. The impact of a lottery on voluntary accessions to enlisted ranks, officer procurement programs, and reserve units must be assessed. A comparison of the lottery and the present Selective Service System is clearly beyond the scope of this paper.

[2] House of Representatives, Eighty-ninth Congress, Second Session, "Review of the Administration and Operation of the Selective Service System," Hearings before the Committee on Armed Services (June 22, 23, 24, 28, 29, and 30, 1966 [hereafter abbreviated *House Hearings*]), pp. 9923-55. See especially pp. 9936-40.

[3] In the last decade, reservists were recalled to active duty in significant numbers only once. During the Berlin crisis of FY 1962, some 111 thousand National Guard and Army reservists were recalled to raise Army active-duty force strength from 858.6 thousand in FY 1961 to 1,066.4 thousand in FY 1962. This generalization does not apply to officers. In the five years FY 1960-64, an annual average of 1,287 reserve officers were activated, accounting for 3.5 per cent of total officer accessions.

[4] The data in the lower panel of Table 1 may differ from other estimates of accessions for at least two reasons. One is that "first enlistments" include some men with prior service while other data may pertain to non-prior-service accessions. The other is that "reserves to active duty" which I have included with first enlistments, except for the unusual situation prevailing in FY 1962, are often neglected. The remaining discrepancies are, however, quite small.

[5] Draftees have mainly been channeled to the Army. A few delinquents (usually reservists who failed to attend drill meetings) are drafted into the other three services. In 1956, the Navy accepted draftees, while the Marines did so in FY 1966. A two-

year active-duty reserve program was offered by the Army in 1956, but the program was dropped in 1958. Finally regular enlistments are obligated to initial tours of three years in the Regular Army and four years in the Air Force. The length of initial tours is more variable in the Navy and Marines, with some recruits signed to six-year tours.

[6] The draft liability is extended to the age of 35 for men holding occupational and student deferments. However, older liable men are placed in a lower order of call so that few individuals over 26 years of age are drafted. One exception is the draft of doctors and dentists.

[7] More careful estimates of mental and physical rejection rates have been prepared by Dr. Bernard Karpinos of the Department of Defense. His estimates indicate that the physical rejection rate rises with educational attainment. The differences between the estimates of Dr. Karpinos and my estimates are, however, quite small.

[8] Earlier age classes experienced considerably higher participation rates because of the Korean War. Moreover, larger fractions of these age classes entered active-duty ranks between 1953-60. The Reserve and National Guard programs requiring active duty for training only were largely developed since 1958. In the current Vietnam buildup, over 900 thousand men entered active-duty components in FY 1966, implying considerably higher participation rates for the age classes of 1942-45.

[9] The data of Table 5 indicate that 70.8 per cent of the two-year reservists did not have a high school degree. The educational attainment of this group is misleading. Many recruits enlist while they are still enrolled in school but enter active duty only upon graduation. Indeed, the mental distribution of recruits to the Navy's 2x6 program is considerably higher than that of regular Navy enlistments.

[10] The 1960 Census data applied to servicemen stationed in the U.S.; the total DOD force strength in FY 1960 included 2,447 thousand males, but the Census enumerated only 1,715 thousand. The Census figures were expanded to the assumed force strength of 2.65 million by multiplying by $(2,650/1,715 =) 1.545$. This procedure assumes that servicemen stationed abroad have the same age and educational distribution as those stationed in the U. S. I suspect that this procedure leads to upward biases in both the median age and education of the force.

[11] The projected accessions appearing in Table 1 correspond to an assumed strength of 2.7 million men and assume that the civilian unemployment rate will be 5.5 per cent—the average unemployment rate from 1957-64. A lower civilian unemployment rate reduces voluntary enlistments to the Army, thereby increasing the projected number of draft calls.

[12] The qualified manpower pools in FY 1970-75 are projected to be 42 per cent larger than the qualified populations in FY 1960-65. However, the DOD projections indicate that Army enlistments rise by only 26 per cent. If excess supplies of enlistment applicants to other services are channeled to the Army, the DOD estimates could prove to be on the low side.

[13] The education distribution of the male population in FY 1970-75 was assumed to be the same as in 1964. Moreover, the education distribution of voluntary enlistments was also assumed to be the same. These assumptions tend to understate the educational attainment of future military service participants.

[14] The estimates in the fifth column of Table 13 contain a downward bias. Since the other services are expected to enjoy excess supplies of enlistment applicants in FY 1970-75, the figures in the fourth column do not represent voluntary supply responses.

[15] Officer procurement programs are considerably more variable than procurement channels for enlisted men. For example, the Army and Air Force now offer scholarships and stipends for some ROTC students; a similar program is also offered by the Navy. It is likely that in an all-volunteer force, the non-college graduate programs (especially for flight training) will be expanded.

[16] Air Force surveys have attempted to identify the single most important reason for original entry. Two of several possible responses can be interpreted as draft-motivated reasons: these are "choice of service" and "volunteered in preference to being drafted." Follow-up studies reveal that reenlistment rates are considerably lower for Airmen selecting these two responses.

[17] The actual retention rates were taken from a special tabulation prepared by the DOD Statistical Office. Retention rates for the all-volunteer forces were based on responses of officers who stated that they definitely or probably would have volunteered if there had been no draft. Each officer on his first tour indicated whether he intended to remain on active duty after completing his present tour of duty.

[18] Data on voluntary enlistments in mental groups I to III were available by states for FY 1963. Since enlistments of men in mental group IV are limited by recruitment quotas, their omission assures that the data represent supply responses. The number of true volunteers was inferred by applying the reults of the 1964 DOD survey in a manner analogous to that shown in Table 13. The voluntary enlistment rate was expressed in relation to the male civilian labor force, 17-20 years of age, adjusted for physical and mental rejections.

[19] In estimating the complement supply equation, the unemployment rate of youths in each region was included as an additional explanatory variable. The data on enlistment rates, E, relative military/civilian earnings, Y, and unemployment rates, U, can be found in the *House Hearings*, Table 6, p. 9957. A more detailed discussion of voluntary supplies of military personnel is contained in a paper by S. Altman and A. Fechter in the May, 1967 *Papers and Proceedings* of the American Economic Association.

[20] In the mixed force, an annual input of one regular Army enlistee (only 56.8 per cent being true volunteers) produced a sustainable force in which $F = 2.73$ men were in their first term and $C = 2.14$ were in the career force. Since losses during the first term arise from discharges for medical, hardship, and unsuitability reasons, the number in the first term, F, will be unaffected by the move to a voluntary force. However, the number in the career force will climb to $C' = C(33.0/22.1) = 3.20$ men. The turnover rate of an all-volunteer force is then simply

$$\left(\frac{1}{F+C'}\right) \text{ or } \left(\frac{1}{5.93}\right) = 16.9 \text{ per cent.}$$

[21] My estimate of the necessary first-term pay increase is lower than the DOD estimates. The DOD study presented three estimates corresponding to three values of β; the point estimate of β, and the point estimate plus and minus one standard error of the regression coefficient. For the case of a 5.5 per cent unemployment rate, I have reproduced the estimates of percentage increases in first-term pay; see *House Hearings*, p. 9958.

DOD low estimate	80	DOD high estimate	181
DOD best estimate	111	my estimate	68

The discrepancy is probably due to differences in our estimates of the required-accessions rate A. I assume a steady state, while the DOD study appears to use a required-accessions rate applicable to the transition period.

[22] Quarters, subsistence, and uniform allowances are classified as nontaxable income, thereby bestowing a tax advantage to servicemen. The monetary value of this tax advantage accounts for around 5.5 per cent of tax-equivalent income. In addition to these items, many men receive money payments for flight pay, sea duty, jump pay, etc. I have also omitted the imputed value of other forms of income in kind such as medical care, insurance, free military transportation, and PX privileges.

[23] The stock demand for servicemen is not completely inelastic, and at higher

prices fewer men would be demanded by the Armed Services. A consideration which operates in the opposing direction is the provision of rotational billets for men on rotation from overseas and sea-duty assignments.

24 *Statistical Abstract of the United States, 1966*, Table 153, p. 112.

25 The major omissions include pay for flight, jump, sea duty, and hazardous duty. Moreover, the age structure of the force refers to years of active military service, while pay is determined by years of service for pay purposes. The latter is always equal to or greater than the former, tending thereby to deflate my estimate of the pay-roll cost. An error in the opposing direction is present because roughly 5.5 per cent of tax-equivalent income represents the implicit tax advantage. Finally, I had only rough estimates of annual military incomes for officers.

26 In arriving at this cost, I assumed that an enlisted man received $3,900 in his first year of service with yearly increases of $300 for three years. The pay of enlisted men in their fourth and later years of service was raised by 17 per cent. The officers' pay profile was adjusted to eliminate the discontinuity between the second and third years. This resulted in a 20.1 per cent increase in first-term pay for officers.

27 The dynamic adjustments of labor markets are ignored in this analysis. If all servicemen were placed in the civilian labor force, wages would surely fall during the transitional period. Two pieces of evidence suggest that servicemen could, on an average, earn more than civilians. The median incomes of veterans in the 1960 Population Census were around 2.5 per cent higher than those of all civilian males. Second, the 1964 DOD survey revealed that weekly earnings were higher for men in mental groups I and II. The mental distribution of military personnel is, moreover, higher than that of the entire population because of the mental rejections. The incomes of Table 22 can thus be regarded as underestimates of the alternative earnings of servicemen. The median incomes of veterans can be found in *U. S. Census of Population 1960*, "Earnings of Total Civilian Male War Veterans in Experienced Labor Force in 1959," Table 16 PC (2), 8c; "Earnings of Males 25-64 in Experienced Civilian Labor Force in 1959," Table 1, PC (2) 7b.

28 Becker contends that nearly all of the age profile of income can be attributed to investment in human capital via on-the-job training; see G. S. Becker, *Human Capital*, (New York: Columbia University Press, 1964). The second hypothesis could be rationalized by my theory of fixed employment costs. Older men are more likely to be married and to possess other attributes associated with low labor turnover. If hiring and initial training costs are high, it behooves the firm to pay higher wages to men with longer expected periods of employment; see W. Y. Oi, "Labor as a Quasi-Fixed Factor," *Journal of Political Economy*, December, 1962.

29 The complement supply curve for enlistments to total DOD produced an estimate for β of .315 with a standard error of .087; compare equation (1). In the absence of a draft, the enlistment rate for men in mental groups I to III was estimated to be 27.8 per cent of the qualified labor force in an age class. In deriving the supply curve depicted in Fig. 1, I set β equal to .402, the point estimate plus one standard error. The elasticity was +1.04. The upward bias in the supply elasticity tends to understate the magnitude of the economic cost.

30 In competitive labor markets, these rents are included in the cost of acquiring larger supplies of labor. If college professors could be conscripted, or if we could recapture the economic rents from teaching, the budgetary cost of higher education could be sharply reduced.

31 When the value of β is lowered from .402 to its least squares estimate of $\beta =$ .315, the elasticity of supply falls from 1.04 to 0.82. The necessary pay increase climbs from $4,700 to $5,600.

32 Recall that a draftee serves for less than two years. Consequently his average annual military pay is $2,100 as compared to $M_0 = \$2,500$ for reluctant and true volunteers. The annual cost is, therefore, slightly larger than the area $EB'C'F$ in

Fig. 1. If β is set equal to .315, first-term pay must rise to $M_2 = \$7,450$ to attract draftees on a voluntary basis. In this event, the annual cost climbs to \$243 million, and the aggregate cost for an age class climbs from \$333 to \$462 million.

[33] The low estimate of the pay increases ($\beta = .402$) was used to arrive at this cost. Each true volunteer is presumed to receive an additional \$3,100 (the difference $M_2 - M_0$) which is the rent he would receive.

[34] The DOD survey revealed that draft-motivated enlistments accounted for 70.7 per cent of new accessions to reserve and National Guard components. Moreover, the percentage of reluctant volunteers was larger for men with higher alternative civilian earnings, as indicated by the following excerpt from the *House Hearings* (p. 9956):

Annual Civilian Income	Percentage of Draft-Motivated Enlistments
less than \$2,999	54.1
\$3,000-\$4,999	71.6
\$5,000-\$7,499	72.1
\$7,500 and over	82.2

[33] The low estimate of the pay increases ($\beta = .402$) was used to arrive at this cost. ployers placed restrictions on draft-liable males. According to the DOD Survey of 22- to 25-year-old civilians, 26 per cent with draft classification 1-A said that they had difficulty in securing employment. The credibility of this type of question is challenged by the finding that 17 per cent of men with dependency deferments, III-A, also stated that they had difficulty securing employment because of their draft liability. The percentages having "difficulty" climbed with age and educational attainment. Further details of these surveys can be found in *House Hearings*, pp. 10008-10.

[36] Enlistment data on a regional basis were available only for 1963. The recent enlistment experience has been strongly influenced by the Vietnam buildup, with over 900 thousand men entering active military service in FY 1966. An ongoing research effort on the supply of volunteers and manpower utilization practices of the Armed Services is surely needed.

[37] Estimation of the necessary pay increase to achieve this larger force involves an extrapolation of the supply curve beyond the range which I consider to be meaningful. The confidence intervals for predictions from a regression equation become extremely wide as one moves outside the range of the sample observations. Hence, the following estimates should be viewed as indicative of orders of magnitude. In a steady state, Army enlistments for a force of 3.3 million men are estimated to be 185 thousand. According to the complement supply curve for Army enlistments, first-term pay would have to be raised to \$6,350 as compared to the previous increase of \$4,200 for a force of 2.65 million men. If part of the higher pay could be given as initial enlistment bonuses, the defense budget for active-duty military personnel would rise by 8 to 10 billion dollars a year.

23

Voluntary National Service

JOHN MITRISIN

The war in Vietnam, with its increased military manpower needs, plus the extension of the Selective Service Law in 1967, has raised a storm of controversy about the fairness of the draft. Inequities which passed unnoticed before have now become prominent both because more men are being drafted and because of the increased concern over equality nurtured in the civil rights movement and the "war on poverty." Why should some be deferred and remain safely at home while others are exposed to the danger of death and disfigurement abroad?

A number of proposals have been made which attempt to remedy this problem. This paper will evaluate them, and then describe a voluntary national service program which avoids the problems posed by the other alternatives.

PROFESSIONAL ARMY

A professional army is one possible solution. It would avoid the question of fairness which centers on deferments, since enlistment would be voluntary. Those who did not want to join would be free not to.

The advantages of voluntary commitment found in a professional army are counterbalanced by the following disadvantages.[1] An army composed of professional soldiers might well engage in conduct, like torture, which would not be tolerated in civilian life. Their actions could be justified on the grounds that in order to win, any means necessary should be used. Unlike a professional army, a non-professional one inhibits unacceptable conduct because of the annual influx of thousands of men for only two or three years. (It does not stop it, as the war in Algeria or photos from Vietnam show.) These men do not accept the values of a professional soldier, since most of them expect to continue in other careers after their service is over, and therefore maintain their civilian outlook.

The use of a professional army would limit public interest and concern about our involvement in small wars. If a professional army were used to fight them, the number of soldiers engaged would be much smaller than if a non-professional army were employed, since the same men would fight the war until the conflict ended. Soldiers would die and families would grieve, but the pressure exerted to end the war would be less than with a non-professional army, since there would not be the annual influx of thousands of men whose families would worry about them and attempt to stop the conflict.

If it was decided that a professional army was desirable, some other inducement besides money would be necessary to attract volunteers. When 16- to 19-

The author is with the Institute for Policy Studies.

year-olds were asked: "If there was no draft, what condition would be most likely to get you to volunteer?" less than 4 per cent said that "equal pay" with civilian life would be an inducement, and only 17 per cent felt that "considerably higher" pay would make a military career attractive.[2] These answers indicate no overwhelming relationship between pay and a desire to make a career of the armed forces.

LOTTERY

A lottery is another proposed alternative to the Selective Service. Under a lottery, all men turning 18 would register. The names of each month's registrants would be put in an electronic hat, and then a certain percentage of names would be drawn. The percentage drawn each month would be based on Defense Department estimates of manpower needs for the year. Since an estimated one-third of those called would be rejected, one-third more names would be drawn than were needed.

Those chosen would be subject to the draft for one year, let us say from the time they are $18\frac{1}{2}$ to $19\frac{1}{2}$. When they reached $19\frac{1}{2}$, those not drafted would no longer be liable for conscription. Those whose names were not drawn would never be liable.

Some of those whose names had been drawn might be deferred, but not indefinitely. Students might be allowed to finish undergraduate school, but upon graduation their names would be placed among those $18\frac{1}{2}$-year-olds whose names had been chosen in the lottery. They would then be eligible for the draft for one year.

The lottery would be an improvement over the Selective Service System. Men would be conscripted on the basis of chance rather than on the decisions of a draft board. Social position and education, which presently help to exempt certain groups from the draft, would play no part. The vagaries of the present deferment "system" would be abolished.

These vagaries arise because deferments are granted by the local boards which are independent from central control. They are composed of community members who decide which men will be inducted into the armed forces, and which will be deferred. The independent nature of the boards means that the criteria for deferments vary from place to place. This leads to a situation where, in certain cases, geographical location can mean the difference between a deferment and wearing Army green.

Independent boards are probably the best way of granting deferments, but why are there deferments at all? Gen. Hershey defends deferments on the grounds that they are necessary for the "national interest." "National interest," in effect, means that the primary goal of American society is to guarantee the continuation of our military might. Every man is evaluated on his ability to contribute to this goal. Those men learning scientific or engineering skills, which will enable them to maintain and advance the complex technological weapons of modern warfare, will be deferred. Those who are doing something else will be drafted. The justice of forcing one man to fight and allowing another to study is not a consideration. According to Gen. Hershey, "Fairness, as a common denominator to the individual desires of each person, does not exist." The concepts of choice and volition are secondary to "national interest."

This desire for deferments, in the name of national interest, seems unwarranted since Secretary of Labor Willard Wirtz, when asked by the President's National Advisory Commission on the Selective Service how a policy of no deferments would affect the labor market, said:

> Not enough to matter. The question is one that ought to be resolved on the basis of the boy and his education. The labor market can readily accommodate itself to whatever is the sensible decision in terms of elevating the human race. . . . We have asked for too long about the needs of the system of things for "manpower" and "womenpower." The question . . . is what opportunities individuals ought to have.

If this is true, there is no reason to continue deferments, since no shortage of trained men vital to defense would occur. With no need for deferments, a lottery would be possible without endangering the "national interest."

A lottery would be more just than the Selective Service in its selection of conscripts, but it would continue to compel men to serve against their wishes. The decision of who would serve would still be made by forces outside the control of the recruit. In a lottery, a machine would pick his name. The number of men picked would still be decided by men older than those in the draft-age population. They have this power because it is assumed they have the experience and judgment to make the "proper" decisions, while 18- to 25-year-olds do not. One consequence of this situation is that our policies are shaped by men whose perceptions and experiences were gained in the past. These perceptions may not be those of the men assigned to perform the task, and may not reflect the actual needs of the contemporary world. Eighteen- to 25-year-olds should have some role in determining what should be done. Their ability to make the "proper" choice is no better or worse than that of others: fools and geniuses can be any age. Since these youths do the work, they should have the right to ratify the decision.

This demand is based on the proposition that we live in a democracy, a society in which the people are the source of power. The majority rules, but the rights of the minority are protected. The minority may disagree and protest the acts of the majority, and attempt to change laws to conform to their view. Their right to dissent extends to the bounds of criminal activity. They may break a law they disagree with to highlight their disagreement, but they may not do so and expect to go unpunished.[3]

A democracy also assumes citizen participation, but it leaves the choice of activity up to the individual. In terms of joining the armed services, this means that those 18-25, who believe that war, in Vietnam or anywhere else is justified, would volunteer to fight. Those who did not believe in it would not join. By no stretch of the imagination could one interpret this to mean that all those 18-25 must join the Armed Forces to defend the rest of society, which *is* the present situation.

Those in positions of power have decided that in order to advance United States policy and protect American interests in the world, military might is necessary. They decided that since the armed forces needs men to operate, those between 18 and 25 must serve, even though this is contrary to the wishes of many. The decision has been rationalized in many ways but the most important of these is based on the rhetoric of duty in a democracy. Rhetoric and reality clash, since those who are drafted have no choice in what they do. There are two possible ways of reconciling this contradiction—change the rhetoric or change the reality. The rhetoric can be altered by telling those 18-25 that democracy is fine, but that, in some situations, its rules are suspended to serve the majority of adults who impose this task on a minority. The majority may say: "The situation is undemocratic, but when you are older it will seem as just to you then as it does to us now."

The alternative is to carry the democratic assumption to its conclusion: allow each 18- to 25-year-old to decide how he wants to serve the state. Even if a majority decided for military service, the minority would be free to dissent and not join.

Conferences on the draft continue the undemocratic process. They either fail to involve those whose fate is being discussed, or when they do, not in sufficient numbers. This Conference has three or four students as panel members and about ten as audience participants. Besides there not being enough representatives present, why are there only students? Student opinion may be solicited because it is felt they are the vanguard of other youths, but how can one be sure the "vanguard" reflects the mood of the entire draft-age population, when the majority eligible for the draft are not students?

COMPULSORY NATIONAL SERVICE

A more "democratic" alternative to the draft proposed by some is compulsory national service. It is viewed as a way to equalize draft inequalities and provide young people with a choice in how they may serve. Most proposed programs are essentially alike. They would require those 18-25 to serve either in the military or a variety of civilian programs for two years. Those who choose the Armed Forces would receive either higher pay, or serve a shorter length of time than those joining civilian pograms like the Peace or Job Corps. All these proposed programs would supplement military manpower shortages through conscription. They assume that there is no practical way of encouraging enough men to volunteer.

Some proponents of this kind of program include Donald Eberly and Morris Janowitz. Others, like Harris Wofford,[4] *speak* of a voluntary national service, but describe a compulsory program.

These programs, in an effort to diminish the inequalities of the draft, make some type of service compulsory for all those not going into the military. By requiring all persons 18-25 to participate in national service, these authors assume: that citizens must serve society; that this service must occur between the ages of 18 and 25; and that there are only certain ways this requirement can be fulfilled. These assumptions are not valid in a democratic society. In a democracy, a citizen does not have to serve if he does not want to even though he does have to pay taxes.[5] One who wishes to enter national service should not have to do so within a seven-year period, since only he himself can decide when his services are the most valuable. National service is not the only valid form of participation. One is constantly participating in a democracy and helping to determine public policy by either accepting or rejecting the status quo. If one feels supermarket prices are too high, one boycotts. If one feels public transportation is too expensive, one walks. Political affiliation and voting are other forms of participation. National service is only one kind of involvement among many possible alternatives.

The proposals of Mr. Wofford and Mr. Eberly reflect their vocational interests. The former is a Peace Corps official, and the latter works for the Overseas Educational Service, which helps recruit teachers to serve abroad. Their belief that service is good and should be encouraged does not mean it should be law. They have no right to impose service on others in a free society.

Support for compulsory national service, even with its many disadvantages, is potentially great. It is seen as a means of reducing draft inequalities without abolishing the draft, or disturbing military, governmental, business, or educational institutions. It satisfies the Selective Service which wants to be able to take men when it needs them. Business would be interested in both compulsory national service and the lottery because it would reduce the uncertainty about hiring young men and losing them to the Army. If there were compulsory national service, its completion would probably become a requirement for employment. In the case of a lottery, only certain men 18½ to 19½ would be draftable. Business would probably exclude these people from employment, and accept everyone else. Students are concerned with the equity of the draft. They feel it is not just that one man has to fight and another is deferred, especially when deferments are based on the ability to afford college. The lottery, alone, or combined with compulsory national service, replaces wealth by chance in deciding who is conscripted. So far, no compulsory national service program has been proposed that would dispense with conscription; that is, replace compulsion with choice. Even if one existed, it would still be a *compulsory program*, and, like the lottery, would not allow for those who did not want to serve in any manner.

All the solutions so far proposed have been unable to solve the question of individual choice because in their attempts to satisfy all the interested parties, they consider only what seems *at the moment* to be politically possible. Fortunately, politically possible solutions are not limited to those plans which attempt to please groups on the basis of present reality, but also include those ideas which make the seemingly impossible possible by bringing in factors which are neglected or disregarded, thereby changing the reality.

VOLUNTARY NATIONAL SERVICE

Voluntary national service is such a politically possible idea. The program would be open to all those between 18 and 25 and participants could undertake service with federal and state agencies as well as with those private organizations exempt under federal law from paying federal taxes. Those people who wanted to serve could choose either military or civilian activities. They would serve two years, and the federal government would pay them a private's wages ($97 a month), would pay for any medical care they might need, and would either supply room and board or make available to the sponsoring private organizations an allowance of $50 a month per volunteer to cover room and board.

The reliance on voluntary commitment would avoid the problems raised by compulsory national service and the lottery. The rights of those who did not want to participate in any kind of service would be protected, while those who wanted to serve would be able to choose the kind of activity they preferred.

This section of the paper will describe how a voluntary national service program would operate. It will explain the military and the civilian programs, project the cost of a voluntary national service program, indicate its possible effects on American society, and discuss the chances of its acceptance by the various groups interested in the draft debate.

Voluntary National Service—Military

The armed forces under this program would rely *solely* on volunteers. This would permit those who opposed the use of violence or disagreed with how military power was used to cast their votes against it by not joining.

A voluntary armed force would be possible only when the manpower pool is so large that under no system of military recruitment would all the men in the pool be used. We have now reached this point. It is estimated by the Department of Defense that by 1974, at pre-Vietnam levels, only 34 per cent of those reaching 26 (18 in 1966) would have to serve. The number would be 42 per cent if military strength were maintained at the three-million man level.

Without a special inducement, even with this large pool, the armed services could not attract enough men to meet their needs. The lottery and compulsory national service would solve this problem by conscription. Voluntary national service would increase military enlistments by offering volunteers a payoff unobtainable in other national service programs: an educational bonus offered to veterans after two years of military service. It would provide them with four years of schooling at any educational institution they wished. The government would pay their tuition, room, board, and incidental expenses.

Critics might argue that an educational inducement would benefit only those who could not afford an education before, and that the Armed Forces would only attract those poor who wanted an education. Veterans' use of the GI Bill after World War II and Korea does not bear this assumption out. If one uses education as an index of socioeconomic status, it turns out that the more formal education a veteran had had prior to entrance into the armed forces, the greater was the chance he used his training benefits.[6] Eighty per cent of the men who used the GI Bill maintain they would have gone to school even if there had been no benefits.[7] This figure is difficult to believe when one considers the economic conditions of the 1930's. The 80 per cent figure might better be considered an indicator of what, on hindsight, they thought they wanted to do after their military service was over.

In considering veterans' use of the Serviceman's Readjustment Act, one must remember that only after World War II were the benefits sufficient to allow one to study without also working. By the 1950's, the cost of education had risen to the point where benefits were no longer sufficient to cover tuition. The Korean Bill and present GI benefits are nowhere near sufficient to allow a veteran to obtain an education without also working. The poor, who would greatly benefit from further education, are effectively excluded from taking advantage of the opportunity offered them because they cannot supplement the $100 a month veterans now get to cover tuition and living expenses. They lack the skills that would enable them to get high-paying part-time jobs to increase their income, and the low-paying jobs which they could get would require working additional hours, with insufficient time left to study.

To attract volunteers, an educational bonus would have to be large enough to permit veterans to study without working, and be more attractive than the opportunities offered by civilian voluntary national service programs. The bonus would probably encourage lower middle-class youths, who now are drafted because they do not have the money to go to college, to volunteer and go to school after their military service was completed. Some of those going to school part-time might decide that they would finish sooner if they went into the armed forces and then studied continuously for four years.

The educational bonus would not be intended to make the student wealthy, but should not be so meager that he would starve, either physically or psychologically. He needs money for clothing, books, and occasional social events. It is unreasonable to expect the student-veteran to watch every penny in order to eat and pay the rent. The educational bonus envisioned would pay:

1) full tuition for four years at any approved school;
2) $150 a year for books and supplies;
3) $50 a week subsistence (this $50 would apply to all veterans in training and would be prorated proportionately for those taking less than a full course load; it would be discontinued when training stopped or the four years had elapsed).

If the average tuition were $1,000 a year, the total cost of training a veteran for one year would be $3,750, or $15,000 for four years. If four hundred thousand men were discharged from the Armed Forces every year, and they all used their benefits for four years, the program would cost:

```
1st year ...................................$1.5 billion
2nd year ...................................$3.0 billion
3rd year ...................................$4.5 billion
4th and every year thereafter .................$6.0 billion
```

This program would not work unless it produced volunteers. At this time it is not certain how many men would be attracted by an expanded GI Bill. The Bureau of the Census recently asked 16- to 19-year-old non-veterans what benefits military service would have to offer to induce them to volunteer. Their responses are given in Table 1.

TABLE 1

Percentage of Non-Veteran 16- to 19-Year-Olds

Who Would Volunteer without a Draft

	Non-Students	Students
If guaranteed training in a job or skill useful in civilian life	29	20
If sent to school or college at Government expense, before or during military service	18	31
If sent to school or college at Government expense, *after* military service	8	12

Source: Thomas D. Morris before House Committee on Armed Forces, Report on DOD Study of the Draft, June 30, 1966.

The first two questions in Table 1 might give the impression that the Armed Forces teaches men skills useful in obtaining civilian employment. It is true that men are giving vocational training, but the applicability of this training to civilian jobs is unclear. Combat specialties, which account for 14.6 per cent of all enlisted men's activities, are clearly non-transferable. There are no jobs in the Armed Forces comparable to those of production workers or sales personnel. Some skills in electronics, mechanics, crafts, and services would seem to be related to civilian jobs, but they are not always so transferable as they appear. The reason for this is that the training period in the military is short. In the resulting courses, much of the theoretical content that is taught in civilian technical institutes is eliminated or curtailed in favor of immediate and practical elements. The specialists produced often have only a limited knowledge of the equipment they work with, which in turn may be specially adapted or designed for military use. There are other obstacles. A specialist like a Navy electrician's mate may not be able to become an electrician: he is not always familiar with local building codes, and union requirements may require that he start as an apprentice. Some military skills, such as radio and radar maintenance, have civilian counterparts, but the number of jobs available in these areas is limited. Practically no concrete data correlating veterans' vocational activities with their military training is available.[8] Studies on this subject would be valuable in ascertaining the feasibility of creating a voluntary armed forces that would use a combination of skilled military training and civilian technical schooling to attract volunteers.

The number of affirmative answers to the third question—volunteering to obtain educational benefits—was low, but considering how meager these presently are, it is easy to understand why. These benefits would have to be on the scale of those outlined above to attract the necessary men. In addition, educational counseling would need to be given to men about to leave the service in an effort to encourage as many as possible to take advantage of this improved GI Bill. Additional information on veterans who did and did not use their benefits would be helpful in judging how practical an educational bonus would be in attracting recruits.

The Department of Defense will probably object to this proposal. It opposed a Cold War Bill of Rights because "it would seriously hamper . . . efforts to retain qualified personnel, particularly those with hard skills, on a career basis."[9] It will probably oppose an educational bonus on the same grounds.

The Department of Defense encourages reenlistments because it wants to create an efficient fighting machine. Men who reenlist have more experience, which hopefully increases their ability to carry out their jobs. The wish of the Armed Forces to improve is natural in any organization that believes in its future. This desire does not mean its goal should come before the desires of the individual or of the society generally. Unfortunately, this was the case with the Cold War GI Bill, and might well be the fate of the educational bonus. The result of this policy is well illustrated by the situation of the Negro in the Armed Forces. Proportionately more Negroes than whites reenlist. (Negro reenlistment rates range from two to three times the white rates.) Negroes are attracted because of the Armed Forces' non-discriminatory policies and the jobs it offers them—possible because of the military's ability to absorb men who have a relatively low level of education.

A Negro may have little chance of becoming an officer, but he will have a secure job and probably a higher standard of living than he could achieve in a civilian occupation.

This situation might seem to reflect favorably on the Department of Defense, since it gives men a chance they would not have elsewhere, but in reality these men have little choice. If they reenlist, they are sure of a job. If they leave the Armed Forces, their chances of obtaining employment are much less certain. An educational bonus would give servicemen a real choice when their term of service was over. Those who wanted to pursue a military career could stay, while those who did not want to would be provided with the schooling necessary to get them otherwise unobtainable civilian jobs.

Voluntary National Service—Civilian

The civilian program would be the place where those who wanted to serve but were either not interested in military service, or unable to join (men who were rejected, and women), could volunteer. The programs offered these individuals would be sponsored by federal and state governments, and tax-exempt private groups, and would cover a wide variety of activities both in the United States and abroad.

At home, volunteers could help solve some of the major problems confronting American society, such as urban blight, unemployment, education, conservation, medical care, and civil rights. Slum youths could participate in programs which would give them marketable skills and at the same time rehabilitate the neighborhoods they lived in. One such program might be an Urban Renewal Corps. Volunteers could renovate dilapidated slum buildings and at the same time learn a trade like electrician, carpenter, plasterer, or plumber. The program could be set up so that the two-year service period would be viewed as an apprenticeship, after which time the volunteer would be eligible to join the appropriate union if he wanted to. Another program might be a cooperative store, in which volunteers could learn the many skills needed to run such an operation—salesmen, accountants, bookkeepers, managers, secretaries, and repairmen. Most of the teachers in such programs would be volunteers like college students. Non-volunteers would be used as instructors when there were no volunteers available with the appropriate training.

Other programs might include professional services offered by highly skilled volunteers. Neighborhood clinics could be set up and operated by medical students who would have their clinic service considered part of their internship. Law students could provide legal aid to those who could not otherwise afford it.

The projects described above involve volunteers working together. A voluntary national service program would also allow volunteers to work on their own. Those who wished to do this would outline their projects and then submit them to one of the many national service organizations. Once approval was obtained, work could begin. The projects involving a single person might include collecting presently unavailable data, writing critiques of present programs, or planning new ones. Volunteers who worked on the last two types of project would be encouraged to use the results of their work to change policy. They could talk to administrators and planners of present programs, publish their material, or try to raise money to start their own projects.

Voluntary national service programs abroad would include a variety of activities similar to the Peace Corps which would offer other nations our experience, skill, and equipment in order to help solve their problems. These foreign voluntary national service programs would include the following activities: a Disaster

Corps to help victims of floods, earthquakes and storms; a Conservation Corps to carry out irrigation, flood control and reforestation projects; an Air Transport Force to provide cargo and passenger service in the underdeveloped countries which do not possess adequate roads and rail networks.

These programs could use surplus military goods such as tools, trucks, tractors, airplanes, and medical supplies. Ships from the mothball fleet could be used as floating hospitals, schools, aid stations, or floating electrical power stations. Volunteers could operate radio stations which would broadcast technical information and act as a communication net which could help bring quick relief in an emergency. These enterprises could eventually evolve into the Unarmed Forces of the United States. They would be the soldiers of an unarmed world where nonviolent competition between nations would substitute for military confrontation. These efforts could help bring about economic development in a democratic context. They would help advance American political and social ideas, but avoid bloodshed, death, and a possible atomic holocaust. Undoubtedly there would be defeats, but not nearly so many as we have suffered using military force to advance American power and prestige.

The private groups would be locally organized. This would enable them to tackle an area's particular problem, and permit activities which a centralized program might shy away from.

The criteria for recognition as a privately run voluntary national service organization would be the same as those applied by the Internal Revenue Service to groups seeking exemption from federal taxation. These require that all organizations be non-profit, while most must be apolitical. These apolitical groups may desire legislation and may even occasionally attempt to bring it about, but they are forbidden from participating in a political campaign for or against any candidate for public office, and their political activities should constitute only an "insubstantial" part of their work. This apolitical stipulation does not apply to lobbyists or political parties which by their very nature are political. In addition, some groups, like scientific organizations and community funds, must make their findings or services available to the public. It must be remembered that a tax-exempt organization is not necessarily a tax-deductible one. Tax-exempt does not mean tax deductible; deductibility applies to several types of tax-exempt organizations, but not to all. (The tax-exempt organizations which allow donors to deduct their contributions from their income are those engaged in functions classified as: charitable, religious, scientific, educational, prevention of cruelty to children or animals, veterans' groups, and cemetery companies.)

The Bureau of Internal Revenue would certify groups. This would mean that no new bureaucracy would have to be created, and complaints of favoritism, which might occur with a specially created commission or board, would be avoided since the Bureau would confer tax exemptions on the same bases used before a voluntary national service program had been created. Its only interest in the program would be to insure that the organizations participating in it were tax exempt.

The federal government's participation in voluntary national service would be in the same vein as its involvement in the Peace, Job, and Teacher Corps. It could expand these present activities, and start some new ones. State governments could initiate programs for welfare recipients as well as use volunteers to improve the quality of education in the public schools. It would be hoped that in the end the government would absorb two hundred thousand volunteers annually.

Voluntary National Service—Cost

The cost of a voluntary national service program to the federal government, assuming an annual influx of seven hundred thousand volunteers (five hundred thousand working with private organizations and two hundred thousand with government) serving for a two-year period, would be six to eight billion dollars a year.[10] The total cost, including educational bonus, would run about $12.5 billion a year.

Some may say that this is too expensive. The question is—too expensive for what? The billions spent on defense are not questioned. Is $12.5 billion too much to spend to break the cycle of poverty and wasted human lives we all decry? Is it too expensive to provide the skilled and professional people we need? To tackle all the jobs that need to be done, billions must be provided.

Voluntary National Service—Effects

The efforts of voluntary national service would be primarily in the areas of vocational training, education, and social services. The effects of these programs would be felt in many other areas of American life, just as the effects of the Selective Service extend beyond the Armed Forces.

Two areas in which possible effects may be seen are higher education and politics. Presently, many students find that college does not offer them the stimulation and excitement they had hoped for. Too often, it is a continuation of high school. The institution acts as a surrogate parent, making decisions for the student and running his life. It decides when he has to be in, and what classes he has to attend. The student wonders if he is a child or an adult. The tragedy is further complicated by the quality and type of courses he has to take. They are often dull and boring, with no relationship to the real world. The student often learns neither content nor method. Knowledge is neatly pigeonholed into compartments. Literature, physics, art, and history are each treated separately. No attempt is made to integrate them into a composite whole.

Attempts to change this educational morass to meet twentieth-century needs run into the wall of tradition, and faculty and bureaucratic intransigence. Any change, even if it helps the student, the supposed gainer from college, endangers the position of those who have created their niche in the organization. Disgruntled students have three choices: they can stick it out, hoping that with their diplomas they can enter these institutions as professors or administrators and induce change by a fifth-column movement; they can leave and join groups which involve them in contemporary society; or, they can revolt, hoping to bring about change now.

The involvement of students before or during their college careers in voluntary national service programs would hopefully increase the number of those who would be dissatisfied. In these programs, students would make their own decisions, regulate their own lives, and deal with problems confronting our world. This experience would hopefully make them more critical of the cloistered classes and paternal atmosphere they encountered when they entered or returned to school. Students could induce changes by demanding a voice in decision making, which would eventually lead college administrators to treat students as adults, and encourage improved courses and more stimulating teachers. College then could become a place where education would be pursued. Students would be judged on their achievements as students. Their personal lives would be their own, to live as they wished.

Also, traditional political patterns would probably be upset by voluntary national service programs. If volunteers succeeded in registering all Americans to vote and, at the same time, helped organize slums, the combined results might lead to a situation in which slum dwellers would begin to use their political rights to advance their own interests. They could compel the government to divert some of the billions spent on defense into projects which would benefit them either by providing needed services or requiring jobs for which they could qualify.

Volunteer programs would focus public attention on social needs and might make the issues debated by candidates for public office more relevant to actual political conditions. The controversy over "Black Power," which was raised by SNCC might be the kind of political question with which voluntary national service organizations would confront the public.

Voluntary National Service—Acceptance

This proposed voluntary national service program attempts to meet the expectations of those groups concerned with the question of Selective Service by introducing new ideas which increase the number of possible alternatives. Gen. Hershey lays down three criteria any proposal has to meet to satisfy the Selective Service: It must provide the armed forces with men when they need them; it must not disturb the civilian economy; and it must guide deferments in the "national interest." Voluntary national service would provide men for the military and eliminate the need for deferments. The expansion of economic activity in presently neglected areas would cause a beneficial disturbance.

For business, the voluntary national service program would permit the hiring of young men without the fear of their being drafted. An employee would be able to stay at his job or leave it to join a national service program at his own discretion. Voluntary national service would be a source of profit to those businesses that provide educational materials or accept government contracts to run programs such as the Job Corps.

Students and educators protest against the draft because it is inequitable in its selection. The lottery and compulsory national service would change the criteria for selection, but only voluntary national service would resolve the contradiction of individual choice and compulsion found in these other proposals.

A voluntary national service program is not a panacea to solve our social problems. It is a way of resolving the Selective Service question. Its acceptance means favoring change in many American institutions, and a willingness to expend money instead of words.

NOTES

1 Michael Waltzer, "Democracy and the Conscript," *Dissent*, Jan.-Feb., 1966.
2 Statement of Thomas D. Morris, Assistant Secretary of Defense (Manpower)

before the House Committee on the Armed Forces, Report on DOD Study of the Draft, June 30, 1966.

[3] In the area of taxation, the majority has the right to tax all in order to provide services they feel are the state's duty to provide, but how money is distributed should be left up to the citizen. He should have the right to decide which services to favor by voting on the allocation of his tax money.

[4] Harris Wofford, "Toward a Draft Without Guns," *Saturday Review*, Oct. 15, 1966.

[5] The difference between taxation and service is that taxation involves giving the state money which is earned while doing what one chooses while service may require the citizen to do something against his will. The money collected through taxation can be used to pay men to do a job. Those who are hired to do this job have chosen to do so.

[6] "Review of the Readjustment Training Program for Korea Veterans," *Information Bulletin*. Department of Veterans Benefits, March 26, 1958, p. 18.

[7] Amos Yoder, "Lessons of the G.I. Bill," *Phi Delta Kappan, April,* 1963.

[8] Harold Wool, "The Changing Pattern of Military Skills," *Employment and Security Review,* July, 1963.

[9] Colonel Winston Wall, *Cold War G.I. Bill*, U. S. Congress, Senate Committee on Public Welfare, 1963.

[10]
1) Medical treatment averaging $200 a volunteer	$ 140,000,000
2) Salaries for volunteers 2 × 700,000 × $1,164	1,629,600,000
3) Room and board for volunteers (at $600 per man per year) assuming 500,000 wanted this	300,000,000
4) Federal programs at a cost (besides the salary the volunteer received) of $7,000 a man . . . 2 × 200,000 × $7,000	2,800,000,000
5) Federal grants to private groups	2,000,000,000
Total	$6,869,600,000

24

Freedom, National Security, and the Elimination of Poverty: Is Compulsory Service Necessary?

RICHARD W. BOONE AND
NORMAN G. KURLAND

I. INTRODUCTION

Our major interest in the Selective Service System is how it relates to a comprehensive national strategy to overcome poverty in America, a strategy the President has established as number one priority domestically. Therefore, our concern is how the draft affects that one-fifth of our nation having little claim to a promising future; that one-fifth which has had far less than its proportionate share of available political power, secure income, and the broad range of family and community services essential for human growth.

The problem of safeguarding our national security against present and potential external threats is no longer one of achieving an adequate level of military power. As we will point out, that level has been reached, and perhaps even surpassed, according to Defense Secretary Robert McNamara.

Not unlike our unsurpassed successes in meeting our defense goals, our quest for an end to poverty demands a level of national commitment, planning, and mobilization of resources commensurate with the seriousness of the problem.

It is still not too late to ask whether high-level spending for military "overkill" and space exploration might be a luxury when our cities continue to decay, when the national mood is one of debilitating anxiety, when our pluralistic unity is threatened by fear and group hatred, and when experts in race relations have even begun to forecast the possibility of an "apartheid President" within the foreseeable future.

Strengthening individual freedom and the dignity of all men lies at the core of our political system. It is the fundamental objective of all our national efforts —whether to overcome poverty, to maintain national security, or to meet other priority goals here and abroad. DeTocqueville recognized it as the source of our inner strength and our resourcefulness in times of crisis. Yet today's battle between the forces of freedom and those of coercion lies at the root of deep and widespread frustration in this country, especially among our most talented young people and the poor.

The situation calls to mind the warning of the noted jurist Learned Hand in his address, "The Spirit of Liberty":

The authors are, respectively, Executive Director and Staff Associate, Citizens' Crusade Against Poverty.

Liberty lies in the hearts of men and women; when it dies there, no constitution, no law, no court can save it. . . . While it lies there it needs no constiution, no law, no court to save it.

Fortunately, the current debate on the future of the draft offers a unique opportunity to reexamine the current condition of our society, while relating the draft to a much broader subject: Reassessing and effectively pursuing our national goals, including that of national security, within a democratic framework. In fact, we doubt that a productive debate on the draft can be carried on without a perspective which focuses on broader national goals than national security alone. Some of these goals were expressed in a statement developed in 1960 by the President's Commission on National Goals, a group of outstanding Americans from many fields:

The Individual. The status of the individual must remain our primary concern. All our institutions—political, social, and economic—must further enhance the dignity of the citizen, promote the maximum development of his capabilities, stimulate their responsible exercise, and widen the range and effectiveness of opportunities for individual choice. . . .

Equality. Every man and woman must have equal rights before the law, and an equal opportunity to vote and hold office, to be educated, to get a job and to be promoted when qualified, to buy a home, to participate fully in community affairs. . . .

The Democratic Process. The degree of effective liberty available to its people should be the ultimate test of any nation. Democracy is the only means so far devised by which a nation can meet this test. To preserve and perfect the democratic process in the United States is therefore a primary goal in this as in every decade. . . .

Education. The development of the individual and the nation demand that education at every level and in every discipline be strengthened and its effectiveness enhanced. . . . This is at once an investment in the individual, in the democratic process, in the growth of the economy, and in the stature of the United States. . . .

The basic foreign policy goal of the United States should be the preservation of its independence and free institutions. . . ."[1]

Knowing in general where we want to head, how can we begin to move into action? Compared to our revolutionary accomplishments in the technology of human destruction, ideas for advancing toward our basic goals—the technology of human, social, and political development—remain largely unexplored and untested. A national blueprint for social action must be developed which assesses our problems and sets out a timetable, specified program goals and priorities, and a plan for marshaling the national support and commitment which are necessary preconditions for such an effort.

A start in this direction is the recently proposed "Freedom Budget," a plan to inject an average of $18.5 billion annually of additional federal spending over a 10-year period into a broad array of poverty-related programs. This would amount to about 2 per cent of our estimated average annual production of goods and services (GNP) and only one-thirteenth of our projected economic growth between 1966 and 1975.[2]

Today, the question is not whether more public and private spending will be expended to overcome poverty and other pressing national and international needs. It is now a matter of how much, when, by whom, and how. And no one seriously debates any longer whether enough money will be raised to sustain an adequate level of military effectiveness. The more fundamental questions are whether our nation can:

1) Redefine "national service" to cover more than the military and
2) Afford to provide sufficient inducements to meet our combat and other critical national needs without forcing men to risk their lives and limit their freedom involuntarily.

Or, viewed from the opposite direction, can we afford not to structure a voluntary service system which will attract virtually all young Americans?

II.   THE SITUATION TODAY

National Security

Defense Secretary McNamara on August 23, 1966,[3] repeated, as he has on many occasions, that upon assuming his office in 1961, President Kennedy instructed him "to determine what forces were required to safeguard our security, to procure and support those forces without regard to an arbitrary or predetermined budget level; but to do so as economically as possible." President Johnson renewed that mandate and today, the Secretary can say that the United States "has become the mightiest military power in the whole of human history. No single threat, no combination of threats; no single conflict, no combination of conflicts; no single adversary, no combination of adversaries can attack us— or those with whom we have defense committments—and remain out of reach of our retaliatory power." (He went on to talk about the corrosive effect that domestic and foreign poverty has on our national security and our national spirit; this will be discussed at another point in this paper.)

This dramatic military accomplishment has been achieved with a pre-Vietnam military force of only 2.7 million. It is now up to 3.1 million and might go as high as 3.5 million. In 1945, the military included over 12 million men and women. Likewise, defense costs have dropped from 38 per cent of our gross national product in 1945 to 8 per cent prior to escalation of the Vietnam war in 1965. (Today, defense constitutes about 55 per cent of the federal administrative budget compared to 82.7 per cent in 1945.) Thus, far greater military power has been consolidated than ever before in history with about one-fourth of the manpower and about one-fifth of the nation's economic effort required at the peak of World War II.[4] This is a tribute to good planning and the spectacular revolution still underway in weaponry, military technology, and advanced management techniques. It also indicates America's phenomenal capacity to accomplish a national goal to which its leaders are committed.

Most amazing is that only 14 per cent of the 3 million in the military actually fire weapons as their primary duty.[5] We are able to meet our far-flung military commitments with less than 500,000 men having combat assignments. No figures are available on how many of these combat men are draftees and how many are volunteers or careerists. How much this figure can be further reduced with advancing technology and the assumption of greater military responsibilities by America's allies is still uncertain. (The figure for our "international policemen" is about the equivalent of the 334,000 policemen and the 169,000 firemen who provided us "domestic security" in 1965.)[6]

Satisfying our military manpower demands has been made easier by the 26 per cent increase in our nation's population between 1951 and 1966, from 155 million to 196 million.[7] The postwar "baby boom" has produced nearly 2 million men who turn 18 every year compared to about 1.1 million in the 1950's and 1.5 million in the early 1960's.[8] Since 1951, the male population of draft age has increased from 22 million to 32 million.[9] Correspondingly, the number of 26-year-old men in the population with military service experience is expected to drop from 70 per cent in 1958 to 34 per cent in 1974.

On the basis of the above, it seems reasonable to conclude that national security can be adequately maintained, if not strengthened, in the future with far less drain on American manpower.

Other National Goals

The elimination of domestic poverty is only one of our national goals. None, however, is more critical. The "War on Poverty" is now off the ground and, hopefully, significant victories are within reach.

No clearer insight into the problem of poverty has been revealed than in the observations of Defense Secretary McNamara[11] who said that "the growing incidence of internal conflict in the world arises not primarily out of Communist aggression and subversion—as real as that is—but out of the bitter frustrations born of poverty." He spoke eloquently of the self-perpetuating nature of poverty and its debilitating impact on the human spirit and aspirations of those caught in its ever-tightening web. He told of the hidden cancer of poverty within our society, which has entrapped one out of every five Americans, including over 20 million children. Speaking as the Secretary of Defense, however, his central point was that *"poverty in America makes our nation less secure."* He pointed out that the "root of all security is the human spirit and its determination to defend what it believes in." He was alarmed at how the complex syndrome of poverty, particularly in an affluent society such as ours, weakens that spirit and induces tensions resulting in violence and the escalation of extremism. He illustrated his point by recalling that on 59 occasions since the end of World War II, the governors of our states have called upon combat-equipped National Guard troops to quell disorders that could not be controlled by local or state police. Most of these emergencies, he stated, were poverty-related.

Mr. McNamara was concerned with another by-product of poverty—its enormous waste of human talent, "our most essential resource" in the technological revolution sweeping the world. He focused upon the 600,000 young men each year who are rejected for military service, the vast majority of whom are victims of faulty education or inadequate health services.

Like Secretary McNamara, we are also concerned with how poverty wastes human potential and weakens the moral fiber and spiritual strength of our society. His eloquent support should certainly lead to greater public understanding of the dynamics of poverty and thus to greater commitment from the nation to the critical task of conserving the potential of millions of neglected Americans. But this effort will surely fail without a clearer set of action goals, better planning, and greatly increased allocation of our nation's talent and technology to the goal of overcoming the root causes of poverty—powerlessness, insufficient and insecure income, and inadequate access to the wide range of human services essential to effective participation in modern society—from quality education, health care, and legal services to better housing, employment services and police protection.

If the vast bulk of America's young men and women were trained and applied their creative energies to these problems, as well as to many others of national concern, our future and that of the world would indeed be brighter. This reservoir of talent is still largely untapped and will remain so until we structure opportunities to utilize it.

A Profile of Our Nation's Manpower and Economic Potential

An important question is whether our society has the capacity and the manpower to meet its national goals. Based on the 1960 Report of the President's Commission on National Goals, a study of what these goals meant in manpower terms was undertaken for the Department of Labor by the National Planning Association.[12] Simultaneous achievement of goals in 16 specific program areas by 1975, it was reported, would require an estimated national productivity (GNP) of more than $1 trillion measured in 1965 prices,[13] a goal attainable in a virtually full employment economy growing at about 4.5 per cent annually.[14]

Preliminary results of the Labor Department study indicate that achievement of the goals by 1975 would require an employed labor force of 100 million— over 10 million more than is expected at that time.[15] Data are available at present on only two of the 16 areas—social welfare and urban development. In welfare, public and private expenditures are projected to increase from $38 billion in 1962 to $92 billion (in 1962 dollars) in 1975, requiring 8.4 million persons directly or indirectly employed for full achievement of these goals. For urban development, expenditures—mostly private—were expected to increase from $64 billion in 1962 to $130 billion (in 1962 dollars) in 1975; manpower requirements will total 10.2 million.[16]

In a September, 1966, speech in Dayton, Ohio, President Johnson spoke of our *immediate* manpower needs: over one million medical and health workers; over one million teachers and school administrators; more than 700,000 welfare and home care workers; two million workers to help improve our cities; and almost one-half million for public protection.[17] Too frequently overlooked is the need to develop manpower opportunities for community development workers, a key force for overcoming the local conditions that keep the poor powerless. If one such worker is assigned to every 500 of America's 35 million poor, 70,000 would be required.

If we improve our manpower machinery, the predicted labor deficit for meeting national goals would be greatly reduced, particularly in view of our post-World War II population levels[18] which have jumped to the point where about four million young men and women reached age 18 in 1965, one million more than in 1964. Over 26 million youths will enter the labor force from 1960-70. The non-white population reaching 18 between 1970 and 1975—a critical group which can no longer be ignored—is expected to rise 20 per cent, twice the rate increase for whites during the same period. The total labor force under 25 is expected to increase from 13.7 million in 1960 to 19.9 million in 1970, causing a rise in young workers of 45 per cent.

While youth are moving into the manpower pool at an accelerating clip (45 per cent increase, 1960-70) youth employment opportunities continue to lag.[19] While youth from 16 to 21 constitute 12 per cent of the labor force, they total

33 per cent of those unemployed. About 30 per cent of Negro workers from 16 to 19 were unemployed, six times the national average and over twice the rate for their total age group. In some ghettoes three out of every four teenagers out of school are walking the streets without jobs.[20] The employment picture becomes even more depressing for untrained ghetto youths, with white collar jobs (for which many are untrained) increasing twice as fast as blue collar jobs.[21] The uncertainty of the draft and rapidly increasing automation, particularly in goods-producing industries, make the situation even more serious for unskilled men of draft age. While the above statistics are revealing, much more must be known of our manpower situation to develop action goals for the future. But it seems clear that much more can be done to utilize more effectively our vast and growing pool of human potential.

III.   VARIOUS POSSIBILITIES FOR RENDERING NATIONAL SERVICE

Arguments for and against the Present System

Arguments against the present system not too often expressed include the following:

1) *Potential leaders of low-income groups are prime targets for Selective Service and assignments to combat units.* Affected in great numbers are men who have sufficiently overcome their poverty conditions to meet the educational literacy, physical, and moral standards of the military. Many of these men cannot afford college and must work to support their families. Yet these are the very men desperately needed to guide ghetto communities into constructive programs of self-help. The highest induction rates are among those who have completed high school (57 per cent) and those who have dropped out of college or could only afford to attend part-time (60 per cent).[22]

2) *Far too many young Americans, particularly the poor, not only bear the scars of oppression from discrimination but are also branded as "rejects" by the draft.* In 1965, the overall rejection rate of men examined for induction was over 50 per cent higher than during World War II.[23] (The Army adjusts its standards according to its current needs.) Among Negroes, the total rejection rate was almost 75 per cent, over 40 per cent for failing the so-called "mental test" (the Armed Forces Qualification Test). This is over five times the "mental test" rejection rate for non-Negroes.[24] This additional reminder of "failure" and inadequate preparation for life bears out the recent charge of Dr. Kenneth Clark, member of the New York State Board of Regents and Professor of Psychology, that the public schools have deteriorated to where they are "grossly inefficient, criminally inferior, and often do not teach at all."[25]

3) *The draft creates an "evasion mentality"—what President Brewster of Yale recently called "a cynical avoidance of service, a corruption of the aims of education, and a tarnishing of national spirit"—among young Americans.* This in turn has created poor morale on the part of draftees and their families.

4) *Because almost absolute discretion is left to the State in the selection of members on local draft boards and State appeals board, they are frequently unrepresentative of the poor and minority groups.* For example, the American Veterans Committee reported that not a single Negro served on a draft board in Mississippi, Alabama, and Georgia.[26] There is mounting evidence that this has led to using the draft for punishment of "undesirables" of the community, particu-

larly civil rights workers. The drafting of student dissenters in the North is another reflection of the arbitrariness of local boards and their failure to include persons responsive to the views of students.

The most articulate and knowledgeable advocate for the present system is its director, Gen. Lewis Hershey, who acknowledges many of the inequities of the present draft but wants to close its "escape hatches."[27] He believes that Selective Service should be a mechanism for compulsory universal military training. Compulsory military service, which he calls a "privilege," not a "duty," is viewed by him as a primary tool in fostering patriotism and a sense of citizenship, responsibility, and discipline.[28] He also sees it as a key channel for developing skills and professions critical to the Nation.[29] Whether patriotism and other virtues can be best fostered by indoctrination, exhortation, or compulsion, particularly within a system framed by democratic ideals, is the key issue separating the views expressed in this paper from those of Gen. Hershey and other advocates of compulsory universal military service.

We contend that unnecessary compulsion stifles an individual's full sense of participation and the spirit of voluntarism which are preconditions for the fullest development of the capacity of citizens of a free society. We also disagree that a compulsory manpower system is more efficient in developing and utilizing available resources than one based on fair rewards and maximum voluntary choice.

Feasibility of an All-Volunteer Military—Cost Factors

A recent Defense Department study estimated that the additional payroll to maintain an all-volunteer active force of 2.7 million would cost about $5.4 billion per year by 1976, under a 5.5 per cent unemployment rate, and $8.3 billion per year under a 4.0 per cent unemployment level.[30] This amounts to an additional bite of about one per cent of our total national productivity for national security; it is now 8 per cent.[31]

Normal annual military turnover of personnel is estimated at 550,000 to 600,-000.[32] In fiscal year 1966, about 336,000 men were conscripted through Selective Service.[33] (Prior to our military involvement in Vietnam less than one-third that number were drafted.)[34] Another 600,000 enlisted in fiscal 1966.[35] Since the Defense study indicates that 38 per cent of enlistees are draft-motivated,[36] about 564,000 men can be viewed as having been involuntarily inducted during fiscal 1966. As noted earlier, based on Secretary McNamara's figures,[37] a total force of less than 500,000 men in combat jobs are needed in all the Armed Forces to meet all of our military commitments, here and abroad.

Some noted economists claim that an all-volunteer military would be less costly in the long run and view the draft as a "forced labor tax." In that light, over one-half million men entered the military involuntarily, thereby "paying" the government an implicit tax of around $8.3 billion (the extra cost for an all-volunteer military) in fiscal 1965. Viewed another way, all Americans received almost $15,000 worth of free "national security protection" at the expense of a year's liberty taken from *each* of over one-half million young Americans. (It may also be argued that millions of other young Americans also paid part of that tax: those unemployed who are unable to find jobs because they are subject to the draft; those enrolled in college to evade the draft who might otherwise have been employed.) With a gross national product of over $700 billion and federal tax revenues increasing annually by over $7 billion,[38] the price of an all-volunteer military seems small indeed.

No one today seriously suggests that civilians be conscripted for compulsory "domestic" police or fire-fighting duty. We pay the bill for "volunteer" policemen and firemen and are grateful for the security they provide us in the face of daily hazards. It is indeed difficult to see any just basis for different treatment of our "international security force." With the increasing federal revenues available, we can well afford to pay just compensation for the services of our men in combat.

An All-Volunteer Military—Social and Political Considerations

In considering the advantages of abandoning a system of involuntary service, we should also call to mind the words of the late Senator Robert A. Taft, Sr.:[39]

By handing boys over to the arbitrary and complete domination of the Government, we put it in the power of the Government to indoctrinate them with the political doctrines then popular with the Government . . . In wartime it is bad enough; in peacetime it would be intolerable.

There are other advantages of an all-voluntary military:

1) Battle-hardened veterans take well-deserved pride in their chosen career, which exposes them to great risks for the welfare of the rest of society. Just as no experienced policeman or fireman would want to rely on "forced participants" to help them carry out their more hazardous duties, professional military men cannot help but become disillusioned when they are joined in combat by draftees who have a lower level of dedication and sense of duty.

2) An all-volunteer force would reduce the turnover rate of the military, adding to military effectiveness and reducing the high cost of training skilled technicians.

3) Abolishing the draft would:

a) Have a profound psychological effect among young Americans, including conscientious objectors to war, liberating them from a future completely beyond their control and providing them new alternatives for advancing freedom and other national goals.

b) Eliminate the most flagrant remaining source of arbitrary discrimination by government, and the lasting resentment it causes among different groups of draft-age men.

c) Remove the principal source of uncertainty today among young men entering adulthood for making vocational, educational, marital, and other critical decisions affecting their future.

d) Reduce the rate of unwise early marriages induced by the draft and their impact on the birth rate.

e) Free employers to hire on the basis of merit rather than on deferments.

f) Reduce enrollment pressures on universities from persons enrolled to evade the draft.

g) Remove the "crutch" of the draft so that the military will be forced to strengthen its efforts to attract volunteers and devote more time to making the reserve system work.

Responses to Common Objections Raised about an All-Volunteer Military

Objections generally raised against an all-volunteer military, besides possibly increased costs for national security, include the following:

1) *That ground units, particularly combat forces, would become racially imbalanced.* The fear of all-Negro combatant units is predicated on a false assumption: that the military life, or combat, is inherently attractive to Negroes. It is true that Negroes constitute about 18 per cent of the combat units in Vietnam.[40] The percentage of Negroes in some airborne combat units is reported to be over 40.[41] But it is obvious why this is so. An Army career is an effective lure for any young man raised in poverty. It offers him more of what he has been denied by society: genuine equality of opportunity to develop to his fullest potential, adequate and secure income, full personal and family services, a sense of personal identity, dignity and pride of accomplishment, and the promise of promotion based on merit. (These attractions are reflected in first term reenlistment rates for Negroes, which in 1965 averaged 45.1 per cent compared to 17.1 per cent for whites.)[42]

If the racial imbalance objection has any merit, the obvious answer is to broaden the base of opportunities for Negroes in other segments of society, a suggestion which is developed in this paper. Other options include raising combat pay and other incentives so that competition for combat jobs will be keener from other segments of society. Certainly, the combatant way of life has its own attractions for men from all ethnic groups, a fact attested to by the composition of police forces in our cities.

2) *That those who would benefit from a military experience might not be induced to volunteer.* As far as many of the poor are concerned, this point is almost a contradiction of the first objection. If the military is interested in affording more of the poor an opportunity to serve, it could lower its educational, physical, and other qualifications. Experience demonstrates clearly that *opportunities to serve with dignity will be quickly grasped* by youth from our ghettoes. The same can be said for those who are more fortunate.

3) *That an all-professional military poses a threat to political stability.* Many claim that the personnel turnover engendered by the draft assures a continual infusion of civilian sentiment into the military, thus preventing the military from isolating itself and losing touch with the body politic. In view of President Eisenhower's departing warning about the "military-industrial complex," this point cannot be lightly dismissed. But this risk must be balanced, not only against the many weighty arguments against the draft, but against the normal vigilance of a free society in maintaining existing safeguards and inventing new ones as needed. The tradition of civilian control over the military, for example, is a well-imbedded safeguard against a usurpation of power by the military. Other safeguards against this danger could be strengthened, including: shorter terms of service and early retirement for combat troops; routine periodic transfers of personnel among various commands; an improved system of civilian controls and points of interaction at a variety of levels in the military establishment; recruitment of civilians into noncombatant military positions; increased hiring of civilians for technical work, logistical operations, intelligence, etc.; increased use of civilian training programs for training military personnel; independent civilian review boards and evaluation teams; contact with national guard and

reserve personnel on active duty tours; vigilance by independent local police and national guard units. Moreover, the danger recognized is a danger that can be confronted, and it certainly should not stand in the way of repairing fundamental flaws in our society. Compulsory service is such a flaw.

4) *That combat units operate most effectively with young men and therefore need a constant turnover.* Better pay and incentives, plus an early retirement program for combat troops (e.g., after ten years), could insure a constant flow of young men into combat positions. Broad training opportunities and liberal transfer rights for combat men would also help.

5) *That severe and sudden emergencies might arise where additional combat troops would be required.* First, it is assumed that emergencies, for the most part, are taken into account in the contingency plans and active duty and reserve manpower levels of the military. Second, Secretary McNamara has assured us that our retaliatory force is more than ample. We assume that our military actions abroad will rely more and more heavily upon our advantages in military technology, strategic retaliatory powers, and the combat troops of regional allies for defense against aggression in other parts of the world.

If a great emergency were to arise and our civilian population were convinced of the immediacy and seriousness of the threat, Americans would voluntarily rise to the occasion, as they have in the past. Whether strength and alertness will be generated, as some suggest, by a "territorial instinct" or from the powerful attachment of free men to a free and just society, we are confident that *when our domestic security is really in grave danger, volunteers will be plentiful and conscripts unnecessary.*

A Voluntary National Service System

There is nothing impractical about Secretary McNamara's idea of asking every young person in the United States to give two years of service to his country—whether in one of the military services, in the Peace Corps, or in some other voluntary developmental work at home or in other countries. Some new social inventions would be required.

But, whether one proceeds from the standpoint of military needs or from social, political, and long-range economic costs, a strong case can be made that the present system is an anachronism within a society whose primary goal is freedom. Based on our previous analysis, we suggest that immediate steps be taken to plan for the termination of involuntary conscription—whether in the military or otherwise—at the earliest possible date. Concurrently, replacement machinery must be devised and phased into operation to implement, on a volunteer basis, a comprehensive national action strategy.

In a certain sense, hostilities in Vietnam make such planning difficult. Yet there are underlying pressures surrounding this situation—including the scheduled review of the draft—which suggest that there is no better time than now to reorient the Selective Service System to a new and broader set of national goals and a time-table for their achievement. Ideally, this step can be structured to establish a system of voluntary national service that would afford all young men and young women—but not excluding qualified middle-aged and elderly persons—a wide range of alternatives, both in the military and nonmilitary areas, to work toward achieving national goals, particularly those directly related to strengthening freedom and individual dignity.

Good ideas are abundant on how such a system could work. More ideas will be generated once we secure enough national commitment on the general objectives. Specific details and mechanics of operation of a voluntary service system—being secondary to program goals—could be worked out once we know the problems the new system itself would create.

As a first step, comprehensive planning and an inventory of our manpower potential and action mechanisms is required. Such planning would include a fresh reassessment of our national needs and problems—our gaps in education, health, housing, and other areas of basic human needs. These problems must have the highest priority because of their immediate and direct personal impact on the quality of life for each individual and his family life. Another look must also be taken at the supportive areas that make essential human services possible, such as national security, agriculture, conservation, communications, power, transportation, industry, finance, police and fire protection, and other supportive arms of society. It would be a tragic failure to concentrate on supportive service areas and continue to neglect basic human needs and services. To fill existing gaps in human services, massive inputs of America's manpower, technology, and resources are needed. More rational planning is needed to decide how much of the total input should be channeled to meet world poverty at the same time we are making progress in overcoming the sources of domestic tensions. Plans for volunteers must be linked to our future manpower needs in the service fields, so that volunteer training and work will serve as a bridge to new career lines. Safeguards must also be developed to insure high quality service by the volunteers and by the institutions to which they are assigned.

Once specific national action goals and priorities can be formulated and resource commitments are made, the national service program can become operational. Actual program implementation can be phased in gradually through qualified existing agencies (like the military, the American Friends Service Committee, the Red Cross, the Peace Corps, VISTA) to the extent that these agencies could absorb volunteers as they were made available. As new agencies develop to train and effectively utilize volunteers, the overall program could expand. Control of this "building block" process must be placed in the hands of an agency like the present Selective Service System, if it became a voluntary system with broadly expanded powers and resources.

Eventually, service opportunities should be provided for all who want to serve, particularly young men and women. However, during the phasing-in period, when openings are limited, the selection process should minimize unfairness and the "creaming" phenomena. This can be achieved by instituting a universal registration and evaluation system applicable to all young men and women upon turning 16. (This will uncover educational and health defects that remain largely undetected today.) Since, in the beginning, there will undoubtedly be more volunteers than openings, a lottery can be instituted assigning all registrants to priority categories for entry into the voluntary system. After all the sponsoring or training units fill their annual quotas, entry for that year can be closed to those holding lower entry priorities on the registration lists. Sponsoring groups should be required to receive certification and program approval by the National Service Commission or an independent body of citizens. Sponsors should be encouraged to set flexible qualification standards but must be permitted to make their own selections among volunteers. The government will therefore remain responsible for directly or indirectly providing training, rehabilitation, and action programs for volunteers who are not accepted by existing sponsoring groups.

A mechanism should be devised for continual and independent evaluation of the program, so that experiences can be fed back to the system for its improvement. Reports should be made public to provide citizens with a full understanding of the overall program. This should be part of a general educational program to prepare the public for the unavoidable criticisms that such a broad-scaled undertaking can expect to encounter.

It is important to understand in advance the limitations and powers of the federal government in maintaining a voluntary service system. A renewed national emphasis on the individual and his freedom necessarily entails limitations on excessive concentrations of power which might subvert this primary goal. This would mean that, where alternatives are available, the federal government's responsibility for direct operations should be curtailed. Government—particularly the federal government through its centralized taxing powers—can and should maximize and promote opportunities for freedom, both here and in other countries. Control over the purse-strings does not necessarily lead to restrictions on freedom—not if the spending is for lifting barriers to freedom, or for providing personal security within which individual freedom can flourish, or for providing the mechanisms through which conflicts can be resolved amicably and efficiently, or for limiting excess concentrations of power. When necessary, greater safeguards should also be developed to offer prompt remedies where government officials overstep the limitations on their powers. Consistent with this thesis, government, in financially supporting a voluntary service system, should diffuse decision-making as much as possible to individuals affected or, where relevant, to their communities.

Hence, a federal national service program should provide "seed money" and "idea channels" with "gap-filler" funds provided only where local resources cannot otherwise be raised.

Although some volunteer service programs operated directly by the federal government would certainly be justified, a monopolization of control over programs and volunteer resources in most program areas, particularly in the non-military area, is detrimental to those served. A national service system should, therefore, give a preference to sponsoring groups that would improve competition in the offering of services. Viable private groups, local governments, or quasi-public bodies should thus be favored over federally operated programs in requests for volunteers.

The ideology of freedom has no national boundaries. This program should, therefore, also provide opportunities for international service, in any capacity and in any place in which the cause of freedom in the world can ultimately be served. The types of service can be as varied as the problems to be tackled. Some may do research for international bodies. Others may teach or develop industry or improve agricultural methods. Some may serve in the military, some in hospitals. Others may help organize unorganized segments of society into effective and viable cooperative units. Retired businessmen can be recruited to provide financial and management help to businessmen in ghetto areas. In short, the nature of the work is virtually as unlimited as mankind's needs and ingenuity. Opportunities can be fashioned for the most highly skilled professionals and technicians as well as energetic but generally unskilled 18-year-olds.

These and other recommendations listed in this paper are designed to show how the idea of universal national service could be made an essential part of our definition of citizenship. In so doing, we would be adding a new dimension to American education in its responsibility to develop effective citizens for a free society. This strategy would provide opportunities to bring together, in what McNamara and the President call a "community of effort," much of the coming generation—all those born in poverty, all those born in prejudice, and all those born with fortune on their side. It would produce what Kingman Brewster of Yale has called a "moral manpower policy."

Conclusion

Freedom remains the ideological springboard and catalytic force that has produced our nation's most significant advances. Compulsory service cannot be squared with this ideology, which still overshadows all of our other exportable assets. The feudalistic institution of forced service has been handed down from past generations and no longer serves any of our national interests. Freedom here and abroad, however, can be served by new social institutions which promote opportunities for all to serve the nation. But compulsory service—whether in the military or in pursuit of other national goals—should not be passed on to another generation. It is inconsistent with our heritage and our future.

IV. SUMMARY OF RECOMMENDATIONS

1) Compulsory service in the military, especially for combat positions, should be terminated as soon as an adequate manpower level for military combat positions can be sustained on a voluntary basis. Increased effort should be made to recruit more civilians for noncombatant military needs.

2) Congress should appropriate whatever funds are required to recruit, train, and maintain an all-volunteer military at the earliest possible date.

3) The Selective Service System should be converted into a mechanism for:
   a) registering all Americans of high school age;
   b) providing each young man and woman an evaluation of his or her educational, health, and other deficiencies;
   c) counseling and recruiting for voluntary public service tours of duty, of a military and non-military nature;
   d) establishing priorities, through a lottery, for all registrants to determine access into available national service opportunities, until adequate resources are produced to absorb all potential volunteers.

4) The President and Congress should establish a permanent commission on national goals to reexamine our national goals and formulate:
   a) *A national blueprint for action*—a comprehensive plan of specific action goals, potential funding sources, programs and priorities, an action budget and timetable, a current and projected national inventory of manpower and other public and private resources, relevant technological advances, and public and private action mechanisms.
   b) *A national human investment budget*—to recommend future levels of

federal spending to meet national goals and to reffect the costs of past public and private human investments as compared to increases in national productivity, reduced social costs, and other benefits attributable to these investments.

5) A commission on national service should be established within the Office of the President to:

a) Stimulate and develop national commitment to the idea of national service as an integral part of the education, development, and citizenship of all Americans.

b) Develop broad and meaningful opportunities for all citizens, particularly young men and women, to render voluntary military or non-military service in pursuit of national goals, whether in this country or overseas, under public, private, national, or international auspice.

c) Promote the widest feasible expansion of service opportunities and rehabilitation programs outside of government in order to develop each citizen to his fullest potential for effective participation in society.

d) Directly provide resources and opportunities for voluntary service and rehabilitation to the extent they are not produced without government support.

e) Utilize the Selective Service for registering, evaluating, and counseling young Americans, maintaining a national volunteer roster, and recruiting for critical national manpower shortages.

f) Evaluate, on a continuing basis, the various phases of the national service system, particularly at the local level, measured in terms of specific yardsticks reflecting national program goals. (At least 2 per cent of the total national service budget should be channeled to independent evaluators and evaluation teams.)

6) Until the draft is terminated:

a) Congress should recognize alternative forms of voluntary national service as equivalents of military service.

b) Educational deferments should be limited to four years.

c) Involuntary induction should be limited to filling combat positions.

d) A national lottery should be used to establish priorities for involuntary inductions.

NOTES

[1] *Report of the President's Commission on National Goals*, U.S. Government Printing Office, Washington, D. C., November 1960.

[2] A. Philip Randolph Institute, *A "Freedom Budget" for All Americans; Budgeting Our Resources 1966-1975 to Achieve "Freedom from Want,"* New York, October, 1966, p. 10. If federal spending for the military, space technology, and international programs were added, a total increase of only about $35.5 billion annually would be required over our present federal budget. The total increase would amount to 4 per cent of our average annual GNP or one-seventh of our projected economic growth for the period. *Id.* at 9.

[3] Robert S. McNamara, Speech before National Convention of Veterans of Foreign Wars, New York City, August 23, 1966.

[4] *Statistical Abstract of the United States*, U. S. Government Printing Office, Washington, D. C., 1964, pp. 254, 261, 321.

[5] McNamara, *supra*.

[6] Hearings . . . Committee on Armed Services, House of Representatives, *Review of the Administration and Operation of the Selective Service System*, 89th Cong., 2nd Sess., June 22-24, 28-30, 1966, p. 9879.

[7] Id. at 10003.

[8] *Ibid*.

[9] Id. at 9878.

[10] Id. at 10005.

[11] McNamara, *supra*.

[12] U. S. Department of Labor, *Manpower Report of the President and Report on Manpower Requirements, Resources, Utilization, and Training*, U. S. Government Printing Office, Washington, D. C., March 1966, pp. 45-46.

[13] *Ibid*.

[14] See *"Freedom Budget"* . . . , *supra*, pp. 69-70, 76, 80-84.

[15] *Manpower Report*, *supra*, p. 95.

[16] *Id*. at 46-47.

[17] National Service Secretariat, *Newsletter*, Oct. 1966; *cf. Technology and the American Economy; Report of the National Commission on Technology, Automation, and Economic Progress*, vol. 1, U. S. Government Printing Office, Washington, D. C., Feb. 1966, p. 36.

[18] *Manpower Report*, *supra*, p. 95.

[19] *Ibid*.

[20] Unofficial report of discussions with officials of Watts Labor Community Action Council in October 1966.

[21] *Manpower Report* . . . , *supra*, p. 95.

[22] Hearings, *supra*, p. 10011.

[23] *Id*. at 10031.

[24] *Id*. at 10032-33.

[25] *Washington Post*, Oct. 26, 1966.

[26] Report of American Veterans Committee, Oct. 1966.

[27] Hearings, *supra*, pp. 9627, 9629.

[28] *Id*. at 9620, 9647, 9656.

[29] *Id*. at 9621.

[30] *Id*. at 10042-43.

[31] *Op. cit. supra* note 4.

[32] Hearings, *supra*, p. 10037.

[33] *Id*. at 10001.

[34] *Ibid*.

[35] *Ibid*.

[36] *Id*. at 10039.

[37] *Op. cit. supra*, note 5.

[38] *"Freedom Budget"* . . . , *supra*, p. 68.

[39] Quoted in *Hearings*, *supra*, p. 9799.

[40] Gene Grove, "The Army and the Negro," *New York Times Magazine*, July 24, 1966, p. 5.

[41] *Ibid*.

[42] *Ibid*.

25

Memorandum for the Conference on the Draft

ERIK H. ERIKSON

Having read the material sent to me on the University of Chicago Conference on the Draft and having had a series of conversations with young people in recent weeks, I have come to a few conclusions which I offer here as illustration of a psychological point of view, and without detailed discussion.

Most of the arguments for compulsory military and other national service seem to be bogged down in the imagery of past national emergencies (as is to be expected if and when a deadline for decision is to be met): "past" in regard to *type of warfare*, "past" in regard to the *technology of armament*, "past" in regard to *manpower needs*, and (most relevant for the social psychologist) "past" in regard to what Kenneth Boulding calls *a sense of legitimacy*. Without committing myself to his statement in its entirety, I find this concept of a *sense of legitimacy* very fruitful, especially in its individual manifestation, that is, a high sense of identity as a member and defender of what is accepted as a legitimate social system, and the resulting increase of energy in the service of what is felt to be a legitimate organizational demand. This has always been the essence of a good morale. It cannot be manufactured or enforced, however, and rather than asking ourselves how much we can get out of our young people by a coercion legitimized with the values of the past, we may ask ourselves what we can see developing in them spontaneously at this point in history so we may help to maximize their potentials, as we lead, guide, and teach them.

I would see three legitimate areas in which youth can feel its energies activated or at least not misspent in organized service at this time.

1) An emergency in national security convincingly calling for an all-out mobilization. This is the pattern of the world wars which called for large expeditionary forces. Considering the safety of American borders and the distance of the fighting fronts, this has been the American pattern of warfare. It is important to specify this because Swedish, Swiss, or Israeli conditions are not applicable to it: there the single citizen is so aware of the all-around exposed borders of a society which maximizes his sense of democratic legitimacy, individuality, and welfare that the defense (and I emphasize *defense*) of his security and of national security coincide psychologically.

At this moment in our history, under the conditions of nuclear threat and counter-threat, the semblance of national emergency must be avoided, wars must

The author is professor of Human Development and Lecturer on Psychiatry, Harvard University.

remain undeclared, and warlike enthusiasms restrained even while the individuals are to be prepared to be *selected* for faraway service in middle-sized wars.

In a selective draft under such conditions, the government wants it both ways: it wants the right to draft all and maintain a sense of universal urgency, but it also wants to select only a few, and leave the others at home. But the draft of a few is no draft at all; and it is experienced by many as a selective sentencing, if as yet more or less legitimate.

The limited emergencies now typical for undeclared war, however, are really police actions secretly sanctioned by large powers who want to avoid attacking each other with nuclear weapons while attacking each other with propaganda. That, I assume, is progress under nuclear conditions. But it is not the kind of legitimacy which will, *in the long run*, arouse a sufficient sense of participation in a sufficient number of young individuals to expect them to be more than passively and fatalistically compliant to any draft or coercion. Such compliance may do for a while as a minimum of necessary morale—that is, as long as the military ideals and identifications of previous wars survive. Otherwise, with the shrewd prolongation by our adversaries of fighting conditions which rarely promise decisive small victories and forever postpone any hope of final victory (not to speak of that total surrender which, according to George Kennan, has so far been the questionable trophy of foreign wars), the military morale on a national scale necessary for an inspired "citizens' army" will, I am forced to predict, sooner or later suffer.

I see no other way, therefore, than a voluntary army composed of men who by ideological choice, by personality, by fortune, or by misfortune find some meaning or some advantage, and preferably both, in military life. To a large extent, this is already the case in our military forces in Vietnam: the sooner the enlisted and reenlisted volunteers are given sufficient status in the national imagery and sufficient reward during their service and especially also at the time of their rejoining the employment at home, the sooner will we have a legitimate expertly trained military force. This will be also available for international ventures, such as actions for the United Nations, which seem already more legitimate to many Americans than does the Vietnam war. Whatever disadvantages are feared in such an army (such as its totalitarian potential, its mercenary character, or the proportion of volunteers from the less privileged classes) are really matters of national education and civil rights which must be discussed in a much larger context.

It is possible, of course, that a *volunteer expert army*, as I would prefer to call it (because it really answers the training requirements of a modern army in a way in which a short-term recruitment of "citizens" cannot possibly answer it), will not provide sufficient reserves for wider emergencies. I think that these reserves, also, should be established on the basis of voluntary enlistments, maybe partially in auxiliary training, such as in the ROTC.

I am opposed to the lottery system for psychological reasons: I do not believe that an abdication to Fate, administered by men, or by man-made machines, is a modern way of utilizing the potentials of a youth trained to think, to predict, and to choose. It can only lead to a more helpless sense of unfairness in those who are thus tapped, because there is nobody on whom they could vent legitimate gripes. By the same token, the guilty discomfort of those who escaped must not be underestimated. And again, if middle-sized wars are to have the legitimacy of national and international police action, then, surely, education as well as tradition should permit a large number of dedicated or adventurous young men to find such service worthwhile.

2) The second legitimacy felt strongly by our youth is humanitarian service. This, however, is more and more internationally or, rather, supranationally oriented. I like the spirit of Margaret Mead's proposal for national service because she makes it clear that it is not enough to be not military. But I would have liked to hear her discuss the question of how the nation, confronted with a sudden oversupply of compulsory services, would find the informed, equipped, and dedicated army of teachers and leaders, without whom such service could be a constant source of nationwide malcontent and disappointment. I could well also see that "elite" organizations (i.e., organizations dependent on a special spirit) like the Peace Corps would shudder to think of being supplied with volunteers by organizational and bureaucratic means. Just because ideological commitment to hardship under accustomed and extreme conditions is the only legitimate counterpart to the rigors and dangers of Army service, a volunteer army of young men and women ready for clearly necessary national as well as international service would, I think, be more desirable. The question of inculcating in our youth the wish to serve in this manner (without being intolerant of those who must develop their own individualized type of "service") is again a matter of education, and of a nationwide awareness that many values once linked to the military posture (discipline, service, and duty) must survive their demilitarization.

3) There is a third legitimacy which I will mention only in passing because it may as yet seem remote to the middle-aged middle class which we represent. I mean service in movements of civil disobedience, on a large and different scale from that of Thoreau's, to be sure, and under very different conditions from Gandhi's. I believe that there is an enormous potential for such action in many of our young people, and especially in our students, a potential which we must not belittle because it is as yet largely leaderless and devoid of a unitary discipline and philosophy. We have, in fact, no right to belittle it, for what is sometimes ridiculous and obnoxious in it is really the result of our ethical hypocrisies as parents and as teachers, which go with the attempt to make youth adjust to outmoded values. We must not overlook the fact that many of the youths now finding some kind of legitimatization in what to us looks like sensory, sexual, and behaviorial excesses of all kinds, will be wiser, but I would hope, not altogether subdued adults, parents, and teachers in the not too distant future. I can only indicate, then, that any aggravated and seemingly corrupt alliance of government (and especially the military) with advancing technology will necessarily lead to a new kind of rebellion which, in fighting "super machines" of all kinds, can only fight by refusing services. What once was loudly voiced dissent must, where there is no way of being heard, become non-cooperation. I know that such a consideration is far from the immediate realities of the draft situation, not to speak of a deadline for a draft law. Yet, if we are really interested in educating, rather than bypassing or resisting, the best potentials of youth, we must, I think, seriously attend to a trend which may provide a high sense of legitimacy, even where it touches on the illegal. How much we can (or should) legalize non-cooperation not sanctioned by past C.O. standards I do not know. But we cannot bypass the problem as one of transient freaks.

This brings me, finally, to the matter of education. I am appalled at the alarmist undertones of many of the reports which try to bolster any particular plan with sinister threats of totalitarianism here and the lack of volunteer spirit there, not to speak of the necessity to advance literacy, discipline, health, love of country, and decent haircuts by governmental regimentation. This, I feel, is the payoff in the whole abdication of the older generation which can face the future squarely only by interposing a mirror reflecting the past, always a prime sign of a weakening sense of legitimacy. All in all, I think that what is over-publicized as the dispirited, or merely conformist, or sometimes riotously obnoxious youth of our day is, rather, the potentially most dedicated, because most informed, or better *informable*, youth in history. The draft law calls for immediate action, but between the lines of all the reports submitted there are questions which call for a clearer formulation of traditional and emerging values—those which give our generation the right to recruit youth, and those which would permit youth to insist on alternatives.

PART 2

The Discussions

Charge to the Conference

Sunday Evening, December 4, 1966

Chairman, SOL TAX

Sol Tax. We begin this evening, after some remarks from Mr. Patterson of the National Commission on Selective Service, with a major part of our program. To open the deliberations, we sought a lawyer who would read *all* of the papers that were made available to the Conference, as the evidence that had been placed before us, and analyze what are the relevant issues and what might be the limits of discussion. We have called this a Charge to the Conference. This evening, after Professor Hazard gives us this charge, we will discuss it and agree upon the intellectual rules for our discussion.

The Committee assumed that in the days to follow it would be relevant to look first at the present system of Selective Service, which is the law of our land, and then at proposals for modifying the System. In each session we will begin with the facts which are before us; we want to get them straight. Then we will have a period of questioning and clarification so we can understand together what the facts are. Then, we will begin to talk about advantages and disadvantages more systematically, and end with general discussion. The Committee proposes that the first part of the discussion be carried on by the experts and specialists who have written papers: facts about the advantages and disadvantages of the present system and of new proposals should be handled by those who have become especially knowledgeable about the system that we have. Later general discussions will of course bring in other questions and clarifications. After these sessions devoted to the advantages and disadvantages of various proposals, on Tuesday evening we will become more explicitly scholarly and ask what we know and what we don't know, what are the facts, and what research is needed. We hope that during the next few days some new proposals will emerge, presented briefly and factually, to be discussed.

Now I would like to introduce Mr. Bradley Patterson, Jr., the Executive Director of the National Commission on Selective Service.

Bradley H. Patterson, Jr. The Commission was established by President Johnson in July, 1966, and I will read you a couple of sentences from our charter which are important to keep in mind as our instructions from the President.

"The Commission shall consider the past, present, and prospective functioning of selective service and other systems of national service in the light of the following factors: fairness to all citizens, military manpower requirements, the objective of minimizing uncertainty and interference with individual careers and education, social, economic, and employment conditions, and goals and budgetary

An Edited Transcript of the Plenary Sessions, December 4-7, 1967.

and administrative considerations. The Commission," the President went on, "is also authorized to evaluate other proposals relating to selective service including proposals for national service. The Commission shall make a final report to the President on or about January 1, 1967, setting forth its findings and recommendations."

The Commission is a group of twenty very distinguished American citizens chaired by Burke Marshall, former Assistant to the Attorney General for Civil Rights, and includes such people as former HEW Secretary Oveta Culp Hobby; George Reedy, former Press Secretary to the President; Anna Rosenberg Hoffman; John McCone of the west coast; and Jean Noble of New York University. It is a very diverse group drawn from all corners of our country and all segments of public and private life, with tremendous experience in back of them. I am confident, from the very membership of this group, that the recommendations to the President will tap the best experience and judgment of their many years in public life.

The first thing the Commission did was to seek advice from beyond its own circle. We wrote to every one of the fifty-five governors of states and territories. We wrote and asked for the opinions and writings of 121 national organizations—student, professional, scientific, educational, civil rights, women's—every major national organization that had an interest in military manpower problems. We talked with forty college presidents. We invited the views of eleven agency heads in Washington, four of whom appeared before us in person. We asked nine universities to designate students to travel to 40 different campuses to select, in an admittedly unscientific, but candid way, the views of fellow students and tell us about them personally. We wrote to seventeen mayors of cities about the problems and possibilities of national service in the nation's cities. We consulted representatives of the National League of Cities, county officials, and the Governors' Conference. A group of us spent an hour with General Eisenhower in his office at Gettysburg, discussing his ideas of universal military training and manpower requirements. The President invited all citizens of the United States, particularly students, to write him about their views on the draft, and we have so far received about 600 letters. We have sent observers to all the major conferences: the one in Washington held by the American Veterans' Committee, the conference in Yellow Springs at Antioch, and this one.

The Committee also conducts a research program. We engaged in taking the first "photograph" in its 26 years of the Selective Service System as it really operates. First we wanted to find out about local draft board members; there are about 16,000 draft board members in the United States. Who are they? How old? What are their characteristics, their experience, their education, their ethnic background, their length of service, and so forth? We sent a questionnaire covering all these items to all 16,000 members.

There are 4,087 local boards in the Selective Service System. What are their views about the system? They are in the "front lines" of it. How do they feel it could be improved? What are the judgmental questions that give them the most trouble? We sent a 14-item questionnaire to every one of the 120 appeal boards and panels, because they again are a part of the "front lines" of responsibility in the system. What are their judgmental problems? What are their ideas on how the Selective Service System might be changed? We sent a 5-item questionnaire to every one of the 50 state headquarters, and we also have engaged in a field survey of Selective Service records. We took a 5 per cent sample of all the boards, roughly 200, and with the help of the Bureau of the Census, which is noted for its impersonal and trained enumerators, paid a visit to each of the boards in the sample, went through 100 files of each of the 200 boards to determine what's in them and what kinds of documents do or do not substantiate a claim for one or another kind of classification. All of the material that was gathered with the help of the Bureau of the Census has been put into computers and is giving us information cross-correlated with the kinds of boards—metropolitan, rural, and so forth. So we are achieving for what I am sure is the first time in its history a scientific photograph of the Selective Service System. I mention this in order to try to assure you that we are trying to go about our job objectively and scientifically, not on the basis of allegations, or pressures, or just charges. We are going on the basis of facts.

The Commission then organized its work around some 67 different issues and has been meeting on these issues. We have had about six meetings, totaling about 80 hours; we have more meetings ahead and our report is not yet written. I say this in order to assure this Conference that the results of your discussions and, almost more important, the arguments I expect to listen to, are really going to have a high probability of making a deep impact on our own discussions, deliberations, and recommendations. The Commission, not having written its report yet, considers that all options are open. We have pursued some of these matters for a long period of time in deep discussion and at great length. We have, however, only pursued them seven-eighths of the way; the last eighth is open and our minds are still very receptive to suggestions. The report has not been written; nothing is final.

Mr. Tax. Thank you very much. And now I would like to introduce Professor Geoffrey C. Hazard, Jr., of the University of Chicago Law School, discussing "The Task before Us"—The Charge to the Conference.

Geoffrey C. Hazard, Jr. There are four basic questions presented:

First, do we need a large Army and, if so, why?

Second, if we need at most a "middle-sized" Army, one of roughly its present magnitude, could we provide it with volunteers?

Third, if we don't rely exclusively on a volunteer Army, what are the proper characteristics of a system of involuntary conscription?

Fourth, if we have a system of involuntary conscription that will take substantially less than the whole cohorts from which conscription is to be made, should there be some complementary system of national service to distribute a parallel burden on those not conscripted into military service?

These four questions provide an oversimplified structure for what is going to be an overcomplicated discussion. Moreover, I will discuss these questions didactically rather than with the measure of restraint they properly deserve, because didactic statement makes for clarity. It should be understood that the positiveness of the statement of the propositions in no way diminishes their debatability.

Let me say a word first about the report we have just received on the President's Commission on the Draft. We are told that the Commission has been studying the question intensively for the last seven months, that this is the first comprehensive official study of the subject, and that, although the Commission is due to report in less than a month, it has not yet reached conclusions and will therefore be open-minded to what is said here. This is truly extraordinary. In the first place, it is outrageous that we have had a "peacetime" draft for about twenty years, and for more than ten years since the Korean War, and yet only now has anyone in the government undertaken to subject the draft system to serious analysis. In the second place, it is difficult to accept the idea that a Commission that has looked into this complex subject for seven months has not yet formed any conclusions but will do so, and write them up, in the next three weeks. While it is comforting to think that this Conference's deliberations may be given heed by the Commission, it is not clear how in fact that is going to happen. Nevertheless, the Commission's work will certainly not exhaust the subject and we may be confident that what is said here will be given some heed somewhere.

Coming now to the problem of the draft itself, we ought to recognize that the draft is a great question in the most proper sense of the term. The draft invites attention to general problems of political morality. These problems are not merely domestic, contemporary ones but ones of significance in comparative and historical dimension. Deuteronomy reminds us that conscription is an old problem. The draft is the kind of question that would and did in fact interest both Napoleon and Tolstoy. At the same time, it has operational reality in the daily lives of every citizen today, another characteristic of a great question. We should treat it with that respect.

Let us now turn to the four questions I suggested were involved. First, the problem of the size of the Army. The size of the Army is a function of foreign policy. For the last twenty years we have had a foreign policy notable for the ambition and the ambiguity of its aims. It is not surprising that the question of the proper size of our Army should likewise be ambiguous and, in the eyes of some, ambitious. For this reason, the discussions here cannot proceed without some reference to our foreign policy, though of course that is not the principal concern these next few days.

I am mindful that President Beadle [University of Chicago] has pointed out that we are not convened to talk about foreign policy in general or Vietnam in particular. Still, we cannot ignore that question in talking about the draft. Two points make this clear. The paper presented to us by Colonel Bar-On of Israel is one. Colonel Bar-On is an officer of an army of a country of fewer than three million people surrounded by something like ten times that number of dedicated enemies. The Israelis don't have any doubt what their foreign policy has to be, or any doubt that they need an army, or any doubt that they need a conscription system. I doubt that there has ever been a draft demonstration or protest in Israel. And the clarity of this view shows in the moral fervor of Colonel Bar-On's paper.

If, for example, we had on our northern borders Red China rather than Canada, I suspect our attitude toward our Army and our draft would be similarly clear. That is of course not the case. On the contrary, the dangers to us posed by our antagonists, both geographically and causally, unlike those of Israel, seem remote and speculative. This is true of our involvement in Vietnam; it was true of our involvement in Lebanon, in Santo Domingo, and probably of some of our involvement in the Berlin Crisis twenty years ago. Apparent remoteness and speculativeness indeed seem characteristic of any involvement of a great power such as ourselves—any involvement, that is, except total war. Hence, unlike the Israelis, we have a foreign policy that is uncertain and unclear in its aims to some people most of the time and most people some of the time.

This uncertainty is very relevant to attitudes toward the draft. The draft is a system of compulsory exaction. How one perceives the rightness of compulsory exactions depends on how one perceives the rightness of the ends to which the compulsory exactions are applied. This means-ends problem is unavoidable and should not be avoided. Our foreign policy and specifically our policy in Vietnam is thus relevant to the present discussion. But it is not determinative. This Conference and its participants cannot ignore the ensuing questions about the draft simply because it or they may have clear views on the immediate ends of the draft system under present circumstances.

The second point that indicates the relevance of the question of our need for an Army is this: If we clearly needed a mass Army, the question of the draft would be academic. We needed such an Army in World War II and we took practically all able-bodied men of eligible age. The draft was clearly the most practical way to do the job. On the other hand, if we needed only a very small Army—one, say, of the relative size it was before World War II—the question of the draft would also be academic, because we could all agree that a volunteer system would do the job. Unfortunately, we find that our needs are for a "middle-sized" Army, one smaller than that for which draft recruitment is obviously appropriate but larger than that for which volunteer recruitment is obviously appropriate. That is the way it was even in the Korean War and that is the way it is in Vietnam now.

Thus, the second issue is: If we need a middle-sized Army, could we provide for it with volunteers? In assessing this question, it is appropriate to consider direct economic costs and benefits. These calculations are of course difficult to make and the notion of "direct" versus "indirect" costs is essentially arbitrary. It is clear, however, that one has to do more than count the Armed Forces payroll in order to figure the cost involved. And one has to do more than compute the average I.Q. of Army inductees to know what the benefits are.

Beyond economic cost, consideration must be given to social costs and benefits, which are economic costs but which also have moral and political attributes. These social costs, and benefits, include such matters as ethnic balance and democratic spirit in the Army—whatever they are—vis-à-vis the military mind—whatever that is. One might consider, for example, whether we would want a volunteer system such that large numbers of our ablest young men would want to enter the military service. On the other hand, there is the question whether we want a society with large numbers of young men so committed to passive virtue as to make a draft necessary to raise an Army.

Let me charge you that consideration of a volunteer Army not be constrained by a narrow conception of cost, nor let it be narrowed by preoccupation with cost. It is important to know the price tag in dollars of something, and to know it in a sophisticated sense. It is also important to know some other things.

Third, if we do not rely exclusively on a volunteer Army, what are the problems of a compulsory selection system? One ought to begin consideration of this question on the common ground from which I know of no dissent: The size of the annual intake required in the Armed Forces will always be a fraction of the age cohort, or any set of cohorts, from which the draft is to be made. Being drafted is going to be a minority proposition.

This creates all kinds of problems: First, what should be the risk group by age and by competency, physical, mental and moral? Bear in mind that military specifications define minimum standards of the risk-eligible group. Second, of those eligible, who should be excluded from liability either temporarily or permanently?

Consider the notion of "essential occupations." Since last year we have had a labor-short economy. We struggled along somehow—at higher costs to be sure—with a lack of "essential" workers. This suggests that we could probably draft into the Armed Forces all of the people that are under some criteria regarded as "essential," and the economy would still work. In World War II, we wiped out the effective trained labor market by yanking it into the Armed Forces, and then had to re-create a labor force; and we did so. Obviously, we could do the same thing on a smaller scale. Quite apart from the foregoing question, consider the definitional problems: What is an occupation? What makes it essential? In a rapidly changing technology, does the concept make any sense at all?

Consider more specifically the question of student deferment. The theory is that being a student is an essential occupation. But what is essential about students? What skills do people have at the draft age of 18 or 19 or 20? What skills are being lost to the nation? Not the skills of the machinist, or of the skilled manager, but skills, as we discover upon turning our products out, that have to be retrained upon entering into industry. Moveover, if draft eligibility were distributed evenly among a given age cohort without regard to enrollment in college, only about 25 per cent of students would be drafted. Finally—even if students are essential—if we assume only a short period of service, say two years, we are only talking about a two-year disruption of this essential activity. At the end of two years, the problem would cease to exist.

In this connection, I understand that General Hershey always uses the case of medical students. I don't know how one reasons from the education of medical students to the education of pre-law students and to others. May I suggest that the justification for deferring students while in medical school is to legitimate drafting them as doctors when they get out.

Consider next the problem of the exemption of conscientious objectors. I will pass the question of religious belief in the traditional sense because there is a political consensus on that: Nobody is proposing to draft Quakers as far as I know. The problem arises about political belief and quasi-ethical convictions not founded on explicit references to a Supreme Being. What about the problem of belief that war in general is wrong? Or, more particularly, the problem that a particular war, for which the draft is providing men, is wrong, for example, the attitude toward Vietnam?

If moral and political convictions are considered broadly, and if the existence of a strong conviction of this kind is ground for exemption, then doesn't the following kind of question arise: Should not a member of the Ku Klux Klan or the Black Muslims be entitled to exemption because induction into the Armed Forces results in compulsory racial integration, a matter on which these groups have strong negative convictions? If they assert their belief to be ethical and political—and some of them do—doesn't this raise questions about the cogency of political and ethical grounds of exemption?

Another exempt group under present law are the reserves. Why? The reserves are not being called up and there seems little prospect that they will be, for reasons not very well explained. If they are not going to be called up, why should they be exempt?

It is important, too, to view the problem of eligibility and exemption in its comprehensive aspect. Specifically, you should address the proposition that the present system is preferable to a lottery. Why is it so? If I understood General Hershey's paper correctly, he said that it would not be possible to program the basis of decision of the present induction pattern. This has curious implications. It is possible to program a lottery. This being so, it seems to follow that the present system lacks even the rationality of a lottery: It is random in an un-random sense. Doesn't the present system have the unpredictability of a lottery without the decency of true unpredictability? Unless you are satisfied that there is an explicable and tolerably uniform pattern of decision by the 4,000 draft boards that are administering this law, doesn't the present system have the objectionable characteristics of a lottery without its virtues? The question is whether the system as it stands is characterized by an insupportable range of discrepancies.

Finally, if we must have a draft, should we establish complementary demands on the time and service of those who are not going into the military forces? National service is conceived alternatively and simultaneously as betterment of the society by educational improvement of the individuals drawn into service, and betterment of society through the work efforts of those conscripted to service. On the one hand, there is projected a kind of post-high-school training program chiefly designed to benefit its enrollees; on the other hand, there is projected a massive program like VISTA.

This is a new idea. Its institutional possibilities, good or bad, have not been identified by experience, and therefore require assessment by conjecture rather than by retrospection. We probably could agree there are many social problems of very considerable magnitude to which the energy and attention of young people could be properly addressed. The question is whether they should be conscripted to the task.

It is an interesting idea. Perhaps one need not assume that an ill wind, if the draft is an ill wind, can blow no good for the general social order. On the other hand, it should not be assumed that necessity is a good mother in all of her inventions.

Mr. Tax. I would like now to open the discussion of the issues facing the Conference. We have heard the Charge to us, which is open for discussion, Mr. Hazard's statement of what is relevant and what should not be considered relevant. I would like to hear discussion on these broader issues rather than on any of the particular points that Mr. Hazard brought to our attention, while leaving us still with all of our problems.

Morris Janowitz. First without questioning the four-point division that was presented to us, I think it might be well to recognize that although it has been very recently that we have started to gather the comprehensive data relevant to understanding the present workings of the Selective Service System and its possible inequalities, we have known about this matter for a long time. If one looks at the printed record as early as 1952, and according to academic protocol I do not cite my own works at this moment, the rigidities of the Selective Service System dating from the end of the Korean War were already known. It took a long time before these issues came into the public attention. Certainly one thing is clear—that among the establishments that exist it is the academic establishment which should have had the responsibility of investigating these subjects at an earlier date, and, because of its particular relationship to Selective Service, it turned its attention in other directions. Whatever we have to say about the tactics and techniques of the student revolt, and I don't like the word revolt, it must be recognized that it was the students who brought this issue so dramatically to the attention of their professors.

Mr. Tax. Thank you, we all understand that we begin by attacking something that is presently with us, but that in the long run we must replace it with something better, so that it doesn't mean anything if we begin in our sessions by saying that there is something that needs correction: it will only count at the end to find something with which to correct it. Is that a fair statement? I would like to hear a discussion of either Mr. Hazard's or Mr. Janowitz' comments.

Wayne Booth. The form of your four topics really suggests that you don't consider each succeeding topic unless you have answered the first one in a given way. You say that we do need a certain kind of Army; the job can't be done by volunteers: we will find a kind of conscription which will therefore leave us with the question of fairness. Did you mean that implication? Are you, in spite of your very skillful and necessary job of balancing this hand with that hand, are you really committing yourself to definite answers for these three stages or at least the first two? The job can't be done with volunteers?

Mr. Hazard. I tried to arrange the points in order of narrowing focus, because I think there is some kind of logical order to them. But I recognize, with Justice Holmes, that general propositions do not decide concrete cases. Although there is a certain order to the questions, as you begin to think through the implications with respect to the fourth question, you will make reference again to issues involved in the other three. I think that that is unavoidable. It is the essential circularity of reasoning that is necessary to consider related propositions.

Erwin L. Kelly, Jr. I would like to address myself to the first point made by Mr. Hazard, that is, this Conference cannot really get anywhere unless we discuss explicitly the issue of our military manpower requirements. We have the experts here. It seems to me that this is our logical starting point. I am here representing the Conference which was held at Antioch, and was one of the people organizing that Conference. We did not confront the problem, but we found that it rose continuously throughout our discussion. I really think that there is something to be gained by making this our first topic, rather than starting with the present Selective Service System. The basic issue would seem to be whether 2.7 million is a reasonable figure for our projected military manpower requirements in peacetime.

Richard Flacks. I would like to add what seems to me at least a related matter which is: what are the purposes of Selective Service in the foreign policy framework? Are we, for example, all agreed about under which circumstances conscripts should be used overseas? This is, as the charge was given to us, quite central to any program that we eventually would propose.

Mr. Tax. I would like to take up the question that Mr. Kelly raised of the size of our Armed Forces. You said, Mr. Hazard, that you were assuming that we were dealing with a middle-sized armed force; if we had almost no need of soldiers, they would be volunteers; if we had an all-out war, there wouldn't be a problem for us. Now what is the middle-sized Army that we are thinking of? Is it something like 3 million? Will somebody here posit some figure? Mr. Kelly, you raised the question; did you have an answer in mind?

Mr. Kelly. Well, it seems to me that the central discussion which we are hearing in essence is—Do you or do you not need a draft? Whether you need or don't need a draft is entirely the function of the size of military you are going to have. Therefore it seems to me that this represents an extremely fundamental question. If we are going to have 2.7 million or 3 million people in the military (one is the Defense Department figure and the other is the *New York Times* figure), this greatly changes the whole direction which our thinking takes. I find, in going through the various kinds of issues that are involved, volunteer versus non-volunteer, national service, universal service, that always in the back of one's mind is this question—Do you really need such a large militia? Is this really that important?

Mr. Tax. Could we ask first, what is the size of our military forces now?

Mr. Kelly. Now, 3.4 million.

Mr. Hazard. I would suppose you would have difficulty in conducting the Conference if the question were regarded as open whether the necessary military force were as small as a million or as large as 10 million. I suppose a military force of a million or less would be intelligible only if we had a vastly different set of foreign policy assumptions than we have now. So, also, with an Army of 10 million—there are many people in this country who believe that we ought to have a foreign policy that would imply that size military force. I am not sure, however, that this Conference could go forward satisfactorily if you wanted to discuss the question of what kind of a world it is in which one could think usefully of having a million-man army. I suggest you ought to recognize that there are differences of opinion about our foreign policy and therefore by implication about the size of the military force, but you should begin with the assumption that we are talking about 2.5 or 3.5 million men. I would doubt that there is any possibility of our military establishment being less than 2.5 million in the next 15 years.

Colonel Samuel Hays. I would think that we would probably get farther if, to back up Professor Hazard, we could make a basic assumption taking judicial notice, if you will, of the foreign policy being as it is, and the world being as it is, and of our national purpose as being what it generally appears to be. Then we should give ourselves as much flexibility on the size of force as we possibly can. It would not do to develop a system which would hold only if the size of the force went up to 3.5 million and be invalid if it went higher. Not knowing what is going to happen tomorrow, we don't know what size force we are going to require. If one could say that the situation in South Africa or Rhodesia or the Near East or the Far East is going to remain as it is, then we could estimate the size force required. If one assumes some different situation, then one would require a different kind of force. I would conclude that we should take a liberal view of the possible scope of our manpower requirements, setting it up possibly higher than 3.5 million with a center around 2.5 to 3.5.

Mrs. McAllister. It seems to me that the size of the Army may in turn determine the foreign policy, and similarly, the number of veterans that we have in Congress may affect our foreign policy.

Donald J. Eberly. Mr. Hazard's fourth point seemed to imply that the avenue to national service was through the draft, and yet there are a number of us who feel that 85 to 90 per cent of the rationale for national service is quite apart from draft inequities. Now this is a Conference on the Draft; perhaps you would wish to consider national service primarily in that context, or as the President's charge to the National Advisory Commission implies, would you wish to consider national service on its own—quite apart from whether or not the draft exists?

Mr. Hazard. I am not sure that this states a real problem. I suppose most of the reasons that one would adduce for or against national service on its own merit would have to be reconsidered in relation to the draft, and in relation to the draft there is the additional problem of equity.

Bruce K. Chapman. The people who are not here would have some better judgment on the question of size, which is certainly critical. Mr. Wool is one of them and of course Dr. Oi from the University of Washington. Dr. Oi believes that under a voluntary system you would need fewer people because your turnover would be lower, because you would have fewer people engaged in the military, in training recruits and so on, so he projects a force smaller than 2.7 million, but 2.7 is the Pentagon figure they are dealing with for the present situation, assuming a new system in 1970, if the Vietnam war has changed materially for the better at that point.

Harry Marmion. I think that a realistic assumption can be made, as Mr. Hazard indicated, that the size of the Armed Forces in the foreseeable future will be either what we have now, or it will go up somewhat as this war, or another war, escalates.

C. Arnold Anderson. I should like to support Mr. Kelly and Mr. Flacks and dissent from Colonel Hays if I understood him. It is, I think, quite superficial to say we take foreign policy as given. First of all, none of us knows what it is. Second, there isn't any. Thirdly, we wouldn't agree on it if we could state it. It seems to me that in the context of this Conference we have to examine what are the implications for the formulation and implementation of the foreign policy of one or another form of raising military forces. Now with regard to the size, we can follow one of two courses; both, if possible. We could discuss what would be the case with a small force or with a large force. Or, we can conveniently fix the figure at 2.5 to 3.5 million because most of the issues that we will have time to discuss can be adequately discussed around these figures. Nonetheless, we must keep in mind that we will want to consider the feedback upon foreign policy.

Leon Bramson. I would like to introduce the fact—well known to most of you—that in the American Army the ratio of men who are in actual combat in relation to support units is one to six. I would like to raise the question as to whether or not a ratio of one combat man to six men in support units, who are doing the jobs essentially done by civilians elsewhere, justifies an army of 2.7 million?

[Unidentified Speaker]. I would like to reinforce Mr. Bramson's point by citing an authority, Defense Secretary McNamara, who used the figure of 14 per cent of the military that are in combat positions. If we take a 3.4 million size military, this leaves us with 476,000 people who are in combat-type positions. Then you can relate the question of conscription, if we are forced to talk in terms of conscription, to a combat force of less than half

a million, and then begin to think in terms of the parallel in civilian terms where we have about half a million policemen and firemen in the country, and whether we think of considering conscripting these domestic security forces.

Gibson Winter. I would agree that we want to talk about method, but how you deal with method always depends on your basic principle. It seems to me important to keep in mind that the norm for service in a democratic society within our tradition is voluntary. Some might argue against this but I think that it is very important. In reading a lot of these papers I noticed a kind of enthusiasm for various kinds of compulsion, as though it was taken for granted as a good thing. I grant that there are points at which there are reasons for compulsion of various types, but that the guideline *is* compulsion, in our tradition, has to have a warrant. No matter what program we talk about, if we are really thinking in terms of a free society, of voluntary movement, then if we start talking about various kinds of compulsion, national service or whatever, the burden of proof is on us, to demonstrate that this is really necessary.

Milton J. Rosenberg. I would like to add a word in response to Col. Hays and Mr. Marmion. What they have said and some of the responses to what they said identified an important question that is going to come up a good deal in these deliberations, namely: Ought we to approach problems of military manpower, or a movement for some sort of national service act as based upon a given and persisting foreign policy commitment? The ultimate business of foreign policy and our ultimate orientation in pursuit of foreign policy goals is some kind of conciliation of international tensions—the achievement of a more pacific international order. In dealings between nations, where conciliation possibilities are at issue, one way in which to proceed is by general recourse to the possibilities of disarmament. These days certainly this involves restriction of nuclear stockpiles, etc., but conventionally it has also involved reduction of armed forces in terms of their actual size. I would think that the bearing of further foreign policy developments on the manpower commitment ought to be considered, particularly if we are interested in fostering further international conciliation.

Mr. Tax. I understood that it was only for the purposes of the Conference that we were imagining this size in order to see how we could resolve some of the problems more equitably.

Colonel Hays. That's about the size we are likely to have with the present circumstances; I don't think we should make our picture or our visualization of what kind of machinery we would set up depend on that alone. We should be flexible enough to go either lower or higher. However, it would appear that we should set some bounds just for the purpose of setting up a model and seeing what it looks like.

Granville Ridley. This is a discussion of the Selective Service System. Shouldn't we talk of a system that is elastic enough to provide a million-man Army or a 10-million-man Army? I know we have had more than 12 million men registered at one time and I don't know how many we have registered right now. We need an elastic system of manpower procurement.

Donald Rumsfeld. It has been my feeling that a voluntary career military was a possibility. Mr. Winter said that our society has tended to avoid compulsion unless there was a need, and that the burden of proof rests on establishing the necessity for it. The question of flexibility has come up. Even with a voluntary system there would need to be a compulsory system above it so that the military could be expanded as the requirements were demonstrated. I don't think that any who may favor a voluntary system should rule it out as being inflexible. We all recognize the fact that you would need, above any voluntary system, a compulsory system of Selective Service that would bring the U. S. military up to the capabilities needed in a given situation.

What bothers me is that I came here with a belief that a voluntary system was possible. Professor Hazard, in following through these four questions, dismissed it very quickly by suggesting that really, after all, none of us would want to live in a society where there were a sufficient number of people who would voluntarily serve in the military, and that this sort of a desire on the part of American citizens would be sufficiently distasteful that we really wouldn't want to have a voluntary system because it might encourage people to be of such a mind. The subject of policemen and firemen was raised here, and there is an analogy. People in the law, very few actually, send people to the electric chair. Very few of the military actually are involved in combat; very few policemen are actually arresting individuals. It would be helpful to me to discuss here a bit, if Professor Hazard would, why he so easily concludes that we would not want a voluntary system because we wouldn't want a society where people would want to be in the military. Why is compulsion a better value for a society than voluntarism?

Mr. Hazard. Well, I don't think I asserted that as a proposition; I think I posed it as a question. What I had in mind was the following—and I don't regard the answers as obvious: I can imagine a society in which, for a variety of reasons, one might want to reinforce the direct monetary rewards made available to people in the military establishments by a series of designed and undesigned systems of encouragement that would attach very high value to military service. I think it's fair to say that that was the case in Prussian Germany. The fact of the matter is that it was very honorific to be in the army. I do not mean to say that it follows that you can have a voluntary army only when you have those social conditions. You can't assume, however, that you may not be paying some kind of social price if you have that reward system. If I suggested that I was making this a statement of fact, I didn't mean to do so; I meant to say that it's a very interesting and important question.

Paul Lauter. I want to raise a few small points, mostly on the basis of the one document that I'm fairly sure all of us have read—namely the Conference program. The program itself raises some questions about the balance of items to be discussed and the time allocated for them. Some of these have been raised already and I want to raise them a little bit more sharply perhaps. I was struck in what Mr. Hazard said, by a certain disjunction between the time that he allocated to discussing certain items and the time for the discussion of those items allocated on the program. For example, the question of conscientious objection, about which I've already heard two misstatements tonight, is allocated 30 minutes on the program. It would probably take a good 30 minutes to correct those two misstatements, let alone do anything else. My understanding of this conference was that at least one of its origins was in the student protest against ranking, yet the question of ranking and of student, and other, deferments is taken care of also in 25 minutes. The question that Mr. Flacks raised about the conditions of service, which seems to me a very crucial one indeed—

one, for example, that the French had to face during the Algerian War, in a very serious way, that is, whether conscripts could be used in a war like the Algerian conflict, and a question which was raised by some of our congressmen when they tried to introduce into the Congress a bill forbidding the use of conscripts in Vietnam—is allocated no time at all that I notice. This, for me, raises certain points and I'd like to throw out a procedural suggestion. The experience I've had in the past has been that there's a tendency for a great deal of repetition in the course of the discussion that takes place in the center of the circle, a great deal of summarization of papers, a great deal of cross talk between the presumed limited number of experts on the subject who sit in the middle. We could spread our agenda a good deal if we finessed that altogether or at least in a great measure. Perhaps, rather than start out a discussion among those people who have written papers, we should try to broaden and spread the discussion immediately to the total assembly right from the beginning.

Mr. Tax. Is this now understood, that first in each case there will be a relatively brief period for a statement, then there will be questions and clarifications, and then we throw it open to general discussion in each case? Now, the second proposal that Mr. Lauter made: do you want to state it yourself?

Mr. Lauter. Yes, I think we have to devote somewhat more time to reconsideration of the present law as it exists, particularly with reference to deferment practices and conscientious objection.

Mr. Tax. We have four different proposals to consider, including the deferment policies, conscientious objection, duration of liability for service, the lottery, and perhaps some that are unmentioned in the program.

Lloyd Anderson. I would appreciate it if Mr. Lauter would briefly state his concern about why, among all of the topics we need to discuss, conscientious objection needs more time?

Mr. Lauter. For two reasons. One is, that practically speaking, as I understand it, one of the main problems in terms of rewriting the law is to try to make some decision about changes in the provisions regarding conscientious objectors. There are issues, secondly, that are involved in *that* that are really complicated and that don't lend themselves to summary. The second reason is this: the whole question of conscience is one of the very few places in which Mr. Hazard's first questions—do we need a large Army and if so, why—really come into focus, so one can grapple with the issues rather than talking in general about foreign policy. I think for those two reasons: first, that it helps to focus what I take to be ultimately the moral issue behind this, and second, that it is a specific and rather complicated issue, that one would want to devote a good deal of time to it.

Sister Thomasine Cusack. I can't see that there's any great discussion to be had on conscientious objection on religious grounds. I think the problem is conscientious objection on political grounds—that is the "thorny" one, and there we are back to a political issue. It's the degree and the reason for conscientious objection—not conscientious objection per se—that should be discussed.

Mr. Anderson. On the subject of foreign policy, we have to find some compromise because of the interactions of foreign policy and our discussions here on the draft, as Mr. Hazard and others have pointed out. I would like to suggest just one specific way in which information from our military colleagues can help us. While we accept that foreign policy cannot change very rapidly, but that it may change, we might like to push it a little bit. A specific example of this would be the Dominican Republic. Will we be involved in such things in the future? If so, would this be appropriately handled by the *same* type of military as is handling Vietnam? If it is a different type of military, would different numbers be required? Would a specially trained force for keeping people apart be required? Such questions as this would deal with what Representative Rumsfeld was worrying about. My basic point is that I think we have to use what information we can from our military colleagues on some changes, some relevance to national policy; we can't throw it completely open, but we can't close it.

Mr. Tax. We have changed the program, then, for tomorrow, and we can worry about the rest of the program later. I suggest that we have two choices —either somebody will think that it is critical that we crystallize some notion of the size of the Armed Forces with which we're dealing, or we will adjourn and not worry about that. It may not be necessary to settle on a generic size at all, is this possible?

John de J. Pemberton, Jr. Professor Hazard suggested on this subject that it could neither be regarded as determinative of our discussion nor wholly irrelevant. I take it that that means that it may be relevant at any point in the discussion, so we need not determine it right now. I was shocked by the description of the terms of reference and procedure of the National Commission that we heard at the beginning of the evening. It seemed on the one hand to be a very casual public opinion poll among assorted individuals, and on the other hand an efficiency audit of an existing system. There seemed to be no statement of any procedure for eliciting serious analysis of issues by some procedure.

Mr. Tax. The Commission, you understand, has had available to it all of the papers that you have read that have been prepared for this Conference, so there is at least that amount of data, and I think we have understood that the discussions would be carried to the Commission, is that right? Professor Hazard wanted to say a word before we adjourn.

Mr. Hazard. I just wanted to suggest to you that there probably are as many central issues as there are conferees. It is to the benefit of the group to recognize that one person's conception of the central issue might not always be somebody else's conception of the central issue.

Mr. Patterson. I want to assure the members of the Conference that there are at least 40 major policy papers before the Commission, in addition to the research which I described, and that I am most grateful to be here for the four days and will make a very prompt and full report to the Commission on the proceedings here.

[Unidentified Speaker]. I have a question for Mr. Hazard. I don't understand where we're going to discuss this question of "Do we need a large Army?" You imply that it is going to have to be discussed sometime, and somehow it has been assumed we are not going to discuss it now. Do you have a specific suggestion about this?

Mr. Hazard. I think you could discuss the points that would be relevant to the question, "Do we need a large Army?" I suppose ultimately we might say what our foreign policy ought to be. The reason you conceive of having a large Army, or a small one, is because you make certain assumptions about foreign involvement. It seems to me that the focus of the discussion ought to be on what I have described as a middle-sized Army, while recognizing that, as Colonel Hays has suggested, there might be an eventuality—I don't think it's going to realize itself—that in the next five years we'll need a 10-million-man Army. Similarly, it is imaginable that we would have a foreign policy in which Armed Forces of a million men might be adequate. If you had that kind of foreign policy, and therefore that kind of an Army, then all the problems we are talking about here would be put into a quite different context. But if you talked political probability, bearing in mind that the Conference is about a Selective Service System and not about foreign policy, then the zone described is a good working one, particularly for the purpose of assessing the relevance of propositions. The focal point ought to be an Army of 2.5 to 3.5 million, but you have to think about the possibility of its being larger or smaller. If I understand the point it would go like this: the size of the military is one of the determinants of short-run foreign policy. I underscore the term *short-run*. If you tried to manipulate foreign policy by manipulating the size of the Armed Forces, you've got it quite backwards; if the Congress or the Executive thinks the foreign policy ought to be different, they'll manipulate the Army's size. I would simply say that it is unlikely in the extreme that you could induce Congress to reduce the size of the Army in order to constrain the Executive on foreign policy. It is a very interesting point made —Army size does affect short-range foreign policy, but I don't think it's really sensible to say that it affects long-range foreign policy.

[*Unidentified Speaker*]. How not, then, to discuss that point? I mean, I don't see how this foreign policy thing comes in unless that's the question you're going to ask.

Mr. Hazard. The point I want to make is this: Some of the difficulties with a selective system for a middle-sized Army arise *because*, whatever the foreign policy is, there is not a substantial consensus about the foreign policy. This affects the moral assessment of the rightness of the compulsory conscription system. I simply posit that with a middle-sized Army, and small, fractured confrontations, you are not going to have continuing political consensus on each one of those confrontations. You're always going to have some people who think any particular confrontation is politically wrong and they might even say, morally wrong. What are you going to do about that group of people when you are confronted with the problem of compulsory conscription?

The Present System of Selective Service

MONDAY MORNING, DECEMBER 5, 1966

Chairman, MORRIS JANOWITZ

Mr. Tax. All day today we will be discussing the present system of Selective Service and proposals to modify it. We will begin with Colonel Ingold and questions and discussion. Immediately after the hour on the present system, we will move into the three major alternatives which were originally scheduled for this afternoon. That would give us an hour and a quarter for questions and discussion about the Selective Service System and these various changes which can't always be separated.

In the afternoon from 2:00 o'clock we have scheduled an hour to understand what is meant by the proposal for the lottery; there will be somebody here able to give us the general idea. We shall then have from 3:00 to 5:00 o'clock for our discussion of the system of Selective Service and *all* of its proposed changes, so that we can go on tomorrow with the alternatives that are larger, that is, that change the system entirely.

Now, I would like to introduce the Chairman for the morning, Mr. Janowitz.

Mr. Janowitz. I take it that this morning, in the presentation on the Selective Service, Colonel Ingold will not address himself to the totality of the System, but will address himself to those problematic issues which are at the center of public discussion at the moment. A steady stream of questions have been coming to me which I have tried to assemble and reduce to a minimum. In your remarks you may want to take a few moments to make certain that you cover some of the concerns of the conferees. Let me just take two out of six or seven. First, there is a good deal of concern about the question of local versus national manpower pools. Do we in fact have a national Selective Service? What are the consequence of each draft board having its own information system, its own procedures for responding to requirements from a national system, with the result that it is presumed, that differential exposure rates are to be determined in considerable degree by administrative practices of not operating a national system but operating a series of local systems?

The second question which comes up repeatedly regards the flow of information from the Selective Service to the registrants, the parents, the counsellors, and the various institutions, to make certain that people are fully aware of their rights and privileges. What we're concerned with here is the relative performance of the Selective Service in different parts of the country, in contrast to other agencies, such as Social Security Administration and the like.

Colonel Dee Ingold. Some of these thoughts may not be as complete as I would like, but I'll at least touch upon many of the things that have been indicated. First of all, I'd like to report on what Mr. McGill, our statistician, has told me as to the results of his sample survey during the last week or two: One, more than one million men entered the Armed Forces in one capacity or another during the last fiscal year; it could well be close to 1.1 million. That was at a time, incidentally, when the registration was 1.8 million. His sample survey shows, among other things, that proportionately college students contribute more to the Armed Forces than non-college students, that the whites contribute more, proportionately, than do the Negroes, and that the non-poor contribute more, proportionately, than do the poor. So much for statistics.

We have been criticized as an agency for a lack of popularity. We were never intended to be popular. I've heard of surveys asking people whether they considered Selective Service to be popular, and, amazingly, a lot of them responded in the affirmative. This is utterly ridiculous—this isn't intended at all. Selective Service is here as an agency presumably because it is necessary. I don't think anybody wants to continue Selective Service one minute after it doesn't have to exist. Personally, I think we would—I certainly would—want any form of compulsion removed if it could, at any time, be removed.

I would like to speak to the question of unfairness and inequity. So frequently people say Selective Service is inequitable and unfair because it is not uniform. Then they invert it and say that in order to create equity and fairness we must have uniformity. This doesn't, I think, follow. Take for example the income tax. If you had a flat income tax of $2,000 for everyone, this certainly wouldn't be equitable or fair, but it certainly would be uniform. I'll grant you that there's some difference between Selective Service and the income tax. Selective Service works more in the area of a quantum, because we have a two-year versus nothing situation, whereas, of course, you have a sliding scale in income tax. But I never have been able quite to understand this philosophy of fairness being translated into uniformity. It seems that fairness is more in the area of a concomitant variation that fits a series of variables.

This feeling of somebody being given an unfair situation is so often translated into his going into the military, which indicates a feeling that there's a dirty end of the stick and that it's the military service. To us, this is difficult to understand. Many of the local boards try their best to get people into service who would like to get into the service and they consider it unfair because they cannot. Are there two dirty ends to the same stick? In a small group, you'll find that very frequently everybody agrees on which end of the stick is dirty; but you get into a large group and this isn't nearly so clear.

The variables about which I spoke a moment ago are something like this, and they're not always alike. First of all, there is the variable of the size of the Armed Forces and the varying need for manpower. This is a backdrop against which the local boards must do their classifying. And in spite of all of the efforts of the services and the Department of Defense to make this uniform, it just is not. And the local boards have to anticipate the situation in the future as well as look at it the way it is at the moment. The next variable is the degree to which an individual has capacity, or skill. A third variable is in the industrial activity area in which he uses his capacity and how it translates into the national interest. A fourth variable is the local situation, and how *it* fits into the national interest. Now, I don't say that every occupational classification involves all those four, but most of them do. So that the test of fairness is the relationship between what the nation needs of a man's time at the moment and his availability at the moment, rather than some flat scale that says you either go in or you don't and everybody conforms. One of these variables in the field of student deferment is the inability to get uniform evidence with which to operate.

Many local boards have complained to us that they would like to be much more uniform, but how can they, considering the variety of evidence that comes to them? One university says that a full-time student is a 12-credit student, another says 14, and another one says 15: some have 5 years for a course and another 4. There is variance. We admit this. The poor local board, though, is up against a situation which is extremely difficult to handle. One way to create better uniformity between local boards would be to create greater uniformity in the evidence. I don't know whether this is possible or not. If the evidence could come in more uniformity it certainly would be a big help to the local board.

As to the question of uncertainty—I don't see how you can write certainty into the present situation. The Department of Defense in setting up calls for the future—as an indication of what's going to happen in the next six months—does its best to try to indicate what certainty there is, and yet it's highly uncertain. Just consider what's happened in the last year. Consider, too, the Berlin buildup, the Cuban situation and all the other varieties of crises. Variation is a reflection of our times, not uniformity. It's up and down, up and down, and up and down. Any kind of program that attempts to convince people that they have a certain future would certainly be misleading, because it's not in the cards.

There's another factor that puzzles me in reading these papers that have been presented: there seems to be a tendency in some of them to try to find a blemish on Selective Service in order to put a "patch job" of a new program on. Many of these programs could stand on their own two feet and be presented as distinctly separate issues. Occasionally people go out of their way to find a reason, other than the inherent value of their programs, in the Selective Service System for creating a new type of procedure or program. This I don't think is necessary and, I think, to some degree it clouds the issue in regard to the type of program and its benefits. Not all crusades have to be in the nature of patchwork on Selective Service. I admit it's an excellent vehicle for a number of reasons: chiefly because it's coming up for extension very shortly, and because it has to do with manpower. But it could be let alone just for the single purpose for which it was created.

I think the best work on national service was done by the War Manpower Commission under Paul McNutt at the time of President Roosevelt. The objective was a little different from the one you people are working on now. It had to do with the 4F's. Why were millions of 4F's running around doing nothing in time of war? The question was whether or not through some kind of a program of "work or fight" we could put these 4F's to work. Now, however, the emphasis seems to be to compete for the same people that the military wants. In that respect, the two periods are different. Aside from this difference, I think that the papers on this subject in 1942 and 1943 were as exhaustive as these today.

There are two schools of thought on criticism of Selective Service. You may not be aware of that, some of you who don't hear the other side of it. There are many people who accept this criticism without analysis, and there are a lot of people who don't understand what the criticism is all about. May I point out that during two or three years of intense criticism of Selective Service, all of our calls have been filled. That's our primary obligation to this country. All of the local boards, 4,100 of them, are in operation—registrants are responding to calls without objection. Delinquency has not increased proportionately during this period, if that's any indication as to the degree to which any of this criticism has effected the American public. Frankly, I think it's time that the criticism of Selective Service was analyzed carefully, both qualitatively and quantitatively. There seems to be an inclination on the part of many people, as soon as Selective Service is criticized, to find something wrong with Selective Service without finding out whether there's something wrong with the criticism. If a criticism of classifications is made, we call in the files. General Hershey has a standing policy: If anybody complains about a file and asks that he look at it, he will look at it himself or have somebody do it. We have a division in the national headquarters specifically for that purpose. We find that the biggest failure in files is a lack of evidence. A man will very frequently write to a congressman and complain that he was not deferred. Then when we call in the file we find he hadn't told his local board about it.

Selective Service is a flexible organization. This I think you should be aware of. It met the situation in Korea, in the Berlin crisis, in Cuba. It met the situation reasonably well when the calls went down to zero and practically stayed there. I'll grant you these transitions from one to the other are difficult. Among other things, they make boards different in their timing. One local board will start something a little sooner than another will. If we could have everything done at the same time, we'd have a lot more apparent uniformity in Selective Service, but you can't do that because everything cannot be done at the same time.

I just want to say one more thing. If you find that Selective Service has done a pretty good job of the assignment it's been given, and you can't agree on something better, I hope you'll have the candor and courage to say so at the end of this Conference.

Mr. Janowitz. Thank you, Colonel Ingold. I would particularly like to invite the Conference's attention to the announcement by Colonel Ingold that the Selective Service, through its statistical section, is now preparing a new sample survey on who serves. We look forward to receiving the information on Selective Service reports based on such sample surveys.

We have available the still incomplete studies of the National Opinion Research Center done for the Department of Defense as to who has served during the last 15 or so years. Let me very briefly set the context by reporting some of these findings. There are two variables which determine exposure to military service: race combined with income or education, Negro and white vs. high and low income (or education). The exposure rate of Negroes with low income is in the lowest category; the middle categories of white and middle-level education have the highest exposure rates; white and high education again have lower exposure rates to Selective Service and military service. These are the facts of the last 15 or 20 years, no matter what approach you use, whether you use the sample surveys or other inferences. In addition, one of the interesting observations from the state is that Selective Service, to a considerable extent, has already achieved a "meritocracy payoff," that is, exposure to Selective Service is much more a function of the education that you yourself are able to achieve than the education or social position of your parents.

Milton Friedman. I'd just like to ask one question. One of the final recourses in a free society for somebody who does not feel satisfied with arrangements is to emigrate. Now I have been told that under present arrangements a young man, or even a resident alien, who is subject to the draft and wishes to emigrate permanently to another land, must get permission from his draft board or from somebody if he does. I don't know what the actual facts are and I wonder if Colonel Ingold would indicate two things. First, whether this is, in fact, the case, and second, if so, whether any suits have been brought or any attempts have been made to test the constitutionality of prohibiting emigration.

Colonel Ingold. There is nothing prohibitive at all. A registrant at the present time does not need permission from his local board to go anywhere. Whatever regulations there may be on that are entirely in the Department of State. There is a form for it: a permit to leave the country from the local board, but it's not a binding thing; it is merely some degree of assurance to the registrant that while he is absent the local board knows where he is and what he is doing and will probably not take action in his direction while he is gone. But this doesn't prohibit him from leaving the country.

Mr. Chapman. I'm rather concerned about the attitude of the Selective Service which has been quite dominant in this whole discussion—that all the ideas that are presented are presented by the same people—while the fact of the matter is that the last time the bill came up, hardly anybody spoke out against it and certainly no conference like this was called and Congress certainly gave the bill little attention. I am also concerned that the Selective Service System seems to think that it has its own justification for every possible procedure, that it has thought everything through. I know that in one of these papers somebody gave the statistics that fewer than half of the young men tested even understood the basic procedures of the Selective Service System, and this is no accident. At no time does a young man who is 18, or turns 18, get a brochure that explains how the Selective Service System acts. He gets a little teeny flyer, if he asks for it, at the Selective Service Board, telling him that if he wants to appeal he has 10 days in which to appeal—but it doesn't tell what an appeal is or how to appeal.

Mr. Janowitz. Thank you, Mr. Chapman, we hear you loud and clear on the question of how adequate the public information system of Selective Service is. Congressmen have for many years reported that questions about the draft constitute perhaps the second or third most frequent queries on the part of their constituents. If I may intervene here—would someone like to talk about the question of information concerning appeals?

John Beal. I think that the situation concerning appeals is very similar to the situation concerning initial registration. For instance, right now I'm 1A and I'm appealing to my local board to have that changed to 2S, and I have no concrete information as to what they want as a basis for this appeal. The only information that I have is based on what I've read in the newspapers, what I've heard by rumor. I've sent in my class standing and there are test results, but I write my board and they never write me back, and all I can do is wait for the mail and see what comes from them in terms of their decision.

John Hope Franklin. I have a question that's related to the question of appeals as well as to the observation by Colonel Ingold that students as prospective draftees have responded to the call without criticism. It seems to me that the whole question of appeals is relevant. Obviously persons who make appeals are not satisfied, they have some criticism in some way, but my question has to do with the observation that Colonel Ingold made regarding the national headquarters' review of files that come from various draft boards. How extensive is that review? For example, how many files come up in the course of a year from the draft boards to the national headquarters?

Colonel Ingold. I can't very well give you that figure on a yearly basis, but I would say that probably there are always about one hundred files in national headquarters at any one time in the process of review. What the turnover is, I can't at the moment say.

[*Unidentified Speaker*]. Colonel Ingold, I would like a further definition of what is meant by national interests. When you read General Hershey's fact paper you talked on national interest but did not define it, and you did not in your own talk, and I would appreciate it very much if you did.

Colonel Ingold. National interest is a variable thing. We have no intention of clarifying it so exactly or drawing such tight strings around it that you cannot interpret it differently according to local area needs. In any locality it's different from what it is somewhere else. I happen to come from Wisconsin where there is a tendency to defer the machinist at a crossroad because he takes care of a lot of farmers' machinery. In the national interest this wouldn't appear perhaps in any other state. In Alaska, for example, an opthalmologist would always be deferred because they happen to have a lot of eye trouble up there. In any place else in the United States he might not be. These are variables which are indigenous to areas, and they've got to be accommodated by people who understand the locality and can apply them, and are free to express their own judgment.

Norman Kurland. Colonel Ingold, it appears from the information that I've gotten that, in fact, the 10-day appeals period presents a difficult problem for many people who want to appeal. There are procedural delays between the board's decision and the mailing. And lags in the mailing process particularly affect students who may be at school away from home. These delays adversely affect the appeal procedure.

Colonel Ingold. In 25 years of operation this is the first time the subject has come up. The local board has the authority to extend the time and if the local board doesn't grant it, the man can see his government appeal agent who has authority to take appeal at any time up to time of an order to report for induction. In addition to that, he has access to local autonomy within the state headquarters. I don't know—it's an arbitrary figure, of course—10 days. I think that perhaps, if anybody insisted, it might be extended.

Mr. Kurland. I was disappointed that the presentation on the Selective Service System was a defense of the System rather than a presentation of facts, which was supposed to have been the intent. My particular question is: How does Selective Service feel—or how does the Colonel feel about the actions of Swarthmore College and, I believe, Wayne State University, with regard to eliminating the ranking system?

Colonel Ingold. Well, I can't respond without defending Selective Service; I hope you'll pardon me for that. Originally, when this came up, the educators of the United States asked Selective Service to set up some criteria. Dr. Trytten and a group of educators and scientists got together for the purpose of recommending to the Selective Service System a method of setting up criteria which the universities presumably would follow. This was not a Selective Service idea, it was theirs. It was offered to Selective Service by them. In the recent adoption of the same plan, it was recommended to Selective Service by a large group of educators. Personally I don't like it particularly. I wish there were a better system. And if anybody will suggest a better system we'd be delighted to look at it, but in the last three years, while there has been considerable criticism of this, not one person, not one agency, to my knowledge, has recommended any system as an alternative, with any degree of unanimity in the educational fraternity.

Mr. Janowitz. Well, we certainly appreciate the candid statement that the ranking system is a creation of the universities and Mr. Marmion later will want to comment on that, I'm certain.

Mr. Flacks. On the local autonomy of draft boards, would you assert with confidence that draft boards are representative of the communities that they are in?

Colonel Ingold. There's no doubt about that. They are certainly more representative than anybody else would be, but they're not completely representative of the whole nation. This is impossible, unless you get a group, for example like the one here, and then you'd never reach any conclusion.

Mr. Flacks. Is my information correct that there isn't a single Negro on the draft boards in Mississippi?

Colonel Ingold. I have to say I don't know, but I think this is so, that there are none.

Mr. Flacks. Do you know that draft boards there have been harassing civil rights workers?

Colonel Ingold. You're talking about the two registrants who were rejected at the Armed Forces Examining and Entrance Stations and later were accepted. The decision in these cases was strictly an Armed Forces examining station decision and had nothing to do with persecution by local boards. And, incidentally, I found in one paper here people recommending both sides of that question. They suggested that everybody be compelled to serve, and at the same time they were complaining because they assumed that some people were being railroaded into service. This kind of meets itself coming around the mountain. No, I think there should be representation. I don't think it has anything to do with discrimination—I don't think it's got anything to do with people being railroaded in—but it does have something to do with representation.

Mr. Janowitz. The question of representativeness leads us back to the question of information. It may well be that the better information levels in the rural areas have to do with the fact that the boards are more representative than in the urban areas. When we are looking for the meaning of "representative" boards we are not even talking about mechanical or statistical criteria, but we're talking about a reevaluation of the meaning of the "local" board. We do know that most of the local boards are no longer local—on the South Side of Chicago they are are overwhelmingly absentee; and that we will be looking forward to reports to the President's Commission which will give us a lot more information. The whole notion of what constitutes a local board will have to be rethought in the light of a rapidly changing society.

Colonel Ingold. Incidentally, the National Headquarters of Selective Service is disproportionately Negro.

Mr. Janowitz. Well, I'm not in favor of any disproportion and I disassociate myself from the view that you have to have a completely statistically representative board in order to have justice. In order to broaden the discussion—

this question of how Selective Service is operating is a source of endless questions. I do think at this moment it would be relevant to broaden our discussion in terms of some of the consequences of the Selective Service System. Among the things that we are concerned with are the issues raised in Mr. Biderman's paper— "What Is Military?" What are we selecting for? This came up yesterday and I think Mr. Biderman would like to address himself to what the Selective Service is selecting for and whether or not there is a proper articulation between Selective Service and the military establishment.

Albert D. Biderman. I cannot summarize my paper "in three minutes, not more," as I was asked to do. Since my paper is a cryptic statement as is, this is quite difficult for me to do. I want to get away from the very immediate questions of right now, right here, 1966, Vietnam, etc., to the general questions of the nature of the military roles that society wants performed—has to have performed, presumably, in the current context—how these change with changes in the nature of warfare and with the implications for the nature of military establishments that have been determined by changes in the world order and changes in the way society as a whole is organized. Now one of the conclusions I reach is that what traditionally was "military" defines to a very small extent what most people do most of the time in our Armed Forces. The essential definitions have been first of all people putting themselves in a position of being killed and of killing other people. And this, certainly has applied to fewer and fewer people, proportionately, in military forces, in recent years—I'm talking now in terms of a couple of centuries or so, and it continues to move in that direction. Another differentiating thing from the standpoint of the individual is the surrender of his liberty. And, here, too, there has been some lessening of constriction of people's liberty when they put on the uniform, but there is a great deal of differential surrender of liberty. Now, some people surrender much more of their life chances than do others. The existence of the Selective Service System, I think, has generated pressures on the military establishment in both these directions. That is, how promiscuously it uses military manpower in terms of acceptance of risk, and the extent to which it demands surrenders of liberty, subjection to military authority in various degrees of rigidity, from people.

Mr. Janowitz. Thank you. This is very valuable to us; we do not want to be limited to the existing definitions. I think this subject will come up again, especially when we talk about a purely voluntary Army. When we talk about Selective Service Systems we're talking about changing definitions for "civil" and "military."

William R. Keast. I wanted to ask the Colonel a question about the relative autonomy of the local board. We are frequently presented with the following problem: We are informed that the local board has virtually complete autonomy within the guidelines which are suggested to them administratively by Selective Service headquarters, not by law, but by administrative interpretation, as for example in the matter of class ranking. Then, we are often also told when we raise specific questions with the local board that they are operating under constraint and do not enjoy the kind of autonomy which we are told operates at the local level. I think many students in many institutions are confused about the extent to which local boards do in fact have a substantial measure of autonomy, treating the guidelines as merely guidelines, and the extent to which, on the other hand, the guidelines are thought to be or are intended to be relatively firm policy determinations of the directions in which the local board shall proceed. I wonder if we could have a comment on this?

Colonel Ingold. Yes, the local boards are autonomous, and I've heard General Hershey say many times, and I think very properly, that when he gets about as much criticism from the local boards for telling them too much as he does for not telling them enough he thinks that he's administering about where he ought to. How else can you sense these things?

Mr. Keast. I wasn't concerned so much about how difficult General Hershey's job was, but what we were supposed to infer as to the course of action pursued by particular local boards. In General Hershey's statement the following two sentences occur. "Local Boards do not place men in Class 1A in order to fill calls. Instead, calls they receive are based on the number of registrants they already have in Class 1A." Now, one interpretation of his statement, allowable under your response to my question, Colonel Ingold, is that a given local board could, in theory, persistently have no 1A registrants at all. Now, I assume that this would be a somewhat unusual circumstance, but as I understand local autonomy and the breadth of variation permitted the boards, any number of local boards, if properly constituted, or improperly constituted, could always fail to have people in 1A. What would happen in that case?

Colonel Ingold. This is the responsibility of the state director. In the original planning, prior to 1940, we attempted to create a balance wheel where there would be just as much inclination to take issue with a 1A as there would with a deferment. And the government appeal agent was set up for that function —to take issue with any deferment he opposed. So you'd still have in the locality, you see, the other side of the 1A. Now, I'll grant you that in many cases this hasn't functioned too well. They have been reinforced by what are called auditors out of state headquarters. The National Advisory Commission on Selective Service has just made a survey, incidentally, as to how many times local boards are audited from state headquarters. A few hundred of the reports reached me through misdirected mail, so I had an opportunity to see them, and it looks as if boards are audited on an average of about once every two months . . .

Mr. Keast. . . . to insure that a proportionate number of men are, in fact, being classified and drawn . . . ?

Colonel Ingold. . . . that there is a reasonable degree of uniformity within the state, yes, sir.

Loren K. Waldman. One of the questions that the Chairman raised at the beginning was the question of local pools versus national pools and the resulting differential exposure to Selective Service. I'd like to make a statement to Colonel Ingold and ask him to comment on that. My understanding of the way Selective Service operates is that there is essentially no national pool and there is no statewide pool, but there are some 4,100 local pools. We know that when the calls come down from the Defense Department that there is a so-called national pool which is then prorated to the state. And then that the states prorate their shares to the local pools, but from reading the transcript of the testimony before the House Committee in June, I get no evidence that there is any sort of national pool in the sense that all men of 19 years of age are exposed in the same way to Selective Service, or all men who are students are exposed to Selective Service. I think there are two other considerations that have to be brought in in talking about differential exposure. Mr. Janowitz mentioned earlier the findings of the NORC report to the effect that education and race are major determinants of exposure to Selective Service; I think it's appropriate also to mention that it seems that the size of the local board is also a determinant because a different mix, a different combination of individuals will be gathered in by boards of differing sizes. One locality might have a very high proportion of people who have a high amount of education; another board might have a large number of people who are underprivileged.

Mr. Janowitz. I think the question is clear. You want to know what Selective Service is doing about the fact that there are differential characteristics in the population at the local level which, therefore, creates an inequity.

Mr. Waldman. Well, there's one other aspect and that is that I want to bring out the differential size of the local boards. . . .

Mr. Janowitz. Both size and social characteristics are differentials as they affect the local exposure rates of Selective Service.

Colonel Ingold. We have local boards so that their local differences can be represented. You'll never get that out of an average, out of national headquarters, out of state headquarters, or anywhere else.

Mr. Janowitz. It gives me great pleasure to introduce Mr. Marmion, who is going to deal with the question of deferment.

Mr. Marmion. I want to bring up the question of deferment. I think it might be said to be a sad commentary on the American educational system that the major proponent of deferment in the United States today happens to be General Hershey. But the fact remains that there is an argument for deferments, and the only argument really that one can give for deferments is that they serve the national interest. How do we define the national interest? Obviously, it is a very difficult concept to define. I will be happy to define it at the same moment that someone else in this room defines for me inequality, equity, fairness. What do they really mean? The national interest in my opinion is a very pragmatic consideration. It has to be determined by those people in the government that are, primarily, elected. I think it was terribly unfair for Mr. Friedman today to indicate that we should shut off the debate, that there was unanimity with regard to the question of deferment. I will predict that despite what this conference does, despite what the President's Commission on Selective Service does, that come June 30, 1967, there will be a modified system of Selective Service, another patch job on the current law, for the simple reason that we are in a war in Vietnam and the national interest would best be served by some system of deferment. Now, certainly I think that Selective Service is somewhat at fault here. I think that guidelines, rather than advisory, should become mandatory. If necessary, the Presidential Executive orders should become so. I think that we have the ability to discriminate between a physical education major and a physicist. I think, however, when we get down to distinctions between a humanist, a philosopher, and so on, that this is very difficult. Deferments are necessary if we are going to supply educated people for the future of the nation. During World War II it was very easy to determine whether or not a person was deferred: it all had to do with his position vis-à-vis the war effort. We don't have a war effort today in the country, so I think that the same kind of consideration must be given to the future needs of the nation. I may not be prepared to define the needs at this point, but I think that's the only way that deferments can be looked at, and the only real argument—not that it provides officers for the Armed Forces, not that it keeps educational institutions in existence—merely that it serves the national interest.

Mr. Keast. In view of the statement so frequently made that the educational deferment system is currently in effect because the educational establishments have made so convincing and heavy a case for it, it seems to me that we won't get our discussion along very well unless Mr. Marmion tells us what case he thinks can be made for educational deferment.

Harold Wool. I think the word *deferment* needs very careful definition. Deferment has been construed as postponement of service, and certainly during the wartime mobilization period occupational deferment (there wasn't any specific student deferment) was very definitely construed in that way. Now, we have some facts which reflect the operation of the System in peacetime —which show that deferment for large numbers of men has meant exemption from service because of the very way the System has worked. In this context, the statistics which were briefly alluded to in a totally non-statistical fashion are terribly important. I want to cite two types of data which the Department of Defense attempted to collect from whatever sources it could on the effects of the whole complex of selection and deferment policies as they operated over the past decade.

First of all, I think we should clarify several references to the proportion of men who serve, according to educational level. Colonel Ingold referred to some data, unspecified, that college men have served more than non-college men. I don't know what is meant by college men—it could mean a man who has had one semester of college, or one with a Ph.D. There are tremendous differences in the incidence of service among these categories, as well as among non-college men. Two types of statistics are available. One, the Department of Defense itself, in cooperation with Selective Service, analyzed in detail a sample of Selective Service registrants as of 1964. This showed that for men then 26 years of age, in broad groupings, 50 per cent of the non-high-school graduates had seen some form of service by age 26; 57 per cent of the high school graduates with no college; 60 per cent of those with some college, but no college degree; and only 40 per cent of those who were college graduates had seen some service by age 26. Subsequently, we have obtained more detail from another source. The Department had commissioned the National Opinion Research Center to develop a survey. The survey was conducted by the Census for the civilian population and by the Department of Defense for the military population. The composites showed an interesting variation for a somewhat different age group. These were men who were ages 27 to 34, as of 1964, and therefore reflected the cumulative effect of the operation of these policies over a longer period of time. The composites showed that the percentage of the population who had served, ranged from 30 per cent of those with less than an 8th grade education to 74 per cent for those who were high school graduates but had had no college. Seventy-one per cent of those with a bachelor's degree had served, but only 26.6 per cent of those who had some graduate work. When one combines all college graduates one gets a pattern which shows that in fact the college graduate group had a lower percentage because a significant proportion of all college men do go on to some graduate work. The survey shows that the young men who, after a bachelor's degree, does go on to graduate work, has a far lesser exposure to service for two reasons. One is that graduate studies, stretching on to age 26, create a de facto, although not legal, exemption, for this period of time. The second is that this is the group which has the highest incidence of occupational deferments as these have been granted. I am reasonably convinced that this pattern is an accurate one, even though statistics may be variable.

As to the matter of proportion of Negroes and proportion of whites serving, the Selective Service System, in checking on this, Colonel Ingold, collects no information at present as to race in its statistics. Therefore, I'm not at all sure how your statistician could say that from his survey, from Selective Service Sources, he could provide information on that. The only data available were obtained from these other indirect means which, generally speaking, show this: Because of the very high rejection rates of the Negro, the proportion of Negroes serving has been less. Among those qualified to serve, the proportion has been higher because, generally speaking, they have been less eligible for deferment. Among those who have served, the proportion serving as inductees has been higher, much higher, because they have been much less eligible to serve in other ways, as officers or in reserve programs. Among those eligible to volunteer for service, the proportion of those volunteering has been quite high, for active service, because military service has meant a positive step upward for them.

Finally, there are no data from Selective Service as to rich or poor because I do not believe that the Selective Service System gets income statistics from their registrants. There again, I'm not quite sure as to the source.

Mr. Janowitz. Mr. Wool, we have the reference to the National Opinion Research Center study; could you give us a reference to the Department of Defense....

Mr. Wool. The Department of Defense Study was included in the record of the Congressional Hearings held in June, 1966, on the review of the administration's operation of the Selective Service System and the testimony of Assistant Secretary Morris.

Mr. Pemberton. Mr. Marmion's paper elaborates his concern about the concept of channeling. I would like to invite Colonel Ingold to respond to that expression of concern and state a defense of the Selective Service System's concept of channeling and its usefulness in our society.

Colonel Ingold. I think this concept springs from the preamble to the act which, until it's changed, represents the thinking of the American public. It reads as follows: "It is further declared that adequate provision for national security requires maximum effort in the fields of scientific research and development and fullest possible utilization of the nation's technological, scientific, and other critical manpower resources." To the best of our ability we acquire whatever information we can from the Department of Labor, Department of Commerce, the scientific fraternity, and other places, to indicate where people should be deferred. This is the basis for the channeling. If an individual goes into an area that is presumed by some of these expert agencies to be important or critical to the national interest, the man is then likely to be deferred. This induces him to stay there; at least it doesn't pull him out.

Mr. Marmion. I think the channeling is an administrative interpretation of very broad language in the act, for which I can find no justification in the legislative history of the act. On the one hand, Selective Service talks about the decentralized function of the local board. Yet, on the other hand, they are making highly centralized decisions to keep people in particular fields for what

I consider to be absolutely the wrong reasons. I think that this must be looked at very, very carefully. General Hershey is constantly using the example of the medical student and doctor to talk about his concepts of channeling, and he transfers this to other fields and other occupations and it goes against the de-centralized decision-making responsibility that Selective Service says the local board really has.

Mr. Friedman. Whatever may be the arguments for educational deferment, there are also arguments against it. Both arguments depend on the percentage deferred. The arguments against deferments become stronger as the percentage inducted goes down, and the arguments in favor of deferment become weaker. But, more important, I believe, this is an issue on which opinions have by now pretty well settled down. My own judgment is that *if* conscription is to be retained, there should be no educational deferment, and I think that this is a view widely shared here. If it is, we might get it on the record and off the table for discussion and move on to other topics. Would it be in order for me to move that it is the sense of this meeting that *if* conscription is retained, there should be no educational deferment?

Mr. Janowitz. Whether it is in order to call the question I leave open, and I shall have a session with Mr. Tax to discuss that matter.

Mr. Winter. I'm not very happy with the idea of taking this vote. I'm mainly interested, along the same line, in Mr. Marmion's making some answer to the feeling of many of us in higher education that this whole tie-up with an educational deferment is contaminating the educational process. It seems to me this is a very fundamental part of the national interest and I'd be interested in his response to this.

Mr. Janowitz. In the interest of getting an expression, wherever possible, but at the same time, not converting us into a legislative group, we are going to circulate a paper on which you can if you wish sign your name as indicating agreement with this proposition. This will be part of the record. There will be no formal vote on anything, but it will be an opportunity for you to express your opinion on the series of propositions that come up.

John Naisbitt. On the question of channeling, I think it's interesting to see how the Selective Service System sees itself in its evolving role as the arbiter of national manpower policy, and I should like to quote just two sentences from the Selective Service System: "Delivery of manpower for induction, the process of providing a few thousand men with transportation to a reception center, is not much of an administrative or financial challenge. It is in dealing with the other millions of registrants that the System is heavily occupied, developing more effective human beings in the national interest." And the Selective Service System has come to perceive itself as an arbiter of manpower for the nation rather than as they say, merely batting up men to examination stations.

Mr. Janowitz. We will now have Mr. Pemberton make a presentation on conscientious objectors. Then we will go on to the question of changes in the duration of service.

Mr. Pemberton. My function is solely as an advocate of a particular proposition that I have put before you in a paper, which I will summarize very briefly. The first point I would like to make is that the importance of this topic is not to be gauged by the number of people who are involved in it. I think it goes, much as the Charge we heard last night suggests our subjects should go, to the quality of the system we are administering. The degree to which the Selective Service System represents our democratic aspirations is measured by the quality of the provisions we make for individual conscience. They relate to our concept of the priority of the individual in our democratic order. In defense of the exemption for the conscientious objector (which the courts have largely assumed is an act of legislative grace and not something that permeates all law as a matter of constitutional principle), it should be said that the exemption of the conscientious objector makes a great deal of sense. Were the conscientious objector not exempted, men would be subjected to an unwarrantedly heavy destructiveness on the part of their government, making them choose between violation by forced induction of that which they hold most important, or forced punishment. Moreover, military services do not profit from the forced induction or forced jailing of a man for whom the whole enterprise constitutes a violation of conscience.

The proposition I advocate relates to this rationale for the conscientious objector. It is that the present definition of the exemption is too narrowly phrased. The concern for individual dignity, the lack of warrant, and the demeaning effect on the government which would act without warrant for being thus destructive of a single human individual, and the ineffectiveness of seeking to punish or induct such an individual, applies, I suggest, as well to the two classes of individuals who are presently excluded from the definition. I ask you to imagine three men, not just one, standing before you at this moment. Each of the three says, in effect, "I cannot participate in the enterprise that the government, through the Selective Service law, commands me to participate in, and I cannot excuse my doing so on the basis that government has commanded it. It is wrong for me to do it, it is wrong for me to yield control over my actions to government's command. I will *not* be excused in terms of what I consider right and wrong by the fact that the government made a command."

One of these individuals is a religious pacifist. He says, in terms of the present act, that his convictions were informed by reason of his religious training and belief, and, that he is opposed to participation in war in any form. The man on his left says that he is not religious. He denies that the basis for the decision that he has made is informed by religious training and belief. I don't believe we know what the difference between the two is. But, he asserts that he knows the difference, and that his belief that it is wrong for him to yield his will to government on the matter is formed on some basis other than religious belief. So there's a difference between man A and man B over what they believe about other matters, but there is no difference between the two of them in terms of what they believe about the rightness or wrongness of obeying the present command. The third man may be religious, but he denies that he is categorically opposed to war. He knows only that he is opposed to doing what is commanded of him right now. And he knows that he cannot do it in the same terms that the first man knows that. He does not know what would happen if he were asked to defend his family, his community, his nation, against a foreign invader. This is not something he faces at the moment. And he's a young man and he's not had occasion to face it in the past. He doesn't know what he would have done in World War II, were he asked to fight Hitler's legions, to fight with violence that form of evil. All he knows is that the present command is something he cannot obey.

The questions that the present law requires be asked of each of these three men, that distinguish them—What does he believe in matters religious? Does he believe in God? Does he believe in some other religious orthodoxy?—are irrelevant to the reasons for the Selective Service exemption. The distinction between the first man and the second has no bearing upon the administration of the Selective Service law. I submit secondly that the questions put to the third man that would distinguish him from the other two are irrelevant to the exemption we are administering. They are hypothetical questions about another war, another situation, one that he doesn't face right now. There is no warrant in the rationale of our present exemption of the conscientious objector for distinguishing between those three men, and yet, on the face of the law, and as it is administered, the first man would be entitled to exemption, the other two would not.

Now that leads me to the kinds of questions that Professor Hazard put to us last night. What about the Black Muslim? What about the Ku Klux Klanner who would find it an affront to his conscience to be asked to serve in an integrated force? It's like the question that Kenneth Greenewalt, when he was arguing the Seeger Case before the Supreme Court, was asked by Mr. Justice Black to answer. What about the Epicurean who finds it an affront to his religious conscience to be asked to go through the discomfort of military life? I suggest that the thing we are talking about is an act of Congress dealing with the subject matter of human killing. We are talking about whether it is fairly limited in terms of what it deals with. I might be willing to defend the proposition that conscience in any matter—serving in an integrated armed force, an Epicurean conscience, or any other subject that law deals with—is similarly to be respected. But this is not the case before us. The law we are dealing with is the law that deals with conscience on the subject of human killing, and the law that we are seeking to test for its fairness deals just with that. A footnote could add that the Epicurean and the Black Muslim might well satisfy both of the collateral requirements that I have called irrelevant, if we were not talking about human killing. Both are religiously informed and both are universal and we might be compelled to respect their religious concerns as much as we respect those of a Quaker or a Mennonite or another religious pacifist. But the examples, I think, do not test the subject with which we're dealing. The thing that does test it is the variety of bases for conscientious objection to human killing that come before us. I suggest that the two present limitations ask us to determine entitlement to exemption on irrelevant considerations. I would ask Mr. Tatum to address himself to experience under the present law with the exemption of conscientious objectors.

Arlo Tatum. The law which the United States has is based on religious training and belief, which, incidentally, is rather similar to the law which the Soviet Union had under Lenin. It is different from most of the provisions for conscientious objection in other countries in that they rely exclusively upon sincerity. Sincerity admittedly is a very difficult, if not impossible, thing to determine.

One of the difficulties with the Selective Service forms, and this applies not only to conscientious objectors but to all, is they seem to be predicated on the assumption that the less the registrant knows the better off he's going to be. In other words they don't indicate what classification you're applying for on the "150"; they don't indicate it on the "100" when they're getting information on other deferments. The forms are never changed by court decisions and regulations seldom are. In the conscientious objector procedures, now the courts require that the conscientious objector receive a résumé of the Department of Justice investigation before his Department of Justice Hearing Officer appearance. The regulations have not been altered to require this; it's simply done by practice.

There's a great deal of clearing up of due process needed in that connection; for example, the extraordinary prohibition against having an attorney at a personal appearance applies to all registrants. I found the President's Commission quite concerned about this, and I look forward to a recommendation that at least a witness be present throughout the personal appearance, because from my desk I can see the different manner in which a local board treats a registrant if there is an adult present.

In determining "sincerity," one must bear in mind that even where the present law permits one to say he is a conscientious objector, it doesn't require that he would have been had he lived in a different time, and he's not prognosticating whether he would have been a conscientious objector if he had been born twenty years later. The law is in the present tense. Selective Service at the present time tends to expand it, to expect a person to be perfectly clear that he would not have fought Hitler and that he would never fight in any other war, whatever that might be. I would say this is not so much required by the regulations as required by the Selective Service System, and the regulations could be altered to reinforce the fact that all the law requires is that at this time, in this situation, as this person, the individual be conscientiously opposed to induction into the Armed Forces.

While in a sense the Supreme Court has sought to define away the religious test, it nonetheless stays on the form; there is no alteration. The first question is —Do you believe in a Supreme Being, yes or no? And there are many people in this day and age who could answer yes or no with equal sincerity, because they don't know what is being spoken about.

There has been no effort on the part of the Selective Service to inform registrants of anything, although the right to appeal is on the classification card. If a man is denied his request, then obviously he should be supplied more information, but there's no such help. It's interesting to watch the development of the classification cards. Ten years ago they said, "If you need advice, go to your government appeal agent." Two years ago they said, "If you need advice, go to any local board" (and of course, if you do, you'll be referred to your own, but they don't say that). Now they have eliminated any suggestions as to how a registrant gets advice on anything, conscientious objection or otherwise, and simply put down the threat of what will happen to you if you mutilate or destroy your draft card. There's an honest statement from Selective Service which doesn't pretend, as the regulations do, that the government appeal agent does, in fact, address himself to the rights or concerns of the registrant. The registrant is left alone without advice. I spend sixty hours a week doing, in my opinion, a a great deal of what Selective Service should be doing, which is informing registrants of their rights and obligations under the law. The law should be expanded. The religious test most certainly should be dropped. It's an anachronism, it serves no purpose, no function whatsoever. It's a confusion. I most heartily support the contention that an unjust-war objector, which everyone seems to consider to be purely a political thing, actually represents the most orthodox of Christian theology. For the unjust-war objector on a religious basis, you have the peculiarity of violation of the First Amendment among other things. A person who takes a more orthodox religious position and applies the moral-religious criterion to the current war and finds it to be unjust, and therefore against his religion to participate, is excluded from the law, but the man who takes the more far-out theological position of the pacifist is included in the law. I consider that a compliment to those of us who are pacifists but I also consider it to be unconstitutional.

Mr. Flacks. I want to say briefly now that broadening the definition of conscientious objection would not only protect the right of individual conscience, but shift the burden of proof to a certain extent from individual objectors to the State, with respect to justification for compelling people to serve in the Armed Forces. Several objectors now are claiming the Nuremberg Trials as a precedent for their objections. I wonder if Mr. Pemberton has any opinion about the validity of that as a basis for making a claim. I would like to throw out a suggestion, which is that we consider the possibility that there should be an independent board to make judgments with respect to CO claims, a board that would have a different composition, perhaps one that would emphasize the interest of religious and other groups in insuring the rights of conscientious objection.

Mr. Pemberton. In answering the first question,-my own view about the Nuremberg Trial's defense is that it is different from what we are talking about and therefore not included in what I have advocated or properly a part of what I conceive to be the exemption for conscientious objectors. As I understand the defense, it is that a higher law, not in the sense of higher than man-made, but another man-made law, interposes itself between the power of my government to conscript me and my unwillingness to be conscripted. It seems to me that is a purely legal argument and I am not qualified to express an opinion on the legal validity of it, but I see some difficulties with it just as I see difficulties in the concept that the Nuremberg court proceeded on. It is not the same as the objector who says something higher than man-made law interposes itself between me and the command that I be inducted. I believe the conscientious objector exemption is, and properly should be, confined to that kind of non-legal objection to war—an objection that is totally personal to the individual's own concept of his duties to himself and his fellow man.

Mr. Tatum. I don't think we should confuse the defenses that conscientious objectors who don't qualify now are using in court with their positions. These men are "unjust-war" objectors and if they come to us for some kind of legal defense, then we have to experiment with novel defenses in order to find some possibility of both making their points and possibly keeping them from being sent to prison. The men who are using the Nuremberg principles for the most part would not accept induction to fight in the war anyway, but they're excluded from recognition. They can't use the Selective Service regulations to defend themselves in court so they find something else. So don't confuse the legal arguments with the man's position.

The second point I think is a very good one. I do a lot of counseling of attorneys and I love to get a court-appointed attorney who has never had a CO case before because he's astonished to discover that unlike someone who has robbed a bank, this conscientious objector is considered guilty until he proves himself innocent. It's the only place in law where this is the case, and he has much less access to defense in court. I think that any system for approving conscientious objector claims is going to run into difficulties so long as the people who make the determinations are primarily military and are primarily, if I may say so, the type who would be acceptable and willing to serve on a local board. I don't think that you're going to get pacifists to serve on that national board you've established, whether a man is a conscientious objector or not. The system we have worked quite well in my opinion, and fairly, for those who qualify with the present system of the Department of Justice investigation recommendation until the last three months when T. Oscar Smith, who's the key man in the CO section of the non-criminal division of the Department of Justice, went sour, and the last fifteen recommendations he's made have been negative. What can you do? I've never had fifteen in a row that were negative in the four years I've been with the Central Committee. In each case the man was accused of insincerity. We'll be spending probably $250,000 in court next year with about 100 cases, 75 of which are cases in which the man would have gotten his 1O classification two years ago. What kind of system can you devise that will prevent this kind of situation when our country is involved in a war as unpopular as the one in Vietnam? I don't think you can do it—I think that there should be a different investigative body from the FBI, partly because when the FBI comes around the person being interviewed wants to be on the right side and wants to think of something derogatory he can say about the conscientious objector. I've discussed this with the Presidential Commission lawyers—who could do the investigation of sincerity—and I was unable to make a proposal that even I found to be satisfactory.

Mr. Lauter. I want to spread slightly the context of the discussion because it seems to me that the problem of exemption has to be looked at not only in terms of conscientious objection but also in terms of student deferments and the like, from the point of view of draft-age men. It's been perfectly obvious in our experience that, as Mr. Keast implied, many young men seek education deferments in order to avoid the draft; many seek ministerial deferments; many seek conscientious objector deferments. It seems to me that one of the criteria that we have to keep in mind here is not whether or not the rationale for seeking deferment is compatible with the procurement of military manpower, but whether opportunities for deferment ought to be made available and indeed broadened for the sake of democratic institutions and also for the sake of the young men who have to confront the problem of exemption. Now, one of the reasons that so many young men are thinking about going to Canada, or stay in school when they want to drop out, or become ministers or ministerial candidates, one of the reasons that the divinity schools have increased pressure of enrollment, happens to be that many young men feel that they can't qualify under the law as conscientious objectors, and indeed feel they ought not apply for conscientious objector's status, that there's something immoral in doing so even if they can qualify, because there are so many of their brothers who are excluded from that law the way it's presently posed. One of the problems we face within the context of a continuing conscription is trying to propose ways of making exemptions like conscientious objector exemptions sufficiently available so that young men do not have to find ways of avoiding the draft like student deferment and going to Canada and a great variety of other ways that we find somewhat less acceptable socially. The problem that we have to confront is not the narrow one about whether an individual is a religious or non-religious objector, but simply one of finding the broadest grounds on which it is possible for any kind of democratic society to provide that kind of exemption. Let me point to the fact that England provided exemption pretty much for anyone who said and could establish in even a moderately credible way that he was a sincere objector to the war that was going on.

Colonel Hays. I have about four basic concerns: one is the continued effectiveness of our Armed Forces in performing the missions that may be prescribed by the government; the second one is the quality of the manpower produced for us to perform these missions; the third, the motivation of that manpower which to me is a very critical point; and fourth, how this manpower and its organizational structure is related to our society as a whole. I have a proposal which was spelled out in my paper. I do not pretend to be an expert in the administration of the draft or to have any of the wisdom or experience of Colonel Ingold or General Hershey in this regard. However, if the Armed Forces were to get what they need, if I could describe the kind of officers and men my sons should serve with, I would say that they ought to get the best. The very best we could provide.

With that in mind, I tried to look at what kind of procedure would provide us with the right kind of human material, and at the same time how far we could go in making certain adjustments which would fit the difficulties which our young people face at the present time. Equity, I'm afraid, is one of those things which we might always chase and never catch up with. There are some modifications, however, that appeared to be possible. One of them was restricting the vulnerability to the draft to a relatively limited period of time in order to increase the chance for a young man to plan his career and to determine what he wants to do. With that in mind, it seems possible (I would have to rely on Colonel Ingold and his Selective Service System to check on this) to examine all of our youths on or about the time they become 18, exposing them to the draft, first during their 18th year or on their graduation from high school, whichever came sooner, for a year. In case the draft calls exceed normal expectations this exposure could be extended a second year. After such a period we could excuse them and say: "If you weren't caught, you're free." Now, from the strictly military point of view this has a number of disadvantages, not the least of which is that these young men are not necessarily our best soldiers. They're not as stable, they're not as reliable, they don't have many of the skills, they obviously in many cases don't have the education that their older brothers do. We might be able to accept these handicaps in return for providing some degree of advantage to our youth.

With regard to deferment, I must confess that I would like to see a certain number of deferments, one for students taking ROTC. If we are to have officers we should have a few of these on the campus. Certain others, such as General Hershey's doctors, we'd like to see educated as early as possible. There are others like pharmacists and those in various skills which we would probably want to defer. However, regarding these deferments, from a military point of view, I would suggest that any man deferred would continue to be deferred until the time when the purpose of deferment was fulfilled, after which he would then do his service so we would have the benefit of his increased skills or knowledge. Now, I'm not a strong advocate of this proposal. I merely offer it as an alternative to the lottery, or to assuming that you have to keep the draft liability open to age 26 or 35.

Mr. Janowitz. I have one point of clarification. Did I hear you correctly when you said that your preference would be a one-year term for a maximum number, to be followed up with a second-year term, depending upon manpower requirements?

Colonel Hays. I mean one year of vulnerability to the draft, not one year of service. For service, I think, two years is minimal.

Mr. Waldman. Colonel Hays, what about the possibility of changing the period of service for enlistees so as to attract a greater number of enlistees? I understand that the military sociologists and psychologists have come to the conclusion that delinquency rates increase greatly in the third year of service, and that it would be wise, strictly from the point of view of efficiency of the military, to reduce that third year of service and make Army service for enlistees equal in length to that of inductees. Secondly, can you confirm for us the fact that there have been some studies done which suggest the possibility of reducing the amount of training time necessary for basic training, which might make it possible then to reduce the time of total service, either for enlistees or for inductees, to under two years, possibly to as minimal a period as one year?

Colonel Hays. Regarding the question of equal time for enlistees and inductees, one of the problems lies in the training of specialists. A continually growing group in all the Armed Forces must go to extended school after basic and advanced individual training: schools for everyone from cooks to military policemen. The percentage of school-trained personnel increases every year. The result is that the initial schooling of a young man, say in the Corps of Engineers as a demolition expert, may not be confined to two months; it may turn out to be six, and for some specialists it could be as long as nine. With this in mind, it's not very practicable to reduce the time of the regular Army enlistees to equal that of the draftees. Now, with regard to time and training, this is not an easy question to answer, because a lot depends upon what kind of training we are talking about. If we are talking about the individual combat soldier, I know personally of no studies that have reduced the time it takes to train this young man; it depends on how well-trained you want him. When he gets in a position to be shot at, no matter how much training he has had, he doesn't feel he has had enough. If you're talking in terms of a specialist, we have reduced the training as much as we can, and we use pretty sophisticated educational techniques to do this.

Mr. Biderman. The draft currently is both directed toward producing what amounts to a military force in reserve and it's also being used to produce troops for combat and combat support right now. The question of the amount of training time needed is much more pertinent, at least from the standpoint of equity, to the procurement of troops for combat right now, than to the training of a pool of reserve military manpower. The figures released recently by the Department of Defense indicate that draftees with presumably a very short period of training are being committed to the active theatre. The probability of a draftee's going to Vietnam is much greater than that for a regular. I raised this in the paper I presented in connection with the thesis that those people who have the most "military" occupations in the Armed Forces, that is, combat, the ones for whom a special military identity is held up as an absolute necessity, are the ones who seemingly are given the least amount of training as compared with those in non-military kinds of specialties.

Colonel Hays. I'm not sure of the facts in this case, but I would suspect that there may be some truth in the statement. The draftee goes to his basic training, and then he moves to an eight-week advanced individual training. Then those designated for combat elements in Vietnam go directly there. Regular Army soldiers make up the bulk of those taking specialist training. This is an opportunity afforded every draftee when he goes into the reception center. The draftee has the option to become a volunteer by extending his enlistment to three years and, if his scores are high, to be assigned to a special school. After such individuals leave advanced individual training they proceed, in many cases, to the specialist schools in which we train radio operators, radio mechanics, and the various other specialties. Thus, the regular Army volunteer tends to get a longer training. This training is in different items, however. The volunteer doesn't get any more combat training but he may get more specialist training. Since the bulk of our specialists come from this regular Army or volunteer component, a larger percentage of them do get, in all probability, more training before they are actually exposed to a combat situation.

Richard Virgil. I have been concerned with an assumption in the presentations of both Colonel Hays and Colonel Ingold, and I believe it was Colonel Ingold who stated it, that the Selective Service attempts to match up the availability of a man's time with the nation's need. Up to now we haven't really discussed, or clarified, the aspect of need, and until that's taken care of, I cannot in my own mind really determine what is the right of the Selective Service to infringe on the time of *any* man, so that when you have a proposal such as Colonel Hays', of the one- or two-year possibility, I really can't conceive of it as an advantage to youth because we still have the matter of compulsion, but it's only at a different time, and I think we have to come to grips with this.

Mr. Naisbitt. Colonel Hays, why is it that the mental standards for volunteers are and have always been higher than the mental standards for inductees? The only reason I can find is tradition.

Colonel Hays. I think one basic answer stems from their utilization in training. If you will recall, we said that the volunteers enlist for at least three years and hence they provide the pools of all the people who get special training, that is mechanics and the advanced training beyond the individual combat training levels. Since they do provide this pool from which we are drawing our specialists the general tendency has been to try to set their mental level higher.

Mr. Wool. First of all, it isn't true that the volunteer standards have always been higher than the draft standards. In fact, there was a standing policy of the Department of Defense for a considerable period in the 1950's which required that they be identical. What happened was that with a growing manpower supply the services, such as the Air Force, Navy, and Marine Corps, which required relatively fewer recruits in relation to the supply were in a position to raise their standards and greatly facilitate from their standpoint their training job. Now, in the case of the Army, the problem was something like this: At any given minimum draft standard, they had to accept whatever distribution of men became available above that minimum standard. Since other services did not take the lowest groups, the proportion of draftees in the lowest acceptable group tended to increase. The only administrative control the Army had was over its enlistment quality, since they could not control the distribution of quality of draftees above a minimum standard. This is the historical explanation of why the enlistment standards have been higher. Currently the Army has reduced its enlistment standards to the same level as the reduced draft standards, so that this is not true at the present time.

Mr. Kurland. I would like to ask two questions. First, what percentage of people in combat roles are volunteers as against the percentage that are inductees? And second, in World War II the Armed Forces recruited civilians for the Merchant Marine's and for the Seabees' vital military missions, and I'd like to know from Colonel Hays, from a military standpoint what are the disadvantages in having civilians replace military men in noncombatant roles?

Colonel Hays. One major difficulty lies in the conditions under which the civilian sees himself as being employed. I'll refer to the same situation that you talked about in the Merchant Marine. I had occasion to talk to an officer the other day who served in the Merchant Marine. The problem ran something like this: during World War II they hired all of the civilian crews for the ships that went into the combat zone. Civilian radio operators, however, wouldn't work 24 hours a day, so they had to sign military people on the ships to work the required 24-hour day. There were some places where the ships got actual refusals from the crews to go any further. They had to pay excessive bonuses for certain areas. Drivers in the military, while they are doing in effect a civilian-type job, are exposed to dangers and rigors and from time to time must perform in the combat role. It's very difficult to predict in each case whether the driver, construction worker, or soldier is going to be required to shoot or not. Even positions which appear on the surface to be noncombat very frequently, even in Vietnam, turn out to involve some combat.

Mr. Kurland. Is it not true that of the entire military, including the Air Force and all the other factions of the service, only 14 per cent are in combatant positions? In the speech that Secretary McNamara gave before the Veterans of Foreign Wars on August 6 in New York City, he said that 14 per cent of the entire 3 million men serve us in this way.

Colonel Hays. I am unable to support or to argue against this percentage. It depends largely upon how you define the combat role. If you define it as applying to those belonging to infantry battalions or tank battalions or similar organizations, I would suspect that this number is probably quite sound. Let's take, for example, the combat role in clerical work, say in the Pentagon. During the crises that they've had there, particularly the Cuban crisis, at a certain time of night all the clerks went home except soldiers. The soldiers had to stand by on duty all night, and fill in the gap when the civilians weren't present for duty. This same kind of thing occurs in other areas. The man who unloads the ship, the longshoreman, for instance in Vietnam works around the clock; he doesn't go on strike, he's dependable, and he can man a gun if he has to. Essentially you could say he is doing a civilian-type job. I doubt very seriously if we would be very successful in recruiting civilians to do these jobs on the same terms you could expect military personnel to do them.

Mr. Janowitz. The question of the replaceability of military by civilian personnel is something, of course, which is very close to Secretary McNamara's heart, and he has a staff working trying to find wherever it is possible to bring about this replacement. At the present time the Secretary hopes that over a period of about three years 60,000 additional military jobs might be made civilian. I do not know if that is definitive, but with his predisposition for civilianization, that is his estimate. I think one of the things that must be borne in mind in the logistical system is the high ratio of personnel in transit from one area to another.

Mr. Kurland. This question is very relevant to Mr. Friedman's point and that's why I'd like to get any factual information I can from Mr. Wool on the two questions; one being the percentage of people in combatant roles who are draftees, if you know that. . . .

Mr. Wool. Well, I don't know that. First of all, the key question is definition. When Secretary McNamara spoke about 14 per cent or so in combat occupation, he was actually talking about the man whose primary occupational specialty is being an infantryman or a tanker or an artillery man. This is totally different from the number of men in combatant roles. In an infantry division you have a huge variety of occupations, and his context was occupational crossover in training. You have clerks, you have cooks, and truck drivers, all within a combat organization, and in that broader sense, their percentage of men who are exposed to combat situations is far higher. . . .

Mr. Janowitz. We could use the words "combat support" for that notion.

Mr. Wool. You can use many words for this thing, but you're really talking about men who are vulnerable in one way or another to hostile fire or whose assignments over a period of their career make them vulnerable to that.

[Unidentified Speaker]. What is your estimate?

Mr. Wool. It's well over half of the total, in that context. Now, the problem is, and this gets us to the "civilianization" issue, Secretary McNamara has not talked about a hope of converting 60,000 jobs in three years' time; he is in the process of converting 74,000 military jobs in this year, replacing them with 60,000 civilians, and that process is virtually complete. In addition, there are an additional 40,000 military positions scheduled for this coming fiscal year.

Mr. Janowitz. We may be converting 60,000 and may be creating another 100,000. . . .

Mr. Wool. Now, that is very true in one sense. There are these positions which have been identified as replaceable and they are being replaced with civilians. We're dealing with a dynamic structure, and the balance may not always show it because our total military strength is growing for quite different reasons. Now, the long-run problem is closely related to the viability of a career military force which has to be deployed world-wide. The career man, at least, has to be assured of some opportunity to get back home, and overseas you do have a variety of civilian-type occupations required in a deployed force. When these people come home, the work that they do at home could, in many cases, be done by civilians—in many cases it is—and the problem is to be sure that you do safeguard an adequate rotation, career development, and training base. We're not convinced that we're at the end of the road in terms of ultimate potential, even after allowing for all these things. It is a difficult problem and it's been given a good deal of study and we're still working at it.

Mr. Kurland. What is the long-range projection as to the percentage of the military force required by 1970 that could be assumed by civilians? Do you have any projection at all on this?

Mr. Wool. No, I don't have anything beyond the current program objectives which do include replacement of—well, 60,000 positions—actually we are able to say 74,000 by the first installment this year, because there is a training pipeline-saving associated with it, plus another 40,000; that's as far as we've gone so far. We have no further projection.

Mr. Kurland. Would you agree that the present Selective Service itself creates attitudes which become a restraint on the potential replacement of military personnel by civilians? Would you say that it is restraining the opportunity of the Defense Department to replace military men with civilians?

Mr. Wool. No, on the contrary, I'd say that this program was one of the by-products of the study of the draft conducted by the Pentagon. We did look into the possibilities of reducing our reliance upon the draft, and one of the things we did look at was this whole utilization complex. The principle should be that we only take military men for jobs that need military men, and we want to see that that is in fact what is being done.

Paul Weinstein. If you really want to, you could change the whole concept of what the military is willing to do, and also redefine the nature of the hardware, so you could cut down training time mechanics, and redefine the old concept of the blackbox mechanic—having somebody plug in one thing and plug out another module. In fact, there's a very, very broad spectrum of policy that has to be considered here, in terms of what occupations you want in the military and what in the civilians. We could probably cut down a great many of the mechanics and just farm out to contractors all the repair work that is now done. Which just means a larger hardware budget as a substitute for internal manpower outlays.

Mr. Janowitz. The question of technology is certainly another very important one. I think at this point we should broaden the discussion, and we ought to leave some time for the interrelations between these different parts. So the floor is now open for general discussion.

Sister Cusack. On conscientious objectors—I would like for Messrs. Pemberton, Tatum, and Biderman to give their views on this point. Granted that the broader definition is desirable and that the religious test is dropped; granted also that A, B, and C categories are reasonable; even D, headed by the Epicureans could be admitted; I would like to add an "E" class and then ask this question to be thought about but not answered now. The E class would be composed of sincere conscientious objectors who still prefer escalation without participation. That is, they would like to be excused, but they're not so anxious to have others excused. That this is conscientiously held by many is apparent today. Then, I would ask of all five groups, including the Epicureans, is it right that such an attitude be considered (and I'm in sympathy with their asking, and in sympathy with their being excused, especially the A, B, and C—I have some doubts about D and E—but nevertheless, I think they have the responsibility and we have the responsibility of their declaring their position publicly), is it right that they have objected, they have been exempted, and why? That is another reason I think they should stand by their position and be accorded whatever is accorded to them.

Mr. Janowitz. Thank you, Sister Cusack, for entering the notion of the rhetorical question into this type of conference. It is really a social invention.

[*Unidentified Speaker*]. On the same issue of conscientious objection —I wonder whether Mr. Pemberton was considering the defense of conscientious objection simply within wartime or in peacetime, and whether there might be some differentiation between conscientious objection during war and during peace. If one considers it during peace, I wonder whether Mr. Pemberton would consider category "F"—an American democrat who, too, we might grant, might have conscience and not *just* that he states his own conscience. I think that he might be able to offer good grounds. Now, suppose he holds that it's wrong for him—perhaps it's wrong in general—to fight in a war when there's been no declaration of war, and the grounds he offers are that the notion of need, which is referred to by Colonel Ingold, Colonel Hays and, before that, in the working paper of General Hershey, the notion of need in wartime is determined by a Presidential declaration of war, ratified by the Senate. Then individuals in the country, through their election process, vote for representatives and vote for the President. During peacetime there is none of this availability. Consequently, the American democrat might allege that it's wrong for him to go to war and fight when there has been no declaration of war, and you are told this quite sincerely. . . .

Mr. Pemberton. I would relate category E, the objector who speaks escalation without participation, to the Epicurean and Black Muslim and so forth. I am prepared, I think, to contemplate the possibility that law would exempt people on grounds of conscience generally—would assimilate the conscientious objector into all other forms of law; that we would be able to administer a law in which an objection of conscience of the same degree that we are now administering in the Selective Service law would be applied to traffic laws and everything else we can imagine. But that's not the question before us. The question before us concerns objection to participation in human killing. As long as that is the only question before us, I think that any defense of other kinds of conscientious objectors ought to be ruled out of order. It doesn't belong in the consideration of conscription and therefore all we really have to face is— What should we do for the man who objects to participating in human killing? In those terms, the speaker's objector, category F, I think fits. I'll state my formulation. He regards it as wrong for him to do this act which government commands of him and considers it wrong for him as well to yield his conscience on this matter to the direction of government. Most of us comply with laws that we disagree with as well as laws that we agree with, and we don't consider ourselves violating our conscience when we do that. The function of law is, in the area where it's competent, to substitute for our personal opinions in determining our conduct, but there are areas I think all of us consider beyond the competence of government to determine. When human killing is that area, and when human killing in the here and now, whether it be peacetime, preparation for future human killing, or wartime participation in human killing, but without a congressional declaration of war, the ground isn't important except that it will be examined in determining sincerity.

Richard Duffee. Mr. Lauter discussed the idea that often avoidance of the draft was based on sound moral principles. When I turned 18 I felt that I objected to killing and that I did not want to kill. However, I did not feel that I could register as a conscientious objector because I would be putting myself in the position of saying that I am not willing to be damned for killing but I will allow other people to take on the responsibility of killing. Now, what can be done about this position? What should I do or what should any person in this position do to be able to state his beliefs that while he cannot kill, he cannot command other people to kill, and he cannot have people killing in his place, since there is a war going on. I was wondering if there was any alternative to conscientious objection. I know that several people in this position have refused to register for the draft. Is there any legal alternative for conscientious objection?

Mr. Pemberton. I would personally advocate that we should offer the same defense to the conscientious objector who expresses his objection by refusal to register as we do to the one who registers on File Form 150. Obviously, there must be a forum in which you do it and the forum under the present law is the Federal District Court, in which he is tried for the Selective Service law offense of refusal to register for the draft—a criminal offense. I would assert that there ought to be a legitimate defense to that, that the same grounds of conscience that warrant exemption to a registrant who applies for CO exemption should exempt from criminal punishment the man whose conscience leads him to refuse to register. I do not see how this relates to the problem you put to me, however, because this man is in the same position as the registrant who applies for an exemption with respect to somebody substituting for him. As Colonel Hays has pointed out, the Selective Service System has always gotten its quota and when I or you refuse to register, or get exempted as a conscientious objector, Colonel Hays is still going to get his quota. I feel that you are taking the whole world on your conscience, and I think that is a kind of playing God that is beyond your competence. I think this is what law exists for. This is what democratic processes exist for. All I can do as an individual citizen in a democratic society is to seek to influence the ultimate decision that that society makes, and if my conscience rebels at that decision, to refuse to participate in it.

Colonel Mordechai M. Bar-On. I thought it would be appropriate for me to give you some of our experience in Israel on this one question. And I don't refer at all to the moral or political decorum because they are so different. Now the point I'd like to raise here is that in our experience, a very large number— some 95 percent of the people, serve only at the ages of 19 or 18 to 20, and the question of instability of this age does seem very pertinent in our situation. We found, however, that the very fact that the young people of age 18 joined the military brought for them much stability after a very short period of time. After being placed in a military situation, within three or four months they seemed to be operating very well at this age. On the other hand, it seemed to us that it was very desirable to have most of the military of the low ranks, privates and corporals and even second lieutenants, of the same age group. We had some occasions in which college graduates came and served together alongside others and this was quite disruptive. The fact that you are 22 or 23 years of age and you serve alongside much younger people, brings about many social and psychological questions. So, the fact that we have primarily one age group in the service seemed to us to be very useful. Also, it seemed to us that disruption of further education was much less at the age of 18 than at the age of 22. At the age of 18, they have just finished high school. They don't have exact plans as far as marriage is concerned. Later disruption is very much more acute to the individual.

Mr. Janowitz. Your feeling is that the 18-year age group in the Israeli situation did not show instabilities, which would then lead us to questions about command structure. There might also be cultural differences which would be very worthwhile to explore. I'm very much interested also in your observation that a military group of the same age group was not disruptive. On purely theoretical grounds I have been thinking in terms of some optimum mix of younger people and older ones—but I take it that what you're saying is that relatively homogeneous categories with proper NCO's do respond in a meaningful way.

Mr. Wool. It is important on this question of age to be rather explicit about what the Department of Defense has testified on. The question was reviewed with each of the military services and the Joint Chiefs of Staff; it is not an unconsidered judgment; after giving it, I will be prepared to discuss some of the considerations. Now, in this area, I will quote from the testimony of Assistant Secretary Morris before the Congress this past June. He says, first of all, that "looking to the future, the draft selection system should be redesigned to concentrate military service among the younger age classes and order of students when they leave school, when force levels are reduced and stabilized." In supporting this conclusion he notes that, in fact, combat commanders have preferred recruits for their combat organizations of a relatively young age. Secondly, we prevent the undesirable effect of creating a long period of uncertainty for those young men who do not choose to volunteer for longer periods of service. We saw no offsetting benefits to the military resulting from that situation; we, therefore, definitely recommended a younger and more stable age. Now, keep one thing in mind— we're talking first about the age when people enter service rather than the age of the force as a whole. I am sure that military commanders would not want a force composed entirely of 18- or 19-year-olds. We're not talking about that. Secondly, given the fact that enlistments are for longer terms, and are where we get most of our technicians, a large proportion of draftees, under normal conditions, don't have the option of enlisting into the more technical skills. They're more likely to go into combat skills. And when we have a situation in which the draft age is as high as 24 it does mean you're getting men already more settled, taken out of civilian life, at that age, to fulfill their two-year tour, with a greater proportion going into the direct combat assignments.

Mr. Janowitz. I'll invite any further discussion of the question of age grading, because I think it's a very vital question at the moment.

Mrs. McAllister. I have some questions about putting people into a non-civil situation at an early age—accustoming them to life within a rigid hierarchy and being subject to the military law where they do not have the advantage of a jury of their peers in case they are accused, and in general becoming accustomed before they have even had the experience of voting, to this kind of autocracy.

Mr. Kelly. My question stems from the reading of the Defense Department testimony. Clearly the manpower requirements of the Defense Department are bi-modally distributed. It requires young people on the one hand; on the other hand it needs people who are college graduates. The one thing that I've never quite understood is how it is possble for the Defense Department to say we should increase certainty by taking younger people, and yet insist that, somehow, the system is also going to pull out college graduates. How do you reconcile this position?

Mr. Wool. Our statements referred to not getting all men in at an age class. We recognize the possibility, if not desirability of some form of college student deferment. At a minimum, from the Department of Defense standpoint, the present system does provide deferments—in addition to general deferment of college students—for those college men who do elect to enter certain officer training programs such as ROTC and certain other programs. This provides an assured source of men with college education to meet our officer requirements. It's necessary, too, to look ahead towards the completion of professional schooling and obtaining such critical occupancies for the military. We believe it's possible, as one alternative, to have a system where one could have men who have completed their schooling enter at some age such as 19 or 20, if they do not choose to volunteer earlier, and at the same time, to permit those who are deferred under whatever rules are established to continue their schooling and enter at later ages, as long as one establishes the principles of equity of exposure to service, irrespective of age at completion of service. This does give us a distribution in terms of educational backgrounds, and so forth, which is desirable.

Mr. Kurland. It is our understanding, in light of what we've done earlier, that the Defense Department is committed to the student deferment. This is a necessary requirement in terms of fulfilling your manpower wishes.

Mr. Wool. We cannot justify in terms of our requirements for about 40,000 officers a year, a blanket deferment of all students. In other words, it seems to me that that has to be considered more broadly in terms of whether or not deferments for all college students are required for other values, in terms of the effectiveness of the educational process and when it is least harmful to interrupt it in terms of the entire civilian economy and the educational system as such. We do feel that deferment at least for those men who have established officer commitments is essential.

Mr. Chapman. I'd like to take up a point in regard to occupational deferment and the national interest. I have two associated points which I'd like Colonel Ingold, perhaps, to respond to. First of all, he has said earlier that the concept of occupational deferments in the national interest is vague; it is admittedly vague. And yet, even a vague interpretation is not given to registrants. In other words, there are men who have occupations which would warrant a deferment, but they do not know that, and so they go ahead and accept the draft. The flyer that is put out does not explain what is in the Dictionary of Occupational Titles or whatever. Also, Representative Curtis has pointed out—and I'd like some response to this—that the Dictionary of Occupational Titles is out of date, and also that the Selective Service System and the Labor Department do not regularly meet to discuss what is an essential occupation and what is not an essential occupation.

And then, secondly, it has been my observation, and I think there are many specific papers that will support this, that deferments of all kinds, including occupational deferments, are easier to obtain when there is a large pool of registrants in the Selective Service than when that pool is small. In other words, it seems that deferments are a means of controlling the pool, and, to me, the only conclusion can be that human beings are being used more to meet current manpower flow problems of the Selective Service System than to meet its own poorly defined concept of what is in the national interest.

Colonel Ingold. The Selective Service System is a service agency. It has no end in itself. It supplies the demand. The demand comes from the services and is translated by the Department of Defense. And when the calls are high the pressure is upon the local boards to develop a larger 1A pool. I don't like the word "pool" for several reasons, but this is what it is called. And then when they cut down calls, as has happened—this is an up-and-down proposition—it periodically leaves a surplus of class 1A registrants.

Mr. Chapman. But doesn't that situation directly affect what is considered by the local boards to be in the national interest? Doesn't a man with the same occupation wind up being deferred in one case when he is not so much needed by the Selective Service System, while he would be taken at another time?

Colonel Ingold. Not needed by the Selective Service System, needed by the Armed Forces. The answer is yes. We create a sliding scale to meet the demands for men in the Armed Forces. It's entirely possible, under different circumstances, that a man would be differently classified. And intentionally so— that's what we're supposed to do. We're not supposed to create a tremendous amount of manpower when there's no need for it. As a matter of fact, in wartime that would immobilize the whole country, to put too many people in class 1A.

Mr. Chapman. So, in other words, essentially the national interest is a *very* flexible thing.

Colonel Ingold. There's no doubt about it, and this is closely associated with this paper that's being distributed about no student deferment. There's a logistic problem in here that everybody should be aware of. Even if you deny deferments to students, they can't be inducted.- There isn't room for all of them in the Armed Forces. So if they can't be inducted, they're going to be deferred in class 1A. Which do you prefer, the honest 2S or the dishonesty of class 1A and being deferred? They'll stay in school in 1A.

Mr. Chapman. I don't see how it's honest to defer just because you don't need them and then give as your rationale that they're "essential."

Colonel Ingold. It isn't the question of us needing them, it's the demand from the Armed Forces. If there isn't room, they can't be put in. We can't order any more people for induction than calls prescribe.

Mr. Chapman. How does their not being needed make them "essential"?

Joseph S. Tuchinsky. I generally distrust statistics, but since there are a great many of them flowing at this Conference, I want to add a couple more to the supply. These have at least the saving grace of being admittedly subjective. An avocation which takes a large portion of my time these days is counseling young men with draft problems, the largest part of whom are seeking to be classified as conscientious objectors. I'd estimate that during the last 14 months, I've probably talked with about 150 men who are exploring the possibility of applying as conscientious objectors. I suppose that my ability to gauge sincerity is about average and about as good as anybody's on the draft board, and since the sincerity of those who apply is so frequently questioned in the public press and has been perhaps indirectly raised here, I'd like to comment on those 150, with each of whom I've had discussions of, oh, perhaps two or three hours or more. I think, of the 150, there have been three—the statistic would then be 2 per cent —about whose sincerity I had real questions. The other 98 per cent impressed me very strongly as men who were doing something which they internally had to do.

Mr. Janowitz. I do think that as part of the discussion the extent of conscientious objection should be clearly noted, recalling also the Charge last night from Mr. Hazard that the question is not significant statistically, but it is a moral question. There are about 9,000 in class 1O at the present time, which would just be an infinitesimal number, over the history of the age groups subject to exposure.

Mr. Tatum. You are giving the impression that this is the number of men classified as conscientious objectors.

Mr. Janowitz. I certainly apologize if I gave that impression.

Mr. Tatum. It's approximately 20,000 who have the conscientious objector classification. This is the 1O's, the 1W's and 1W's-released. The Selective Service statistics are that one registrant out of a thousand was classified as an alternative service-type conscientious objector in the 1940 draft. Between '52 and '62, Selective Service says that one registrant out of 600 was a conscientious objector. Colonel Omer, who's Deputy Director of National Selective Service, agreed with me on a radio broadcast in June that one out of 400 is now a recognized conscientious objector. I would say that about one out of 200 or 300 registrants is now making a conscientious objection claim.

Mr. Flacks. There are a couple of points that I would want to raise. First, with respect to the sort of question that Mr. Duffee raised before, it seems to be part of the problem with conscientious objection that there is, in a sense, an inequity about who is exposed to the moral problem. College students who are involved with the peace movement, or are on campuses where there are active peace movements, are to a certain extent tested with respect to their own conscience about fighting; the general population is rarely confronted with the question. It seems to me that there ought to be some independent mechanism for judging claims of conscientious objection. Broadening the definition would expand the possibilities for youth to test their own consciences about whether they were going into the Armed Forces. It seems to me socially desirable that young people ask themselves the questions: Can they in good conscience fight? Can they in good conscience refuse to fight? And we ought to try to increase the mechanism by which this can be made possible. I also feel that we should spend some time discussing this question of ranking since that was one stimulus to the Conference. I hope I'm not putting him on the spot with this, but I understand that Mr. Keast's university is one of the few that has decided not to rank students for deferment. I'm wondering if he would want to talk at all about his experience in that regard since that decision was made.

Mr. Janowitz. I think I have to pass that on to the next Chairman.

THIRD SESSION

Proposals for Modifying the Present System

MONDAY AFTERNOON, DECEMBER 5, 1966

Chairman, ARNOLD R. WEBER

 Arnold R. Weber. There was one unfinished element of business which I think we should take up and that was the question of educational institutions' policy regarding ranking or the submission of ranks in connection with student deferments. Mr. Keast, President of Wayne State University, indicated that he would be willing to tell all, or almost all, and I was reflecting that there were three high administrative officers from major educational institutions who intended to come, and of the three, Mr. Keast is the only one who has come because the other two were kept home as a result of present or incipient demonstrations. And now we learn that Mr. Keast comes from an institution that does not have student ranking, so, although we might not have any lessons from Mr. Patterson or the Congress, the message in terms of insuring the tranquillity of educational administrators is clear.

 Mr. Keast. We adopted in June of this year the university policy that class rankings for students, male and female alike, would not be determined and since they were not being determined, would not be supplied to local boards. This policy was enunciated after extended discussion in the university faculty and in the university administration, and represented then and continues to represent the manifest coincidence of the preponderant views of both the faculty and the university administration. We did not have, at the time we undertook to make this policy determination, the opportunity to solicit extended student discussion. But such discussion as there had been and such registration of student views as at that time occurred obviously went in the same direction. And since that time we have received overwhelming student endorsement of the university policy. We also have unanimous approval of this action by the Board of Governors of the university, which is a public institution, numbering this fall 32,000 students. We have an elected Board of Governors and they saw no particular difficulty, in view of exposure to electoral reprisal, in approving unanimously the university's policy. The question has been raised a couple of times of how a public institution finds itself in the position of pursuing a policy which appears to flout the requests or requirements of duly constituted governmental bodies. I won't go into that question at the moment. The fact is that we have not received any particular backfire. On the contrary, there is general approval of our policy from the press in Michigan and from radio and television, and such citizen comment as I have received. The exception is the customary small number of people who have indicated that we are being unpatriotic and that they propose hereafter to divert their contributions to the university to some other philanthropic purpose.

 There has been no evidence of reprisal against our students from local boards, although we have made it a particular point to insure that we are kept closely informed about the position in which our students find themselves. A consequence of our position in view of the current operations of Selective Service is that our students are virtually required to take the Selective Service test. We adopted our policy fully realizing that this would be the case. I have not myself made a thorough study of the Selective Service test. I have been informed that in some respects it is thought to be defective by experts. It has this merit, that it is uniform, whatever the variations of performance that may derive from differences in cultural or educational background.

I circulated a 12-page memorandum, indicating the reasons for our taking this step, to all the people I could think of who might be in a position to take similar action in their institutions or influence their institutions to do so. So far I haven't had any particular luck. The Michigan Council of State College Presidents took note individually of our action. They said that it was very interesting, but that they were going ahead with their class rankings and reporting them to local boards. It had already become clear that the official position of the American Council on Education and certain other national educational groups was not only to follow the Selective Service guideline but indeed to do so because these groups were themselves instrumental in securing the adoption of these guidelines in the first instance. So it wasn't at all surprising to me that none of these groups saw fit to undertake an extensive modification of their draft policies.

I won't go into details on why we decided that class rankings are not to be supplied to local boards, but our principal reason was that we didn't think they ought to be made in the first instance. They are educationally unsound, useless and counterproductive of significant educational development, both for students and for curricula. If the educational community has painted itself into a corner by continuing to carry out class rankings on the supposition that they had some meaning for a certain number of years, it's no particular surprise to anybody if for once the community at large has taken the academic community seriously and said, "if you people think you can rank students, then we'd like to use those rankings for other purposes." It seems to me the best thing we can do, generally, is to acknowledge that we shouldn't have been trying to separate the 247th from the 248th student in a class in a complex institution with high variations in the program of study. If we would acknowledge this frankly and candidly to ourselves, and cease doing internally what has no particular educational merit in itself, I think we would not have any great difficulty persuading the Selective Service System and the community at large that this is a measure which doesn't really measure anything and that to present it to hardworking, serious-minded local boards as an instrument by which they can confidently make comparisons among students at different stages and in different educational programs in vastly different educational institutions, is in fact to perpetrate a fraud upon the local boards, Selective Service, and the student. And I, for one, hope that this group, whatever else it does about the far more significant problem that we're dealing with, and the National Commission on Selective Service also, will as promptly as possibly signify at least this small part of the silliness in which we now seem to be engulfed can be stopped without any serious consequences to the overall effectiveness of the draft. Indeed, if the universities would withdraw themselves, at least to this extent, from acting as agents for the Selective Service System in ways in which they cannot properly be agents, then I believe reform of the whole system would be more rapidly stimulated, because it would be seen that other measures than those now being relied upon have to be developed.

Mr. Weber. Mr. Keast has very articulately presented a position which as I understand it would be an amendment to, or supplementary to, Professor Friedman's resolution, which apparently is now in the process of being revised and amended and rewritten. I wonder if we would want to talk to Mr. Keast's motion, which I would accept as a formal statement, that this group should indicate that the practice of ranking is undesirable. As I understand you, your arguments are twofold: one, ranking is undesirable because it's inconsistent with good educational practice; and, two, it involves cooperation in a system which has other basic defects, and one of the ways that you inspire revision and amendment is to not cooperate to the extent that you have such discretion. Is that a fair statement?

Mr. Keast. I'd like to make it three, then, because I hadn't quite wanted to put my second point as you have put it. So if you'll make yours as number three, then I will insert a number two: Whatever one wishes to say about cooperating in the execution of a system which one may wish to see amended in other respects, it is, I believe, an unsound policy for us, as educators, to pretend to local boards, each of which is dealing with a large number of students coming from different institutions, that the measures which are submitted by those institutions are comparable. Third, then, is that I don't believe the universities ought to put themselves in the position of acting as agents for the Selective Service System in this respect, perhaps in others.

Mr. Booth. The issue we'd like to underline is the educational indefensibility of rank as the mode of indicating quality. Anyone who has ever done any careful educational testing of the validity of grades which go into ranking, particularly in the humanities or the social sciences, but also even in such seemingly hard-and-fast subjects as mathematics, knows that they're only roughly valid, at best. One test of validity in mathematical grading shows that professional mathematicians grading freshman papers at Haverford College on a seemingly objective scale couldn't agree closer than plus or minus ten on a hundred-point scale. These imprecise grades are then set into a system with even more imprecise grades and then averages are calculated out to three decimal points and used for positioning in Phi Beta Kappa nominations, graduate admissions, and whatnot. The educational community would benefit if the group here could dramatize the fundamental unreliability of the data the draft boards are asking for, so that it would be recognized that they aren't really asking us for information which would be useful but that we don't want to give. Really, it's no use to them if it's looked at closely.

[Unidentified Speaker]. I'd like to say about this theory that it sets forth in almost complete detail the same position precisely that Haverford College has taken. They have taken the position for precisely the same reasons as Wayne State.

Judy Barrett [Mrs. Hal Litoff]. But I want to ask Mr. Keast two questions. What about the students who don't want to take the Selective Service test, and what about the A-B student who takes the test and just doesn't score well on it? What provision has been made to protect this type of student?

Mr. Weber. I subscribe to the theory that progress takes place in small steps. And I think Mr. Keast has pinpointed the particular issue of ranking grades. You have introduced the supplementary issue of participation in the test, and although that might be important, I was hoping you'd reserve it for the two hour free-for-all scheduled for later this afternoon.

Gregory Craig. I have three questions. What is your response to the attitude that the university discriminates against the student who wants his rank in order to participate in the Selective Service System, the argument being that as soon as one student wants his rank in class, in order to comply with the law, the university is obliged to give it to him? What about the legal problems coming out of that one student's request for his rank? Can the university be enjoined to compute rank, the injunction being prevention of breaking the law by the act of not computing rank? And the third question, do you furnish students Form 109, which is the first involvement of the university in the Selective Service System and philosophically would be the first element in the participation of the educational process in the Selective Service System.

Mr. Keast. Back to number one, we've taken the position that the statement on the part of the university, when requested by the student, that he is enrolled, that he is a full-time student, and that his grades are such and such, are the student's property. We submit them to employers and so on. We have no proper ground on which to refuse to submit them to local boards if the student requests, and only if he does. With respect to rank in class, however, we do not regard the student as having anything like a quasi-property right in his class rank, since it cannot be determined except by a procedure which involves the rights and purposes and privileges of a large number of other students. So we simply say, we're terribly sorry, if you want your rank you can't have it. This gets us into Mrs. Litoff's question, which is a hard one. With respect to the legal problem, we are not, I think, in a position of disobeying a law. There is an administrative guideline which suggests that local boards use rank in class as one, but only one, means by which they determine deferment. We are simply not providing that information. They have to use what information they have. This creates some other problems of course. For the third question, we sumbit Form 109. It has a place in which to say something about class standing; we simply say that Wayne State University does not rank classes and class standing is not available.

Mr. Craig. Does the statement that comes from the university that says this particular student is a member in good standing of that university in fact constitute the first compromise that the university makes in participating in a Selective Service policy?

Mr. Keast. We don't regard it as a compromise. We regard the university as having an obligation to provide to the local board, if the student asks for it, a statement that he is registered in the university as a full-time student. This, I think is not a compromise, at least in the terms of reference that I customarily use. Now I realize there are those who regard any communication with Selective Service as outside the bounds. I don't myself believe you can maintain this position and still say that the university ought to provide student transcripts for graduate school, etc.

Mr. Marmion. Does Wayne State in any way rank students for admission to graduate school, other graduate schools?

Mr. Keast. We have for a long time ranked students at graduation. And this has the effect, of course, of providing a basis for ranking for applications to graduate school as well as for employment. And obviously, therefore, it will, under the circumstances currently prevailing, provide a basis, if we wish to use it, for giving local boards information concerning standing in the upper quarter of the class for purposes of continued deferment as graduate students. We have not yet decided whether to cease to make these determinations or not. We are in the process of considering it now.

Mr. Marmion. The point is that ranking is utilized every day by educational institutions to provide adequate information for admission to graduate school.

Mr. Keast. Right. Mr. Booth's view and mine would be that class ranking, in the sense in which it is used by Selective Service, requires a degree of refinement which is incompatible with any of the measures that we know about. If we did it by quartiles or something, it would be better.

Mr. Booth. I'd like to add to Mr. Keast's answer to these three questions that they are questions which arise only so long as the law remains as it now is. And we have two questions before us. I think that the university's resistance is really subsidiary to this meeting, and the hope is that we might get the law changed, so that these questions wouldn't even have to come up.

Mr. Weber. Well, I'm a little torn because this seems to be one of the few occasions on which there's general agreement, if you want to pursue it.

Mr. Wool. I think we're jumping a bit too quickly at the general agreement. I think we have to recognize the implications, assuming for the moment that Professor Friedman's recommendation is not followed, and that you have some students being drafted and others not. Now, the dilemma of Selective Service or anybody who has to select is this: if you establish national test criteria, you must recognize that a national test will mean that in many of the least selective colleges of the country, and particularly in the segregated Negro colleges in the South, a very large percentage of these students will not pass that test. We have to look at the adverse effect of complete elimination of some form of measure of relative progress within an institution. It would certainly mean that there'd be no measure of the differential performance of those who for various reasons have not had the same ability to do well on these national tests but have shown competitive progress in their institutions. Now that's a very important consideration in terms of social implications. A second implicaton, it seems to me, has been touched upon. I wonder how many of the selective institutions in this country will accept a high school graduate into their institution without looking at his high school class standing. I don't know of one which does not consider that as a criterion, imperfect as it may be. They consider test scores, but they certainly also consider the latter.

Mr. Friedman. I agree with Mr. Keast on both parts of what is now under discussion. He and I agree that it would be in the national interest not to have special student deferments. I do not agree with him that it would be desirable for universities to follow the practice which Wayne State follows. In fact, I believe this is a "rank herring." Far from it being a situation in which sending in ranks involves letting the Selective Service System interfere with education, it's the other way around. The resolution of the kind he has proposed involves doing that. The reason is, that we issue, as Mr. Marmion has suggested, transcscripts for many purposes. Now these transcripts are not self-explanatory. I get a piece of paper from XYZ University which says an individual has had

18 A's and 16 B's. I may know whether that university is a good university or a bad university, but I don't know whether 99 per cent of the marks are A's or 80 per cent of them are B's. And I think everyone here would agree that it adds to our knowledge of transcripts, if in addition to the transcript we have, let us say, a statistical classification of grades. If, in addition to a Wayne State transcript, we have a statement that statistical studies reveal that 28 per cent of all marks are A's, 33 per cent are B's, and so on, I think Mr. Keast will agree that that improves our knowledge and our ability to evaluate that transcript. Now a ranking is nothing more than a more statistically complicated transformation of such a distribution of grades. And it seems to me that in the interest of universities giving full information about the meaning of their grades, it would be perfectly all right for them to provide the statistical distribution instead of ranking students. I would have no objection to that. But I do think that to say no, we're not going to let you know what our grades mean for this particular purpose, although we're going to continue to do it for graduate schools, for employers, and so on, is close to asking for special treatment for the university.

I believe that the most important issue here is how we keep the university free from being involved in the political decision-making process, in order that we, as individuals, may be as free as possible. I want to be able to take any political position I want, and therefore I don't want my university to be in a position of trying to take a position as a corporate body. I would not want my university, as a university, to come out against student deferment, although I personally am opposed to it. Similarly, I do not want my university, as a university, indirectly, to come out with a particular position about the draft, in the form of refusing to give information that will make its transcripts meaningful.

Mr. Keast. I think Mr. Friedman is a very much better reader of transcripts, with or without the supplementary information he asks for, than we can reasonably presume local boards to be. Point two: he is considering the use of transcripts for judgment of students' further academic work. The validity of the transcript and of the educational program that it testifies to, and the student's rank in it has some kind of valid relation—at least we hope it does—to Mr. Friedman's willingness to take him on as a graduate student in the Department of Economics. When you convert this, however, to a totally different setting in which whether one stands just below the 60th percentile or just above the 60th percentile determines whether or not one should continue with one's education in a particular program, or go into the Army, I think you have so different a setting that Mr. Friedman's objections largely fall to the ground. I don't believe we're in a position of withholding information which is validly related to the purposes for which Selective Service is organized. Rather, we are not pretending that information which we could, with I think grave difficulty, make available, is of any use to the judgments which are in fact being made.

Mr. Friedman. But do not as a corporate body make a judgment about what's relevant to the Selective Service administration. That is a case in which you are entering into the political arena and not acting simply as an educational institution.

Mr. Keast. There isn't any way in which you can easily submit or not submit class rankings except as a corporate body. If you do it, everybody is involved in doing it. If you don't do it, everybody is involved in not doing it.

David Bakan. On the ranking question, I'm really appalled at the degree to which a society that considers itself rational has been acting quite irrationally. I'm now about to underwrite the point just made by Mr. Keast. There seems to be a presumption that there is a relationship between grades and the future performance of an individual, or a relationship between his grades and the degree to which he will eventually make a contribution to the national welfare. Such data as we have on this question all characteristically indicate that the correlation between grades and future performance is around zero. I refer you to a book by Eli Ginsberg called *Talent and Society*. A study in the *Journal of Medical Education* on the relationship between undergraduate grades, graduate grades, medical grades, *and* future performance on a large number of different criteria concludes that there is no relationship whatsoever.

Mr. Rosenberg. So far, we have touched essentially on whether ranking will enable adequate and effective rational discrimination of potential talent as this bears upon the question of who is and who is not to be drafted. I agree with Mr. Friedman that educational institutions should not presume too far, if at all, into the political realm. I think one must note, however, that the contrary is also a legitimate stricture, that political power should not presume too far into the operation of educational institutions. I would like to point out that yet another set of disfunctions associated with ranking concerns what the influence of the ranking procedure is upon the day-to-day operation of educational institutions. Those of us who do some college teaching have noticed, certainly in the last half-year since the ranking issue has become this salient, that many male students are more nervous about the grades they are getting than they might otherwise be, and in fact sometimes seem to be jockeying into position to get the easier instructors, or get into the easier courses. At least, in private conversations, students sometimes confess to just this kind of strategy. Which means they may not be getting the courses they need or may not be exposing themselves to some of the instructors they ought to be seeking out. A second disfunction, and one I can speak of with greater certainty because I myself have experienced it, is a kind of apprehension, indeed a kind of moral concern, felt by many teachers. This is due to their recognition that, however indirectly, the ultimate effect of the grades they give to their male students is to exert some influence upon the basic decision of who goes to war and who does not. In fact, one is thereby exerting influence upon the question of who lives and who dies. This will tend to make a sensitive or concerned college professor a little bit wary about grading low, particularly for males; and this means that he is going to misperceive or misreport the actual quality of his students as he formulates their grades. And this, by the way, contributes still further to the already remarkable degree of invalidity in the grading process—the sort of thing that Dean Booth was talking about before. I don't suggest that these considerations are the only salient considerations. I suggest, though, that as educators we must view the ranking problem in terms of the disfunctions it generates within the academic community and in terms of the ways in which it invalidates our commitments to some of the basic purposes of the educational enterprise.

Mr. Tuchinsky. I want to add to Mr. Keast's three objections to the use of rank a fourth one provided by the registrar at my university, who points out that when Roosevelt University initiated the rank for Selective Service this year it had to take a considerable amount of money the university badly needed for educational purposes and transfer it into that. She had no comment to make on the educational effect of it or the validity of it, and possibly Mr. Ingold could overcome her objections if he paid for it instead of making us pay for it, but I think until that happens we have four objections.

Mr. Weber. It is clear that many people here are opposed to rank as such. We find two positions, at least, that I could detect, generally in support of it, given the existing circumstances: namely, non-participation with respect to rank is an intrusion by the university into the political process, and if you don't participate in ranking this will discriminate against those persons whose classification in terms of intellectual potential and ability falls back upon the Selective Service tests, and in so doing penalizes persons in institutions of lower quality, primarily the segregated Negro schools.

Having said that, there are two other options for modifying the present system that we want to get on the table. One—university military training, and the lottery. One statement describing UMT in some detail was an article written by President Eisenhower for the *Reader's Digest*. We've asked Professor Little to present not General Eisenhower's position on UMT, which you can all read, but rather his understanding of what the UMT approach would be.

Roger Little. We might call this "the Little Eisenhower Plan." I think that President Eisenhower's proposal has the real virtue of attacking the essential problems of the Selective Service System today. These are (1) the declining rate of participation and (2) the failure of the implicit promise of universality in the preamble to the act. There is only one proposal that will actually eliminate those two defects: universal military training. I would also remind you that all of the discussion of the draft and Selective Service that I have heard has been preoccupied with the way in which manpower is procured. I suggest there's another problem and that is the agency demanding manpower and how it uses it, and that we turn our attention now to military organization, military manpower policies, and adapt them to the problem of Selective Service, rather than fussing around with Selective Service in relation to manpower problems.

As I read General Eisenhower's proposal, it has two major objectives. First, to fulfill the implicit claim of universality—this is not in a sense that it's completely universal and that everyone will serve—the existing criteria and selection will continue to be used, and secondly, to enhance participation rates. We've heard a great deal about reducing participation, either by the lottery or by some other system. This neglects the fact that the military institutions have a very pervasive role in our cultural tradition in American society, and increasingly, as participation declines, these symbols of integration, these aspects of our cultural tradition, will deteriorate and ultimately be utterly meaningless.

So, I would suggest two alternatives: First, that we manipulate the term of service to correspond with the number of men available and qualified for service each year. That is, the term of service should be related to the number of potential entrants to military service. Even minor increments in enlarging participation would help the problem of the surplus in the manpower pool today. Reducing the terms of service of all first-term enlistees by 8 months, or by 12 months, would have some effect. Completely eliminating the three-year term of service for regular Army men would mitigate the problem by approximately one-eighth. These contributions would expand the opportunities for service.

The second aspect of the plan would be to adopt new internal military manpower policies. I don't mean such things as spending more money to train poor boys, but rather spending more money to train more men of all kinds, whether they are college-bound youths or high school dropouts, and this can be done. Mr. Waldman alluded this morning to a study of Army basic training. That study was completed in 1956—and for some reason has disappeared in the last decade. It demonstrated something that needs no demonstration to any of us who have gone through basic training: that the 8 weeks of basic combat training can be cut in half and that many trainees will learn just as much in 4 weeks under an intensive training program as they now learn in 8 weeks. This will make a major contribution. Other possibilities would be to give added credit for combat tours, thus reducing the overall terms of service for hardship areas. An increasing degree of flexibility in military manpower policy should allow for the fact that time is most important to youth. It's not the amount of money they will get, it's the few moments, a few hours, days, months, or years of their lifespan saved. To the extent that you provide this reward—a shorter term of service for hazardous exposure—it will be more important than a monetary increment.

Finally, the practical values of UMT are these: first, it will enlarge the universe of selection, and consequently minimize the effect of the self-selected enlistees who are relatively inefficient as entrants in military service. A second major value is that performance in the initial term of service will provide a basis for further selection into the career service, a more adequate basis for selection than the AFQT, the aptitude tests, and the various gimmicks that are currently being used.

Mr. Weber. I can't say that your remarks were wholly consistent with the spirit of President Eisenhower's article, but they certainly are provocative. Would anybody like to respond to the various points that have been raised within the framework of the UMT system?

Mr. Bramson. I'd like to know why it is that the only two people I've ever heard go on record in favor of universal military training are General Eisenhower and my friend Roger Little? Why is it that no one in the military establishment, to the best of my knowledge, no one in the Department of Defense, either, has come forward with a plan for universal military training?

Mr. Little. UMT is needed to eliminate the problem of the lack of universality, to emphasize the equity of service to all citizens. It has an entirely different purpose than to build character, or to build up the reserves, as was originally proposed in the immediate post-World War II period. But, I don't think that because the Department of Defense hasn't mentioned this that it makes it invalid. I think that there are many great ideas that do not emanate from the Department of Defense, and many great ideas die because they do emanate from there.

Joseph Leo. Is it true that basic training can be cut in half with the increase in technology that the Armed Forces relies on today, even for the basic infantrymen who must master many of the new weapons that the Defense Department has put out? Does this correspond with Mr. Little's plan for a reduction in serving time in the military?

Colonel Hays. I'm not aware of the paper or the study to which Mr. Little refers. Having spent time trying to train basic infantrymen and others, I have serious doubts whether the effectiveness of training in a shorter period of time would be as adequate. There may be a possibility of devising some kind of test which one might try, and I've tried to devise various kinds of tests to determine progress in basic training. I'm afraid, in answer to your question, that my own personal opinion would be no.

Mr. Little. I say there are two reasons why this can be accomplished, very fundamental reasons. First, recruits today are smarter than they were 20 years ago, when I first came in. They know more about technology—much more —and consequently basic training can start at a much higher level than it did in 1940–45. Second, is that they don't have to learn *more* technology—they learn *different* technology. The old weapons are gone and, really, the old weapons are not remarkably different from the new ones in many cases, so that there is not that much difficulty in shortening this term.

[*Unidentified Speaker*]. I question the overall quality of the inductee who would come into the Armed Forces under the UMT program, in that the UMT program would seemingly become unnecessary and perhaps an unwanted program because service in the Armed Forces would then be an obligation, and it would be looked upon as something that would be completely unacceptable and promote more conscientious objectors or be completely subject to the military service.

Mr. Little. I doubt very much if it would *become* completely unacceptable because to a large portion of youths today it is already unacceptable. This would not make much of a change. The positive point is that it would establish a youth's civic responsibility to defend his country. This sounds like a Fourth of July oration, perhaps, but it's something that is gradually being lost sight of in terms of military service.

[*Unidentified Speaker*]. Well, I just wanted to say that right now it seems as though defense of the country, to the youth—maybe they're less patriotic, but the fact that they'd have to serve in the Armed Forces would make them even less patriotic, because it would be an undemocratic kind of thing and it would be perhaps against the principles that they are taught in high school and grammar school; it would be more of a compulsory, dictatorial thing.

Mr. Little. Do you mean the internal characteristics of military organization itself, rather than the method of selection?

[*Unidentified Speaker*]. No, the method of selection.

Mr. Little. What could be more democratic than that everybody serve?

Mr. Lauter. I want to make a very furious objection to Mr. Little's remarks to the effect that defense of one's country is equivalent to serving in the Armed Forces. I mean, this seems to me to be very narrow, both in what one understands about defense and in terms of the way in which one serves and what one serves—people, humanity, society—what society? One's country? You know, these are not all identical, and it seems to me that this kind of equation is right at the root of the problem with that sort of proposal which identifies service with military service. And the other point that is very strictly in error, I think, is the evidence that you use to suggest that trainees can go through basic training faster because they're more clever, and that they have had a higher degree of training beforehand, and what one might call a greater sophistication of a certain sort. It seems to me that one of the fundamental problems of basic training is to get people into a command and control structure and that basically they don't ask questions which a more sophisticated young man might be more liable to ask, and that *that* is the sort of thing that takes place only over a course of time. Those of us who've been looking into problems of what we call brainwashing know that you don't do it overnight. What you do is not a matter of training people to their weapons but a matter of getting them to accept certain kinds of control structure and to fit into those patterns and, you know, that goes on and on. That again relates to the basic objection to this universal military training procedure. Do we, in fact, want young men—all of the young men in this country—to be subjected to that kind of training uniformly and to that kind of concept of what constitutes service uniformly? I dare say we don't.

Mr. Little. I have the feeling that you're advocating a very familiar argument—that participation in military organization has certain persisting adverse effects. May I remind you that the public opinion polls have consistently demonstrated that the veterans who have escaped this bondage think that their sons should have military service, think that it does have some value. What benevolent bastards we are to endow our sons with this bondage if it is really that adverse. It doesn't have that persisting effect.

Mr. Eberly. Is there somebody who is keeping track of the main principles that are put forward? It may well be that there is more of a consensus on the various principles than on certain elements of the particular proposals.

Mr. Weber. You have to keep in mind that we really have, you know, two frameworks. One is an agenda and the other is Mr. Hazard's statement, or articulation of principles. Then we have Mr. Lauter's revision of the agenda. It's my understanding that there are two broad approaches to dealing with the problem. One is that we've got a system, and we must call forth the Thomas Edisons or Rube Goldbergs as the case might be and attempt to determine how we might change the shape of the camshaft and provide for better carburetion so that it runs better, given the situation of a non-voluntary system of military conscription. We've talked about four or five alternative proposals which accept this framework and UMT is one of them. Then, beginning tomorrow, we'll talk about other broader alternatives.

Dr. Margaret Mead. We've had several statements here today; one is that being in the Armed Forces for even a short period of time produces all sorts of evil effects. People become authoritarians, they're gradually brainwashed, they become the sort of people we don't want. Now, as someone who has taught students from 1928 to the present, and therefore had an opportunity to teach a group of students who had very little contact with the armed services, and then had the opportunity of teaching the immediately post-World War II group, I saw no signs of this brainwashing. I saw no signs of this acceptance of authority, of having been molded into some kind of a military docility. My general experience has been that young people who have been in the Army for a brief time all come out disliking authority on the whole, very often disliking order. And all the things that people are fearing don't happen. If you have a small professional Army, or an Army that's restricted to particular classes or parts of the country, over several generations they may develop a style of mind that's extraordinarily different from the rest of the population. I think that's true but one of the ways of insuring that the Army is just like the rest of the population and just as unaccepting of most kinds of order, is to have a rapid turnover. I'm not supporting Mr. Little's suggestion, but I think this assumption ought to be very well examined. If anybody has any proof whatsoever that being in the Army for two years against your will produces this unfortunate docility, I'd love to hear it.

[*Unidentified Speaker*]. I had a question on Dr. Little's point about democracy; you're saying that many of the students don't want to serve in the Army and that's the whole reason that they protest against the draft. And yet you say that universal military training is good, that all men should go into the Army, and that means that you're making a choice, that these people don't have the choice of making a decision on their own, that you've made the decision for them. I think that if you do this then you take away the whole democratic process which you're talking about in the first place.

Mr. Little. Did I make any comment about student protest?

[*Unidentified Speaker*]. Well, it was brought up that many young people might not want to serve in the Army. I mean, I think you said that.

Mr. Little. I think that what you're suggesting is that compulsion is still inherent in the system. Is this right?

[*Unidentified Speaker*]. Yes.

Mr. Little. I'm merely contending that the variations in the pool to which compulsion is now applied are inequitable. I'm not suggesting we eliminate compulsion in this respect at all. I think it's essential in procuring military manpower under present conditions, that we have compulsion.

[*Unidentified Speaker*]. I'd like to throw another comment in the hopper which might be helpful in our analysis of the whole question of the draft, especially as regards the black man in this country—the fact of what the system does to a Negro who lives here. It castrates him. It takes away a man's power, a feeling of manhood—inability to feed your family—in the South, especially. I'm sure you're acquainted with our society—how white it is—how anti-black it is. And how can we expect a Negro to be willing to serve in the Army and kill somebody for this country when he is treated like a dog in this country? I think we ought to think about that when we are analyzing the whole process.

Mr. Weber. Roger Little has raised UMT as an option, and one of the specific arguments he indicated is that it would reinforce certain democratic or egalitarian or at least equitable notions. There's been the counter-argument that it will make Prussians out of all of us, and Margaret Mead has indicated that available empirical evidence doesn't sustain that view.

Dr. Mead. I said there was no evidence to support what is being said on the other side. . . .

Mr. Weber. Now, the additional point which has been raised by the system of UMT, or one like UMT, is especially difficult to defend, where there are gross inequities associated with particular segments in the population at large. And this, in a sense, would not make these inequities better but worse, by forcing these segments to serve a society that is hostile to them and, in your term, suppresses them.

Mr. Arnold Anderson. Miss Mead's comments suggest, and so does much of the rest of the discussion, the desirability of distinguishing and dealing separately with the effects of military service or any other program, national service, etc., on individuals, and so the effects on what we may call the institutional structure, as discussed, for example, very ably in Mr. Flacks' paper. If we keep crossing over between these, we are, I think, going to muddy the situation, to put it mildly.

Mr. Winter. I'm sorry that Mr. Little left; his general point about universal military training is an inadequate one—it goes on the assumption that because there are inequities in imposing compulsion on a few, it becomes more just to impose it on everyone. And it seems to me that it's a contradiction— I find it hard to take it very seriously.

Dr. Mead. I'm sorry, too, that Mr. Little has left, but he did raise two issues. One was the sharing of responsibility. If something is an unpleasant duty, everybody ought to be made to do it, and if everybody's made to do it, then all suffer alike, all run the same hazards, and we've found over and over again, in studies of disaster, for instance, that if a whole community is subjected to a disaster they bear it with psychological fortitude and think it's part of life. In both the United States and Great Britain, the minute you begin to discriminate among people, select some and not others, give some people's children shoes and others not, the cry of inequity is raised. When the equity problem is presented in line with an unpopular idea—which UMT is—then everybody more or less stops thinking, in one way or another. And Mr. Little, as I understand it, was suggesting two things: one, that it would solve the equity problem if we were going to continue to conscript; and, two, that it would be done by various forms of efficiency, all of which were very much in question.

Mr. Weber. What you are really talking about is universally applying the principle rather than endorsing UMT as a universal. . . .

Dr. Mead. Yes, but because a lot of people here don't like *any* military service, they say it wouldn't be equitable to give it to more people, which is again illogical, you see.

[Unidentified Speaker]. I'd like to raise a question here. Beyond simply the unpleasant duties, the facts of war in recent generations have raised serious ethical and moral problems for people, and Dr. Mead has suggested this, you know, in one way. The question I think is this: What would the pressure of universal military training do for those people who choose to take the witness, if you will, against any form of military service at all? We already see that there's a pressure, particularly as the war escalates, on those persons who for one reason or another are called, at one time, conscientious objectors and another time "draft dodgers." Now, what pressures would be present if we take a more intense stand and say that we want universal military training? I'd be interested in hearing this.

[Unidentified Speaker]. I think, Dr. Mead, that one point is that we are all facing disaster, and we're all living under the threat of destruction, and the question is—how do we move to a situation in which that can be eliminated? The question is whether a program such as universal military training would not contribute further to hastening that total disaster. The second point is whether it would not be, in fact, an admission of something that Dr. Boulding suggests in his paper, that is that the nation state as we know it is in decline and the institution of something like universal military training would be a confirmation of the fact that the society cannot command loyalty, it can only compel duty.

[Unidentified Speaker]. It seems to me directly relevant at the moment that perhaps we are in general agreement that the national interest transcends the military needs of the nation. I think that one of the problems that we're confronted with here when we talk about universal military training, is compulsion. I suggest therefore, the possibility that this will tie into our discussion of national service, in which we might consider military service to be just one aspect of

national service. I would almost like to make it a motion that it become a recommendation of this Conference that the President, upon the termination of the present National Advisory Commission, appoint a national advisory commission on national service with any questions of selective service to be included under that heading, which will give it a broader societal framework.

Mr. Weber. I think that approach could best be considered tomorrow, within the framework of the general concepts of national service. We have now one more alternative to lay on the table. This is the lottery. The lottery, at least at this assembly, is being proposed and supported by Senator Edward M. Kennedy of Massachusetts, who, I understand, will come tomorrow. However, we have from him a brief statement on the lottery and how it would work, which he read over the telephone.

Senator Edward M. Kennedy. In an age-class lottery system, all men reaching the age of 18 would be examined by their local draft board. Those found physically and mentally qualified, and *only* those, would be assigned a number by their local board. After these numbers were assigned, the Selective Service System would conduct a national drawing. It would put into a fishbowl as many numbers as the largest local draft board had registered, then draw out each number and make a record of the order in which it appeared. Each local draft board would receive a copy of this list. The men whose numbers were selected first and were therefore higher on the list would be called first by their local board.

Let us assume that the first number chosen in the drawing was 508. Every eligible draftee in every local board who held the number 508 would know that he would be called up first in the next draft call. Every eligible draftee who held the number near the bottom of the list would know that he would be drafted only in the event of a national emergency. Each number would, of course, represent a different quota of men; 508 would be held by fewer men than 35, because fewer local boards have 508 men. Before issuing the draft call, the Selective Service would decide how many men were needed, then compute how many numbers would have to be called to supply that many men. Registrants whose numbers were not reached during the year of their draw would go to the bottom of the next year's list. They would remain eligible for the draft but it is not likely that they would be called unless military manpower requirements increased enormously. They would merely be in a better position to plan their future. Thus, all physically and mentally qualified men would stand an equal chance of selection at the time the lottery was held for their age-class, presumably during their 19th year. No deferments would be made for marriage, fatherhood, dependents or occupation, except in cases of extreme hardship. Retention of the deferment of extreme hardship would enable local boards to decide pressing hardship cases on the merits of a particular case, thereby retaining flexibility and compassion in the system. Educational deferments might be granted for a limited period of time of up to four years, but they would be in reality merely postponements. Those students who wish to finish college before participating in the lottery would have to take their chances when they completed college, with the 19-year-old age group in that year's lottery. There would be no deferments for graduate school and it would no longer be possible to compound a deferment in order to reach the age of 26 and, in practical effect, escape the draft altogether. Continuation of the doctor's draft would be the only exception to the rule. The problem of physicians has been handled as a special case under our draft laws for many years, and I see no reason for not continuing to so treat it. Those graduating from college who go on to medical schools would not go into the lottery. They would be called, if at all, after completion of their studies under a special doctor's draft. Under this system the average age of induction would remain about 20, which, as I understand it, is desirable both from the viewpoint of the Armed Forces and from that of those eligible for the draft.

Mr. Marmion. I think it's fair that in any discussion of the lottery, the proposal by Congressman Reuss of Wisconsin receive some mention. His system is basically the same as Senator Kennedy's, except that it is a complete program for Armed Forces recruitment in the nation. On the one hand, for example, he would call for increased benefits for servicemen, to increase enlistments and then spur reenlistments, reduction in the number of military, replacement with civilian jobs, and so forth. Once all the possible reductions had been achieved, and the enlistments had been increased, he would then abolish the present Selective Service System and revert to a lottery. Reuss would abandon all student deferments. He explains that this would not determine whether a man goes to college or not, it would simply determine at what point he goes. The basic distinction then, between Kennedy and the Reuss proposal is that Reuss abolishes deferment, Kennedy is sympathetic to deferments on a limited basis, as long as at the end of college the student take his chances in the lottery for that particular year. Basically, the distinction between the two concerns deferment.

Mr. Weber. The question of educational deferment?

Mr. Wool. I think it would be helpful to distinguish between two notions of what has been termed the lottery. One notion, which the word *lottery* itself conveys, is a lack of rational judgment, a system where there are practically no deferments or no distinctions among individuals in any way. This is a very extreme position because people normally recognize that at a minimum you have to discard those from the lottery who are physically unfit or perhaps mentally unqualified. Much of the image of a lottery has been in that context. There is a much more limited way in which a random method of selection could be used to supplement any degree of deferment policy which is considered desirable and necessary. At present, after the Selective Service System completes its classifications of registrants and determines who is deferrable and who is exempt, they then have the problem of those who are in Class 1A. That sequence, except for the delinquents and the volunteers for induction, is essentially an age sequence, where the oldest men in the age group 19 to 25 are selected first. As our historical requirements declined following Korea and as the population of eligibles grew, two things happened. It was possible to liberalize deferment policies, in fact to some extent this may have influenced the decision to liberalize them. Yet in spite of that, the draft age did grow from about 21½ years in 1954 to nearly 24 years in 1963. A further measure was then taken which was simply to place all married men in a lower order of call by sheer possession of a marriage license without any critical review of hardship, as such. This was the only device which had the effect of substantially reversing the trend toward an older age of induction. The mere fact that young men typically marry at age 21, and that by age 24 or 25 something like 70 per cent are married, means that you sharply narrow the prime vulnerable pool by this device. This is what has happened.

Looking into the future, we see a possibility, assuming that we have future military strength levels following the present situation similar to those of the recent past, of needing an average of about 600,000 to 700,000 men per year for voluntary service, in relation to an age class of about 2 million men per year as we move into the early 1970's. Now, the choice would be to continue the existing system, but unless we find drastically new ways to liberalize deferments even beyond "deferring" married men, this age would creep up. The procedure of simply placing married men in a lower order of call is one which we did not find desirable, either from the standpoint of its social impact or from the standpoint of what I personally believe is considered equitable, as long as there is no hardship associated with a married man's situation. It clearly stimulated early marriage among those age groups most vulnerable to the draft when it was in effect, and our data prove this.

Now, this produces a dilemma with some alternatives. We go beyond the point of rationality and public acceptability in finding ways to select people out, we permit the draft age to go up under these conditions, or we must face some other alternative to establish an order, or sequence, of call if we want to maintain the draft at a relatively stable age. At least some of the staff people working on the defense study could think of no other logical, impartial sequence, other than a random one, after having exhausted the acceptable reasonable selection policies based upon deferment. We thought we couldn't, for example, keep on raising our rejection rates to 50 per cent or 60 per cent in order to whittle away this population. We thought that would be unreasonable and not acceptable, just as a marriage policy would be. And this, in effect, would not be a "lottery," in the sense of a grab-bag, but what you do in establishing a sequence of calls after applying rational deferment policies—whatever they may be. For that purpose we felt that some random selection, without going into the mechanics of it, deserved the most careful consideration.

Let me explain the dynamics of how the past system has worked. There are two key facts. As the age of vulnerability—the age of induction—has gone up, it was possible for many individuals to obtain a deferred status in several ways. The college student, after the completion of college, had time to establish an alternative form of deferment, typically through marriage, fatherhood, or occupational deferment. The system worked to select individuals out from vulnerability simply because of the demographic facts of life. At a younger age, such as 19 or 20, you have a more representative cross-section of young men, among whom there is no rational basis for selection other than by simply giving them individual ways to select themselves out, or channel themselves out, if you will, between that age and age 26.

[*Unidentified Speaker*]. I take it that the lottery and random system that you are talking about within the limited frame become the same thing, don't they? What do you mean by a random system? You don't mean the random opinions of a draft board.

Mr. Wool. I'm trying to get away from the concept of a lottery which means lack of selection, lack of rational choice, because this would apply only after application of any reasonable classification procedures. Unfortunately, an image has been conveyed that the two are totally incompatible, but when one finishes rational choice one is still left with the dilemma of choosing among those people equally available for service.

[*Unidentified Speaker*]. I've read that concept in Selective Service literature, but aside from that, would you propose a national random process or a system that would be carried out by each local board, or state?

Mr. Wool. I think that you're getting into the mechanics of this and at that point the objective would be to assure that the system would work nationally in an equitable way. In other words, I think there would have to be some national sequencing of numbers rather than an internal one within a local board, but obviously it would be totally compatible with a continued operation of the local board system.

[*Unidentified Speaker*]. You're *very* close to Senator Kennedy's proposal, then, aren't you?

Mr. Wool. The main questions would be the important details as to what deferment policies would be considered which we haven't any recommendation on.

Mr. Beal. I'd like to ask Mr. Wool how under either his system or Senator Kennedy's system, or both, the Armed Forces would be assured of having sufficient officers so the system would work?

Mr. Wool. That gets to the related question of what types of deferments would be allowed for those individuals who are going on to college and particularly those who assume an officer commitment. There'd be nothing at all in any selection sequence of the type I'm mentioning which would not permit, as would Senator Kennedy's proposal, a continuation of certain types of student deferment, particularly if there is a specific commitment to enter an officer commissioning program at the end of the period of education, so that this does not in any way imply that everybody goes in at age 19.

[*Unidentified Speaker*]. One of Senator Kennedy's remarks suggests a problem which we should keep in mind as we go on in this discussion. He mentions that in the lottery proposal it is not likely that people would be called unless military manpower requirements increase enormously. This suggests that almost all of the alternative proposals that we're beginning to consider have in mind a certain type of emergency situation. Many of the comments made earlier referred to the sense of obligation, civic obligation, etc., which again assumed a certain defined situation. It is important whether we consider the lottery or other alternatives more and more removed from the present system, that we do not feel we need to keep in mind a *single* alternative system which is suitable for all possible conditions. We should keep in mind that it is possible to design different systems which have different advantages and disadvantages in relation to certain situations. This would in a sense lead to a clearing up of present ambiguities in the system, which stem not only from the nature of the Selective Service System but also from the lack of political clarification as to what is the nature of the emergency for which the system is being used. A citizen's obligation can only be invoked if political leadership has taken responsibility to define the national interest. Under the present system this is simply not done.

Mr. Biderman. The alternative to the solution of the problem which comes from the presumed insufficiency of volunteers and the presumed superfluity of eligibles for compulsory service can also be solved by elevating the standards for induction. It would seem to me that in relation to most ethical considerations, as well as rational and functional deferments, this would be much the preferable course. When the country faces a situation where it feels that it should compel people to surrender, to use Mr. Lasswell's terms "income, deference, and safety" in the national interest, then the situation presumably is one of great social importance and the society at large is not entitled to take a very casual attitude toward it. The demand on certain people does put an ethical burden on all the rest of them. The solution of elevating standards then allocates these risks and sacrifices in accordance with criteria derived from the nature of the need and the best way to meet the need—the old "Uncle Sam needs YOU!" kind of rationale. I think this has very important implications for the morale of the persons selected for military service.

Mr. Bakan. I would like to comment on the side comment by Mr. Wool and also refer back to an issue which was raised by Mr. Ingold this morning. I want to raise the question of the so-called draft delinquent. As I understand it, the Selective Service law has a section in which it says that anyone who violates the Selective Service Act shall be brought to trial and face a possible five year imprisonment and a $10,000 fine. Associated with the latter, of course, is due process. But over and above this, the Selective Service regulations also indicate that the Selective Service Board should, when it is filling its call, take draft delinquents first—I'm quoting General Hershey on this. This, it seems to me, is really beyond due process, in that there is no way by which an individual can make his case when there is no trial. It is exclusively up to the draft board to decide whether he is or is not a draft delinquent. Worst of all, the draft is taken as a punishment. I notice, rather interestingly, that Mr. Wool uses the term "vulnerable" in connection with being drafted. Perhaps that really speaks to a truth which we all need to recognize, in spite of the noble comments which were made about drafting in the first place, i.e., that somehow it is not an injury to be drafted.

Mr. Weber. Let me try to put this into the framework of the discussion. We're talking about the option of a lottery and there are really two levels at which the discussion has proceeded. The first is a philosophical level associated with—"Is this the right way to do it, given our goals in this area?" The second concerns the mechanics of the lottery, in a sense saying it's the old system cleaned up, and you indicated that there's a priority of call that's established, this is a device. Mr. Bakan is asking whether draft delinquency is viewed as a criterion in determining priority of call in your statement of how a lottery would work.

Mr. Wool. I would think he is *describing* the existing Selective Service regulations. If more information is needed about the meaning of the term "delinquency" I think Colonel Ingold could clarify that.

Colonel Ingold. The regulations provide that delinquents are at the top, volunteers come next. I do not know the historical background for that specific sequence so, unfortunately, I can't answer.

Mr. Friedman. I want to get the discussion back along the line that Mr. Wool was suggesting, and try to see if we can see the issue more clearly about the lottery. What Mr. Wool emphasized is that arithmetic dictates that so long as we have compulsory conscription we must use chance to select. The only open option is the form the chance takes. The specification that all those who get married before a certain date are eliminated is a form of chance. We have the basic fact that we have too large a pool: we're only going to use a third of them. Therefore, some mechanism or other has to decide which man goes and which two or three do not. The crucial question, therefore, is, do you want to use open chance or do you want to conceal the operation of chance, in various ways, through various devices? And the answer to that is not as obvious as it might seem. My first impression was to think that if you're going to use chance you ought to use open chance. Walter Oi in a letter made a comment that persuaded me that that wasn't nearly so clear as I first thought it was, because one of the major effects of using open chance is that you reduce the indirect pressure on people to volunteer, and therefore you end up drafting, or inducting, through conscription channels, a larger fraction of your Armed Forces than you now do. That has both advantages and disadvantages, but it really raises some very important issues.

If, like myself, you believe that the optimum structure of the Armed Forces is that which would be obtained by voluntary means alone, then it turns out that concealed chance gives you a closer approximation to that structure of the Armed Forces than open chance does. By open chance, people know immediately that they are largely relieved from having to be conscripted and therefore they have no inducement to volunteer. The argument people would make for concealed chance is that you make everybody uncertain and therefore some people go ahead and volunteer and those people are induced to volunteer for whom it is the least costly. This is the argument. I am trying to clarify the issue and see that we discuss what I think is the real issue between the open and the concealed lottery.

Colonel Hays. I would like to add one other thought that has bothered me about the lottery, and that has to do with its effect on the motivation to serve. I've gone over many questionnaires over the years on the matter of what makes a man want to join the service or stay in once he's there. Although there may be some who know the answer, I'm not included among them. It is a delicate matter and one, I'm sure, that draft policy can very substantially affect. I would suggest that one of the factors that causes men to volunteer is the perception that it is a popular thing to do, that it is an "in" thing to do, that other people of their particular kind of group are there. Hence, to the extent that we could follow Dr. Biderman's suggestion by increasing the caliber or quality of personnel selected for service, you would induce additional volunteers and thus reduce the requirements for drafting. To the extent that one makes it a matter of chance, I suspect one is likely to reduce the motivation to volunteer. This reduction of motivation would snowball and we would end up having much less motivation in our armed services among those already serving.

Mr. Weber. In a sense these comments here are really directed at the consequences of the lottery, given some objective of developing an Armed Forces primarily through voluntary means. Milton Friedman and Colonel Hays have identified what we might call a "lottery backlash," in the sense that by making for open chance you would reduce the incentives or motives for people to voluntarily enlist. This would then be not a philosophical objection but really a technical objection. Assuming certain philosophical rules, it just wouldn't work in the sense that you'd want it to work. This would presumably cancel out some of the other advantages, for example, equity and fairness.

Mr. Keast. I think it's a most interesting and difficult problem, especially since I agree with you that we ought to have a largely volunteer force. First, do you think you could qualify the extent to which this effect would occur? Second, could the volunteers who would be eliminated be replaced by other volunteers whose presumptive grounds for volunteering would not have been merely to get something done now that they knew they were going to have to do anyway? These are not, in my judgment, the best grounds for volunteering or the highest kind of motivation. Could we supply some new and better methods of voluntary recruitment than we are now talking about? In other words, are the effects you describe with respect to lottery paralyzing only if one assumes that you're not going to change any other part of the system?

Mr. Friedman. But they're independent. Change the other part of the system as you should, and you'll still have the effect of the lottery we have been discussing. Now on the quantitative matter, either Walter Oi or Harold Wool can speak much more knowledgeably than I can about the quantitative magnitude of this effect because they've worked on it.

Walter Y. Oi. Well, on the quantitative magnitude of the effect, it's a tricky problem and I don't think we've really come to any decision. My opinion is, that the lottery will reduce voluntary enlistments if we don't change pay or anything else, for the simple reason that we'd lose a large fraction of the reluctant volunteers. I couldn't say how much of a drop this would be. My hunch would be in the neighborhood of about a 20 to 35 per cent drop in voluntary enlistment, but I just don't know. There's one comment I would like to make. If you're going to have a lottery, why not do it in the cheapest way? Physical and mental rejections are highly predictable. Simply utilize the order of birthdays—everyone born on May 8, January 15, etc.—and don't examine the entire population. Then draft boards don't have to worry about registering people, all birth dates are on record, somewhere.

Mr. Weber. I don't understand how that would work.

Mr. Oi. You just draw out dates from a bowl and list them, and that's the order in which they're going to be called, people born on May 8th go first, December 25, second, and so on every year. It's a sensible system—the Australians are doing it.

Bill Mauldin. There was some conversation a minute ago about whether military service was an injury or not. Unless people are actually hurt in it, I don't think it really is so much of an injury. There's no doubt that it is an inconvenience, though, which is why they have to have drafts. Now, as far as a lottery is concerned, my feeling against the lottery really is based more on morale than anything else. I rather hate to think of an Army that's largely made up of men who consider themselves losers in a monumental crap game, you know. I would think that as far as their morale is concerned, they could go one step further and say, "Well, I've lost the first pass, who's to say I'm not going to lose the second one?"

Mr. Weber. Then we would add this sort of objection on the basis of technical feasibility: first, the reduction of voluntary enlistments; and, second, the effect on morale of those who in fact were selected using this chance procedure.

Harris Wofford. But it doesn't seem to me that the issue is whether it's a birthday lottery, or number lottery, or a lottery. It's really the reverse of the order of call that invites the backlash you're talking about. If I follow this, it's the fact that the uncertainty that now hangs over people's lives for six, seven, eight years would be ended by being called while you're 18 or 19, or immediately after you come out of college. I think the uncertainty ought to be carefully weighed. If I sense any major damage in the present system, it comes from this frontlash of uncertainty that keeps people from being able to go on with their lives, including Peace Corps, job or marriage, or anything else. I would go further, therefore, and say that to really remedy this, you need to make the selection time the last term in high school, so that they know before the middle of summer whether they can start college or not. If we do have student deferments, it ought to come in the last term in college—no graduate deferments but college deferments, so again they could know what to do at that point. If you took that step, I think you would lift a great shadow from many people's lives.

Colonel Ingold. One of our primary objectives in Selective Service is to get as many people as possible into the Armed Forces through a volunteer or a quasi-volunteer method. This may sound peculiar to you, but this is so. We try to diminish in every respect possible all degrees of compulsion and the number of people to whom it applies. Now, there's a simpler way of getting at this thing if you wish to, and that is to reduce the age from 26 where we call them now to, say, 24, 23, 22, 20. But it's still going to be a question of escape. The term *escape* ought to be defined a little bit. It's got to do with the size of the Armed Forces. The only reason people escape from the draft is because there isn't room in the Armed Forces for them. If anyone is going to escape it would be much better to escape on grounds of judgment than on the basis of lottery. Now, the next charge will be that lottery, as distinguished from deferment, produces escape. We do allow for uncertainty, there's no question about that, and we acknowledge that it has a specific purpose—uncertainty produces volunteers.

Dr. Mead. In considering the point that Dr. Janowitz made in his paper, which was the same point that Colonel Hays mentions, the effect on morale of being a loser, does put into any kind of service the element of chance which results in either this loss of morale, which is bad from the point of view of the military, or a generally corrupt, gambling, "fix-it" position. Now, all Americans, or almost all Americans, think that almost anything that is slightly wicked will also be fixed—prize fighting, horse racing, all forms of gambling are going to be fixed—and to use the lottery element, therefore has certain dangers. It seems to me, however, that what Mr. Wool was saying was that if this group were tested—selected, chosen—as those who would be suitable members of the Armed Forces, and the lottery was moved further along in the system of choice, but also providing against uncertainty, possibly this should be weighed against these other arguments. I don't agree with Dr. Friedman about this concealed chance business. It isn't a concealed chance that you're going to get married—it's open, and plotted.

Mr. Kelly. We've talked about national manpower policy in terms of national interest, in terms of military manpower needs, and in all sorts of terms except those of the individual. It's about time the individual got dragged into this conference. I find it very difficult to discuss many of the issues with which we're having some philosophical difficulty because my question is what policy maximizes the freedom of choice for the individual. In a democratic society, that must be one of our considerations. And no one, to this moment, has utilized that terminology. With respect to Mr. Mauldin's point, those of us who were drafted in the post-World War II period all considered ourselves losers. We knew everyone didn't get drafted. My next-door neighbor didn't get drafted—I did. I have been very disturbed by the whole philosophy of the Selective Service System, particularly as it has been expressed to us today. I find it highly undemocratic. I find it highly alien to the kind of society in which I believe to create uncertainty for eight years in a man's life in order to induce him to volunteer. Then to hear this statement made public shocks me—just simply shocks me. I hope that perhaps in the next few minutes someone will talk about some of these issues in terms of what individuals want to do with their lives, and how we can organize our military manpower selection system in such a way as to minimize the impact on the individual while serving the "national interest." Although I don't know what "national interest" means, I do know the Defense Department has manpower problems, and our system has to solve their problems. That's our big constraint.

Mr. Weber. I think your remarks serve as an appropriate introduction to the next part of this discussion session. Now we're confronted with the task of bringing together all these proposals as they relate to each other. What we should do now, I feel, is to turn our attention to this "general equilibrium" problem. I suppose there are alternative ways of formulating the questions. I suppose these would be—assuming that we continue to adhere to some form of non-voluntary conscription—what modifications should be made and what should be the mix? How do the various proposals relate to each other in a consistent and efficient, and perhaps even a compassionate way? I suppose some of you might say, following this discussion, that this merely verifies the need for a complete overhaul of the system. Some of the other alternatives will be presented to you and discussed tomorrow. So, I would put to you in those general terms: Given that we will have some system and assuming that it will be a system providing for involuntary conscription, which of these five proposals that we've talked about—deferment practices, conscientious objection, change in the duration of liability for service, UMT, and the lottery—should be incorporated, and in what way?

Robert Bird. I'd like to question the assumption with which you opened this session that there must continue to be conscription. It staggers the imagination to contemplate what would happen if conscription were abolished June 30. It's not just a matter of doing without; there would be all kinds of alternatives. For instance, abolishing conscription would immediately decrease the military stance of this country. It would permit national service without having to deal with this nasty question of compulsion. National service could really develop, and all the other programs such as OEO and Peace Corps would open up. Tension would decrease throughout the world because the nation with the greatest military power was taking steps toward demobilizing. It would force the President and the Department of Defense to think in terms of other than military solutions to world tension. It would eliminate all the dissatisfaction that is an undercurrent at this conference.

What would the Department of Defense do under such circumstances? I don't know. But I haven't noticed that they lack either flexibility or resourcefulness, and I think they could deal with this problem.

Mr. Weber. I was suggesting we somehow try to draw on the preceding analysis. In a sense you are feeding into this discussion variables of a different substantive nature and magnitude. I think certainly you may do that, and I would interpret it to mean that for other statements for the national interest, as

Mr. Marmion indicated, you would junk the entire system and not accept my assumption. That might be picked up by other participants but it should be clear that this is my understanding of the frame of this discussion, and we would move on from there.

Mrs. McAllister. During World War II, I had a friend who came to lunch one day with a very sad look. He had seen the new list of national priorities and he was very low—just below the artificial flower makers—he was a bond salesman. We still have this kind of problem as to what is the national interest. Since World War II I've been seeing enough of what goes on in Congress and in colleges that I'd like us to have a first priority for the national interest. Those who should be deferred first would be teams of persons qualified to consult on values—to consider what is important, what is American, where we are going and how we want to get there. I think that, unfortunately, there has not been much of that kind of deferment in the draft. Rather, deferment has gone to those who had expertise in computer systems. I'd like us to turn about, have a look at what would happen if the first kind of deferments were for those who care about what happens, and have qualified themselves in scholarship.

Mr. Arnold Anderson. One thing we need badly is some information on the profile of deferment. We have practically no information; we don't know whether it is equitable considering whatever criteria you want to apply. We know nothing about it. This is again a deficiency in the information that the nation should be getting from Selective Service. On the other hand, I would agree with what Mr. Hazard said last night, that, except for short-run and certain very specific occupations in the present and anticipated level of military induction, there are no essential occupations, in the sense in which that word has been used, that is, none that are more essential than others. We are trapped if we try to deal with this issue substantively in other terms than we have. We badly need information.

Mr. Marmion. As a part of the national service that you mention, I'm merely saying that to have over 4,000 local boards determine what is the national interest is incorrect and not valid. I would agree with Mr. Anderson that we don't have a profile. You'd have to take 4,051 profiles to find out the deferment situation in each local draft board.

Mr. Rosenberg. I agree that we need to be concerned with the national interest. I'm rather surprised though that in these deliberations no one has yet mentioned the international interest or perhaps the human or humane interest. It surprises me too that in a body composed of social science scholars, as well as others, we've had very little recognition up to this point of the fact that military policy, though it may be developed to serve prior aspects of national policy, will, in turn, have quite considerable effect upon the structure of our society and upon the further alteration or stabilization of foreign policy. What is implicit in our deliberations is the question of whether our current foreign policy is, in fact, a defensible one and whether stabilization of our military establishment at the level of 2.5 to 3.5 million may not in some way freeze our overall foreign policy or at least reduce possibilities for corrective alteration of that policy. I would suggest that though we've skirted this again and again it will become necessary for this body to address itself to the question of the effect upon American foreign policy and upon prospects for international conciliation of the kinds of military recruitment and national service policies that are here being examined.

George H. Watson. I want to take issue with Mr. Marmion on the question of student deferment and make two points. First, that it seems to me the delay is the only real problem here and that for a great many students, in my experience, this is not a serious problem. An interruption in college career is not likely to be disastrous for most. In the second place, student deferment is extremely difficult to make equitable for a reason that I don't believe has been brought out by anyone yet: the problem of the student who has to support himself, at least partially, while in college. The urban student who is partly self-supporting is coming to be a larger and larger fraction of our student population. I work in an institution with a great many of them. One of their problems is that they have constantly to be discouraged from carrying too heavy a combination of work and courses. The effect of the Selective Service deferment system is to force them to carry too heavy a load, with consequences that are often quite disastrous. I don't really see any practical way of "jiggering" the system so that it will not have this effect, so it seems to me the best solution to this problem as well as to others, is to abandon it.

Mr. Pemberton. Mr. Chairman, we've paid a great deal of lip service to voluntarism during today's discussion, but I think I've got an issue in the deferment problem that tests the lip service. We've heard even the Selective Service System state its preference for voluntarism, but it prefers the deferment system so it can channel voluntarism into activities and occupations that it finds to be in the national interest. Now, I suggest that our loyalty to real voluntarism is twofold. First, we define the national interest in terms of what people voluntarily and individually do with their talents and their opportunities and their resources—without "channeling"; we decide that a John Dewey or a Thomas Edison is important in our society because he decided to do what he did with his life. Second, we favor voluntarism as an end in itself. I don't think the case has been made for the preservation of more than a few occupations from the ravages of the draft. Certainly the case has not been made that a substantial portion of our population would have less formal education if there were no student deferments. Their education might be postponed. I suggest that what we have said about voluntarism has this application to deferment: it should impel us to reject every possible deferment we can reject, and particularly the student deferment.

Eugene Groves. I think the problem of student deferments has been reasonably well handled. It is certainly apparent that there is really no justification which has been presented in any conceivable definition of the national interest for student deferments per se. I think Mr. Marmion's basic justification essentially rests on an occupational consideration. Certain types of students are more vital to the national economy because they are studying, perhaps, physics; correct me if I misunderstand you, Mr. Marmion. I think that the question of occupational deferment—its justification—rests basically on the fact that the present system drafts people at the oldest age first, thus disrupting the economy or disrupting certain vital services of these people. The only answer, it seems to me, is that the draft ought to seek them out at the earlier age, before they are trained and thus considered to be in a vital occupation. I think this gets around most of the problems. I think this is basically what we have to do. We have to start talking about people being subject at an earlier age, before they get into college, with no student deferment, perhaps in a few exceptional cases, but basically no student deferments and no occupational deferments, and taking them at an early age.

Mr. Chapman. I imagine Mr. Marmion would agree that there should be some sort of system by which they would be actually told that they were going to be drafted when they were 18, and allowed to finish their school and then inducted. But what to me seems critical here is that we abolish the Selective Service practice of drafting some students—because we not only have differences in deferments from time to time, but we have differences in place to place. These tests and the ranking are given to local draft boards on advisement and that means that a man with a rank of 120, let us say, out of 200, could be deferred by one board and drafted by another. It just obviously is an inequity.

I think a similar inequity which hasn't been touched on is in the Selective Service test. Now, there are a lot of problems with this test and I would like to hear some people who are in the testing field comment on the usability of tests. I think someone mentioned that there isn't a correlation between future success and success on these tests. I also would like to make the observation that Dr. Banesh Hoffmann, of Queen's College, who is a testing expert, pointed out that the sample test for the college qualification test of the Selective Service itself contained numerous errors of fact and certainly many areas of dubious interpretation. At one point they quote a poem by Housman and at the end of the poem, is the question: "How old was the poet when he wrote this poem?" None of the answers was the age of Housman when he wrote that poem. In another case, they ask a question which requires a particular answer and one was *a kind of gas* and one was just the word *gas*. Now obviously either of these words was correct. If the sample test has that many errors in it, there ought to be some sort of review of the tests that are given.

Mr. Robert Van Waes. I represent the AAUP. I've been disturbed by two things during the conference, as I've listened. One of them is that the members of the defense establishment have been among the most active here and at the conference that was held under the auspices of the American Veterans Committee in Washington, in defending student deferments, while people from the educational community sit like stones, mute on this important issue. Second, I'm a little surprised to see a petition circulating so early in our deliberation that there should be no educational deferment at all. Now, the educational community was one of the strongest groups in originally urging student deferment. I would suspect that there may still be some good reasons for deferment. In addition I would like to add that it seems to me that the educational community in its dread of abuses during the past year may be running the risk of throwing the baby out with the bath. We all recall the abuses connected with the handling of students who were reclassified at the University of Michigan. These produced a very substantial hullaballoo in the world of higher education, and properly so, inasmuch as the view of the educational world was that the local draft boards ought not to get involved in what was essentially a judicial finding and an act against the students that seemed to represent reprisals for demonstrations that they had participated in. There have been a good many comments today which would suggest that there could be improvements in the student deferment program, all of which probably bear very close inspection. I would like to suggest that it might be to our advantage to walk around the quarter of student deferment at least three times before we decide to jettison it so lightly.

Mr. Rumsfeld. I'm not a member of the defense establishment or the academic community and I've been trying to listen very carefully, and as yet I've not heard a good defense of student deferment. Mr. Marmion has taken what sounds like a rather polarized position and certainly did not argue the points which Professor Hazard raised in his opening statement. I would agree that possibly there could be an argument made if we were talking about taking all students. But we're not; we're talking about a small fraction. We're not talking about denying education, but simply postponing it. I would like to hear some good arguments favoring educational deferments.

Mr. Marmion. In the early Fifties when the original deferment plan was evolved, the scientific community wanted deferment to mean exemption and many of them still do. There was a portion of the original Tryten Plan which was not adopted, and it was as follows: After graduation, students would be given four months to secure essential employment. Those who at the end of that period were not eligible for further deferment would then be inducted. There are still people in the scientific community who feel that people in their area do their most productive work before they are 30, or almost immediately after they are out of school. They feel that their fields move so fast that a period of interruption after education is completed leaves them far behind their field when they come back. The only argument really for deferment is what I've tried to articulate, the "national interest." It is a difficult term to define. If there is no national interest, *if* the Selective Service System is scrapped and we go to a lottery, or another form, then there's no reason for deferment. Deferments can only exist under this present Selective Service System, as I see it.

Mr. Rumsfeld. It sounds like you've argued against the position you took a minute ago when you suggested that there would be a deferment and not a complete escape, by saying that it would be harmful to their most productive work if they served in the military immediately after education which is just what you said a minute ago they would be doing.

Mr. Marmion. I'm trying to give you *their* side, and I'm trying to indicate that when the Tryten Plan was originally introduced, the final part of it, which would transform deferment to exemption, was not included. Deferment should not mean exemption, but in fact it probably does because the pool gets larger and these people pick up other deferments by the time they're 26.

Sister Cusack. Going back to the Tryten Plan, the whole psychology or psychosis, whichever you prefer, of people at that time who were under the Sputnik fear, was to bow and scrape to the scientists. I admire scientists immensely and think they are very necessary, but they are not completely essential. In any case, I think we in the educational establishment are not really so irrational as we seem. We've lived through a lot since 1957, and we've seen so many obvious abuses of students and of the word "student" arising from this deferment plan, that because of our dedication to students we object to the plan.

Mr. Arnold Anderson. There's a point which underlies several of the discussions that I believe has not been made. All proposals to even out non-uniformity and remove inequities by imposing more control over local boards or by replacing local boards by a national pool will have the effect of strongly encouraging more centralization of our whole governmental system. I think this is an issue that does have to be faced. People who want compassion, who want flexibility, who want attention to needs, ought to think twice before they kick at the small inequities today and favor a system that would become rigid and would obviously have more inequities concealed behind *seeming* uniformity.

Mr. Weber. Is that a general point or related to the question of occupational deferment?

Mr. Arnold Anderson. It's related to the question of occupational deferment, student deferment, and the various criticisms about social and educational and racial inequality.

Mr. Weber. Are you saying that inequality or inequity is a necessary consequence of localism?

Mr. Arnold Anderson. No, that is the question of fact about which, as I said earlier, we have no information. But if it is true that we get inequities, we might remove them by getting another kind of system which we would like less and which might have more inequities.

Mr. Lauter. I want to take a different tack on the whole question of deferment because it seems to me that one of the ways in which people get at this question is to say that, in effect, current deferment policies produce inequities; therefore, what you have to do is to eliminate certain things like student deferments in order to eliminate that particular kind of inequity. No one would question that student deferments do produce inequities between those people who can afford to go to college and those who can't and between, generally, white middle-class kids and Negro working-class kids. If you are going to retain a system of Selective Service with deferments, I don't think it follows that what you do is throw away such things as the student deferment, but rather you begin to look at the operation of the System itself and to find out whether there are ways of correcting inequities by expanding other sorts of deferments that should be made available to other people who are being injured under the present system. I want to point specifically, for example, to something I would like to have more information about but such information as I do have indicates that it is really an inoperative system. There is a deferment theoretically granted to the young man for hardship, and yet I know that in the ghetto, in the operation of draft boards, that deferment is something that is *very* difficult for the young man to get, although in very many cases there's no question that they deserve it. But the draft board looks at them and says, "Well, you're not married to the woman who is bearing your children, and therefore you go." It seems to me that the case for such things as student deferments can be made. First, you ask not how you can eliminate those causes of inequity, but, rather, how you can provide other opportunities for people to seek deferment. Second, you ask who is to decide about when the student performs his service. The third question is what's the nature of that service: Is it service in the military or some other kind of service, and who's to make that kind of determination?

Finally, let's face it, one of the reasons that certain deferments are retained or are in the form they are is because of certain kinds of political pressures that help to obtain them. For instance, conscientious objector status was, at least in part, a result of political pressure of church groups when the law was written. It seems to me that one of the things that we have to contend with is the reality of where young people are and what that is as a political force. I wonder what would happen, actually, if all such deferments were eliminated and you faced the prospects of that kind of counter-political pressure being developed.

One other thing I want to toss in here is something that Mr. Marmion takes up in his paper, and which relates again to the operation of the board. You raised the question of appeal procedures and Mr. Bakan raised the question of how a determination is made with respect to who's delinquent and who isn't. I would like to raise the question of how a determination is made, what sort of alternative service job is approvable. All of these questions seem to go down to one real basic problem which is that the draft boards themselves are given a large number of tasks to do for which in many respects they are notably unfitted. One of the suggestions was that perhaps we ought to seek other kinds of mechanisms for determining who is deferred, and who isn't, if deferments are to be retained, and other kinds of mechanisms for deciding what form of alternative service fits and what sort doesn't.

Mr. Eberly. In my distant and quick reply to Representative Rumsfeld, I listed three hard cases for student deferment. All of them are linked to future service contracts: One is for the doctor or dentist—they have to be drafted, apparently, so we have to defer them. The second is for future military commitments—presumably, officers require some training, so we defer people at West Point and Colorado. The third would be if we get into some kind of commitment for non-military service. It would be clear that some people can serve better with a background of a college education than without.

[Unidentified Speaker]. I'm also interested in the establishment or the expansion of individual choice. If you argue in defense of a student deferment, you have the choice being made for the student by the Selective Service System, or by those individuals in the government who chose to determine the national interest, instead of placing the burden for the decision to participate in the draft system squarely on the shoulders of the individual and making it his choice of whether or not he can participate in the Armed Forces. I would also like to raise the question of why there has been no consideration of the possibility that many of the jobs being performed by men in the Armed Services now can be performed by women. I don't know whether that is too politically explosive to be considered or not, but if you're going to talk about a Selective Service System that is going to draft people, women should be considered in that system.

Mr. Naisbitt. I think basically the answer to your question is that we have a large pool with a moderate demand, and the numbers just work out conveniently. When deferments were considered we had a standing Army of a couple of million and the number worked out right and the rationalization has followed. Now, with greater demand on the pool, yet quite a bit short of the full pool, we have to suggest other arrangements in order to manage simply the numbers. I suppose that's why we're here, to suggest other ways of simply managing a system that has a pool that is too great for the need.

[Unidentified Speaker]. It seems to me that Mr. Marmion's proposal or idea was actually on the definition of essentiality, and that in turn seems to reflect some definition of national emergency. This concept of national emergency must be redefined to meet what is going on in Harlem, parts of the South Side in Chicago, and Watts. This is as much a national emergency as what's going

on in Vietnam, as what's going on in the plants that develop a supersonic transport plane. Now, we're not going to get any ultimate decision as to what a national emergency is, or complete agreement on the problem of essentialness either. Perhaps the nub of the question is one that Mr. Marmion hinted at, and that is—Who is going to decide? I for one challenge the competence of the Selective Service System to decide what is essential and what is not. I challenge anybody's competence to do this. I think we have two very real, sharp alternatives for us: either to throw the question of what is essential open periodically, to let it go through due legislative, democratic process at given periods of time—two years, four years, it's difficult to say—or eliminate the concept altogether, in this context, and eliminate, therefore, all occupational and educational deferments.

Dr. Mead. I'd like to go a little further on this question of the overall ethical frame that is now being raised. I don't think that we can only talk about the national interest. The major thing that has happened since World War II is that there is no national interest that is not also in the interest of the world. And this is one of the points we're not clear about. As we talk about maximizing individual freedom in this affluent society of ours, and worry about what's happening to particular groups of students here, we must take into account that every decision we make here will inevitably be copied or reacted against all the way around the world. All of these questions have to be put in a worldwide framework today. Any discussion of the national interest which doesn't take that into account tends to have either an archaic or, in a sense, a trivial flavor, not because many of the people here who have been discussing details most intelligently are not conscious of this, but because it isn't built very systematically into what we're saying.

We talk about the need of rapid movement of military forces—this is true. But also, we have to realize when, for instance, to introduce the question of "peacetime." We've entered into a period in the world when war and peace, as they were known, are historical terms. The day we have a declaration of real war from this Congress is probably the last day any of us will ever see. Now the framework was meaningful, but it's got to be transformed. I agree with what Dr. Janowitz says, that this whole draft system has remained rigid while the world has changed, and many points like the Tryten Plan, and the worry after Sputnik, and the report that no scientists ever had original thoughts after 35, come into the picture and get pickled there. Somehow the task of this Conference is going to be to place this whole question in a context of the safety of the human race, the safety of all societies within it and then the role of our own society within this picture. And then the problems of who will work for whom, and when, will assume slightly better proportions.

Maurine Neuberger. But all through this discussion I've been interested in the fact that we're talking about revising the Selective Service from many angles; but nothing has been said about revising the Army that these people are going into. If you're going to draft women or have women volunteers (and I see many points in its favor), or people who are not in school, or who are eligible in so many other ways, I do think that you have to take a new look at the Army, consider whether it should provide more education and physical training, and so on. We did pass in the Congress another GI Bill and I'm one of those who think that there are some people for whom the Army might be good. I'd like to see the Army continue education, and recognize why, as a country, we have so many people deferred for physical reasons. Here's an opportunity. And, I'm somewhat the devil's advocate here, but, nevertheless, this has to be considered as we discuss this whole problem.

[*Unidentified Speaker*]. I'd like to speak very briefly on the positions represented by Dr. Mead and Sen. Neuberger. I think that, except in the case where an overwhelming portion of the people are required for wartime service, I would ask how is the compulsion of any universal service anything but incompatible and utterly hostile to the values of a free society? I think the point is that freedom of choice is worth preserving and my own personal opinion is that equality in slavery is not necessarily the most rapid route in that direction.

Mr. Weber. Senator Neuberger, would you care to exercise your prerogative?

Senator Neuberger. I never heard of anybody who was enslaved by being in the Army.

Recruitment of Military Manpower
Solely by Voluntary Means

TUESDAY MORNING, DECEMBER 6, 1966

Chairman, ARISTIDE ZOLBERG

Aristide Zolberg. Let me just mention the division of labor we've worked out: a discussion by Mr. Chapman of the advantages of the system, a contribution by Mr. Oi on the practicality of the system, a continuing discussion by Professor Friedman on some of the possibly undesirable aspects, and then a return by Mr. Chapman to the problems of transition. We will give the participants a very brief opportunity to add some points and then we will open up for general discussion.

Mr. Chapman. Abolition of the draft will have numerous salubrious effects on our society, ending injustices that are now experienced and precluding others that are now developing. It would be sound morally, militarily, and fiscally. Conscriptive service, when unnecessary to the national defense, is totally antithetic to a free society. In these days when apologists for the draft and other systems of coercion are embarrassed by what they call the "problem" of abundant available manpower, a volunteer system is the only proposal that keeps faith with the primary tradition of personal liberty. It is remarkable that people with a sense of justice and concern for freedom should turn their backs on the blatant unfairness of the draft.

Only a volunteer system deals with concern for each human being. It does not traffic in vague and dubious generalities of local, national, and international interests such as always are the justification for robbing people of their liberty. Only a volunteer system terminates the problems of conscientious objection. Only a volunteer system protects the dissenter from the threat, real or imagined, of reprisal. Only the voluntary system makes first class citizens of the first-term soldier, many of whom are now coerced into uniform and paid an outrageously low wage which is in fact a discriminatory tax imposed by older people and by their own luckier peers. Only the voluntary system, with the exception of UMT or compulsory national service, would end the anxiety that now is the characteristic of late adolescence for men. UMT and compulsory national service are rejected of course, because, for the individual whose services are not needed, the fact of conscription is even worse than for the victim of a necessary gamble.

Similarly, draft abolition would end the inequities attendant upon all the student deferment problems, and all the problems of other deferments, by the simple expedient of obliterating the need for deferment.

The false concept of "channeling" would be buried, as would the evasion mentality. Also, the problems of variations of interpretations of draft eligibility, which now obtain in the draft system from board to board and from time to time, would end. And of course, we would preclude the Russian roulette idea of a lottery whose abstract virtues would be not particularly palatable to the individual who was chosen by such a system.

Now, some of the military advantages: A volunteer system would raise living conditions and morale in the general life situation of the military man. Career men would know that their co-workers were with them by choice. They would enjoy greater regard in the eyes of the general public. With the voluntary service would come a lower manpower turnover, and the Army's most persistent problem, according to General Lynn D. Smith—that of personnel manpower—would be eased. General Smith has said that just as soon as men seem to get trained in the Army, they leave. And this is also the consideration of the people who prepared the Cordiner report for President Eisenhower, and others. Also, only a volunteer system with fair pay would provide opportunity for those good men who now leave the services for lack of decent financial prospects, or who fail to join at all for the same reason. We focus on the punishment a draft places on the unwilling inductee, but we often forget that it closes doors too in the faces of would-be careerists. As an economic advantage, because of a lower turnover, the volunteer system would free to productive civilian enterprise several hundred thousand men at any given time who otherwise would only be contributing to the inefficiency of the military.

Finally, as a footnote, I'd like to observe that all drafts, in situations where they are unnecessary, seem to adopt a very patronizing attitude, and usually it's the older people who express it, toward the abilities, concerns, plans, and hopes of individual young people. But there is no value served by a system of compulsion that is not more appropriately served by voluntarism, neither military skill in handling complex problems, nor Peace Corps assistance, for example, in civic action. This generation is not lacking in patriotic or humanitarian concern. It has reached out and is reaching out, region to region, and race to race, and class to class, and nation to nation, more than previous generations. It wants to make real contributions to world peace and progress. But it has grown increasingly cynical about certain institutions in the power structure manned by persons who were tutored in depression and world war, who want all young people put in prefabricated niches, even though that means round pegs in square holes. Any system of compulsory service, where compulsion is not intrinsically necessary, only aggravates the prevailing suspicion and cynicism of youth toward the power structure, and ultimately can only lead to apathy toward social roles. But purge compulsion, and free young men, provide them a wide range of voluntary outlets for service and give them positive incentive for service, and they will respond. And you'll get your strong defense, and you'll also get a healthier, more dynamic and progressive society, and a freer one.

Mr. Zolberg. Now Professor Walter Oi, who will speak on the practicality of the system.

Mr. Oi. Let me preface my remarks by saying first, that these are my own opinions and conclusions based on the available data which I've examined, and not those of the Department of Defense. In the six years prior to Vietnam, the average strength of the active and reserve forces was just under 3.7 million men, of which 2.6 million were on active duty. To maintain this active duty force, 535,000 men were actually conscripted and recruited into active duty service. An additional 110 to 130 thousand a year were enrolled into the reserve and National Guard units. For the decade of the 1970's, to determine the need for a draft, we have to first estimate the number who are likely to volunteer. The voluntary enlistment rate has been found to respond to the relative attractiveness of service life, especially in relation to alternative civilian job opportunities and to the threat of a draft. Whenever we begin to draft more people under the gun, so to speak, more also tend to enlist.

Now, according to the DOD study reported to the House Armed Service Committee in June of this year, if unemployment can be expected to be at the level of 5.5 per cent, about 417,000 men will enlist annually. On the other hand, if unemployment should fall to its current level of about 4 per cent, we can expect voluntary enlistment to fall by about 50,000. With a high enlistment projection, an annual average draft call of about 55,000 can be expected under a low unemployment of about 100,000. If we should eliminate the draft, the first impact is obvious. The Armed Forces would lose the draftees who accounted for 21 per cent of accessions to enlisted ranks in the period of 1960–65 and are projected to account for between 10 to 20 per cent of accessions to enlisted ranks in the decade of the seventies. In addition to this loss of draftees, we can also expect that the reluctant volunteer, no longer coerced into service by draft liability, would remain in civilian life. It is estimated that about 43 per cent of regular enlistments in the Army would not have entered in the absence of a draft liability. Consequently, the initial accession to enlisted ranks during the decade of the seventies can be expected to fall to levels of about 260,000 a year with the low unemployment figure and to even lower levels if unemployment should drop to a full-employment level. The loss in initial accessions is, however, offset to some degree by improvements in retentions. If we can assume that the reluctant volunteer has the same reenlistment rate as the draftee (about 7.5 to 8 per cent), then we can expect that the Army first-term reenlistment rate will jump from about 22 to 33 per cent.

Now, to achieve the prescribed force-strength objective of about 2.7 million men we tried to estimate the responsiveness of supplies of voluntary enlistment to pay changes. On the basis of a statistical supply equation, albeit a bit shaky, my estimate is that first-term Army pay would have to be increased by 68 per cent. The regular Army enlisted man today can expect to earn about $2500 a year in each of his first three years of service. With the pay increase, he will receive about $4200 a year. Now, I'm using the '63 pay scale; all the figures are a bit higher now. If we apply the higher pay profiles to the active duty force on a voluntary basis, it is estimated that the defense payroll budget for active duty personnel would rise by about $4 billion annually. If I use the lower unemployment figure, which means fewer voluntary enlistments and better civilian alternative job offers and opportunities, the estimated pay increase would be in the neighborhood of $5 billion per year over and above the $12.7 billion needed to pay the force in 1965. (In arriving at these estimates—and I should point out they differ from the DOD estimates—I neglected the factors of the transition period, the saving from lower personnel turnover, and the possibility of civilian substitution. These are discussed in detail in my paper for this Conference.)

In addition to analyzing the cost of staffing 2.7 million men in the Armed Forces, I went through a rough exercise of estimating what it would cost to maintain a force of 3.1 million. My estimate here is that first-term pay would have to be advanced, not to $4200 but to about $5300 per year. If one includes this calculation, plus the fact that you now have more labor resources allocated to the Armed Forces, the cost of a voluntary force would climb by about $8 million over and above what it would have cost us in 1965. As I pointed out, my estimates are on the low side. I estimate a first-term pay increase of 68 per cent. However, I think that a lot of my built-in assumptions tend, if anything, to blast it upward. The DOD best estimate to achieve a 2.7 million armed force required a first-term pay increase of about 111 per cent to a level of about $5000-5200 a year. Then their range of budgetary pay increases from $4 to $17 billion.

I must question some of their high estimates. Econometrics is still more of an art than a science when it comes to this game of projection: for example, their high estimate implies that the first-term enlisted man must be paid an initial entry-level pay of about $7500 which, to me, seems extremely high when less than one-third of the qualified population would be required to staff the Armed Forces. Perhaps more important, the major objection to a voluntary force is its inflexibility, its inability to adapt to short-term fluctuations in force strength. One recommendation is to build flexibility into a voluntary force by rigging entry-level pay—in fact, career-force pay—to provide excess supplies of enlistment applicants in most periods. Thus, when a period comes in which we must rapidly increase strength, we can take up the excess supplies both at the point of initial entry and at the reenlistment point. In the professional armies of Canada and England, the voluntary recruits sign up for rather extended tours. In the Royal Navy, the initial tour of duty was about 12 years the last time I looked at it, with the option of discharge by purchase. Yet the concept of short-service officers as applied in these services—men who can receive retirement benefits of up to a year's pay after completing 8, 10, or 12 years of service—seems to me an entirely feasible program for a voluntary force. Moreover, most evidence suggests that the number who remain beyond the retirement point of 20 years, especially in the enlisted ranks, is smaller than the number who would like to continue in service life. If we had retirement and retirement benefits at the 10th or 12th year, then during any period of rapid buildup we could again extend the tours of these men. All of these considerations, I think, would allow us to fluctuate force strength within a 5 per cent to 10 per cent range. Of course, if you're talking about raising forces from 3 to 4.5 million men, then I say we're in an all-out war, and to talk about a voluntary system here is academic.

Mr. Friedman. My main assignment was to discuss the political effect, if any, of a volunteer force. But, before doing so, I want to supplement what Walter Oi said in one respect. He was talking about the costs in the government budget of having a volunteer army, and came out with estimates of about $4 billion to $8 billion, which is clearly within the range of what seems feasible. I would like to emphasize that we are now paying larger costs than that. The costs he estimates are the budgetary costs. They are not the real cost, because the situation now is that we have two kinds of taxes. We have taxes that you and I pay in money, and we have taxes that the young men who are forced to serve pay in compulsory services. When a young man is forced to serve at $45 a week, including the cost of his keep, of his uniforms, and his dependency allowances, and there are many civilian opportunities available to him at something like $100 a week, he is paying $55 a week in an implicit tax. And it doesn't make that any less of a tax because you exact it in the form of service than if you exact it in the form of money. If you are going to get a real accounting of what the Armed Forces are costing us, in my opinion you must include and should include, not only the taxes in money, but the taxes in kind. And if you were to add to those taxes in kind, the costs imposed on universities and colleges; of seating, housing, and entertaining young men who would otherwise be doing productive work; if you were to add to that the costs imposed on industry by the fact that they can only offer young men who are in danger of being drafted stop-gap jobs, and cannot effectively invest money in training them; if you were to add to that the costs imposed on individuals of a financial kind by their marrying earlier or having children at an earlier stage, and so on; if you were to add all these up, there is no doubt at all in my mind that the cost of a volunteer force, correctly calculated, would be very much smaller than the amount we are now spending in manning our Armed Forces.

Is there any offsetting disadvantage to a voluntary army? I think there are two classes of people with respect to the volunteer army. Most people say, well, the volunteer army would be fine but it isn't feasible for some reason. That subject Walter Oi has handled very well. There is a second class of people who say: A volunteer army certainly sounds fine, but it has great political disadvantages. The political disadvantages that are alleged are that it somehow threatens political and individual freedom. Individual freedom on the part of the draftee, and so on, is obviously strengthened. The great virtue of the voluntary army is that it is responsive to the individual desires and preferences.

So what I want to talk about is the broader political issue. Now, when anybody starts talking about this he immediately shifts language. My army is "volunteer," your army is "professional," and the enemy's army is "mercenary." All these three words mean exactly the same thing. I am a volunteer professor, I am a merceary professor, and I am a professional professor. And all you people around here are mercenary professional people. And I trust you realize that. It's always a puzzle to me why people should think that the term "mercenary" somehow has a negative connotation. I remind you of that wonderful quotation of Adam Smith when he said, "You do not owe your daily bread to the benevolence of the baker, but to his proper regard for his own interest." And this is much more broadly based. In fact, I think mercenary motives are among the least unattractive that we have. But let me put it in another way. As Margaret Mead instructed me last night about the right rhetoric, and quite rightly, if you want to you can emphasize the fact that men join the Army or do other activities for a great variety of motives, but whatever those motives are, they ought, at least, while they're in the Army and doing other things, to get paid for it. And, it's unconscionable that we should impose on these young men, as we now do, the heavy burden of underpaying them as grossly as we do.

Let me go more directly to the question, "Is there any political threat from a mercenary, professional army?" The answer is *yes*. There is such a threat also from a conscripted army. The elementary fact is that a large military force, with the attendant industrial complex, does represent a very real threat to our liberties and our freedom. We would be vastly better off if the state of the world were such that we could afford to dispense with them. I happen to be one of those who believe we cannot afford to dispense with them, and that we must have a large military force and a strong one. The question then comes, "Which way of organizing that force will minimize the threat to freedom which any such force does offer?" The argument that is made against a volunteer army is that a conscripted army, because it is a citizen army, involves closer contact with the community at large, and therefore you're less likely to have a separate military class which will try to take over, or which will try to exert political influence.

My main answer to that is that it's a real problem but it doesn't have anything to do with how you recruit the enlisted man. It has to do primarily with the officer force. I call to your mind the record of history on this. I was amused when Mr. Hazard, in answer to a question from Mr. Rumsfeld about the problems connected with a volunteer force, cited Prussia, which, of course, had a conscript army. And, the interesting thing is, most of the cases people cite are cases where you had a conscript army. France, the republic after the French Revolution, had a conscripted army, and Napoleon rose to power at the head of a conscripted army. Franco, to take a modern example, rose to power at the head of a conscripted army. Argentina has just had a take-over by the military; Argentina has a conscripted army. Now, I am citing these examples because they go against the widely held view. I am not citing them to say that a conscripted army is more of a threat to freedom than a volunteer army. It isn't, because I could cite examples on the other side.

What I would like to emphasize is that in my opinion, the record of history suggests that whether you have a conscripted enlisted force or whether you have a volunteer enlisted force is largely irrelevant to the question of the political danger offered by an armed force. The reason for that is that in all cases you have an essentially professional, mercenary—whatever word you want to use—officer corps.

The problems that have been raised are problems of the structure of the officer group. Here, I think, the crucial question is not conscription or volunteering, but what are the social and institutional arrangements whereby that officer corps is recruited? What arrangements will see to it that the officer corps is in contact with the population at large, is fairly representative of the population at large, and does not constitute a separate military caste? I think we have, on the whole, been very fortunate in this country in having a set of institutions which have achieved that objective to considerable measure. I believe the broad geographical origin of the recruitments for the service academies, although, undoubtedly they mean that we don't necessarily get, in some senses, the best people, have had the great virtue of keeping the Armed Forces closely connected with the grass roots and the population at large. I think lateral recruitment, through the ROTC officer corps, and the like, has had the same effect.

Thus far, some of this has been accomplished through the conscription machinery, but in my opinion could equally well be accomplished in a volunteer force. I would hope that in a volunteer force there would be great emphasis upon lateral recruitment into the officer corps, because I think that's really, in many ways, the more essential need rather than anything that happens with the enlisted men. The need is to keep the officer corps, the people at the top, in touch with the rest of the population. And the way to do that is to have relatively short-term officer assignments with people coming into the Army and going out of the Army, the same way we do in the universities, in the government, and in the industrial complexes. In many countries, the academic group has formed a rather separate independent core-group that has had very little contact with the rest of the community. That sometimes happens in this country too. But insofar as it does not, it is primarily because of the movement of people in and out of the academic world, into the business world, or into the government, and it seems to me the same thing is true on the score of the officer corps. So I would stress that we are and should be enormously and deeply concerned about the possible threat to freedom from a large military establishment. But that threat does not arise in any way from the use of a method that is utterly repugnant to our basic values to get men for the Armed Forces. It arises from the possibility of having an insulated officer corps. And that's a danger we can and should try to avoid in other ways.

Mr. Zolberg. Mr. Chapman, would you like to speak about the transition now?

Mr. Chapman. The draft has been the military's crutch for antiquated manpower policies and recruitment policies for some 15 years. We would remove that crutch, but not overnight. Emerson said, "if you cannot be free, be as free as you can," and so that would be the principle of the transitional draft which would probably have to obtain for a couple of years. This is what I would consider an outline.

The goal of an all-volunteer military force would be established by Congress this next year. It would become a national goal, and our manpower policies in the military would be directed toward meeting that goal. Pay would be raised during the transition, living conditions and other aspects of military life would be improved, and possibly some enlistment bonuses during the transition would be introduced. Also, during the transition, I would recommend that volunteers be paid more than conscripts. This traditionally has gone against the grain in the United States, but it's a sensible way of priming the pump of volunteers. Perhaps we could give some sort of tax break in terms of a deduction on income taxes for a conscript later in life to compensate somewhat.

The Selective Service System under the transition would be reformed in its operation. The local board would qualify registrants, but actual selection would be from a national pool. It would not, as I see it, be a lottery. Hence, a priority of call on a national basis would be preserved as it is now in local boards, but uniformity of standards would be maintained so that the same kinds of people would be called at any given time. The draft-vulnerability pool would be lowered to age 18 to 22 with the oldest drafted first. This is to get the average age down, as we all seem to agree should be done, but at the same time keep it high enough so that there would be some pressure for volunteering continued during the transitional period. Because the system is temporary, the present Selective Service System would also retain the deferment aspect, except that students would be selected for induction at the same time as other people were selected. However, they would be allowed to finish college before actual induction. Data processing would speed paper work at national headquarters and would continue to keep track of registrants and a standby Selective Service System skeleton, after the volunteer systems were instituted. There would be no Selective Service prosecution of draft protesters or draft-card burners. If they broke laws they'd be tried in real courts. Registrants would be treated with respect and consideration. Complete brochures explaining obligations and rights in full, and possibly high school seminars, would assure maximum understanding by young people of the Selective Service System regulations and procedures.

After abolition, the Selective Service network, as I said, would continue to inventory manpower and to register 18-year-olds and possibly to give physical and mental tests as well. And for that reason I think it would be nearly as flexible, in terms of getting into a massive land war at some future point, as is the present system.

This transitional system, I believe, would be a more efficient and truly compassionate system on a permanent basis than is the present Selective Service, or than a lottery or a national service or UMT would be. But the main virtue of this transitional draft is that it would be transitional. It is designed to dismantle itself and conclude, once and for all, the injustice that is inevitable under any draft setup.

Mr. Arnold Anderson. I want to underline one of the most important by-products of the line of arguments presented to us this morning, namely, that it forces us to begin to use this formidable armament of techniques that in recent years have been increasingly elaborated by the economists for dealing with opportunity costs, indirect costs, real costs, and so on. And I think the advantage of a volunteer system, above all others, perhaps, more than equity, is specifically that it forces us to face the question of what are the costs and who is paying them.

Mr. Weinstein. I want to point out the failure in some of the arguments to add in the benefits that come about through the military. The military is a substitute training organization, and people who are highly trained are not going to stay in the military; this implies that training is then going to have to be supplied by some other institution. Then there's a question, and a very legitimate question, of how to estimate the cost of supplying specific human capital in various sectors of the economy. The question of reducing VA benefits really implies that these services are not going to be picked up at all. There is also the question of whether, on the medical care, we are then going to establish some other technique to supply the services. So, what you're really saying is that you're going to eliminate the real flow of services that are going to be produced in the economy.

Now, I would like to get on to a question that is really a technical point; that is, whether the reenlistment rate is tied to the level of unemployment, for this is given as a constant. Secondly, there is the assumption that all of the individuals in the service are essentially perfect substitutes for one another. But, in fact, there is a high range of skills in the military. In your papers you say that going into the volunteer service will give you an older and a less educated group in the military. If the technology in the military continues to change in the same directions, then what you're really saying is that an older, less educated group is perfectly capable of performing all of the tasks that can now be performed by a younger, more educated group in a more sophisticated environment. Assuming that these people can perform these tasks, there must be a real cost involved—I would like to see a specification of what the real cost of substitution of these factors would be—not of an aggregate force, but in the performance of some functional activities within the military.

[Unidentified Speaker]. There are several points I would like to make on this. First, I think that the proposals of Mr. Friedman and the others are frequently said to be unrealistic because in fact we're not going to abolish the draft in any near future. I would like to say that there are several types of realism and one I would call crackpot realism. Crackpot realism says that we can maintain an Army of the size that we have through conscription and involve ourselves

in wars of the type that we're now involved in and are likely to be involved in, in South Africa, in Thailand, and in other places in the Third World, using conscripts, and that while this is going on, our society can be stable. Young men can continue to have a sense of dedication to that society and, in general, that this sort of system can operate smoothly.

My own view is that the draft has to be abolished, but that along with that, these types of military goals have to be abolished. I would support a volunteer army, particularly if that meant a redirection of our military goals or that it would contribute to such a military direction. One reason I am concerned about the draft is that it seems to permit the President to make unilateral decisions about military adventures overseas without an effective check by the Congress, without assuring popular consent. My own hope is that abolition of the draft and the necessity of recruiting people through voluntary means would require more popular consent. I am not sure that that's true, in the sense that the rest of Mr. Friedman's remarks seem to indicate that he felt it wouldn't make any difference, but I certainly would not want to support any military proposals that facilitated the present policy, or want to support a military structure which is in fact more rigid than the present one, which prevents flexibility on the part of the President in the ways which I have described.

Secondly, it would seem to be essential, if there is a volunteer army, that there also be a program of voluntary non-military service to compete with that volunteer army, and to ensure that we do not develop a caste system in which young men are essentially faced with the choice of going on to a higher education or going into the Army. Rather, there should be other alternatives that are equally attractive so that the Army does not become composed, more than it even now is, of particular groups within the population.

Mr. Oi. Let me respond to the first position. In a year spent at the Pentagon I picked up a lot of little bits of information, one of which was that the highest "occupational cross-over" was that of bakers, and that this could perhaps account for the quality of American bread. Let us take the problem of training. If I were Boeing Aircraft and training machinists, I would certainly rather train them myself (and would do it much more efficiently), than farm them out to the Air Force Academy and then have to retrain them. This is well established in almost every discipline—that a layoff from a job necessarily entails a short period of retraining. If you believe that the individual doesn't know what's best for him and that training must be forced down his throat, that is your value judgment. But I don't think we can force military service simply as a vehicle for training. In Mr. Weinstein's paper he mentions the need for police. If you really think this, why not conscript men into the police force, rather than go through the inefficiency of teaching them to use the Browning automatic rifle and then bringing them back to the city—what are they going to do with a Browning automatic rifle?

Mr. Weinstein. I am not suggesting that we force people into careers. But, in fact, the military does engage in training and this training is used and there are many people who enter the military because they believe, and in many cases rightly so, that they will receive training that is useful in the civilian sector.

Secondly, the training of police happens to be a very, very complicated business. It is not just learning the use of a Browning automatic rifle. One of the problems that we have observed in many of the communities of the South is that obviously the police have some difficulty in getting trained, and the military does a very sophisticated job of training police. There is a question of efficiency, and whether it might be—*might be*—more efficient to use the military, or at least to consider the benefits that are added into the civilian economy by using the training institution of the military.

Mr. Friedman. If the military does in fact provide people with occupational training that is subsequently useful, that will reduce the price you have to offer people coming into the military. That is one of the advantages of a military career, in addition to the direct military pay. So, I believe that your factor has already implicitly been taken into account. But remember, civilian jobs also offer this opportunity. People who are hired by Boeing and are going to be trained get a lower wage because they are going to get on-the-job training. So our question has to be, is there a further advantage in calculating the equivalent civilian pay? We want to have a program that has roughly the same makeup as occupational training.

[*Unidentified Speaker*]. Liking the idea of a voluntary military myself, I'd like to ask four questions.

First, an old one, philosophically: How does one reconcile opposition to compulsion in the draft with the apparently accepted notion of compulsion in education? Secondly—this would be more for the military men—if we have a volunteer army, how can we judge sudden things which may come up (for instance, there might be a massive attack sometime in the future against a relatively small, although well-trained voluntary army), taking into account the apparent unpreparedness of reserves and other present reserve forces as back-up strength? Third, one danger that appears to me in separating the military from society is that if we have a situation like Vietnam, two or three years ago, a relatively small war, where is the involvement with the rest of society in this war? Might there not be a danger of having this small, mercenary, professional army in Vietnam doing the fighting and the rest of the citizenry feeling, "Well, it's just a small war, they signed up to fight such small wars, it's not going to affect us, so why should we become concerned with it at all?"—and then, having this rather neglected war suddenly develop into a much larger one, as has been the case since 1962? My last point is in economics. I assume that the volunteer system would also apply to doctors, engineers, and this type of person. Now, in order to attract a sufficient number of doctors and engineers into a volunteer army, you would have to pay them more, I would assume, than other occupations. Your military pay scale would have to reflect the civilian pay scale. This would mean, I assume, that we would have to have doctors all at the rank of colonel or general; engineers all at the rank of major, colonel, or general; and perhaps instructors at the rank of second lieutenant! I would like to know if this wouldn't require some major alterations in the officer structure of the Army, and if so, how it is to be dealt with. I realize these are long questions but I think that all four of them do have some application, and since I am, more or less, for a volunteer army, I would like to know how to answer when people ask me.

[*Unidentified Speaker*]. Whatever the virtues of a volunteer army, and I think there are many, I think it's politically naïve in the extreme, and we should be aware of that. In fact, the administration staged an event to make this clear. When the Defense Department's long-awaited report was made by Assistant Secretary Morris last June, the whole thrust of the report was that we couldn't afford a voluntary army. The only other point made of course was the coming of a younger age. If there was anything the administration has said flatly that it will not consider, it is this. This is not to say we shouldn't consider it. It's just to say that the case to be made for it would have to be very strong.

Dr. Mead. I'd like to go back to Dr. Friedman's point that a volunteer, a professional, and a mercenary army are all the same thing; it just depends on how honorific or pejorative you want to be. If we use the word voluntary, and then a "career" army, instead of the word professional, that will probably help a little bit, but a mercenary army, which I'm quite sure a large number of people here shudder at the thought of because it's been historically pejorative, is an army that fights for anybody for pay, and is not concerned in any ethical issue whatsoever. It's only concerned with people who like fighting and if they are paid well enough, they will fight. Now, I don't think that this is what Dr. Friedman is suggesting, and we're not really discussing a mercenary army. We don't expect to hire it out to other people, I assume, and I also assume we probably aren't going to hire other nationals if they're cheaper, though last night Dr. Friedman said he might consent to that.

If we consider this question of pay, the point I attempted to make was that you cannot get people into any occupation that requires any ethical or dedicated qualities whatsoever by pay. You can *keep* them in by pay. We've found this for teachers, for nurses, for social workers. Just raising the pay won't get the kind of people you want in—*ever*. But paying them decently will *keep them in*, will make it possible for them to stay there, when otherwise they will be attracted out because they can't afford it. So, I completely support Dr. Friedman's notion that we pay the Army well. I think we should. Not that this will give us a good Army; it is a necessary pre-condition of a good Army.

Furthermore, a voluntary Army can be regarded as an Army with more or less return to civilian life, the point that Mr. Craig made, and we could envisage enough interpenetration and lateral recruitment in a volunteer Army possibly to correct for what I regard, and I think Dr. Janowitz regards, as a major objection to a volunteer Army, that is that it might have an ethos that was different from the rest of the society. If we have sufficient forms of transfer back and forth, which would mean the possibility of civilians entering the Army at different stages as well as leaving it, and we didn't think of this as mercenary and with too large a career army group, then these objections would be overcome.

Mr. Wool. I have the highest respect for Dr. Oi's technical competence, as evidenced by the fact that he directed certain aspects of our study at the Pentagon.

I can agree with two generalizations which Walter Oi made: one is that as we moved into a shooting-war situation, with a strength of about 3 million, there's no great argument as to the impracticality of trying to procure a volunteer force of 3.3 million which we need at present. I've heard no argument which alleges that we could.

Secondly, I think that the basic point is the statement that econometrics is still an art rather than a science. I think it's an art at present, which unfortunately lends itself in some cases to wishful thinking. We have used, in our judgment, the same techniques, often starting from the same data and the same premises as Dr. Oi, and we felt that it was only fair and responsible not to state estimates in convenient rounded numbers such as $4 or $5 million, but to at least convey some image of the uncertainties involved in projections of this type by using some of the probable ranges of error of the assumptions themselves. In that process we arrived at a range, rather than a convenient single billion-dollar figure, from as low as $3.7 billion, if we maintain 5.5 per cent unemployment for an indefinite period of years, to as much as nearly $17 billion if we had a 4 per cent unemployment level which we now do, and if our estimates of the recruitment yield of a given pay raise, in fact, proved to be low, as compared to some other set of estimates, I think we should realize the very important limitations of the guesswork which we have been compelled to use to answer questions that people have a right to ask. We're trying to judge the reactions of millions of young men to what they would do with their lives under a set of hypothetical conditions which are not those which necessarily exist today, but which might exist 5, 10, or 15 years in the future. To do this, we used whatever data we could develop, but I'm convinced that the amount we don't know is far, far greater than what we do. For example, the knowledge available collectively here as to what makes young men choose an occupation or a career is still very limited indeed. We do know that there are a tremendous variety of factors, psychological and sociological, as well as economic. We do know that we have to try to get as many as one out of three qualified young men in this country by some pay inducement (perhaps $5000-$7500, which Dr. Oi thought was tremendously high) to choose a career of military service rather than some other kind of career, at least for a period of years.

Now, I'd say that under some conditions we might get all the volunteers we needed right now, if we had a depression, or if we had the kind of economy which many other countries in this world have. Under other conditions, I think we'd fall flat on our face, and we haven't tried to conjure all of these conditions up. One of them, hopefully, would be a type of economy in which the overwhelming majority of young men leaving school would have available to them a clear-cut opportunity for using their skills in a civilian job. The experience we've had available during the past 10 years was one where we had not merely an average unemployment rate of 5.5 per cent, but a deplorably high unemployment rate for young men, and a rate for young Negroes of over 20 per cent. This was the labor market situation in which our recruitment experience developed. We found some relationships which existed within a limited range of variation of unemployment, of civilian earnings differentials, and then we had to begin extrapolating. We have some insight from the cases of other countries which have had very high employment and very low unemployment rates. For example, Australia has had among the lowest unemployment rates in the world. In Australia, their force in relation to their population has been far greater than ours, yet they were compelled, when they had to increase it even slightly, to go back on the draft, in spite of the fact that they had the highest military pay relative to civilian pay that we've observed in any country we could study. In other words, we're dealing with many massive uncertainties.

Secondly, we do know that the mechanism by which pay influences young men to choose an entry job is far from direct. One can't push a "pay button" and suddenly generate overnight an extra 50, 100, or 200 thousand men, as is conveniently implied by some of these supply curves. Men get conditioned to the careers they wish to choose by a vast variety of factors. We found, that in fact, the knowledge as to the real relation between military pay and civilian pay, among young men, was very limited, and that pay in fact was one of the less important or visible factors which motivated them in terms of an immediate choice as to jobs. All this implies that the responsiveness, both in terms of time and in terms of degree, could be far different from what some of our estimates suggest. There's no question that a substantial amount would be needed to elicit even some response, but on how much more of an increase would be needed, we're still largely guessing.

Given this inevitable massive uncertainty, as to the yield, whether one-third of our young men would, in fact, choose military service, with its inherent risks, under a high employment economy, is a darned good question. I think many here would come to a different judgment than some of the economic projections would suggest. A very fundamental uncertainty is the type of economy and the type of society we will have. Beyond that point, there are still greater uncertainties as to what our requirements would be. I think we just have to face up to the fact from our recent history that there can be very substantial fluctuations in military strength requirements, short of an all-out war. There can be a very welcome contingency of a much better organized labor market for which we have to plan, and our military policy planning must assume that we're going to be successful. We can't assume we're going to have a continuation of a 10-15 per cent unemployment rate of youth as a convenient recruitment source. When we add these things up, plus some of the real qualitative implications of a more technological world, where everything is getting more complicated, we find we might have a volunteer force which would increasingly consist of older men whose education would be far less than average, as compared to the civilian society, and somehow have this force be effective. I think this is naïve.

Other factors are the fact that we've ignored the further cost of maintaining a reserve force, where we know that a large percentage of men in that force is draft-motivated; we still need it as a second line of defense for us. We've also ignored the very difficult problems of the top range of the quality spectrum, the professional and highly intellectual skills which are needed in military service. All of these considerations, when added together, mean, first, that a continued system for selective service will be needed as long as the active force is about 2.5 million, certainly, rather than 3 million; and second, that as far as the probability of "buying our way out" of military service goes, if we're talking above the 2.5-million range, I think we're much too optimistic in terms of the estimates we've heard here today.

Mr. Zolberg. Mr. Wool, you've raised some very serious issues to which we will return in a few moments.

Sister Cusack. I'd like to make a brief comment on the insulated officer corps to which Dr. Friedman referred, and to the fact that insulation might be offset to some extent by rotation and exposure to the outer world. Now, I presume, that exposure, to use his term, is lateral. That is, you'd move from being a general to the head of a university. I belong to an organization that as a volunteer force has a longer history, I suppose, than either the British or the American Army; and we've learned a few things, I hope, over the centuries. One of the things we've learned is that vertical exposure is of great help. That is, a dignified demotion into the ranks not only helps the individual officer, or a Mother General, but also helps the ranks because a new point of view is found. I can envisage a world in which Brigadier Generals and Bishops were all alike given vertical leave.

Robert W. Kastenmeier. I just wanted to express a general agreement with the three panel members supporting a voluntary army. I think it does raise questions even for those who support it. One thing that is not clear to me from the three panelists is where we proceed from today, being involved in the Vietnam War. Professor Oi indicated that beyond, I think, 3.5 million, his projections go out the window as far as the voluntary army is concerned, and Mr. Chapman indicated Congress might start this coming year with a transition, with the voluntary army as a goal. But I'm wondering, in view of Vietnam, whether we start now, or do we literally have to wait for the end, a resolution of the conflict and a more normal requirement, in terms of force, before we proceed on to a voluntary army? It's clear that we can't really predict what requirements will be in the future. It may be that there will be a resolution in Vietnam, and it may be that we will have a meaningful UN peace force in time, that our NATO troop commitments will be less, and that a really lower figure and possibly a fairly stable one will be necessary in years ahead. I think we ought to move on to a voluntary manpower system as soon as possible. It may not be now.

Mr. Rumsfeld. I also find myself in general agreement with the three panelists, which is interesting, since Mr. Kastenmeier is a Democrat and I'm Republican, and the presentation of these three gentlemen was called politically naive.

There are three or four points that I would like to comment on very briefly. One, the question was raised as to how you resolve this question of compulsion in education with the concern about compulsion in the military. I think the age differential, in part, answers that. In the case of the military, you're dealing with people between 18 and 26. Young adults and adults as opposed to younger people.

On the question of alterations that might be required in the present military structure, certainly one of the first would be a change in personnel policies. The personnel policies of the U.S. military are based on the crutch of compulsion, and therefore they can be as good or as bad as the individual desires, because they still have the conscripts to deal with. Different personnel policies within the military would make a great deal of difference, just as different personnel policies within different companies make a great deal of difference as to their success or failure. Certainly, under present personnel policies, a voluntary force would be absolutely impossible.

The question of the age of the force that would be generated by the proposal our panelists have presented also could be determined by the personnel and recruiting policies and how they planned the force to be designed, just as a corporation would set up its policies, to see that the mix was desirable.

The matter that gives me the most concern is Mr. Wool's repeated response saying the panelists have ignored certain problems. If blame is to be assigned for ignoring problems, it falls on the Department of Defense and the administrations in the past two decades, none of which have really looked at the Selective Service question, at the manpower requirements of this country, at the manpower availability in the country, and that's *their* job, and it's the Congress' job. Congress also has failed to hold adequate hearings. I'm the first one to admit it. To simply say that some problems have been ignored doesn't really answer it at all. On the one hand you say that your present circumstance is based on monumental uncertainty. By the same token, your opposition to these three panelists is based on monumental ignorance and the ignoring of the need for greater information. To my knowledge, the back-up material, at least, and the full report have never been fully disclosed to the public. We don't even know what's in it. We've not heard what, if anything, will be made available of the information that the Marshall panel is presently accumulating. So, it's our job in this Conference to try to evaluate these things on the best information we have and certainly if some things can't be answered, government bears a responsibility for seeing that the questions are answered as precisely as possible.

Finally, a question came up as to possible insulation of a voluntary military. Mr. Flacks touched on a subject that Miss Mead raised yesterday. It concerns this question of the control of the decision-making process in foreign policy and national security areas, and this is a proper concern in both cases. I, on the other hand, don't believe that a solution to this fundamental and constitutional question can necessarily be found in what we're discussing here. Congress has voluntarily, on a piecemeal basis, over many decades, yielded up what amounts to something approximating total authority to the Executive to function in the foreign policy and national security decision-making area in practically any situation ranging from total war to total peace. The words "declaration of war" are almost meaningless. It's not useful any more. And the Joint Committee on the Organization of Congress, notwithstanding recommendations by me and others that they give attention to this question, refused to give attention to this question. We must see if there are differing degrees of authority that the Executive should have in the differing types of emergency situations that the country finds itself in. They've not done this and they should do this. Certainly the academic community and the rest of our society should bring enough pressure to bear on the Congress to see that it does give attention to deciding what the desirable degree of involvement by the legislative branch should be in the foreign policy and national security decision-making process. I don't know precisely what it should be. I do know that it's wrong to have arrived where we've arrived without giving systematic thought and attention to where we were going. I recognize that the Executive does need greater flexibility in emergency situations. Because of excessive Executive power, we are presently denying the areas of foreign policy and national security decision-making the benefit of that check between branches of government which is built into our system, and we're denying it unnecessarily and unwisely.

Mr. Tatum. If the reserve programs in the United States do not give flexibility to the Armed Forces to deal with an emergency in a military manner, then they should be abolished instantly. We'd save a lot of money and have a lot more people to draft. The second point is that I think we'd be hard put to it here without the very concrete contributions of Dr. Wool, particularly in view of the dearth of information from Selective Service itself; but I find Dr. Wool much more convincing when he's quoting figures from studies which are being presented to Congress than when he's quoting from a top-secret report. If I announce that I'd made a two-year study and determined that if we eliminated the draft there would immediately be a million volunteers, I think it would be rather suspect. I think that it's highly suspect when Dr. Wool is placed in the position that he is by the government of needing to pull specific figures from a secret report not available to Congress or anyone else in order to support the decision that is being taken by the administration. I hope that all of us will share this lack of conviction, and will add to this the belief as democrats that if we are going to have a compulsory system of conscription for military purposes, the burden of proof rests with the government, and we will not have that proof unless this secret report is released.

Mr. Virgil. I wanted to address myself to one of the concerns that Mr. Cullinan raised. How much of a factor is the conscription Army in producing a large war in Vietnam? Given the hypothetical situation of a strong Executive dependent upon a volunteer arrangement, it would seem to me that if he's to commit the nation to an involvement which is certainly dubious, and that involvement grows out of hand, with a volunteer army he is then somehow going to have to "sell" it to the American public. This certainly raises some questions about relationships with the press. It seems to me, however, that a volunteer army may be worth considering, rather than committing a conscription Army to a foreign involvement, and then having this serve as a factor in saying that it is now a part of this nebulous thing called the national interest. In other words, if I remember correctly, John Kennedy said at one time that it was a Vietnamese war for the Vietnamese to win or lose. Somewhere there was a transition and it became a matter of national interest. I don't know if this would take place with a volunteer Army. I think it would be a safe or a better check system than what we have now.

Mr. Friedman. I ask for permission to break in because I hate to see us diverted on what I think is a fairly false issue, the one that Mr. Wool raised. Mr. Wool, in his comments, illustrated one of the best-established generalizations in all political economy: that an existing administrator is always against change; it is always unfeasible. I have observed this time and time again. I'm sure I would do the same if I were in his position. But the issues he raises are strictly speaking irrelevant to our consideration and can be put to one side, because we do not need an estimate. What we need to do is start in the direction of a volunteer force by raising military pay, raising conditions of service, getting the Army to try to use some sensible personnel policies, and then we'll see how many come along. If he's right, and it turns out that this produces very few people and we can't really get rid of Selective Service very quickly, we will have to go further. If he's wrong, we'll find that we have a considerable number of volunteers that we're able to manage, and that then we can dispense with Selective Service earlier. As Mr. Chapman pointed out, you do have a transition problem, and the reason you have a transition problem is because you must use actual experience to eliminate the range of uncertainty that inevitably resides in the best informed estimates.

I mention this only in order to suggest that we not let our time be diverted by pros and cons about whether the right budgetary number is 17 billion or 3 billion or 27 billion. I only want to make one other point, in order to keep our discussion on the track. Mr. Wool, unfortunately, and no doubt unintentionally, misquoted Mr. Oi. Mr. Oi said when you got up to a range of 4.5 million a voluntary force was not feasible. Mr. Oi did not say that it was not feasible to procure our present size of Armed Forces, and Mr. Oi can check me on this. He did not say that that was out of range of feasibility with a volunteer Army.

Mr. Arnold Anderson. There's one aspect of volunteer service which has not been raised. If the occupational remuneration were the same for people in civilian or military service, with a slight advantage for attracting them into military service, would a certain psychological type who volunteers be inclined to develop traits while in service which we do not wish to have representing American society, domestically or abroad? Now, this is a very important question; I need to refer only to Algeria. I think it is one which can be resolved, but it does take formidable amounts of research to resolve it.

Mr. Kurland. The speakers, up to now, have raised the basic issue of compulsion versus a voluntary system. I think it's quite clear that there are people in government who favor a compulsory system. They can array the full range of resources of government researchers to justify their position, and it's quite clear that other people, the advocates of freedom, have not done as extensive a job in researching the possibilities of a free or voluntary system. I would like at this time to try to take up two of the questions raised by Mr. Cullinan because I think that they've been ignored up to now.

One, on the question of reconciling compulsory education with compulsion in the military, Representative Rumsfeld touched on one point. I think we have to raise an additional distinction relating to compulsory school laws: whether or not society has any alternatives to compulsory education. Here we are discussing whether there are feasible alternatives to a compulsory military system. This is the essential issue of this panel.

Another question that was raised was how you could recruit a sufficient number of doctors, and the related question, had we taken the costs into account for recruiting additional doctors and officers? I think if we examine the officer question, we'd probably find that in terms of total numbers, the amount is relatively insignificant. We can also say that the doctors and officers, particularly those recruited through the ROTC program, have been recruited with scholarships and other financial inducements. This raises an interesting point about subsidizing people who are not going into college now because they can't afford it, some of whom might wish and be well qualified to become officers and doctors. This might be a response to your question.

But the more important question that I have is—What price freedom? I'd like to put this question in the perspective of the total resources that are available and will be available to pay for this freedom. There would be disagreement by different economists, but I think most economists are willing to say that with a five per cent growth rate in this country we ought to have a GNP of about $1 trillion by 1975. Leon Keyserling suggests that, at this growth rate, between 1966 and 1975 there will be a GNP growth increment in this country of $2.4 trillion. If we accept the highest figure for a cost of an all-voluntary service that Dr. Oi has suggested, that is, $8 billion a year, this would be $80 billion out of the total growth between now and 1975, which is a cost for freedom of 3 per cent of the total growth of this country between now and 1975. I would like to pose the question: "Can the government justify not asking for these resources to pay for freedom?"

Mr. Flacks. There has been something of a debate lurking between Mr. Friedman and Mr. Wool which I want to make explicit. What Mr. Wool knows is that you can't get one-third of the youth to volunteer to fight the sort of wars that they're being asked to fight. That is, some of us feel that we want a volunteer force even if we can't get one-third of the youth to participate in it, precisely because we feel that a volunteer Army is appropriate for the national defense, but not appropriate for the alleged requirements that we now seem to have. It's not simply that the requirements are unpredictable. We can decide that there are certain ends for which we do not want to have young men conscripted and furthermore that we do not want to have the size Army that permits us to engage in that type of military activity. So I think it's not quite relevant to argue that a volunteer Army is impracticable because we need one-third of our youth. We also have to argue that those military ends for which we need one-third of our youth are inappropriate and decide that we want a volunteer Army because it's in the national interest and because it dictates military requirements that are genuinely in the national interest. I think that the reason that Mr. Friedman sounds unrealistic in his statement is because he's ducking that aspect of the situation. Furthermore, I think Mr. Wool is unrealistic if he thinks that in the next 20 years we can continue to conscript one-third of our youth for the sorts of wars which they are likely to fight in and continue to feel that the draft will be legitimate for that kind of war.

Senator Neuberger. I think that there is a certain political naïveté in this room if members of this Conference think they can ignore the political questions that come up before the Congress. I was glad Mr. Tatum referred to the reserve, because I thought maybe we should be reminded that we do have two voluntary organizations, the reserve and the National Guard. But I'm always offended when I drive along highways in Oregon and see our scenery desecrated by big signs which say: "Sleep well tonight, your National Guard's awake," because I don't have that kind of faith in them. During recent debate on the reserves, when the questions came up about whether reserve members should be called up by a lottery, really sporadically, or as units, much heat was generated among these people who are in the reserves. They fought like steers about any consideration that they be called up. And yet this is what we've been supporting them for, and this is the kind of a reserve situation we've been dependent on. So, we do have a voluntary situation.

Then I just wanted to ask one other question of the panel group. I got the implication that, if we had a voluntary army, once a volunteer you turn into something else. Do you continue to be a volunteer and after you're trained and inducted can you just up and leave any time? Or do we have the impression I did during the discussion—that once you volunteer then you're conscripted, and that it's understood that you're going to stay there?

Colonel Hays. As the sole representative of the isolated and rigid mentality that has been so adequately described here, I throw myself on the mercy of the court. I would really in many ways like to see a voluntary Army. I would like to see a situation in which the Army would be attractive enough to attract young men to it, and which would make everybody in it happy and willing to serve. Unfortunately, my experience gives me little reason to believe that this is likely to be the case in the foreseeable future. One factor which Dr. Mead very carefully described is this matter of military motivation, with which I'm considerably concerned. There are many aspects in military motivation that are similar to the motivations of teachers, preachers, and social workers. There are many intrinsic values developed, largely after men enter the service. Both in ROTC programs and on active duty, we tend to receive a number of volunteers and reenlistments from men who initially did not intend to volunteer. On the other hand, many who volunteer initially do not reenlist.

I'd like to suggest a few problems in this connection. First, I may assume that the suggested pay raise would affect officers as well as men. I would be delighted to have my own pay escalated. One difficulty connected with such a general expansion of military pay stems from the principle of equity. When my pay is escalated this way, Dr. Wool, a civil servant, wants his pay escalated also. He works in the Pentagon and everyone there wants his pay raised just like the military they work with. This feeling moves across to the Postal Department and other government workers. Then Senator Neuberger and the Congress have problems on their hands. That relates to the next problem: How high should the pay levels be? When we get into the special categories of engineers, doctors, and lawyers, we're talking about more than a small pay raise. When we talk about the pay given a commanding general in Vietnam matched against a comparable civilian pay, we may be talking about adding maybe $100,000 to his paycheck. And if we're going to do it equitably, you cannot consider that initial man in isolation.

Another problem: Anybody who lives near a military post has some idea of what the soldier does with his pay. He spends it as rapidly as he can. Our civilian communities have been very helpful indeed in assisting him to do this. But I submit that it may tax their abilities to absorb the much larger sums involved with $5,000-a-year privates, and equally escalated corporals, sergeants, and colonels. It might be a boon to the automobile industry, but the traffic problems would be rather more than I care to envisage.

The problem of living conditions has not been considered by the panel. I do not believe that we can expect the $4500- or $5000-a-year private to live in the type of housing we offer him now. Off-post housing around most of our installations is deplorable. The initial impact immediately around many posts would be to raise rentals, forcing many civilians out into the substandard housing that soldiers are now occupying. This might be good for the landlords. But on-post housing and transportation facilities would require some attention to support the substantial increase in living costs in the local communities. This involves an additional substantial sum, one which at the present time the Secretary of Defense apparently feels is too great.

There are other facets of the pay scale problem which, as Dr. Wool has pointed out, are exceedingly complex: problems of differential pay for different kinds of skills, problems of differential pay for different kinds of responsibilities. I'm not sure that we're going to solve the problem merely by saying we're going to raise the pay. I'm convinced, with Dr. Mead, that it isn't pay that motivates the man in the first place. I don't think we can buy a soldier for money.

Mr. Biderman. Representative Rumsfeld said the obligation for developing the facts relevant to this question resided with the government. It does to a considerable extent and, as it is, we are dependent upon the Department of Defense, primarily, for most of the information we have about this question. But I think whatever information we are provided with by Defense will continue to be looked at askance by those who regard DOD as having an ax to grind in this and all issues related to defense. This is a problem of the place of military affairs in our national and international life that has to be studied objectively. If we're going to have the kinds of evaluations of this situation that bring various perspectives to bear on the problems, they have to arise from the entire research community, not merely the government part of it.

There is a vast fund of misinformation and a preference for stereotypical impressions and presuppositions about the nature of the military—rather than a reliance upon that little bit of information which is based upon objective and systematic study. I think, for example, the propositions relating to insulation of the military are all naïve. It's not one way or the other way. There are certain ways in which insulation has very clearly protected the civil-political body from interventions by military power. There are other ways in which some influence on military elite from the civilian-political consensus provides this protection.

The motivation for military service is a very elaborate issue alluded to by Mr. Wool, and raises questions that have to be studied a great deal more.

The assumptions about the military mind, I think, are so transparent as hardly to need mention.

Mr. Flacks' remarks about the motivation of people for combat in Vietnam, I think, should be tested against the actual motivation of conscripts in this conflict. To what extent do conscripts who are fighting in Vietnam feel that this is an unjust obligation and that they are suffering an unjust fate? My impression would be that this would be characteristic of only a very small minority, but I don't know that as a fact.

To get this kind of information there has to be considerably more encouragement of the study of the military affairs by social scientists, and to do this requires some establishment of "viable" relations with the Armed Forces for independent studies. It can't be a study of "a culture at a distance." The project Margaret Mead was associated with years ago was a study of Iron Curtain countries when you couldn't observe them directly. We can observe the military directly, but it will require the establishment of relationships with the military for this kind of independent study.

Mr. Chapman. I want to talk on just one of the number of questions that are still outstanding. That is, the assertion that pay alone won't make a man into a soldier or won't attract a man to the military. I think that's so obvious that I'm rather startled that it needs to be said. Of course, pay won't attract anybody to the military, and the suggestion of the DOD report, as given last June in the House of Representatives, that only 4.4 per cent of the interested young men were interested in the pay alone is very deceptive. There are many motivations for entering the service, just as there are many motivations for going into the academic world. Presumably professors by and large think they could get better pay somewhere else, but they stay in because they approve of their function in society. On the other hand, what if some of the professors were offered the kind of pay that the military men are offered? Would you stay in your career if you were offered $45.00 a week? Would you stay when you get wages that are lower than wages paid in other countries that have comparably lower standards of living to begin with? Now in the military that's the situation. The military man gets a base pay of $96.00 here in the United States. He gets $110 in Canada, $110 in Germany, $112 in Australia, and so on. Now there shouldn't be any objection to raising pay—yet we hear an objection to raising pay, because I'm afraid some people who secretly like the ideas of compulsion and of a draft are afraid that if we did raise pay and did undertake these changes in housing and so on, that we would find that volunteer rate would rise and rise and then we couldn't justify this draft anymore at all.

Mr. Lloyd Anderson. There are several points that I don't think we've quite faced yet. First, in reply to Mr. Flacks, I think I'm as firmly committed as he is to the immorality of acting God and policing the world, but isolation is too simple an answer. We may not have acted perfectly in the Dominican Republic, but that doesn't mean we shouldn't have done something there. It doesn't mean that we shouldn't have prevented the slaughter of 800,000 people in Indonesia. As for Mr. Biderman's point on conscripts in Vietnam versus volunteers: I think volunteers may be forthcoming for international police forces restricted to non-involvement in the dispute. But, there is a difference in the Vietnam case between asking the volunteers or the conscripts who are already there and who have cognitive dissonance working for them, and asking someone to go over there to become a volunteer. There might be a strong influence on foreign policy of the kind Mr. Flacks describes, and I agree it's very important.

There's a related element to this which is the question of taxation without representation. It doesn't seem possible to treat it as a legal question here, but to give blanket approval to the Executive, in what we want to regard as peacetime, does violate the principle.

On the possibilities Representative Rumsfeld mentioned of distinguishing cases, we might want to make it very difficult to use conscripts, perhaps by saying that Congress must reapprove a specific limit every month. We might even want a constitutional limit. Of course, it's difficult; of course it's obnoxious. That's the whole point, which gets me to Mr. Wool. He seems to be taking as the norm a system which will give us the maximum military we would ever want to use. Now, this to me is completely the wrong point of view. Let's take the voluntary as the norm and then make it difficult to get away from that. It can be done. There's nothing, save a nuclear holocaust, which could require such instantaneous action that Congress couldn't handle it.

Another question is whether, if the incentives were kept just a little bit higher so that the military could always be refusing certain volunteers, it could start accepting more. It would immediately have them.

One question, finally, on economics. And I think many of the discrepancies in figures between Mr. Wool and other people seem to be due to his simple refusal to take opportunity costs into account, a simple refusal to count them. If I'm misrepresenting him, I apologize, but he gave no specific indication he was.

Mr. Gibson Winter. I think that this career military idea is a good proposal. Any good proposal in our society has to mobilize diverse interests, and this one seems to be drawing together people from different political backgrounds. I never thought the day would come when I would be in agreement with Mr. Friedman on any matter of public policy; yet I find myself much in agreement on this one. I'd like to set this, however, in the context of foreign policy. The style of our military cannot be separated from our foreign-policy stance, and this is integral to my proposal. Let me say first I more or less side with this career military. I don't think it ought to be called voluntary, because it's no more voluntary than any other occupation; but it can be a serious career. Many of us are deeply disturbed by the emergence of a militaristic culture in this country which is engaging more and more extensively in violence. We see some reasons for it, but we see emerging in the society a politics of domination, and I don't mean this in a rhetorical way. Those of us who have a real commitment to this society are deeply troubled by this, and we see ourselves being pushed, also by others, into it. This is something that is being encouraged on a world basis.

Given this context (with which some would disagree, but nonetheless the evidence seems to go this way), the peacetime draft with all of its faults, and I believe that it is a violation of our democratic tradition which we have put up with much too long, this peacetime draft has created for us a *negative politics*. That is, our students and our young people have protested this increasing violence because they have been exposed to it. The professors helped them for a short while and then pulled out to write their papers or to do other things. The Congressman has already pointed out that the legislature has more or less pulled out of it. The fact of the matter is, we have depended upon a negative politics, and the costs of this are increasing, the pain and burden of it are increasing, and will increase, I believe, in this coming year to the point where Kenneth Boulding can write a paper, well-documented, that the legitimacy of the nation-state is really coming into question.

Now, having said this, I'd like to say that if we take on a career military, we are going to have to take on very seriously a positive politics. This is not only a matter of the Congress. Monetary costs will help a bit, but in an affluent society you can assimilate monetary costs rather quickly and they become routinized. I would suggest that we link to this a very extensive program of voluntary services abroad; link it into careers, not maladjusting young people for future careers, but really linking into occupational futures for them.

Mr. Rosenberg. I want to speak to one of the questions that Mr. Cullinan raised. He asked: Won't movement toward a volunteer army lead to our national public losing interest in involvement in the Vietnam war? I think by implication, he was asking: Won't our national public lose interest generally in similar international commitments that we may get involved in, in the foreseeable future? I think the answer to that is yes. However, I view that as a happy rather than an unhappy state of affairs, and I think that perhaps that's where I would differ with Mr. Cullinan. I think it is desirable that our public lose some interest in such matters. Loss of interest in such international armed commitments would tend to work towards a diminution of a kind of garrison consciousness which has, over the last 20 years, developed in this country. This garrison state atmosphere has been growing not merely because we have had conscription but because conscription has been further justified and the whole pattern of national policy associated with conscription has been justified and sold through the mass media generally. This garrison consciousness, I think, is presently one of the main obstacles to what we would otherwise get via our democratic political process; namely, some significant constraint upon our elite as it contemplates military adventures in response to the many difficulties that it thinks it encounters on the international scene.

Congressman Rumsfeld was concerned about the loss of one important check upon the policy-planning elite, namely the congressional check; there is also the possibility of a public-opinion check upon such policy initiatives, particularly when those policy initiatives risk escalation to total war. An important check upon military adventurousness has been lost by virtue of the development of the Cold War consensus, as it has sometimes been called, which has now prevailed for some 20 years. For me, one of the great advantages in moving toward a voluntary force and toward a reduction in the size of the military establishment, which I think is ultimately implicit in a move toward voluntarism, is that it would, in fact, free American public opinion for a renewed and critical analysis of just those kinds of military adventurism to which our present policy planners seem to be growing more and more committed as they lose a sense of the range of other, non-military, options which are available to us as we confront a very difficult international scene.

Mr. Watson. I want to comment on the cost issue, and particularly the comments made by Mr. Wool. It seems to me that he and Colonel Hays have been making a great contribution for us by playing the role of the responsible civil servant who presents all of the practical objections to proposed new policies, so that the policy considerations will be dealt with very carefully, and mistakes will be avoided. But, in this context, it also seems perfectly clear that these objections do not decide the policies, that the policies are decided on through broader considerations, because these things can always be worked out once the policy is decided.

What the facts amount to are that roughly the real economic costs are likely to wash out, and that what we save with one hand, we spend with the other. What we save in not taxing the present conscript we spend for useful purposes, and the soldier spends for useful purposes; if he isn't offered useful opportunities for expenditure close to the base, then there's something wrong with the system already. The only problem left is the budgetary problem from the national government. Since it's pretty clear that the progressive income tax tends to outpace the growth of the economy and embarrass the national government with excess funds, I don't really see any problem in providing the necessary expenditure, even if there is a considerable increase in the budget cost. Everything else I had to say has been said better by Mr. Winter.

Dr. Mead. We've had a good deal of comment here on who's to blame for what. The DOD shouldn't classify things; Congress shouldn't have stayed asleep; the military should welcome social scientists to study them. I'd like to put a certain amount of blame on the social scientists themselves, who progressively since 1950 have been more and more alienated from government. I grant that from the Korean War on, government was very prickly to work with. We had a long period of very bad relations, and we got very bad habits. If social scientists are not willing to go into government and work, even under the uncomfortable conditions, we won't be able to reestablish the sorts of relationships that we need. We're responsible too, and I don't think we'd get anywhere by putting blame in any particular direction unless we take some ourselves.

Mr. Mitrisin. Mr. Wool expresses a fear that a voluntary Army would not be able to get the necessary men to fight our wars. I would say that if we can't recruit the men to fight our wars voluntarily, then we should ask: Why are we fighting wars at all, if men are not willing to die for what we're supposed to be fighting for? I want to add a comment to Mr. Cullinan's comment on compulsory education. It is true that we compel children to go to school, but at a certain point we must assume that an individual is capable of making decisions for himself. I would say that by the time a person is 16 this point has been reached. The draft takes men 18 and over. By this age individuals are able to make their own decisions.

Mr. Janowitz. I have two points I'd like to address myself to. One is this question of National Guard—and the distinction between the National Guard as a part of our strategic reserve, and the role of the National Guard in the society as a whole. At the present time, given the structure of the requirements of law and order in Illinois and the political responsibilities of the two major parties, the local police force is not able to enforce federal statutes without reliance upon the National Guard. We are all very thankful for the high degree of balance between professionalism, voluntarism, compulsion, and political intervention which you find in the National Guard, which makes possible keeping a minimum amount of law and order in the city of Chicago during the summer. We anticipate that the National Guard will have to be a creative institution here in the years ahead while we are trying to change race relations.

On the question of distinction between compulsion and freedom, I quite agree with Mr. Friedman. The national military establishment must make more use of economic incentive systems to manage the military establishment. Step-by-step techniques, including raising wages, are certainly required. However, I would like to emphasize, in this regard, that wages are only one part of this process that I think is very crucial in the modification of the retirement system. There have been before Congress, repeatedly, statutes to have fully vested, fluid retirement systems like any industry, which I think would make the system more competitive, but very little progress has been made in modifying military retirement systems. Likewise, the whole question of dual compensation and the barriers that operate against military people when they seek civil employment, need to be eliminated—some progress has been made in the elimination of aspects of dual compensation.

But economic variables are not enough; the basic notion of military professionalism needs to be changed. We are beginning to see some signs within the military establishment of a changing in its self-conception, because its prestige is derived from its self-conception. And in the long run, I cannot see how, simply by manipulating the economic variables, you get the necessary changes in the professional identity of the military establishment. We must recognize that the variables that we used in the past—to maintain civil supremacy, and to have a military establishment better than that we deserve—will not work in the future. In the past, two factors have been at work in giving us the military establishment to serve our foreign policy. We've operated on a simple principle; there has been a small group of service families who didn't care what prestige they had but who, out of family tradition, supplied the cadres for maintaining our military establishment. In the past, that is during World Wars I and II, our economic and political elites were prepared in times of crisis to send their sons into crucial positions in the military. As a result of the fusion of this leadership and the small group of service families, the professional basis of our military establishments was maintained. There is absolutely no guarantee at all that there will be any continuity and development of professional traditions since these patterns of recruitment do not necessarily work or are currently changing. Both of these things, the service families and the elite, may be passing from the scene. I think the question of how we are going to continue to professionalize our military becomes the question of a bridge between the intellectuals and the military. In part, in the world in which we live, we are creating intellectual, scholarly, and research contacts with civilian universities which are an essential element of professionalization.

Mr. Wool. I'd like to clarify one point raised by Congressman Rumsfeld. There is no secret Pentagon study on the draft. There is a public Pentagon study of the draft. That study is included in over 100 pages of the Congressional Record of the House Hearings on the Administration and Operation

tive Service System conducted last June. The findings have been made available to the extent that they are mechanically reproduceable. Dr. Oi used a great deal of the data made available to him, as well as other scholars interested in this problem. I think, deplorably, the number of people who talk about a secret study, and the number of people who try to get the information are quite different in dimensions.

Now, moving to substance—I want to make one thing clear. The impression has been conveyed that the Department of Defense generally, or I, personally, really don't want a volunteer force. I think the record, in this respect, is somewhat different. There are three military services—the Air Force, Navy, and Marine Corps—which have, with very limited exceptions, recruited their people completely through enlistments. Those limited exceptions were for brief periods when they had to resort to draft calls, this year and a few years earlier. In the Army, the best evidence I can submit is when they could get more recruits, they reduced their draft calls as low as zero. We had zero draft calls in a couple of months of 1960. When recruiting during the past year increased, even with considerable complications for both Selective Service and the Army itself, the draft calls were cut, at short notice, as low as they could be, consistent with the best estimate of how many recruits they could get. They have not turned down any recruits. We spend $70 million a year trying to get them.

Now, having said this, I think that it's an accurate statement that the government as a whole has not embarked upon the approach suggested by Professor Friedman, of saying, "Let's start paying five or more billion dollars more to just see what happens." Will this produce enough volunteering? I think there's been a tremendous skepticism on the part of the professionals concerned with recruiting and on the part of the congressmen as to whether a figure which they might consider within a fiscally realistic range for an experiment would produce the results. I think this, in part, underlies the feeling, because when you're dealing with huge expenditures, with all their fiscal impact, a judgment is needed as to the probability of success for this investment. Now, the judgments here differ somewhat, obviously. First, the probability of succeeding is perhaps lower than some people here might think, and second, even after you got there, you might succeed for a brief time and then fall flat on your face a year later because of the broader consideration of contingencies, even for a "limited war."

I should emphasize that the decision to look at the possibility of an all-volunteer force was not imposed upon the Department of Defense by the Congress. I think I've looked at all the resolutions passed and all the debates and only a very small number of individuals, among all those who criticize the draft and its operation, seriously raised the issue of an all-volunteer force. That issue and the prospect of attaining it were, in fact, initiated in the Pentagon itself, because people like Colonel Hays and many others feel that they could, in fact, have a more professional force. We looked at it hard; we recruited talent where we could. Obviously, estimates in judgment vary as to the specific costs involved, but these, I think are honest, professional judgments. For example, there was a tendency to brush away this transitional problem. The estimates presented by Dr. Oi indicate what the cost might be 10 years later, after this transitional phase is totally completed. Well, unfortunately, we live in a world where we need military forces between now and this 10-year level-off period. Another obvious technical factor is that the supply relationship, the responsiveness of recruitment to pay, which might exist in more normal conditions, would not necessarily prevail under a condition such as the one we are now in. When a great majority of young men can choose various careers in a soft, urban, white-collar-oriented society, let's be very honest as to how many would really choose the career which involves your being an infantry officer in Vietnam now, as a present fact or real contingency, and how much more you'd have to be paid to make that switch in your profession. I'm talking now about feasibility rather than the desirability. I personally think it's totally unrealistic to expect that we could just pay 5 or 10 or 15 billion dollars more to get a 3.3- or 3.5-million force, which, whether we personally like it or not, is there because of the world we live in today.

Now, there are a few other specific points. The question was raised as to reserve: wouldn't they be available for an emergency? Well, honestly, I don't think you'd have much of a reserve if you had an all-volunteer force. You'd have, first of all, much less turnover from the people separating who would enter the reserves; second, those who initially enlist in the reserves we know do this because it involves less of an active service commitment than does active service, so these men typically would not be available.

Mr. Rumsfeld. I'd like to clarify one thing. It's my recollection that there was political pressure for a study on the draft in 1964. The President announced that he was setting up a DOD study group. The results of that study were in fact kept secret for 8 to 12 months beyond the scheduled reporting date. The report that was made public was "a report on the report," and certainly not the study that was made by the Defense Department study group. Now this was essentially what I thought I said. You suggested that the full report of that group was made public. It's my understanding that the full report was not made public.

Mr. Wool. The only report that exists in a real sense is the report of the Secretary of Defense. There were many staff studies. Dr. Oi made some; I made some; dozens of other individuals gave importance to this thing. This is not a study in terms of the government report. What is ultimately the study is what in fact is finally approved and submitted by the responsible official, in this case the Secretary of Defense. That study and a vast amount of supporting material in connection with that study have been made available.

Mr. Oi. I would like to raise the simple question that I think we've been skirting around. I think Congressman Kastenmeier raised it. "What do we do now?" We're in Vietnam; the draft law ends on June 30, 1967. My feeling is that when we had Armed Forces of 2.6 million with age classes of about 1.2 million men, at that point, a minority of Congress felt that a voluntary army was feasible. If we extrapolate this into the decade ahead, then I think the case becomes even stronger that a voluntary Army is indeed possible.

I would like to say my relationships with the Defense Department were excellent and I enjoyed the experience. I disagreed with some of the conclusions that they drew from the papers and the report, but to some extent that is a matter of judgment, and justifies differences of opinion. In terms of moving toward a voluntary force, I think one thing deserves much more attention and study: how have others done it? Australia is one example. Britain is another. They announced in 1956 that they would abolish the draft as of 1960. In between, I believe they had a crisis or two; I believe Suez occurred after the White Paper report on the decision to abolish the draft. I think that this proposition, whether it's adopted or not, ought to be seriously debated and the alternative faced that if we continue the draft, even with 3.3 million, we are forcing from 60,000 to 75,000 men to enter military service, when the same job on a voluntary basis could have been done by 40 to 50 per cent, each man remaining in service longer. In response to Senator Neuberger's question, the mechanism that I would envisage would be one of an initial obligatory tour, expecting about two-thirds of those who reach the reenlistment point to leave the service at that point and not stay on to retirement.

      Mr. Chapman. I'm very happy to hear that there is no secret study of the draft. I was also glad to hear that the DOD started all these studies. It seems to me that the President announced his study approximately three days before the scheduled House special orders by a group of Republicans to blast the draft back in 1964. Of course, there are always studies going on, but the "big study" was then initiated by the President. It was supposed to report a year later. It didn't report. It didn't report until June of this last year and then the report was 22 pages, double spaced, wide-margined and, as a matter of fact, to my surprise later on, there was a great amount of additional material added to the testimony in the printed version which appeared later. But some of the material that's in those surveys contradicts some of the points raised in the report itself. Now, I'm also happy to hear that this material is available, and the findings behind the material are available, and I would like to avail myself of it. Congressman Curtis, who tried to, right after the June 30 hearings, was refused. I'm very happy to hear that this is open now and I look forward to a full exposure of this to any Congressman who would want to have it.

    Also, I am glad to hear that the Department of Defense does want volunteers and that, of course, we have three services that do use volunteers. As a matter of fact, it seems somewhat contradictory on one hand to say that we are able to get volunteers for the Marines and Air Force and so on and yet, on the other hand, ask people how many of them would want to go to Vietnam. Is it really true that we'd have to conscript people to undertake that kind of task?

    It also was mentioned that in 1960 we didn't have a draft for a couple of months in succession; there were no calls. Congressman Curtis has pointed out that a number of people have come to him reporting that recruitment officers discouraged people during that era from enlisting. I don't know if this is true or false, but I'll tell you there's only one way to find out, and that is not through a Defense Department study, it is not through a Presidential commission, it is through an open hearing of Congress where recruitment officers can be subpoenaed to appear and give their testimony. I think that's the only solution to some of these matters of fact—to get Congress, with a select committee, to get this material before themselves and before the public.

    Finally, it was asked why we should pay 5 billion dollars just to see what happens. It seems to me that, as Dr. Friedman pointed out, even if we all agree that the draft is necessary, we would still need to pay these people fairly, and I think that should be a beginning right there. As for the reserves, it seems to me that if we had a similar professional reserve, we would be more able to call them up than we are today. The fact of the matter is, the reserves are not called up today. They can't be called up today for political reasons and because they are filled with reluctant people who do not make good reservists, who do not like the reserves, and therefore are not good soldiers. We'd be doing much better to have a group of willing volunteers who could be used.

Mr. Friedman. In simple justice, in asking who got this Defense Department study started, I think that Mr. Chapman should have mentioned that President Johnson's proposal came one week after Barry Goldwater pledged that he would abolish the draft if elected. Maybe it was two weeks.

To return to the subjects that are more appropriate for us to consider, I want to agree completely with Mr. Janowitz that economic variables alone are obviously not the way in which you establish a satisfactory academic group in running a university; it's not the way we get satisfactory positions. It's not the way we get a satisfactory Army. The point is that mishandling the economic variable can make it impossible to use other variables and other approaches in such a way as to have a satisfactory force. The first requisite for getting a military force on a volunteer basis is to get the economic picture straightened out. That's a necessary but by no means a sufficient condition.

Along these same lines, I appreciated very much Margaret Mead's expansion on the notion of mercenary forces and I apologize if I misquoted her. I didn't intend to, and I agree completely with almost everything she said. I do believe that there is a distinction between mercenary forces in the sense of an army available for hire out to anybody, and a career army, and I think that's a very important distinction, and one that should be made. With respect to hiring foreign nationals if you could get them cheaper, let's not make false issues. We now do. In every country where we have military forces we hire nationals of that country. We hire Germans for duties, some of which are the same as those of military personnel. In Vietnam we hire Vietnamese, and there's no reason why we shouldn't. The question is not one of all or none, that we hire or don't hire them; the question is: To what extent are the Armed Forces constituted of American citizens?

Senator Neuberger's question—Does the volunteer turn into something else? No. The volunteer or the career man makes a contract to do a certain job over a certain period of time. He commits himself for that period of time. As in all civilian contracts, there are termination possibilities. If in some way or another the contract is broken, by one side or another, it may be terminated. It may be terminated at the end of a three-year agreement, just as if a man agreed to go abroad for an American company for three years, that's an agreement for three years, but it's a voluntary arrangement. So the notion that the only strictly voluntary arrangement is between day workers is not one I think that the Senator would want to maintain.

Finally, I cannot resist ending with one comment on the issue of compulsion in the draft versus compulsory education because that's a much broader philosophical issue and one in which the various answers that have been given do not get to the heart of the problem. The argument for compulsory education is not an argument for compulsory conscription for the following reason. The comparison you want to look at is this: We compel an owner of an automobile in some states to have liability insurance to insure other people against his doing them damage. That's not the same as commandeering his automobile for public purpose, and this is precisely the distinction. Whether rightly or not, we now compel parents to school their children on the grounds that otherwise those children will be a danger to the rest of the community. Now that's vastly different, philosophically, from conscripting those children for forced labor.

FIFTH SESSION

National Service

TUESDAY AFTERNOON, DECEMBER 6, 1966

Chairman, WAYNE C. BOOTH

Mr. Wofford. Thanks to the sessions and the papers and the arguments in the past few days, I'm a convert to the idea of a volunteer Army, to the idea of taking as a real goal the ending of the draft and an all volunteer Army as part of the program. It would make voluntary national service a major part of our national life, and especially of our education system. Now I've been hung up between two poles, the idea of universal national service and the idea of volunteering. The values of universal service are great; Margaret Mead's paper lists some of them. Many papers list others. If we want to win the war on poverty, Dick Boone's paper shows that this would be a way to do it. If we want to win the struggle for integration, universal national service—in bringing everybody together for a period of common work—would help do it. If we want really powerful education for the twentieth-century world, this kind of period of experience for everybody would help do it. I've seen this and it worked—in Israel for example, and in Ethiopia. In Ethiopia the only university had made national service the condition for any degree, and it works. Israel is winning its war on poverty, and is integrating and educating its people through voluntary national service. So, I've been on this mountain top and been tempted.

But, I don't think we should have compulsory national service because of the damage it would do and probably the destruction it would cause to another great value, that of volunteering. Suppose that we add that word to the title today: *"voluntary* national service." The definition I'm using is the first definition in the dictionary, that is, doing something of your own will and volition. Another way of putting this is self-government. I'm suggesting that the idea of volunteering taken seriously can give new vitality to what America is all about, to self-government. I've seen this in the Peace Corps, and it works. A period of volunteer service on public problems could be the most appropriate form of education I know for a life of self-government. If at the beginning of your career you have this period when you do something of your own free will, something difficult and concerned with the common good, if you have a variety of alternatives, and you choose one and you do it, maybe the habit is going to stick. What I've seen in the Peace Corps makes me think it has stuck, and that a great part of ex-Peace Corps volunteers want to go on making their own futures as they go. They have become full-time, permanent, life-long volunteers in that sense.

I believe America is ready for a real quantum jump in this kind of volunteering. You see it on all sides. The Peace Corps is one little example of it. The student movement, the 7 million man-days of tutoring that Gene Groves' group estimated went on last year, is another example of it. Participation is the battle cry.

If we try to proceed now, however, by compulsion, while the idea of volunteering for national service is just about to break loose and be taken up by private groups, churches, schools, colleges, and corporations, the heavy hand of compulsion could kill the spirit of volunteering.

Yet, the draft today is crushing that spirit of volunteering. The draft is a heavy hand. The lottery might be a crap game, but the draft today is a monstrous crap game in which millions of young men are forced to play with 4,000 local boards. The draft is indirectly discouraging volunteering in all kinds of ways. Take, for example, the Peace Corps volunteers. Some draft boards treat two years of Peace Corps service as national service, and they don't call volunteers generally until they're through with those who haven't served anywhere or volunteered for anything. Other draft boards give no recognition whatsoever to the period of volunteer service and they draft Peace Corps volunteers. Many have been drafted after they come home for service, and then they go and spend two years at Fort Dix or perhaps in Vietnam. We have some draft boards that draft Peace Corps volunteers who are in service and call them home in the midst of their assignment, after the government has sent them over committed to carry out important work for other nations. Then they go to Fort Dix.

The problem is, how to encourage volunteering so that it becomes as common as going to high school or to college. I would suggest that if the Vietnam war subsides, or ends, by the time of the next presidential election, the following proposal should be part of the platform of a presidential candidate. We will end the draft as soon as possible, and go on to an all-volunteer system of national service including military and non-military volunteering. We are going to devise incentives that will make this realistic for both military and non-military service, and these incentives, although they will include raising pay to a decent, competitive level, will be designed primarily to put this whole field of volunteering in the context of American education. Therefore, the main incentives for the military volunteer will be a GI bill of rights that will really enable him to go on to higher education without working, which the GI bill of rights is not generous enough today to do and for the non-military volunteer the incentives will be a system of educational scholarships that will give the individual a subsistence allowance to enable him to be a volunteer. I would hope colleges and universities and high schools would see this program as an appropriate new stage in American education and encourage it.

There also needs to be an entity, a national commission on volunteer service, that supervises and appraises this program. Their assignment should not be just to appraise the draft but to bury it, and during that transition period, we're going to have to assume the Selective Service System is going to resist its own demise, quite naturally. We have to assume that there will be elements in the Pentagon who will find it easier to keep the draft and keep the pool as large as possible. Therefore, we need a very high level and potent national commission on volunteer service that will have as its task moving to an all-volunteer system of national service.

Secretary Wirtz's proposal for a continuation of universal compulsory registration and health examination might well fit into this program as a form of getting medical and other counseling to the whole younger generation, and providing them with a source of information on available opportunities. As a means of encouraging volunteering, the transitional steps needed are; first, to make the call come for younger people first and end the uncertainty as soon as possible, preferably at 18, and, second, to give deferment automatically as a national rule to those who engage in non-military volunteer service—to the Peace Corps now, so that they will not be called back from service. A new order of induction should be established for those who have engaged in voluntary service, who would be called after those who haven't served anywhere. Finally, as part of universal participation, I think we should go all the way: if we're going to call people at 18 and send them overseas in war and peace on assignments of life and death, they ought to have the right to vote. That would be in the platform of the candidate I'm nominating today.

Mr. Eberly. The 80-page plan for national service that was distributed just yesterday morning tries to outline the operation and scope of national service in some detail and to provide the basis for exploring the subject further, looking into the impact of national service on the economy, on society, on higher education, and trying to set up an operational model for it. It deals with the needs of society, and describes the actual service tasks to be performed. We suggest that the number of tasks at a level which could be met by young people in programs of national service is significant, on the order of half a million within a very short period of time.

The plan makes certain manpower assumptions that were suggested in the Department of Defense study regarding those persons who will be needed by the military in the coming years, and the increasingly large numbers of persons who will be qualified for military service but cannot be expected to be called. We've analyzed this group, together with the medically unqualified, using as a base Dr. Kárpinos' figures and making an approximation of the percentages in the various categories who might qualify for a program of national service.

Mr. Anderson mentioned this morning the cost factor. We've tried to indicate an approach to figuring out the economics of the question, but it's only a very basic beginning in that regard.

The plan, like the one that Mr. Wofford has just put forward, is one for non-compulsory, non-military service. It suggests, on the first page or two, that compulsion would be limited to meeting the necessary military manpower requirements and that no one would be compelled to serve in a non-military activity. The plan approaches national service not through the avenue of military service, but from the needs of society, in terms of education, health, the other jobs to be done, the needs of the individual, and the responsibility of the society and the state to give him opportunities and experience for education, and for service, to better prepare him for the life ahead. I think that any program of national service which has as its primary base the problem of draft inequities will result in a structure for a national service that will fall flat on its face when the draft calls drop to zero. It must be structured properly, and perhaps we should lean over backwards not to introduce the draft question at all until such times as the calls fall to a lower level.

The program itself is outlined starting with the transitional stage. I think it is here that a number of us proposing various forms of national service probably agree that universal voluntary service is a good idea and should be put forward as a national goal, that more information should be made available to young men and young women about the kinds of service opportunities which are open to them, and that perhaps the Selective Service System might do this. We feel that some funding should be available for a wide array of non-military activities through some kind of foundation for volunteer service, so that the real importance of the kinds of non-military service we're talking about might then be expected to evolve.

The transition period would last from three to five years, with the next stage becoming possible as the Vietnam situation subsided, reducing the size of the draft calls. You'd have to identify enough useful tasks to be sure that you have places for everyone who was volunteering for this program. Machinery would have to be developed. There would have to be enough trained personnel to do the training at the sites and to supervise the young men and young women in their non-military service activities, and there has to be assurance of sufficient funds. When this happened you could move to the so-called steady-state stage, the option plan in which when young men register for the draft they would be able to opt for military service or non-military service, or apply for conscientious objector status, or go into the draft pool. The draft pool might be selective, it might be a lottery, or whatever mechanism is needed. But those choosing a particular kind of service would then be under a contract to fulfill that service at the time indicated. People could go in right away at 18 or upon completing their college degrees, so there would be a wider variety of talents and skills in this non-military service program and greater freedom of choice among the individuals who enter it. Here the relationship to the draft would be very much as Harris Wofford described. The liability would still have to be there, and I think this follows from the definition of national sovereignty, but men could be placed later in the order of call so that they would be called, let us say, after the married men but someplace before the 4F's, and normally would be called only in case of emergency. This then would give national recognition to the service which had been performed.

How does this meet the various strong viewpoints expressed? Mr. Kelly and Mr. Houston talked about the individual; I think this program takes into consideration the needs and interest of the individual. Mr. Mauldin talked about morale; a national service program of this kind would give greater morale in both military and non-military activities. Colonel Ingold has indicated a desire for increased voluntarism in the military; probably this kind of system would encourage that, so a higher percentage in the military would actually be volunteers.

Some issues remain which I'm sure we'll get to this afternoon. How centralized should this be? Can we use the basic decentralized approach suggested in this plan or do we need a national service corps with directors and supervisors to control this? Can the local schools and Red Cross really manage these people? What criteria do we use to define approved national service? Should it be simply "the national health, safety, and interest" written into the law now for conscientious objectors? We might have to define that further to include non-profit agencies offering work commensurate with the person's talents, and so forth. What is the relationship to paramilitary operations? The proposal makes brief reference to this and the boundaries that should exist between non-military and military service programs. Would this be a challenge to the military service to give more thought to the kinds of activities they carry on and who should do them? Finally, I would return to the question of the national image of national service. Happily, Secretary McNamara talked about it last May; unhappily he is the Secretary of Defense, and I think that because of the nature of his job, and because it is the National Advisory Commission on Selective Service which is examining the proposal, it is too closely tied to the military and to the draft.

Dr. Mead. When I proposed that national service be universal, I agreed with everything Mr. Wofford said about the desirability of volunteer service and participation in society and its being part of education. But you notice he said our young people in high school and college. And we're repeating in spite of ourselves what we've been doing for the last 50 years, leaving some 20 or 30 million of our population dispossessed. The only way that we know how to include everyone is to coerce not the people, but the government—federal, state, or local, as you wish—into making something universal. These are the grounds on which I propose that this should be universal. It should be *available* to everyone.

I tied it to the draft here because this is a conference on the draft, and I was asked to come and discuss national service here. When I proposed it originally I didn't tie it to the draft. I agree very much with Mr. Eberly that it shouldn't be tied to the draft, except at the moment when the draft is what the country is thinking about, and what college students are thinking about. The only connection that I would make with the draft is that if all young people were given opportunities to be looked at again by the country, to be assayed for their potentialities and defects, to be given a chance for help and education, or a chance for the widest possible choice of volunteer services, I think we could probably fill the needs of the military most of the time.

Many of the feelings about the draft are that it's inconvenient, it interferes with your life, and it interrupts your life. If, instead, say at 18, all young people in this country could have a second chance to participate in what the country regarded as important, I think this would be very valuable. Now, there is such a prejudice against anything that is done today, any new rules, new suggestions, new law, that would suggest anybody is forced to do anything, even the government. I imagine this is the reason that this has been interpreted as a picture of coercion, that I would draft every man and woman and haul them up. Also, they say I said I was in favor of women in combat units because they were such good, fierce, defensive fighters, when actually I said I was *not* in favor of women in combat units *because* they were such fierce fighters. Men have all sorts of nice rules, like you don't fight on Christmas, you know, and they're willing to make them—but never trust women to make rules like that if they are fighting. This is my analogy from the animal world, but so far we know of no human society that has given women weapons for any length of time that survived, and I think doing so may be slightly dangerous. This statement got translated in the Press into my wanting to have women in combat units because they were so fierce—it's very curious, you see? My suggestion really, was that we give all young people a chance to choose—to serve their country for about two years, and in that period we make up to them for anything that they've lost, and we give them a chance. And from within this group what military forces are necessary may be drawn.

There's a crucial issue here that I think is going to be very important, and it relates to how we feel about the draft and how we're going to feel about any kind of universal voluntary service. There is some feeling not that anything voluntary puts a demand on our government, but that anything universal puts a demand on us. It depends on whether you think of compulsory education as a way in which children get an education and that every community has to provide a school, or if you think it is a way of keeping their parents in order. If you've ever been to the new countries, you know that compulsory education is the first step for literacy for all the people, and without it you won't have literacy, and you won't have the budget to apply it. We've learned a great many lessons through the years from the piecemeal way we handled Social Security; one lesson is that sometimes universality is the simplest way of guaranteeing something for everyone. But it's only in that sense that I'm proposing that the service be universal. If it gets defined as coercion, or authoritarian regimentation, this is the dilemma that we face in our society. I'm not advocating the unfeasible. I'm advocating that we move towards as full a voluntary service as possible, only I would see, as a long-term plan, some way of including *every* young person in this country. Some way should be found in which all our young people can see service to their country as complete instead of partial, not only being asked to go out to kill on behalf of their country, but being asked to do positive and constructive things.

Mr. Wofford. Another crucial thing would be that there ought to be real effort to get volunteer service opportunity to parts of the young population not covered today by the Peace Corps or by *Vista*, to the high school dropouts. This will take some special provision for fellowship programs that come up with good designs, that bring those young people together with others in teams or other ways.

Mr. Eberly. I think recently some $16 million was authorized for a Senior Citizens Service Corps of some sort, and I would see that fitting into national service. Many of these people could be the supervisors, the administrative personnel. With the expansion of voluntarism and the greater number of volunteers that the various community service agencies, schools, and hospitals have, they would need some of the older people to manage it, and I would see them fitting in, in that kind of way.

Mr. Naisbitt. I'm thoroughly confused about Miss Mead's position. When you say you want to give everyone a chance, every young person a chance, does that mean only those who volunteer, or that everyone will be not drafted, but everyone will sign up?

Dr. Mead. No, I would like everyone to have a chance as they now have a chance at a public school education.

Mr. Naisbitt. But if they choose not to take the chance—do they have to go?

Dr. Mead. They'd have to do something or I suppose we'd have a new breed of conscientious objectors and we'd have a new set of ethics to deal with them. They're all right—we can always have them. But most people would choose, if they had the degree of choice. Only people who regarded anything that was done by the federal government as an anathema, I think, would choose against the kind of program that we ought to move toward. I don't think we're going to have it next year.

Mr. Eberly. I want to make it clear that that is not what I mean by voluntary.

Mr. Booth. Mr. Eberly, in what sense were you using the word *voluntary* when you said a voluntary national service?

Mr. Eberly. That a person would volunteer for a non-military service activity and that that activity would be recognized by placing him later in the order of call.

Mr. Booth. But he would be required either to do that or be drafted, is that it?

Mr. Eberly. No, no, his option would be to go into the draft pool, which is where everybody else is now, or to become a CO. It is simply adding on the "voluntary" as an additional option.

Dr. Mead. I think I ought to add one more point: Within this system we would give a wide range of choice. There are two definitions of "voluntary" —one is that you're able to choose within a condition, such as being alive, or being an American; the other means that you do something for nothing, or for very poor pay, out of nobility. Those are the two usual positions.

[Unidentified Speaker]. I expected you to say something quite different, but it keeps coming out that everyone's going to have to sign up, which is kind of a draft.

Dr. Mead. I don't think our children are drafted to go to school; I've spent too much time in countries where no one could learn to read and write. And I'm using that analogy.

Mrs. McAllister. I would like to know if the intention is that these voluntary, obligatory, what-not services must be performed under a government agency or, as with the education system, may be done through such parochial institutions as Crossroads Africa, or the UWCA.

Mr. Booth. I think that all three speakers did suggest that they could be done by other organizations. Am I right in that?

Mrs. McAllister. Administered through a national agency?

Mr. Booth. I think that all three suggested otherwise? Mr. Eberly?

Mr. Eberly. The agency would have to say: This is going to be the housing arrangement; these are the administrative personnel, and so on. The person then would report directly to the school or to the Operation Crossroads or the service agency, and the funds for providing a subsistence allowance for the volunteer would be channeled through it. The agency could, of course, refuse federal funds.

Mrs. McAllister. But it would still qualify to meet national needs for services of youth?

Mr. Eberly. Yes. There'd be two separate organizations: the national foundation which would be the funding group, and a national service system, which would establish the criteria for meeting the manpower needs in the military sector. Now, when that goes to zero, the national foundation and the non-military service activities would continue.

Charles Sherrod. Could activities which are carried on by civil rights organizations be included in this voluntary service?

Mr. Booth. Would the three speakers accept SNCC or CORE activity? Are you thinking of those specifically?

Mr. Sherrod. Civil rights activity, voter registration . . .

Dr. Mead. I think civil rights activity is too general. I would like, contrary to some of the other statements that have been made here, to reserve the right of civil disobedience for people who strongly object to anything that is going on, including accepting civil punishment as the way of bringing that to people's attention. I don't believe that taking all the sacrifice out of civil disobedience is an answer. Some civil rights organizations could go in, but it would depend on their methods, not their aims.

Mr. Wofford. I would like to turn that question back to Mr. Tatum or someone else who knows about how the provision for conscientious objectors is worked out. The language reads well in terms of the answer I would give. Civilian work contributing to the maintenance of national health, safety, or interest has been defined to be "work with a non-profit organization, association, or corporation which is primarily engaged in a charitable activity, conducted for the benefit of the general public or in carrying out a program for the improvement of the public health or welfare, including educational or scientific activities in support thereof, when such activities or program is not principally for the benefit of the members of such organization or for increasing the membership thereof." Now, that's fairly good language. I'd like to know how it's worked out. Has it worked out to include working in Negro voter registration, or for SNCC or for NAACP?

Mr. Tatum. No, these organizations have not been acceptable for alternative service.

Mr. Wofford. Some variety has been accepted.

Mr. Tatum. Well, it's pretty good. I'd say that we have the best alternative service in the world, of those countries that have provisions for conscientious objection. The Peace Corps type of work with volunteer organizations is approved as alternative service, a good many of the men do their work abroad.

[Unidentified Speaker]. With church groups?

Mr. Tatum. Principally with church groups, international voluntary service and other organizations—not necessarily religious. Domestically, we're now running into some difficulty with what you might call domestic Peace Corps work. Actually, at this particular point, as in everything in the field of conscientious objection, there's a pulling in. But up to this development of the social tension that's resulted from the war, there have been fairly good opportunities, but civil rights organizations have always been excluded.

Mr. Chapman. I have some of the same questions about interpretation of what's universal and what's coercive. It seems to me that Mr. Wofford is looking forward not only to a volunteer national service but also a volunteer military, and in fact they're part of the same system. Mr. Eberly is saying that he would prefer to separate the draft question from national service. For example, he'd take it through a different committee in Congress, but his system of voluntary service assumes and finds it necessary to go to the draft. Is that correct?

Mr. Eberly. When the option plan goes into effect, say after five years of transition period, then those in the draft pool could be taken, as necessary, by the military by lottery, or by Selective Service. It is not an integral part of the plan to have either one or the other.

Mr. Chapman. In other words, you are equally at home with a draft or no draft. It makes no difference to your concept of national service?

Mr. Keast. May I clarify? In Mr. Eberly's plan there is no longer a draft pool. It is fully voluntary, as I understand Mr. Wofford's to be. That is to say, the 18- or 19-year-old either volunteers or doesn't, as he chooses, is that right?

Mr. Eberly. That's right, but there would be a national foundation for volunteer service which would only be a funding outfit, anyway, and it would continue just as it is.

Mr. Keast. But there would be no obligation on anybody to serve?

Mr. Eberly. That's right.

Mr. Wofford. Could I clarify it another way? I want volunteer service to become the thing to do. I want to get it considered the most interesting part of one's education, and I think to get that to happen, you're going to have to put this in the context of true volunteering.

Mr. Winter. It might be helpful this afternoon, although you can't get too neat uses of language, if we would agree on the term *voluntary* as meaning something like an internal principle, that is, self-choosing, self-initiation, self-determination. The word is ambiguous and it's being used in several ways. If we could agree that it usually means the will, and it means one acts out of one's own will as a principle of determination, that would really help a lot.

Mr. Booth. And you're pointing out the radical difference between a situation in which an 18-year-old must choose one organization or another, in which case voluntary means . . .

Mr. Winter. Forced options, acquiescence, consent, these are all different from choosing. This is all I'd argue.

Mr. Arnold Anderson. If some people need rehabilitation, literacy, improved health, and so forth, and this takes so long that their period of "service" is exhausted before they ever do any service, is their rehabilitation still embraced in your proposal?

Dr. Mead. It would be in mine. Very definitely. That's the reason I think it's hard to ask the Army to do it, because they never can get it done in time.

Mr. Wofford. I would say, "Yes, *but.* . . ." If the Job Corps, or the rehabilitation programs, do not really include an element of service, if it's all having things done to you, to rehabilitate you, I don't think rehabilitation would be genuine. So I believe that the Job Corps has got to be somehow merged into a volunteer service program so that participants really do feel that they are contributing something to the country.

Mr. Eberly. Mr. Anderson suggested that for those who've received least from their society in the form of education, most of their time in national service would be in educational rehabilitation, and for those who have had the greatest benefits, most of their time would be in the actual service function. Now, the Job Corps has some 88 conservation centers at which there is a service component, and my understanding is they find this better in many respects than others which are totally for the person. This service element would be expanded in a program of national service.

Mr. Booth. Does any one of the three speakers want to offer any final points of clarification?

Mr. Eberly. I would have one on "phasing" here—Would it be possible to talk about what we would like to see happen in 1967? I think there is more agreement among us as to what the right next steps are, than on what might be the condition 10 years from now.

Mr. Booth. If we can fit it in I think we should.

Colonel Bar-On. One word to second what Mr. Wofford said. We experimented both with deprived people who were drawn for educational purposes only, and those who were drawn for education and service. We failed completely with those who were drawn only for education. But success was considerably greater with those who went in for actual service and education came only as a secondary purpose.

Mr. Bramson. I want to say that I think this Conference is very fortunate to have as a representative of the Selective Service System a gentleman with as much candor and intelligence as Colonel Ingold. Colonel Ingold said that Selective Service creates uncertainty deliberately, so that people will volunteer. I think that's what we're talking about now, when we talk about national service. I think we're hung up on the problem of whether or not it's practically possible to affect the situation of Selective Service now and the draft now. In short, I'm referring to a problem that's related to the political feasibility of the national service scheme, in which non-military alternatives have parity with military alternatives. I'm very concerned that it will not be possible to change this system, and I'm personally committed to a system of national service alternatives which are non-military. I believe that our national interest demands an expansion of the concept of narrow military service to a much broader field. It seems to me that we approach a fork in the road: this is the question of whether or not we're going to press for a program which is morally immaculate, which is unattainable, as opposed to a program which might be pragmatically feasible. I have not yet resolved that question in my own mind. I am not sure how I can answer the problem of creating uncertainty deliberately, so that people will volunteer not only for military but for non-military service. Anyone who considers the problem of national service alternatives has to face this question.

If you believe that the Congress will not do anything about the draft, it seems to me that you have to look at the real possibility that next year and two years from now we will again be faced with what is, to me, the ludicrous situation of, for example, Peace Corps volunteers who lay their lives on the line in the Dominican Republic and Northern Nigeria contrasted with the man back home in the Quartermaster Corps; or the ratio of support to combat of 6:1 in the United States Army where a man is not laying his life on the line, but sitting in an Army post. I propose, in short, that the concept of what is military is indeed crucial to this question.

Finally, I want to suggest that before this Conference is over we should take a close look at the data which are presented amply in the papers. Professor Janowitz' paper deals very poignantly with the issue of the differential quality of participation of individuals in this society. There are statistics presented there. Dr. Karpinos' studies document the fact that the condition and the situation of the American Negro, in relation to military service, would deserve a conference all by itself. If the study by the Department of Defense which revealed that 67 per cent of all American Negroes in the 18-year-old bracket failed the AFQT is relevant to this Conference, it is also a symptom of a larger social issue. That issue needs to be attacked. I think it is connected with the problem of the college student in a way which I will suggest. In this country we're facing, socially, a crisis which hasn't yet risen to the surface; which we haven't yet defined. I'm interested in how social problems become defined, and I think we're facing a problem about the isolation from one another of different groups within a country where groups used to be in close touch with each other. It's possible for college students, for example, to grow up in one-class, one-race communities without having any contact with people who are different from them. I deplore this situation and I think it's contrary to the American heritage. This is one of the great opportunities that I see in terms of the educational value of non-military service alternatives.

Mr. Cullinan. We seem to have avoided at this Conference the combination of our idealistic goal with a pragmatic short-run approach for June 30, 1967, when something is going to have to be done. Just to summarize, very briefly, my own studies, including a survey that I recently carried out at Stanford University: People from every walk of life, and from every level of life, can benefit a great deal by a break in their formal educational program (if they are going on to college), or by an extension of their educational experience if they do not plan to go on to college, if they dropped out of high school, or if they were deprived of a complete high school education because of race, poverty, or any other reason. I refer you first to the statistics on the acceptability of national service among the younger age groups, specifically high school and junior college. Dr. Bramson has presented a paper here which, he tells me, is the only statistically supportable survey of high school attitudes on the question of national service which has ever been carried out. The annual convention of California Junior Colleges heard several recommendations from area groups that in June, 1967, the present draft law should be changed to provide a system of national service which would include non-military alternatives, on a voluntary basis, to military service.

We must realize that this Conference represents an extremely skewed representation of the American population. The lower levels—the non-college levels of the American population—are unrepresented here except perhaps in Dr. Bramson's paper and in this statement. I think that the feeling against the draft is *not* something that is widespread throughout the country. I think it exists widely among vocal groups on most of the "prestige" college campuses, and that's just about all. I think also that this Conference has to accept one fact: as has been pointed out, on June 30, 1967, there is going to remain a compulsory draft in the United States. The question is: Do we want to do something to change this, or to point it in the direction which I think we all would accept in the long-run—a voluntary system of national service, including both military and non-military options? I believe this is a consensus of this Conference. (I'm not sure—I'll probably be challenged by 124 people.) I would suggest, therefore, (1) that we first make a positive statement as a Conference, rejecting conclusively the concepts of compulsory *non*-military service, (2) that we consider coming out in favor of the abolition of compulsory military service by, say, June 30, 1971, or by *x* years after the culmination of the Vietnamese war, and (3) that we come out in favor of the establishment of a voluntary, alternative, non-military national service at the earliest possible time, under either a national foundation for voluntary service or some other organization similar to that suggested by Don Eberly or Harris Wofford. I would like to suggest that for the interim period (during which military service is to be retained), we urge adoption of an alternative, non-draft service as part of the law which will be passed on June 30, 1967, which would enable any individual, by his own choice, prior to receiving a draft induction notice, to state that he will do an equivalent service term in non-military alternative service. Such service could be either private or public. Each private agency participating (again on a voluntary basis from the agency standpoint) would be able to set whatever prerequisite criteria for national servicemen it wanted, and utilize the servicemen in any way that it chose. The only requirement would be annual certification that the serviceman actually had contributed a year's service. I would suggest that, for the present, this program could be accomplished within the scope of existing public and private organizations. It is something that could be done practically *now*, without sacrificing the long-range goal of a voluntary, non-military *and* military service under an umbrella of overall national service.

John Mitrisin. I'd like to agree with Dr. Mead on one point, at least. We should give all Americans, when they are 18, another chance to take advantage of educational and training opportunities. I do not think they should be compelled to participate in national service. We should give them the choice of not doing anything if they want to. You should not try to make national service into a compulsory system and then add a provision for conscientious objection. The program should be created so that people would have to volunteer to join. It can be argued that some of those individuals who would not join are the ones most in need of such a program. This group's failure to participate would mean that they would waste their lives and fail to reach their potentials. This argument has a basis in fact, but I would say that this is the price that has to be paid for freedom. When is a person able to make his own decisions? I say 16. Requiring people when they are 18 or 19 to go into national service denies the idea that people at this age can make decisions.

Mr. Keast. I don't quite understand Mr. Cullinan's proposal to us. Do I understand you to be advocating the following: That as long as the draft must be continued, for whatever reasons, and against whatever objections we may think there could be, that every registrant will have a choice of military service or some other form of alternative, approved, non-military service. Is that correct?

Mr. Cullinan. That is correct. The registrant would have to make that selection, however, before he had been tapped for the military draft. He would have to opt for *non*-military service before he was put into the military service pipeline.

Mr. Weinstein. I want to raise a question in terms of the feelings that I have about the acts of giving and what is given or received by the rest of society. As an economist I am fairly parochial, and am interested in the flow of resources and the real goods available. Can a person go on to become a lawyer, a doctor, a physicist, and put in his service using the specific skills that he has achieved; or must he fit into a rigid category which, from what I've heard, sounds more like social work? To what extent can an individual fulfill this alternative and the society still achieve the benefits of the higher-priced talent?

Dr. Mead. I think we could have any number of different plans, and I'm not trying to lay down a blueprint here. This is something we're going to be working toward. And I don't think we know yet. I *do* think we ought to have all young people register in some form and we should find out who they are, and where they are, and what they need. But whether national service should be within high specialties or low, the important thing is that it should be given as part of activity in the country.

Mr. Cullinan. To answer Mr. Weinstein specifically, I think his human resources—the professionals—could, at the termination of their various edu-

cational programs, find something in the broad spectrum of non-military alternatives which would both qualify as national service and be professionally
and personally stimulating and satisfying. I would prefer, however, that at some
time in the course of their education they take a break and do something which
might not be specifically related to their field, at an early enough time so that it
would not interrupt their professional preparation.

Mr. Booth. But for you, working as a lawyer, or working as a
teacher, would not qualify. This certainly is one of a large range of questions
we'll all have on our minds about just what *is* service, and how broadly do we define the category? Mr. Bakan?

Mr. Bakan. I don't understand what Mr. Cullinan has in mind. Consider the situation in which the draft call exceeds the number of volunteers.
What happens under his proposed plan? This is a conference on the draft, but
somehow we find ourselves right now judging it appropriate to discuss national
service. I've heard it said that we're going to consider a plan in which we are going
to provide individuals with alternatives: you either take defense or you take
non-defense. Now I'm concerned with the very simple situation which we are
originally confronted with and which we have been discussing up till now—What
happens in the event that the call for military defense exceeds the number of
volunteers?

Mr. Cullinan. The answer is that, assuming that there is some kind
of compulsory military retained, it would have the first priority. If there were
not enough people left in the military draft pool (an almost 100 per cent im-
probable situation, by the way), some of those who had volunteered for non-
military service would have to be selected to make up the difference.

Mr. Bakan. But will we be taking people out of the Peace Corps, say,
and putting them into the Army?

Mr. Cullinan. That would be correct.

Mr. Bakan. That's the problem we're confronted with at the very
beginning here.

Mr. Cullinan. This would only occur, of course, if the entire military
draft pool had become exhausted, if there were nobody left, and everybody was
either doing military or non-military service. A certain percentage of the non-
military servicemen would then have to be taken into the military, since that
would have first priority.

Mr. Bakan. Then it becomes obvious that your non-defense service is
not really an answer to the problems posed by the draft. It has other advantages,
as we have heard, but it does not direct itself to the original question, namely:
Where are we going to get manpower when there aren't enough people willing
to volunteer to fight the war?

Mr. Cullinan. The only ways that can be handled are by compulsion
or by just not filling the gap.

Mr. Bakan. Then, from what you say, non-defense service is only
remotely related to satisfying the need for military manpower.

Mr. Booth. I do think that this discussion possibly should be postponed until we get the clarification. Or have you got the clarification and now
it's becoming controversy?

Mr. Marmion. I'd just like to ask about the effect of these national
service plans on our society. For example, Mr. Anderson raised the problem of

people spending their whole time being rehabilitated. This supposes that we would have a lot of teachers in the program. The Job Corps has some 88 centers. We have Upward Bound, Headstart, etc. These various programs have had a terrific impact on public schools in various parts of the country. They have created teacher shortages. For example, this year, very surprisingly, there was a shortage of industrial arts teachers; some of it has been attributed to these programs. I'm wondering if any of the panelists have thought about what effect a national service program would have on the number of teachers available in elementary and secondary schools as just one impact of a program like this on our economy?

Mr. Booth. Mr. Eberly . . .

Mr. Eberly. The accusation was made six years ago about the Peace Corps—that it would drain off teachers badly needed here in the United States. The result is that service in the Peace Corps has almost doubled the percentage of those who had originally intended to go into teaching as a career. Now, national service would have the same kind of effect, but at various levels. Some would go into it after college as teachers' aides, the Peace Corps kind of operation. Others with only a high school education, could perform certain educational tasks under proper supervision, and would get acquainted with education, maybe getting some aspirations for becoming teachers themselves. Their availability would open up a wide array of experimentation with some of the new educational techniques being talked about, again breaking away from the 30 people in a classroom.

Mr. Cullinan. One question wasn't answered earlier: whether or not teachers could qualify for alternative national service. I think the answer would be that they certainly could. Anybody could, depending on how such service was defined. I personally would be in favor of having teachers qualify. That again would be up to the President and/or Congress, to define exactly what alternative service is. But it could be anything; even service as an astronaut.

Mr. Booth. I think we have now twice subtly crossed the line between clarification and controversy. Let's open up now for any kind of questions but let's try to remember not to give speeches, but to discuss with each other, so that we really get maximum understanding.

[Unidentified Speaker]. I would like to ask those who advocate a national service if there isn't a problem here concerning how young people who would be out of this program would feel about their country's foreign policy. In fact, the person serving in the Peace Corps may be involved in promoting American foreign policy, and may have certain ethical ideas which contradict this policy. He may be really opposed to it. I wonder if in some way we would be better served by a program like Mr. Cullinan's, where a person might feel conscientiously that he's freer, in terms of his own opinions and his own attitudes relative to foreign policy, in serving in a voluntary service program.

Mr. Bird. I do want to state that, as far as I can tell, every private voluntary youth agency that has a concern with national service has been omitted in the list of agencies consulted, except Operation Crossroads. There has apparently been some consultation with Girl Scouts and Boy Scouts, who I believe really wouldn't be called service agencies; they are a different category of agency. I am from the American Friends Service Committee. It seems surprising to me that the AFSC, which is celebrating its 50th anniversary next year, and the IVS, which is an old and honored service, particularly known in southeast Asia at this time, shouldn't have been invited into this discussion. I don't suppose it would matter particularly except for certain lapses in the concept of voluntary service, which I judge come from the inexperience of the people who are advocating national service.

There is a false impression in the latest national service statement that national service people have consulted with these agencies. Specifically, there's mention of having made contact with the American Friends Service Committee. Now if this is true, I do not know who it is in the Committee, and I've asked around. Also, IVS is mentioned and if this is true, I do not know who it is, and I've asked around there. I just wonder how it came about that the know-how of these agencies should not have been brought in, in discussing a subject which affects their very existence.

Now if these agencies had been asked, or will be asked, I think these are some of the things that they might contribute. One of them is that two concepts have been confused: military draft and voluntary service. It *still* remains confused, and we have the amazing paradox, if not contradiction, of universal voluntary service. You cannot combine these two concepts satisfactorily, even if you're doing it on a pragmatic basis. This is one thing I think the voluntary agencies would be saying. Now, I'm not an official spokesman for any of these agencies, but I predict that if the compulsion element is put into national service, all the private youth agencies will oppose it. This would be a shame because it's a great idea. Fundamentally, the idea of making voluntary service open to many, many people is one that has a strong attraction for such agencies.

There ought to be some sacrificial element in this kind of service. There are many reasons for this, but one could state two points. First of all, if there isn't this element, then you simply have low-paid, exploited workers, or else you have highly-paid professionalism. It was the idea of service that made such agencies as the Peace Corps exciting.

It wasn't necessary for anybody to do any research about the jobs that might be available, except to ask volunteer agencies whether they thought that there were jobs. They would have given a tremendous, loud "yes."

Mr. Booth. Is it true that all of these private organizations will oppose national service eventually? Does someone want to talk about that?

Mr. Leo. I would like to add something in response to Mr. Bird, and I am very much in disagreement with Mr. Cullinan and Miss Mead. Also, I find myself in complete agreement with Mr. Wofford. Young people today have demonstrated that they are concerned with the problems of this nation. The people who propose a national compulsory system are robbing young people of their freedom. These people who have created the inequalities throughout the past generations are now telling the youth, "We're going to put you in one of these categories. You can choose between five or six, and then you're going to straighten up the mess that we've created." The people you mention are not even allowed to vote. You're dictating to these high school students that when they complete high school they're going to go into some type of national service. I think you're going to take away what Mr. Wofford has called the spirit of wanting to do something. I think that if you demand that young people serve with national legislation, they will go against you.

Richard W. Boone. I'd first of all like to reemphasize my position and that of my colleague on a completely voluntary national service—compulsory in no way.

I'd like to go back to Mr. Bakan's position of what could be done if not enough people can be recruited through the draft call. Let me break it down into two parts and suggest that it is not only a logistics problem, but an ethical problem as well. I don't know of any case in the nation's history where we have not responded with a substantial number of volunteers to a clear and present danger. I suggest that the present condition in which we find ourselves may not be interpreted by the American public as a clear and present danger. Going to the question of voluntary national service, a problem has been posed by Mr. Bird when he says that many, or some, national service organizations may very well oppose a national service program. I think he's completely correct. There is the danger that national service would be seen as a monopoly on service. In addition, that monopoly might tend to be presided over by those who identify themselves as "professionals." I'm deeply concerned that we look at the question of service without being too concerned about trying to professionalize it or suggesting that service must be based upon sacrifice. Sacrifice, in this context, is based upon a concept of scarcity. We are now living in rather affluent surroundings, and I suggest that service should be equated with opportunity, opportunity for the most effective use of human beings, the human use of human beings. In any attempt to consider national service and its feasibility, a basic question is the *quality* of service to be offered. I think that it's dangerous and somewhat trite to talk about national service, either voluntary or compulsory, without facing very squarely and very quickly the problem of quality. One of the great problems of voluntary service today is that its bounds are sorely limited by professionals and their demands for credentials. Possibly one of the most valuable ways to loosen up the definition of who "can" and who "cannot" offer service would be to open up the service professions to competition—lowering the often arbitrary barriers which have been put up by many professionals to preclude other people from entering into important person-to-person service. I am not sure what this change would do to, say, the teaching profession. But seeing education operate in the slums, almost anything you do to it would be an improvement. For instance, at the moment I see no reason to demand a system of credentials for teaching in the slums.

Finally, in relation to quality, let me say something else. Many young people in the slums, if given an opportunity to perform effective tasks there, would be very happy to move into a service system. One of the great problems facing any national service system is the possibility that young people in the slums would be denied the opportunity to perform those tasks. We talk about social change, but social change is a threat. One of the great dangers in setting forth recommendations for a national service system is that we will get it, but on terms which preclude many from having the opportunity for real quality performance. And without that commitment to quality very soon, we shall find the system suffering from "hardening of the arteries," and becoming a national liability rather than a national asset.

Mr. Booth. I find this discussion so far vague and frustrating. Is there anyone who would like to define a particular issue, which could then serve as a basis for brief discussion, and then we'll go on to another sharply defined issue?

Mr. Lauter. I listened to Mr. Wofford and to the remarks that Mr. Boone just made and I had a sense of exhilaration, of possibility. And then I listened to some of the other remarks, and read some of the papers, and I had a sense of deep gloom and depression and indeed something of the feeling that I have in reading George Orwell. Earlier in the conference, we've been told that war is peace, and now we seem to be told that slavery is freedom. It seems to me that the problems that Mr. Leo raised and Mr. Boone raised really are crucial. They had to do with definitions and with power.

For example, it seems to me very clear that the option plan is not in any sense a voluntary plan; rather it is a choice that is presented in the framework of compulsion. If that is what we are to understand is voluntary, it seems to me it exemplifies precisely the lack of credibility, the lack of clarity that is the problem that we're trying to deal with here.

Another thing is this. We talk about the spirit of voluntarism, and we harken back to the time when Sen. John Kennedy posed the Peace Corps idea. We wonder why youth doesn't seem to be responding at this point to similar inventions like national service. I would suggest that again that has to do with ambiguity in purpose, and ambiguity in the application of power to which Mr. Boone has referred. I would like to refer to Mr. Eberly's paper, where he talks about paramilitary activity and says: "It would be consistent with the national service concept to accept as one service activity participation in the United Nations Police Force, in police apprenticeship programs, wherein a development corps within the U.S. Armed Forces would work constructively in places such as Vietnam, where the presence of the Peace Corps is not feasible." Now that sounds lovely; but it can be very easily interpreted as being the other end of a pacification program. This sort of ambiguity is one of the reasons that youth does not respond to a federal program. It has to do with the lack of credibility in the application of policy by the federal government, in respect to the war and in respect to the elimination of poverty. One of the factors that we refuse to face all the time here is that we cannot separate an idea of national service, let alone *compulsory* service, from the way in which it's going to be applied, from who is going to make the decisions about how people are going to be used, from who is going to make decisions, as Mr. Sherrod tried to say before, about whether somebody can in fact work for SNCC, or the American Friends Service Committee. We're having a lot of problems in getting alternative service work with the American Friends Service Committee approved by the Selective Service System. It seems to me that is a function of the war and of those people and of those interests who define what national interest is in their terms. The two issues that we have to deal with are keeping clear what voluntarism really means, and that, in turn, means working against the kind of established national interest that is manifest in war and is manifest in our cities.

Mr. Booth. It seems to me that these are two extremely good issues on which to focus discussion. I propose that we talk now for a while about the definition of voluntarism in relationship to the various proposals.

J. Timothy McGinley. I think we've fallen into a trap by talking about national service in terms of military service. Because the military requires registration at 18 and service shortly thereafter, we have considered national service only as it relates to young people. Every remark today has been in terms of the 19-year-olds serving, or the youth serving. Why should national service be limited to the youth of this country?

Perhaps Americans of all ages should take a sabbatical from their current role in education, industry, or government, and participate in national service. The problem lies in the fact that we are discussing volunteer service along with the military draft. The military draft is for young people. National service may not be solely for young people.

Mr. Chapman. The key words seem to be "volunteer" and "service." I'd like to develop the idea of service. I think it would be discriminatory to defer people who were in the government-approved service programs, and to draft other people who also are making real contributions to society. What is service? Is the doctor performing service? Is the postman performing service? Is his service something that you can put into these programs that are largely of a social work nature? Is the writer? Is the civil rights worker?

The case of the civil rights worker is very interesting because some national service proponents would like to have the civil rights worker included; but if you're going to include him, whom do you include? CORE? SNCC? The NAACP, the Black Muslims? Where do you stop? I don't think you can define service; it's largely a personal matter. And that's really what the voluntary idea is. I'm very much afraid that if we set about, as Mr. Cullinan and Mr. Bramson have suggested, putting together a national service system on top of an existing draft, the result would be to institutionalize that draft permanently, and especially if you don't enhance the competitive advantage of the military in terms of wages and so on. Now, of course, you can say that certain people get paid for service; the doctor for example, the poet, in the civilian economy, but that the VISTA worker doesn't. You can say that the man who goes into the military should get higher wages. We're for that. But isn't the man who goes into the national service program, goaded by the draft, also getting a quid pro quo? Isn't he getting rewarded directly by his deferment? And so the idea of voluntarism and the idea of service are being poisoned. They're being corrupted, just as every other deferment we've talked about at this Conference we have seen has become a corruption.

Mr. Flacks. I was extremely exhilarated by Mr. Wofford's presentation and Mr. Boone's presentation. But I'm also concerned, because in connection with the Peace Corps I was in Ann Arbor when John Kennedy came there at two in the morning during the election campaign, and about 5,000 students greeted him. At that point he said, "Let us create the situation where youth can serve the country through non-military means. Go to Africa not with guns, but without guns." And everyone there had the impression that what he was suggesting was what is being suggested now again—that is, genuine alternative to military service. I think that that spirit was sold out because of political necessity. I'm very afraid that the people who are advocating a genuinely voluntary program of national service—not tied to the draft—will, when faced with the choices, end up tying it to the draft as they did with the Peace Corps. So I hope that we can get some kind of assurance that they are not going to stir the enthusiasm of youth with this program, and then turn around and make it part of the military system.

I want to go on from that and suggest that we have been presented really with two models. One is Margaret Mead's model, which she says is based on the notion of compulsory education. The other model, which I take Mr. Wofford's to be, is more like the system of higher education. That is, instead of having a national legislative mandate which says that everyone is obliged to serve, he's talking about a norm of service which should be decentralized. There should be a tremendous variety of ways in which this can be realized, and they should be created from below, in a sense, with government subsidy and assistance and so forth. Now that's the program I would advocate. I hope that that is not sold out. And I think the first way it would be sold out is if it becomes a gimmick for legitimizing conscription.

It will serve that function if people are led to believe that this service is a way of reducing the inequities of the draft. It is not a way of reducing the inequities of the draft. Nothing can reduce the inequities of the draft, but it can be sold to the public on that basis. Secondly, this should not be a program that increases surveillance over youth. We should not have a situation in which every youth has to register and then get assigned for rehabilitation or something of that sort. Third, it should not be structured so that youth are placed in regimented situations, such as large-scale camps for underprivileged youth where they allegedly will be rehabilitated. Finally, I don't think it should be seen as a substitute for ending segregation and transforming the educational system itself. It is a mistake to think that by giving a second chance to youth we have solved the problem of slum education and segregation in society.

Mr. Lloyd Anderson. There were two issues brought out which made me wonder a little bit. One is Mr. Cullinan's point about the stratification in our society. In the long run, if this system were to become stable, it might reinforce itself and continue so that individuals would serve willingly, among groups of people from different socioeconomic backgrounds, and the system could maintain itself. However, I am very much afraid that that's not quite the situation at the moment. And maybe it needs a little push.

Now, I am just as afraid as Mr. Flacks of any government interference, even Mr. Wofford's version of this. In the transition period, he mentioned acceptance or approval by a government agency of programs for the service system. This, I think, is extemely dangerous. However, that's not the same as saying that under no conditions would we want national service. It is somewhat justifiable to say, as Mr. Friedman did about education, that we cannot afford to have individuals growing up who do not have some feeling for voluntary service to others. Therefore, social necessity dictates that the complete freedom of the individual must be overridden to the very slight degree, in this case, of requiring voluntary service. The *only* condition, however, under which this is acceptable is one in which we do not have a feedback system through the government—this produces real political questions. Could the courts, for example, be responsible for the decisions whether or not the activity involves a large element of service and interaction with others? A criterion such as this is administratively difficult, but that's the only condition under which compulsion of this kind would be acceptable. The precise method of application is extremely important.

Mr. Keast. I'm deeply grieved to discover the readiness—and here I share Mr. Flacks' views and those of Mr. Lauter—the readiness with which a good many of us seem prepared to accept quite a monstrous amount of system, of bureaucratic intervention in human lives, non-voluntary voluntarism, when we happen to be talking about a program which, to be sure, has socially approvable ends, but which is open to this same objection that many of us have to the compulsory features of the draft and its inequities. I find it infinitely discouraging that we should so readily throw away all of our strong objections to bureaucratic centralization, as long as we are personally deeply convinced that we're doing so for a good purpose. I'm sure a view can be elaborated that under some circumstances, some kinds of use of military force are, in fact, highly desirable and socially productive, and that under those circumstances you might very well wish to make the same points that some poeple have been making here. I don't want my objections to many features of the draft, or its administration, to be undercut by the supposition that I'm willing to put up with precisely the same kinds of morally unacceptable alternatives, only provided that they don't involve danger or risk, or provided that they involve doing good. We should be talking about a voluntary non-system; it can't be a voluntary national system. The terms are essentially self-contradictory. I feel very strongly about this, despite the fact that we had developed up to this point, I thought, a substantial amount of agreement on other featuers which, in my judgment, we might have extended if we had kept our terms of reference roughly comparable. But we haven't done so.

Colonel Bar-On. I want again to make clear that I don't think it appropriate for me to express any opinion on the issue at hand, being an outsider. But I think that we have some expertise on voluntarism, and I would like to say a few words on that concept, drawing from our own experience. Much of what we have been doing in Israel in the last 80 years came out of voluntarism, yet our entire military service is compulsory. In my opinion, there are two different levels to approach this problem. One is the philosophical level and the other is the psychological, practical level. I'll give an example of the second. We give compulsory elementary schooling for those who haven't had it before entering the service. If I took a vote among the soldiers on whether they wanted to study during the last 3 or 4 months of the service, I think I would have only about 20 per cent who would want to do it; however, if I took a vote only 3 days after they had started these studies, I would have a consensus of 95 per cent who want to study. It is a complicated question—whether voluntarism means just a certain free choice made at a certain point of time by a certain person, or whether one can define a deeper concept. For another example, girls' service, according to the law, is compulsory in Israel. However, there is a clause by which a girl can be excused, if the service is objectionable to her religious or traditional background. As a matter of fact, every girl can easily be excused, and many are. This means, in fact, that girls' service in Israel is voluntary for all practical purposes. However, I think if we were to reverse the procedure and ask for volunteering, we would have many fewer girls in the service. And a third example—the entire youth in the Jewish community in Palestine, before the creation of the state of Israel were members in a voluntary-underground military movement. Now, there was neither compulsion nor any formal sanctions whatsoever, but I don't think that anyone would have dared not to go simply because of social pressure, and in actuality it was quite compulsory. So, there are many, many other variables that go into this concept of voluntarism.

Mr. Booth. We've had several statements in favor of a national service, all of them defining themselves as voluntary. We have now had a good deal of talk on the issue about what is voluntary, and although obviously, we're not agreed upon any concepts, I think it's clearer now than it was a few moments ago.

[*Unidentified Speaker*]. There's an assumption that women are only peripherally interested in national service. We're very definitely interested, but I want to say something about voluntarism. It seems to me that in our society, voluntarism has not only meant the individual's right to choose but it has meant recognition of the fact that the strength of our society grows out of the pluralism of points of view, of approaches, of solutions to problems. The right of dissent is terribly important to our system. And in a period of revolution and social change, it's terribly important that all of us be involved in the revolution. I don't know whether we have fully comprehended what it might mean to have national service which opened up to all young people the chance to be in the revolution, to bring to the solution of our great problems in our society a variety of points of view about how that society was to be ordered. One of the things that's distressed us about the way the poverty program is working out is that the minute you begin to get into the political arena or into the controversial areas, then there's a tendency to put the lid on. I would hope that voluntary service would mean that we would not have a kind of big brother who was screening out the appropriate kinds of national service or ways of serving your country which would make it impossible to have this dissent, this controversy and the variety that makes America what it is.

Richard Mendes. I have a strange and uneasy feeling here that we are dealing with a mythology superimposed upon a metaphysical pathos and interlaced with semantic confusion. I notice a strong trend running through our conversation: anti-government, anti-big government, in particular; anti-bureaucracy—yet I think a strong case could be made to the effect that government, as it has gotten bigger, has worked toward ensuring more and more freedom of more and more people in the United States over the past recent history. I think that bureaucracy has its problems but it also remains a rather effective device to deal with certain societal matters. I don't consider the bureaucrat to be a lost soul. I know that in my own contacts with government bureaucracy I have found some of the most creative people and programs that I know. This is the mythological aspect that I'm talking about. The problem about who is going to decide what is national service is a very real one, but I'd like to remind everyone here that we do have a mechanism, a social mechanism for deciding questions of this type, and that's the political process. The political process is not necessarily going to come up with the right answer; it's going to come up with the democratic answer; and that's probably the very best we can do at this particular time.

Finally, I think that the idea of national service is somehow being put forth as a solution to all of our problems, or as a major mechanism for solving our most pressing social problems. I don't think the exponents—Mr. Eberly and company—have particularly put forward this idea; but the critics have sort of superimposed it. It's not going to be the answer to the civil rights problem. Its not going to be the answer to the problem of poverty. It may help. We don't know what the total consequences of this program are to be on these particular programs, but there are other avenues available to us. For example, SNCC does not have to join national service, does not have to be "accredited," in order to continue. We do have a way in our society of maintaining these other types of programs.

There's one further point: the idea of voluntarism itself seems to me to be a two-edged sword. Perhaps in the term *voluntarism*, we have put our finger on something great about our society. That's perfectly possible. However, I think that there are also aspects of voluntarism that represent an abomination. It has been one of the factors, defined as the "American Way," which has prevented creative planning, which has prevented in many instances planning of any type and from any source. The great struggle for a Medicare program offers an example, where the doctors in fighting it have told us that the voluntary way is the American Way. There are many consequences to voluntarism. As a nation we have been blessed by the fact that we have not been wedded dogmatically to a single ideological proposition. We have been a pragmatic society. Maybe that's our salvation.

Mr. Eberly. The discussion has shifted so rapidly between long-range national service programs and short-range, that I would just like to renew my suggestion that we talk about the short-range. What can we recommend for next year? This may bear no relationship to the draft. A recommendation of compulsory non-military service? A recommendation for some kind of foundation for volunteer service that could receive public and private funds? Distribution of information about service and educational opportunities of a completely voluntary nature?

Mr. Bakan. As you know, there is a "Resist the Draft" conference across the street, about the same time that this Conference is going on. One of my young radical friends, in a discussion of national service, said to me that national service is to the draft as showers are to the gas chambers. Mr. Hazard indicated that one of the major questions associated with this Conference is the matter of the war. I think that this is right. The background of the war really conditions everything that we say here. Associated with war is a special kind of condition of involuntary servitude, the draft. We don't say it is the finest expression of our democracy. We tolerate it for the sake of the greater good. I was very troubled reading some of the papers on national service. Although I usually don't like to take a conspiratorial approach to history, I got a terrible feeling that these papers, perhaps unintentionally, may have the effect of taking the very pleasant atmosphere of the Peace Corps and the like, and using it to mask the ugliness associated with the involuntary-servitude feature of the draft. And somehow I had a sense that the advocates of compulsory national service would make the whole thing good by making everything equal. So if we take everybody and impose involuntary servitude of a kind, somehow it's not as bad as just having the kind of involuntary servitude associated with the draft.

I think that we really need to pursue, rather tough-mindedly, exactly what is being proposed for the relationship between the draft and national service. On the one hand, we hear from Mr. Eberly that he is proposing that in some way, if you engage in non-defense service, you're going to get extra credit as far as draft liability is concerned. Mr. Wirtz was very, very explicit when he said that non-defense service will not exempt anybody from defense service. We have to take him at his word. The realities of the situation are such that they are going to make those people who will be engaged in non-defense service prime eligibles for being drafted. If they are illiterate, they will be made literate, and then you can draft them. Certainly, a young man who is engaged in, say, some kind of non-defense work, if he is unmarried, without dependents, and healthy, will certainly be drafted before, say, a man who is older, has children, and is engaged in some kind of critical occupation. If this is the case, I think we have to look at it. I would ask those people who are advocating national service to explicate exactly what they intend to be the relationship between the draft and the non-defense national service.

Mr. Eberly. That has totally to do with the longer-range plan, a plan that I would not advocate for adoption now. There is more reason, I think, for talking about the short-range future and the kinds of things we can do within the next year or two.

Mr. Booth. We'll go into short-range. Before we do that, is there somebody who'd like to talk directly to what Mr. Bakan has said?

Mr. Mitrisin. I agree with Mr. Bakan that we should not make national service an alternative to the draft. I would think that national service would be possible only when there was a voluntary army. Making national service a way to avoid the draft or to put off going into the army avoids the whole issue of compulsory service.

Colonel Ingold. A point of terminology—the last time I heard this conversation, nearly a quarter of a century ago, they used national service for compulsion, and alternative service for the voluntary part. If you don't mind adopting a real old term for a very modern thought, you might wish to adopt this for clarity.

Second, I've heard the term draft "pool" repeatedly. This draft pool is subject to very great misinterpretation and should be clarified. I think we're talking about the pool of availables, ordinarily 1A classification. This is a very friable outfit. About 15 to 20 per cent of it dissipates every month. And at any time that you take a photograph of it, it isn't there to use the following day, the following week, or the following month. It is made up of different people, and over a very short period of time it's an entirely different group. You must keep this concept in mind. These are not the same people a little later on, even though the total figures are identical.

Third, the Peace Corps: the two people who were classified in 1A while overseas in the Peace Corps were so classified because of what was in their files—in both cases. Their local boards put them in Class 1A. They both appealed to the state appeal board because the Peace Corps will not take their own appeals. There they were also placed in Class 1A. The case was then brought to the attention of the Director of Selective Service by the Peace Corps, and he appealed both cases to the President, where they were again placed in Class 1A, indicating, I think, that automatic uniform deferments violate good judgment and are recognized as doing so on a national, state, and local basis.

Mr. Biderman. I think a great deal of the difficulty here revolves around the presentation of ethical and moral issues other than the way these are presented through what's been referred to as the political genius of the country. There are many people here who think the political genius of the country is political imbecility, but that's using two different meanings of the term.

We have to confront the question of why a large majority of the public agrees very heartily with a proposition stated to them by pollsters, or applauds political speakers enthusiastically when the idea is presented that *all* youth should devote some period of service or sacrifice to their country. I suspect the reason they do is that it's presented in a context of persistent military mobilization, where some people have to do this in terms of military service. In much of the discussion there's been implicit assumption about a diminution of the necessity for the United States to have a high level of military strength in the future, and this includes military in the other senses I tried to mention in my paper. The public and the "political genius" operate on another assumption, however: that there will not be, in the foreseeable future, a diminution of the role of military power in world affairs in which the United States, like it or not, is going to be involved. This forms an assumptive *mass* from which national service is considered, and from which the draft is considered, from which UMT and all of these things are considered. And to ignore that, I think, is to ignore the central reality and central questions posed here.

Mr. Booth. Did you want to make clear whether you agree with this assumptive mass yourself or do you think that's clear enough already?

Mr. Biderman. I think that it's irrelevant, that I think a lot of what the public decides about these things is imbecilic. That's quite apart from the point. One of the difficulties I have with presentations of national service, viewed in this kind of social and political context, is that the public does indeed relate it to compulsory military service; and to be acceptable to the public it would have to have some of the same features that compulsory military service has. It would have to relate to the central values of the American public. Many of the things that are put into the national service package do not have that element; they're what many people would regard as very non-essential kinds of social work that don't relate to the same kind of value dimension as a threat to the very existence of the nation, whether from war, from very extensive national disaster, or from insurrection. I think the Peace Corps was assimilated to this kind of ethic only by virtue of the idea of international service in relation to an international crisis, a chronic crisis, which affects the very centrality of the values of this country. So I think for national service to have equivalent significance it would have to involve, for the individual, similar kinds of purposes, and also a similar kind of sacrifice, to use that term that was derogated a while ago, as that which is demanded of the person who has to perform compulsory military service. That is, the person must be surrendering income, he must be surrendering safety, by choosing this alternative.

Mr. Wofford. I'm going to try to answer Mr. Bakan. I hope this Conference and the Marshall Commission and the President and Congress and —failing them—the next presidential platforms of both parties will commit themselves to the goal of ending the draft and taking the steps necessary to bring that about and trying the various incentives. But I don't think we can dodge the transition period and what we do about this issue so long as there is a draft, which will be for some time to come. There, it seems to me, we should want to add to religious conscientious objection. A new recognized category of conscientious preference, because the deep inner dissent to war or to this war which can only now be expressed, as Margaret Mead says, in civil disobedience, by a "No," also ought to be able to be expressed by a "Yes," by enabling those who'd rather "build than burn," to build. We should recommend that there be a deferment, automatically, for those who are accepted into the Peace Corps or into VISTA, or into other approved programs, possibly approved by some new entity like a foundation for voluntary service, but handled in a way that conscientious objectors' alternative services are handled. Secondly, these people should not be fully exempted from military service so long as there is a draft, but they should go in a new order of induction that recognizes that they've given some service; therefore they ought to be called after the main categories who have not given any service at all, but before fathers, let us say. Third, the age of call should be early and the call certain, so that a majority, hopefully two-thirds of the men, would know at an early age or before they leave college that they are not going to be called to military service. This majority of men would be free to be recruited, to enroll, to join in voluntary services without any compulsion at all. It seems to me that's a plan that would increase the range for volunteering during this interim period which, if linked to a serious move to end the draft and to end compulsion altogether, would make sense.

Mr. Booth. I'd like to give Mr. Bakan a chance to answer, but Mr. Bramson has to leave and wants to make a concluding statement.

Mr. Bramson. I want to associate myself with Mr. Wofford's remarks. I think that we're going to have to face the possibility that although many of us would like to see a voluntary Army—which would remove a great many of the problems that have been discussed here—because of Congressional opposition, the draft may continue over an indefinite period of time. In the face of that continuation, I wonder whether we can't help to legitimize, within that system, the concept of serving your country without carrying a gun, a very important concept.

Mr. Bakan. What you're proposing, Mr. Wofford, is that by virtue of the fact that somebody has already given some non-defense service, he would be getting an "extra credit" toward draft deferment. And you suggested that he be placed in a category, say, just before fathers. The question that I would ask, and this is just a question of fact, is whether this would really amount to very much. That is, I don't think there is much slippage, in terms of bodies who are available for the draft, between students who are in college and fathers. But there are people around the table here who, I am sure, know about that. Perhaps Mr. Wool would tell us how much "extra credit" one can get for serving in the Peace Corps the way the draft is operating at present.

Mr. Wool. In the lower order of call, under normal conditions where you have an average requirement for all kinds of service, volunteer and draftee, of about 600,000 a year, it would be tantamount to not being called at all unless there were a major emergency.

Mr. Wofford. Let me also point out, though, that the fathers who are exempted and are not called before the Peace Corps volunteers, are people who haven't engaged in any national service other than fatherhood.

Mrs. McAllister. Assume that I am a 19-year-old conscientious objector to national service organizations. I would prefer to spend my two years in service with a local neighborhood organization which is helping mothers whose husbands are in prison. Am I to have any better position in delaying the awful day, or am I to be given credit as a conscientious objector? Am I a citizen just pursuing my private purposes?

Mr. Tatum. One of the characteristics of alternative service is that it can't be done in your own community. So you would be booted out of that. There's also a tremendous resistance on the part of local boards to approve anything that a person would do anyway.

Mr. Booth. As I understand, the question was not about the present, but about any one of these plans for a national service, wasn't it?

Mrs. McAllister. I think this is the most preposterous thing: some people can serve much better in their own communities than they could by going a hundred miles away.

Mr. Booth. I think there's no question but what your person would not be deferred under the present setup.

Mr. Tatum. I'd like to address myself both to the short-term and the long-term on this.

Mr. Booth. I think we should begin to turn to the short-term if we can.

Mr. Tatum. I've experienced voluntarism of the Margaret Mead variety. The first time was when I listened to the orientation when I was entering federal prison and they said, "Work is a privilege and you damn well better do it." I think those who are proposing universal voluntary service which is compulsory should set what the penalty is for not volunteering. Alternative service should not be used to mean national service, because it is a current term for the conscientious objector program. At present if service requires approval, then you can't say that it's voluntary. Conscientious objectors do have a wide selection, but if they don't select something, they're subject to being sent to prison for up to five years. I have clients who are going to prison because there isn't the kind of provision for conscientious preference that's being suggested. I would like to see an expansion of opportunities for alternative service which I think should continue to be used as it is at present. I would also like to see instituted now, without waiting to see what happens to the draft, and not related to the draft, a nationwide service rather than national service, to indicate the breadth of variety, to give encouragement to all volunteer organizations, to the school boards, and so forth.

You cannot damn the concept of volunteer service by starting it out as alternative service. Keep the two separate. Acknowledge the difference between them. I see no reason why alternative service provisions could not be expanded, why the provisions for conscientious objection could not be extended to conscientious preference. I would like to see this conference recommend it. Let us also recommend nationwide service and encouragement for the private sector, for all the volunteer organizations, for schools and so forth, to really present a breadth of opportunity so that our young people begin to volunteer now, even while we apparently are obliged to keep compulsion when it comes to the military.

Mr. Chapman. I, personally, approve of the idea of voluntary service, although I don't think that you can define it too closely; that's why I oppose deferment. Conscientious preference would be all right to the extent that in the next year or so it defers those people who choose the Peace Corps or VISTA; I wouldn't extend it much beyond that.

But I want now to challenge these public opinion polls. First of all, all the public opinion polls that I've seen either preface their questions with remarks like, "Assuming that we're going to have to have a draft, do you approve of national service?" I haven't seen one that says, "Assuming we could get rid of the draft, would you approve of that?" They merely present the idea of national service to people who have been led by 25 years of conditioning to believe that we *can't* get rid of the draft. And no wonder they find it attractive. I think that the political reality hasn't been established yet. Some people who have come to this Conference have decided to change their minds one way or another, and this is some progress. It is an especially good sign inasmuch as there has not been anything published on the possibility of abolishing the draft, so that alternative hasn't been offered as yet. The only point I want to make is that the political reality in this next Congress is very much up in the air at the moment.

Mr. Arnold Anderson. It seems clear to me that the country is not going to go pacifist and abandon an army. We can try to abolish conscription; we would then have to shift to an employed army. That's one situation.

Now, we talk about national service. It seems to me there is an effective demand, in any realistic sense, for only a very limited number of people in useful, productive kinds of national service, except as they are in some kind of employment. So you then have another demand scale and supply-price curve to work out in that situation. Now the people who object to compulsory service want volunteer service, but it seems to me that there is little place for very many volunteers. You therefore will have to put them into employment and it may even be discounted employment. Now, the argument that we used when we were talking about a hired Army this morning and the arguments that we are using this afternoon do not seem to me to run parallel.

Mr. Oi. The only comment I make is that if we do offer these programs, we're providing another avenue of employment to these people. Once we do that, the cost of raising an Army will become higher. Certainly the cost of a voluntary Army will be increased by coupling it with an expanded program of voluntary national service. But this is a choice we make.

[Unidentified Speaker]. I have an example to place before those who are interested in a voluntary service, a national service. Suppose an individual prefers a peaceful national service but he doesn't meet the educational standards required for VISTA or the Peace Corps, I'm thinking of the poor people and particularly the Negro poor. Will those who are interested in national service undertake to provide other educational scholarships for these people so that they will be able to meet the standards of VISTA or the Peace Corps, or will the other national services be provided with the same standards as for entry into the Army?

Mr. Marmion. I would say yes. I want to raise a question along the very same lines. I have no fixed opinion about national service, but I hear some of its advocates saying that national service can become another white middle-class organization, an elite organization like the Peace Corps. I want to know how the minorities feel about this, and this is part of the question that was just raised. For example, people say that Negroes in the military are a good thing. This is upward mobility for them. But I have heard Bayard Rustin of the H. Phillips Randolph Foundation question this. He says that taking those Negroes who are able to pass the physical and mental requirements into the service skims off that element in the ghetto and in the large cities and makes it even more difficult for the people in these communities to make any headway. So, I think one of the questions that has to be answered is how the minorities feel about this. Can the proponents of national service reassure people that this is not going to become another middle-class, white organization?

Mr. Wool. I think that the question Mr. Anderson asked deserves more explanation. It seems to me, and personally I'm very sympathetic to the educational objectives of truly volunteer service, to be a way of really breaking down many of the divisive aspects which I think we see presently among youth in our society. But, if we get away from the educational aspect and think in terms of a hypothetical program employing as many as 5 million persons at any one time, then we have to think of the service aspects rather than the purely educational aspects and thus of national needs. We're talking about a program which would cost a tremendous amount of money. Volunteers are very expensive, as Mr. Wofford, I think, will testify. I think it costs about roughly eight or nine thousand dollars to support a man in the Peace Corps. Other programs could be less expensive, but this is not free service. Now, given the goals, the national needs to be met, it becomes reasonable to ask, again in economics language, how can we most effectively meet these goals in our society?

Then we come back to the paradox. This morning, in talking about the volunteer versus draft army, many individuals said that perhaps it's more socially efficient to have a volunteer "professional" army. Here we're talking about a volunteer non-professional mass of services. Now what are these services? These are services which do constitute existing professional and semi-professional disciplines. In education we complain now about teachers who aren't too well trained in teaching, about those who don't have the right training and the right motivation. Somehow we think that if we got twenty times as many individuals involved in teaching, they will have the right motivation and training. They're coming out of the same population. I think we have to look at that. In health services we have a highly advanced medical technology that will become more so, but if we think of massive numbers, we must recognize the fact that in these fields, as in military service, as in other parts of society, we do have the need for highly trained professionals. We need a balance between semi-skilled and skilled people. These are areas of current employment which we are trying to staff with people dedicated to careers, and we do have some real need for defining sharply what we mean by volunteer service, as distinct from the needs of the society which demand a re-allocation of human expert resources in some other way.

[*Unidentified Speaker*]. To speak to the question that was raised by Mr. Marmion, I think that it would be very difficult to convince many Negroes that in some sense national service would not comprise just the problems that you were hinting at, that it would not be simply an agency for upper middle-class orientation. It seems to me, that even more important than this, is the structural problem that somewhat enforces this upper middle-class orientation. The other problem is the values that are implicit in national service, if national service is to be compulsory. What would a person be able to do about community organization in a city in which a political organization opposed the person's efforts to organize the poor in the community? What would a person be able to do—even about simple things like schools and health problems—if he were faced with organizations that felt this was a threat to their own control of the community and they, then, became the source of feedback to the larger governmental agencies? All of these things would have to be considered. And then on the international level, I still say that some people have some real questions about American foreign policy; are you going to guarantee international service, freedom, in the real sense of the term, to express, and to identify, with interest other than the interest of our country alone?

Mr. Booth. I wonder if we shouldn't turn to Mr. Eberly's questions about the possibilities for the short range. We have several plans for the long run, and we haven't said very much about what's to be done immediately, given the assumption that the draft is going to be eliminated, but that we could extend, in one way or another, current possibilities of voluntary service.

Mr. Eberly. The short range is the transition plan, which would simply encourage the development of volunteer service. It would create a national foundation for volunteer service which would be a funding operation so that these programs could go into effect, and it would provide information for young people about the kinds of service opportunities open to them. The option plan would come after, I should think, five years or so, but it's only put up as a model, so that we can examine what the ramifications of a plan of this magnitude would be on the economy, society, etc., but at the beginning it would obviously be experimental.

Mr. Virgil. Regarding the short-range possibility, one idea is that national service would be aligned with the draft; that if a guy is drafted, he's got the alternative of going into the military service or he goes into some non-military two-year service. I believe it was Mr. Wofford who presented this as a viable possibility in the transition period. I'm questioning whether the promotion of this idea is in any way transitional. It would seem to me that once this system was established, the military would be able to get the amount of manpower it wished and those people who did not want to comply with that would go into some other type of service, but I don't see where in any way this would work to reduce the compulsory nature of the draft, nor would it in any way offer possibilities for a change toward what I would argue would be a better foreign policy.

Mr. Boone. Going back to Mr. Wofford's presentation on a short-run strategy, I find it both appealing and dangerous. I'd like to concentrate for just a moment on what I consider several dangers. First is the danger of assumed political realities to which Mr. Chapman referred. A great deal more attention must be devoted to an analysis of those realities. Second, there is danger in overemphasizing the need for political compromise related to the Vietnam situation. Indeed, if one were to assume a resolution of that problem within the short-run, the political realities for a kind of position which we might want to adopt here would be quite different. We have to be careful about establishing a compromise position based upon the immediate political situation, even if we judge it correctly. Third, if we do compromise and wish to expand the opportunity for voluntarism within the existing system, let me again bring up the danger of low-quality opportunity current in that voluntary system, and what that may mean for any major expansion of that system.

Let me emphasize: We cannot separate our goal of voluntarism, even in the short run, from a concern for the quality of service-opportunities to be offered. If opportunities are poor, then the possibility of attaining our long-range goals becomes much more difficult because of the bad experiences people have in going through a voluntary system—initially thinking they will have the opportunity to be people, and then finding out that they have only the opportunity to be things or tools.

Mr. Wofford. Would you suggest that the program we focus on is a post-Vietnam program and that *that's* what we should propose to the country?

Mr. Eberly. No, I'm just suggesting at this point that whatever we want to propose as good for the nation in the long run may be compromised unduly by a short-term political strategy.

Mr. Wofford. It's really an interesting possibility—coming up with the program which we say would make sense as of the time that the shooting war stops in Vietnam. It might have a lot of values. Let's hold that as a possible question for us all. Another solution to this that I think has been constructive and interesting is Mr. Tatum's. He says that the two ideas can be separated if you move toward conscientious preference, in the context he's familiar with, in ways which would increase the degree of freedom and volunteering in the present system. It would help his clients—some of them are going to jail. It would help others. We could then treat what Don Eberly calls the transition plan toward increased volunteering as an entirely separate proposition. We could create another committee of Congress, and a volunteer service foundation that promotes volunteering primarily, or especially in the areas where opportunities are low today. I don't know what you mean by the downward trend in the Peace Corps, since the Peace Corps in any case only offers opportunities for 15, 20, 30 thousand people, and we're talking about 200,000. The Peace Corps is largely a college corps, and we're now talking about two-thirds of the people who don't go to college. So, I would say that the transition plan would have written into the law that maybe 50 per cent of the funds for financing volunteer programs would go to programs or fellowships to people now left out by existing volunteer programs.

[*Unidentified Speaker*]. Mr. Boone, is it possible that Mr. Wofford just this minute slightly misunderstood your point? You were not talking about the numbers of opportunities available, but you were talking about the quality of opportunities available. Then you are suggesting that Mr. Eberly's national foundation idea might contribute to the proliferation of what you consider to be low-quality opportunities, which may—in turn—have an effect on any future planning for a really viable service program. It that correct?

Mr. Boone. Correct. Young people are told that they can join a particular organization and perform an extremely valuable service in, say, community development, whether it's in this country or abroad. Then, because of bureaucratic, political, or of other kinds of limitations, they find there are extreme limitations on carrying out the functions of community development. A disenchantment sets in. I am deeply concerned about the repercussions of that disenchantment as you attempt to extend the system.

Mr. Wofford. I think it's not true in the Peace Corps. I have the impression that VISTA, for the first time, is really designing programs that use people from the slum communities themselves as volunteers in joint teams.

[*Unidentified Speaker*]. Realistically, I speak both from within and without now, the present effort is very small and personally I don't feel that it's going to expand very much in terms of the criteria that have been set up for such service.

Mr. Boone. On this, I refer back to Mr. Marmion's question. In terms of quality considerations he poses a very deep and very meaningful question.

Mr. Arnold Anderson. All societies, including our own, and at all times, have some people able to do more of what the people whose opinions count will approve of. Now, if there are so many useful, appropriate kinds of volunteer service that the, shall we say, "less advantaged" people in our society can do, why in the devil aren't they doing them? They aren't being kept from doing them. I think we're muddying the waters by some of this discussion.

Mr. Lauter. It strikes me that to the extent that a short-term movement toward national service is tied into the draft, and it becomes in some sense subservient to the idea of national interest that the draft carries out, that in itself begins to raise in the minds of many young people something about the character of that national service. That's another way the problem of the war affects this short-term question. I share Mr. Boone's combination of exhilaration, perhaps, and apprehension. The apprehension leads me to think that ideas of national service of this sort really ought to be postponed if they can't be detached from the draft. My sense of it is that they be postponed entirely separately, that the opportunity for national service be offered entirely on a voluntary basis, and people who volunteer for national service be entirely exempt from military service. What would constitute a reasonable set of criteria might be what Arlo Tatum has suggested, that if a man is willing to spend two and a half or three years doing some sort of volunteer service, that willingness to spend that extra time would be a testimony to his sincerity and value.

[Unidentified Speaker]. You can't call that disconnecting it from the draft.

Mr. Lauter. It's disconnecting it in a sense of presenting a package which in the short term says, "You have to go into something, but you have some reasonable sort of opportunity to choose some voluntary program or some nonvoluntary program." What I'm getting at, you see, is if it's all put in that compulsory package and the compulsory package is in turn tied to the national interest defined in military terms that we're seeing in Vietnam, or defined in white middle-class terms as we see frequently in poverty programs, that begins to corrupt the other elements of the package, which I think everybody here would like to see implemented.

Mr. Pemberton. I would like to suggest to Mr. Wofford that I think the only way we can disconnect the two is to abandon the seeming equity of deferment or draft advantage from alternative service. If voluntary service is good in and of itself, let us promote voluntary service. Let us devote our energies, if we believe in voluntarism, to replacing the draft. Let us at the same time, if we believe the draft is going to be with us despite those efforts, devote some energies to improving the equities of the draft. At this point, the proposals that would reduce the average age of induction in a period of low inductions would tend to give an advantage to voluntary service, but the end would be improving the equities of the draft, not promoting voluntary service. Once we tie the two together—and this is where I feel emotionally torn, because I lean toward this notion of conscientious preference—once we do that, I think we then have the Selective Service System back in its role of channeling, and here I think we have the other side of Mr. Boone's "quality" coin. There are going to be some approved forms of alternative services and there are going to be some disapproved ones. The genius of voluntary activity, if there is any, is that some people find out for themselves a better thing to do than any kind of authority provides for them.

Mr. Eberly. I respond first to Mr. Anderson. If there are jobs for the disadvantaged—service kinds of opportunities—why aren't they filling them? There's a parallel here with the situation the Peace Corps faced a few years ago. There were opportunities. I was in Nigeria myself. There were hundreds of teaching positions there, but America was only sending over a trickle until the Peace Corps came. Now, what did the Peace Corps have? It had money and it had information. It had visibility on a national scale. It had the machinery, the money with which to get these people over there into the service task. Similarly, a survey of Washington, D. C., about opportunities for national service volunteers, indicated that about one-fourth of the some 1,300 openings required college experience, about half were at the high school level, and about a quarter at below high school level. This is roughly the way our spectrum is now among 18-year-olds, so that developing these, setting up the machinery, getting the funds, is the key to it.

Finally, on the separation question, it may well be that if the questions relating to the national foundation, to the ideal of volunteer service, to sending out this information, are dealt with by education and labor people in Congress, their action could be taken quite independently of anything that the Armed Services Committee may decide to do about the draft.

Mr. Flacks. I think what the advocates of national service should do in the short run is to tell young people that there really is a barrier to a positive vision of the way their lives can be developed; that that barrier is war and militarism. If it can be reduced, then there is a great chance that we can begin to develop racial and economic integration, situations of service, situations in which their creative impulses can genuinely be used; and reducing militarism really is the strategy for making all this politically possible. Otherwise, I think you will be presiding over a situation in which we will have an Army which is increasingly black and poor, and a parallel system for the middle class in which they believe they are serving the country and sharing the troubles and inequities of the poor and the black, but in fact they're not. This is the very situation which many of us are frightened about.

Mr. Rumsfeld. I find myself very much in agreement with many of the arguments against an attempted link-up between the concept of national service and the draft system. I quite agree that it's undesirable to extend the compulsory system. What I think is leading people in this direction was highlighted by Mr. Eberly. He said the key to it is getting the money and setting up the machinery, and he cited the Peace Corps. One of the problems I've found in Congress, when a piece of legislation is being considered, is the difficulty of determining what is already being done in a given problem area. I would suspect that the number of people who have voluntarily been involved in what we today call Peace Corps-type activities dwarfs what the Peace Corps has done. Yet, I support the Peace Corps; I voted for it. I think the problem we're having in this discussion is that we're going from a discussion of the draft into a discussion of national service. A better approach would be to discuss the problems of our society, which admittedly is not the purpose of this Conference, and then determine the best ways to effectively solve some of those problems through existing structures, or organizations, or activities, or through new ones that might supplement or substitute for some existing errors. If you look at the column inches in the newspapers that have been devoted to poverty programs and compare the total number of dollars that the poverty program has had with what is raised door-to-door through voluntary contributions, the latter is many, many times greater than poverty program funds. We have to look at the whole picture.

Mr. Cullinan. I've heard three suggestions now as to what a short-term program for improving the draft could be. One came from Professor Flacks, who in essence wants to oppose the military system. A second was from Don Eberly, favoring the provision of more information on voluntary services and the establishment of a foundation to encourage it financially. The third was from myself, subsequently improved upon by Harris Wofford, who suggested the inclusion right now of a procedure which would in effect give immediate de facto exemption to alternative service. I'd like to ask Mr. Wofford what he means by the term "conscientious preference." If I preferred to do alternative national service, would I still be able to take this way out even if I didn't oppose war?

Mr. Wofford. Yes, but you left out the fourth alternative, Mr. Pemberton's, that would call the younger group and not have any connection between military and alternative services. I'm with him all the way until he finishes, and then I think of my colleagues, Peace Corps volunteers, who are being drafted right now and being brought home from overseas. About thirty cases are pending right now before the Presidential appeal board. A number of draft boards have vowed that they're about to go out and get Peace Corps volunteers back. I see the possibility now of a real proliferation of this around the country, with conservative draft boards drafting Peace Corps volunteers back. I think of Mr. Tatum's clients who are going to jail, and despite the strong case for the total separation, I come out in favor of a "yes" answer to the President who asks the National Commission "Is there a practical way of providing non-military alternatives without harming our military security?"

Mr. Pemberton. My proposal is inconsistent with the first two. I simply suggest that there is long-range disadvantage to a short-term program that would tie the two by giving any authority, whether it is created by the House Labor and Education Committee or by the Armed Services Committee, the opportunity to channel by designating approved alternative service.

Mr. Booth. Let's call that four. Is there a fifth?

Mr. Kelly. I'd like to reinforce what Mr. Pemberton is saying. I think that we're really making a mistake if we tie up national service with selective service. The national service, no matter how we construct it, given the operation of our governmental system and the purposes for which it is established, is again going to be a shelter for the middle-class student. I don't see this as any movement forward. My suggestion is for an improvement in the conscientious objection provision of the present Selective Service act, because what most of us are worried about is alternative service, and Colonel Ingold did us a great service by pointing out that distinction. We want some kind of alternative service for certain kinds of people. I think this has to be very limited as to who these people should be. It should not be someone who simply got a degree in education or economics and therefore can function for society in some other way. I really think if we're going to have military establishments, and if we're going to have wars, we must distribute death. That's the whole point of having a draft versus a voluntary army, the distribution of death, and I consider that extremely important in a democratic society. When the society itself determines foreign policy and has a military, and then carries out that foreign policy, the risk of that foreign policy must be shared by as many segments of that society as possible. This is another of what I consider to be fundamental issues that just has not been expressed. I am very much in favor of national service. I think we need a national service foundation. I think it should have nothing—absolutely nothing—to do with Selective Service, and I'm in favor of expanding the conscientious objection provision to include those people who have a rightful claim on alternative service.

Mr. Rosenberg. I want to suggest that there's a specter haunting this conference and it is, I think, the specter of compulsion. I find in Secretary McNamara's Montreal speech, and in a recent statement by Secretary Wirtz, considerable evidence that within important sectors of our policy elite there is the notion that though one may start with voluntarism, one goes ultimately toward compulsion in setting up a large-scale national service program. I think that the drift toward statism, which our conservative friends have so long warned us about, is something that liberals are just beginning to catch on to, and it is a problem with which they ought to be very concerned if they remain grounded in basic humane values. There is, I think, in the kind of talk we are now hearing about national service possibilities something quite frightening: namely, the possibility of a further movement toward a complex, bureaucratized, and thus disguised garrison state. Though I've simplified it tremendously, I think this is something we must remain wary of and this Conference and its participants must keep in mind at every point in considering the whole national service question.

Mr. Booth. May I associate myself with that question after I cut you off?

Dr. Mead. I'd like to state over again, I am not in favor of Selective Service. I am not in favor of the kind of draft that we have. I do believe that we're going to have some kind of military service. I believe that the more that can be made voluntary the better. I'm not proposing "voluntary service" in the sense that people go and work voluntarily in their community. It is a very important thing in this country and they should be doing it for the rest of their lives. I'm simply proposing, *and I'd like to get this clear*, that all young people be given, and give, the kind of two years to their country which will benefit them, benefit the country, and will make what military service has to be done one of a series of types of service, not segregated as it is now, so that the only thing that young people are asked to do for their country is, if necessary, to kill, and all other things are left in this quite different category. I just wanted to make this clear. I didn't expect anybody to be in favor of this. I just thought it might clear the air on a few issues.

[Unidentified Speaker]. Most of the arguments for national service, and particularly the very last and glowing paragraph of Miss Mead's paper, are based on the assumption that all the institutions that we have in this country for educating people, compulsively and non-compulsively, do not produce good citizens, and that we need something—a new layer of bureaucracy; we have to realize this is 2 million people a year and it will be run by a bureaucracy, and we need something new to do it. I am reminded of a book, also written by a quasi-cultural anthropologist, called *Middletown;* the point of that book was that this was the way that Americans have traditionally tried to solve their problems, by looking away from the problem, which is the fact that our schools are segregated, or schools are not good enough. I'm not agreeing with these positions, necessarily, but just pointing out that everyone else seems to be, and simply adding a new structure. Now, the question then becomes, does this have the least thing to do with resolving the inequities in the draft? Perhaps it could be argued that most Americans would simply not accept an idea of a massive new program of national service unless somehow they were convinced that this would

reduce inequities resulting from another system. One last point about all this is that in making any further gestures towards resolving these inequalities, we have to remember that essentially we're dealing with a very small part of the population. There just aren't a great many conscientious objectors, maybe 20 thousand, maybe 40 thousand; but we shouldn't be railroaded into thinking that we have to provide for all of these people.

Mr. Sherrod. I don't think I can remember any proposal that has been made about national service which, used as an alternative to the draft, was working for a group that was dominated or under the authority of black people. And just one mention has been made of the fact that in the South —in fact in a lot of other places—the draft boards are peopled by whites. Again, I don't know what this group can do about the situation. I do know that it seems that people here are insensitive to it. I could probably say it a thousand times and there probably wouldn't be any response to it. Maybe there should be more Negroes here so that their presence could be felt. That's one of the problems in our whole country. I think one of the problems, too, is that we can't be seen, so you hear one voice and then you go on, and go on, and go on, and the word is just not heard. Thank you.

Mr. Janowitz. I think that we must be careful that we're not creating a new ideological problem when we talk about "volunteer." I see as many weak volunteer programs as I do strong ones. The criteria of performance are important. Formal definitions are not enough. I look at national service as a device concerned with the limitations of the existing educational system. I do not see it as a device for redistributing income in the United States, of fundamentally changing problems of law and order, birth control, abortion, political action, and the like. These must be dealt with through the political process in its entirety. I see national service as uniquely trying to overcome the defect of the present educational system which believes that the process of socialization of the young takes place in the classroom, takes place in a purely verbal, formal situation. What we are interested in doing is extending a variety of circumstances which make it possible for young people to grow up. This is particularly important in a period in which we are moving so rapidly towards the meritocracy, and in which the skills and capacities of the educational establishment to bring up humane, well-rounded, decent human beings, are pushed to the limit, and in fact unable to cope with the situation. So, I see it mainly as an educational device in its broadest, richest and most John Dewey-ian sense.

Under these terms, I have two criteria which I'd like to have entered into the record. When we develop national service we do not want to develop any new islands of privilege. It would be very easy to make special arrangements, through national service, which would give those who have the most, the greatest access to the benefits of national service. In some respects, the Peace Corps already begins to be an island of privilege. I am against all-voluntary institutions in the sense of an all-voluntary military and an all-voluntary Peace Corps. All institutions need outsiders. I do not know what a draftee into the Peace Corps is, but I think a few of them would be very useful to give it the necessary heterogeneity and prevent it from becoming an island of privilege. If one takes this perspective, one does not come to the conclusion that national service will use people at their maximum skills, but rather that they will be used to compensate for the limitations on their educational experience.

Issues and Areas Requiring More Data

TUESDAY EVENING, DECEMBER 6, 1966

Chairman, ALLISON DAVIS

Allison Davis. A conference is an outpouring of many things: First of values, which by definition are always ethnocentric. We have had values of a national type, of an age group type, of a political type (conservative or liberal and majority or dominant group) expressed. Secondly, human beings are driven by emotions, either conscious or unconscious. This research meeting is supposed to be devoted to facts and how to get more pertinent facts. I would say that this is the one area which has been poorly represented in our meetings because there are very few published studies on Selective Service.

Selective Service itself, however, has published excellent studies. For instance, its study of the relative standing of northern Negro officers in World War I, as contrasted with white southern officers, on intelligence tests was one of the major contributions to the field of intelligence testing. In this case, of course, the northern Negro officers had higher IQ's than the southern whites. This is something that we didn't know and we needed to know. Also, Selective Service published special studies after World War II in Monograph No. 10, a comparison of the standing of southern whites and northern Negroes on the minimal education requirements test. We learned what we needed to know, that in every southern state, the rate of white failure on the minimal education requirements was higher than the rate of failure of Negroes in Illinois, in New York, in Massachusetts and Connecticut. So, there really is a place for facts and knowledge in this sphere.

I learned something which was most helpful to me from Colonel Ingold who said a day ago that no one really evades Selective Service. It is just that Selective Service can't use him or doesn't need him at the time. But if they need him, they will get him. And this helped me understand many of the things that I had not understood before.

Now, I make no apologies because this session deals with the interests and aims of social scientists. I feel that human beings should be studied in the way a physiologist studies the central nervous system, or the way a biochemist studies molecular structure of nucleic acid. What we want to ask ourselves is: How does this system really operate? What more do we need to learn about this operation? How does it influence the men and the institutions of this society? And that means how does it influence this country? A simple example, perhaps not so simple, from the second World War: A great deal of talk appeared then in all the papers about what was happening to the American family as men were taken from their families, their children and their homes, and as the mother, certainly in the working class, was often left without adequate support. No one doubts today that the toll of war upon the American family in the Forties was tremendous. But we learned nothing about it. I would like to introduce the first of five people who will talk for five or ten minutes. For those in the academic world, I shall use the honorific title "*Mister*," which owing to my long experience in the deep south do I know is the most jealously guarded of all titles. Mr. Mark Abrams of Research Services, Ltd., London.

Mark Abrams. I am going to keep myself to what you call the broad issues, the issues which really lie right at the back of the whole question of Selective Service. I will not deal with the day-to-day operations, where I am sure we need, if I may say so, a great deal more research. These comments are in the order in which the issues came up in the course of debate, not necessarily in the order of their importance.

The first thing that struck me was the remark thrown out, and allowed to settle as an established fact until it was challenged, that compulsory military service is socially dysfunctional. That, in a sense, the men who come out of military service are undemocratic in their outlook. They are excessively submissive and, at the same time, excessively aggressive, and that this corrupts in some sense the values of a democratic society. This was in fact challenged by Margaret Mead, who said, "What is the evidence of this?" but no one answered her. I think that this is an important point and should be researched and studied. We do know of several Western-style democratic societies which have had compulsory military service under peace conditions and where one would say that the quality of democratic society is reasonably high: Australia, New Zealand, the Scandinavian countries, Switzerland, England. It doesn't seem that compulsory military service automatically produces undemocratic men. It may well be, however, that it does produce such men in the United States. If this is so, then one would like to know what the specific values and institutions in American life are which have this effect on men, but don't have this effect in Australia or New Zealand. That is one point where I think any competent research worker could produce reliable findings, reasonably quickly.

The next one, and here I have to disagree with my friend Morris Janowitz, concerns the whole question of the socialization of adolescents. It seems to me that throughout the debate on the national service system, all sorts of ends were thrown out as being possible benefits. For example, it would train the minority of middle-class people in the skills and habits of philanthropy, and so on. I would have thought that the most useful end that one could pursue through such a system is, in fact, the socialization of American adolescents; this seems to have failed in some cases, and national service might help. But then Janowitz went on to say that the schools are the most effective institutions for the socialization of the young. Now, if this is so, it is rather surprising, because in every other country, the school does not undertake the task of socializing people in their late teens. This task is undertaken by the work place, by the factory, by the workshop. This is where, in fact, young people make their first entry into adult life, learn to accept the rules of adult social life, participate in adult life. I would have thought that we should do research to see if, in fact, the prolongation of education in schools, or school-like institutions, does in fact help or hinder the socialization of young people. If I were guessing at an answer, I would say that it hampers the socialization of young people, in some countries.

Another point, which we have only touched on occasionally, was how does the draft affect schools rather than universities? And how does it affect school pupils rather than university students? Here there is the beginning of some evidence in other countries which ought to be looked at. I think that we have over-emphasized the impact on the university student and we should go further back, because children in their early teens obviously are aware of a future which contains compulsory military service. What effect does it have on them? What effect does it have on the functioning of schools? There is some limited evidence from England that when you have, under peace conditions, a draft or compulsory military service, this raises the rate of dropout, or the number of what we call, in England, "early leavers." As long as we had compulsory military service in Britain, we had a very high rate of early leavers. As soon as conscription ended, the dropout rate fell. It would be interesting to know under what circumstances that happens. Does it happen only in England and Australia? Does it happen in America? If it happens in America, too, why does it happen? I would suggest as a possible explanation that these young people who were early dropouts—in England anyway—were anxious to participate as soon as possible in the adult world, and to do this before they went into military service. This then is another area where I think that we should do some research.

Another discussion dealt with what sort of selection system might be used as a substitute for the present methods of selection. Here I think that what research would seek for is to discover what, among the population at large, are the concepts of fairness which politically limit the application of ideal solutions. This seems to me a realistic problem. We do know that no matter what publicity and other devices politicians and political parties use, they are in the last resort prisoners of the values of the people who elect them. One of these values is the everyday sense of fairness held by the population at large. Can we identify this in practical terms? There are various non-market areas of social life where the resources are so scarce that, in fact, people who do not have them, suffer, and suffer drastically—for example, the access to kidney machines. Could we not find out what people would regard as a fair solution of the problem of access to kidney machines? We have had, since 1948, selection in one area of British life which is extremely important—selection for access to high school education. But we know that today any attempt to discriminate on grounds of academic achievement or on grounds of the applicant's potential usefulness to society is widely regarded as unfair. In a typical response in one survey in this field, a woman said, "The whole process of selection by examination for entry to high school is unfair, because only the intelligent children can win." Now, that may seem to you absurd. In fact, it is not an absurd situation, given the values, and therefore the political constraints, of English life. I think that we should find out here what are the limits set on ideal solutions for a situation where selection seems inevitable.

Again, a very simple point on which I think research could be useful is why, in the absence of a draft, do some men volunteer and others not, and who are these men who do volunteer? If we can find this out, and I think that we can, we can start to predict with reasonable accuracy what will happen to total enlistments in the Armed Forces if we abandon the draft, and we won't have to guess. There are other countries where it has been done and where decisions have been made either to retain the draft, or to abandon it. But they knew, roughly, what was going to happen, because they had already made some attempt, through research, to identify the sort of people who would volunteer, and under what circumstances they would volunteer.

Finally, one other area: many speakers used the phrase "the national interest."

This may not be a research problem in the conventional sense, but I think we need to define and test much more clearly what lies behind this phrase, especially in the context of military service. Is it not possible for researchers to look at these definitions, these assertions about national interest, and test their reliability? Again taking recent English history as an example, in the name of national interest it was decided that medical students should not receive military deferment or exemption. They were regarded as almost the most expendable of university students. This turned out to be a very poor definition of the national interest. We are today grossly under-doctored. Again, it was decided that in the national interest coal miners and farm workers should be exempt or deferred. Both of these decisions turned out not only to be wrong, but almost disastrous from the point of view of technical advance in the British economy. We now are still, in both these industries, using out-of-date techniques, because today we have too many coal miners and farm workers. If we decide at the end of this examination that, in fact, past decisions about national interest don't hold up historically, then I think that we are some way toward saying we will not allow this consideration to intrude into our argument as to what should or should not be done about exemptions and deferments in any selection system.

Colonel Bar-On. I already noted in my paper, before knowing how correct I was, that there is a fantastic difference in the conditions prevailing in our country and in the background to your problems here. After spending three days here, I know that it is much more than I thought it was. My main conclusion is that for me this was an excellent study in human and national differences. I know, of course, that our *answers* may have little relevance to your problems; nevertheless, maybe some of our *questions* may be of interest to you. What I will try to do is to tell you briefly about a few investigations that we did in Israel that I thought might be interesting and relevant to you and might suggest further research to be done here. You will have to bear with me if I bring up some ideas that were already tried here and were not brought to my attention.

One more word about the difference between Israel and the United States is in order to hint at the magnitude of that difference. In Israel, the ratio between regulars, or what you call reenlisted people, to draftees is one regular to eight draftees. I think that the ratio in the American Armed Forces may be the reverse. I heard here a lot about compulsion and voluntarism. In our society, compulsion, the need for compulsion, is so apparent that we almost don't have to use compulsion. We had a questionnaire given to boys at the age of 17, that is, one year before coming to the service; the question was asked whether they would volunteer if the law of draft were abolished, and 85 per cent said yes. Now I said that one could almost do without compulsion; it is only for those 15 per cent who said no that we have to have compulsion.

Before going deeper into the various research projects we did, I want to make one comment on the general nature of this research. We found out over the years that the research on these problems *has* to be longitudinal. There is very little you can get from research that takes a picture at a certain point in time. You get much more benefit out of research that goes on for ten years or fifteen years and measures the dynamics of the problem and the changes that occur. I think that one project that is being done currently may be of interest. This is on the attitude of young people to the military service itself. We try to handle it in six or seven different stages. One I just mentioned—that is, one year before reaching the draft age, the age of 17. Another stage is in the induction camp, that is, one or two days after induction; the process is repeated after the end of the basic training, this would be five months after induction; then again upon their discharge; and finally three or five years after discharge. We tried to look at it from many variables like social status, social class, cultural origin, and then even through political outlook, like the approach of the individual to the main security policy problems. And I found that there is in the United States, in this Conference, much need for such research. It would be very interesting to find out what are the different and changing variables in each case.

Then the next phase in the same research was to try to see the change in out-look, attitude, and orientation toward the basic values of the country and of the society—for example, toward the state as such, toward discipline, toward friend-ship, toward liberty, etc. And we ran immediately across a difference between regulars and draftees. Of course, cognitive dissonance had a lot to do with many of the differences here. I think it was Mrs. McAllister who brought out the ques-tion of how much the long period of service in the military bears upon the psychology of the individual. Even in our condition and moral environment, which is basically defensive, we are concerned with this question and we do a lot of research in this direction. I must say that we found out with the draft laws that there is hardly any change at all. Nobody that goes through the draft has become more autocratic in his outlook. Yet there is some change among the regulars; it is not alarming, but there is a change. One has to look out in the years to come, I guess, for the question of whether a "military mind" may be created in the country or not. I don't think we have it as yet.

With regard to regulars, we ran across a phenomenon that may sound very similar to yours: that in the range of first sergeant and sergeant-major we have a high proportion of people who come from deprived backgrounds, namely, those that we call the mid-Eastern Jews. They are about 50 per cent of the com-munity but they run as high as 70 per cent on these two rank levels. We also thought that it is a line of mobility for them, yet we now try to look at it in a more sophisticated way—is this only a positive social mobility, or are there other variables involved, like the problems arising from the new expectations of these people or the sudden sense of frustration that may show up in their handling of their subordinates? We try to give them general education as a preventive mea-sure. There is a famous story in Israel that a sergeant-major of Moroccan origin who went to one of our schools and studied on primary school level, spoke to his soldiers and said: "Water boils at 90 degrees." So one egghead said, "No, sir, you made a mistake, boiling is at 100 degrees." So he ran back to his office and looked at his books quickly and came back and said, "I am sorry, you are right; 90 degrees is a square angle."

We have a lot of interest in Professor Weinstein's study. I don't know how deeply he went into the question of how far vocational training in the military is relevent and helps the economy. In Israel, of course, the turnover of soldiers is very large. Our people come into the military and go out every two years and, as far as quantity goes, it is all beneficial, since so many have the opportunity to acquire a vocation and skills. Yet, one has to look more into the details of the relevancy of the vocation taken in the military, to the placement problems of the individual in civilian society. If he is in aviation electronics, of course, we know he can go into aviation industry. But on a broader scale of more diffused skills, it calls for a good deal of longitudinal research to find out, for example, what happens to a man who became, let us say, a quartermaster or a sergeant or occasionally a second lieutenant—how this affects his life later, in ten or fifteen years.

Special, marginal, but interesting research was done with juvenile delinquency. I cannot go into details here, but the basic answer was that the more severely delinquent juveniles were before the service, the more they were delinquent in the military and finally dropped out of service, which meant that it doesn't pay to draft them. On the other hand, we still draft some of them, for the sake of those who may find a remedy in the service. We try to refine the criteria because we feel that for those delinquents who did adjust to military life, it may have been beneficial. We try to find predictive criteria for this difference. For the lower levels of felony and delinquency, the dropout rate was much lower, and we found that the military service in this case was quite beneficial to them.

I think that it was Senator Neuberger who spoke about changing patterns in the military itself. I think that the military in Israel is, on the whole, very democratic as far as relations between ranks go. Nevertheless, we experimented in the last four years with bringing more democratic patterns of behavior to the military. There is a gentleman here in Chicago, Professor Dreikurs, who is a super-liberal Adlerian psychoanalyst. He came to Israel and we tried his methods—which were extremely revolutionary for most of our people—in a school preparing boys for technological positions in the Air Force. We tried to make it a "free society," so to speak, where everyone was expected to act by his free will and motivation, and where almost all disciplinary measures were waived. We failed. We failed because we tried the extreme. We tried to do it too fast. When we tried it again with a gradual approach in the OCS course, we succeeded. After half a course, we introduced the so-called "self rule." The candidates there ran the whole show and it was very successful. I suppose that this is one example of changing patterns within the military itself.

Maybe the last thing that I should bring up here has to do with the problems of deferment. Basically in Israel we draft at the age of 18 only. There is a certain group of people whom the Army selects after induction, to be sent to the universities and to come back for their term of service. We tried to look at this problem and we tried to ask a few questions: first, whether the draft that comes between the ages of 18 and 20 is by any means a handicap to people who go into higher education—does it make any change in their prospects for continuing their studies? The answer was no. On the contrary, in the university community professors found that in most cases it was beneficial for people to have a break and come back to their studies after they matured in the service. Then we asked the reverse question, about the changes that occur among the young men who go first to the university and then come back to the military. The answer there depends on how you place them within the service. As to the conclusion I incorporated in my paper, in Israel at least, with our mentality and our social conditions, the age of 18 to 20 is the proper age for the service.

And if I may, for one more minute, say one particular thing that maybe I should have said at the beginning—in Israel we utilize the military to perform non-military functions in the national interest because of the lack of other competent agencies. In a fully developed society, many of these functions may easily be performed by other types of national service, or in institutions other than the military. The fact that it is in the military is not that important. This brings me to the last point I want to make. Everything I mentioned was relevant primarily for boys. The situation with girls' service is different. There is a universal service law for girls, too. But in reality we do not draft girls with less than primary-school education. There is very little we can do with them in the military. Girls in the Israel Defense Force serve as clerks, or perform other functions which call for a certain minimum of education. However, we tried to bring into the military groups of semiliterate girls—with a thought to educate the mothers of the next generation. And the mothers will become more and more vital in the process of breaking through vicious circles of deprivation. We did it a few times with quite an amount of success. It was very costly, but we believe that we should move very fast toward better conditions in the social structure; nevertheless, our experience shows that it is a problem that one has to think of in terms of solving within three or four generations. No one can hope to do it faster.

Mr. Arnold Anderson. Tonight I want to outline some topics on which I think we need analysis, empirical facts, or speculations. But I am not being critical of Mr. Eberly's report. It was an impossible task to undertake in the first place, and I will keep the two modes of discourse separate.

Let me begin with the finance and administration package. Now we are being told that it is desirable to find a way to persuade private agencies to muster the staff and resources for their share of the financial burden, to take on assistants, understudies, interns, and so on; that there is to be a system of local boards to assign, administer, and supervise. There is a problem of keeping one's finger on the people who are assigned to service, and, since they will cover a wide gamut of abilities, temperament, and personalities, a problem in obtaining accountability from them in their self-assumed duties. There is a proposal about something like the GI bill, and there are proposals about conscientious objectors. Now, I submit that before we propose a package of that kind, we ought to try and figure out which are the crucial elements, for how many people, for which kinds of activities, and which ones are manageable with a staff that can presumably be found to coordinate or administer such a program?

Second topic: The specification of needs. It seems to me that when one tries to speak about the needs for national service workers, or I would prefer to call it citizens service workers, we should take warning from the miserable mess that the poverty program is in. It is difficult to find in even three, four, five, or six years the staff who can handle these programs. This is one side of it. The other side is to find activities in which these people can be sufficiently useful to warrant the expenditure of time and money on the programs. In other words we need some kind of a curve of demand for these different kinds of activities and national service and we have also to plot, so to speak, the demand in relation to what you can call, by analogy, kinds of prices. There is no need, there is no demand for services in any generic sense. There are scales, or orders of priority, and these have to be worked out with some insight. We also have to face, it seems to me, very clearly, pragmatically as well as analytically, the task of not undermining the ongoing programs and various things in the private sector. For instance, there are glittering statements about how these people can be used for urban renewal. Now, this is fine, but I have heard about labor unions which have so far stultified in the city of Chicago a large part of the OEO program. And there are going to be other kinds of groups with legitimate interests, and these have to be dealt with. A related problem is, what will be the attitude of the teachers, whether they are or are not unionized, to proposals to inject a flood of amateurs into the operations of the school or paraschool program.

Third category: The incidence of national service. There are some very ticklish questions, as we have seen, with respect to equity: To what degree is the program going to be a remedial program? Who is going to rehabilitate whom? And for how long? And where? I find very disturbing the descriptions about placement centers. They do not sound like very constructive activities, if one is seriously concerned about equity. Equity, you can say, is merely a value. But equity can be dealt with analytically as regards its impact on different groups in different situations. Then there is the question of whose skills are going to be used for what activities. There are some people who don't have any. There are others that have some but we don't know how to use them. There are others who have skills that perhaps would be more effectively contributory if they were used in non-volunteer ways, and so on. There are going to be very difficult problems about assessing competence. If the military has difficulty and creates endless snafus with its assignment job, as we are always being told, I shudder at the task of assigning people to the most effective appropriate activities in civilian programs. And self-choice is not necessarily the last word. Then again there is the question of in what situations you can use amateurs. This bears on the question of the incidence of National Service. There are some sort of things, for instance the YMCA street workers in Chicago, where there has been some very effective use of people with very little professional competence. The question of the relation of national service and military service we have discussed sufficiently. But there are very complex questions about the incidence of national service and the ramifications into the equity and efficiency domain and the freedom of choice domain which seem to me need to be thought through before we start drafting big programs, even five years hence.

Fourth topic: The whole question of "obligatory." I find it difficult to think through, in the short time that we have been together, how one is going to create a service which meets the stipulations that it be, in some major way, voluntary. Taking into account also the parallel situation of the military service, the needs that people talk about and so on, I don't quite see how all of these things are going to be made compatible without injecting a major portion of direction and authoritarianism into the program, which I think many of the strongest supporters of national service would not welcome. There is also a related topic that was not discussed today, but seems to really deserve extensive inquiry, and I am sure the military themselves have a great deal of work which bears on this: that is the relation between national service and the civil action kinds of activities of the military or paramilitary organizations operating parallel to the military. That ranges over the Peace Corps, AID, and so on. All the way through the discussion I find it very difficult to find who is defining what in the discussions about voluntary service. Now you can say that the problem is equally great in military service, and I can see that it is. We do have certain patterns that we have lived with, and once somebody gets into the clutches of the military or the Selective Service System, we have been managing to squirm around and adjust to the situation. But in opening up this whole new sector, I think that there is a problem of who is defining the kind of thing that is going to be. Who is going to serve in what kinds of capacity? Whose lower level skills are going to be regarded as ready for application rather than meriting remedial work, which is another kind of compulsion. Who is going to decide which organizations and activities are legitimate? Who is to decide what is a reasonable contribution from the organization if it is to qualify for receiving these people? One could go on endlessly.

Now all that I am really saying, I suppose, is that any particular paragraph in Mr. Eberly's report, or section of it, really, is a nest of one problem inside of another, all of which badly need some disentangling. On some of the topics, we have some precedents from analogous programs or from the military itself. For others, we can get strong precedents in the operation of our school system. On others, we will have to figure out a whole series of issues including some constitutional issues, as well as what, to me, is the most onerous of all: the very ticklish problem of who's going to push whom around. And all of these programs, unless they are strictly voluntary, are going to involve somebody pushing somebody around. And this, I think, calls for a considerable amount of fresh thinking and sharp analysis before we begin to lay programs on the desks of the congressmen.

Mr. Marmion. Very quickly, I would like to cite some eight areas of the current Selective Service act which need to be studied. Some of these have already been studied. These are the major areas of controversy, as I see them, within the current legislation.

First, there is considerable confusion over the principle behind the legislation in question. The act itself is misnamed: The Universal Military Training and Service Act. Second, there is the question of the decentralization of the present Selective Service System and the absence of national standards. On the one hand, it can be said that the essence of democracy is in the decentralization of the Selective Service System. However, this decentralization, with about 4,000 draft boards—called "supervised decentralization" by the Selective Service—has been criticized because it apparently creates some undemocratic situations. There is a lack of uniformity and interpretation. There are people on both sides of this particular issue. Third, and personally I think most important, there is the whole concept of the Selective Service channeling people into fields of endeavor where there are shortages of trained personnel—unfortunately, sometimes for the wrong reasons. Fourth, there is the matter of the high standards, both physical and mental, for induction into the Armed Forces. I recognize that Mr. Wool has spoken to the question of the reduction of some of the standards, but the fact remains that since 1950 over 3 million men have been found not qualified; in fiscal 1965, 50.5 per cent of those given preinduction physicals were found not qualified. Fifth, there is the question of the entire selection and induction process, essentially, the question of "who goes first?" Sixth is the question of deferments, deferments of students in particular. The seventh is a mechanical question, but one that is causing far more trouble than people realize: the question of appeals procedures. And eighth is the question of draft quotas and the allocation of calls. The selection burden is falling unevenly upon the states; the more men that are processed and reported qualified by the state, the higher the quotas in that state. You've all heard the argument that in 1966 Michigan drafted 17,200 men, while Texas, a state with a comparable population, inducted 15,000.

These eight areas, then, appear to me to need study. Finally, I would like to say that we should be aware that if we are going to select an alternative system of producing military manpower, we should all be quite aware that this will create other new problems with regard to equity and fairness.

Mr. Oi. I would like to address my remarks toward the desirability of research on the problem of meeting our military manpower requirements, and Harold Wool is probably in a better position to evaluate some of the ongoing research.

Foremost is the reevaluation of the current level of pay structure now being carried on by a paid study group in the Pentagon, under Admiral Hovel. This study should receive careful outside review as well as review by members of Congress.

Second, if we are to move toward a voluntary force, then I think continued study of the supply of voluntary enlistment (which we did in the draft study, and which was done subsequently by the Defense Department staff) should examine the characteristics not only of those who volunteer for military service, but also of those who are inducted, to obtain a better estimate of the real cost of the draft to these individuals. How much disruption of civilian life is there?

Third, there is the question of reenlistment, retention, and assignment. It is often alleged that the military, given its constraint, does a pretty good job of finding personnel—that comparatively few Ph.D.'s are out digging ditches, and the like. I tend to agree; but, again, the evidence has never been fully documented. More important; did the assignment policy, the rotational policy, influence those who chose to remain and to make a career in the military, as opposed to those who left the military with an adverse opinion of it?

Fourth, the possibility for civilian substitution should, I believe, be carefully examined. What is the necessary force-strength to exceed the desired levels of military preparedness? How many civilians can we substitute? This is especially important in the case of doctors, where it is anticipated that shortages will occur if we abolish the draft.

Finally, fifth (and indirectly related to the question of military manpower policies), I believe we should make a careful cost-benefit analysis, similar to those given to water projects but, I hope, correcting some of the errors made there, to determine what are the costs and the benefits, the real economic cost, of various national-service alternatives being proposed. How much are they going to end up costing? If we're talking about 5 million people in these programs, as Harold Wool mentioned, you have to remember that figure constitutes close to 7 per cent of our labor force and is an enormous number of people. What are the costs of these people and what are the benefits that society receives? I think these questions should be asked and thoroughly examined. The planning of research and the anticipating of the kinds of problems to be encountered should be very carefully done.

Mr. Davis. We're now ready to open the meeting to discussion.

Mr. Flacks. Mr. Hazard, when he described the problems before the Conference, mentioned the first one as relating the draft to the foreign policy context; I'm somewhat disturbed that none of the panelists referred to that as an important area for research. It seems to me that we said a number of things about this, all of which are problematical, all of which I think are capable of being studied. About 25 years ago, Harold Lasswell wrote a paper called "The Garrison State," in which he suggested that it was possible that societies which were involved in perpetual international conflict would move toward a social structure characterized by the merger of civilian and military elites, the sacrifice of civilian goals for military ones, a breakdown of democratic political institutions, peacetime conscription and compulsory labor, and the tying-in of voluntary organizations to the state, among other things. Now, how does the institution of a permanent peacetime conscription contribute to that trend in our society? Second, a question which we had some exchange about and which Congressman Rumsfeld commented on: How does the draft contribute to undue autonomy on the part of the executive branch? Does the draft contribute to military adventurism? Does it detract from searches for peaceful resolutions of international conflict? Alternatively, would restrictions and constraints on the use of conscripts, and on the use of conscription, enable Congress and other portions of the political system to control the Executive? Would such constraint facilitate search for peaceful resolution of conflict? All these are problems which I think are central, and as far as I know, very little research is done on them, for fairly obvious reasons.

I wanted to raise a second minor point for research, but perhaps Colonel Ingold could comment on it. That is, what are the effects of uncertainty? Let me give one instance. It seems to me that there is some question as to whether there was an intention to draft students this year or in the immediate future, but the draft boards began to create the notion that in fact there was going to be an immediate draft of students. I wonder whether that was done because Selective Service believed in fact that students had to be drafted or because they believed this was necessary to increase the rate of volunteers. If the latter is true, then we've had a whole series of serious disturbances on the campuses because students believed they were going to be drafted, when, in fact, that was not in the cards.

Colonel Ingold. When I pushed the button I had something else in mind here; I wanted to speak to Marmion's statement. In regard to his eighth point, the Michigan and Texas variation, this was called to our attention by several members of Congress and a special study was made of it. By combining all of the factors that have to do with the military, including the membership on active duty, and the reserve, and the veterans of comparable age, and adding all of these together, the two states were almost identical, and the differences in calls and delivery by Selective Service were merely making up the differences between the two, and therefore, were bringing about almost exact statistical uniformity.

Now, as to the other question, the effects of uncertainty. Generally it amounts to this: the uncertainty that is created by international circumstances and by the method in which we select men to meet them, results in the enlistment for more than two years of pretty close to 30 or 35 thousand men a month. This was not intended for the purpose of making students uncertain. It's because if the rate of call continues to go up as it has recently, we will eventually have to take some students in a greater number than they've been taken in the past. It is something we have to do to meet fluctuations, and it was not for the purpose of creating uncertainty.

Mr. Flacks. The thing I can't reconcile with that is the leveling off of the draft calls and the decline in the draft calls.

Colonel Ingold. We do not control that.

Mr. Flacks. You thought that there was going to be a steady increase in draft calls and that students would have to be drafted in the near future.

Colonel Ingold. We certainly did, and if they continue as they did prior to a very recent cutback, it will still be necessary to call more students than we have in the past—not to *start* to call students, that is a misnaming of the thing. We've *always* called some students.

Mr. Flacks. Are the Selective Service tests and the ranking procedures that were adopted this year going to be used to establish deferments of any students? I mean, are they really relevant to the induction of anybody?

Colonel Ingold. Yes, very definitely. They're part of the regulations. You understand, however, that there is in the act a prohibition against requiring any local board to defer people on the basis of either of those grounds. They are advisory.

Mr. Wofford. The case for decentralization is that the local boards know the boys, have a more intimate knowledge, and can make better decisions. Apparently when you register, if I'm right, Colonel Ingold, at a board when you are a senior, or in high school, or 18½, you stay with that board, even if for years and years thereafter you have no connection with the town at all. How many Negroes, for instance, in districts in the black belts of the South—where it was stated earlier there are *no* Negroes on draft boards—are getting decisions made about them by boards in towns that they left years ago and have no connections with? I know of one sharp case of a Peace Corps volunteer in Ethiopia who was a Negro. He came back and went to law school and suddenly was redrafted while he was at law school by a board in the deep South that never had a Negro on it. You assured us this morning that it was your impression that no discrimination resulted from there being no Negroes on these boards. We were assured in this case by a man in Selective Service that he happened to know that board well and there wasn't any discrimination, but you could never convince this volunteer that they didn't find it easier to draft him, who had no connection with that town, than to draft somebody that they did know intimately and locally. So, I think there's a statistical question of how many people are affected by boards who have no knowledge of them at all, or no connection with them. And particularly there is a question of whether, in these areas where boards have no Negroes on them, there's discrimination against Negroes.

Colonel Ingold. I'd be glad to speak to both questions. On the question of transfer, there are more than 3 million people away from home at all times. If we are to protect the national interest, as we're expected to, we have to have some degree of solidity in regard to files, or we'll have that many files en route somewhere at all times. So, we have arrangements for transfer for classification. We also have full arrangements for transfer of appeals to the locality in which the man is currently located. This takes the case completely out of the area in which he is registered and transfers it to the state appeal board in the state where he is currently working or residing. As to the question of discrimination, I do not consider induction into the Armed Forces to be a penalty.

[*Unidentified Speaker*]. It's a penalty to the Negro. It's discrimination.

Colonel Ingold. On Monday I made an introductory speech in which I pointed out that the whites serve more than the colored do, percentage-wise.

Mrs. McAllister. My question has to do with the matter of centralization and decentralization and making accurate reports or predictions. As early as March of 1964 some draft boards had gone so far as to set up standards which meant that any student with less than an A average in his senior year, or less than a B average in his junior year, and any grades below a C in his sophomore year would be immediately subject to call. There was no notice given to students or teachers, there was just a decision that was made by the board and they acted on it without any kind of notice to the selectees that they were choosing, and they broke up terms of school in doing this. I know that it happened because I sat in the draft board office and watched the students' utter amazement as they came in every afternoon for four days. Now if this was done to confuse, at a time when generally throughout the country it was assumed that students were not being called, I'd like to know just what the purposes were?

Colonel Ingold. Well, I can't very well respond to that without knowing the complete facts. I'd be glad to look into it. I would like to say this, though. If we have bureaucratic action there, it was on a local level where it could be taken care of instead of in a centralized area where it would be more difficult.

Mr. Brenman. In answer to what Colonel Ingold said about people not being able to transfer from one board to another, it seems to me there's a contradiction between this and what he said earlier as the reason for having local boards. As I understood it, the reason for local boards, over 4,000 around the United States, is because in a national emergency large numbers of people would have to be called up at a snap. People who are in transit cannot be called up by their local boards at a snap, so the contradiction is, if you don't allow people to transfer boards, then you might as well have a national board and hence uniformity of standards, which is a big problem as has been admitted. One local board is not the same as another in its standards.

Colonel Ingold. I think I said that there would be about 3 million *files* in transit. The people have gone somewhere and the problem is trying to get the materials to them after they notify you where they went. As to uniformity, if you have national uniformity, you will not have local uniformity, because as I indicated before, an opthalmologist in Alaska would be deferred, but it would be ridiculous to defer all opthalmologists all over merely to accommodate a situation in Alaska, or to deny them deferment all over because Alaska happens to be in the minority. So local option does produce uniformity within the local area.

Mr. Davis. This panel is to be devoted to the gathering of data and I hope that we will try to stick to it.

[Unidentified Speaker]. I think that what discussions heretofore have brought out is that we need a study of whether there is discrimination from board to board and how it operates. The Michigan case was mentioned. I disagree with Colonel Ingold that it has been properly answered, because discriminations according to my records are still continuing. Along that line, I think it would be very interesting if we could find out what is the easiest board in the country to belong to? What are some of the easiest boards? I understand there are some very good ones in Texas and that there are some people there that just never get drafted, because there are plenty of volunteers, so if you really want a "cushy" board you go to a certain town in Texas. And, conversely, Michigan has some really tough boards, I think it would be interest-

ing to really compare these boards and how they operate, from state to state.

Second, I think that Mr. Flacks' question about student deferment and the uncertainty that General Hershey's alarm created in terms of deferment and inducing volunteers is definitely a good one. I think that General Hershey has admitted, from time to time, that these alarms that he puts out do have that effect.

If that's untrue, then we need to determine to what extent the Selective Service System has a good statistical research division which does understand what conditions are going to be. Last March they made a projection that the pool of 1A men would be completely exhausted by June, and therefore they had to go through with this student change. First of all, the report they gave the House Education and Labor Committee had an error of 100,000 men and had to be returned for correction. Then, it was returned, and six months later, or four months later, there was no reduction in the pool, there was no exhaustion of the pool at all. So, I would like to have an examination of the research that the system does undertake.

On a more sociological nature, is there an evasion mentality in relation to the draft which we haven't touched much upon yet? If there is an evasion mentality, what is its source? What is its nature, and what are its lasting effects? Such a study I would think would go into the psychological effects on the individual and the social effects on his peers, his family, etc.

Another question is—How does the Selective Service System locally and nationally use deferment to control manpower flow, and how do induction centers change, or regulate consciously or unconsciously, officially and unofficially, the physical standard for induction? I happen to know people who get deferred for asthma and their buddies went down a year later and they didn't get deferred for asthma, and the situations were identical. I'm sure that there are a great many people who suspect that the induction centers—which we should acknowledge are not run by the Selective Service System, which is getting its lumps tonight, but by the Army—change their own attitudes. And if this is so, we need to know exactly how they do change their tactics.

Mr. Davis. Speaking of evasion and tactics, the subject here is the gathering of data and research.

Mr. Keast. I have one or two others to add that I hope someone will undertake appropriate studies of; they are not, I think, of quite such broad reach as some of the items already covered, but I think they're relevant and worth mentioning. We have not discussed the Selective Service test, which has been reinstituted in recent months, but which was used in another form, I guess, or perhaps in the same form, between 1961 and 1963. I think we ought to know how good this test is for what purpose. I think despite the vigor of my approach to the subject of class ranking, there is a researchable subject here. It might be undertaken by universities in connection with the normal conduct of their work. It would be worth finding out what we can do about the reliability of class-ranking mechanisms of various types and their relevance to various reasons for student deferment, or the grounds on which student deferment is offered.

I believe it's relevant for us to raise the question of what the effect of the deferment system has been upon the decisions of young people regarding college, or graduate studies. Here again, I think we're in the position as we are with so many of these items: of having to make policy decisions or recommendations, but in the virtual absence of systematic data and controlled studies which would give both those of us who are in this position and the Selective Service System a better and more legitimate warrant for the things we all have to do. I'd like to underscore the point made by Mr. Marmion, that a full-scale investigation of the system of channeling, occupational deferments, adequacy of the analysis of job titles and so on, and the propriety of the entire undertaking as a function of the Selective Service System would also be a very valuable subject for intensive study.

Mr. Davis. I don't know whether anyone else here has done work on the tests. I have, and I can tell you that the correlation between such tests and performance on the job runs around $+.3$, which is significant but much too low to predict, and is the best a test can do. For instance, the Educational Testing Service made, among many other tests, a test to predict efficiency as a torpedoman's mate, a man who helps a torpedoman, and it also correlated .3 with success on the job, and that's as good as anybody can do using tests.

Mr. Naisbitt. On the subject of tests, I'd like to talk to Mr. Flacks' suspicions about inducing anxiety in college students. The Selective Service College Qualification Test has been given 32 times. It was given 4 times this past year and 800,000 college students took it. The previous 28 times—1951 to 1963—a total of only 600,000 took it. And yet, to date, as of December 5, virtually no students in good standing have been drafted.

Mr. Winter. We've talked a good deal in this meeting about the comparison between the present Selective Service System and the possibility of a career military. I think one of the key things that we haven't talked much about is the problem of morale. Perhaps some of the experts in the military who are here will know the answer to this, but you hear a good deal now, at least sort of sub rosa, about the desertion rates during this particular Vietnam conflict. This is probably characteristic of the kinds of conflicts we'll be involved in and I think this is an area where some comparative studies could be done—Korean conflict versus this one, etc. What are the desertion rates and how serious is this? Is it a real morale problem?

Mr. Tatum. I would like to make one quick point, in case there was any misunderstanding in what Colonel Ingold said. It is true that an appeal to the state appeal board can be transferred under certain circumstances, though most registrants are not informed of this, but the first step, a personal appearance before your local board which was the point being discussed, is not transferable and that was not made clear. I want to quickly get on Colonel Ingold's side and go against my two friends and say that not only Selective Service, but I, thought that students would be drafted, and it looked like a pretty good bet at the time. I don't think, both from my personal knowledge and contact with Selective Service at the time and from their own bulletin, that there was anything phony about this. I would like to agree with you, but I don't. It cuts across what Mr. Naisbitt said, because since the beginning of the year a good many students in good standing have been drafted, not those who lacked the rank or didn't pass the test, but because of a further qualification which has been added by Selective Service and not nearly so much publicized—that of continuous study. For example, men who took a year out for work in civil rights in the South and then came back to go on to school found themselves being drafted. This was simply clarification of what I consider to be facts.

The points of research that I would like to see are two. One is on the treatment of men in the Armed Forces who become conscientious objectors and qualify for discharge as such, under Department of Defense regulations, where the percentage has gone from 80 per cent granted in 1964 down to virtually none at present. I think that this is a very serious situation which relates directly to morale and does in some cases involve desertion after the request for discharge has been denied. I think a second point for research, which is a tremendous problem in court, is that while local boards have very wide discretion, except for mandatory deferments (there has been no differentiation at this Conference but there are two kinds) the law requires that they treat all of their own registrants in the same manner. Now the difficulty in court is that this is an inapplicable standard. In other words, there is no way on this earth to know how they treat their other registrants, and most local boards don't know themselves, don't remember. I think it would be extremely useful and fascinating to take a random sampling of local boards, go through their files and determine whether they are, in fact, obeying the regulations in this regard.

[*Unidentified Speaker*]. This seems to be one of the ending sessions of the conference, and one might be given the false impression that the issues which are to be discussed and studied are issues which simply require gathering and tabulating data. I think that would be a misconception and I think it's acknowledged by most of the social scientists who have spoken on the panel this evening in that they've incorporated in their summary remarks words like: How important is this issue? How serious is the effect of such and such? I think it is probably worthwhile to acknowledge that there are some issues that don't need more data. And some of the issues which require more data, require more than simply tabulating the data. One might rephrase some of the issues as not just studying the effect of inducting into military service during peacetime, but studying the fairness of it; not studying the effects of peacetime drafts on executive power, but studying the justice and the fairness of it. Now, this may be within the purview of social science, but I'm inclined to think it's not. Similarly, the fairness of inducting unenfranchised members of the society should be studied. There has been very little said about this, and that's probably because we're not concerned with such issues as voting. I don't know whether there's some sort of reciprocal relationship between obligation and responsibility on the one hand, and rights—rights as citizens of the country to express their views in some minimum way through the electorate. Finally, one might study not just the effects, but the fairness of granting, as we said before, deferments exempting elected officials and exempting ministers of religion. I don't know whether one wants to raise issues about whose purview this is, but I do suggest that it's somewhat beyond, although included in, the purview of the social sciences.

Mr. Rosenberg. I'm in partial agreement with the speaker. I would say that the panel has raised a number of good questions, but not particularly pertinent questions. The mistake they have made, I think, in asking what the effects of continued conscription might be, is the mistake of looking largely to individual psychological effects. I don't think psychology and psychological questions irrelevant; in fact, I must confess that I am a psychologist. But I do think that for the kinds of problems we're discussing now, where the independent variables concern the maintenance of some kind of conscription system, or some alteration of that system, the dependent variables we might well begin to examine are social systemic ones. Mr. Flacks is the only one I've heard in this discussion tonight who has touched upon some such possible dependent variables In the main, I endorse the significance of the problems that he's noted, as worthy of investigation.

I would like to suggest one or two more, along the same lines. If we agree that public opinion has some bearing upon the policy process, that policymakers are to some extent influenced by, or at least constrained by, public opinion as they decide on certain foreign policy issues or innovations, it then becomes important to ask what the determinants of public opinion are. In this context it becomes important to ask what the influence of recourse to a conscription system has been upon public opinion in this country and other Western democratic states, and whether public opinion has been changed by abandonment of a conscription system. I had hoped that Mr. Abrams would tell us something about the effects upon British public opinion when Britain abandoned its conscription sys tem. Did British public opinion begin to open up a bit more to the possibilities of international conciliation when the British state seemed, by disestablishing the conscription system, to be saying: We now enter a new phase in international relations, one in which we need not rely upon the maintenance of an armed force of a certain constant size? I think it is a researchable hypothesis, that where governments abandon conscription and, for that matter, where they reduce the total size of the military force, the message, to those portions of the public who watch what their governments do, may be that the world is changing, that more specific opportunities are available, that international conciliation of significant, outstanding issues may yet be possible. If such public opinion changes occur, this may well free members of the policy elite for innovations in conciliatory directions, innovations which very often they would like to pursue, but in fact are constrained not to pursue because of apprehensions about electoral punishment, apprehensions based more often than not upon the actual content of public opinion polls. In this whole area, I think we have the possibility for some very interesting research, research as far as I know that has not been done very often.

I would suggest just one other researchable topic. What do we know about the attitudes within the military elite concerning their recourse to policy deliberations, or about their right to attempt control or influence over foreign policy decisions? I would suggest it is conceivable—it is only again a hypothesis—that where conscription affords a military elite the vision of themselves as holding power over a large system filled with constantly recruited or constantly commandeered personnel, this may, in fact, foster aspirations toward more effective influence in the policy process than would be the case where one has an army based upon volunteer enlistment and perhaps an army which is, at points, diminished in total size. Again, one might find some evidence by looking to those nations, largely within the Commonwealth I gather, in which conscription has prevailed for a while and then has been undone. And one might ask: What changes did occur?

Conclusions of the Conference

WEDNESDAY MORNING, DECEMBER 7, 1966

Chairman, ARNOLD R. WEBER

Mr. Weber. We now intend to present brief statements dealing with each of the topics that were raised during the course of the last two and a half days. I understand that each speaker or set of speakers will attempt to do two things: one, summarize the conference discussions, and in that sense act as a reporter; and, two, indicate in a supplementary fashion how the negative aspects of each of the proposals that were raised during the course of the Conference might be minimized—in other words, how each of these specific programs or proposals might be made operational. The first topic is "Recruitment by Voluntary Means." We have two speakers on that topic, Representative Kastenmeier of Wisconsin and Representative Rumsfeld of Illinois.

Mr. Kastenmeier. I think that this has been an important conference, not only because the Congress is undertaking the question of what to do about the draft law which expires this year, and the President has appointed a committee to reappraise the draft, but because of other reasons. First among them are those relating to Vietnam. We're not only asking young men for two years of their lives but also subjecting them to hazardous duties. Yet American military involvement in Vietnam does not have overwhelming popular support within this country. One further point which makes this Conference different from those in former times, is, I think, the fact that American youth has awakened itself and become politically active, politically involved in these questions.

We discussed the Selective Service System and the inequities that we said existed there, and we discussed alternatives. The one alternative that seems to have a reasonably broad amount of support, including my own, is the volunteer army. It seems to meet better than any other proposal the question of what we can do about compulsion. How can we get rid of coercion? The volunteer army meets this completely. It certainly has the appeal of returning to a former way of life in this country, that known before 1940. Furthermore, all the administrative problems of deferments and exemptions would be washed out if we had a voluntary system. It would eliminate the uncertainty in the career planning of many young Americans. There are many other reasons advanced for returning to volunteer systems.

However, a number of cogent objections have been submitted at this Conference, as well as certain reservations about what returning to volunteer service would mean. Even advocates of the plan admit that the budgetary costs to the government would be substantial, because part of the major inducement for enlistment would have to be a substantial increase in salaries. Advocates of the program estimate that it might cost 4 to 6 billion or even perhaps 8 billion dollars a year, depending on the force maintained, on the condition of the economy, and on the relative state of unemployment and the manpower pool. This figure is more or less doubled by the Defense Department; it feels that such a plan could cost up to 17 billion dollars a year. Now, the actual cost is minimized in at least a couple of arguments. One argument is that this differential is offset exactly by relieving the tax imposed on each youth who is supposed to serve. That is, the difference between what he is paid under the present system, and what would be required to maintain the given force system would be a tax on the man who is required to give a subsidy to the state. It is also submitted that since we will have less turnover, and greater reenlistment, we will need less training, and we will probably need less manpower in terms of the standing American force.

There are objections of course, one being that an all-volunteer army is sometimes equated with a professional army, and that this is something we should avoid or at least be aware of the difficulties it may create. To this objection it is stated that it is not whether a man is a volunteer or a conscript that poses a danger, but rather the officer corps. It is submitted that the officer corps essentially would be selected in the same way it is now, and this would not be substantially altered. Another serious criticism of the volunteer system is that the conversion to it would mean a loss of flexibility in moving from one size force to another. I think this has to be freely admitted. In the volunteer system, there would be less elasticity. If we are speaking of the ability of the military to respond to crisis, the answer members of the Conference have given to this is that we still do have a National Guard and a reserve system, whose essential function is to respond to such crisis and to provide some elasticity in force. It is said that the objections made have been reasonably met, and that we must move forward.

Another question, of course, is posed: When can it be done if it is done at all? Can it be done now in the middle of a bloody conflict in Vietnam, or must it be deferred to a later time? Perhaps to the end of that conflict? I don't think this Conference, or the sense of it, provides an answer to that, but I do think the very least that the Chief Executive and the Congress should be called on to do is to make a resolution assuring the American public that the goal of a free and voluntary service will be achieved and that they will take some steps to move in that direction when they consider the entire draft question. For indeed, if it is not done now, within the next six months, this may be our last chance for freedom in these terms.

Mr. Rumsfeld. When one accepts the political reality that during this period of our history we will require a military capability, then the question arises as to the best mechanism for recruiting that manpower. The present system has to be evaluated in terms of whether or not it is the most desirable and efficient method of procuring military manpower. I would suggest that a reasonable conclusion is that it very likely is not. Not only is the present system subject to the inequities and uncertainties discussed at the conference, but it is based, as Representative Kastenmeier has indicated, on the principle of compulsion, and certainly during the overwhelming majority of our history we, as a nation, have not had a compulsory system. There is broad agreement that for compulsion to be acceptable in a free society there must be a demonstrated need for it.

On the question of the need for compulsion, or, conversely, the feasibility of a voluntary system, there were differing viewpoints. However, the discussion demonstrated, I believe, a lack of factual information sufficiently serious to prevent final conclusions. Those favoring a voluntary system, or at least favoring a serious study of the feasibility of a voluntary system, suggested the following advantages of such a system: preserving freedom of individuals to serve or not to serve avoids the compulsion inherent in any of the other proposals—the present system, the lottery, or universal military training—avoids the discrimination and inequities among different groups under the present system, eliminates the uncertainty problem, and eliminates questions relative to conscientious objectors as well. Further, a necessary advantage of a voluntary system is that the military personnel would be properly compensated for their service. They deserve no less.

There were two potential difficulties of the voluntary system that were discussed extensively, and properly so. The first was the question of feasibility, especially with respect to cost. This resulted in differences in opinion based on an admitted lack on both sides of sufficient information. Next, the argument was made that a voluntary, and therefore professional, army could conceivably develop into a potential threat to established political institutions. Such a threat, however, could be expected to come from the officer corps, rather than enlisted personnel; and officers are currently, and have always been in this country, recruited voluntarily. Further, our proper tradition of civil control of the military has, thus far at least, always been sufficiently strong so that there has been no serious threat of military takeover. History seems to show, however, that such threats have come from conscript as well as volunteer armies. I believe that such a threat is a concern, but with attention and care it can be as readily avoided in a voluntary system as it could be, and has been, in a conscript system, by building possibly some turnover into the system.

To conclude—and these are personal observations—during the discussion, I was impressed that very few valid arguments, supported by documentation, were put forth against the voluntary system. I also felt that there were numerous and significant advantages to the voluntary system which were not specifically rebutted. Further, I was struck by the apparent degree of support for a voluntary system and also the diverse political and personal viewpoints of the individuals who seemed to be uniting in agreement on this question.

My view is that a reasonable course of action would be for the Congress to give prompt attention to establishing as a goal the institution of an all-voluntary system and phasing out the use of the compulsory draft system as a device for maintaining any size army other than that which would be required for a major conflict or a massive land war. It is recognized that above a voluntary system it would be necessary to have a compulsory system available to raise the military capacity that conceivably could be necessary in something more serious than the current situation. Second, the ninetieth Congress, early in the first Session, should establish a joint committee to determine the feasibility of a voluntary system, try to fill existing information gaps, and at the same time study improvements and alternatives in any compulsory system which would serve as a secondary mechanism for raising manpower. Third, if a voluntary system is found to be feasible, a joint committee should recommend to the Congress a transitional system designed to move toward this goal. Under present circumstances, and with the information available to me, it seems that the case for such a course of action by Congress and by the Executive is indicated.

Mr. Weber. The next topic is an evaluation of the present system and of military manpower procurement. That issue will be handled by Professor Little.

Mr. Little. First, I'll assume that some system of conscription is still necessary to maintain effective force levels either by direct induction or by impelled enlistment. The question is how this can be done in a way that will eliminate or minimize objections that now threaten its legitimacy in a democratic society. Our concern is with means rather than with ends.

What is right about Selective Service, not only today but since World War I? First, it has been an effective means of manpower procurement. Second, it has distributed the risks of service throughout the society, with greater universality than would then have been possible by purely voluntary recruitment. Third, it has attempted to minimize interference with other activities of the larger society and with individual careers by using the strategy of classification and deferment. But what is *right* with Selective Service has been concealed by barriers of secrecy which have forbidden, hampered, and confused public examination of its activities. A vast amount of psuedo-knowledge has developed and discredited what are often positive features of the organization. The best example of this is quota allocation. The formula was not revealed until the Armed Services Committee Hearings. When it was made known that it is based on registration data, which are relatively more current than census data, that it allocates the quota according to the jurisdiction's ability to provide the manpower rather than the number of people who reside there, it made sense. It's a fair and equitable formula. It also explains the Texas-Michigan canard that is so frequently introduced. It is not because Texans are favored; it is because they have a higher rejection rate—perhaps because they are taller, so tall that they fail to meet the anthropometric standards.

What are the problems of Selective Service? The first one is accessibility. I think that the barriers may be a by-product of the military image that is fostered by the military staffing of national and state headquarters and their affiliation with the reserves. The military image tends to justify a defensive posture and secrecy about routine operations that are perfectly susceptible to public examination. I might say that is also promotes, to the disadvantage of the Selective Service System, a spurious identification of Selective Service with the Armed Forces. If General Hershey is blamed for exempting a prominent athlete, rather than the Armed Forces examining station, it is because he is called a General.

Second, the actual operation of the local boards presents problems. Boards are reported to have widely different criteria for deferments. Allegations of the ambiguity, arbitrariness, and capriciousness of the local boards are direct results of the representation of local boards by the Selective Service System as functionally autonomous, independent units which exercise independent judgment. However, in reality the board is a rare entity—it meets only once a month for three to four hours and processes such an enormous number of cases that it couldn't possibly be performing the tasks that are attributed to it by Selective Service. Most decisions are so routine in nature, and fit explicit criteria so exactly, that adjudication is required in only a small fraction. The classification decisions, however, are delayed precisely because they have to wait until the board comes once a month to ceremonially validate what the clerk has done earlier in the month. The real importance of the local board clerk should be recognized and established legally.

Third, the local boards are not representative of their jurisdictions, especially in metropolitan areas. First of all, they are not responsive to a changing community. Tenure is almost indefinite. Replacements are recruited by remaining members rather than by the external appointing authority. They are unrecognizable by name or position in the community, especially in a metropolitan area, and I might say that in Chicago and some other metropolitan areas registrants are denied the names of the local board members. Also, the jurisdictions vary widely in demographic characteristics. In Chicago, again, the registrant load varies between 4,500 for some boards and 13,500 for others. Obviously, a registrant before a local board with a case load of 4,500 has a much better chance of having his appeal heard than before one that is rushed by the processing of 13,000 cases. In addition, the rejection rates in contiguous areas in Chicago vary from 23 per cent in one to 74 per cent in another.

Fourth, the appeals system requires an excessive amount of legal knowledge by young registrants; it depends on a system of appeals agencies that is practically inoperative in most areas. All registrants are now apprised of legal aid and there are agencies and instruments by which all registrants could be provided with legal assistance in appeals agencies.

Fifth is the matter of occupational deferments. (I will omit education deferments because they will be covered subsequently.) The flexible criterion, which is so highly spoken of, permits boards to base decisions on their own interpretation of criticality, and this interpretation is easily influenced in the local board by the prestige of the employer in the community—the economic importance of the industry to the community rather than the individual field of the registrant. I would suspect there are as many administrative assistants to university presidents and public relations officers for industries as opthalmologists and space scientists who are deferred for occupation.

Sixth is the problem of the interfering with life plans. The order of call of older men interrupts established careers, procures more expensive manpower more expensively at a greater loss to the community, and is inefficient because relatively more must be called before the quota is met as more are disqualified with increasing age.

Seventh, prospective registrants have inadequate information as to their legal rights and responsibilities in the System. There's no organized program of education and information.

Finally, what recommendations for change could emerge? First, enlarge the universe of selection at least to the state level. A national pool, as has been suggested here, would penalize those states with educational systems that produce a larger number of qualified men. The routine nature of most local board classifications suggests that it is perfectly feasible to automate registrations and classifications at the state level, and this would also permit the transfer of registration to the area of domicile—a simple automative process.

Second, redefine the organizational functions of the local board to make them more compatible with reality. This could be done, for example, by upgrading the role of the clerk to the position of registrar, with functions comparable to those of a local magistrate. Reconstitute the local board as a local appeals agency with truly representative members, residents of its jurisdiction and domiciled in its jurisdiction, fully known to all registrants, with limited tenure, not more than one war removed from that for which the registrants are being inducted. Define the area of jurisdiction in terms of population characteristics and census tracts, and perhaps adjust them periodically in the same way that congressional districts are adjusted to correspond with population changes.

The third change would be to restore the principle of universality and to distribute the chances of service fairly and equally by eliminating student and occupational deferments.

Fourth, modify the order of call in order to call 18- and 19-year-old age groups first and then reach into the older age groups to fill the quota.

Fifth, establish an informational and guidance system oriented less toward defending the existing system and more toward informing potential registrants what it's all about and how to do it.

Finally, open the doors to research and consultation, first by eliminating the military image and second, by recognizing that if research is indeed a search for truth, Selective Service has nothing to hide.

Mr. Weber. The next topic is conscientious objection. We have two speakers, Sister Cusack and Rabbi Ticktin.

Sister Cusack. Conscientious objection, in the eyes of someone formally committed to religion, has taken on a new importance in the last decade or so. We now have, to quote Mr. Hazard, the "middle-size war." The middle-size war has ruled out the complete acceptability of the draft, but it has not ruled in, as yet, the volunteer army, so we are in a quasi-state, and I think that accounts for the so-called confusion of this Conference. But I'm one who thinks confusion is a good thing if it's supported by thought.

The second change has been in the field of religion and morals. Even those formally committed to religion realize now, particularly since Pope John, that formal commitment, church membership, by no means separates the good from the bad or the religious from the irreligious, and that religious conviction may be very strong, however vague. Similarly, the ongoing moral revolution has broadened moral convictions and, some will say, weakened them until they encompass many things for many people. The particular resolution that was passed last evening said that moral conviction constituted a reason to object to killing. In my opinion, and in the opinion of many here, the three grounds discussed earlier make a very salutary postscript to the Supreme Court decision, so that the conscientious objector is not nearly so objected to as he thinks. However, I can only speak for myself, of course, and I am for a broadening of the concept of conscientious objection.

I think you will find out that there is a fourth class of moral objector present today who is a conscientious objector to killing, and is a sincere person, but he seems, on the surface at least, to have no particular political objections to other people doing the killing. He may wish escalation without participation, and it never occurs to him that when he is to be sincerely treated as a conscientious objector, his objections, his conscience, are subject to some scrutiny. And I think they should be. All groups of C.O.'s, however, should be subject to two things: one is the obligation which in my creed accompanies every right—the obligation or responsibility to declare oneself and stand by one's position. In addition, it may be that they all should be offered other opportunities to serve their country, opportunities without one touch of disrepute being added. In that way, I think, we may put the subject in focus and in outline form.

Rabbi Ticktin. The consideration of the question of conscientious objection is a unique vantage point for dealing with all of the central issues raised here. I see three or four major issues that are unresolved but deserving of continued treatment: one, compulsion and its limits versus individual freedom and its limits; two, inequity and arbitrariness in the present draft system; and, three, the recognition that we have abdicated our responsibilities in the political process over a period of 25 years. (Congress has done so also in permitting the draft to become a kind of sacred cow.) All of this has convinced me of the desirability and the eminent feasibility of a volunteer career army.

I have been struck here by the fact that persons with quite different ideologies and life styles yet seem to have somewhat similar approaches to these three issues and a similar faith that a volunteer career army is in the direction of the best solution.

We pride ourselves on America's providing access to higher education to over 5 million young people. The major premise of that whole venture is that we should present the broadest possible range of choices in schooling, training, and value formation to young people. Because of this I think those young persons who are considering conscientious objection should be permitted a broad latitude for expression. Our educational goals call for the greatest open-mindedness, not simply an uncritical extension of traditional religious training and belief, but rather a critical outlook. An expansion of conscientious objection was indicated in the Seeger decision, and here the judiciary entered into the process in ways some of us were not able to find for ourselves.

The implications, as I see them, are that followers of America's spiritual and cultural heritage can no longer relegate conscientious objection status to a group of persons whom we have regarded in the past as having an exotic religious or moral position. I think that we must grant recognition to those citizens who have conscientious preferences, even unpopular ones, even to those whose present positions may not seem morally superior. (I, for one, believe that a classical pacifist position is not always morally superior.) Such recognition granted to these individuals permits the growth of personality and the maintenance of personal integrity. Thus, present exemptions should be broadened because of our concern for personal integrity. Furthermore, on purely pragmatic grounds, I fail to see how inducting those who seek conscientious objection status is going to help the effectiveness of the Armed Forces, however that is to be defined. I also feel that it is practically impossible to describe all conceivable war positions or situations for the purpose of defining the status of conscientious objection. A volunteer career army and the abolition of the draft solves this problem as well as a number of others.

Mr. Weber. We deal next with changing the practices of deferment. We have two speakers, President Keast of Wayne State and Professor Flacks.

Mr. Keast. It is important to recall that our discussion of modifying deferment policies occurred as an aspect of our treatment of Mr. Hazard's third question, namely—If we do not rely on volunteers what system of conscription should be used? First we assumed that for the indefinite future, annual military requirements would continue to be substantially smaller than the total number of men potentially available for military service. Consequently, some scheme would have to be found for eliminating, at least temporarily, larger numbers of men from call-up. We assumed that a significant number of improvements in the administration of the present system, of the kind that Mr. Little has so admirably characterized, could and probably would be made. I believe our discussion of deferment may be said to be characterized by the conviction among many that some other means, lottery or voluntary procurement, might in time replace, in whole or in part, the present system.

With this general background, we should note that the Conference did not, in fact, systematically examine the entire deferment picture, but concentrated its attention on some components of that picture. For instance we gave no consideration in detail to hardship dependency. It is probably fair to infer from this fact that no one regarded these deferments as constituting a problem of equity under the current administration of the act, provided that Mr. Little's proposals are taken seriously and improvements made in this direction. We gave some consideration to what may be called occupational deferment, in the non-student sense. Reference was made, I think, without any significant attempt at rebuttal, to the probable inadequacy or inaccuracy of the current list of occupational titles used for establishing occupational deferments. It was suggested that communication of authoritative and up-to-date information on critical manpower requirements between the Selective Service System and local boards and sources needed to be improved to ensure that if, in fact, occupational deferment was to be regarded as an important component of the system, it should be carried out on the basis of the freshest and most accurate information available.

In general, our attention was directed in very large measure to educational deferment and to the deferment of students, and it should be noted that the deferment of students is a kind of occupational deferment in the current regulation. Our discussion of the deferment of students was notably abbreviated, owing perhaps to Professor Friedman's uncommon and remarkable ability to ascertain the sentiments of the group before they had in fact been uttered, and his proposal that we substitute, on a trial basis, circulating the document indicating the number of people who favored the elimination of student deferment. He then passed on to some subsidiary aspects of the problem. I am left, therefore, to report that it appears from the circulation of an informal poll that many members of the Conference believe that if conscription is to be retained, educational deferment as such can be and should be eliminated.

I would like to explicate some of the grounds on which this sentiment seems to rest. The opposition to general student deferment seems to be linked to a number of convictions. First, student deferment as such is inherently inequitable, given the uneven distribution of opportunities for higher education in the United States. Student deferment cannot be demonstrated to be in the national interest. Deferment, as currently practiced, amounts in effect to exemption because of the possibility of extension and pyramiding beyond the age of 26. Student deferment increasingly seems to require from university administrations objectionable or unreliable methods of class rankings. The elimination of student deferment would end many present difficulties which arise from the lack of uniformity and from the problem of part-time students. Eliminating student deferment might also alter the undesirable motivation of students both in respect to the values and purposes of university study and those of military service. If student exemption as such were to be eliminated, this could probably be best done if it were linked with the initiation of call-ups at an earlier age. Uncertainty would thus be minimized and education, if it had to be interrupted, would be interrupted at an earlier rather than a later point. In the event that it is necessary to retain certain features of the present educational deferment system, those relating to a steady supply of clearly identifiable trained technical people—dentists, doctors, and pharmacists were mentioned, but there are doubtless others—and officer candidates engaged in ROTC programs, a condition of deferment could be some explicit contract to serve a designated period of time after the completing of the educational program for which the deferment had been originally given. The general tone of the Conference seems to indicate that many members of the Conference who favor eliminating student deferment would take the view that occupational deferment should be either eliminated entirely or defined as rigorously as the proposed deferment for the ROTC student. The administration of occupational deferment should be governed similarly by uniform standards followed by all local boards and there should be some form of later service requirement.

Mr. Flacks. This Conference is in part a result of intense student protest over the system of educational deferment and the use of class standing as a basis for educational deferments. They began to question not only the desirability of students in the university competing for educational deferment, but also the special privilege of students with respect to deferment. The fact that such privilege exists is confirmed by the statistics we heard at this Conference showing the shockingly low participation of college graduates, particularly those with advanced education, in the Selective Service System. I think the protest also had an impact on college faculties. They too began to question more openly the desirability of continuing educational deferment. It is particularly interesting that many of those students who are most vociferous in opposing the 2S classification are also most active in opposing the war. I call your attention, for example, to the statement issued by the University of Chicago Chapter of Students for a Democratic Society which has as its conclusion three demands: oppose 2S; oppose the war; and resist the draft.

Many conferees expressed concern about the effect of student deferment on higher education and on the students. In particular, the use of class standing as a basis for deferment was criticized on a number of grounds. First, rank in class is not a measure of future competence in careers; the correlation between grades in college and future performance in careers is zero. Grades themselves are too unreliable an index to serve as a basis for deciding whether students should be inducted or not. Second, professors should not be put in a position of being judges of who should or should not be drafted. This is personally distasteful for faculty who oppose the purposes of the draft, and it is also distasteful for faculty who believe that their grading policy should not be criteria for induction. Third, the use of class standing interferes with educational experimentation designed to reduce competition for grades. Using class standing increases competition for grades. Fourth, it is educationally and psychologically undesirable for students to compete with each other in order to avoid the draft. Fifth, it is our impression that students' choice of schools and courses of study are being affected by this competition. Some students are likely to choose schools where they believe they get higher grades and are unwilling to risk certain courses that may lead to lower grade-point averages.

Furthermore, with respect to educational deferment generally, strong feeling has been expressed at the Conference and also in the academic community that educational deferment prevents students from rationally deciding whether they belong in school at all. These are impressions and deserve further study. Applications to graduate school have increased markedly in the past year or two; this is not solely attributable to the population explosion.

Interestingly enough, there were few arguments presented that justify educational deferment. Mr. Keast mentioned the desirability of channeling certain people into critical occupations. A second justification that I heard was that since there is such a large pool of young men, students could not be used in the Armed Forces anyway, so we might as well defer them.

My feeling is that many people at the Conference support the abolition of student deferment. If student deferment is retained for any reason, strong sentiments were expressed against basing deferment on class ranks or tests. The use of tests without class rank presents a very serious problem, in that it creates a situation in which students at less selective institutions are more vulnerable to induction than students at highly selective institutions. As far as I am concerned, if deferments are to be retained, the only solution would be a random procedure such as a lottery in which students were notified before entering college what their probability of induction would be upon graduation. In general, however, our sentiments have been to abolish these deferments and put students into the general pool for inductees. There is a problem that has not been mentioned which affects, I would say, several thousand students: One virtue of student deferment is that it alleviates the compulsory nature of the Selective Service System for those students who have very strong and deep moral objections to participating in a war, such as Vietnam. I would say that if student deferment were dropped, provisions for conscientious objectors would have to be broadened.

Mr. Weber. Walter Oi will present his discussion on the lottery.

Mr. Oi. I will try to present the argument for and against the lottery without expressing my position on it. The lottery begins with the basic premise that only a fraction of our population will be needed in the military service in the future. Somewhere between 30 and 45 per cent of the men who will come of age in the decade ahead will be needed by the Department of Defense to fill manpower requirements. Given this probable participation, the lottery is designed to remedy two shortcomings of the present Selective System: the first is induction at older ages: 23, 24, and older; the second is inequity in the incidence of military service. The House hearings amply showed that the high school graduate and the high school dropout, once exemptions are made for disqualification, are considerably more likely to enter military service than is the college graduate. This is what one would expect, since military service is more attractive for those whose alternative job opportunities are inferior. Even under a lottery there will be this uneven distribution. Senator Kennedy's very succinct statement on the mechanics of operating a lottery was presented. Given that one wants to examine and register all individuals—an assumption not shared by everyone in this society—one finds that Kennedy's solution, using modern data-processing systems, is likely to be as efficient as any other. A cheaper system which I suggest would be one of random selection by birth dates. These are mechanics. A question was raised as to whether such a policy would assure a supply of officers and persons with civilian skills useful in the military. I believe that with sufficient ingenuity the mechanics of the lottery system can be made to accommodate all of these. Obviously, the lottery as applied to doctors will be different from the lottery applied to others, given current manpower practices. The remedies that the lottery would provide include, first of all, shortening the period of draft liability. The lottery would replace a Selective Service System with a system of random chance, with the aim of equalizing the incidence of military service.

The most crucial question to the lottery was raised by Miss Mead and Mr.

Abrams: Is this what our society wants? Do we want to play a game of Russian roulette, or do we prefer the present system, inequitable as it is? This question I am not capable of answering.

Finally, the greatest merit of the lottery is that it does allow very rapid changes in force strength, for once large numbers of men are conscripted in a hurry, there will be an even incidence of service across age classes—people born in certain years will have all served, while in other years, none will have.

Mr. Weber. The last proposal to be summaried is national service. The first speaker for that topic is Mrs. Hal Litoff.

Mrs. Hal Litoff [Judy Barrett]. I would like to discuss one major concern of some of the participants, and that is the concern over voluntary national service. When arguing for voluntary national service, the first point that was made was that compulsion in a democratic society is wrong. This would include compulsory military service or compulsory national service. College students in particular have stong feelings against compulsion, and one of the main reasons for the success of national service organizations such as the Peace Corps and VISTA is that they are voluntary. Therefore, it was concluded that one of the main stipulations for national service is that it must be voluntary. But there are many, many problems in assuring voluntary national service. For instance, it has been proposed that voluntary national service be an alternative to Selective Service. In other words, if an individual belonged to a national service organization, he would no longer be subjected to the draft. But this, in effect, would produce compulsory national service, for, if the individual did not wish to be drafted, he would be forced to choose a national service organization, or else face a jail sentence. Many young people would no longer join organizations such as the Peace Corps, or VISTA, because they felt a desire to fulfill the goals and purposes of such organizations, but rather in order to be exempt from the draft. It was also argued that the problems in determining which national service organizations would qualify as alternatives to Selective Service would be innumerable. For instance, what role would SNCC and CORE and other civil rights organizations play in this? Therefore it was concluded that in order to have truly voluntary national service it is necessary to have a voluntary army.

Mr. Weber. We will now turn to Professor Anderson.

Mr. Arnold Anderson. If you have grown up in non-metropolitan America, the kinds of communities alluded to by Miss Mead, the concept of a variety of programs for youths as well as adults, concerned with benefiting others, seems natural and normal. It is only natural that as we try to find a way to remove alienation and restore participation in the giant cities—even without the complications of pairing the issues with military service—we face the problem of how to institutionalize new ways of participation in programs. Mr. Sherrod pointed out the difficulties of trying to design a system of civilian citizen service—like the one we have in military service—which would provide constructive opportunities for service to others, as well as benefit the individual. And the problem of making people better, which we are now belatedly confronting in a dramatic form in our schools, we also face in our concept of national service. We are going to make other people better, whether they like it or not. Now this is, I suppose, unavoidable, and I have complimented the Peace Corps and the poverty program.

In the discussion of voluntary service as against compulsory citizen service, we face the problem of pricing—whether you use money or some other system of prices—and of figuring out appropriate scales of priorities and the incidence of benefits and costs. We should, in considering national service, not get caught in this cloudland of good intentions. Most of us, I think, would agree on that, though we do not agree as to how one sets up the priorities or how one adjusts the volunteer. Here we come around again to the matter of compulsion. How do we adjust our insistence that the institution—national service or military— shall take in people and remake them? How do we decide whether we should focus on using those people who are most adept for the particular activity and let the others linger in that strange kind of half-world that we now summarize by the word "disadvantaged." There are also the very complex problems of linking up prestige processes and the diffusion of good activities with the requirements of universality and effective administration. As one tries to spell those out for national service, I think that we will discover that all the apparent, or alleged imperatives of Selective Service are going to haunt us again in national service.

Mr. Weber. That completes our summaries. I will now throw the session open for discussion.

Mr. Winter. A perplexing concern lies behind the things that we have talked about. We have repeatedly seen in the urban ghettos that government and voluntary programs benefit the white middle class and have a reverse effect when they reach the ghettos. I am sure this applies in different ways in the rural ghettos. Most of the programs devised assumed that they develop in middle-class cultures. When these programs develop in segregated cultures, the presuppositions no longer apply and the programs defeat their purposes. It's a very general statement, and we could argue it, but I'll just draw your attention to our very bad experience with programs like Aid to Dependent Children, public housing and, more recently, the struggle we've been having with the poverty program. There is a deep discontinuity in our social process which is the result of institutionalized racialism. This discontinuity has effects that reverse our best intentions when our programs cut down more deeply.

I raise this problem in relation to two issues which we have considered, and I urge that support of legislation and voluntary programs take into account this discontinuity. Selective Service may be giving some upward mobility to ghetto youths, but as Bayard Rustin has already been cited as saying: it is siphoning off potential educable leadership out of the ghetto where it is desperately needed, and the Selective Service provides no substitute for adequate education in the ghetto. Second, they increase the opportunity of the privileged classes, whereas such programs if they were really designed for the undervalued sector would have to be people's colleges for the development of indigenous leadership. The issues that we have considered require representation by those for whom the planning is being done and, as we've seen here, they simply are not represented.

Colonel Ingold. There is a tremendous amount of basic misunderstanding of what Selective Service is doing and how it operates. We have a terrific bibliography—and a tremendous library—and we do our best to distribute information, but apparently it isn't read. I am concerned about a number of things: The question of uncertainty with regard to the 18- or 19-year-old: He is actually in suspense and if the calls should become higher, which is always possible, he would be called later. So it actually extends a period of uncertainty rather than eliminating it. If you eliminate the student deferment, you have to increase the Armed Forces sufficiently to accommodate the numbers that the elimination record put in class 1A, or it's dishonest and purposeless. And if you do increase the Armed Forces by that amount, you don't have to eliminate the deferment. On the question of the lottery: we talk about the need for doctors and make special provisions for them. But we also have calls for dentists, pharmacists, and allied specialists, and others, even male nurses, and yet no provision is made for them. There's no provision for late registrants to be integrated into the lottery, or foreigners, for that matter, or those who emerge from a hardship deferment, and there's a tremendous number of people constantly emerging from all kinds of deferments. Last, no thought has been given to the fact that while the Selective Service is criticized now for providing an escape by deferment, isn't it quite evident that the next thing will be called escape by lottery? It's merely a change in semantics.

Mr. Kelly. I'd like to register a very strong dissent to what seems to be the consensus of the Conference, and this has to do with the voluntary service. One group is in favor of voluntary service because it provides choice, and I have complete sympathy with them—freedom of choice. There's a second group, however, who see this as a foreign policy device. If you have a voluntary military, one of two things will occur: either the President's hands will be tied because of the difficulty in raising calls for military manpower, or, alternatively, taxes will have to be increased, and thus the effect on our pocketbooks of military involvement will be felt immediately. I am not sure about these last two points. Indeed, I think that if one is concerned about foreign policy, and if one is concerned with what Professor Boulding called the "legitimization" of decision-making by the body politic, the most important thing you can do is to have the most widespread kind of military obligation possible. If we are going to maintain a military of 2.7 to 3 million, it seems to me that it is absolutely incumbent on us to have a manpower selection system that will include the President's son, the professor's son, the garbage collector's son, the mechanic's son—every single stratum of society. I feel strongly on this point. The essential issue is as follows: Either we have a change in our foreign policy position vis-à-vis the military; that is, we have a smaller military establishment (in which case I'm a thousand per cent in favor of voluntarism), or we maintain the present large military force, in which case we can only maintain conscription *if* we want to be a democratic society which *makes* legitimate the decisions of the body politic.

Mr. Arnold Anderson. I do beg you to stop talking about middle-class values. This label merely confuses the issue and irritates discussions. Second, Colonel Ingold does not seem to have understood that what many of us object to is receiving ad hoc Selective Service information on particular issues as they may be raised. It is the absence of systematic inquiry and research on Selective Service that confounds conferences such as this, and needs something done about it, though I can see that it does call for some appropriation of money.

Colonel Ingold. Will you help us, please, by outlining what you have in mind? This could be a very constructive thing and we'd like to do it, if you'll tell us how to go about it.

Mr. Arnold Anderson. If you will formalize the invitation to a group of people who are competent to advise you, I would be happy to add my nickel's worth at such a consultation session.

Mr. Mendes. I feel that our sessions with respect to data gathering, etc., received somewhat short shrift. There are a number of researchable questions that have been asked and some that haven't been. Not all questions before us are researchable. However, whatever decisions are going to be made, I think it's possible to predict with a little greater accuracy than we have the capacity for at the moment what the consequences of some of these decisions are going to be. For example, what are going to be the consequences of differing definitions of national service? Let's put it up as a hypothetical case: this can be researched. Instead of asking ourselves the question with respect to voluntarism versus compulsion, can we find out—and I think we can—what might be the consequences of different *degrees* of voluntarism? The experiences in other nations and some of our own experience can furnish us with data for research into these particular kinds of questions. With respect to the voluntary army, what kind of people will be recruited into it? Will it be essentially an army of black enlisted men and white officers? I think that's a distinct possibility. Will it be like the police forces in our major urban areas? I think that's a possibility to be carefully considered. These are just some of the questions that should be raised and can be at least partially answered. Therefore, I recommend that Congress institute a massive research effort that could be as significant as that required to launch a supersonic transport or to put a man on the moon.

Mr. Marmion. The thing that has surprised me most about this Conference is the position that has been taken concerning the voluntary army. In the past it has not received any support in the public sector and I think the reception given here to the voluntary army is a compliment to its proponents who are here.

There are problems—first, the provision for an officer corps. You can say that this can be handled. But very specifically, how are you going to provide 90 per cent of the officer corps for the Armed Forces? Second, the National Guard and the reserves will be an absolute necessity for a backup force under a voluntary army. It would be absolutely a catastrophe to depend on these components in their present state. Third, the cost would be astronomical. Fourth, the black-white possibility raised by Mr. Mendes is a very real one. Fifth, a transitional program of going from the present Selective Service System to a voluntary army during the Vietnam war may be desirable but not feasible.

To turn to Mr. Little's constructive criticism of the Selective Service, his point about the military flavor of Selective Service is quite well taken. Many people do not know that the first director of the Selective Service System was President Clarence Dykstra of the University of Wisconsin, who served as head of the Selective Service System prior to the appointment of General Hershey. I think that Congress should take a very close look at the possibility of making the Selective Service System a civilian agency (obviously after General Hershey retires), returning it to the concept that it was originally given in the legislation when President Roosevelt selected Dr. Dykstra as the Director.

Mr. Bird. There are three problems with regard to national service, aside from that of compulsion, which have received little or no attention. The first is the relation of the voluntary agencies to a federally subsidized system, especially when you consider that a good many of the voluntary youth agencies are church sponsored or supported. The same problem that we have in education with regard to the church-state relationship would certainly be present with national service. This is important and should be considered in setting up such a plan.

Second, the problem of discrimination in employment. In the plan proposed by Donald Eberly, the statement was actually made that upon appeal, a potential volunteer would be required to be taken on as a volunteer by his agency. Although on the surface this appears to be a good idea, it means that a volunteer agency would be forced to take some people who do not fit into their program. This would be a very serious problem for the agency.

The administrative snarls which are inevitable in any large-scale federal operation constitute a third problem. The snarl-ups now, which have been alluded to in several ways, would certainly continue in an exponential fashion. For instance, in regard to Selective Service, I know, at the moment, of five states which have turned down perfectly valid alternative service projects on what appear to be arbitrary grounds—the CO's would move around too much, or, as the state director said, "We don't need any more of this kind of project, we have enough in the state already." This kind of bureaucratic administrative fiat would be multiplied, I believe, in national service, and some means have to be built in to prevent these things happening.

Mr. Wool. I think the discussion and summaries of an all-volunteer force left us with more hope of attaining such a force in the near future than the available facts can justify. First, even the proponents of an all-volunteer force scarcely predicted the feasibility of doing so during a period when we are engaged in active hostilities in Vietnam and require a force of 3.3 million. Secondly, I think there was much too short shrift given to the whole question of what we know now about what makes men volunteer for service and what makes them choose a career. In this area the wish was father to the econometric thought. There was too much willingness to accept assumptions which made the cost and the mechanics look easy. We ignore the fact that some of the estimates presented say that in ten years' time this might be the cost—not the cost tomorrow and the day after, when we need these forces. We must reluctantly face up to the fact that there is very little probability of attaining the kind of all-volunteer force we would want as a nation, a force in which men served at a reasonable and equitable rate of pay, not one which would create a symbol of a mercenary force attracted purely by huge bonuses. We might be rich enough to afford to pay $10,000 or $20,000 per man to get that last marginal man we need to fight in the infantry, but I don't think we'd want that force in the nation. Now, having said this, I agree fully that all responsible agencies, public and private, should continue to study this problem in the hope that if our situation does change, we may at some future date arrive at that force. I agree that the American tradition as well as the desire of the military services is for a voluntary force. I think there is a profound question as to its feasibility.

[Unidentified Speaker]. We may be forced to some real dialogue on the kinds of priorities that our nation needs to have here. The discussion at this Conference may compel a reassessment of our foreign policy, it may compel some real attempt to evaluate what it means for us to attempt to engage in what I think Lippmann has called "ideological globalism," to be world policemen, and all of the massive commitments that that entails. As we look at a world that

we call one world, we will have to look at our priorities and compel some reassessment of our foreign policy and its large implications in terms of a world that we now live in.

Colonel Hays. I would like to say a word supporting Mr. Marmion and Mr. Wool in approaching the problem of the volunteer army with a certain amount of caution. While I am wholly sympathetic with its purposes and its ends, and would be most happy to serve in such an organization, we would need a high degree of assurance in a few areas before we move in this direction. The first lies in the caliber and quality of the personnel for our organizations. The second deals with the speculation as to whether we would be able to procure the specialists and officers which our Armed Forces are demanding in higher percentages every year. We would want to have some ability to maintain the reserve forces at adequate strength and with adequately prepared and trained men to support the standing forces. We would want to have the kind of program which would continue the general concept that a citizen owes certain duties and responsibility to society. And, finally, I think that we would need some assurance of the commitment of the public to the purposes, to which the Armed Forces are committed. We should ensure that there is no alienation between those Armed Forces and the public which supports them.

Mr. Eberly. I think it's interesting that there were more papers on national service and more panelists on national service than any other topic. Some of the polls that have been taken in the last few months indicate that there's a tremendous move in this direction. The notion that a young person is responsible to his society and—in reverse—the society is responsible to the young person is gaining wide support. There are very crucial questions about the administration of the program, as has been pointed out. Attacks were made on the educational system. Attacks have been made on Selective Service. Yet the need for military manpower and the need for teaching our children how to read and write are so overwhelming that we do it anyhow. I'd like to suggest this may be the framework that is developing with regard to national service. Replying to Mr. Bird, the report we have submitted suggests, within the framework of our model, what the relationship would be between the individual volunteer and the receiving agency, which could be a school or a service agency of some kind: "The receiving agency would have full administrative control over national service participants and would maintain its rights to select or refuse persons who applied either directly or through a placement center for one of its programs. If an individual felt the agency rejection was in violation of criteria established by the national foundation—for example, for reasons of race or religion —he could appeal the case. If the youth's objection were substantiated, the agency would be considered for removal from the list of approved organizations." There's nothing to require a person to stay with an agency.

Mr. Tuchinsky. Some, but by no means all, of those who have advocated a volunteer army have made a point which was left out in the summaries of that position. That is, relative inflexibility might be seen as an advantage in that it would force a megalomaniacal President like Mr. Johnson to obtain a popular mandate before undertaking an escalation like that in Vietnam. On the subject of conscientious objection, if the draft were to be retained, many of us would see a need to expand the definition of conscientious objection to include a broader range of belief, including the non-religious conscientious objector and the objector on conscientious grounds to a specific war. The best system and the easiest to administer would be to grant alternative service to all of those who apply. If they express a willingness to perform the alternative service for a longer period than is given in military service, perhaps 2¼ or 2½ years, as in Scandinavian countries and many others, this could be done without any religious test or any ultimately arbitrary attempt by a draft board to evaluate a person's sincerity. If we retain the draft, I believe that the Congress should provide funds and require that the Selective Service System undertake an ambitious educational program about rules and alternatives. At present, this educational job is being done very inadequately by volunteer agencies. The government has a responsibility to do in this area what, for instance, the Social Security Administration does extremely well in its area.

Mr. Biderman. The tendency of much of the discussion has focused around three value positions, rather than by consideration of the many alternative value positions that are strongly held in relation to the issues, the realities in question. The value positions are, first, the desire for a constriction of the role of military force in the world, achieving this by unilaterally constricting the power of the United States. The second is a privatized, individualistic, ethical point of view as opposed to general communal, societal, or other kinds of social ethics. The third involves race relations, a matter on which I think there is more consensus. The discussions consequently failed to distinguish military force for training versus that for utilization, either at this particular moment or in the long haul in military confrontation. Mr. Tuchinsky's remark on escalation indicated the lack of consideration of what alternative policies with respect to the draft meant, or how a given kind of military force would then be entered into the world arena. I assure him that without adding one man the President could escalate things as big as he wanted to. He could do it with considerable contraction of manpower, as a matter of fact. Discussion failed to come to grips with the effects of the composition of the enlisted ranks on the nature of these Armed Forces. The relation of the military leadership to the enlisted personnel was hardly considered. Implicit assumptions in the attempt to constrict violence by unilateral means might be suggested by thinking of the possibility of a draft-ban treaty.

Mr. Lauter. On the voluntary army, it seems to me that whatever else has been overcome by Professor Friedman's, Chapman's and Professor Oi's presentations, the Conference also reflects a desire to restore the principle of voluntarism, and that carried over into the discussion of national service, where one of the strongest imperatives that I felt, was the necessity for the advocates of the national service to be clear on the principle of voluntarism. There seems to be an incapacity to clarify what is meant by voluntary, and what is not. A lot of us would be much more comfortable with the idea of national service if in the present system there were any indication that possibilities for alternative service would continue to be present and, indeed, would be broadened in the direction that Mr. Riddick proposed. I don't see any reason, for example, why it would not be in the national interest, as defined by the law, for alternative service people to serve with the United Nations, for example, or with other international agencies. It is not my impression right now that that's permissible, yet it seems to me that proposals for national service would be much more satisfactory to those of us who think of ourselves as members of a world society if those proposals indicated very clearly that national service would involve world service—not just world service administered by the United States for the good of underdeveloped countries, but world service administered through a world organization like the United Nations, both for its symbolic and its physical possibilities.

Mr. Kurland. As an advocate of an ideology of freedom that would promote maximum choice in all areas of concern to the individual, as an advocate of the all-voluntary military, as an advocate of national planning which would bring this about, I am very much disturbed, as this Conference comes to a close, at the atmosphere of cool rationalism, of short-range pragmatism and of misplaced levity. Some people have made comments about the existence of poverty and the effect it has on the security of this country. I think we ought to take a closer look at the effect of a continuation of the draft on the freedom of the poor in this country. One of the most understanding people in terms of the effect of poverty on our national security is Secretary McNamara. Secretary McNamara said that the growing incidence of internal conflict in the world arises not primarily out of communist aggression and subversion, as real as that is, but out of the bitter frustrations born of poverty. He spoke eloquently of the self-perpetuating nature of poverty and its effect on the human spirit. He talked about the 20 million children who are entrapped in poverty, and he said, "Poverty in America makes our nation less secure." In my view, a system which attempted to deal with these frustrations would have little difficulty being defended voluntarily by the poor.

I think there's a conflict here between those who are "goal-oriented" people and those who are "mechanics-oriented." The goal-oriented here are seeking to promote freedom and extend it into our system. My concern is that the institution of the draft not only skirts the problems of poverty, but, in fact, reduces the respect the poor have for our system and thus, our national security. Even today, the poor have little influence over basic decision-making processes, such as that which will decide whether they will be forced to fight against their will.

Mr. McGinley. I happened to sit down next to a few students at lunch today. We had just completed the panel discussion on the volunteer Army, so I asked them what incentives they would need to volunteer. My question was met with a smile, and after some hesitation one of them finally replied, "Are you kidding?" My point is obvious. The people who are going to volunteer are probably not in this room. One could almost accuse this group of conspiring to develop a system to exclude themselves, and include those who aren't represented here.

In considering a volunteer army we must consider who will volunteer and what will happen to these people. What will exist, in fact, is that those people who are excluded from other opportunities in our society will join the military. We will have a widening of the opportunity gap between the haves and the have-nots. Many people have advocated a volunteer Army on the basis of freedom of choice. I want to raise the issue that this perhaps clashes with another basic democratic principle called equality of opportunity. I don't think that should slip from our minds.

Mr. Tatum. If Mr. McGinley had asked the same group how many of them are going to be drafted, you would probably have gotten the same answer. But I am one of a number here who feel that regardless of whether the draft continues, or in what form, it is grossly unfair and immoral to take advantage of it. It is bad enough to have compulsion, but to take advantage of it in financial terms seems to me especially reprehensible. In other words, let us spend the 4 billion. What is that? The war in Vietnam for two months? In a year? Let us increase the pay in any case. Let us not save this money, whether we keep the draft or not. Mr. Weinstein's valuable contribution, about the cross-over in training in the Army, stands on its own merits and certainly requires more serious attention than it is being given. I would say that we should think of it in reverse too. This point has been admitted with regard to the voluntary Army: we are also concerned about replacing military men with civilians who have already had their training.

We should separate the concept of alternative service and citizens service very sharply, but there is no point in not proceeding with either or both, whatever we may determine. I would be in favor of both extending the provision for alternative service, not necessarily confined to CO's, and of launching a decentralized, indigenously controlled, funded program of volunteer citizens service.

Samuel P. Huntington. It seems to me that in principle everyone should be and quite obviously has been in favor of a volunteer force. The problems which come up are: What prices are you willing to pay for a volunteer Army? Some very basic differences have been expressed here in the Conference and exist outside the Conference. Perhaps the most basic difference is on the question of whether we wish to pay the price, or gain the benefit, however you wish to phrase it, of changing our foreign policy. Quite obviously some people are in favor of a volunteer Army because it will require a change in our foreign policy. If you set that group aside, there are those who in principle would still be in favor of a volunteer Army, but given current foreign policy, or current involvement, the question then becomes what other price do we have to pay? When we consider specific problems of the balance in the force composition, turnover, the officer problems, it seems to me that the social cost of a volunteer Army gets very high. The whole discussion of the draft in recent years, I think, springs from the situation in which we found ourselves in the spring of 1964, when it looked as if we were exhausting all possible ways of deferring people and still had too many people coming into the pool. At that time it looked as if a volunteer Army might be practical. The Pentagon's study group assumed the desirability of a volunteer Army, investigated rather carefully the practicability of it, and concluded that it might be practical in the future. But by that time the situation had changed and we were more deeply involved in Vietnam. It had become impracticable for the present and for the foreseeable future.

[*Unidentified Speaker*]. You have to ask yourself just what it is that is so attractive about the idea of a voluntary Army. It says, you have a lot of forces here; let's find a way to put them in some sort of equilibrium. In other words, get them all going so that all of the people are relatively happy, or happier than they are now. You take the best Negroes that you can get of those who haven't been college educated, and give them a relatively better opportunity than they have now. You give them some extra money. But, this is essentially a very short-term proposition. You stabilize the situation now; you eliminate pressure on college students; you don't have SDS people angry; you don't have professors getting up at meetings and saying they will not judge whether someone should go to Vietnam. But the problem is what have you done for the society in any kind of long run? It is reasonable to suspect a volunteer Army will stabilize, it is fairly clear that you could rig it so that the Army wouldn't take control. Still, you would have created a situation in which a certain amount of very productive social agitation is completely choked off. This is fine if you are not interested in social change, but underlying this whole Conference is a very big problem and to take a solution that simply stops people from talking and more or less bribes them is what you are talking about here: giving some people money so they will be happy or happier and won't get angry at you. It seems to be a very unproductive idea.

Mr. Rumsfeld. There have been some comments made concerning the proposed voluntary system which I don't believe have as much merit as it might seem. We should think of it in terms of the military competing in the manpower market, and ignore current military personnel practices. It is said that the mix is going to be bad and that there is going to be some serious imbalance or possible harm to the society. I contend that it is not useful to call something as fundamental as establishing personnel policies designed to meet a specific goal as bribing. The suggestion that society might be imperfect if we had a volunteer system ignores the fact that society is imperfect today, and I would suspect that society will be imperfect in varying degrees tomorrow and tomorrow and tomorrow, regardless of whether we have a voluntary system or an involuntary system. We should think in terms of an approach to the policies that will achieve a goal that is desirable and reasonable. I don't know that it can be achieved, I don't know if it is feasible. I do think that, at the minimum, the Congress has a responsibility to try to determine the feasibility because there are compelling arguments favoring such a program.

[Unidentified Speaker]. I would like to register my statement in the form of a lament, based on a series of statements that I have heard that make the assumption that the national interest must be preserved through the establishment of a large military—2.5 to 3.5 million men. My lament is that we have come to the point of seeing the national interest preserved by the establishment of a large military force. I think that it is a tragic situation for our country and for the world and bodes serious and frightening possibilities in the future. I hope that in some way in the future for my generation we can see our way to world peace.

Mr. Chapman. I think that a number of people came to this Conference who had not seriously considered the possibility of a volunteer military; some of them have changed their minds and that's to their credit. But the fact of the matter is that Mr. Eberly can quote all the polls he likes, but the people have not had an opportunity to hear why a volunteer system is practicable and desirable. I would even say that the commission that the President has appointed has not had that opportunity. They haven't even read Dr. Oi's paper and they have three weeks to go. I think the reason for this is that there were two studies, both instituted by the President, both held in secret, and both have led a gullible public into accepting some outrageous general cost figure of the Department of Defense. I believe that if the DOD had been conscripting for the police for the last fifteen years, they would now be telling us that voluntary hiring was impractical and naïve and maybe we would go along with it. Mr. Wool reminds Dr. Oi that econometrics is an art. Presumably it is an art for the DOD, too. Mr. McGinley says that he had a meeting with some students today, or yesterday, and he asked them if they would volunteer and they smiled, so he doesn't believe this is possible. These are very interesting scientific data. I also have some observations. I notice that Colonel Hayes is here in uniform and Mr. Wool is working in the Defense Department. Presumably they were not drafted; presumably they are volunteers. So perhaps some intelligent people do desire a career in the military service. I would like to say to those who are offering this very speculative, conjectural opposition to this idea that the burden of proof against voluntarism is on you. The first answer is voluntarism. If you want compulsion, you have to find proof against voluntarism. I would also like to ask why you would oppose paying what would be the fair wage, quite apart from the justification or the desirability of volunteer service. Why would you be opposed to paying an honest just wage for work in the military? A transitional military draft system which would work toward getting volunteers would be a fairer system than we have now and a fairer system than the lottery or the national service. If nothing else, let's get that started, then see what happens.

Mr. Patterson. The President's Advisory Commission on Selective Service has had an excellent paper on the subject of a voluntary service prepared by one of Dr. Oi's colleagues, Dr. Stuart H. Altman, an economist from Brown University. This paper has been before the Commission for some time.

[*Unidentified Speaker*]. Professor Bramson cited some evidence from a public opinion poll of high school students. They were asked what careers they would like to enter, and I believe the military was the second most popular choice, even under the present conditions of the military. We might keep this in mind because of the arguments stating that we would lack volunteers. I think we need more information on the popularity of the military as a career choice.

Mr. Weinstein. This is an extremely complicated question in which the burden of proof is totally inappropriate. Somewhere between the middle-size war in which we can afford monetarily 3.5 million men, and cannot abide the thought of the compulsion, and the large war, where suddenly we cannot bear the cost but we can bear the compulsion, there has to be a point at which there is a trade-off. There have to be comparable values equating notions of equity and compulsion as well as the cost. As long as the various participants here are going to maintain positions where one single value cannot be altered, we will not be able to get a very clear idea of what the real choices open to our country are in terms of dealing with compulsion, dealing with equity for various minority groups, and dealing with the cause. Maybe we should all recognize that our absolute values are going to be subject to trade-offs after all. Are two medium-size wars the equivalent of a big war? Somehow somewhere this question must receive an appropriate answer.

Mr. Patterson. Just an observation, if I may. I remember the late President John F. Kennedy in discussing the office of the Presidency before he was elected in 1960 made a statement that has remained with me. He pledged his office to "reopen the channels of communication between the arena of thought and the seat of power." As I leave this Conference today, I would like to express my own personal appreciation to Dr. Tax and the committee, for having provided the arena of thought. I know I speak for myself and all those who visited here from the seat of power who will take back to Washington a great deal of benefit from the ideas, the propositions, the controversy, and the outcome of these three days, in stressing our great appreciation to the University of Chicago, the Ford Foundation, and to all of you.

PART 3

Epilogue

The President's Message on Selective Service to the Congress

MARCH 6, 1967

THE BACKGROUND

The knowledge that military service must sometimes be borne by—and imposed on—free men so their freedom may be preserved is woven deeply into the fabric of the American experience.

Americans have been obliged to take up arms in the cause of liberty since our earliest days on these shores. From the militiaman who shouldered his musket to protect his community in the wilderness, to the young recruit of today who serves the common defense and then returns to civilian life, we have known the price of freedom as well as its glory.

In 1940, the mounting threat of Axis aggression was poised against us. The Seventy-sixth Congress responded by making compulsory military service a legal obligation in peacetime as well as war. Although this was the first peacetime draft in our history, it was an action consistent with our evolving traditions and responsibilities. As President Roosevelt said on that occasion:

America has adopted Selective Service in time of peace, and, in doing so, has broadened and enriched our basic concepts of citizenship. Beside the clear democratic ideals of equal rights, equal privileges and equal opportunities, we have set forth the underlying other duties, obligations, and responsibilities of equal service.

Americans ever since then have come to know well those "broadened concepts of citizenship" of which Franklin Roosevelt spoke. Little more than a year later, war began. The Selective Service System established by that foresighted Seventy-sixth Congress mustered the greatest military force in the history of the world.

After the end of World War II, in the face of new hostile threats, the Eightieth Congress met its obligation by enacting new Selective Service legislation. Six times since then, succeeding Congresses—the Eighty-first, the Eighty-second, the Eighty-fourth, the Eighty-sixth, and the Eighty-eighth—have kept it alive as an indispensable part of our defense against an aggression which has taken different shapes but has never disappeared. Twice—in Korea, and today in Vietnam—we have borne arms in the field of battle to counter that aggression.

Thus, for more than a quarter of a century, through total war and cold war and limited war, Selective Service has provided the nation with the ability to respond quickly and appropriately to the varied challenges confronting our democracy.

THE PROBLEM TODAY

The Selective Service Act under which men today are drafted into our Armed Forces is now almost two decades old, about the age of many of the men who stand watch on the frontiers of freedom throughout the world.

That generation, whose lifetime coincides with our draft law, has grown to maturity in a period of sweeping change. We are in many ways a different nation—more urban, more mobile, more populous.

The youth of the country themselves have added most heavily to our growth in numbers. In 1948, when the present act was passed, less than 1.2 million male Americans were 18 years old. Today that number has increased about 60 per cent to almost 1.9 million, and will exceed 2 million in the 1970's.

Because of this population increase, many more men of their generation are available for military duty than are required.

A decade ago, about 70 per cent of the group eligible for duty had to service with the Armed Forces to meet our military manpower needs.

Today, the need is for less than 50 per cent, and only about a third or less of this number must be involuntarily inducted—even under the conditions of war. When the firing stops, as we all fervently hope it will soon, the requirements will be for fewer still.

The danger of inequity is imbedded in these statistics. It arises when not every eligible man must be called upon to serve. It is intensified when the numbers of men needed are relatively small in relation to the numbers available.

Fairness has always been one of the goals of the Selective Service System. When the present act was passed in 1948, one of its underlying assumptions, was that the obligation and benefits of military service would be equitably borne.

The changing conditions which have come to our society since that act was established have prompted concern—in the Executive branch, in the Congress, in the nation generally—with whether the System might have drifted from the original concept of equity.

That concern deepened as young men were called to the field of combat.

A Selective Service System, of course, must operate well and fairly in peace as well as in times of conflict. But it is in the glare of conflict that the minds of all of us are focused most urgently on the need to review the procedures by which some men are selected and some are not.

Last July, by Executive order, I appointed a National Advisory Commission on Selective Service, composed of twenty citizens, distinguished and diverse in their representation of important elements of our national life.

I asked that Commission, headed by Mr. Burke Marshall, to study these questions, and indeed whether the need for the draft itself was ended or soon might be.

I instructed the Commission to consider the past, present, and prospective functioning of selective service and other systems of national service in the light of the following factors:

—fairness to all citizens;
—military manpower requirements;
—the objective of minimizing uncertainty and interference with individual careers and education;
—social, economic, and employment conditions and goals;
—budgetary and administrative considerations;
—and any other factors the Commission might deem relevant.

The Commission undertook this responsibility with seriousness of purpose, and a clear recognition of the abiding importance these issues hold in American life today. It consulted with or sought the opinions of national leaders, governors, mayors and officials of the federal government; educators and students; business groups and labor unions; veterans organizations, religious leaders and others broadly representing every sector of our society. I asked people across the land to send their thoughts to the Commission, and many did.

The Commission's work is now concluded. Its report has been made available to the American public. I have studied that report carefully.

I have also had the benefit of two other recent studies relating to the same problems. Another distinguished group of leading citizens reviewed the Selective Service situation for the House Armed Services Committee. Its conclusions have been made available to me. Earlier, at my direction, the Secretary of Defense conducted a study of the relationship of the draft to military manpower utilization policies. It was completed in June of last year.

These reports have confirmed that continuation of the draft is still essential to our national security. They have also established that inequities do result from present selection policies, that policies designed for an earlier period operate unevenly under today's conditions, creating unfairness in the lives of some, promoting uncertainty in the minds of more.

To provide the military manpower this nation needs for its security and to assure that the system of selection operates as equitably as possible, I propose that:

1) The Selective Service law under which men can be inducted into the Armed Forces be extended for a four-year period, upon its expiration on June 30, 1967.

2) Men be inducted beginning at 19 years of age, reversing the present order of calling the oldest first, so that uncertainties now generated in the lives of young men will be reduced.

3) Policies be tightened governing undergraduate college deferments so that those deferments can never become exemptions from military service, and providing for no further postgraduate deferments except for those in medical and dental schools.

4) Firm rules be formulated, to be applied uniformly throughout the country, in determining eligibility for all other types of deferment.

5) A fair and impartial random (FAIR) system of selection be established to determine the order of call for all men eligible and available for the draft.

6) Improvements in the Selective Service System be immediately effected to assure better service to the registrant both in counseling and appeals, better information to the public regarding the System's operation and broader representation on local boards of the communities they serve.

7) A study be conducted by the best management experts in the government of the effectiviness, cost and feasibility of a proposal made by the National Advisory Commission to restructure the organization of the Selective Service System.

8) The National Commission on Selective Service be continued for another year to provide a continuing review of the system that touches the lives of so many young Americans and their families.

9) Enlistment procedures for our National Guard and reserve units be strengthened to remove inequities and to ensure a high state of readiness for those units.

CONTINUATION OF THE DRAFT LAW

The United States must meet its military commitments for the national security, for the preservation of peace and for the defense of freedom in the world. It must be able to do this under any circumstance, under any condition, under any challenge.

This fundamental neccessity is the bedrock of our national policy upon which all other considerations must rest.

To maintain this ability we must continue the draft.

The volunteer tradition is strong in our Armed Forces, as it is in our national heritage. Except for the periods of major war in this century, it has been the chief source of our military manpower since the earliest days of the republic.

It must remain so. Our Armed Forces will continue to rely mainly on those who volunteer to serve. This is not only consistent with the American tradition. It is also the best policy for the services themselves, since it assures a highly motivated and professionally competent career force.

Improving the quality of service life and increasing the rewards for service itself encourage volunteering. We have taken a number of actions toward this end and will initiate still others:

—Four military pay raises in each of the last four years, averaging a total increase of 33 per cent in basic pay. I shall shortly recommend another increase.

—A military "Medicare" program which expands medical care for the dependents of those on active duty, as well as for retired members and their dependents.

—The Cold War GI Bill of Rights, which provides education, training, medical, and home loan benefits to returning servicemen.

—The Vietnam Conflict Servicemen and Veterans Act of 1967, which I proposed last month, to provide additional benefits to members of the Armed Forces and their dependents.

—I have asked the Secretary of Defense to submit to me this year a comprehensive study of the military compensation and retirement system.

—To attract more physicians, dentists, and other members of the health professions to volunteer for military service, I am directing the Secretary of Defense to develop a broad program of medical scholarships. Students taking advantage of these scholarships would commit themselves to longer terms of obligated service.

At the same time that we have been increasing the incentive for volunteer service, we have also taken steps to reduce our requirements for men who must be drafted.

I have directed that the services place civilians in jobs previously held by men in uniform wherever this can be done without impairing military effectiveness. During fiscal 1967, 74,000 former military jobs will be filled by civilians. During the next fiscal year, an additional 40,000 such jobs will be so filled. If these measures were not taken, our draft calls would have to be much higher.

Starting last year, under Project 100,000, the military services have revised mental and physical standards to admit young men who were being rejected—more than half of whom had sought to volunteer. As a result, the services will accept this year 40,000 men who would have been disqualified under former standards. Next year, the Defense Department's goal is to accept 100,000 such men.

Finally, the Secretary of Defense is taking steps to expand opportunities for women in the services, thus further reducing the number of men who must be called involuntarily for duty.

But in spite of all we can and will do in this regard, we cannot realistically expect to meet our present commitments or our future requirements with a military force relying exclusively on volunteers.

We know that vulnerability to the draft is a strong motivating factor in the decision of many young men to enlist. Studies have shown that in the relatively normal years before the build-up in Vietnam, two out of every five enlistees were so motivated. Since then, the proportion has been considerably higher.

Research has also disclosed that volunteers alone could be expected to man a force of little more than 2 million.

Our military needs have been substantially greater than that ever since we first committed troops to combat in Korea in the summer of 1950. The average strength of our Armed Forces in the years between the end of hostilities in Korea and the build-up in Vietnam was 2.7 million. Today, we have 3.3 million men under arms, and this force will increase still further by June, 1968, if the conflict is not concluded by then.

The question, whether we could increase incentives sufficiently to attract an exclusively volunteer force larger than any such force we have had in the past, has been subjected to intensive study.

That study concluded that the costs would be difficult to determine precisely, but clearly they would be very high.

Far more important is the position of weakness to which an exclusively volunteer force—with no provision for Selective Service—would expose us. The sudden need for more men than a volunteer force could supply would find the nation without the machinery to respond.

That lack of flexibility, that absence of power to expand in quick response to sudden challenge, would be totally incompatible with an effective national defense. In short, it would force us to gamble with the nation's security.

We look to, and work for, the day the fighting will end in Vietnam. We hope —it is the most profound hope of this Administration as it is of this generation of Americans—that the years beyond that day will be years of diminishing tension in the world, of silent guns and smaller armies. The total efforts of this government will be constantly directed toward reaching that time.

But although we are hopeful, we are realists too, with a realism bred into us through long and lasting experience. Any responsible appraisal of world conditions leads inevitably to this conclusion: We must maintain the capability for flexible response which we have today.

The draft is one of the essential and crucial instruments which assures us of that flexibility.

I recommend legislation to extend for four years the authority, which expires on June 30, 1967, to induct men into the Armed Forces.

THE ORDER OF CALL

The general procedure today for the selection of draft-eligible men is in the order of "oldest first"—from 26 downward.

In the period prior to the Vietnam build-up, when draft calls were small, the average age for involuntary induction was between 22 and 24 years.

All three of the recent studies of the draft reveal that the current order of call is undesirable from the point of view of everyone involved—and is actually the reverse of what it should be:

For the young men themselves, it increases the period of uncertainty and interferes with the planning of lives and careers.

For employers, it causes hardships when employees are lost to the draft who have been trained, acquired skills, and settled in their jobs.

For the Selective Service System, if proliferates the number of deferment applications and appeals. Claims for dependency and occupational deferments are much more frequent for men over the age of 20.

For the Armed Forces, it creates problems. The services have found that older recruits are generally less adaptable than are younger ones to the rigors of military training.

The time has clearly come to correct these conditions and remove the uncertainties which the present order of call promotes.

I will issue an Executive Order directing that in the future, as other measures I am proposing are put into effect, men be drafted beginning at age 19.

DEFERMENT INEQUITIES

Almost 2 million young men—and soon many more—reach age 19 each year. The foreseeable requirement is to draft only 100,000 to 300,000 of them annually. We must ask: How shall those relatively few be selected? As the National Advisory Commission on Selective Service phrased it, "Who serves when not all serve?"

Past procedures have, in effect, reduced the size of the available manpower pool by deferring men out of it.

This has resulted in inequities.

Two separate groups of men have been selected out of consideration for military service:

1. *Rejectees*

In the past, many thousands of men were rejected—and put into deferred categories—who could have performed satisfactorily, sharing the burdens as well as the benefits of service. Most of these were disadvantaged youths with limited educational backgrounds or, in some cases, curable physical defects.

We are taking action to correct this inequity. I referred earlier to Project 100,000 established by the Secretary of Defense. Under this program, the services are taking in men who would previously have been disqualified because of educational deficiencies or minor medical ailments.

With intensive instruction, practical on-the-job training, and corrective medical measures, these young men can become good soldiers. Moreover, the remedial training they receive can enable them to live fuller and more productive lives.

It is estimated that about half the men who enter the Armed Forces under this program will come as volunteers, the other half as draftees.

This will be a continuing program. The nation can never again afford to deny to men who can effectively serve their country, the obligation—and the right— to share in a basic responsibility of citizenship.

2. College Students

The National Advisory Commission on Selective Service found the issue of college student deferments to be the most difficult problem for its consideration. The Commission could not reach unanimity. This is not surprising, for it was sufficiently representative of the nation itself to reflect the healthy diversity of opinion which centers on this subject.

Student deferments have resulted in inequities because many of those *deferments* have pyramided into *exemptions* from military service.

Deferred for undergraduate work, deferred further to pursue graduate study and then deferred even beyond that for fatherhood or occupational reasons, some young men have managed to pile deferment on deferment until they passed the normal cut-off point for induction.

In this regard, a recent survey revealed that only 27 per cent of one age group of graduate school students past the age of 26 had served in the Armed Forces— contrasted with approximately 70 per cent of men of the same ages with educational backgrounds varying from college degrees to some high school training.

There is one group of postgraduate students to whom this condition does not apply—men who are studying to be doctors and dentists. About half of them later serve as medical officers in the Armed Forces.

Their service is vital. Because their studies are essential to military manpower needs, students engaged in such programs must continue to be deferred until their education is completed.

I have concluded, however, that there is no justification for granting further deferments to other graduate school students.

To correct the inequities in the deferments of postgraduate students, I shall issue an Executive Order specifying that no deferments for postgraduate study be granted in the future, except for those men pursuing medical and dental courses.

Undergraduate students present a different problem for consideration.

Many citizens—including a majority of the members of the National Advisory Commission—hold that student deferments are of themselves inequitable because they grant to one group of men a special privilege not generally available to all. Their concern was heightened by the belief that a student deferment in a time of conflict might be an even greater privilege.

They contend that such deferments cannot properly be justified as being in the national interest. Moreover it is their conviction that the elimination of a student deferment policy would have no harmful effect on the educational process in this country. Indeed, they believe that the nation's experience with the returning veterans of other wars indicates that interruption of college studies for military service actually results for many men in a more mature approach and a greater capacity for study.

Others—including a substantial minority of the Commission—believe just as strongly that college deferments from service are not unfair—however manifestly unfair are the conditions of life which permit some to go to college while others cannot.

They agree that the unpredictability of world conditions could conceivably work to the advantage of students who were able to defer their service. But they point out that the same unpredictability could work just as easily to opposite effect, that men who were deferred as college freshmen in 1963 would be graduating this spring into a world in which they could face the hazards of combat. Finally, this point of view calls attention to the fact that the elimination of student deferments would unduly complicate the officer procurement problems of the Armed Forces, for almost four out of five officers who come into the Services each year come from the nation's colleges.

An issue so deeply important, with so many compelling factors on both sides, cannot be decided until its every aspect has been thoroughly explored.

I hope and expect that the Congress will debate the questions this issue poses for the nation's youth and the nation's future.

I will welcome the public discussion which the Commission report will surely stimulate.

I shall await the benefits of these discussions which will themselves be a great educational process for the nation.

I will then take the Presidential action which, I believe, will best serve the national interest.

A FAIR AND IMPARTIAL RANDOM (FAIR) SYSTEM OF SELECTION

The paramount problem remains to determine who shall be selected for induction out of the many who are available.

Assuming that all the men available are equally qualified and eligible, how can that selection be made most fairly?

No question has received more thoughtful attention or more careful analysis.

There is no perfect solution. For the unavoidable truth is that complete equity can never be achieved when only some must be selected and only some must serve.

But a decision cannot be avoided. It is due. The question will become more urgent with the passing months and years.

I have concluded that the only method which approaches complete fairness is to establish a fair and impartial random (FAIR) system of selection which will determine the order of call for all equally eligible men.

That FAIR system would operate generally as follows:

—At age 18, all men would be examined to determine their physical and mental eligibility.

—All eligible men reaching age 19 before a designated date would be placed in a selection pool.

—The FAIR system would then determine their order of call.

—They would be selected in that order of call, for induction at age 19, to fill draft calls placed by the Department of Defense.

—Those not reached during this period would drop to a less vulnerable position on the list with the entry of the next year's group of eligible men into the selection pool.

—All men would retain their vulnerability to the draft, in diminishing order by age group up to 26, in the event of a national emergency. Those who had received deferments would continue liable, as at present, until their 35th birthday.

This system, giving young men a clear indication of a likelihood of being drafted, in conjunction with the "youngest first" order of call, will further reduce uncertainty in the planning of futures and careers.

I am instructing the Director of Selective Service, working in collaboration with the Secretary of Defense, to develop a fair and impartial random (FAIR) system of selection to become fully operational before January 1, 1969. This system will determine the order of call for induction of qualified and available 19-year-olds and older men as their deferments expire.

SELECTIVE SERVICE ORGANIZATIONAL STRUCTURE

The proposals I am presenting in this message have one common objective: Insofar as it is possible to do so, to make certain that men who must be called to serve their country, and fight and die for it if necessary, will be chosen equitably and justly.

The governing concept I propose for selection is one of equal and uniform treatment for all men in like circumstances.

The National Advisory Commission has reported that in order to achieve that objective in all its dimensions, the Selective Service System itself should be restructured.

The Commission presented its conviction that the System's decentralized operation, with more than 4,000 neighborhood boards, 56 State headquarters and 95 appeal boards—all functioning under general and sometimes inconsistent guidelines—is not responsive to the requirements of our nation today. It believed that uniformity of treatment would be difficult to achieve through that System.

The Commission recommended that the Selective Service System be consolidated. It suggested a coordinated structure of eight regions, embracing from 300 to 500 area offices located in major population centers and staffed with full-time government employees. It proposed a System modernized by means of new management techniques, communications technology and data processing equipment.

I believe these recommendations should be exposed to further searching analysis and study by management experts building on the work the Commission has done.

The Selective Service System has done a good job for America. For a quarter of a century those who have been responsible for its operation have provided the nation with an inspiring study of patriotic citizens volunteering their time and devotion to demanding tasks vitally affecting the national welfare.

Moreover, as I have already observed, the System itself has been flexible and responsive, meeting the widely varying calls for manpower placed on it over the past twenty years.

And beyond these considerations are others more difficult to measure, but deeply important nonetheless.

The Selective Service System is a part of America, a part of the process of our democracy, a part of our commitment to a full regard for the rights of the individual in our society. Because of the large number of registrants they must classify, many local draft boards in large cities cannot fulfill completely the function intended for them. But nonetheless the draft board concept is built on a uniquely American belief—that local citizens can perform a valuable service to the government and at the same time personalize the government's procedures to a young man fulfilling one of his earliest and most serious obligations of citizenship.

We cannot lightly discard an institution with so valuable a record of effectiveness and integrity.

Neither can we afford to preserve it, if we find that in practice it cannot adapt to the new controlling concept of equal and uniform treatment.

These counter-balancing considerations highlight the need to subject the System's organization to intensive study by experts skilled in management techniques and methods on the basis of the Commission's work.

I am instructing the Secretary of Defense, the Director of the Selective Service System and the Director of the Bureau of the Budget jointly to establish a Task Force to review the recommendations for a restructured Selective Service System made by the National Advisory Commission. This review will determine the cost, the method of implementation, and the effectiveness of the System the Commission recommends, in view of the changes in the System I am proposing in this message.

In the meantime we can make certain changes to strengthen the System.

The Commission study brought into focus areas where immediate improvement can and should be put into effect.

I am instructing the Director of the Selective Service System to:

—Assure that advisers and appeal agents are readily available to all registrants.

—Examine the System's appeals procedures to insure that the rights of the individual are fully protected.

—Improve the System's information policies so that all registrants and the public generally will better understand the System's operations.

—In conjunction with Governor Farris Bryant, Director of the Office of Emergency Planning, work with the governors to assure that all local boards are truly representative of the communities they serve and to submit periodic reports on the progress in this area.

RESERVE POLICIES

The National Advisory Commission focused attention on the administration of enlistments into reserve and National Guard units. The Commission expressed concern over the inequities it saw in the enlistment procedures of these units.

The reserve forces are essential to our military posture and are an integral part of it. My first concern is that these forces be maintained at their authorized strengths, and in a state of readiness for deployment, if and when they are needed.

I also believe that the reserve components should, like the active forces, be manned primarily by volunteers.

Two steps have recently been taken by the Secretary of Defense to assure greater equity in the enlistment policies of the reserve components:

—Men who meet qualification standards must be accepted into reserve units in the order of their application.

—Reservists who are not satisfactorily fulfilling their obligation will be ordered to active duty for up to 24 months.

Authority to order such reservists to duty is provided in the Department of

Defense 1967 Appropriations Act. *I recommend that such authority be incorporated in permanent legislation.*

I have concluded that two additional actions should now be taken:

First, I am directing the Secretary of Defense to give priority to reserve enlistees who are under draft age (those young men 17 to 18½ years of age) to encourage a maximum number of volunteers who are not immediately draft liable. Reserve deferments for men who are draft liable will be authorized only to the extent required to fill specific vacancies in reserve components.

Second, I recommend that the Congress enact standby authority to allow the Department of Defense to draft men into reserve and National Guard units whenever the authorized strength of these units cannot otherwise be maintained.

THE NATIONAL ADVISORY COMMISSION ON SELECTIVE SERVICE

The work of the National Advisory Commission on Selective Service represents the most comprehensive study of this system since it began twenty years ago. Any citizen who reads the report of the Commission—and I urge all citizens to do so—will recognize that the distinguished members have provided the most penetrating analysis of Selective Service in our history.

To provide the American people with a continuing review of a system which touches every American family and to assure the diligent pursuit of the actions I have discussed and approved in this message, as well as other suggestions in the Commission report, *I am extending the life of the National Advisory Commission for an additional year.*

CONCLUSION

Service performed by the youth of our nation honors us all.

Americans have good reason to respect the long tradition of service which is manifested in every flight line and outpost where we commit our bravest men to the guardianship of freedom.

We have witnessed in our day the building of another tradition—by men and women in the Peace Corps, in VISTA, and in other such programs which have touched, and perhaps even changed, the life of our country and our world.

This spirit is as characteristic of modern America as our advanced technology, or our scientific achievements.

I have wondered if we could establish, through these programs and others like them, a practical system of non-military alternatives to the draft without harming our security.

Both the National Advisory Commission on Selective Service and the group reporting to the Congress posed this question for study.

Both found the answer to be that we cannot.

But the spirit of volunteer service in socially useful enterprises will, we hope, continue to grow until that good day when all service will be voluntary, when all young people can and will choose the kind of service best fitted to their own needs and their nation's.

We will hasten it as we can. But until it comes, because of the conditions of the world we live in now, we must continue to ask one form of service—military duty—of our young men. We would be an irresponsible nation if we did not—and perhaps even an extinct one.

The nation's requirement that men must serve, however, imposes this obligation: that in this land of equals, men are selected as equals to serve.

A just nation must have the fairest system that can be devised for making that selection.

I believe the proposals I am making today will help give us that system.

LYNDON B. JOHNSON

The White House

Résumé of Recent Developments
Affecting Selective Service

LT. GEN. LEWIS B. HERSHEY

Public Law 90-40, 90th Congress, was passed by the Senate on May 11, and by the House, with amendments, on May 25. The Senate agreed to a conference report on June 14, and the House accepted the report on June 20. The President signed the bill into law on June 30, 1967.

The principal changes made by this law are summarized as follows:

The name of the Act was changed to the Military Selective Service Act of 1967.

The authority of the Selective Service System to induct men between the ages of 18½ and 26 was extended for four years.

The President's announcement in his Message to Congress that he intends to call 19-year-olds first was endorsed by the Armed Services Committees' reports. No new legislation was needed. Executive Order 11360, June 30, 1967, authorizes call by age group or groups. The Secretary of Defense has no plans now for implementing call-ups by age group.

The use of a lottery for selection purposes was prohibited by Congress. Specific legislation will be required to put a lottery into effect.

Undergraduate college student deferment was made possible to all who request it and who satisfactorily pursue a full-time course until graduation or twenty-fourth birthday, whichever comes first. Regulations have been issued by the President putting this provision of the law into effect.

Congress rejected recommendations that graduate deferments be ended and provided in the law that critical areas of study be identified by the National Security Council. Regulations were issued to put the new law into effect.

Congress clearly expressed the view that apprentice deferment should be continued on same basis as undergraduate deferment. It also dismissed the concept that the national interest no longer requires occupational deferments, and, in the awareness of the position taken by the Department of Labor, provided that the function of advice in this area be given to the National Security Council. Selective Service Regulations have been amended to delete hourly requirements for apprentice deferments.

Committee reports noted the proposals for a national manpower pool and national quotas and calls. Congress specifically reaffirmed provisions of Section 5(b) for setting up the present system of state and local board quotas.

Congress eliminated the referral to the Department of Justice of conscientious objector cases to eliminate delay and the opportunity for a volume of frivolous claims to hinder Selective Service operations.

Congress also eliminated the reference to "Supreme Being" in the definition of religious training and belief in an effort to express congressional disagreement

477

with the rationale of the Seeger decision. (The original House Committee bill, as reported, would have inducted *all* conscientious objectors, providing for furlough of total objectors for civilian work.)

The President created a special study group to examine further the structure of the Selective Service System, and announced this action to Congress. Hearings, reports, and floor discussions are replete with evidence of congressional awareness of proposals and current studies, and of total opposition to any change in the organization or procedures of the system, including changes in the authority of boards, in the methods of appointment of uncompensated personnel, and in the system of compensation of paid employees of local boards, as well as in other aspects of organization and operations.

The Congress specifically considered the matters of "uniformity" and the discretionary authority of the local boards. The President proposed repeal of the so-called Kilday Amendment, restating local board autonomy in classification. The proposal was rejected by Congress, although the House had adopted an amendment deleting it. Concurrently, a House Committee Amendment, authorizing the President to issue uniform criteria and to require its uniform application as the national interest dictates, was modified in conference to limit the President's authority to one of recommendation.

The Congress actually tightened provisions for drafting aliens by extending to age 35 the liability of physicians, dentists, and allied specialists. This provision affects aliens in these fields who enter the U.S. after age 26.

Congress liberalized deferment to the extent of authorizing enlistment in the National Guard and Reserve up to the day of induction when a governor has proclaimed, or the President determined, that unit strength cannot otherwise be maintained.

The President requested standby authority to induct men into the National Guard or Reserve. Congress declined to provide this authority.

Congress endorsed a program of improved service and counseling by Selective Service, provided for greater local control over local board clerks, limited the tenure of members of local draft boards to give greater flexibility in appointments, and authorized the use of reserve officers as government appeal agents and counselors.

The House Committee announced their intention of conducting a "watchdog" operation, and have, at their request, been kept informed of educational efforts and other recent operational actions.

Both Congressional Committees oppose universal military training, all voluntary-force proposals, national service, etc., and so stated in their reports.

Objections to the Selective Service Act of 1967

SEN. EDWARD M. KENNEDY

[On June 14, 1967, Senator Edward M. Kennedy of Massachusetts objected on the following grounds to the report of the Joint House-Senate Conference, which nevertheless eventually became law.]

I would like briefly to review [my objections to the conference bill], taking them in the order in which they appear in the statement of the Managers on the part of the House, in the conference report.

OCCUPATIONAL DEFERMENTS

The National Security Council is required to advise the Director of the Selective Service System on the establishment of occupational deferments. Under existing law, the National Security Council is charged with advising the President on broad matters relating to national defense. Its staff of 50 comprises experts on foreign policy and national security. It simply does not have the staff or the expertise necessary to weigh the manpower needs of specific industries or employers and to process the many hundreds of petitions for deferment status. Policy on occupational deferments is presently made by an Interagency Advisory Committee, which has performed its task well and which has the resources to do so. I think it a most unwise precedent to require the National Security Council to concern itself with matters other than those broad issues of national security and defense which it has traditionally focussed upon.

RANDOM SELECTION

The President cannot change the method of determining the induction without the passage of legislation authorizing him to do so. Thus the existing system, drafting the oldest first, will continue in force and effect. This would preclude adoption of a random selection system, which was recommended by the Marshall Commission, the Defense Department, the Selective Service System, and the President, as the House Committee has consistently made its opposition to any random selection system very plain. Thus even if the Senate were to pass a bill approving a random selection system, we would—for four years—be faced with adamant refusal by the House to approve it. It is my understanding that the Director of the Selective Service System has already prepared regulations for implementing a random selection system.

PUBLIC HEALTH SERVICE PHYSICIANS

Presently, medical officers of the Public Health Service are deferred from the draft. Small numbers of Public Health Service doctors have in the past been "detailed out" to other federal agencies, as this is the only way these agencies can be assured of a steady supply of able physicians and dentists. Under the conference bill, only service in the Coast Guard, the Environmental Sciences

479

Services Administration, and the Bureau of Prisons will constitute draft deferment for Public Health Service doctors "detailed out." This shuts off the supply
of physicians to such agencies presently receiving them as the Peace Corps, the
Office of Economic Opportunity, the Food and Drug Administration, the Pan
American Health Organization, the Department of Agriculture, the Department
of Interior, and so forth. This is, I think, a very serious matter. To illustrate, the
Public Health Service physicians assigned to the FDA have been performing
research and testing of new drugs, and they will have to curtail this vital activity
if the flow of Public Health Service physicians is cut off.

STUDENT DEFERMENTS

There are two troublesome aspects of the conference bill's student deferment
provisions. One is the mandatory provision for the deferment of undergraduate
students, without any provision for apprentice or vocational students. In other
words, those who have the means—intellectual and financial—to stay in any
college are assured of a deferment. Those without these means, who may be
engaged in on-the-job training or vocational skill training, are subject to the
draft. I would only point out that both groups are learning to become productive
citizens—but one group, the less privileged, has no protection from exposure to
the draft.

The other troublesome provision concerns graduate deferments, the subject
of the sharpest criticism in the national debate on draft reform. The conference
bill continues the President's authority to prescribe graduate deferments, and
thus continues the loophole which has generated the greatest cynicism. The Bill
contains a so-called "anti-pyramiding" provision, but it very plainly points out
that the procession from college student to graduate student to occupational
deferment, until the cut-off age of 35 is reached, will provide the means for many
young men to beat the draft.

These two provisions are worse than the present law because present law
gives the President wide discretion; the conference bill does not.

CONSCIENTIOUS OBJECTORS

Again there are two separate and objectionable provisions. One would over-
rule the 1965 Supreme Court decision, *United States* v. *Seeger*, by striking from
the statute the language upon which the Court relied. In its place, the statute
requires that conscientious objection be based on "religious training and belief,"
not including "essential political, sociological, or philosophical views, or a merely
personal moral code." This raises the prospect of denying conscientious objector
status to those not members of religious sects, which would raise the issue of
equal protection.

The other objectionable provision eliminates the present requirement for a
hearing by the Department of Justice whenever an appeal is filed against a local
board's denial of conscientious objector status. This would terminate the procedure in effect since 1940, whereby conscientious objection appeals are referred
to the Department of Justice for FBI screening and investigation, hearing before
a volunteer lawyer hearing officer, and written recommendation by the Department to the Selective Service appeal board. The purpose of eliminating this
procedural step was announced as an intention to reduce delays in prosecuting
conscientious objection appeals. It has the effect, however, of giving each appeal

board the authority and discretion to set its own rules, without uniformity and without the investigative expertise of the FBI and the Department of Justice.

JUDICIAL REVIEW

The conference bill would prohibit judicial review of local board classification except as a defense to a criminal prosecution. In other words, no appeal lies against a classification—either as 1A, student deferment, conscientious objector, or any other—until and unless the registrant has agreed or disagreed to report for induction. Thus, one can only petition for judicial review of an administrative decision—classification—as a criminal. There is no civil judicial remedy. This is surely an extraordinary situation.

COURT PROCEDURES

There are two troublesome aspects of the conference bill's interference in Federal court procedures. One is a requirement that selective service cases—both trial and appeal cases—be given absolute precedence on the dockets of federal courts. There is no room, under the terms of the bill, for the exercise of discretion by the courts. We can all be sympathetic with a desire to avoid delay in the decision of selective service cases, particularly in a time when we are engaged in combat operations. Yet to permit absolutely no flexibility, no discretion, to the courts in the management of their dockets seems most unwise. There are other cases, civil and criminal, which compete with the importance of selective service cases, and courts should have some breathing space.

This is particularly so when coupled with the other objectionable provision. This second provision would require the Department of Justice, on the Selective Service Director's request, to prosecute a given selective service case or advise the Congress, in writing, the reasons for its failure to do so. The judicial doctrine of prosecutorial discretion in the federal courts has, down through our legal history, uniformly permitted U.S. attorneys absolute discretion both in bringing and dismissing criminal prosecutions. The reasoning is particularly applicable to this case: only experienced prosecutors can make the judgments of whether the evidence is sufficiently strong to merit the expenditure of public funds in the prosecution. This provision of the conference bill is a novel and virtually unprecedented interference with the court system. And I do not think it belongs in the law.

DISCRIMINATION ON LOCAL BOARDS

The conference bill would prohibit discrimination by sex in determining the composition of local boards. It does so in these words: "No citizen shall be denied membership on any local board on account of sex." Despite the fact that the issue of racial discrimination has already been raised in court cases and with the Justice Department, there is nowhere mentioned in the conference discrimination on account of race, or of religion, or of creed. Are we to interpret the positive legislative mandate against discrimination by sex to mean an implied neutrality of the Congress on discrimination in other ways? Surely, this should be clearly spelled out in the law, unless it is intended to preserve the composition of totally white local boards in states with populations thirty to forty percent Negro (which have not one Negro on local boards) or similar discrimination against Spanish Americans, Puerto Ricans, and other minority groups.

Overhauling the Draft System:
Hard Times for the Reformers

ROBERT J. SAMUELSON

The draft has absorbed more than its share of criticism in the last twelve months. A presidential commission has studied it, students have damned it, and Congress has debated it. Almost everyone talked of overhauling the present setup, perhaps even eliminating it. Yet, when the President signed a new Selective Service Act last month, the draft hadn't changed very much. (For what has changed, see the accompanying Summary.)

The existing system exhibited extraordinary resilience. Between July, 1966, and July, 1967, proposals to revamp the draft ranged from replacing it with a volunteer army or universal service to diluting it by allowing draftees to serve in the Peace Corps or Vista. The very abundance of revisionist ideas was significant: criticism of the present system was plentiful, but agreement on what to do about it was not.

The debate was also a victim of conflicting circumstances. The controversy arose because the war and increasing manpower requirements drew attention to the draft; but the war—and the demand for a continual flow of men—also reduced the incentives for the military, its spokesmen in Congress, and even the Administration to experiment too boldly with the existing system.

The story of draft reform, 1966–67, then, is one of a large supply of ideas put through a fine filter, which, at every stage of public debate, eliminated the most controversial schemes. The process started a year ago when the President appointed a special commission, headed by former Assistant Attorney General Burke Marshall, to conduct a thorough study of the existing system. The commission itself did a heavy job of refining by discarding a number of highly publicized proposals. It rejected alternate service ("no fair way exists, at least at present, to equate military and nonmilitary service"), a volunteer army ("no flexibility in crisis . . . the sudden need for greater numbers of men would find the nation without machinery to meet it") and universal service (unnecessary and impractical). The commission's rejection robbed these schemes, and the prospect of radical reform, of whatever slight chances they had.

The Marshall Commission concentrated instead on the most prevalent complaint about the draft: that it was unfair. This criticism caused the President to establish the commission in the first place and permeated the panel's final report. It said that: (1) all student deferments were an example of "special treatment" and ought to be eliminated; (2) the order of induction ought to be reversed, taking nineteen- and twenty-year-olds first instead of taking the oldest in an

Reprinted from *Science*, July 21, 1967, pp. 290–94, by permission of the publisher. © 1967 by the American Association for the Advancement of Science.

eligible pool of men between nineteen and twenty-six (the present order, it was argued, forced men to wait too long, often impairing employment and career prospects or delaying family plans); and (3) a lottery should be introduced to select the men in the nineteen- to twenty-year-old pool who would serve. (Between 1.9 and 2 million men turn nineteen every year; at present rates of induction, the Defense Department needs to draft only one out of two, and after Vietnam it estimates draft needs at one out of seven.)

The President supported many of the commission's ideas—specifically, the lottery and the reversal of the age of induction. But he, like the Commission, narrowed the scope of reform. The Commission had found wide variations in the classifying procedures of the more than 4,000 local, largely autonomous draft boards; it wanted the system drastically restructured and the lottery pool made national instead of local. The President, probably sensing congressional attachment to the present decentralized system, recommended only a management study of the current setup. Likewise, student deferments seemed too controversial; the President committed himself to end only graduate school deferments. (Significantly, a minority of the commission had also recommended that graduate school deferments alone be ended.) Reform had reached its most difficult hurdle, Congress, and already two major proposals seemed dead: ending undergraduate deferments and restructuring the Selective Service System.

The scene now shifted to the House Armed Services Committee. It, too, wanted reform, but reform of a different sort. If the concept of "fairness" dominated the Marshall Commission, the war in Vietnam and opposition to the draft evaders preoccupied this committee. The Armed Services Committee, chaired by L. Mendel Rivers (Dem., S.C.), had authored a recent law against draft card burners, and its impatience with dissent was clear. F. Edward Herbert (Dem., La.), the third-ranking Democrat on the committee, put it this way:

"Let's forget about the first amendment. I know that will be the refuge of the Supreme Court, I recognize that. But at least the effort can be made and the demonstration given the American people certainly that the Department of Justice and most assuredly the Congress is determined to eliminate this rat-infested area in this country."

The bill that emerged from Rivers' committee bore the marks of this anger. It required that the cases of draft evaders be given priority by the Justice Department. It struck the Supreme Being clause from the section on Conscientions Objection in an attempt to narrow the definition of C.O. status. It eliminated Justice Department hearings for C.O. applicants who receive adverse decisions from local boards. Apparently in the same mood, the committee curbed exemptions for doctors in the Public Health Service, the Food and Drug Administration, or the Office of Economic Opportunity.

Yet, Rivers' bill did not necessarily block most of the Administration's major reforms. The crucial setback came in the conference called to reconcile the House and Senate bills. The House Committee had opposed a lottery until it saw a concrete plan from the administration, which had simply asked for authority to establish the new system. Consequently, the committee had required that the President give Congress sixty days to disapprove of the lottery before putting it to use. The restriction, though unwanted by the administration, was not necessarily crippling: a disapproving resolution would have to pass both branches, and the Senate, which was more friendly to the lottery, would probably not go along. But the conference replaced the sixty-day veto with an absolute ban against a lottery until new legislation had passed both houses. The change, surprisingly, was made at the urging of Sen. Richard Russell (Dem.— Ga.), the bill's Senate manager, who disliked congressional vetos. As he told the Senate: "I am well aware that there are some circumstances in which the so-called Congressional veto is applicable, but I do not like to extend this practice generally."

Of such idiosyncrasies is history made. The conference bill—which cleared both houses, but not without a lengthy floor debate in the Senate—apparently destroyed the administration's plans to announce a shift to the nineteen- and twenty-year-old pool. Without a lottery, the Defense Department thought there were too many problems. The administration will introduce a lottery next session.

What happened to the reformers and the pressure for change? Despite the proliferation of proposals to alter the system, there was little support for the plans offered by the Marshall Commission and later endorsed by the President. It may be true, as the Harris poll indicates in *Newsweek*, that only 40 percent of the public thinks the draft works fairly. But other polls also say that a majority is opposed to a lottery, although it is not clear whether most people really understand the President's proposals.

Much of the discussion of the draft was stimulated by uneasiness about the war in Vietnam or outright opposition, feelings that hardly bothered either Armed Services Committee. Some leading proponents of reform of the structure of the Selective Service System were Republicans (relatively junior ones at that) and their criticism was labeled "political." From the committee's vantage point, as from the military's, the main objective of the Selective Service Act is to get men for the army. The calls for a volunteer army, for example, made little impression not only because they originated both from critics of the war and from Republicans, but also because a volunteer army was unacceptable to the military.

The Administration, as advocates for the Marshall Commission, did not help very much. The President, or his aides, did little to push the proposals. He may not have thought they needed pushing—after all, up until the conference the framework of the administration's plans had survived. Or, faced with what has generally been a reluctant Congress, the President may have been content to let nature take its course. The Defense Department, formally entrusted with bearing the package to Congress, was not very persuasive. The Department was not a long-standing lottery advocate, and, as recently as early 1966, had not favored the idea in public testimony.

The anti-lottery, anti-reform forces also had a powerful, if silent ally, the Selective Service System. Though Lieutenant General Lewis B. Hershey, the head of the system since 1941, had publicly reversed his long-standing opposition to the lottery, there was no question where his, and the system's, heart lay. As Senator Russell noted once while defending the conference bill on the floor: "It is significant to me, in reading these communications [against the conference bill] here today, that we have not had anything from General Hershey objecting to this bill. He has not expressed any displeasure with it."

The main opposition to the lottery was in the House Committee where the lottery was viewed as inflexible and "change for the sake of change." In contrast, the Senate included nothing about the lottery in its bill. There were a variety of other differences between the two bills, but most were settled in favor of the House. Nothing is more significant to the shape of the new draft legislation than the fact that the Senate version, generally leaving much more discretionary authority to the President than the House bill, was virtually destroyed in conference.

Just why this happened is difficult to explain. Conference committees have always been mysterious, holding executive sessions and keeping no records. A number of factors, however, seem to have been at work. The Senate was under time pressure: the censure of Sen. Thomas J. Dodd (Dem., Conn.) was a few days off, and Russell, fearing extended controversy, reportedly wanted to get the draft bill approved before the Dodd debate began. Moreover, the positions of the House and Senate committees were not so far apart as their bills indicated. (For example, the House had written a guarantee of undergraduate student deferments into its bill; the Senate made a similar recommendation in its report. The House included the lottery veto in the bill; the Senate noted several misgivings about the lottery in its report.) Finally, the House Committee's interest in draft legislation was more thoroughly established than the Senate's. The House Committee held two sets of hearings on the bill and appointed a civilian panel, headed by retired General Mark W. Clark, to make recommendations. The House conferees, drawn from the committee, were stubborn: they knew what they wanted and were determined to get it.

This setback to reform, however, may have obscured the draft debate's more lasting significance. Most fundamentally, the debate spotlighted a long-ignored subject and gave public currency to such ideas as the volunteer army. Once the war in Vietnam is over, there may yet be another reconsideration of Selective Service and proposals rejected this time may fare better then.

The debate also seemed to make some subtle changes in existing assumptions about the draft. The old assumptions favored educational and occupational deferments on the grounds that the draft was not simply a device for supplying men to the military, but one for serving the nation's manpower needs in many areas. The Selective Service System calls this "channeling" and believes it has helped—through deferment policy—direct men into scientific, engineering, and teaching careers "which are essential to national interest." Regardless of the impact or desirability of this concept, it has become increasingly—though not thoroughly—discredited during the current debate.

The present controversy may also foreshadow the downfall of the local board. Although local boards were strongly supported in both the House and Senate, the new legislation does away with the bulk of board duties, the classifying of undergraduate and most graduate students. The board will still have jurisdiction (and discretion) on remaining graduate deferments, occupational deferments, hardship deferments, and the cases of conscientious objectors, to name a few. But there is no doubt that its job has been diminished. In a few years, it may seem foolish to keep the boards alive for so little work.

In fact, even the reports of the administration's defeat may be premature. The lottery, which seems to have been pushed aside, is not dead. The administration plans to present a lottery plan to Congress next session. This commitment reflects more than attachment to the recommendations of the Marshall Commission.

The Defense Department has always wanted to keep the average age of induction low, between nineteen and twenty-one. With draft calls high and with most graduate school deferments in effect next year, the average draftee will remain, as he has been, relatively young. Because of this, the department saw no need to shift now to the nineteen- to twenty-year-old pool. Next June, however, two new groups—this year's college graduates who go on to graduate school and have one-year deferments, and next year's college graduates—will join the pool simultaneously; this influx will presumably force up the average age of induction considerably.

As a result, the Defense Department would like to shift to the nineteen-year-old pool and mix the younger boys with older college graduates. The fairest way to do this, it believes, is the lottery. If it can't get a plan through Congress, it will face a difficult choice: switching to the 19-year-olds with what it considers an unfair selection system (but one actually preferred by the House Armed Services Committee); or, staying with the present order of inducting the oldest first in the nineteen- to twenty-six-year-old pool. Because of the department's preference for the nineteen-year-old pool, the push for the lottery may be undertaken with more fervor next session.

Regardless of what happens, the most important consequence of this year's debate may lie somewhere else entirely. By eliminating most graduate school deferments next year, the new law enlarges the size of the 1-A pool significantly. In twelve months, the Selective Service System will be able to efficiently draft many more men than it has in the past. The ultimate effect of the draft debate may be to give the administration more flexibility in increasing the size of the army—and, if desired, the size of the U.S. commitment in Vietnam.

SUMMARY OF DRAFT LAW CHANGE

The new draft law and implementing regulations will be almost identical to the old for at least a year, when a sharp curtailment of graduate deferments will be announced. Specifically:

1) All college undergraduates are guaranteed a deferment while in "good standing." Though not guaranteed a deferment under the old law, few undergraduates were actually drafted (boards often asked for a student's class rank or his results on a national draft test to determine his status—both measures are now eliminated).

2) Graduate students in 1966–67 will keep their deferments—M.A. candidates for one year, and Ph.D. candidates for no more than four. A candidate for a professional or doctoral degree *who was in school last year* has a total of five years, including those he has already had, to earn his degree.

3) Last June's college graduates entering graduate school this fall will be deferred for only one year.

The most sweeping change in the new statute—the eventual elimination of most graduate school deferments—does not go into effect for a year. In the interim, the National Security Council will advise the President whether any deferments should be given other than those for medical and dental students. The council will also review occupational deferments. The current assumption is that graduate deferments which are extended by the council will be for scientists and engineers, though there is no indication which areas will receive continued grace.

During the next year, draft boards will continue to take the oldest men first in a pool of eligibles from nineteen to twenty-five years old. However, there is a good chance that in a year the Defense Department will reverse the order of induction by taking men in the nineteen- to twenty-year-old group first. In that case, men older than twenty who had previously been deferred would probably be mixed with the nineteen-year-old group; or, a transitional arrangement would be worked out so men in both age groups would be equally vulnerable.

In either case, a man's period of maximum eligibility would be about a year. The Defense Department would probably not need all the men in the eligible pool—at present rates, the need would be for about one out of two. At the end of the year, the man would drop into a pool with a lower eligibility, and, unless draft calls rose drastically, he would probably never be called.

Other important changes in the new law include:

1) Conscientious objection: The so-called Supreme Being clause has been eliminated in an attempt to narrow the definition of C.O. status. Under the new law, as the old, anyone who by "religious training and belief" is opposed to war can qualify as a C.O. The old law interpreted "religious training and belief" as "an individual's belief in relation to a Supreme Being involving duties superior to those arising from any human relation. . . ." This clause is considered important because the Supreme Court relied on it for the 1964 *Seeger* decision, which included as conscientious objectors anyone who could demonstrate "a sincere and meaningful belief which occupies in the life of its possessor a place parallel to that filled by God of those admittedly qualifying for the exemption. . . ." The Selective Service Administration has told local boards that the change means a narrower definition of C.O. status, though some legislators and lawyers—including a representative of the American Civil Liberties Union—believe the courts will still uphold *Seeger*. A court case will almost certainly be necessary to clarify the impact of the new law.

2) Exemptions for doctors: Doctors will no longer be able to receive credit for military service by serving in the Peace Corps, the Office of Economic Opportunity, or the Food and Drug Administration as members of the Public Health Service (PHS service normally carries an exemption). The new provision will not affect those now serving or scheduled to serve in these agencies.

Contributors of Papers and Participants in the Discussions

Mark Abrams
Research Services Ltd.
London, England

C. Arnold Anderson
Professor, Departments of
 Education and Sociology
The University of Chicago

Lloyd Anderson
Student
The University of Chicago

David Bakan
Professor, Department of Psychology
The University of Chicago

Col. Mordechai M. Bar-On
Chief Education Officer
Israel Defense Forces

John Beal
Student
The University of Chicago

Albert D. Biderman
Senior Research Associate
Bureau of Social Science Research
Washington, D.C.

Robert Bird
Director
American Friends Service Committee
Philadelphia, Pennsylvania

Richard W. Boone
Executive Director
Citizens' Crusade Against Poverty
Washington, D.C.

Wayne C. Booth
Professor, Department of English and
 Dean of the College
The University of Chicago

Kenneth E. Boulding
Professor, Department of Economics
University of Michigan

Leon Bramson
Associate Professor and Chairman, Depart-
 ments of Anthropology and Sociology
Swarthmore College

Marc J. R. Brenman
Student
The University of Chicago

Bruce K. Chapman
Author and Editor; The Ripon Society

Gregory B. Craig
President, Undergraduate Council
Harvard University

Terrence Cullinan
Stanford Research Institute
Menlo Park, California

Sister Thomasine Cusack
Professor, Rosary College
Lake Forest, Illinois

Allison Davis
Professor, Department of Education
The University of Chicago

Richard Duffee
Student
Evanston (Illinois) High School

Donald J. Eberly
Executive Director
National Service Secretariat
New York, New York

Erik H. Erikson
Professor of Human Development and
 Lecturer on Psychiatry
Harvard University

Richard Flacks
Assistant Professor, Department of
 Sociology
The University of Chicago

489

John Hope Franklin
Professor and Chairman, Department of
  History
The University of Chicago

Milton Friedman
Professor, Department of Economics
The University of Chicago

Raymond L. Garthoff
U.S. Department of State
Washington, D.C.

Eugene Groves
President
United States National Student
  Association
Washington, D.C.

Col. Samuel H. Hays
Director, Office of Military Psychology and
  Leadership
United States Military Academy
West Point, New York

Geoffrey C. Hazard, Jr.
Professor, The Law School
The University of Chicago

Lt. Gen. Lewis B. Hershey
Director
Selective Service System
Washington, D.C.

Samuel P. Huntington
Professor of Political Science
Harvard University

Col. Dee Ingold
Special Assistant to the Director
Selective Service System
Washington, D.C.

Morris Janowitz
Professor and Chairman, Department of
  Sociology
The University of Chicago

Bernard D. Karpinos
Special Assistant for Manpower
Office of the Surgeon General
Department of the Army
Washington, D.C.

The Hon. Robert B. Kastenmeier
Representative from Wisconsin
United States Congress

William R. Keast
President, Wayne State University
Detroit, Michigan

Erwin L. Kelly, Jr.
Assistant Professor, Antioch College
Yellow Springs, Ohio

The Hon. Edward M. Kennedy
Senator from Massachusetts
United States Senate

Norman G. Kurland
Staff Associate
Citizens' Crusade Against Poverty
Washington, D.C.

Paul Lauter
American Friends Service Committee
Chicago, Illinois

Joseph Leo
Student
Western Illinois University
Macomb, Illinois

Judy Barrett (Mrs. Hal Litoff)
Student
Emory University
Atlanta, Georgia

Roger W. Little
Associate Professor, Department of
  Sociology
University of Illinois at Chicago

Mrs. Frances B. McAllister
Friends Committee on National
  Legislation
Pasadena, California

Timothy McGinley
Special Assistant
U.S. Department of Labor
Washington, D.C.

William H. McNeill
Professor, Department of History
The University of Chicago

Harry A. Marmion
Staff Associate, Commission on Federal
  Relations
American Council on Education
Washington, D. C.

Brig. Gen. S.L.A. Marshall
Author, military analyst
Detroit, Michigan

Bill Mauldin
Cartoonist and author
Chicago Sun-Times

Margaret Mead
Curator of Ethnology
American Museum of Natural History
New York, New York

Richard Mendes
VISTA
New York, New York

John Mitrisin
Research Associate
Institute for Policy Studies
Washington, D.C.

John Naisbitt
Special Assistant to the President
Science Research Associates
Chicago, Illinois

The Hon. Maurine B. Neuberger
Senator from Oregon
United States Senate

Walter Y. Oi
Professor of Economics
University of Washington
Seattle, Washington

Bradley H. Patterson, Jr.
Executive Director
National Advisory Commission on
    Selective Service
Washington, D.C.

John de J. Pemberton, Jr.
Executive Director
American Civil Liberties Union
New York, New York

Judge Granville Ridley
Security Commission, American Legion
Murfeesboro, Tennessee

Milton J. Rosenberg
Professor, Department of Psychology
The University of Chicago

The Hon. Donald Rumsfeld
Representative from Illinois
United States Congress

Charles Sherrod
Church Society for College Work
Albany, Georgia

Arlo Tatum
Executive Secretary
Central Committee for
    Conscientious Objectors
Philadelphia, Pennsylvania

Sol Tax
Professor of Anthropology and
    Dean of University Extension
The University of Chicago

Rabbi Max D. Ticktin
Director, B'nai B'rith Hillel Foundation
The University of Chicago

Joseph S. Tuchinsky
Counselor on the Draft
Roosevelt University
Chicago, Illinois

Robert Van Waes
Associate Secretary
American Association of
    University Professors
Washington, D.C.

Richard Virgil
Student
The University of Chicago

Loren K. Waldman
Student
The University of Chicago

George H. Watson
Dean of Students
Roosevelt University
Chicago, Illinois

Arnold R. Weber
Professor, Graduate School of Business
The University of Chicago

Paul A. Weinstein
Associate Professor of Economics and
    Director, Military Training Study
University of Maryland

Gibson Winter
Professor, The Divinity School
The University of Chicago

Harris Wofford
Associate Director, Peace Corps
Washington, D.C.

Harold Wool
Director for Procurement Policy
Office of the Assistant Secretary of
    Defense (Manpower)
Washington, D.C.

Aristide Zolberg
Assistant Professor
Department of Political Science
The University of Chicago

Index of Persons

492

Subject Index